Encyclopedia of
*American
Women and
Religion*

Encyclopedia of

American Women and Religion

June Melby Benowitz

ABC-CLIO

Santa Barbara, California
Denver, Colorado
Oxford, England

Library of Congress Cataloging-in-Publication Data

Benowitz, June Melby.

   Encyclopedia of American women and religion / June Melby Benowitz.

     p. cm.

   Includes bibliographical references and index.

   ISBN 0-87436-887-1 (alk. paper)

   1. Women and religion—United States—Biography—Encyclopedias.

2. United States—Religion—Encyclopedias.   3. United States—

Biography—Encyclopedias.

BL2525.B45   1998

200'.82'0973—dc21   98-25706

                                                   CIP

04   03   02   01   00   99   98   10 9 8 7 6 5 4 3 2 1

ABC-CLIO, Inc.

130 Cremona Drive, P.O. Box 1911

Santa Barbara, California 93116-1911

This book is printed on acid-free paper. ∞

Manufactured in the United States of America

To Dad, with love
(Harold Eugene Melby, 1919–1998)

Contents

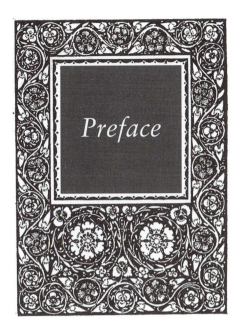

Preface

Since colonial times, women have been in the majority in most American religious denominations. Yet until the resurgent women's movement of the 1960s and 1970s, most knowledge of the history of American women and religion remained hidden. If asked, a college student might be able to name a few female religious leaders, such as Mary Baker Eddy, Aimee Semple McPherson, or Anne Hutchinson, but virtually none would be able to identify Jarena Lee, Alma Bridwell White, Henrietta Szold, or numerous others who have made important contributions to the history of American religion. The growth of women's studies during the 1970s and 1980s has led to the uncovering of valuable information regarding American women's involvement in religious activities.

In addition to recognizing female leaders in American religious history, historians have uncovered a broad story of ordinary women and their contributions to this country's religious past. What they have found is a story of women striving to answer "God's call" through service to their churches and their communities. Frequently, these women faced obstacles far greater than those encountered by men. Despite their normally fewer numbers, the men in religious groups usually dominated. Until well into the twentieth century, most church authorities were male. At present, many religious denominations in the United States continue to be patriarchal: Roman Catholicism, Mormonism, Islam, and Orthodox Judaism, among others. Although some women have been willing to accept the status quo, others have struggled to achieve equality in religion as well as in society at large. The majority of women in this study sought greater influence and power within their religious denominations, but others were content to maintain subordinate roles. Nevertheless, the latter also contributed to the expansion of women's sphere by joining with others of their gender to work in church-related activities. The acts of organizing and learning fund-raising and leadership skills expanded a woman's experience and brought her closer to the "male" world than she realized.

Included in this volume are women who influenced American religion during their time and some whose influence continues to be felt. This encyclopedia covers religious denominations, with their positions on the roles of women; women's religious-based organizations, such as sisterhoods, deaconess orders, charitable associations, missionary groups, and reform-oriented groups; and individual women who have managed to overcome many obstacles and attain positions within church hierarchies or founded religious sects of their own. The reader will find that I have defined "religion" rather broadly and have included groups that some might consider quasi-religious, such as witches and ecofeminists.

During the course of researching the topic of American women and religion, I have been curious to learn what caused women to choose religious work as a career. Most of those who became leaders were inspired to embark upon religious careers because of their individual experiences. A conversion experience, the death of a loved one, a recovery from a life-threatening illness or injury, or an encounter with persons suffering from economic hardships could motivate a woman to devote her life to religious work and to aiding other human beings. Although they seldom had the opportunities available to men, women embarked on a variety of religious occupations. Some sought to evangelize and became preachers or missionaries or joined the Salvation Army. Many joined or created charitable organizations that were associated with their churches or enlisted in causes to reform and purify American society. Others combined other talents, such as art, music, or writing, with their religious enthusiasm. They created religious-centered artworks, composed hymns, entertained audiences by singing gospel music, or authored inspirational or theological works.

The reader will find that the entries in this encyclopedia focus heavily on the nineteenth and twentieth centuries. The dearth of information concerning women of the colonial period accounts for some of this problem, but it is also true that the nineteenth century saw an enormous outpouring of women from their domestic spheres into church-centered activities. In fact, the tremendous growth of women's influence in religious enterprises during that period has led some historians to consider the nineteenth century to be a time when American religion was "feminized." Since then, women's involvement in most areas of religious activity has increased, though the mid-twentieth century has seen a decrease in the number of women becoming deaconesses and Roman Catholic nuns. Also, some religious denomina-

tions such as the Mormon Church have placed restrictions on women's participation in their churches that were not imposed during their formative years.

There have been numerous women involved in religious work during the course of American history. In addition to those women who have made valuable contributions to religion in America, I have included a few whose religious prejudices have had a negative impact on American society. This volume also contains entries on several men in religion who have influenced the history of American women. I have endeavored to provide a balanced picture of American women and religion, drawing from diverse religious faiths, races, and ethnicities. There are many more women who have made valuable contributions to American religious history than have been included in this volume, and as further investigation is made into women's history, more details of women's involvement in religious activities will be uncovered.

For their help in completing this volume, I am indebted to many people. I wish to thank the host of librarians and archivists without whose help I could not have completed my research in a timely manner. I am particularly grateful to the employees in the reference section of the Selby branch and the interlibrary loan section of the Venice branch of the Sarasota County Library system, who have graciously and rapidly processed my many requests for books through interlibrary loan. Without their assistance, many months and miles would have been added to my project. I also wish to thank the representatives of the many women's organizations who responded to my inquiries and willingly provided me with information about the histories of their associations. To Todd Hallman of ABC-CLIO, I wish to express my appreciation for commissioning this book and for his supportive words and suggestions. I am grateful also to my friend Janice Daigle, who helped with some last-minute research via long distance. Most of all, I wish to thank my husband, Elliot Benowitz, who has patiently proofread my work and offered other valuable assistance.

Encyclopedia of
American Women and Religion

Abortion

The issue of abortion has been a concern of the clergy in America since colonial times. Until the nineteenth century, it was the tradition in most churches that "quickening," or the moment when the mother first perceived fetal movement (usually in the third month), marked the point at which the child acquired a soul. Thus if an abortion was performed early in the pregnancy, it was not a sin. Although abortion was not prohibited by law during the colonial era, ministers preached that deliberately terminating a pregnancy after quickening was equivalent to murder.

Some states became involved with the abortion issue during the 1820s, declaring that the deliberate termination of pregnancy after the fourth month was illegal. Among the states passing such laws were Connecticut (1821), Missouri (1827), and Illinois (1827). By 1840, ten of the twenty-six states had enacted similar laws. In the spirit of moral reform that began in America during the mid-nineteenth century, the churches reversed their tradition of condoning abortions performed during the first trimester. States too were placing stricter limits on the practice, many outlawing abortions at any stage of pregnancy. However, scholars have found that legal restrictions on abortion in the nineteenth and early twentieth centuries were instigated more by physicians and legislators than by pressures from the public or religious leaders. In his research into the history of abortion, James Mohr found that by 1900, largely through the efforts of the American Medical Association, abortion was virtually outlawed throughout the United States.

Despite the legal restrictions, women of all social classes continued to obtain abortions. Historians believe that prior to the 1840s, most abortion recipients were single women. However, the following decades found a great increase in instances of white, middle-class, married, Protestant women undergoing the procedure. Between 1800 and 1900, the fertility rate for white American women dropped by almost half—from 7.04 to 3.56 children per mother. Much of the drop has been attributed to abortion. Until the 1920s and 1930s women knew little of other methods of birth control in large part because the Comstock Law (1873) had labeled "obscene" most educational materials about birth control and made the mailing of such literature and devices illegal. With the lifting of federal bans against the distribution of birth control devices during the 1930s, more women were able to prevent conception and avoid abortion. Meanwhile, more laws that prohibited abortion were passed, until by 1965 all fifty states had anti-abortion laws in place. States did permit abortion if the mother's life was in jeopardy, and some state laws also made exceptions if the pregnancy resulted from rape or incest, or if the fetus was deformed.

With the 1973 Supreme Court decision in *Roe v. Wade,* holding that laws restricting abortion during the first trimester of pregnancy are unconstitutional, abortion became a central issue for a number of religious denominations. Some took the position that a woman had the right to make her own decision with regard to having an abortion, especially during the first trimester. At the same time, a number of conservative religious groups who were angered over the court decision began organizing in protest. Their strong opposition to abortion caused many religious and political conservatives to set aside their differences and to cooperate in support of a common goal. One of the most active anti-abortion groups was Operation Rescue, founded in 1984. Friends of the group's leader, Randall Terry, say that Terry began organizing his crusade after experiencing a religious vision. Operation Rescue has held large-scale demonstrations in opposition to abortion and has blockaded women's clinics where the procedures are performed.

A minority among those abortion opponents who describe themselves as "pro-life" have resorted to violence against abortion clinic personnel. Claiming that they have been directed by God to save babies from being killed, they have committed murder or attempted murder themselves. When three abortion clinics were bombed on Christmas Day, 1984, the four people who were tried and convicted of the crime identified themselves with Gideon, from the Old Testament, who slew those who sacrificed first-born infants to the god Baal. The perpetrators called the bombings "a birthday gift for Jesus" (Blanchard and Prewitt, 1993, p. ix). Within the churches themselves there is conflict regarding how far pro-life advocates should go in their demonstrations. In the mid-1990s a Roman Catholic archbishop, Bernard Cardinal Law of Boston, called for a moratorium on all protests outside abortion clinics. But, in 1995,

the archbishop of New York, John Cardinal O'Connor, said he would only call for a moratorium on protests if a moratorium was called on abortions.

See also: Birth Control; The Clergy Consultation Service on Abortion; Comstock Law
References: Dallas A. Blanchard and Terry J. Prewitt, *Religious Violence and Abortion: The Gideon Project* (1993); Marie Costa, *Abortion,* 2nd ed. (1996); Kathryn Cullen-DuPont with Annelise Orlick, *The Encyclopedia of Women's History in America* (1996); Elizabeth Frost-Knappman, *Women's Progress in America* (1994); Linda Gordon, *Woman's Body, Woman's Right: A Social History of Birth Control in America* (1977, reprint 1986); James Mohr, *Abortion in America: The Origins and Evolution of National Policy* (1978); Glenn H. Utter and John W. Storey, *The Religious Right: A Reference Handbook* (1995).

Ackerman, Paula (c. 1894–?)

Little is known about her early or later life, but Paula Ackerman was in the public spotlight for a brief time during her late fifties when she became the first woman to perform the functions of a rabbi. In 1951, she was chosen by the trustees of Temple Beth Israel, a Reform congregation in Meridian, Mississippi, to serve in place of her rabbi husband, William Ackerman, who had died in November 1950. The one-hundred-member congregation was the second-largest Jewish congregation in Mississippi. Ackerman held the position from 1951 to 1954, when a "regular" rabbi was selected and had all the authority and duties of a rabbi. This meant that she was preacher, counselor, teacher, and manager. The state of Mississippi gave her permission to perform marriages. Ackerman realized the significance of her position, writing, "If I can just plant a seed for the Jewish woman's larger participation, perhaps it will open a way for women students to train for congregational leadership, then my life would have some meaning" (Umansky, 1979, p. 345).

See also: Clergy; Jews; Priesand, Sally Jane
References: Tina Levitan, *First Facts in American Jewish History* (1996); Phyllis J.

Read and Bernard L. Witlieb, *The Book of Women's Firsts* (1992); Ellen M. Umansky, "Women in Judaism: From the Reform Movement to Contemporary Jewish Feminism," in Rosemary Radford Ruether and Eleanor McLaughlin, eds., *Women of Spirit: Female Leadership in the Jewish and Christian Traditions* (1979).

Adler, Margot (1946–)

Margot Adler, a major figure in the neo-Paganist movement, was born in Little Rock, Arkansas, on April 16, 1946. Margot was raised in a nonreligious family in New York City. Her father, Kurt Alfred Adler, was a psychiatrist and an atheist, and her mother, Freyda (Nacque) Adler, was an educator and a Jewish agnostic. Margot's grandfather was world-renowned psychiatrist Alfred Adler.

Margot became interested in Paganism at an early age. It was an interest that grew out of her fascination with ancient Greek gods and goddesses. While in high school, she sought to learn about a variety of religions, and she visited various churches. During her college years Margot developed an interest in politics, and she earned a bachelor of arts degree in political science from the University of California at Berkeley in 1968. She participated in the civil rights movement in the mid-1960s and joined the demonstrations at the Democratic convention in Chicago in 1968. From 1969 to 1970, Adler attended Columbia University, earning a master's degree in journalism. Her pursuit of a career in broadcast journalism led her to work for radio station WBAI from 1968 to 1977.

In the early 1970s Adler found a way to combine her interests in journalism, politics, and religion. She was particularly interested in the environment and saw a connection between environmental issues and religion. Adler found the Judeo-Christian belief in humankind's right to dominate the earth unacceptable and discovered that she agreed with paganistic and animistic religions that considered humankind a part of nature and the equal of all parts of nature. This discovery led her to explore Paganism and neo-Pagan organizations, and soon she was drawn to neo-Pagan witchcraft. Adler entered the Craft in 1972, originally through a study group in Brooklyn that was run by the New York Coven of Welsh Traditional Witches. When some members broke off from that coven to form a coven in the Gardnerian tradition (named for Gerald Brousseau Gardner, the person chiefly responsible for reviving witchcraft in the modern West), Adler followed. She was initiated as a first-degree Gardnerian priestess in 1973 and remained with the coven for about three years. Adler then established a Pagan Way Grove in Manhattan, which has served as an informal recruiting center for persons interested in neo-Paganism and witchcraft. In 1979 Adler completed and published *Drawing Down the Moon*, the first major work to chronicle in detail the emergence of neo-Paganism in the United States. An expanded and revised edition was published in 1986.

When Adler married her longtime companion, John Gliedman, on June 19, 1988, in a handfasting ceremony officiated by Wiccan-Pagan high priestess Selena Fox, it was the first Wiccan handfasting to be written up in the society pages of the *New York Times*.

Adler lectures and conducts workshops throughout the United States on Pagan spirituality, Goddess spirituality, and the polytheistic perspective on the modern world. She prefers to be called a Pagan rather than a witch because, although modern witchcraft has little or nothing to do with the witches and witchcraft of earlier times, the term "witch" continues to carry many negative associations.

See also: Fox, Selena; Handfasting; Wicca; Witchcraft

References: Margot Adler, *Drawing Down the Moon* (1986); Rosemary Ellen Guiley, *The Encyclopedia of Witches and Witchcraft* (1989); J. Gordon Melton, *Religious Leaders of America* (1991); Charlene Spretnak, ed., *The Politics of Women's Spirituality: Essays on the Rise of Spiritual Power within the Feminist Movement* (1982).

African Americans

Blacks came to America with their own religious traditions that were deeply embedded in their culture and expressed in everyday life. Although their religions were diverse, most were inclined toward monotheism. Animism, ancestor worship, and Islam were among the various beliefs to arrive in America with the Africans. The first blacks to arrive in British North America immigrated to Jamestown, Virginia, in the early seventeenth century as indentured servants, but the white settlers' need for labor soon led to the importation of black slaves from Africa. Separated from their roots, the Africans found it difficult to maintain their religions and other traditions, though throughout their history, African-American women have devoted considerable energy to maintaining tradition, especially religious tradition. Aspects of African culture did survive in some areas, especially in parts of South Carolina and Louisiana. Recently, black Americans have been seeking to restore African traditions to their culture. One result has been the observance of Kwanzaa, a family festival celebrated by some African Americans from December 26 through January 1.

The first black Christian women to settle in North America were probably Roman Catholic. The first known community of free black men and women, which dates from the end of the seventeenth century to 1763, was settled by blacks who arrived with the Spanish and was located just to the north and east of St. Augustine, Florida. The Spanish in Florida allowed escaped black slaves to remain as long as they converted to Catholicism. However, the Catholic clergy throughout the colonies usually accepted slavery and maintained a low profile on the issue. In 1763, Spain ceded Florida to Britain, and all Spaniards, black and white, migrated to Cuba. The Spanish returned in 1784, following the British defeat in the American Revolution, and remained in Florida until 1821, when the territory became a part of the United States.

During the seventeenth and eighteenth centuries, some African Americans converted to Christianity. However, it was not until the outburst of revivals during the Second Great Awakening (about 1795 to 1835) that blacks began converting to Christianity in large numbers. In addition to the revivals, missionaries and clergy conducted missions to the plantations, reminding slaveowners not only that it was their Christian duty to convert the "heathens" but that slaves would be more honest and submissive once they accepted Christianity. Masters often placed limits upon slaves' worship practices, as they were uneasy when blacks gathered without white supervision.

Rarely treated as equals in mixed churches, free blacks in the North began founding their own churches early in the nineteenth century. Preaching in black churches was usually reserved for men, but there were several exceptions, particularly among the Methodists. One notable exception was free black Jarena Lee, who was perhaps the first female preacher for the First African Methodist Episcopal Church. She began a long career as an evangelist in 1818. Later, Sojourner Truth, a former slave who converted to Methodism in 1827, became well known as an itinerant minister and for her advocacy for both abolition and women's rights.

The post–Civil War era of Reconstruction found large numbers of blacks leav-

Nannie Helen Burroughs and other African-American women formed the Women's Convention Auxiliary of the National Baptist Convention in the early 1900s.

ing white-dominated churches and founding their own denominations and congregations. This led to the rapid growth of the African Methodist Episcopal Church and the African Methodist Episcopal Zion Church and to the formation of the Colored Methodist Episcopal Church, Colored Primitive Baptists, and the Colored Cumberland Presbyterian Church, among others. The biggest growth was among black Baptist congregations, though it was not until 1895 that they united to form the National Baptist Convention. In the last quarter of the nineteenth century, the Holiness crusade enjoyed much success in the black Baptist and in the black Methodist churches, most of which had devotedly held to the traditional Wesleyan teaching on the second blessing of sanctification. A leader of the Holiness movement was Amanda

Berry Smith, a freed slave, Methodist, and attendee at Phoebe Palmer's "Tuesday Meetings for the Promotion of Holiness." The Holiness movement stressed the achievement of a state of perfection through "sanctification," a religious experience that followed conversion.

African-American men and women played an important role in the Pentecostal movement (c. 1890–1920), an outgrowth of the Holiness movement. Women in Pentecostal churches could become evangelists or missionaries but not pastors or bishops. However, elder Ida Robinson of Philadelphia was an exception. Upset over men's domination over women and their refusal to ordain women into the ministry, she founded the Mount Sinai Holy Church and became America's first black bishop. Most of her pastors and bishops were women.

Throughout the twentieth century, African-American women have struggled for opportunities to hold responsible positions within the hierarchies of their churches. To overcome the limits placed upon them by black males, significant numbers of African-American women have sought alternatives to the mainline black denominations. Some black Baptist women have joined the integrated but white-dominated American Baptist Convention, which favors female ordination. Others have chosen to join black spiritual churches. Studies have found that approximately two-thirds of the members of the black spiritual churches are female. A recent examination of spiritual congregations in New Orleans found that about three-quarters of the pastors were women.

Despite the barriers to full participation in many of their churches, African-American women compose the majority of the population in black denominational churches. They are also heavily involved in church-related programs. According to one estimate, women represent 75 to 90 percent of the participants in all varieties of black religious activity.

See also: Harris, Barbara Clementine; Kelly, Leontine Turpeau Current; King, Coretta Scott; Lee, Jarena; Truth, Sojourner
References: Hans A. Baer, *The Black Spiritual Movement: A Religious Response to Racism* (1984); Hans A. Baer and Merrill Singer, *African-American Religion in the Twentieth Century: Varieties of Protest and Accommodation* (1992); Cyprian Davis, *The History of Black Catholics in the United States* (1992); Leslie H. Fishel, Jr., and Benjamin Quarles, *The Negro American: A Documentary History* (1967); Cheryl Townsend Gilkes, "'Together in Harness': Women's Traditions in the Sanctified Church," in Micheline R. Malson et al., *Black Women in America: Social Science Perspectives* (1990); Evelyn Brooks Higginbotham, *Righteous Discontent: The Women's Movement in the Black Baptist Church, 1880–1920* (1993); Susan Hill Lindley, *"You Have Stept Out of Your Place": A History of Women and Religion in America* (1996); Vinson Synan, *The Holiness-Pentecostal Tradition: Charismatic Movements in the Twentieth Century,* 2nd ed. (1997); Delores S. Williams, *Sisters in the Wilderness: The Challenge of Womanist God-Talk* (1993).

Aitken, Jane (1764–1832)

An early woman publisher, Jane Aitken was probably the first woman to print the Bible in the United States. Born in Paisley, Scotland, on July 11, 1764, she emigrated to Philadelphia with her parents, Robert and Janet (Skeoch) Aitken in 1771, where her father established a bookbinding, publishing, and stationery business. Robert Aitken published the first English Bible in the United States in 1782. (It had been illegal to print Bibles in colonial America, since only firms granted permission by the King could print English Bibles and these firms were all in England.) Little of Jane's early life is known, but it is likely that she assisted her father with his work. Upon Robert Aitken's death in 1802, Jane inherited a $3,000 debt plus the care of two younger sisters. Apparently, she had been trained in her father's business, for she immediately carried on with his work. The most important among the more than sixty books that she published during her career was the four-volume Thomson Bible. This Bible, published in 1808, was a translation by Charles Thomson of the Septuagint (the Greek version of the Old Testament).

Although she was known for her exceptional skill at bookbinding, Aitken was unable to overcome the inherited debt and was forced to sell the business in 1813. She was briefly jailed for debt in 1819 before bankruptcy laws were revised to disallow imprisonment for debt. Although she was able to lease back her bookbinding business, her listing disappeared from the Philadelphia city directory after 1820. From then on, little else is known of her life. Aitken died in Germantown, Pennsylvania, on August 29, 1832.

References: Edward T. James, ed., *Notable American Women, 1607–1950* (1971); Frederick E. Maser, "The Day America Needed Bibles," in *Religion in Life*, vol. 45 (1976); Phyllis J. Read and Bernard L. Witlieb, *The Book of Women's Firsts* (1992).

American Missionary Association

Founded in 1846, the American Missionary Association (AMA) was the most influential of the northern religious associations to work among African Americans after the Civil War. Prior to the war, the AMA promoted the abolitionist cause and served as a vehicle for northern Protestants to use Christian gospel in the fight against slavery. After President Abraham Lincoln's Emancipation Proclamation of January 1, 1863, declaring that all slaves in the rebellious South were "forever free," the AMA began sending missionaries southward to work with the freed African Americans. By the end of the Civil War, the AMA had employed more than 250 teachers and preachers, black and white, male and female, to participate in what it called the "ecclesiastical and Christian reconstruction" of the South (Queen, 1996, p. 24). Most of the organization's administrators and supervisors were men, whereas women usually served the AMA as teachers. By 1870 several thousand northerners had journeyed to the South to educate the emancipated blacks, and more than 90 percent of the volunteers were female.

The vast majority of women going South were white and of the middle or upper classes. They were usually young and single or widows of men who had lost their lives in the war. Some historians have speculated that the white women chose to serve the AMA because it offered them the opportunity to escape the limits placed on women by nineteenth-century society. Black women frequently enlisted in the cause for the purpose of "uplifting" their people. Sara G. Stanley, one African American who answered the AMA's call, did so because she felt that work among the freed people would bring her closer to God.

Once they reached the South, many women found that the path they had chosen was not easy. Some had difficulty adjusting to the hard work and harsh climate. Many became ill, and a few of the women died. Black women teachers found that despite their pretensions of empathy for the freed slaves, some white AMA associates were racist and treated their black coworkers as inferiors. Black women also found that the AMA had a double standard, employing white women if they supported a child but disqualifying blacks who were in similar circumstances. After 1870, the majority of the white women returned north, although black women remained in the South, determined to "uplift" their race.

During Reconstruction, the AMA staffed and funded primary schools as well as several black colleges, including Hampton Normal and Agricultural Institute in Virginia, where the famous African-American leader Booker T. Washington studied. Other schools established for blacks by the AMA included Atlanta University, Fisk University in Nashville, and Howard University in Washington, D.C. Once the AMA's focus turned to black colleges, the role of women within the organization diminished. Missionary work was abandoned in the South after Reconstruction ended, and the AMA began to focus primarily on home missions work among Native Americans. The AMA's work was not limited to the United States, however; it also employed agents in Canada and overseas. In the twentieth century, the AMA lost its autonomy and was absorbed into what is now the United Church of Christ.

See also: Missionary Societies
References: Thomas F. Armstrong, "The American Missionary Association," in Angela Howard Zophy with Frances M. Kavenik, eds., *Handbook of American Women's History* (1990); Linda M. Perkins, "The Black Female American Missionary Association Teacher in the South, 1861–1870," in Darlene Clark Hine, ed., *Black Women in United States History,* vol. 3 (1990); Edward L. Queen II et al., *The Encyclopedia of American Religious History* (1996); Judith Weisenfeld, "'Who Is Sufficient for These Things?' Sara G. Stanley and the American Missionary Association, 1864–1868," in *Church History* 60, no. 4 (December 1991), 493–507.

Amish

One of several religious groups evolving out of the sixteenth-century Anabaptist movement, the Amish emerged following a split with the Mennonites during the late seventeenth century. At that time Jacob Ammann, a young Swiss elder, broke with the Mennonites when he perceived that there were impurities in the church and that the Mennonites were not upholding the doctrine of strict separation from the world. Those who followed Ammann became known as the "Ammann-ish," and soon "Amish." During the eighteenth century, the Amish, like hundreds of thousands of other Europeans, saw North America as a land of opportunity to escape religious persecution and begin a new life. Between 1736 and 1770, about five hundred Amish immigrants settled in eastern Pennsylvania. After the American Revolution, until 1810, several more families settled in the Midwest. A larger number of Amish immigrants—about three thousand persons—arrived in North America between 1817 and 1860. Some settled in Pennsylvania, but most eventually moved to Ohio, Illinois, Indiana, New York, Iowa, or Ontario, Canada.

Most of the Amish arriving in America were farmers. Men worked in the fields, while their wives performed the domestic duties. If a wife was left a widow, her children who took over the management of the farm were obligated to supply their mother with ample produce for survival.

During the Great Awakening of the mid-eighteenth century, many Amish left the church when they were drawn by revivalists into Methodism, Baptism, the United Brethren, or the German Baptist Brethren. It has been estimated that less than 40 percent of the first-generation Amish retained the Amish tradition. Divisions among the Amish themselves resulted in congregations taking separate paths during the nineteenth century, when some chose to adapt (to some degree) to modern American society by wearing more mainstream clothing, enjoying a more formal and extended education, and holding government office. The tradition-minded Amish became known as the "Old Order Amish," and those who were change-minded became known as "Amish Mennonites." Later tensions led to the creation of more branches of Amish believers.

The plain clothing of the Old Order Amish men and women physically demonstrates humility and separation from the world. Women wear prayer coverings on their heads as a sign of obedience to the Bible. Amish women are taught to obey their husbands but usually feel free to express their opinions within their households. Mary Swander, who wrote of time she spent among the Amish in *Out of the World: A Woman's Life among the Amish,* concluded that Amish women are valued for their cleverness, muscle, and hardworking nature more than for their looks. Though Amish women seldom have careers, they frequently supplement the family income by making and selling quilts and other crafts. Sue Bender, who also spent some time among the Amish, noted in *Plain and Simple: A Woman's Journey to the Amish* that everything in their lives is a

Amish woman raking hay (1975)

ritual, including household responsibilities and work on their farms as well as churchgoing and daily prayer. Their entire lives reflect their faith.

The church hierarchy is entirely male. During Sunday services women and men sit on opposite sides of their church, or if services are held in a home, they frequently sit in separate rooms. Amish children sit in the room with the mothers, and since the women normally have eight to ten children, the women's room can become crowded. After the morning church service, the worshippers gather for a feast that is prepared and served by the women.

Since the 1972 Supreme Court decision in *Wisconsin v. Yoder,* the Amish have had the right to educate their own children. Formal schooling in Amish communities typically ends after the eighth grade. This is because the Amish fear that education beyond that level might lead the student toward a feeling of self-importance. Often their teachers

are young Amish women who have recently completed the eighth grade themselves.

During their youth, Amish boys and girls are often allowed to experiment with practices considered to be of the world. These might include smoking or driving an automobile. Amish elders hope that after some exploration of the larger world, the young will realize the value of Amish belief and tradition. When the young man or woman feels ready to completely accept the Amish way of life, he or she is formally baptized into the faith.

Louise Stoltzfeus, in *Amish Women: Lives and Stories,* concludes that, at least on the surface, Amish life thrives for three reasons: People who are born into the Amish community find it difficult to sever ties to their church, family, and community; church members learn to submit to the absolute will of the community; and church leaders extend a severe form of punishment—shunning—to those who digress. She also found that members do not blindly submit to the decisions of their leaders but take time to discuss new ideas. Although women have no vote in church affairs, when they are together at quiltings or reunions, they often discuss matters relating to the community. However, once a decision to adopt a new rule has been made, both men and women are expected to conform.

See also: Mennonites
References: Sue Bender, *Plain and Simple: A Woman's Journey to the Amish* (1989); Steven M. Nolt, *A History of the Amish* (1992); Louise Stoltzfeus, *Amish Women: Lives and Stories* (1994); Mary Swander, *Out of the World: A Woman's Life among the Amish* (1995).

Barbara Andrews (December 1970)

Andrews, Barbara (1935–1978)

Barbara Andrews was the first woman to be ordained a minister in the American Lutheran Church. She was born with cerebral palsy on May 11, 1935, in Minneapolis, Minnesota, and lived her life in a wheelchair that she did not have the strength to propel. Throughout her life, she relied upon family, friends, and caregivers to meet her basic needs. Nevertheless, Andrews was an independent woman and performed on her own every task she possibly could.

While serving on the staff of Lutheran Campus Ministry at the University of Minnesota at St. Paul, Andrews studied at the Lutheran Theological Seminary in the hope of becoming a Lutheran minister. In 1964, the seminary accepted Andrews as its first full-time female student and granted her the right to take homiletics and other preordination courses. Andrews graduated from the seminary in 1969 but was not ordained until December 22, 1970, two months after the American Lutheran Church approved the ordination of women.

Within two months of her ordination, she was invited to be pastor at Edina Community Lutheran Church in Edina, Minnesota. She received and accepted a call to serve as chaplain at Luther Haven Nursing Home in Detroit in 1974, even though this required her to move away from her support network in Minneapolis-St. Paul. The elderly people she served at Luther Haven found in Andrews a pastor who, like them, was physically frail and who sat in her wheelchair at their bedsides, speaking to them eye to eye. Andrews became known for her good listening ability and her playfulness. After two and a half years at the nursing home, she resigned to accept a call as interim pastor at Resurrection Lutheran Church in Detroit.

On March 31, 1978, Andrews died in a fire in her Detroit apartment. Her contributions as a woman who overcame her disabilities to become the first female Lutheran pastor were not forgotten. Barbara Andrews was posthumously awarded the Faithfulness in Ministry Cross by Luther Theological Seminary on January 5, 1995.

See also: Clergy; Lutheran Church
References: Gracia Grindal, "How Lutheran Women Came to Be Ordained," in Gloria E. Bengtson, ed., *Lutheran Women in Ordained Ministry, 1970–1995* (1995); Phyllis J. Read and Bernard L. Witlieb, *The Book of Women's Firsts* (1992); Susan Thompson, "Barbara Andrews," in Gloria E. Bengtson, ed., *Lutheran Women in Ordained Ministry, 1970–1995* (1995); Caroline Zilboorg, ed., *Women's Firsts* (1997).

Andrews, Lynn V. (1945–)

Author, teacher, and medicine woman Lynn V. Andrews was born in 1945. Although much of her writing is autobiographical, she has kept details of her early life to herself. In *Medicine Woman* (1981), her first autobiographical account, Andrews details how she, a wealthy Beverly Hills wife, mother, and art collector and dealer, began a search for personal spirit guides. She became fascinated with a Cree Indian marriage basket she saw in a photograph at an art exhibit and was determined to possess it.

While searching for the mysterious basket, Andrews met two Cree medicine women, Ruby Plenty Chiefs and Agnes Whistling Elk. She remained with them for six months and shared their simple lifestyle while they taught her their shamanic secrets. Under their guidance, Andrews acquired the determination and the courage to enable her to recover the basket that Plenty Chiefs and Whistling Elk told her was woven from the dreams of all women and represented female wisdom and the power of creation. But the basket was in the possession of a man, the male sorcerer Red Dog, whom Andrews would need to fight to retrieve it. In a battle in a world outside physical reality, Andrews fought Red Dog, defeated him, obtained the basket, and thereby freed her powerful spiritual self. She then learned that it was her calling to help correct the imbalance between male and female energies that is disrupting the world.

Andrews wrote several best-selling books in which she recounted a series of fantastic adventures. Eventually she was initiated into an ancient, secret organization of native women known as the Sisterhood of the Shields and was given the responsibility of revealing the teachings of the sisterhood to the outside world. Since then she has led seminars in which she spreads her newly found knowledge. Andrews told Beth Ann Krier, who interviewed her for the *Los Angeles Times,* that she was attempting to fulfill her destiny to be "a bridge between the primal mind and white consciousness" (Trotsky, 1992, p. 11). When she is not teaching, Andrews spends time with shamans around the world, learning various mystical techniques for use in her practice.

Although critics have praised Andrews's exploration of shamanism, her claim that the events recounted in her books are true stories has become controversial. Criticisms have come from scholars and from Native Americans who question the authenticity of her accounts. Although she has been a popular figure within New Age circles, she has even drawn criticism from members of that group for the same reasons. According to Krier, Andrews's detractors "find her adventures too strange or plentiful to have occurred in a relatively short length of time" (Trotsky, 1992, p. 11). Professor Buck Ghost Horse, a specialist in Native American culture and spirituality, agrees: "You talk to our medicine people and they say you have to study years and years" (Trotsky, 1992, p. 11). Nevertheless, Andrews has continued to insist that all the tales of her experiences are true.

In addition to *Medicine Woman,* Andrews's many writings include *Flight of the Seventh Moon* (1984); *Jaguar Woman* (1985); *Star Woman* (1986); *Crystal Woman* (1987); *Teachings around the Sacred Wheel* (1990); and, most recently, *Walk in Spirit: Prayers for the Seasons of Life* (1996).

References: Lynn V. Andrews, *Crystal Woman: The Sisters of the Dreamtime* (1987); Lynn V. Andrews, *Medicine Woman* (1981); J. Gordon Melton, *Religious Leaders of America* (1991); Susan M. Trotsky, ed., *Contemporary Authors,* vol. 129 (1990).

Anti-Semitism

Anti-Semitism, or prejudices displayed through hostile utterances or negative behavior toward individuals or groups because of their Jewish faith or tradition, has existed in America since early settlement. For centuries Christian Europeans made Jews scapegoats in times of trouble, and they carried that tradition to an overwhelmingly Christian America. During the course of history, anti-Semitism has surged and waned, usually coinciding with unrest and calm, respectively, within American society. Anti-Semitism reached a peak during the economic depression of the 1890s, a time when Jews were immigrating to the United States in vast numbers. Overt anti-Semitism declined over the next two decades but rose again during the general unrest following World War I. After a short respite amid the prosperity of the 1920s, anti-Semitism peaked again during the Great Depression and was strong during the early stages of World War II. By the closing days of the war, there were signs that some people were intent on denying the Holocaust: Extreme isolationists like Freda Utley were arguing that during the conflict the United States committed atrocities of as great or greater magnitude than Nazi Germany's.

American women have been both victims and instigators of anti-Semitism. For many years Jewish women (and men) faced discrimination in the workplace, were restricted from social clubs and various recreational facilities, and encountered prejudice within educational institutions. For instance, in 1939 three young Jewish women who were students at the Dental Hygienist School at the University of Minnesota were encouraged to drop out of the program since, as Jews, they would be unlikely to find work in their chosen field. Fanning the flames of anti-Semitism in the late 1930s and early 1940s were women such as Elizabeth Dilling and Agnes Waters. Waters, a rabid anti-Semite, attempted to convince Americans that there were hundreds of thousands of Jews waiting in Mexico with intentions of invading the United States and raping the country's women. Since the close of World War II, overt anti-Semitism has waned. Christian churches, especially since the war, have themselves denounced anti-Semitism. It continues to exist, as evidenced by small groups of Holocaust deniers circulating propaganda materials on college campuses during the 1990s, but blatant discrimination against Jews appears to be no longer acceptable to the American mainstream.

See also: Dilling, Elizabeth Kirkpatrick (Stokes)
References: June Melby Benowitz, "Speaking Out: Right-Wing American Women, 1933 to 1945" (Ph.D. diss., 1996); Leonard Dinnerstein, *Antisemitism in America* (1994); John Higham, *Send These to Me: Jews and Other Immigrants in Urban America,* revised ed. (1984); Frederic Cople Jaher, *A Scapegoat in the Wilderness: The Origins and Rise of Anti-Semitism in America* (1994); Deborah E. Lipstadt, *Denying the Holocaust: The Growing Assault on Truth and Memory* (1993); Charles Herbert Stember, *Jews in the Mind of America* (1966).

Antislavery Movement

In the 1830s and 1840s, a time when an increasing number of Americans were seeking to reform their society into one that was as morally perfect as possible, many men and women became caught up in the movement to abolish slavery. The question of manumission had been raised in the past, particularly during the years after the signing of the Declaration of Independence, when freedom for slaves was mentioned in conjunction with rhetoric propounding liberty, equality, and justice for all, but it was not until the second third of the nineteenth century that the concept developed into a movement.

Women's roles within the movement might have remained passive had it not been for William Lloyd Garrison, a leader of the relatively small radical wing of the antislavery movement. When Garrison established his abolitionist weekly, *The Liberator,* in 1831, he issued a call to both men and women to participate in the antislavery crusade. Although nineteenth-century society deemed it inappropriate for women to become involved in public affairs, their religious faith motivated a number of women to answer his call. Contending that God would punish a nation that allowed the institution of slavery, Maria Stewart, a free African American, lectured on the sins of slavery and published articles in *The Liberator.* Other women to respond included two prominent Boston Unitarians, Maria Weston Chapman, a founder of the Boston Female Anti-Slavery Society in 1832, and Lydia Maria Child, who authored *Appeal on Behalf of That Class of Americans Called Africans* (1833). Quakers had a lengthier history of opposition to slavery than most other religions, and women of that faith made up a large proportion of the abolitionists. Lucretia Mott, a Quaker minister, led in the organizing of the Philadelphia Female Anti-Slavery Society in 1833, which, like the Boston society, included both black and white women. Sarah and Angelina Grimké, South Carolina sisters who had moved north and converted to the Quaker faith, became the first white agents for the movement. They created

considerable controversy, especially among New England clergy, when they drew audiences of men as well as women on their lecture tours.

Female activists in the antislavery movement found that despite their dedication to the crusade, they were rarely treated as equals. Few men joined Garrison in support of women's full participation in the movement and, largely due to that issue, in May 1840 a split developed in the American Anti-Slavery Society. Later that year, women were refused seats at the World Anti-Slavery Convention in London, England. Their rejection from the convention was not soon forgotten and was a major motivating factor in the decision of Lucretia Mott, Elizabeth Cady Stanton, and others to call the first woman's rights convention in 1848. The women's rights movement that followed is seen by many historians as being directly linked to the antislavery campaign.

See also: Garrison, William Lloyd; Grimké, Angelina Emily; Grimké, Sarah Moore; Mott, Lucretia Coffin; Perfectionism; Stanton, Elizabeth Cady; Woman Suffrage
References: Eleanor Flexner, *Century of Struggle: The Woman's Rights Movement in the United States* (1970); Blanche Glassman Hersh, *The Slavery of Sex: Feminist Abolitionists in America* (1978); Susan Hill Lindley, *"You Have Stept Out of Your Place": A History of Women and Religion in America* (1996); James Brewer Stewart, *Holy Warriors: The Abolitionists and American Slavery* (1976).

Arendt, Hannah (1906–1975)

Philosopher and political theorist, Hannah Arendt was born in Hanover, Germany, to Jewish parents, Martha Cohn Arendt and Paul Arendt, on October 14, 1906. She received an excellent education, culminating in her graduation from the University of Heidelberg with a doctorate in philosophy in 1929. During Hitler's rise to power, she was arrested for being a Jew. In 1933 she fled to Paris, where she soon became active in the newly created Youth Aliyah, a division of Hadassah that was devoted to the relocation and care of Jewish children. When France fell to Hitler, Arendt escaped to New York. She became a naturalized citizen of the United States in 1951.

While in New York, Arendt wrote essays for Jewish magazines, taught history at Brooklyn College, and was director of research at the Conference on Jewish Relations. From 1946 to 1948 she was an editor at Schocken Books. She also worked for several other publications during the 1940s. In 1951 she published what would become her most widely read book, *The Origins of Totalitarianism,* which traced the history of anti-Semitism, imperialism, and totalitarianism. It was the first post–World War II study of totalitarianism and was tremendously influential. In the book, Arendt compared the Soviet Union and Nazi Germany and drew some controversy over her assertion that Communism and Nazism were similar. In 1961 Arendt, as a reporter for the *New Yorker,* attended the trial of Adolf Eichmann for his leading role in the extermination of European Jews. She later wrote a book, *Eichmann in Jerusalem: A Report on the Banality of Evil* (1963), in which she questioned the legality of the trial, portrayed the convicted Nazi war criminal as an average bureaucrat, and placed blame upon Jewish leaders for forsaking their fellow Jews. The book proved highly controversial and cost her many friends. Other works by Arendt include *The Human Condition* (1958), *On Revolution* (1963), *Men in Dark Times* (1968), *On Violence* (1970), and *Crises of the Republic* (1972).

In addition to writing, Arendt continued her teaching career. She was invited to Princeton as a visiting professor in 1959 and was the first woman to become a full professor at that institution. She was a professor of political science at the University of Chicago from 1963 until she left to accept a teaching position at the New School for Social Research in New York City in 1967. Arendt died in New York City on December 4, 1975.

See also: Hadassah; Jews
References: Hannah Arendt, *Eichmann in Jerusalem: A Report on the Banality of Evil* (1963); Hannah Arendt, *The Human Condition* (1958); Hannah Arendt, *On Revolution* (1963); Hannah Arendt, *The Origins of Totalitarianism* (1951, 1973); Seyla Benhabib, *The Reluctant Modernism of Hannah Arendt* (1996); Kathryn Cullen-DuPont, with Annelise Orleck, *The Encyclopedia of Women's History in America* (1996); Elizabeth Frost-Knappman, *Women's Progress in America* (1994); Phillip Hanson, *Hannah Arendt: Politics, History, and Citizenship* (1993); Barbara Sicherman and Carol Hurd Green, eds., *Notable American Women: The Modern Period* (1980).

Armstrong, Annie Walker (1850–1938)

Cofounder and first corresponding secretary of the Woman's Missionary Union (WMU) of the Southern Baptist Convention, Annie Walker Armstrong was born July 11, 1850, in Baltimore, Maryland. Her father, James Dunn Armstrong, died when Annie was two, but the family was left in comfortable circumstances from money made in tobacco. Mary Walker Armstrong, Annie's mother, was a devout Christian and a member of the early Southern Baptist women's missionary group, Woman's Mission to Woman. Annie, however, had little interest in religion and did not convert until she was nineteen years old, at which time she was baptized into the Seventh Baptist Church of Baltimore. In 1871, she left that church to join the Eutaw Place Baptist Church, where she taught the infant class for the next thirty years. Armstrong took up missions work in 1882 when she became involved in efforts to aid a school for Native Americans. From then on she worked wholeheartedly in missions programs and was soon known as a powerful advocate of home missions.

In 1886 Armstrong answered the call for women to help a group of Maryland Baptist ministers publish literature that would inform the convention of various missionary projects and opportunities. She became the secretary and editor in chief of the Maryland Baptist Mission Rooms and quickly built it into a major publisher of missionary literature. In 1887 Armstrong and Martha E. McIntosh of Charleston, South Carolina, proposed the formation of a national organization of Southern Baptist women. Their plans were realized in 1888 when Armstrong chaired the organizational meeting of the Woman's Missionary Union of the Southern Baptist Convention in Baltimore. McIntosh was the group's first president, and Armstrong became the WMU's first corresponding secretary.

Over the next eighteen years, Armstrong worked to help not only the missionary cause but also the entire Baptist convention. Her work was full-time and without remuneration. As head of the WMU, she led fund-raising campaigns, began a statistic-gathering program, and corresponded with missionaries and pastors on the frontier. She also developed the idea for a church building loan fund. Armstrong launched a number of missionary efforts, among minorities in particular, instructing local members on how to organize missionary societies. Working closely with Nannie Burroughs, she helped to form an organization for African-American women that was similar to the white WMU. Through her work with WMU, Armstrong became one of the most knowledgeable persons on the condition of the Southern Baptist Church, both at home and abroad.

Despite a dislike for travel, Armstrong made several trips to Oklahoma to meet with and preach to the Native Americans there. However, even if invited to do so,

she refused to speak to mixed audiences, and she was adamantly opposed to women appearing in the pulpit or in a ministerial role. Although she firmly believed that women had a right to perform volunteer work in missions, she dismissed as absurd any suggestion that her work contributed to the cause of women's rights. Her thoughts on femininity put her into conflict with other women leaders. When the Woman's Missionary Union proposed a training school for women, Armstrong vehemently opposed it. Her position brought on such strong criticism that she resigned in 1905, although she remained at her post for another year to allow time for the WMU to find a replacement. But in 1906 she closed her office in Baltimore and passed the work on to some volunteers. Her resignation did not end her missionary work, for she participated in local activities. Despite the conflicts at the end of her tenure with the WMU, the convention appreciated her many years of service and honored her in 1934 by naming the annual home mission's offering after her.

Bedridden during the final years of her life, Armstrong died in Baltimore on December 20, 1938.

See also: Burroughs, Nannie Helen; McIntosh, Martha E. (Bell); Missionary Societies; Woman's Missionary Union
References: Catherine B. Allen, *Laborers Together with God: 22 Great Women in Baptist Life* (1987); Clifton Judson Allen et al., eds., *Encyclopedia of Southern Baptists* (1958); O. K. Armstrong and Marjorie M. Armstrong, *The Indomitable Baptists: A Narrative of Their Role in Shaping American History* (1967); Paul Harvey, *Redeeming the South: Religious Cultures and Racial Identities among Southern Baptists, 1865–1925* (1997); J. Gordon Melton, *Religious Leaders of America* (1991).

Ashbridge, Elizabeth Sampson Sullivan (1713–1755)

Autobiographer and renowned Quaker female minister, Elizabeth Sampson Ashbridge was born in England in 1713. She was the only child of Thomas and Mary Sampson, who raised her in the Anglican faith. Ashbridge's elopement at the age of fourteen against her parents' wishes left her estranged from her father, so that when she was widowed a few months after her marriage, she was not permitted to return to her childhood home. Instead, she went to live with relatives in Ireland. Ashbridge emigrated to New York as an indentured servant in 1732. She soon found herself in the service of a cruel master whom she had initially believed was a religious man. This brought her to have doubts about all religions. Her exceptional skills at needlework allowed her to earn sufficient money to buy herself out of her last year of indentureship. Not long after gaining her freedom, Ashbridge married a man named Sullivan who was impressed with her dancing abilities. He turned out to be an abusive husband.

During her marriage to Sullivan, Ashbridge began to explore other religions and worshipped briefly in the Baptist and the Presbyterian churches. While visiting relatives in Philadelphia, she became familiar with the teachings of the Society of Friends and soon converted to the Quaker faith. Her adoption of the Quaker religion changed her life. Her husband disapproved of her conversion because, like most Americans of the era, he considered Quakers a peculiar people whose language, dress, behavior, and beliefs were outside the mainstream. He dragged her from town to town as he sought to sever her from her new religious beliefs. On one occasion he attempted to test her conversion to Quakerism by forcing her to dance with him at a Philadelphia Tavern. The persecution she suffered as a result of her religious convictions only served to strengthen her faith.

Following Sullivan's death in 1746, Ashbridge married for the third time. Her new husband, Aaron Ashbridge, was also a Quaker, and he encouraged her work as an itinerant minister. Elizabeth was apparently a skillful rhetorician who was able to adapt her style of delivery to fit the audience and the occasion. In 1753 she carried her preaching to England and Ireland and died in Ireland two years later. By the time of her death, her preaching had earned her great respect among Quakers in America, England, and Ireland. Her autobiography, which appeared under various titles, including *Remarkable Experiences in the Life of Elizabeth Ashbridge* and *Some Account of the Fore-Part of the Life of Elizabeth Ashbridge,* which was published in 1774, gives a narrative account of the trials she faced in the American colonies, both as a woman and as a convert to Quakerism.

See also: Society of Friends (Quakers)
References: Cristine M. Levenduski, "Elizabeth Sampson Ashbridge," in Angela Howard Zophy with Frances M. Kavenik, eds., *Handbook of American Women's History* (1990); Cristine M. Levenduski, *Peculiar Power: A Quaker Woman Preacher in Eighteenth-Century America* (1996); Daniel B. Shea, *Spiritual Autobiography in Early America* (1968).

Asian Americans

Asian Americans are a broad and diverse group of people that include many different ethnicities, practicing many different religions. Asian Americans encompass Chinese Americans, Japanese Americans, Korean Americans, Vietnamese Americans, Americans from India, Pakistan, Iran, the Philippines, and Pacific Islands such as Guam, and others. Among each of these various peoples several religions are practiced. For instance, many Chinese practice Confucianism, which is a moral code and pattern of social organization. But Taoism, Buddhism, and, to a lesser extent, Christianity, are also important. All of these were present in

China and were carried and maintained by Chinese who came to America.

For the most part, Asian American women come from male-dominated cultures. In the United States the self-definition of ethnic groups and their relations to each other has been slowly shifting. The same is true of male-female relations. As Fumitaka Matsuoka says in *Out of Silence,* women in church are in a double bind. Asian Americans suffer racial discrimination, but Asian American women also suffer sexual discrimination. Yet Asian American women also find greater opportunities for development in American society. For example, among Korean Americans, who are largely Christian and self- or family-employed, the church serves partly as a center for developing business contacts. Since many Korean American women are self-employed, the church serves in this way as a vehicle of self-development for them.

As the number of immigrants from Asia has increased, Asian religions have grown in their importance in American culture. The United States is basically a religious country, and religion is an accepted way of maintaining one's own group identity while doing as Americans do. Asian religions in the United States are dynamic and adapting. Some non–Asian Americans are adopting Islam, Hinduism, the Parsi religion, Sikhism, and Buddhism. For instance, American Ruth Fuller Everett Sasaki, who was raised in the Presbyterian faith, converted to Buddhism as a young woman and was a major popularizer of Buddhism in America during the late 1930s to early 1940s.

For many of the Asian societies the very definition of "woman" has been different from that in the West. These concepts of womanhood and their evolution in American society are a complex, mutually enriching, and ongoing process.

See also: Buddhists; Muslims; Sasaki, Ruth Fuller Everett
References: Louise H. Hunter, *Buddhism in Hawaii: Its Impact on a Yankee Community* (1971); Victoria Hynchu Kuron, *Entrepreneurship and Religion: Korean Immigrants in Houston, Texas* (1997); Karen Isaksen Leonard, *The South Asian Americans* (1997); Fumitaka Matsuoka, *Out of Silence: Emerging Themes in Asian American Churches* (1995); Charles S. Prebish, *American Buddhism* (1979); Paul Rutledge, *The Role of Religion in Ethnic Self-Identity* (1985); Steve S. Shim, *Korean Immigrant Churches Today in Southern California* (1977).

Association of Southern Women for the Prevention of Lynching

Founded in Atlanta in 1930 by Jessie Daniel Ames, the Association of Southern Women for the Prevention of Lynching (ASWPL) was an association of white women who worked through church organizations to protest the lynching of African-American men. These women pledged that their association would do everything in its power "to create a new public opinion in the South which will not condone for any reason whatever acts of mobs or lynchers" (ASWPL Bulletin No. 4, p. 2). In the 1930s an increasing number of southern women were taking a stand against lynching. As they became more educated, sophisticated, and independent, many came to realize that what they had once considered male chivalry was in many ways a means of controlling and repressing women. They now understood that lynching, which was often based on false charges of rape, was not only immoral but was an extension of male domination. Although many of the women had not previously participated in political activities, their hatred of lynching inspired them to publicly deny the truth of the idea that black men were lynched because they had raped white women.

With much of its initial backing coming from the Methodist Church, the anti-lynching movement grew until the women of the ASWPL numbered in the thousands. In 1934, the Southern Methodist Woman's Missionary Council voiced unanimous support for a federal law that would outlaw lynching. Probably referring to the ASWPL, in 1935 the editors of *Woman's Home Companion* announced that seventeen thousand women had organized in eight southern states and were "actively working to stamp out lynching and the perverted sentiment that inspires it" (*Woman's Home Companion*, August 1935). The ASWPL disbanded in 1942 after several years of a marked decline in the numbers of lynchings.

See also: Reform Movements
References: Association of Southern Women for the Prevention of Lynching, "The Business of Lynching," Bulletin No. 4, no date; June Melby Benowitz, "Speaking Out: Right-Wing American Women, 1933 to 1945" (Ph.D. diss., 1996); "The Drive against Lynching," *Woman's Home Companion* (August 1935); Jacqueline Dowd Hall, *Revolt against Chivalry: Jessie Daniel Ames and the Women's Campaign against Lynching* (1979); Susan Hill Lindley, *"You Have Stept Out of Your Place": A History of Women and Religion in America* (1996).

Ayres, Anne (1816–1896)

Anne Ayres, the first woman to be consecrated an Episcopal sister and the founder of the first American sisterhood, was born to Robert and Anne Ayres in London, England, on January 3, 1816. Little is known of her background and early life. Ayres emigrated with her parents to New York City in 1836. Shortly after her arrival, she became a teacher to the daughters of wealthy parents. Through her students, she met and became acquainted with the Reverend William Augustus Mühlenberg, the head of a church college on Long Island. In 1845, she was inspired by one of his sermons to devote the rest of her life to serving Christ. At that time, no sisterhoods existed in either the Episcopal Church or the Church of England. Thus, when she took her vows as Sister Anne, she became the first Episcopal sister. In 1852, she founded the Sisterhood of the Holy Communion in New York City, an organization that became attached to Mühlenberg's church. Ayres became "First Sister," the leader of the sisterhood.

Members of the sisterhood did not take lifetime vows but signed a renewable contract every three years. Included in their contract was a pledge not to marry during their terms of duty. The sisters did not adopt a nun's habit but wore a style of secular dress. In 1858 Sister Anne became "House Mother" of St. Luke's Hospital in New York City, an institution she had helped to establish. Her position put her in charge of the administration of nursing and household matters at the hospital. After the Civil War, the sisterhood aided Mühlenberg's St. Johnland project, a Christian industrial community that served the poor, disabled, aged, and orphaned. The sisterhood soon changed its name to one that would associate it with its major projects, becoming known as the Sisterhood of St. Luke and St. John.

At about the same time, Ayres published *Evangelical Sisterhoods* (1867), a work that discusses the emergence of the sisterhood and its rules and raison d'être. Apparently, not all the sisters were happy with Ayres as their leader. Some members of the sisterhood found her rule too autocratic and erratic, and some preferred a more conventlike style of organization. In the winter of 1862–1863, four sisters, led by Harriet Starr Cannon, left the hospital and formed a new Episcopal sisterhood that more closely resembled Roman Catholic orders. Nevertheless, the board of trustees had faith in Ayres's administrative abilities. In 1876, they voted her "Sister Superintendent," giving her administrative powers equal to those of Mühlenberg. After Mühlenberg's death in 1877, Ayres worked to edit his essays and wrote his biography. Sister Anne died in New York City on February 9, 1896. The sisterhood was never large, and it was discontinued in 1940. Nevertheless, Ayres has been remembered as a pioneer in the modern revival of monastic life in the Episcopal Church in the United States.

See also: Episcopal Church
References: Anne Ayres, *The Life and Work of William Augustus Muhlenberg* (1880); Edward T. James, ed., *Notable American Women, 1607–1950* (1971); J. Gordon Melton, *Religious Leaders of America* (1991); Phyllis J. Read and Bernard L. Witlieb, *The Book of Women's Firsts* (1992); Alvin W. Skardon, *William Augustus Mühlenberg* (1971).

Bagby, Anne Luther (1859–1942)

Anne Luther Bagby, who for sixty-one years served as a missionary in Brazil for the Southern Baptist Church, was born in Kansas City, Missouri, on March 20, 1859. When she was about eighteen years of age, she moved with her family to Texas, where her father, John Hill Luther, began thirteen years of service as president of Baylor College. Anne became attracted to foreign mission work after meeting a missionary from Africa. She chose to work in Brazil, and her support as a missionary was guaranteed at a meeting of the Texas Baptist Convention in 1880. On October 21 of that year, she married fellow missionary William Buck Bagby. Together they sailed for Brazil in January 1881.

During the years of the Bagbys' mission work in Brazil, Anne bore nine children. Two died in infancy, and two others passed away in young adulthood. The remaining five children all became missionaries, four going to Brazil and one to Argentina. A school at Saõ Paulo, Colegio Batista Brasileiro Ana Bagby, was named in their mother's honor in 1902. Anne Bagby died in Recife, Brazil, on December 23, 1942.

See also: Missionaries
References: Clifton Judson Allen et al., eds., *Encyclopedia of Southern Baptists* (1958).

Bailey, Alice La Trobe Bateman (1880–1949)

Noted Theosophist and founder of the Arcane School, Alice La Trobe Bateman Bailey was born into a wealthy family in Manchester, England, on June 16, 1880. She was an unhappy child who on several occasions attempted suicide. Alice grew up as a member of the Church of England and was a church schoolteacher for her local parish, but she frequently felt drawn toward mysticism. She claimed that one Sunday, when she was fifteen years old, a mysterious man in a turban entered her home and told her that she was destined to perform an important mission and that she must prepare herself. For years Bailey thought the man was Jesus Christ.

When Bailey was eighteen, she attended a finishing school in London. After graduation she went to work for the Young Woman's Christian Association, which resulted in her traveling throughout the world. While in India, she met her future husband Walter Evans at a soldier's home. She married him in 1907. They moved to Cincinnati, Ohio, where Evans studied for the Episcopal priesthood at the Lane Theological Seminary. After Evans's graduation, the couple moved to California. Their marriage was an unhappy one, however, and they separated in 1915. Four years later, they divorced.

In 1915 two friends introduced Bailey to Theosophy when she accompanied them to the Theosophy Society in Pacific Grove, California. There she was surprised to see on the wall of the society's quarters a picture of the man who had come to see her when she was fifteen. He was Koot Hoomi, one of the mahatmas, or spiritual leaders, who had communicated with Helena Petrovna Blavatsky, cofounder of the Theosophical Society. Bailey's discovery spurred her to become an active member, and she moved to the society's headquarters in Krotona, near Hollywood, California, in 1917. There she edited the organization's magazine, *The Messenger,* and began teaching classes. In 1919, while she was walking in the hills, another member of the spiritual hierarchy contacted Bailey. (The spiritual hierarchy comprises mahatmas, or spiritual masters, who theosophists believe live on through the centuries in various incarnations. They guard their knowledge, teaching it only to worthy students.) Djwhal Khul, popularly known as D. K. or "the Tibetan," asked Bailey to become his amanuensis. He would dictate to her, and she would produce a series of writings that would be released to the world. In 1920, she began writing *Initiation: Human and Solar* (1922), launching an arrangement that was to last almost thirty years and produce nineteen books.

But conflicts were rising within the Theosophical Society. The movement's national leader, Annie Besant, had disagreements with the organization's national secretary, Foster Bailey. Alice, who had a romantic interest in Foster, also came into conflict with Besant, both over Alice's book and her charge that the society was dominated by the Esoteric Section. Both Foster and Alice were removed from their positions within the organization. They moved to New York City and were married in 1921. Within two years the Baileys had launched the Arcane School, a new spiritual school for their disciples, and soon were producing a magazine, *The Beacon.* They also established the Lucis Trust for the publication of Alice's books. Bailey's teachings were similar to regular Theosophy in

that they accented a divine plan for the world, karma, reincarnation, the evolution of humanity to higher levels, and a spiritual hierarchy whose teachings and energies could be put to use.

For the remaining years of her life, Bailey continued writing with the Tibetan and working to build the Arcane School. In 1932 the Tibetan encouraged the founding of the New Group of World Servers, who would become goodwill ambassadors in anticipation of a coming new age. Several of Bailey's works with the Tibetan foretell a future world religion that will unite the East and the West. The Arcane School developed special prayers and meditations to hasten the achievement of this goal.

Bailey died in New York City on December 15, 1949. After her death, Foster Bailey remained the head of the Arcane School and the Lucis Trust until his own death in 1977. Nevertheless, conflicts erupted within the organization after 1949, which led to its splitting into several groups.

See also: Besant, Annie Wood; Blavatsky, Helena Petrovna
References: J. Gordon Melton, *Biographical Dictionary of American Cult and Sect Leaders* (1986); J. Gordon Melton, *Religious Leaders of America* (1991); Leslie Shepard, ed., *Encyclopedia of Occultism and Parapsychology,* 3rd ed. (1991).

Bakker, Tammy Faye (1942–)

Tammy Faye Bakker, along with her now ex-husband, Jim Bakker, was one of America's most popular televangelists from the late 1970s until their PTL (Praise the Lord) Club was brought down by scandal in the late 1980s. She was born Tammy Faye LaValley in International Falls, Minnesota, on March 7, 1942. Her parents divorced when she was a child, and she was raised by her mother and a stepfather in a family of eight children. Tammy was brought up in the Pentecostal faith, and at the age of ten she had the profound experience of speaking in tongues as she lay on the floor of her church. This experience normally would have brought her into the Pentecostal church as a full-fledged member, but since her mother was divorced, Tammy was denied insider status.

After graduating from high school, Tammy entered North Central College, the Assemblies of God school in Minneapolis, with intentions of eventually becoming a missionary. It was at the college that she met Jim Bakker who, like Tammy, belonged to the Pentecostal faith. Student marriage was against school policy, so when they decided to marry in 1961, the couple left the college and began their life together as itinerant evangelists.

In 1966 televangelist Pat Robertson invited Jim Bakker to host a Christian talk show on Robertson's newly established Christian Broadcasting Network (CBN). Bakker remained with the network until 1973, when he resigned and cofounded Trinity Broadcasting Systems, headquartered in Santa Ana, California, with Paul Crouch, the former assistant pastor of his home church. However, the business relationship lasted only a few months, and Bakker left for North Carolina. In November 1974, he began hosting a preexisting talk show on WRET-TV, which he renamed "The PTL Club." This grew to become a new Christian television network, the PTC or Inspirational Network. Tammy became a cohost of the talk show, and when Jim was away, she hosted it alone. Although as the years passed, Jim and Tammy stretched some of the strict rules of Pentecostalism (most notably, in Tammy's case, the proscription against wearing makeup or jewelry), they remained true to the teachings of 1 Corinthians 11:3, that "the head of the woman is the man." There was no question but that Jim Bakker was in charge of PTL.

In 1976 Jim Bakker purchased 25 acres in Charlotte, North Carolina, which became the first Heritage Village, a religious retreat that eventually became a giant Christian theme park. Two years later, he acquired land and began building a new Heritage Village (later Heritage U.S.A.) near Fort Mill, South Carolina. He also raised hundreds of thousands of dollars by fund-raising on television and by selling shares in the PTL corporation that would allow shareholders to stay at Heritage U.S.A. for several days each year.

With one of the highest-rated religious television shows of the 1980s, the Bakkers became national celebrities. But despite their outward success, there were problems within PTL and the Bakkers' marriage. First, they had begun living an opulent lifestyle that alienated them from colleagues in the ministry. Second, much of the money that was pouring into the PTL ministry was being diverted to the Bakkers' personal use. And third, Jim Bakker had become involved in various sexual encounters, including one with PTL secretary Jessica Hahn. In the case of Hahn, PTL funds were used in an attempt to keep her quiet about the incident. Likely aware of her husband's sexual infidelities, in 1980 Tammy became romantically involved with Nashville recording artist Gary S. Paxton.

As tales of Jim Bakker's sexual escapades became public, the fall of PTL appeared imminent, and Jim turned the corporation over to fellow televangelist Jerry Falwell. The Assemblies of God church defrocked Bakker. Meanwhile, the PTL corporation had gotten deep in debt. Eventually, Heritage U.S.A. was sold to help cover the debts. While stories of her husband's indiscretions were unfolding in the public eye, Tammy was suffering from a growing addiction to prescription drugs.

Meanwhile, Jim and Tammy attempted to found a new ministry, and in November 1987, Jim Bakker received ministerial credentials from Faith Christian Fellowship International. When these credentials were not renewed the following year, he received credentials from the New Covenant Christian Church of Cranesville, Pennsylvania. The Bakkers attempted to launch a new "Jim and Tammy" show in Charlotte in early in 1989, but after a few months they moved to Orlando, Florida, to establish the new Covenant Church of Orlando. Legal problems stymied this attempt to launch a ministry, however. Jim Bakker was eventually convicted of a number of charges stemming from his manipulation of funds at PTL and was sentenced to a lengthy term in a federal prison. The Bakkers subsequently divorced.

Despite the problems that led to the downfall of the PTL ministry, through her television ministry Tammy Bakker opened the way for new freedom for Pentecostal and Holiness Christian women. Although strict Pentecostal teachings considered self-adornment sinful, and although critics ridiculed her excessive use of makeup, Tammy showed women of the faith that they could wear cosmetics, wigs, and jewelry and still remain devout Christians. In addition, she and Jim overlooked Pentecostal restrictions and allowed "mixed bathing" in the swimming pools at PTL's Heritage Village U.S.A.

References: Joe E. Barnhart, *Jim and Tammy: Charismatic Intrigue inside PTL* (1988); Jeffrey K. Hadden and Anson Shupe, *Televangelism: Power and Politics on God's Frontier* (1988); Hunter James, *Smile Pretty and Say Jesus: The Last Great Days of PTL* (1993); J. Gordon Melton, *Religious Leaders of America* (1991).

Baptists

Although the history of the Baptists dates back to early seventeenth-century Europe, it was not until the Great Awakening revivals of the mid-eighteenth century that the faith began to draw a large following in America. During the seventeenth century, Baptist men and women faced persecution in New England. Upon intervention by the King of England, Puritan authorities grudgingly granted them toleration in 1691. As in a number of religions in the early stages of their history, the Baptists offered women opportunities to perform roles that most established religions proffered only to men. Baptist women were not permitted to become pastors, but in some congregations women participated in business meetings and could even vote on election or dismissal of clergy. Occasionally they led prayers at religious meetings. At the end of the eighteenth century, as the Baptist church moved from the margins of religious life toward the mainstream, women were disenfranchised from church politics, and their voices were usually ignored or silenced.

There had been mission societies for women since the beginning of organized Baptist life. In the last half of the nineteenth century, Baptist women were caught up in the burgeoning missions movement. Baptists established three regional women's missionary associations in the 1870s, the Woman's Baptist Home Missionary Society, the Woman's Baptist Foreign Mission Society, and the Woman's American Baptist Home Missionary Society. The Woman's Missionary Union (WMU) of the Southern Baptist Convention (the denomination's nongoverning central association) was established in 1888 by a small group of women who felt called to missionary work. Its membership has since grown to over a million women.

Because of the Baptist Church's organizational structure that gave local churches the final decisions in respect to appointments of their pastors, several Baptist women had been ordained to the ministry by the late 1800s. So, although women's roles within the mainstream

Baptist churches remained limited, by opening up the pastorate to women in a few local parishes, Baptists led other denominations in offering opportunities of authority to women. Unlike the women's mission societies of many of the other mainline denominations, Baptist women were able to resist male takeover of their major societies. Baptist Helen Barrett Montgomery became the first woman to head a major American religious denomination when she was elected to the presidency of the Northern Baptist Convention in 1921.

The greatest gains for women within the organizational structure of the Baptist Church did not come until the 1970s. During the 1960s, Baptist women, like women in other religious denominations, began to reassess their roles in church and society. Baptist women were moving into the workforce and embarking on careers. Some of these women, particularly those who had participated in church activities such as the Girls' Auxiliary (a branch of the Woman's Missionary Union aimed at girls in fourth to twelfth grades), became interested in pursuing religious careers. In 1964, the Southern Baptists ordained a woman to the ministry for the first time, but ten years later only about fifteen women had been ordained within that denomination. Although the more liberal Baptist congregations, especially the Northern Baptists, are ordaining substantial numbers of women in the 1990s, Southern Baptist women are experiencing greater difficulties in achieving ordination. Those Southern Baptist women who have been ordained have found that many parishes will not accept female pastors. Although the National Baptist Convention and the other major black Baptist conventions have no specific policies against the ordination of women, they have been resistant to female ordination. Generally, more liberal congregations accept women as pastors, and conservative and fundamentalist congregations do not.

While most mainline churches are liberalizing their positions regarding women's roles in the church and society, the Southern Baptists are taking a more conservative stance. At their June 1998 convention in Salt Lake City, the Southern Baptists amended their essential statement on beliefs to include a declaration that a woman should "submit herself graciously to her husband's leadership." The amendment is based upon such biblical passages as Ephesians 5:22–33, which compares the husband-wife relationship with Christ ruling the church. With nearly sixteen million members, the Southern Baptists comprise the largest Protestant denomination in the United States.

See also: Montgomery, Helen Barrett; Woman's Missionary Union
References: Nancy Tatom Ammerman, *Baptist Battles: Social Change and Religious Conflict in the Southern Baptist Convention* (1990); Evelyn Brooks Higginbotham, *Righteous Discontent: The Women's Movement in the Black Baptist Church, 1880–1920* (1993); Susan Juster, *"Disorderly Women": Sexual Politics and Evangelicalism in Revolutionary New England* (1994); Susan Hill Lindley, *"You Have Stept Out of Your Place": A History of Women and Religion in America* (1996); William G. McLoughlin, *Soul Liberty: The Baptists' Struggle in New England, 1630–1833* (1991); Gustav Niebuhr, "Wives Urged to Follow Lead of Husbands," New York Times News Service, in *Sarasota Herald-Tribune* (June 19, 1998).

Barr, Amelia Edith Huddleston (1831–1919)

Christian writer and novelist Amelia Edith Huddleston Barr was born in Ulverston, Lancashire, England, on March 29, 1831, the daughter of William Henry and Mary (Singleton) Huddleston. Her father was a Methodist minister who had an independent income apart from his parish salary, which enabled the family to send Amelia to private schools. William Huddleston lost much of his private income when Amelia was sixteen. His wife responded to the financial setback by enlisting her two older daughters to help her open a school for girls. Amelia prepared to join her mother and sisters by first teaching at a private school in Norfolk for a year. The family's fortunes improved, but Amelia decided to continue teaching. She worked for the Wesleyan Board of Education while attending the Normal School in Glasgow, Scotland, in preparation for employment in Methodist schools for the poor. Amelia did not complete the course, however. Instead she married Robert Barr, a prosperous businessman and the son of a Scottish Calvinist minister, on July 11, 1850. During this time she met American Congregationalist minister Henry Ward Beecher, whom she would encounter again later in her life.

Robert Barr declared bankruptcy in 1851. Two years later, he, Amelia, and their two children emigrated to the United States and settled in Chicago. Robert began work as an accountant, and in January 1854, Amelia opened a school for girls. Over the next several years, the Barrs lived in Chicago, Illinois, Memphis, Tennessee, and Galveston, Texas, before settling in Austin in 1857. The family spent nine years in Austin, where Amelia opened a girls' school and gave birth to five more children of her own. Four of these children and another born in Galveston in 1867 did not survive childhood. As British citizens, the Barrs were relatively unaffected by the Civil War, but like most people in the South, they suffered from shortages of foods and material goods. In 1866 the family moved to Galveston, where Robert found employment in a cotton house. He died a year later of yellow fever.

Amelia Barr operated a boarding house in Galveston during the next two years but then moved to Ridgewood, New Jersey, in the fall of 1869. Throughout these hard times, Barr's faith in God gave her comfort. During her brief stay in Ridgewood, she became a teacher of the sons of a Mr. Libbey, and Libbey became her first literary agent. Encouraged by the sale of an article she wrote describing Texas after the Civil War, Barr moved to New York and began a successful career as an author.

Upon her arrival in New York, Barr became reacquainted with Henry Ward Beecher, who urged her to write for the *Christian Union,* of which he was editor. Over the next ten years, Barr supported herself and her surviving family by writing more than a thousand articles and poems for the *Union,* the *Christian Herald,* and Robert Bonner's *New York Ledger.* The New York religious weekly, the *Working Church,* serialized her first novel, *Eunice Leslie,* during this period. In 1875 Barr published her first book, *Romances and Realities: Tales of Truth and Fancy.* By the late 1880s she had become one of the most popular novelists in the United States. She eventually published eighty-one books in addition to numerous articles, poems, and short stories. Most of her novels were historical romances, sentimental, folksy, and characterized by strong religious undertones. Among her most popular were *Cluny MacPherson* (1883); *Jan Vedder's Wife* (1885); *The Bow of Orange Ribbon* (1886); *A Daughter of Fife* (1886); *Remember the Alamo* (1888); and *The Lion's Whelp* (1901). Her novels were usually set in places that she had lived—Scotland, England, Texas, and New York. In 1915 Barr published her autobiography, *All the Days of My Life,* in which she tells of her lifetime of spiritual experiences and urges young readers to not be ashamed of their own religious sentiments.

Although she frequently spent summers in England and Scotland, Barr spent most of the last years of her life in New York state. She died in Richmond Hill, Long Island, on March 10, 1919.

References: Amelia E. Barr, *All the Days of My Life: An Autobiography* (1915); Edward T. James, ed., *Notable American Women, 1607–1950*, vol. 1 (1971); J. Gordon Melton, *Religious Leaders of America* (1991).

Barrett, Kate Harwood Waller (1857–1925)

Kate Harwood Waller Barrett, cofounder of the National Florence Crittenton Mission for unwed mothers, was born January 24, 1857, in Falmouth, Virginia. She was the eldest of the ten children of Withers Waller and Ann Eliza (Stribling) Waller. The coming of the Civil War in 1861 created extreme turmoil in young Kate's life. Not only was her father's life in jeopardy as a Confederate colonel, but the family plantation, Clifton, with its location along the Potomac River, was an open target for Union gunboats. Their land and the surrounding county frequently changed hands as one army gained an advantage over the other. The Wallers became wandering refugees for much of the war. Kate, or Katherine, as she had been christened, received most of her education from governesses, though she spent two years at the Arlington Institute for Girls in Alexandria. On July 19, 1876, she married the Reverend Robert South Barrett, a rector in the Episcopal church located in a poor section of Richmond, Virginia. The Barretts had seven children.

Four years after her marriage, Barrett's life was changed when an unwed mother and her baby arrived at the rectory door. After spending some time talking with the woman, Barrett was surprised to discover that the woman's background was not unlike her own. She found that those commonly described as "fallen women" were not so degraded and depraved as she had been taught to believe, and from that moment on, she dedicated her life to helping this "outcast class" (Wilson and Barrett, 1974, pp. 154–156).

When Reverend Barrett was called to a parish in Henderson, Kentucky, in 1880, Kate joined him in pastoral work among prostitutes in the area. When in 1886 he became dean of St. Luke's Cathedral in Atlanta, Georgia, Kate took on the social responsibilities required of a dean's wife. She also became president of both the auxiliary of the Young Men's Christian Association (YMCA) and the Woman's Cooperative Club. Later she enrolled in the three-year course at the Women's Medical College of Georgia, receiving a medical degree in 1892. A year later she opened a home for unmarried mothers age eighteen and under in Atlanta. The home, however, met with considerable hostility from the public, who feared that the establishment would attract loose women. It was not until the city council received notice that the local ministerial association was supportive of the project that the home was finally approved.

Meanwhile, Barrett had become aware of Charles N. Crittenton, a millionaire who after the death of his daughter Florence had set aside his business career to devote his life to preaching and to rescuing "fallen women." When she wrote him to tell him of the home she wanted to establish, he sent her $5,000 of the $7,500 required for the building, and her home in Atlanta became the fifth of the Florence Crittenton Homes. In 1894 Reverend Barrett was appointed general missioner of the Protestant Episcopal Church, a post that took him to Washington, D.C. A year later Crittenton and Kate Barrett founded the National Florence Crittenton Mission in the nation's capital.

When Barrett was widowed in 1896, she began devoting more time and energy to the rapidly growing mission, which was chartered by Congress in 1898. By this time there were more than fifty local homes. Although Crittenton was the mission's financial backer and president, his principal interest was in preaching. Therefore, the running of the mission was in the hands of Barrett, the vice president and general superintendent. She organized the annual conferences that began in 1897, edited the *Florence Crittenton Magazine,* and wrote a book, *Some Practical Suggestions on the Conduct of a Rescue Home* (1903). In her book Barrett offered suggestions on aspects of operating a rescue home, examining issues ranging from the layout of the facility (preferably an old-fashioned, roomy house) to the evaluation of an "unfortunate girl's" potential for leading a productive and moral life. She advised mission workers to avoid listening to the life stories of the women taking refuge in the homes but to guide the "fallen women" to renounce their sinful pasts. Barrett soon realized that it was impractical to put too much effort into converting prostitutes and focused instead on the requirements of young, unwed, expectant mothers. She argued in favor of the mothers keeping their children but encouraged the women to move to new areas, where they would be less likely to bring shame upon their families.

When Crittenton died in 1909, Barrett became president of the National Florence Crittenton Mission. During the Progressive era of the early decades of the twentieth century, Barrett's work received general acceptance as a worthwhile philanthropy, and she became a well-known spokesperson on women's issues. She was a delegate to the White House Conference for Dependent Children in 1909. In 1911 she was elected to the presidency of the National Council of Women, a group she had been active with since 1899. She had also served in the International Council of Women, attending conferences in London (1899), in Toronto (1909), and in Rome (1914). For eleven years, from 1909 to 1920, she served as vice president of the Virginia Equal Suffrage League, and she was president of the National Women's Auxiliary of the American Legion from 1922 to 1923.

Barrett retained the post of president of the National Florence Crittenton Mission until her death in Alexandria, Virginia, on February 23, 1925. Her son Robert South Barrett succeeded her and was president of the mission until his death thirty-four years later. In 1927 the Kate Waller Barrett Hall, a dormitory for women, was dedicated in her honor at the College of William and Mary in Williamsburg, Virginia.

See also: Reform Movements
References: Kate Waller Barrett, *Some Practical Suggestions on the Conduct of a Rescue Home* (1903, reprint 1974); Edward T. James, ed., *Notable American Women: 1607–1950,* vol. 1 (1971); J. Gordon Melton, *Religious Leaders of America* (1991); Otto Wilson with Robert South Barrett, *Fifty Years' Work with Girls, 1883–1933: A Story of the Florence Crittenton Homes* (1933, reprint 1974).

Bat Mitzvah

The Bat Mitzvah, the ceremony that celebrates a young Jewish woman's religious coming-of-age, was first performed in America in 1922 when Judith Kaplan was called to read from the Torah during a Sabbath morning service. The Bat Mitzvah was established to give young women a ceremony equivalent to the Bar Mitzvah that had for centuries marked the religious coming-of-age of young men. Although Jewish tradition had long acknowledged that girls reached religious maturity at age twelve, there had been no specific ritual to signify this coming-of-age. In the decades that followed Kaplan's Bat Mitzvah, a number of Reform and some of the more liberal

Conservative congregations adopted a form of Bat Mitzvah that nearly paralleled the young man's Bar Mitzvah. Although sometimes the ceremony was modified for young women, it was still an important and formal occasion.

At present, a Bat Mitzvah equivalent to a Bar Mitzvah is observed in almost all Reform and Reconstructionist congregations and in a majority of Conservative synagogues. Many congregations offer one course of instruction, attended by both boys and girls, that culminates in either a Bar or Bat Mitzvah. Still, some congregations distinguish the young woman's ceremony from that of a young man by holding the Bat Mitzvah on Friday evenings rather than on Saturday mornings and having the young woman read from the Prophets or develop other creative alternatives to the traditional chanting of the Torah and Haftarah.

See also: Jews
References: Charlotte Baum, Paula Hyman, and Sonya Michel, *The Jewish Woman in America* (1976); Jane Lewit and Ellen Robinson Epstein, *The Bar/Bat Mitzvah Planbook* (1982); Susan Hill Lindley, *"You Have Stept Out of Your Place": A History of Women and Religion in America* (1996).

Bennett, Belle Harris (1852–1922)

Southern Methodist lay leader and founder of the Scarritt Bible and Training School, Belle Harris Bennett was born December 3, 1852, at Whitehall, near Richmond, Kentucky. Christened Isabel by her parents, Samuel and Elizabeth (Chenault) Bennett, she was the youngest daughter among eight children. Samuel Bennett was a successful planter and the son of a Methodist clergyman, and he and Elizabeth raised their children in an atmosphere of gracious living and religious piety. The elder Bennetts also instilled in their children a respect for education. After attending local grammar schools, Belle entered a private school in Richmond. She then went on to Nazareth School near Bardstown, Kentucky, and completed her education at College Hill, Ohio. Belle was a voracious reader, especially intrigued by history, but was not particularly concerned with religion until she was twenty-three. At that time she was moved by the preachings of a visiting evangelist to join the local Methodist church where her family attended. Soon after, she and her older sister Sue opened a Sunday school for the poor children of the county.

At a revival in 1884, Belle had a religious experience that gave her a sense of sanctification, a feeling professed by many Methodists who believe that the Holy Spirit has perfected them in love. Three years later, while attending a Methodist missionary meeting, Bennett realized that young women were ill-prepared for their assignments in foreign missions. At about the same time she learned of the work of Lucy Rider Meyer, who had founded the Chicago Training School for Women in the Northern Methodist denomination. In 1888 Bennett met Meyer at a summer assembly in Chautauqua, New York, and returned to Kentucky determined to establish a missionary training school for Southern Methodist women. When she presented her plea for a training school at the 1889 meeting of the Southern Methodist Woman's Board of Foreign Missions, Bennett was appointed the board's agent to collect money and to open the school.

Although initially timid and overwhelmed by the task before her, Bennett began to travel throughout the South, speaking in churches and at camp meetings. She was a gifted orator, and before the end of 1889, Dr. Nathan Scarritt of Kansas City, Missouri, offered her land there and $25,000 for a building, under the provision that the church raise an equal sum. There was some opposition within the church over establishing a school so far west and also over Bennett's and Scarritt's plan for the school to broaden its scope to train home as well as foreign missionaries. But these obstacles were overcome, and the Scarritt Bible and Training School (now Scarritt College) opened in September 1892.

Bennett turned down an offer to become principal of the school but devoted the next three years to raising more funds for it and then worked to establish home missions in the Methodist Episcopal Church, South. After the death of her sister Sue in 1892, Belle was chosen as her replacement on the central committee of the Woman's Home Mission Society. She immediately set forth to carry out her sister's plan for a school in the mountain country of southeastern Kentucky. The Sue Bennett Memorial School opened in London, Kentucky, in 1897.

As president of the Woman's Home Mission Society (1896) and, after 1898, president of the organization's governing board, the Woman's Board of Home Missions, Bennett turned her attention to the social needs of urban areas. In 1901 she visited settlement houses in London, England, with Tochie Williams MacDonnell, general secretary of the Woman's Board. Bennett urged the Methodist Church to establish settlement houses across the South that would incorporate broad social programs. These became known as Wesley Community Houses and Bethlehem Houses (the latter were settlement houses for African Americans). Following the lead of Lucy Rider Meyer, in 1902 Bennett persuaded the General Conference of the Methodist Church to authorize the development of a program to train deaconesses to staff the many projects. Bennett stood up to the church's initial resistance to working among blacks and in 1901 persuaded the Woman's Home Mission Society to establish an industrial department for girls at the church's Paine Institute for Negroes in Augusta, Georgia.

She taught a weekly Bible study class from 1900 to 1904 for black church leaders in Richmond, Kentucky, where she resided, and organized a chautauqua (an educational program that usually consisted of lectures, concerts, and recreational activities) for African Americans. Emerging as a southern leader for black equality, she frequently spoke out against racial prejudice.

Bennett also worked to raise the position of women within the Methodist Church. When early in the twentieth century the church made a move to consolidate its mission work from four scattered organizations into one Board of Missions, Bennett started a movement to open church conferences and boards to women. The Southern Methodist women's home and foreign mission boards were united as the Woman's Missionary Council in 1910, under a mostly male Board of Missions. Bennett was chosen president of the council and remained its leader until her death. In a speech before the 1910 convention of the Methodist Episcopal Church, South, Bennett took a firm stand on voting rights for laywomen. She used the occasion to voice her opposition to the church's long-held prejudices against women's participation in decisions regarding church affairs. At the General Conference of 1914, Bennett debated in favor of equal laity rights for men and women. Her persuasive arguments led to the granting of laity rights to women at the 1918 General Conference. In 1921 Bennett became the first woman elected a delegate to the church's General Conference. Unfortunately, she was unable to attend the conference, which was held in 1922, because she was dying of cancer.

As leader of the Woman's Missionary Council, Bennett was again drawn into foreign concerns. She led in the establishment of new mission fields in the Belgian Congo (now the Democratic Republic of Congo) and Japan, of a mission college (later named for her) in Rio de Janeiro, Brazil, and of the Woman's Christian Medical College in Shanghai, where the Belle H. Bennett Clinical Building was named for her in 1925.

Bennett died July 20, 1922, in Richmond, Kentucky. Two years later the training school she had founded was renamed Scarritt College for Christian Workers and relocated to Nashville, Tennessee. A central group of the school's buildings has been dedicated as the Belle H. Bennett Memorial.

See also: Methodists; Meyer, Lucy Jane Rider
References: Edward T. James, ed., *Notable American Women, 1607–1950* (1971); J. Gordon Melton, *Religious Leaders of America* (1991); Rosemary Radford Ruether and Rosemary Skinner Keller, eds., *Women and Religion in America*, vol. 3, *1900–1968* (1986).

Bennett, Mary Katharine Jones (1864–1950)

Prominent Presbyterian laywoman Mary Katharine Jones Bennett was born in Englewood, New Jersey, on November 28, 1864, the youngest of the two daughters of Henry and Winifred (Davies) Jones. Raised in comfortable circumstances, Katharine, as she was called, received a solid education. She attended the Dwight School in Englewood and then the Bordentown (New Jersey) Academy. In 1881 she entered Elmira College, where she excelled in her studies and graduated with a bachelor of arts degree in 1885. After graduation, she taught in public and private schools in Englewood for several years.

During the 1890s, Katharine became interested in religious and social work, and in 1894 she became national secretary of young people's work for the Woman's Board of Home Missions of the Presbyterian Church in the U.S.A., the foremost Presbyterian denomination in the northern United States. At about the

same time, she served on the governing board of the College Settlements Association, an organization founded in 1890 by alumnae of several Eastern colleges for the purpose of promoting the settlement house movement.

Katharine's work was momentarily interrupted when she married businessman Fred Smith Bennett on July 20, 1898. She resigned her position with the Woman's Board of Home Missions but was soon elected a member of the board. Fred Bennett encouraged his wife in her church career, and she used personal funds to pay for travel on the board's behalf. Katharine also renewed her activity within the secular community. She was the first president of the Englewood Civic Federation (1901–1911); was president of the Woman's Club (1902–1906); and helped found the Englewood Forum in 1916.

Despite her participation in a variety of community projects, Bennett continued to devote considerable energy to church work. In 1909 she became president of the Woman's Board of Home Missions. Under her able leadership, the board effectively raised funds and gradually developed more and more autonomy in its administration. It was incorporated in 1915, no longer tied to the male-led Board of Home Missions but directly responsible to the General Assembly. When in 1923 the Presbyterian Church of the U.S.A. reorganized and allowed the Woman's Board to be placed under the Board of Home Missions, Bennett became vice president of the board. She also served her congregation as a corresponding member of the General Council from 1924 to 1932.

Bennett also participated in the Protestant ecumenical movement. She represented her church at the founding of the interdenominational Council of Women for Home Missions and was president from 1916 to 1924. She served as the first president of the interchurch Board for Christian Work in Santo Domingo between 1920 and 1936 and was a member of several commissions of the Federal Council of the Churches of Christ in America, including the Commission on the Steel Strike of 1919. That commission's 1920 report contributed to the elimination of the twelve-hour day and to other reforms in the steel industry. In 1937 Bennett was a representative of the Presbyterian Church at the Life Work Conference in Edinburgh, Scotland. She remained active in interdenominational work until she was well into her seventies, and in the early 1940s she devoted special attention to the plight of migrant workers and Native Americans.

Widowed in her later years, Bennett died in Englewood on April 11, 1950.

See also: Presbyterian Church
References: Lois A. Boyd and R. Douglas Brackenridge, *Presbyterian Women in America: Two Centuries of a Quest for Status,* 2nd ed. (1996); Edward T. James, ed., *Notable American Women, 1607–1950,* vol. 1 (1971); Susan Hill Lindley, *"You Have Stept Out of Your Place": A History of Women and Religion in America* (1996); J. Gordon Melton, *Religious Leaders of America* (1991).

Annie Wood Besant (c. 1887)

Besant, Annie Wood (1847–1933)

Prominent Theosophist and leader of the Theosophical Society during the period of its greatest growth, Annie Wood Besant was born in London, England, on October 1, 1847. After her father died when Annie was five years of age, her mother raised her in a devout religious atmosphere. Annie married minister-schoolmaster Reverend Frank Besant in 1867, and they had two children. But Annie had become skeptical of orthodox Christianity, and she was outspoken in her dissent. This led to marital problems that eventually resulted in a divorce.

During her marriage Besant had begun to write short stories. After her divorce in 1873, she turned to writing essays concerning her doubts about Christianity. In 1874 her interests brought her into contact with atheist Charles Bradlaugh, the leader of the National Secular Society. She joined the society and began to write for Bradlaugh's *National Reformer.* Besant was a feminist and was soon campaigning for women's rights. In 1877, as coeditor of the *National Reformer* and copublisher with Bradlaugh of the Freethought Publishing Company, she and Bradlaugh were prosecuted for publishing literature that supported atheism and birth control.

Over the next decade Besant was drawn to socialism, which led to an eventual break with Bradlaugh, who disagreed with her adopted politics. Besant championed the strike of poorly paid match girls and was a member of George Bernard Shaw's Fabian Society. A turning point came in her life in 1888 after she read *The*

Secret Doctrine by Helena P. Blavatsky, a founder of the Theosophical Society. In Theosophy Besant discovered a philosophy by which she could lead her life. The Theosophical Society was dedicated to the formation of a universal brotherhood, the study of comparative religion, and the exploration of as yet virtually untapped faculties of the human mind. Besant met Blavatsky shortly after reading *The Secret Doctrine* and was soon caught up in the Theosophical movement. She was certain that Blavatsky and Theosophy offered her a philosophy with which she could be comfortable.

After Blavatsky died in 1891, Besant, who had become very close to the Theosophical Society's leader, became increasingly prominent within the organization. That same year she was promoted to head the society's Esoteric Section in Europe and India, a post second only to that of president and society cofounder Colonel Henry S. Olcott. In 1892 Besant wrote the Theosophical book, the *Seven Principles of Man.* Her second Theosophical work, *Karma,* was published in 1895. The following year Besant made a triumphal tour of the United States. During her travels she spoke to tremendous crowds at the World Parliament of Religion at the Chicago World's Fair.

Later in 1893, Besant moved to Adyar, India, where she set up headquarters and made her home for the rest of her life. During 1894 and 1895 William Q. Judge, a cofounder of the society with Olcott and Blavatsky, challenged Besant's power. Besant won, but the society split. Most of the American members sided with Judge, but Besant gradually restored the American movement's faith in her. When Olcott died in 1907, she was elected to succeed him as president. Besant became the leader of an organization that was enjoying slow but steady growth.

Besant organized the Order of the Star of the East in 1909 to advance her conviction that a new world savior had come to earth in the person of Jiddu Krishnamurti, a child under the society's care. In 1912 the order began publishing the magazine *Herald of the Star* to announce the news. The order lasted for twenty years, only disbanding in 1929 when Krishnamurti himself publicly denied his assigned role.

Besant led the Theosophical Society until her death in Adyar, India, on September 21, 1933. For the majority of her tenure at the organization, the society experienced a period of growth, from approximately fifteen thousand members in 1909 to forty-five thousand members in 1928. After 1928 membership began to decline. During her years as a Theosophist, Besant wrote numerous articles and more than thirty books in her attempts to extend awareness of Hindu wisdom and its spiritual message. In addition to making the riches of Indian religious philosophy available to the English-speaking world, Besant played an active role in the emancipation of women and in support of India's quest for independence from Britain. Her dedication to Indian nationalism influenced several leaders, including Mohandas Gandhi.

See also: Bailey, Alice La Trobe Bateman; Blavatsky, Helena Petrovna
References: Henry Warner Bowden, *Dictionary of American Religious Biography,* 2nd ed. (1993); J. Gordon Melton, *Biographical Dictionary of American Cult and Sect Leaders* (1986); J. Gordon Melton, *Religious Leaders of America* (1991); Leslie Shepard, ed., *Encyclopedia of Occultism and Parapsychology,* 3rd ed. (1991); Anne Taylor, *Annie Besant: A Biography* (1992).

Bethune, Mary McLeod (1875–1955)

Educator, civil rights reformer, federal government official, and founder of Bethune-Cookman College, Mary McLeod Bethune was one of the most influential African-American women of the first

Mary McLeod Bethune (c. 1943)

half of the twentieth century. She was born July 10, 1875, in Mayesville, South Carolina, the fifteenth of the seventeen children of former slaves Samuel and Patsy McLeod. From the time she was a young child, Mary's parents recognized their daughter's intellectual abilities, and they enrolled her in the Mayesville Presbyterian Mission for Negroes. Aided by a scholarship, Mary continued her education at Scotia Seminary for Negro Girls in Concord, North Carolina. She graduated at the top of her class in 1894, and in July of that year she began studying at the Bible Institute for Home and Foreign Missions (later the Moody Bible Institute) in Chicago. With hopes of becoming a missionary in Africa, Mary applied to the Presbyterian Mission Board for an assignment but, because of her race, was turned down.

Disappointed in the Mission Board's decision, Mary decided to return to the South and work to uplift African Americans. In 1895 she joined the teaching staff at Haines Normal and Industrial In-

stitute in Augusta, Georgia. While there she met the school's black founder and principal, Lucy Laney, who became Mary's model for service to humanity. After a year at the school, she moved to Sumter, South Carolina, and taught at the Kindell Institute. While in Sumter she met Albertus Bethune, whom she married in May 1898. Three years later the couple moved to Palatka and then to Daytona Beach, Florida, where Mary held teaching jobs at elementary schools. In 1904 Bethune began her own academy, the Daytona Normal and Industrial Institute for Girls.

From a modest beginning of only 5 students, the school grew to become a large institution. Enrollment grew to 300 by 1923, with a faculty of 25. In that year the school merged with the Cookman Institute, a coeducational Methodist school, and Bethune herself joined the Methodist Episcopal Church at about the same time. For some time Bethune had had hopes of transforming her school into a college, which finally came to pass following the merger with Cookman. The institution was officially renamed Bethune-Cookman College in 1929. With Methodist support, the school grew to become an accredited junior college in 1939 and then a senior college in 1941. Bethune, who was the first African-American woman to found and head such an institution in the United States, remained in firm control of the school until she retired in 1942.

In addition to her work at the school, Bethune became nationally prominent as a result of her efforts to serve blacks in general. After World War I she was active in the antilynching campaign. From 1917 to 1924, she served as president of the Florida Federation of Colored Women, which opened and operated a home for "wayward" and delinquent girls in Ocala. In 1924 she became president of the National Association of Colored Women, an office considered the highest to which an African-American woman could then aspire. She traveled and lectured throughout the country and, by example, inspired thousands of black women to increase their level of service to humanity. In 1936, under President Franklin D. Roosevelt, Bethune became director of the Division of Negro Affairs of the National Youth Administration. In that post, which she held until 1944, she traveled across the nation an average of 40,000 miles a year to supervise programs for African-American youth. She organized the National Council of Negro Women in 1935 and was its president until 1949. Bethune was also an avid supporter of the National Association for the Advancement of Colored People (NAACP) and of the Southern Conference for Human Welfare.

During the final years of her life, Bethune received many honors in recognition of her leadership role. In 1952 she was chosen by President Harry Truman to represent the United States at the second inauguration of Liberia's president, William Tubman. Bethune died of a heart attack at her home in Daytona on May 18, 1955, and was buried on the campus of Bethune-Cookman College.

See also: African Americans
References: Henry Warner Bowden, *Dictionary of American Religious Biography*, 2nd ed. (1993); Rackham Holt, *Mary McLeod Bethune: A Biography* (1964); J. Gordon Melton, *Religious Leaders of America* (1991); Catherine Owens Peare, *Mary McLeod Bethune* (1951); Barbara Sicherman and Carol Hurd Green, eds., *Notable American Women: The Modern Period* (1980).

Biblical Authority and Women's Rights

When the colonists arrived in North America in the seventeenth century, they brought their customs and traditions with them. Most important for many was their religion, which was normally based upon the Judeo-Christian tradition, which has placed males in authority. For centuries, religious leaders have referred to the Bible to support the positions on male authority within their church. Often cited as proof of God's intention that men should dominate women are the creation stories in Genesis and the apostle Paul's Letter to the Ephesians. Church fathers have contended that Eve was an afterthought in God's plan of creation. She was formed of Adam's rib (Genesis 2:20–23) and was therefore meant to serve him. Eve was also perceived as the weaker of the two, for it was she who succumbed to temptation. She compounded her sins by tempting Adam to disobey God's commands. After the Fall, God is said to have stated to Eve, "I will greatly multiply thy sorrow and thy conception; in sorrow thou shalt bring forth children; and thy desire *shall be* to thy husband, and he shall rule over thee" (Genesis 3:16). The Judeo-Christian tradition has taught that all women possess Eve's nature and, therefore, they must bow to their husbands' authority.

Leaders of the Christian church have historically looked to Paul to confirm their position that women are the inferior sex. Frequently cited are Paul's Letter to the Ephesians 5: 22–24:

Wives, submit yourselves unto your own husbands, as unto the Lord.

For the husband is the head of the wife, even as Christ is the head of the church: and he is the saviour of the body.

Therefore as the church is subject unto Christ, *so let* the wives *be* to their own husbands in every thing.

According to Paul, women were by nature weak and in need of protection. He felt that men were the spiritual leaders and, in I Corinthians 14:34–35, instructs women to be silent in church.

Although church leaders have turned to the Bible to support male authority over women, Quakers and others, especially feminists, have quoted the Bible to uphold their position that men and women were created equal. For although Genesis 1:27 begins, "So God created man in his *own* image, in the image of God created he him," the passage continues, "male and female created he them." Those who seek to uplift women's positions within church hierarchies have also looked to biblical heroines like Deborah and Queen Esther as examples of strong, influential women. And in support of women as preachers, many have found evidence in the New Testament, noting that Jesus Christ chose three women: Mary Magdalene; Mary, the mother of James and Joseph; and Salome to publicly announce his resurrection (Mark 16).

Biblical versions of specific events have been studied critically since the mid-nineteenth century for their historicity and reliability. Today most "mainline" churches interpret judgments and mores historically, in terms of customs and beliefs of the times in which they were developed. These new interpretations have led to the opening of positions within church hierarchies that were for centuries closed to women. Historians perceive that despite all the restrictions placed upon them, women have at times been able to develop a sphere for themselves within the church. Possibly the best example of this is the leading role of some nuns in the Middle Ages who established and headed monastic orders, wrote learned works, and ran hospitals. During the nineteenth and twentieth centuries American women of both the Christian and Jewish faiths have created increasingly larger spheres of responsibility for themselves within their churches and synagogues. Women became active in charitable work, which grew to include missions, and some became deaconesses or nuns. The twentieth century

found increasing numbers of women being ordained as pastors in mainline denominations. Throughout American history, and especially since the 1830s, there have been women who have challenged traditional interpretations of the Bible. Among them were Matilda Joslyn Gage, Sarah Grimké, and Elizabeth Cady Stanton in the nineteenth century and, in the late twentieth century, Mary Daly, Georgia Harkness, and Rosemary Radford Ruether.

See also: Clergy; Daly, Mary; Feminist Theology; The "Feminization" of American Religion; Gage, Matilda Joslyn; Grimké, Sarah Moore; Harkness, Georgia Elma; Ruether, Rosemary Radford; Stanton, Elizabeth Cady; *The Woman's Bible*
References: Georgia Harkness, *Women in Church and Society: A Historical and Theological Inquiry* (1972); King James Version of the Bible; Winston E. Langley and Vivian C. Fox, *Women's Rights in the United States: A Documentary History* (1994); Rosemary Radford Ruether, *Religion and Sexism: Images of Woman in the Christian and Jewish Tradition* (1974); Elizabeth Cady Stanton, *The Woman's Bible: Parts I and II* (1895 and 1898).

Birth Control

In 1800 American women were bearing an average of 7.04 children; by 1900 the number of children born to American women had decreased by almost half, to an average of 3.56 per woman. A principal cause of this great decline in the birthrate was an increased knowledge of and use of methods for birth control.

The first American tracts on the subject were inspired by English reformers of the 1820s. Reformer Robert Dale Owen wrote what is considered the first important book on birth control, *Moral Physiology; or, A Brief and Plain Treatise on the Population Question,* in 1831. Owen included a brief discussion of birth control methods and recommended coitus interruptus. The publication of *Moral Physiology* marked the beginning of national debate over the morality and

When Margaret Sanger was arrested in Brooklyn for dispensing birth control, several poor mothers brought their large families to court to support her. Sanger founded an organization that later became the Planned Parenthood Federation of America.

safety of contraceptive use. When the book was distributed to Indiana voters during Owen's campaign for the Indiana assembly in 1836, it won the approval of the local clergy, but not all of the religious community was so accepting of the promotion of birth control.

Charles Knowlton wrote the first popular tract on birth control to be published by a physician. In *Fruits of Philosophy; or, The Private Companion of Young Married People* (1832), Knowlton proposed that women douche with water and a semen-killing additive. As a result of the publication of the tract, he was prosecuted three times under the Massachusetts common-law obscenity statute, with the last prosecution being inspired by a Congregationalist minister.

During the last quarter of the nineteenth century and through the late 1930s, the distribution of birth control tracts was inhibited by what was known as the Comstock Law (1873), which banned the circulation of and trade in literature defined as "obscene." Challenged by birth control advocate Margaret Sanger, the power of this law was gradually lessened. Meanwhile, in the 1920s Sanger became involved in public debate with Roman Catholic Church leaders. She argued for the equality of women in family, society, and the church. Church leaders considered her views antinatalistic and reaffirmed their position that it was woman's duty to stay home and bear many children. Backing Sanger were Protestants who disdained the large families of the foreign-born, a large proportion of whom were Catholic.

Robert Dickinson, a liberal Episcopalian and an important medical advocate of contraception during the late nineteenth and early twentieth centuries, represented another viewpoint held among Protestants. He believed that the sharing of intimate experience with another person was important to the process of human growth and discovery. One of Dickinson's contributions to the birth control cause was his bearing Christian witness that sex was a force to be accepted and enjoyed. A church's position on the importance of the family frequently affects its stand on birth control. For instance, the Mormons, who believe that children provide bodies for waiting spirits who can then work out their eternal salvation, discourage birth control but do not forbid it. In contrast, Jehovah's Witnesses, who emphasize evangelical work, often dissuade young couples from starting families and stress sexual abstinence.

Women have often dismissed the rulings of church leaders and used their own judgment when making decisions concerning the practice of birth control. Among these are American Catholic women, many of whom have defected from the teachings of their church on the subject. Although in 1968 the church reaffirmed its ban on birth control methods other than the rhythm method, the majority of American Catholic women of childbearing age use contraceptives of some kind.

See also: Abortion; Comstock Law
References: Linda Gordon, *Woman's Body, Woman's Right: A Social History of Birth Control in America* (1977, reprint 1986); Susan Hill Lindley, *"You Have Stept Out of Your Place": A History of Women and Religion in America* (1996); M. James Penton, *Apocalypse Delayed: The Story of Jehovah's Witnesses* (1986); James Reed, *From Private Vice to Public Virtue: The Birth Control Movement and American Society since 1830* (1978); Charles F. Westoff and Norman B. Ryder, *The Contraceptive Revolution* (1977).

Black Women in Church and Society

Founded in Atlanta, Georgia, in 1982, Black Women in Church and Society (BWCS) serves both ordained women and laywomen. Its goal is to provide leadership training and support systems for black women who aim to fulfill responsible roles within both religious and secular society in the United States and in the Third World. Also, it serves as a forum for communication between laywomen and women of the clergy. BWCS conducts research into questions of importance to black women and sponsors charitable programs and seminars. The organization has established a research-resource center and a small library with materials relating to black theology, feminism, and women's movements. Its organ, *Black Women in Ministry*, is published quadrennially.

References: Jacqueline K. Barrett, ed., *Encyclopedia of Women's Associations Worldwide* (1993); Harry A. Ploski and James Williams, comps. and eds., *The Negro Almanac: A Reference Work on the African American,* 5th ed. (1989); Wendy S. Van de Sande, ed., *Black Americans Information Directory, 1994–95,* 3rd ed. (1993).

Blackwell, Annie Walker (1862–1922)

Annie Walker Blackwell, a well-known leader in the missions work of the African Methodist Episcopal Zion (AMEZ) Church, was born in Chester, South Carolina, on August 21, 1862. She was the oldest daughter of Mathilda (Potts) and Dublin Isaiah Walker. Her father, who was a minister, became associated with the AMEZ Church after the Civil War and was one of the first presiding elders in the South Carolina Conference. Annie, therefore, had a strong religious background before she attended Scotia Seminary in Concord, North Carolina. She then began a career in teaching but left that profession when she married the Reverend George Lincoln Blackwell on December 7, 1887. George Blackwell, who would later become a bishop, had been ordained to the ministry two years prior to their marriage. Both he and Annie were interested in mission work. George is credited with having established the foundation for the AME Zion Church's missionary department.

Soon after her marriage, Annie Blackwell began devoting considerable time and effort to the enterprises of the Women's Home and Foreign Missionary Society. The society, which had been in existence since 1880, had suffered a slow start. It did not hold its first missionary convention until 1901. At its second convention the following year, Blackwell was named assistant corresponding secretary as well as editor of the women's column in the *Star of Zion,* the denominational journal. She later became associate editor of the *Missionary Seer.*

In 1904 Blackwell drew the attention of the bishops with her report concerning the lack of missionary societies in local churches and her prescription for rectifying the situation. She urged that the society be placed under the sole control of women and that it be considered the women's auxiliary of the Mission Board of the church. Her position was strengthened at the 1904 General Conference, when her husband was elected a bishop and she was elected corresponding secretary of the Woman's Home and Foreign Missionary Society. The society was turned over to the women. During its eighteen years under Annie Blackwell's leadership, the society experienced tremendous growth, until almost all local churches had chapters. She has been credited with implementing the idea of life memberships and the naming of Life Matrons as a means of raising money for the church. The first Life Member was enrolled in 1906, and friends contributed the funds to pay for Blackwell's life membership a year later. Together with Victoria Richardson, Blackwell also established the Young Woman's Society, a missionary organization for youth.

In addition to her work as corresponding secretary of the Women's Home and Foreign Mission Society, Blackwell was editor for four years of the *Woman's Christian Temperance Union Tidings* and was president of the Staff Auxiliary of Douglass Hospital in Philadelphia. In 1911, she served as a delegate to the Methodist Ecumenical Conference in Toronto, Canada, and in 1914 Pennsylvania governor John K. Tener appointed her a delegate to the National Civic Movement Convention in Kansas City, Missouri.

Annie Walker Blackwell died suddenly at her home in Philadelphia, while tending her ailing husband, on her thirty-fifth wedding anniversary, December 7, 1922.

See also: Missionary Societies
References: J. Gordon Melton, *Religious Leaders of America* (1991); Larry G. Murphy et al., *Encyclopedia of African-American Religions* (1993); William J. Walls, *The African Methodist Episcopal Zion Church: Reality of the Black Church* (1974).

Blackwell, Antoinette Brown (1825–1921)

Antoinette Brown Blackwell, the first woman to be ordained a minister of a Protestant denomination, was born in Henrietta, New York, on May 20, 1825. As a child, she attended the local Congregational Church with her family. When she was nine, she went before the congregation to apply for full membership, an action unprecedented for a child of her young age. She answered the minister's simple questions and stated her

*Antoinette Brown Blackwell
(undated photo)*

reasons for considering herself a Christian and desiring to be connected with the church. Despite her youth, the church voted unanimously in favor of her membership.

When she was twenty-one, Brown enrolled in Oberlin College in Oberlin, Ohio. She was among the pioneering women intent on pursuing a college education. In 1847, Brown completed a literary course of study and received a literary diploma, but her greatest interest was in religion, and she remained at Oberlin until she completed the school's course of study in theology in 1850. The college refused to grant her a degree because she was a woman. Twenty-eight years passed before she finally received the degree, and her name was not included on the roster of graduates until 1908.

On September 15, 1853, Brown was ordained a minister of the First Congregational Church of Butler and Savannah, New York, becoming the first woman to be ordained by a nationally recognized denomination. But she had serious theological differences with her congregation and resigned as minister of the church in 1854. She later became a Unitarian. Following her resignation, Brown spent a year as a volunteer worker in the slums and prisons of New York City. She examined causes of mental and social disorders and wrote a series of articles on the subject for the *New York Tribune.*

In 1856, Brown married Samuel Blackwell, and in subsequent years, she raised six daughters and wrote ten books. Among the books was *Studies in General Science* (1869), a philosophical work on religion and science, and *The Sexes throughout Nature* (1875), which argued that Darwin's male perspective limited his understanding of the roles of the sexes. She was also a strong supporter of the woman suffrage movement, giving lectures around the country and writing a number of articles for the cause. Antoinette Brown Blackwell lived to vote in the election of 1920, which followed the passage of the Nineteenth Amendment granting woman suffrage. Throughout her life, she continued to participate in religious activities. From 1908 until her death, she served as pastor emeritus of All Souls Unitarian Church in Elizabeth, New Jersey. Blackwell died in Elizabeth on November 5, 1921.

See also: Clergy; Woman Suffrage
References: Elizabeth Cazden, *Antoinette Brown Blackwell: A Biography* (1993); Blanche Glassman Hersh, *The Slavery of Sex: Feminist Abolitionists in America* (1978); Phyllis J. Read and Bernard L. Witlieb, *The Book of Women's Firsts* (1992).

Blavatsky, Helena Petrovna (1831–1891)

Helena Petrovna Blavatsky, or H.P.B. as her friends and followers fondly called her, was an influential writer of the occult community and a cofounder of the Theosophical Society. Born into an affluent family in Ekaterinoslav (now Dnepropetrovsk), Ukraine, on August 12, 1831, she was known throughout her life for her flamboyant personality. From childhood she was drawn to the occult and the supernatural. She had an extraordinary imagination and is said to have caused hallucinations in her playmates through her vivid storytelling. Her mother died when she was twelve years old, and for the next five years H.P.B. lived with her grandfather. After having threatened to shoot any man who dared to speak to her of love, Helena surprised her family and friends in 1849, when she married General Nikifor Blavatsky, a man in his forties. However, the Blavatskys were married only three months before Helena fled to Turkey.

For the next twenty-five years, H.P.B. journeyed around the world, enjoying a series of adventures while she explored the occult. While staying with her father in London in 1851, she first reported having contacts with mahatmas, or spiritual masters. In 1858 she became acquainted with the famous medium Daniel D. Home while visiting France and became attached to Spiritualism. In 1871 she founded a Spiritualist society in Cairo, but it soon closed amid charges of fraud and embezzlement.

H.P.B. arrived in New York City in July 1873 and was soon actively involved in Spiritualism in the United States. In 1874 she was in Chittenden, Vermont, where the American farmer mediums, the Eddy brothers, were holding seances. From their home, she began writing for magazines, mostly on Spiritualism. Soon she was working with successful agricultural scientist and lawyer Henry Steel Olcott, who was also intrigued with the idea of investigating Spiritualist phenomena. With Olcott she arranged Spiritualist gatherings in New York City, and she translated his articles on Spiritualism into Russian. In November 1875, H.P.B. and Olcott joined with lawyer William Q. Judge to establish the Theosophical Society in New York City. H.P.B.'s home on 8th Avenue and 47th Street became the organization's unofficial headquarters. Olcott lived in the same apartment building. With the help of Olcott and that of the mahatmas who she said continued to contact her, H.P.B. wrote her first book, *Isis Unveiled,* which was published in 1877. On July 8, 1878, she became an American citizen, announcing that she was proud to do so because she was a lover of liberty.

The goals of the Theosophical Society were to promote the formation of a universal brotherhood of humankind; to study comparative religions, philosophy, and science; and to explore the expansion of human powers of mind and spirit. Its founders claimed that the society was being directed by secret mahatmas. The Theosophical Society introduced cremation into the United States when the body of follower Baron Joseph Henry Louis de Palm was incinerated on December 6, 1876, in the town of Washington, Pennsylvania. During the following century, the society grew until it had 150 centers in the United States by the late 1980s. However, the Theosophical Society struggled during its early years, and soon Olcott and H.P.B. left the United States, determined to establish new headquarters in India.

After a slow start, their work in India prospered. Olcott and H.P.B. began a magazine, *The Theosophist,* in 1879, which earned them a living. In 1882 they moved their headquarters to a large parcel of land in Madras. There H.P.B. spent time studying Buddhism and Hinduism, and her philosophical views began to change. She moved away from Spiritualism. Instead of contacts with the spirits of the dead, she placed greater emphasis upon contacts with the mahatmas. Soon she was claiming that letters from these spiritual masters were mysteriously arriving for her. But in 1884, while H.P.B. and Olcott were in London, a close associate in India, Emma Cutting Coulomb, publicly accused Blavatsky of fraud. The mahatmas' letters, it seems, were written by H.P.B. herself and deposited in the file cabinet, where they often appeared, by way of a secret opening from H.P.B.'s bedroom. The scandal hurt the Theosophical movement and caused H.P.B. to leave India and move first to Germany and later to London, where she remained for the rest of her life.

In London in 1888, H.P.B. met Annie Besant, an essayist in search of a meaningful philosophy. In the late 1880s Besant was drawn to both Theosophy and Blavatsky. Before she died on May 8, 1891, Blavatsky used Besant's talents to ignite the recovery and growth of the Theosophical Society.

See also: Bailey, Alice La Trobe Bateman; Besant, Annie Wood
References: Sylvia Cranston, *HPB: The Extraordinary Life and Influence of Helena Blavatsky, Founder of the Modern Theosophical Movement* (1993); Robert S. Ellwood, Jr., *Religious and Spiritual Groups in Modern America* (1973); J. Gordon Melton, *Biographical Dictionary of American Cult and Sect Leaders* (1986); J. Gordon Melton, *Religious Leaders of America* (1991); Gottfried de Porucker, *H. P. Blavatsky: The Mystery* (1974); Leslie Shepard, ed., *Encyclopedia of Occultism and Parapsychology*, 3rd ed. (1991).

Bonney, Mary Lucinda
(1816–1900)

Advocate for Native American rights, educator, and Baptist laywoman Mary Lucinda Bonney was born in Hamilton, New York, on June 8, 1816. Her father, Benjamin Bonney, was a farmer, and her mother, Lucinda (Wilder) Bonney, had been a schoolteacher prior to her marriage. Mary received a solid education, attending the local Hamilton Academy and then Emma Willard's Troy Female Seminary in Troy, New York. Bonney graduated from the latter school in 1835.

Following her graduation, Bonney began a teaching career, holding positions in Jersey City, New Jersey; New York City; DeRuyter, New York; and at her alma mater in Troy. In 1842 she moved to Beaufort and later to Robertville, South Carolina. During her six-year stay in the South, Bonney became acquainted with Thomas Rambaut, a Baptist minister. Under Rambaut's ministry, Bonney left the Episcopal Church in which she had been raised and became a Baptist.

Bonney returned north in 1848, first to Providence, Rhode Island, and then to Philadelphia. Along with Harriette Dillaye, a friend from Troy Seminary, Bonney opened the Chestnut Street Female Seminary in Philadelphia and became the school's senior principal, a post she held until 1888. The school proved to be a success. In 1883 it moved to Ogontz, Pennsylvania, and changed its name to Ogontz School for Young Ladies.

Upon her arrival in Philadelphia, Bonney joined the city's First Baptist Church. She also became associated with the interdenominational Woman's Union Missionary Society of America for Heathen Lands. She served as an officer of the society and, from the 1860s, was a regular donor to this organization that sent female missionaries to the secluded women of Asia. But Bonney's concerns were increasingly drawn to problems closer to home, that is, the plight of Native Americans. She served at her church as the president of a women's home missionary circle interested in Native Americans. Bonney was outraged when, in 1879, she learned that Congress was considering proposals that would allow settlers to take lands in Oklahoma that by treaty had been assigned to Native Americans. She immediately set to work funding a campaign to circulate a petition that demanded that treaties be honored and that white encroachment on Native American lands be stopped. The 300-foot-long petition with thirteen thousand signatures was presented to President Rutherford B. Hayes and to Congress in 1880. Bonney then went to work gathering signatures on a second petition. This one called for the protection of Native Americans' lands.

Meanwhile, Bonney and her supporters organized the Central Indian Committee (later renamed the Indian Treaty Keeping and Protective Association). The women's second petition, representing fifty thousand persons, was presented in the U.S. Senate by Massachusetts senator Henry L. Dawes on January 27, 1881. Dawes also presented the women's third petition, brought before the Senate in February 1882. With double the number of signatures of the previous petition, it urged that Native Americans be given full rights under the law, that tribal lands be allotted to individual Native Americans, and that sufficient common schools be provided to accommodate "every child of every tribe" (Prucha, 1976, p. 135). As incorporated in the Dawes Act of 1887, land allotment became the official policy of the United States. The act also made it possible for Native Americans who owned land to become citizens of the United States. Educational reforms came later, but by the beginning of the twentieth century, most schools for Native Americans were public. The Dawes Act remained in place for fifty years, until unforeseen problems brought about new reforms.

In 1883 the Indian Treaty Keeping and Protective Association changed its name to the Women's National Indian Association. With the Dawes Act pending, the group altered its focus and launched a missionary and educational program with hopes of aiding Native American women by offering child care, instruction in English and religion, and vocational training. Because of her school responsibilities, Bonney resigned as head of the organization in November 1884 but remained its honorary president and a member of the executive board and missionary committee. She also continued to make personal financial contributions to the organization, meeting most of the association's expenses for its first five years.

Bonney, then in her seventies, retired from the Ogontz School in 1888. She traveled to London that year as a delegate of the Women's National Indian Association to the Centenary Conference on the Protective Missions of the World. There she renewed her acquaintance with Baptist minister Thomas Rambaut who, since she had known him in South Carolina, had been twice widowed and had retired from his job as a college president. Bonney and Rambaut married in London and returned to live in Hamilton, New York. Rambaut died two years later. Bonney survived another decade, residing with her brother in Hamilton until her death there on July 24, 1900.

See also: Baptists; Native Americans
References: Edward T. James, ed., *Notable American Women, 1607–1950*, vol. 1 (1971); J. Gordon Melton, *Religious Leaders of America* (1991); Francis Paul Prucha, *American Indian Policy in Crisis: Christian Reformers and the Indian, 1865–1900* (1976).

Booth, Evangeline Cory (1865–1950)

Evangeline Booth was the first woman to command the Salvation Army in the United States and the first general of the International Salvation Army. Born in London, England, on December 25, 1865, Evangeline, who was named for Little Eva, a character in *Uncle Tom's Cabin*, was the daughter of William Booth and Catherine Booth. Her parents cofounded the Salvation Army in the year of Evangeline's birth. From early childhood, Evan-

On the steps of City Hall in New York City, Commander Evangeline Cory Booth salutes as the Salvation Army National Congress celebrates its golden jubilee in 1930.

geline absorbed the Salvation Army's charitable and religious ideals, and she preached her first public sermon at the age of thirteen. When she was eighteen, Evangeline was put in charge of an entire section of the London slums. Her abilities to find food for the needy, to find doctors for the sick, and to reform drunkards, wife-beaters, petty thieves, and brawlers earned her the title "The Angel of the Slums." Captain Evangeline Cory Booth's performance in the slums so impressed her father that he promoted her to the rank of field commissioner and placed her in command of all army operations in metropolitan London. He also made her principal of the Salvation Army's International Training College at Clapton.

In 1896, Booth, who was then directing army operations in Canada, was or-dered to go to New York City. Her older brother, Ballington Booth, who had been leading the Salvation Army in the United States since 1887, resigned as a protest against their father's absolute rule over the organization. Booth arrived in New York with hopes of convincing Ballington to reconsider his resignation and restoring order within the ranks of the army. She failed to persuade her brother to change his mind but, after consider-able effort, did quell much of the dis-sension within the ranks and regained public support for the army. After com-pleting her assignment in New York, Booth returned to Canada.

In 1904, she was recalled to New York to serve as commander of the Salvation Army in the United States. She held that position until 1934, during which time she became a naturalized American citizen (1923). Her tenure as commander ended when Booth was elected general of the International Salvation Army. Under her leadership, the Salvation Army expanded its evangelical efforts, social services, and its program for emergency disaster relief. When she had assumed command of the army in the United States in 1904, there had been very little cash with which to conduct operations, and the value of Salvation Army property there was approximately $1,500,000. When she turned command over to her successor in 1934, the army's bank accounts totaled $35,000,000, and its properties were worth $48,000,000. By 1934, the army had become the foremost social service organization in the United States.

Booth retired from her generalship of the International Salvation Army in 1939 but retained an active role in army enterprises. With the onset of World War II in 1939, her principal interest was in soliciting funds for programs that would provide assistance to soldiers. Only a series of illnesses in the 1940s prevented her from maintaining a busy schedule of army activities. Evangeline Booth died in Hartsdale, New York, on July 17, 1950.

See also: Booth, Maud Elizabeth Ballington; Salvation Army
References: Sigmund A. Lavine, *Evangeline Booth, Daughter of Salvation* (1970); Norman H. Murdock, *Origins of the Salvation Army* (1994); Phyllis J. Read and Bernard L. Witlieb, *The Book of Women's Firsts* (1992); Philip Whitwell Wilson, *General Evangeline Booth of the Salvation Army* (1948).

Booth, Maud Elizabeth Ballington (1865–1948)

Cofounder of both the Salvation Army in the United States and the Volunteers of America, Maud Elizabeth Ballington Booth was born in Limpsfield, Surrey, England, on September 13, 1865. She was the daughter of Reverend Samuel

Beddome Charlesworth, an Anglican clergyman, and Maria Beddome Charlesworth. When Maud was three, her family moved to London, where her father preached in one of the city's poorest sections. Maud reached a turning point in her life in 1881, when she attended a Salvation Army meeting at which Ballington Booth, a son of General William and Catherine Booth, was preaching. She was greatly impressed with the Salvation Army program and joined the group the following year. Soon, she was helping Catherine Booth establish armies in France and Switzerland, before returning to London to work in the slums. In 1886, she married Ballington Booth, adopting both of his names as her own. A year later, the Ballington Booths were assigned the supervision of the Salvation Army in the United States and moved to New York City. They became American citizens in 1895.

Ballington and Maud had difficulty accepting William Booth's autocratic control over the Salvation Army. By 1896 their disagreements with the general had reached a point where they could no longer tolerate their roles within the army, so they resigned. The couple, who had garnered much public support during their years in New York, drew upon that support to begin a new movement. Immediately following their resignation from the Salvation Army, they founded the Volunteers of America, a charitable organization that, unlike the army, elected its leaders.

Prison reform was of great interest to Maud, who centered her work on rehabilitating prisoners through religion. She worked in connection with the Volunteer Prison League, which founded group homes for families of prisoners and worked to provide employment for ex-convicts. Her work is documented in several books: *Branded* (1897); *Did the Pardon Come Too Late?* (1897); and *After*

Prison, What? (1903). In Booth's view, prisons were best used as centers for rehabilitation rather than for punishment. Her reforming efforts influenced the gradual development of the parole system.

After Ballington's death in 1940, Maud was elected general of the Volunteers of America and was active in that post almost until her death. She died in Great Neck, New York, on August 26, 1948.

See also: Booth, Evangeline Cory; Salvation Army
References: Edward T. James, ed., *Notable American Women, 1607–1950* (1971); J. Gordon Melton, *Religious Leaders of America* (1991); Phyllis J. Read and Bernard L. Witlieb, *The Book of Women's Firsts* (1992).

Bowles, Eva del Vakia (1875–1943)

Eva del Vakia Bowles, a prominent leader of the Young Women's Christian Association (YWCA), was born January 24, 1875, in Albany, Ohio. She was the eldest of the three children of John Hawkes Bowles and Mary Jane (Porter) Bowles. Her father was the first African-American postal clerk for the Railway Mail Service. In 1883 the Bowles family moved to Columbus, where Eva grew up. She received her education from public schools, a business college, and some courses at Ohio State University. Her religious affiliation was Episcopalian.

Bowles began her career as a teacher for the American Missionary Association in Lexington, Kentucky. Later she served on faculties in St. Augustine, Florida; Raleigh, North Carolina; and Lawrenceville, Virginia. In 1905 she was appointed secretary of the Harlem branch of the New York City YWCA, the first African-American secretary for that organization. The Harlem branch was the largest branch for blacks in the United States. After three years she left the YWCA to spend 1908–1912 working as a caseworker for the Associated Charities of Ohio. Bowles returned to New York City in 1913 and became secretary for the newly created YWCA National Board Subcommittee for Colored Work, which in 1917 became a full-fledged committee.

When America entered World War I in 1917, Bowles was put in charge of African-American concerns associated with the YWCA's War Work Council. She was given the task of supervising the establishment of recreation and industrial centers for black women and girls in forty-five cities. To help her accomplish this, she enlisted the help of prominent African-American women, locally and nationally.

After the end of the war, the immigration of blacks to northern cities placed pressure on the YWCAs that served African Americans. With Bowles as its leader, in 1920 the Committee on Colored Work became the Bureau of Colored Work, and two years later, it became the Council on Colored Work. In her role as a leader, Bowles set to work to improve interracial relations within the YWCA. She resisted a separatist movement by some younger African-American leaders during the 1920s and promoted changes within the national YWCA that would give black women a greater share of recognition and responsibility. Although Bowles was disappointed in the slowness of the progress in improved interracial relations within the YWCA, she remained devoted to the organization. She retired from the national YWCA in 1932.

Bowles, a woman dedicated to uplifting her race and improving interracial relations within a national Christian organization, died in Richmond, Virginia, on June 14, 1943.

References: Darlene Clark Hine, ed., *Black Women in America: An Historical Encyclopedia* (1993); Edward T. James, ed., *Notable American Women, 1607–1950* (1971); J. Gordon Melton, *Religious Leaders of America* (1991); Dorothy C. Salem, ed., *African American Women: A Biographical Dictionary* (1993).

Brooks, Nona Lovell (1861–1945)

Nona Lovell Brooks, leader of the New Thought movement and founder of the Divine Science Church, was born into a large family on March 22, 1861. While still a child, she moved with her family from her Louisville, Kentucky, birthplace to a farmstead near Charleston, West Virginia, where her father had a prosperous salt-mining business. Both parents were staunch Presbyterians, and Brooks received a solid religious upbringing. She had her first religious experience when she was a young girl, later recalling that she was walking alone in the garden when she was engulfed by a supernatural light. Thereafter, she was determined to be close to God.

Her teen years were a dark period in Brooks's life. Her father's business faltered when rock salt was discovered in New York. The family then moved to Colorado because of her mother's poor health. Brooks's boyfriend became engaged to another girl while he was away at seminary, and in 1880, her father died, leaving the family almost penniless. Since her move to Colorado, Brooks had been suffering from a throat infection. In 1887, at the urging of her sister Alethea Small, Brooks attended classes taught by Kate Bingham, a teacher of Christian Science. Bingham had worked in Chicago with Christian Science teacher Emma Hopkins and credited her newfound faith with curing her of a severe illness. After attending her third class with Bingham, Brooks found her throat had healed. Soon both she and Alethea were using the techniques they had learned from Bingham to heal others. The sisters were so excited over their work that they told their minister. He invited them to speak at the church, but the elders disapproved of their practice and removed Brooks from her Sunday school teaching duties.

Meanwhile, Brooks became concerned about her future. In 1890, at age 29, she enrolled at Pueblo Normal School and then at Wellesley College to prepare for a teaching career. At about the same time, another sister, Fannie James, was in Denver, teaching metaphysical classes in her home. James had been corresponding with Divine Science teacher Malinda Cramer, and her classes were similar to those taught by Cramer in San Francisco. Divine Science is a part of the New Thought movement, which emerged out of Christian Science in the 1880s. New Thought advocates do not accept the ideas of Christian Science founder Mary Baker Eddy as unerring doctrine but insist on the freedom to supplement her writings with other religious works. Brooks began working with James, and Small soon joined them.

The sisters opened the Divine Science College (later the Colorado College of Divine Science) in Denver in 1898, and Brooks went to California to receive her ordination from Cramer the same year. In 1899 Brooks opened and pastored the first Divine Science Church in Denver. It was not long before she was the leader of a growing movement. In 1902 she launched a monthly magazine, *Fulfillment,* which was published until 1906 when it was superseded by the *Divine Science Quarterly.* Brooks added *Daily Studies in Divine Science* (now *Aspire*) in 1915, the first of New Thought's daily devotional studies. The death of Cramer in the San Francisco earthquake of 1906 left a void in the organization there, but Brooks and her sisters kept the movement alive in Denver. By 1918 there were Divine Science churches in cities coast to coast. After James's death during World War I, Brooks became head of the college. In 1922 she carried the Divine Science movement into the International New Thought Alliance (INTA) and became a well-known leader of that organization. Brooks was also a prominent and respected citizen of Denver who served on various boards of civic and philanthropic agencies. In 1926 she became a member of the Ministerial Alliance.

Brooks resigned from her pastoral and college work in the late 1920s and spent the next decade traveling. She introduced Divine Science in Australia and opened two centers there. Upon her return to Denver in 1938, Brooks again presided over the college until her resignation in 1943. She died in Denver on March 14, 1945.

See also: Cramer, Malinda Elliott; Hopkins, Emma Curtis; New Thought Movement
References: Charles S. Braden, *Spirits in Rebellion: The Rise and Development of New Thought* (1984); J. Gordon Melton, *Encyclopedic Handbook of Cults in America* (1986, 1992); J. Gordon Melton, *Religious Leaders of America* (1991).

Brown, Antoinette (Blackwell). See Blackwell, Antoinette Brown

Brown, Olympia (1835–1926)

Theologian and activist for woman suffrage Olympia Brown was born January 5, 1835, in Prairie Ronde, Michigan. Her parents encouraged her to obtain a solid education, and Olympia eagerly followed their advice. She enrolled in Antioch College in Yellow Springs, Ohio, in 1856 and graduated with a bachelor of arts degree in 1860. Inspired by Antoinette Brown Blackwell, whom she heard preach during her years at Antioch, Brown entered the theological school of St. Lawrence University in Canton, New York, from which she graduated in 1863. She was a member of the Protestant Northern Universalists and, within a month after her graduation from St. Lawrence, was ordained minister of the church at their association meeting in Malone, New York. In July 1864, she became pastor at a Universalist church in Weymouth, Massachusetts.

In 1866, Brown, who had long been interested in raising the political and social status of women, became a charter member of the American Equal Rights Association. She moved to Bridgeport, Connecticut, in 1870, when she received a call to become pastor of a church there. While living in Bridgeport, she married John Henry Willis, a merchant, in 1873. With his approval, she did not adopt his last name but continued to use her birth name. They had two children. The family moved to Racine, Wisconsin, in 1878. In 1884, Brown was elected president of the Wisconsin Woman Suffrage Association. Three years later, she resigned her pastorate at a church in Racine, where she had been serving since 1878, to devote all her energy to the woman suffrage movement. Her tenure as president of the Wisconsin Woman Suffrage Association lasted until 1912.

Supported by her Universalist belief in the fatherhood of God and the brotherhood of man, Brown viewed suffrage as a woman's right as well as a means for women to improve their communities and raise the level of political morality. Brown died in Baltimore, Maryland, on October 23, 1926.

See also: Blackwell, Antoinette Brown; Clergy; Woman Suffrage
References: Charlotte Coté, *Olympia Brown: The Battle for Equality* (1988); Lawrence L. Graves, "Brown, Olympia," in Edward T. James, ed., *Notable American Women, 1607–1950* (1971); Phyllis J. Read and Bernard L. Witlieb, *The Book of Women's Firsts* (1992).

Buddhists

Although Buddhism arrived in America with Chinese immigrants in the mid-nineteenth century, the Chinese were usually uninterested in proselytizing. There was some interest in Buddhism among white Americans during this period, but it was not until 1893 that a person was converted to Buddhism on American soil. By the turn of the century, Japanese Buddhist missionaries had begun coming to the

United States. As the century progressed, Buddhists from other parts of Asia arrived with differing traditions of Buddhism. Between 1950 and 1980, American women began converting to Buddhism in relatively large numbers. From that generation came a group of highly respected female teachers.

The first woman to teach in the United States was British-born Jiyu Kennett-roshi, who was raised in the Buddhist faith. As abbess of Shasta Abbey in northern California, she was the only woman to be the leader of a Zen Buddhist monastery in the United States. Founded in 1970, Shasta Abbey is known as a place where men and women train together and are treated as equals. Other women teachers include Ruth Denison, who heads the Desert Vissana Center in California, near Palm Springs, and conducts meditation retreats throughout the country; and Maurine Stuart-roshi, a Zen master who until 1990 headed a center in Cambridge, Massachusetts. They have taught both men and women but have been especially valued as sensitive teachers and role models for their female students.

Women played important roles in bringing Buddhism to the United States. In 1905 Mrs. Alexander Russell and her husband invited the first Japanese *roshi* to this country to teach Zen to Americans. Ruth Fuller Sasaki was a leader of the emerging Zen community in New York City during the late 1930s and early 1940s. She was a major financial backer of the First Zen Institute of America and married the institute's Zen master in 1944. After his death in 1945, she moved to Japan, where she immersed herself in Zen study and eventually became abbess of her own temple. In the late 1950s, Elsie Mitchell and her husband organized a meditation group and a Buddhist library, which later became the Cambridge Buddhist Association. It was one of the first centers of Zen Buddhism for Westerners in the country. Maurine Stuart-roshi headed the center until her death in 1990.

Thousands of Western men and women have converted to Buddhism, most since the end of World War II. Some feminists have been attracted to Buddhism because of what they perceive as the faith's nondualistic, nonsexist philosophy. Sandy Boucher, author of *Turning the Wheel: American Women Creating the New Buddhism* (1993), believes that a "distinctly Americanized, feminized, democratized" style of Buddhism is being created that will appeal to modern American women (p. 1). She feels that the Buddhist tradition of considering women inferior can be broken in the United States, since the religion's history in this country is so short.

Women are rarely found in leadership positions in the Buddhist Church in America, although they can be ordained and serve temples. Nevertheless, other scholars in addition to Boucher have noted that modern Buddhism is undergoing change. Recently Buddhist women, both nuns and laywomen, as well as laymen have assumed more prominent roles within the religion. Problems remain in respect to the roles of nuns because they continue to be required to consider every monk as senior or superior. For example, nuns go to monks for instruction but never the reverse. Most Western converts cannot accept the subordinate position of Buddhist nuns. Therefore, there are very few Buddhist nuns in the Western world.

See also: Sasaki, Ruth Fuller Everett
References: Nancy J. Barnes, "Women in Buddhism," in Sharma Arvind, *Today's Woman in World Religions* (1994); Sandy Boucher, *Turning the Wheel: American Women Creating the New Buddhism* (1993); Rick Fields, *How the Swans Came to the Lake: A Narrative History of Buddhism in America*, 3rd ed. (1992); Susan Hill Lindley, *"You Have Stept Out of Your Place": A History of Women and Religion*

in America (1996); Diana Y. Paul, *Women in Buddhism: Images of the Feminine in Mahayana Tradition,* 2nd ed. (1985).

Buffalo Bird Woman (1839–1929?)

Medicine woman and transmitter of Hidatsa tradition and culture, Maxidiwiac, or Buffalo Bird Woman in English, was born in the Hidatsa village of Sakakawea, along the Knife River in what is now central North Dakota. Her mother, Weahtee, was one of four sisters, all of whom were married to Buffalo Bird Woman's father, Small Ankle. When Buffalo Bird Woman was six, Weahtee died. From then on, her grandmother took primary responsibility for raising her. Buffalo Bird Woman was the descendant of chiefs on both sides of her family, and as a member of a prominent family, it was important for her to be educated in the traditions and beliefs of the Hidatsa. Her grandfather, who was a medicine man, taught her the ways of the spirits. The family's earth lodge held the holy objects of their community and was also the clan's meeting place.

Buffalo Bird Woman grew up during a period when the United States was in the process of tremendous expansion, with thousands of white settlers flocking into the American West. Pressured by the Americans to the east and by the Lakota Sioux to the south and west, in 1845 the Hidatsas and the Mandans moved to Like-a-Fishhook village, upstream from Sakakawea. Buffalo Bird Woman settled in Like-a-Fishhook with her family.

When she was about sixteen, Buffalo Bird Woman and her half-sister married Magpie, who, in accordance with the Hidatsa matrilineal custom, moved into the lodge of the two women. The marriage lasted until Magpie's death from tuberculosis thirteen years later. Buffalo Bird Woman's second marriage was to Son of Star, a Mandan, with whom she had a son, her only child. The boy was named Tskaka-Ssakis, or Goodbird. Over the years, Buffalo Bird Woman became known among her people as a devoted supporter of the old ways of the Hidatsa. She practiced the traditional skills of Hidatsa women, including gardening, food preparation, earth lodge building, and the weaving of mats and baskets. She learned and, in turn, taught the songs and oral literature of her people.

Following the passage of the Dawes Act in 1887, which was intended to end the status of Native American tribes as "domestic nations" and to absorb them into American life by allotting tribal lands as individual holdings, the Hidatsa people were forced from Like-a-Fishhook and onto land that became the Fort Berthold Reservation. Unlike many less fortunate Native Americans, Buffalo Bird Woman's family received allotments of land that were close together. This allowed them to carry on some semblance of their old manner of life. Buffalo Bird Woman raised her son in the traditional ways of the Hidatsa, but he later changed his name to Edward Goodbird, converted to Christianity, and became a Christian missionary. As an adult, Goodbird served as interpreter for his mother and her brother Wolf Chief when they dictated their biographies to Gilbert L. Wilson, an anthropologist who sought to record the beliefs and culture of the Hidatsa. Buffalo Bird Woman passed on descriptions of the Hidatsa lifestyles and philosophies. She articulated the pride and care that Hidatsa women took in their work as well as the power they derived from it. Without Buffalo Bird Woman's detailed report, little would be known of the customs practiced by this particular group of Native American women in the nineteenth century.

See also: Native Americans
References: Gretchen M. Bataille, *Native American Women: A Biographical Dictio-*

nary (1993); Joan M. Jensen, "Native American Women and Agriculture: A Seneca Case Study," in Ellen Carol DuBois and Vicki L. Ruiz, eds., *Unequal Sisters: A Multicultural Reader in U.S. Women's History* (1990); J. Gordon Melton, *Religious Leaders of America* (1991).

Burleigh, Celia C. (1827–1875)

Celia C. Burleigh, an advocate for woman suffrage, was the first woman to be ordained a minister in the Unitarian Church. She began her working life as a teacher in Syracuse and later worked as personal secretary to pioneer educator Emma Willard in Troy, New York. After her marriage to abolitionist William Burleigh in 1865, she pursued her interest in becoming a minister. She was ordained in 1871 and soon after was named pastor at a parish in Brooklyn, Connecticut. Her tenure as minister was short, however. In 1873, she resigned from the ministry because of poor health. Burleigh died in Syracuse, New York, on July 27, 1875.

See also: Clergy
References: Ellen Carol DuBois, *Feminism and Suffrage: The Emergence of an Independent Women's Movement in America, 1848–1869* (1978); Phyllis J. Read and Bernard L. Witlieb, *The Book of Women's Firsts* (1992); mentioned in Elizabeth Cady Stanton, *Eighty Years and More: Reminiscences, 1815–1897* (1898, reprint 1993).

Burroughs, Nannie Helen (1879–1961)

Educator, reformer, and religious leader Nannie Helen Burroughs was born May 2, 1879, in Culpeper, Virginia, the older of the two daughters of John and Jennie (Poindexter) Burroughs. John Burroughs died when Nannie was four, and soon after she moved with her mother to Washington, D.C. Nannie graduated from M Street High School with honors in 1896 but, as a black woman, found it difficult to find a job beyond the menial

Nannie Helen Burroughs (ca. 1900–1907)

level. She left Washington and spent a year in Philadelphia, where she acquired a position as associate editor of a Baptist paper, *The Christian Banner*. Anticipating an appointment to a clerical post as the result of her excellent score on a civil service examination, Burroughs returned to the nation's capital a year later, only to be turned down for the job because she was black.

In 1900 Burroughs moved to Louisville, Kentucky, to become bookkeeper and stenographer for the Foreign Mission Board of the National Baptist Convention. That same year she gave a stirring speech at the organizational meeting of the Women's Convention Auxiliary at the annual National Baptist Convention in Richmond, Virginia. Entitled "Hindered from Helping," Burroughs's speech decried the waste of unused talent among women. A founder of the Women's Convention Auxiliary, a group whose purpose was to bolster Christianity in America and to support missions and help train missionaries for foreign service, Burroughs served as its corresponding secretary from 1900 to 1947 and as president from 1948 to 1961.

Work for this religious auxiliary became the center of Burroughs's life. She used the organization to mobilize campaigns for the development of an industrial school for African-American girls in Washington, D.C. Arguing that missionary work was needed at home, she urged Baptist women to establish and maintain a national school to train black girls to be homemakers and to have respectable careers. In 1909 the National Training School for Women and Girls (after 1934 the National Trade and Professional School for Women and Girls) opened in Washington, D.C., with Burroughs as its president. She was to remain the school's spiritual and administrative leader for the balance of her life.

Since October 1909, when the school opened with seven students, thousands of girls from every state in the nation and from the Caribbean have attended the school. Religion and self-help were strongly emphasized in Burroughs's teaching. The school motto was "Learn to do at least one thing extremely well." Burroughs believed that strong religious character combined with outstanding performance would enable African-American women to overcome stereotypes related to race and gender.

Burroughs was a talented orator who used her skills to solicit financial backing for her school and to urge black Americans to support their own institutions. At the Baptist Women's Convention in 1912, Burroughs revealed how she judged the quality of the clergy by its devotion to social service. She criticized ministers who preached "too much

Heaven and too little practical Christian living" (Higginbotham, 1993, p. 175). Also, Burroughs caused the National Association of Colored Women to recognize the plight of black women in industry and helped to establish the National Association of Wage Earners. In the last decade of her life, from 1950 to 1960, she served as a member-at-large on the executive committee of the Baptist World Alliance. Burroughs died from a stroke on May 20, 1961, in Washington, D.C. In 1964 her school was renamed the Nannie Helen Burroughs School.

See also: African Americans
References: Henry Warner Bowden, *Dictionary of American Religious Biography*, 2nd ed. (1993); Evelyn Brooks Higginbotham, *Righteous Discontent: The Women's Movement in the Black Baptist Church, 1880–1920* (1993); Dorothy C. Salem, ed., *African American Women: A Biographical Dictionary* (1993); Barbara Sicherman and Carol Hurd Green, eds., *Notable American Women: The Modern Period* (1980).

Butler, Marie Joseph, Mother (1860–1940)

Mother Marie Joseph Butler, founder of Marymount College and the first American to head a Catholic congregation whose motherhouse was in a foreign land, was born at Ballynunnery in County Kilkenny, Ireland, on July 22, 1860. Butler, whose given name was Johanna, was the seventh child of John and Ellen (Forrestal) Butler. Johanna was raised on the family estate and received her education in nearby public and parochial schools. She received religious instruction both in the family home and at the local parish chapel. When she was a teenager, she grew interested in leading a religious life and convinced her parents to allow her to enter the Congregation of the Sacred Heart of Mary at Béziers, France, in 1879. The mission of the order, founded in 1849, was to educate daughters of the upper classes. Six months after entering the convent, Butler took her veil and the name Sister Marie Joseph.

In 1879, while she was still a novice, Butler was sent to teach at the order's school in Oporto, Portugal. There, on April 22, 1880, she took her first vows. Within a year, she was transferred to the order's school in Braga, Portugal, to head the English and French departments. She was popular with both the students and their parents and was able to work well with local public officials. Her adeptness at handling her responsibilities led to her appointment as superior of the Braga convent and school in 1893. Ten years later, Mother Butler was sent to the United States to head the order's school at Sag Harbor, Long Island, New York, and to expand the order's work in America.

One of Mother Butler's longtime dreams had been to fulfill the founders' original intentions of establishing a college for Catholic women. Her dream began to come to fruition in 1907, when her cousin James Butler donated some property for a school in Tarrytown, New York. In 1908 Marymount School opened with one pupil and the goal of growing into a liberal arts college that would be academically equivalent to the best of the secular colleges. A novitiate was established on the school site in 1910, and in 1918 the college officially opened. Mother Butler then set out to found branches elsewhere in the United States and in Europe. Marymount College of Los Angeles opened in 1921–1922, and in 1923 Mariemonte opened in Paris, France. Later, two additional branches were established, Mariamonte in Rome (1930) and Marymount in Santa Barbara, California (1938).

The curriculum of the Marymount colleges emphasized social and physical training in addition to intellectual and religious development. Recognizing the changing status of women, students were taught political science and law. Mother Butler expected her students to become leaders in Catholic circles and convincing defenders of the faith. She stressed the importance of charitable work and established a number of Mother Butler Mission Guilds in local congregations. She also organized a retreat movement in the United States that would eventually spread to other orders and involve large numbers of Catholic laywomen.

Mother Butler's achievements led to her election in 1926 as Mother General of the Congregation of the Sacred Heart of Mary. She was the first American to head a Roman Catholic order that was based in a foreign country. A year later she became a naturalized citizen of the United States. Under Mother Butler's leadership, the congregation continued to grow. As Mother General, she traveled extensively, supervising an expansion program that included new schools in England and Brazil and a new novitiate in Ireland. During a trip to Rome in 1939, she became gravely ill but lived to celebrate the sixtieth anniversary of her becoming a nun. Mother Butler died the following day, on April 23, 1940.

See also: Roman Catholic Church; Roman Catholic Women's Orders (Nuns)
References: Katherine Burton, *Mother Butler of Marymount* (1944); Edward T. James, ed., *Notable American Women, 1607–1950,* vol. 1 (1971); James J. Kenneally, *The History of American Catholic Women* (1990); J. Kenneth Leahy, *As the Eagle: The Spiritual Writings of Mother Butler* (1954); J. Gordon Melton, *Religious Leaders of America* (1991); J. Gordon Melton, *New Catholic Encyclopedia,* vol. 2 (1967).

Cabot, Laurie (1933–)

Laurie Cabot, "the Official Witch of Salem" and founder of the Witches' League for Public Awareness, was born in March 1933 during her family's move from Boston, Massachusetts, to Anaheim, California. From an early age, Cabot felt a compatibility with witches. She has maintained that she is descended from a long line of witches and has claimed that she possessed psychic powers of her own since she was six years of age. From her father she gained an appreciation of science, which she has combined with her interest in witchcraft and the occult.

When she was fourteen, Cabot returned with her mother to Boston to complete her high school education. About two years later, she was instructed in Druidic/Celtic witchcraft and was initiated into the Craft by three Druidic/Celtic priestesses. After high school, Cabot attended Fullerton Junior College in California and Massachusetts College of Art. She later received a full scholarship to attend Rhode Island School of Design. Throughout her college years, Cabot continued to study Druidic/Celtic witchcraft. She studied both independently and under the direction of professors and elders and gradually came to link witchcraft with psychic science. As a result, her practice of Druidic/Celtic witchcraft was broadened to include Hermetic science, laws, and magic.

During the 1960s, Cabot developed and privately taught a course entitled "Witchcraft as a Science." She gave her first public classes in 1971 at the Wellesley Adult Education program at Wellesley High School. In the late 1960s, Cabot vowed that she would wear only the traditional clothing of the witch, which she believed was black robes. Soon a friend convinced her that Salem was the best place for a witch, and the two women moved there. For seven years during the 1970s, she taught at Salem State College and at the Cambridge Center for Adult Education. Although she discontinued her public classes in the late 1970s, Cabot has continued to freelance. She has been hired as a psychic consultant and healer for organizations, such as an oil company and police agencies, and for individuals.

In 1977 Cabot was presented with the Paul Revere Patriot's Award in recognition of her work with dyslexic children. Governor Michael Dukakis used the occasion to informally grant Cabot the title "the Official Witch of Salem." In 1988 she established the Temple of Isis in Salem, a chapter of the National Alliance of Pantheists. She was ordained Reverend Cabot by the alliance and may legally perform marriages. Also in 1988, she founded the grove of the Council of Isis Community. (A grove is a group of three or more covens.)

In recent years, Cabot has worked to defend witchcraft against attacks from the media, police, and some mainstream religious organizations. With the belief that witches should do more to defend their civil rights, she founded the Witches'

League for Public Awareness. Cabot published her first book, *Power of the Witch: The Earth, the Moon, and the Magical Path to Enlightenment,* in 1989. She later wrote *Celebrate the Earth* with Jean Miller, which details the traditions of the eight major Pagan holidays.

See also: Salem Witch Trials; Wicca; Witchcraft

References: Laurie Cabot with Jean Miller, *Celebrate the Earth: A Year of Holidays in the Pagan Tradition* (1994); Rosemary Ellen Guiley, *The Encyclopedia of Witches and Witchcraft* (1989); J. Gordon Melton, *Religious Leaders of America* (1991).

Cabrini, Frances Xavier, Mother (1850–1917)

Frances Xavier Cabrini, born in Sant' Angelo Lodigiano, Lombardy, Italy, on July 15, 1850, was the first citizen of the United States to be named a saint in the Roman Catholic Church. It is said that the first evidence of Cabrini's piety appeared on the day she was baptized. White doves were reported to have flitted throughout the Cabrini home on that day. Her family was known for its devotion to the Roman Catholic Church, and her uncle, Luigi Oldini, was a priest and a foreign missionary.

Frances was a pious young girl who began taking an annual oath of virginity at age twelve. When she was eighteen, she swore to remain forever a virgin. In 1870, Cabrini graduated with a teacher's license from a convent school that was under the direction of the Daughters of the Sacred Heart of Arluno. With hopes of serving the Catholic Church as a teacher, in 1874 she petitioned to become a Daughter of the Sacred Heart. She had only recently overcome smallpox and was in fragile health, however, and her petition was rejected on the basis of her poor health. Nevertheless, her enthusiasm was recognized by Father Antonio Serrati, who selected her as supervisor of an orphanage in Codogno. In 1880 Cabrini founded a new religious order, the Missionary Sisters of the Sacred Heart, which established orphanages and schools throughout Italy. The order had established seven convents by 1887, and in 1888 the sisterhood was approved and formally recognized by the Vatican. Pope Leo XIII praised Cabrini's efforts, calling her "a woman of marvelous intuition and of great sanctity" (Estep, 1995, p. 309).

In 1889, the pope sent Mother Frances Xavier Cabrini, as she had become known, to the United States to work with Italian immigrants. Hundreds of thousands of Italians left Italy for the United States during the 1880s and 1890s, and the Vatican had become concerned about their plight. Mother Cabrini traveled to New York to implement plans to establish an Italian orphanage for girls that would be funded by Countess Mary Reid DiCesnola. After much dispute between the countess and Archbishop Michael Corrigan of New York over the role that Mother Cabrini and her order of nuns would play in the operation of the school, the orphanage opened on April 21, 1889, under the control of Mother Cabrini.

Little more than a year later, Mother Cabrini purchased a Jesuit novitiate and moved the Sacred Heart Orphan Asylum there. She and her Missionary Sisters of the Sacred Heart raised funds for the establishment of an Italian hospital, the Columbus Hospital, which was incorporated in May 1891. Mother Cabrini soon became well known for her benevolence. She founded more than sixty-seven charitable institutions in the United States and throughout the world, including Buenos Aires, Paris, and Madrid. Mother Cabrini was also known for her efforts to create opportunities for Catholic women as missionaries. She became a naturalized American citizen in 1909.

On December 22, 1917, Mother Cabrini died in Chicago following a brief

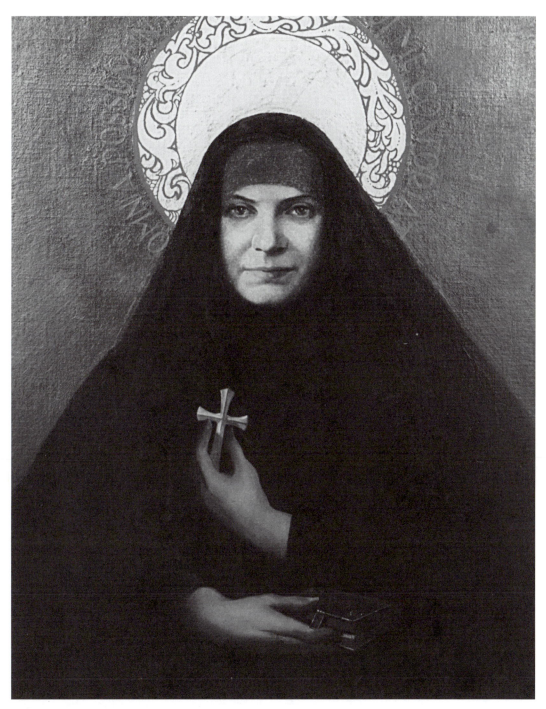

Mother Frances Xavier Cabrini was the first U.S. citizen to be canonized in the Roman Catholic Church (undated painting).

illness. At the time of her death, she was mother general to approximately four thousand nuns. She was canonized on July 7, 1946, the first American to be made a saint. Her feast day is November 13.

See also: Roman Catholic Church; Roman Catholic Women's Orders (Nuns); Seton, Elizabeth Ann Bayley
References: Kimberly K. Estep, "Frances Xavier Cabrini," in Frank Magill, ed., *Great Lives from History: American Women Series* (1995); James J. Kenneally, *The History of American Catholic Women* (1990); Phyllis J. Read and Bernard L. Witlieb, *The Book of Women's Firsts* (1992); Mary Louise Sullivan, *Mother Cabrini: "Italian Immigrant of the Century"* (1992); Caroline Zilboorg, ed., *Women's Firsts* (1997).

Cady, Harriet Emilie (1848–1941)

Popular author of the New Thought movement and one of the first female physicians in the United States, Harriet Emilie Cady was born to Oliver and Cornelia Cady in 1848 in Dryden, New York. Little is known of the early years of her life. As an adult, she spent some time as a schoolteacher and, by the late 1880s, was a practicing homeopathic physician in New York City. A devoutly religious person, from early in her career Cady was attracted to faith healing and was interested in investigating the connections between medicine and religion. After spending some time researching the subject, in November 1887 Cady attended a Christian Science class taught by the independent teacher and founder of the New Thought movement, Emma Curtis Hopkins. As a result of her studies under Hopkins, Cady was able to reconcile her divergent concerns.

Following her lessons with Hopkins, Cady wrote and published a booklet, *Finding the Christ in Ourselves*, which eventually caught the interest of Myrtle Fillmore. Fillmore and her husband, Charles, had also been students of Hop-

kins and had recently begun publishing a New Thought magazine, *Unity*. Charles Fillmore too was impressed with Cady's booklet and invited her to write for the magazine. "Neither Do I Condemn Thee," her first of many articles for *Unity*, appeared in the January 1892 issue. Two years later, she agreed to write a series of lessons that would set forth the principles of divine healing. The twelve lessons were later published in one volume, *Lessons in Truth*, which continues to be a standard text for the Unity School of Christianity (founded by the Fillmores in about 1889). Among the tenets presented in *Lessons* were her beliefs that "God is the substance of all things," and that Christ is the center of humankind's being and consciousness and "the means by which God, the Father reveals himself." Her concept of evil, or the Mortal Mind, was simply "the consciousness of error." She maintained that because humankind has free will, it is possible for Mortal Mind (which is the opposite of the divine Christ) to control one's thinking and actions. Cady taught that it was a person's right, and even his or her duty, to enjoy life.

Her 1912 book, *God, a Present Help*, was also popular. A collection of her articles was eventually published as a book, *Miscellaneous Writings* (later retitled *How I Used Truth* [1934]). Throughout the years that she wrote for *Unity*, Cady continued her medical practice in New York. She died there on January 3, 1941. Through the influence of her writings, Cady was second only to the Fillmores in shaping Unity's thought.

See also: Fillmore, Myrtle Page; Hopkins, Emma Curtis; New Thought Movement
References: Charles S. Braden, *Spirits in Rebellion: The Rise and Development of New Thought* (1984); H. Emilie Cady, *God, a Present Help* (1912); H. Emilie Cady, *Lessons in Truth* (1919); Martin A. Larson, *New Thought Religion: A Philosophy for Health, Happiness and Prosperity* (1987); J. Gordon Melton, *Religious Leaders of America* (1991).

Caesar, Shirley (1938–)

Gospel singer, minister, and evangelist with the Mount Calvary Holy Churches of America, Shirley Caesar was born into a family of twelve children in Durham, North Carolina, on October 13, 1938. Her father, the Reverend Jim Caesar, died when she was a child. He had been a gospel singer with a quartet known as Just Come Four. After her father's death, Shirley was raised solely by her mother, Hallie Caesar. Shirley was eight years old when she first sang in public. At age ten she began singing with the Caesar Sisters, a quartet that included her sisters, Anne and Joyce, and her cousin, Esther. She later sang with the Charity Singers, and in 1958, she joined Albertina Walker and the Caravans, one of the leading female gospel groups in the country. Three years later, Caesar became an evangelist. In the meantime, she had completed some college work at North Carolina Central College and had earned a business degree at Shaw University.

Caesar left the Caravans in 1966 to organize her own music group, for which she was the featured soloist. Her move proved to be a wise one, for she was an immediate success. For her recording of "Put Your Hand in the Hand of the Man from Galilee," in 1972 she became the first African-American female gospel singer to win a Grammy Award. A decade later, she won a Dove Award from the Gospel Music Association. Caesar received the Stellar Award from her peers in gospel music in 1987.

When she married Harold Ivoy Williams, a minister (now bishop) with the Mount Calvary Holy Churches of America, the wedding was a major event within gospel music circles. Over 2,500 people attended the wedding, in which the bride and groom sang their vows to each other. In 1983, after their marriage, Caesar and her husband became copastors of the Mount Calvary Baptist Holy Church in Winston-Salem, North Carolina. During the next decade, her husband became presiding bishop with the Mount Calvary Holy Churches of America, and Caesar became pastor of another of the denomination's sixty churches, the Mount Calvary Word of Faith Church in Raleigh, North Carolina. She is founder and president of Shirley Caesar Outreach Ministries, an organization that provides emergency food, clothing, and shelter for the needy.

In addition to serving as pastor, Caesar remains active in various civic and community affairs. Each year she spends thousands of dollars buying food for the needy.

References: Robert Anderson and Gail North, *Gospel Music Encyclopedia* (1979); Horace Clarence Boyer, "Shirley Caesar," in Darlene Clark Hine, ed., *Black Women in America: An Historical Encyclopedia* (1993); Sherry Sherrod DuPree, ed., *Biographical Dictionary of African-American Holiness-Pentecostals, 1880–1990* (1989); J. Gordon Melton, *Religious Leaders of America* (1991); Shirelle Phelps, ed., *Who's Who among African Americans, 1996/97* (1996).

Calvinism

A theology developed by Frenchman John Calvin (1509–1564), Calvinism was one of the most influential religions of the Protestant Reformation. Calvin's doctrine was explained in his greatest work, *The Institutes of the Christian Religion*. First published in 1536, the *Institutes* grew in length in subsequent revised editions, though Calvin's basic theology never changed. The fifth and final edition, published in 1559, was five times the size of the first. Calvin possessed exceptional communication skills, both as a writer and as a speaker. His legal training enabled him to develop a highly organized theology, and his abilities as an effective communicator helped to ensure the powerful influence of Calvinism in his time and in subsequent generations.

At the core of Calvinist belief was the idea that God was the ultimate being, all-knowing and all-powerful. Because of sin inherited from Adam (original sin) humankind was worthless in the sight of God. Only through the grace of God and the redemptive death of Jesus Christ on the cross were men and women offered the hope of salvation. Like Martin Luther before him, Calvin insisted that humans could not "earn" their way to heaven through "good works" but only through faith. According to Calvin, faith came to an individual at God's pleasure; he or she could neither accept nor refuse it.

The concept of predestination was an important aspect of Calvinism. Calvin believed that God had chosen certain people—the "saints," or the "elect"—to help him to defeat Satan and usher in a new kingdom. Only those among the elect were predestined for salvation, and these numbered only about one in a thousand. All others were foreordained to eternal damnation. Despite these odds, the doctrine of predestination did not lead to fatalism. Calvinists, who believed in Christ as their Redeemer, were convinced that they were among the elect.

That God was the author of Scripture was commonly accepted in Calvin's time. Calvin maintained that the Bible was the only authority in the lives of Christians, but he did not intend that Christians should disobey civil law. Rather, he believed that God had desired two governments for humans—one spiritual and one secular. The first was to be under the control of ministers and was expected to adhere to God's word alone. Calvin proposed that each local church should have a ruling body made up of ministers and elders (or presbyters), who were to hold regular meetings in councils (called synods) with officials from other churches in their district. The civil government was necessary to maintain peace and order in society and was to be obeyed unless Christians found it to be in violation of God's word.

Like Luther, Calvin insisted that there were only two sacraments in Christianity—the sacrament of baptism and the sacrament of holy communion. Baptism, wrote Calvin, "testifies to us our purgation and ablution; the eucharistic supper testifies our redemption. Water is a figure of ablution, and blood of satisfaction" (Calvin, 1957, p. 114). He did not, however, believe that all who died unbaptized were doomed, and he criticized private persons, especially women, who took it upon themselves to perform infant baptisms. Calvin followed Roman Catholics and Lutherans in the belief that Christ was present in holy communion. But, although he agreed that Christ's body and blood were present, he believed that this was so only in a spiritual sense.

For Calvinists the institution of marriage was important, but it was not a sacrament. "Man was not created to live in solitude, but to have a companion somewhat like himself," wrote Calvin. But, he insisted that "companionship outside of marriage between a man and a woman is damned and that marriage has been given to us in order to bridle our lust" (O'Faolain, 1973, p. 199). He acknowledged that people had sexual desires but maintained that they must wait until marriage before engaging in sexual intercourse. However, even in marriage sexual activity must be limited, for he warned couples "not to pollute [their] relationship with unbridled and self-indulgent lust" (O'Faolain, 1973, p. 200). Like most religions of the time, Calvinism was male-centered. Men controlled the pulpit and all hierarchical roles while women were expected to be submissive.

Calvinism spread through western Europe in the sixteenth and seventeenth centuries. Only in Geneva and Scotland by 1560 and in the American colonies in New England in the seventeenth century did the followers of Calvin's teachings compose a majority of the population. Nevertheless, Calvinists were a well-organized minority in other areas. They influenced the Anglican Church, and they gave rise to Puritanism in England, to the Huguenots in France, and to the Dutch Reformed Church. In the United States today, Calvinism is the base doctrine of both the Congregational and Presbyterian churches.

See also: Great Awakening; Hutchinson, Anne Marbury; Puritans
References: John Calvin, *On the Christian Faith: Selections from the Institutes, Commentaries, and Tracts* (1957); Harold J. Grimm, *The Reformation Era: 1500–1650* (1954); Julia O'Faolain and Lauro Martines, eds., *Not in God's Image: Women in History from the Greeks to the Victorians*, 2nd ed. (1973).

Cannon, Harriet Starr (1823–1896)

Harriet Starr Cannon founded the first sisterhood to be officially approved by the Episcopal Church in modern times. She was born May 7, 1823, in Charleston, South Carolina, the daughter of William and Sarah (Hinman) Cannon. Her parents died of yellow fever when she was sixteen months old, and she and her sister Catherine were raised by a maternal aunt. While still a child, Harriet lost an eye in an accident.

Harriet had some talent as a musician, and after she left her aunt's home in 1851 to live in Brooklyn, New York, she was able to support herself by giving private music lessons. In 1855 her sister died. Catherine's death was a tremendous blow to Harriet, who had been very close to her sister, and likely was the principal reason for Harriet's decision to begin a religious life.

On February 6, 1856, Cannon began her career as a probationer with the Episcopal Sisterhood of the Holy Communion in New York City. This was a deaconess-like order, organized by Anne Ayres and the Reverend William Augustus Mühlenberg. Cannon became a full member of the sisterhood in 1857. Mostly, she worked as a nurse in St. Luke's Hospital, an institution founded by Mühlenberg and operated by the sisters.

Cannon and three or four other women left the Sisterhood of the Holy Communion following a dispute over Cannon's insistence that the community be more traditionally monastic. On February 2, 1865, the women founded the Sisterhood of St. Mary, the first new community to be formally established by the Episcopal Church since the English monasteries were dissolved in the sixteenth century. The following September, Cannon was elected the community's first superior. She made her formal vows on the second anniversary of the community's founding, February 2, 1867.

The sisterhood's projects included the management of the House of Mercy, a refuge for young female prostitutes. The sisters also established orphanages, shelters for homeless women and children, hospitals, and convent schools. At first the women met with disfavor from Protestants who associated the women's service with Roman Catholic nunnery, and the sisters were expelled from both an orphanage and a homeless shelter. But their good works in aid of the poor eventually won them public support and fostered the growth of Episcopal sisterhoods. Cannon died at St. Mary's Convent in Peekskill, New York, on Easter Sunday, April 5, 1896.

See also: Ayres, Anne; Episcopal Church
References: Edward T. James, *Notable American Women, 1607–1950* (1971); J. Gordon Melton, *Religious Leaders of America* (1991); Phyllis J. Read and Bernard L. Witlieb, *The Book of Women's Firsts* (1992).

Captivity Sermons

Settlers on the New England frontier during the late seventeenth and early eighteenth centuries lived with the fear of Indian raids. When raids did occur, tales describing Indian atrocities spread throughout the colonies. Some whites escaped the onslaught, but many men, women, and children were either killed or taken captive. For the captives, there was always the chance they might escape or be ransomed, and those who did survive had some amazing stories to tell. Frequently these stories were about women who, through faith in God and personal courage, had managed to return to white society. New England ministers found these narratives to be excellent bases for their sermons.

By comparing the actions of former captive Hannah Duston to those of a Biblical heroine, Puritan minister Cotton Mather used her situation to illustrate God's desire for the New England settlers to prevail over the Indians: In 1697, within days of giving birth, Hannah Duston had found herself a victim in an Indian raid, in which she was taken captive although many others in her settlement were massacred. She remained in the custody of the Indians only briefly, for she soon was able to escape her captors. With the help of another woman and a boy, she killed ten Indians (six were children), scalped them, and returned with the scalps to collect a reward for each. Mather overlooked the payment for the scalps and gave a sermon in her honor at his church. In 1702 he again told her story in his ecclesiastical history of New England, *Magnalia Christi Americana*. Mather compared Duston's heroism with that of the Biblical Jael in the Book of Judges, who had helped to save Israel when she calmly and resolutely murdered Sisera, the military commander of the Canaanites.

Another former captive who became renowned through stories of her survival was Mary Rowlandson, who wrote her own narrative about her experiences among the Narragansett Indians. Rowlandson, a minister's wife, was taken captive in 1676, during King Philip's War, and was forced to become a servant of Indian women. She performed her tasks diligently, including sewing and knitting, but Rowlandson refused to work on the Sabbath, which brought threats of bodily harm from the chief's mistress. Her one solace was a Bible that one of her captors had given her. Meanwhile, Rowlandson prayed. Her prayers were finally answered when she succeeded in making arrangements to be ransomed, and the English obtained her release. When Rowlandson's story reached the public, she was held in great esteem for her faith and godliness. Mary Rowlandson credited God for her survival among the Indians, and the Puritan ministers agreed.

Although Indians were the foremost cause of concern for the whites who settled the New England frontier, the French, battling with England for sovereignty in North America, were also a factor. In fact, many late-seventeenth- and early-eighteenth-century Indian raids on the New York and New England frontiers were led by Frenchmen. Captives taken in these raids were often delivered into French custody and taken to Canada. Women who eventually returned to New England without succumbing to the proselytizing of the French "Papists" were held in great esteem by Protestants who learned of their ordeals.

For the New England settlers and their clergy, both the Indians and the Roman Catholic French represented the powers of evil, whereas the survival of faithful women like Rowlandson betokened the rewards of holding steadfast to the teachings of the Lord. Sermons about the strengths of these godly female captives persisted well into the eighteenth century and served to enhance the image of frontier women.

See also: Puritans
References: James Axtell, *The European and the Indian: Essays in the Ethnohistory of Colonial North America* (1981); Susan Howe, *The Birth-Mark: Unsettling the Wilderness in American Literary History* (1993); Laurel Thatcher Ulrich, *Good Wives: Image and Reality in the Lives of Women in Northern New England, 1650–1750* (1982); Nancy Woloch, *Women and the American Experience* (1984).

Censorship

Throughout American history, religious groups have been alert to denounce or censor information and material that they have not wished their congregations or other members of society to read, see, or hear. From the time of the Puritans, who banished or even executed those who they felt were spreading heretical ideas, to the present-day religious fundamentalists who protest secular humanism in school textbooks, currents of censorship have risen and fallen throughout the centuries. Although censorship has usually affected men and women alike, certain restrictions on access to information have been gender-specific. The Comstock Law (1873), for instance, which prohibited the circulation of materials about male and female sexuality and birth control, greatly limited women's access to information that may have preserved their health or even saved their lives.

With the advent of the movie industry at the turn of the century, moralists, including some religious leaders, began denouncing "sex films." Reverend Frederick Bruce Russell raided any Coney Island peepshows that dared show such "dangerous" films as *What the Girls Did with Willie's Hat* and *Fun in a Boarding House.* Moralists stepped in to prevent the showing of films depicting prostitution, venereal disease, abortion, and birth control. In the early years of the twentieth century, Protestant clergymen led most attacks on the film industry, though priests in local Roman Catholic parishes expressed concern about the influence of movies on American children. The large proportion of Jews in the movie industry, along with the climate of anti-Semitism in America, likely influenced Protestant and Catholic denunciation of films.

One of the most successful pressure groups in the history of the motion picture industry was the Catholic Church's Legion of Decency, founded in 1934. In 1965 church leaders liberalized the association and renamed it the National Catholic Office for Motion Pictures. Fifteen years later it closed down as a result of dwindling interest. Still, individual Catholic leaders occasionally speak out against movies that they consider objectionable. Currently, however, the strongest forces for censorship in film are fundamentalist Protestant groups.

Long concerned with the morals of American youth, women have often joined in censorship crusades. It is a woman's group, the Concerned Women for America (CWA), that has become one of the most influential of the fundamentalist Protestant-based associations. Founded in 1979 by religious activist Beverly LaHaye, the CWA has campaigned against such things as condom advertising on television, violence and vulgarity in the mass media, and secular humanism in classroom texts. Given recent concern over the accessibility of pornography and sex-related information on the Internet, as well as fears about provocative lyrics in popular music and immorality and violence in books, films, video games, and other media, there is no sign that censorship will disappear in the foreseeable future.

See also: Comstock Law; Concerned Women for America
References: Stephen Bates, *Battleground: One Mother's Crusade, the Religious Right, and the Struggle for Control of Our Classrooms* (1993); Lee Jacobs, *The Wages of Sin: Censorship and the Fallen Woman Film, 1928–1942* (1991); Robert O'Neil, *Classrooms in the Crossfire: The Rights and Interests of Students, Parents, Teachers, Administrators, Librarians, and the Community* (1981); David J. Pivar, *Purity Crusade: Sexual Morality and Social Control, 1868–1900* (1973); Frank Walsh, *Sin and Censorship: The Catholic Church and the Motion Picture Industry* (1996).

Charitable Work

Women's involvement in charitable work began in the late 1790s and then began growing at a rapid pace in the early nineteenth century. Two of the earliest women's charitable organizations were the Society for the Relief of Poor Widows with Small Children (1797) in New York City and the Female Humane Association (1798) in Baltimore, which also aided indigent widows. Similar organizations quickly followed in Philadelphia and in other northern cities. By 1812 the movement had reached the South as women of Petersburg, Virginia, petitioned the legislature for the establishment of an orphan asylum.

Scholars have found that most of the women's benevolent activities were associated with their religious beliefs. The first third of the nineteenth century was the time of the Second Great Awakening, during which large numbers of Americans were inspired by religious revivals to strive toward the perfection of themselves and of the society in which they lived. At about the same time, Protestant ministers were pointing to the aftermath of the French Revolution as an example of the dangers of a "godless" society and noticing the growing urbanization, influx of Catholic immigrants, and lack of religion on the Western frontier. They called for funds for the training of ministers to evangelize the unchurched, as well as money for the religious materials they planned to distribute to poor of the cities and the settlers in the West. Women, who made up the largest proportion of most congregations in the eighteenth century and continued to do so in the next, were urged by the male clergy to offer their support.

During the early decades of charitable work, most of the women's benevolence focused upon those who suffered under unfortunate circumstances from no fault of their own. Orphans, indigent widows, the blind, and the deaf were frequent recipients of female charity. Bibles and religious tracts were often given to the poor, along with food and clothing, by groups like the interdenominational Female Bible Society. Jewish women participated in the movement, founding the Female Hebrew Benevolent Society in Philadelphia in 1819. Over the following decades, women found that participation in church-associated charitable societies was one of few ways that they could extend their sphere of influence with the approval of male church leaders and society.

By the middle of the nineteenth century, societies to help the "deserving poor," beyond the blind, the deaf, widows, and orphans, were emerging in major American cities. Middle-class men and women conducted home visits to urban slums, pressing their social and moral values upon the poor. Women's charitable associations began demanding proof of an applicant's "worthiness" before providing the needed relief. As historian Christine Stansell argues, the women's demands for character references and marriage certificates often ruled out those who were in the most dire need, the immigrants.

After the Civil War, women enlisted in such organizations as the American Missionary Association and in home mis-

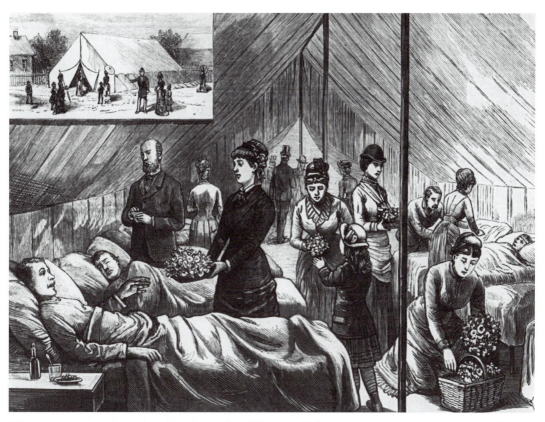

This wood engraving from Frank Leslie's Illustrated Newspaper *depicts ladies of the Flower and Fruit Mission caring for patients in a hospital tent (October 2, 1880).*

sions organizations associated with their churches for the purpose of offering aid to the newly emancipated slaves. Women like Baptist missions worker Joanna Moore traveled to the South to teach reading skills, provide Bible lessons, and help establish orphanages and homes for elderly women. By the end of the nineteenth century, many individual women were founding charitable institutions on their own. Often inspired by religious zeal, women founded places of refuge like Mary Moise's "faith home," welcoming women in trouble. Among the many benevolent organizations founded by women during the nineteenth century was the National Council of Jewish Women (NCJW), established by Hannah G. Solomon in 1893 to further the cause of religious education and philanthropy. In its early years, much of the NCJW's focus was on assisting Jewish immigrants arriving in America, and in the 1930s and 1940s the group aided Jewish refugees. Other women, like Carrie Judd Montgomery, provided substantial support to evangelical/benevolent organizations such as the Salvation Army.

As women's participation in public enterprises became more accepted by society in the twentieth century, women became less reliant on church-associated organizations for involvement in charitable work. Women's social and professional groups began to flourish, and they too provided assistance to the less fortunate. Nevertheless, large numbers of American women continue to be active participants in their churches' and synagogues' benevolent programs.

See also: American Missionary Association; Female Hebrew Benevolent Society; Missionary Societies; Moise, Mary; Montgomery, Carrie Judd; Moore, Joanna Patterson; National Council of Jewish Women; Salvation Army; Solomon, Hannah Greenebaum

References: Nancy F. Cott, *The Bonds of Womanhood: "Women's Sphere" in New England, 1780–1835* (1977); Nancy A. Hewitt, *Women's Activism and Social Change: Rochester, New York, 1822–1872* (1984); Marvin N. Olasky, *The Tragedy of American Compassion* (1992); Christine Stansell, *City of Women: Sex and Class in New York, 1789–1860* (1987).

Church of Jesus Christ of Latter-Day Saints (Mormons)

Since the founding of the Church of Jesus Christ of Latter-Day Saints (or Mormon) in 1830, the women of the church have filled a variety of roles. Like other fledgling religious sects, the Mormon Church was relatively open in providing opportunities for women during its early history. Although only men were authorized to perform the formal religious functions of the priesthood, women, who like men were considered to have "gifts of the Spirit," received personal revelation, healed the sick, prophesied future events, administered blessings, and performed other operations that required spiritual gifts. The Female Relief Society, established by church founder Joseph Smith in 1842 and placed under the presidency of his wife Emma Hale Smith, became a center for women's activity and an integral part of the Mormon Church. In the early years of the church, women were given responsibilities for treating the sick, assisting in the establishment of new communities, and caring for families who were faced with hardships.

When plural marriage was introduced (secretly at first) in the 1840s, the practice altered the lives of many Mormon women. For some, it was their devotion to their religion alone that gave them the ability to accept their husbands' taking additional wives. Emma Hale Smith only reluctantly accepted Joseph's secret marriages to other women. But once the practice of polygamy was made public and outsiders voiced loud opposition to the custom, Mormon women rose to defend their menfolk. The introduction of the Cullom Bill (1869–1870), with its proposal to outlaw plural marriage, and the passage of the Edmunds-Tucker Act (1887), which declared such marriages illegal and disenfranchised Utah's women (who had been voting since 1870) as well as men who practiced polygamy, drew vehement protests from Mormon women. Likely contributing to the women's public support of polygamy was the requirement placed upon them by church leaders that they either support the principle or leave the church entirely.

In any case, most Mormon marriages were monogamous, for before a man was permitted to take more than one wife, he had to prove that he could financially afford to support a larger family. Thus, a plural wife was usually married to a man of relatively high status within the community. Mormons believed that plural marriage also provided benefits in the afterlife, for the highest kingdoms were said to be reserved for the men, women, and children of such marriages. Another advantage for women was the sharing of household duties, which allowed them to have more free time and independence.

Because of their husbands' frequent absences due to their mission work and, in the case of plural marriages, time spent with other wives and children, much of the responsibility for consolidating and strengthening the Mormon Church after its relocation to Utah in the late 1840s fell to the women. Leader Brigham Young supported higher education for women and involvement in commerce, and he encouraged them to vote. The women of Utah were among the earliest female populations in the United States to be granted the vote in a national

Brigham Young, founder of the Mormon Church, and his family appear in this wood engraving from Harper's Weekly *(1857).*

election (as opposed to voting for local officials only) and a number of Mormon women became active participants in the national struggle for female suffrage.

After 1920, with the Mormon Church firmly established in the United States and expanding into foreign lands, women's functions within the church became more limited. Gradually their right to exercise spiritual gifts, especially healings and blessings, was taken from them. In 1946, Joseph Fielding Smith, the head of the church, officially relieved women of the right to anoint for illness or childbirth, and between 1968 and 1978 church leaders moved to effectively strip the women's auxiliary of its autonomy. In the 1970s the Mormon Church took a strong stance in opposition to feminism and the Equal Rights Amendment (ERA), endorsing instead the ideal of women as homemakers, wives, and mothers. Some Mormons, like Sonia Johnson, a founder of Mormons for the

ERA (and who was excommunicated from the church as a result of her political activities), disagreed with the official position of their church on the issue and voiced their protest. In recent years, some Mormon women and men have looked into church history and questioned why Mormon women of the nineteenth century had greater freedom and more powerful leadership positions than they do today. A few feminists and feminist sympathizers have been excommunicated, seemingly as a result of their challenges to authority.

See also: Cullom Bill; Edmunds-Tucker Act; Gates, Susa Amelia Young; Johnson, Sonia Harris; Penrose, Romania Pratt; Rogers, Aurelia Spencer; Snow, Eliza Roxey
References: Martha Nibley Beck, "Roles of Women," in Daniel H. Ludlow, ed., *Encyclopedia of Mormonism*, vol. 4 (1992); Vicky Burgess-Olson, *Sister Saints* (1978); Claudia L. Bushman, ed., *Mormon Sisters: Women in Early Utah* (1976); Sonia Johnson, *From Housewife to Heretic* (1981); Susan Hill Lindley, *"You Have Stept Out of*

Your Place": A History of Women and Religion in America (1996); Barbara B. Smith and Shirley W. Thomas, "Gospel Principles and the Roles of Women," in Daniel H. Ludlow, ed., *Encyclopedia of Mormonism*, vol. 4 (1992).

Church Women United

Church Women United (CWU) is an ecumenical movement of Protestant, Roman Catholic, Eastern Orthodox, and other Christian women. The CWU dates its founding to December 11–13, 1941, when a group of one hundred women from three interdenominational women's organizations met in Atlantic City, New Jersey, to form the United Council of Church Women (UCCW). The UCCW represented women from seventy Protestant denominations who belonged to the Council of Women for Home Missions, the Committee on Women's Work of the Foreign Missions Conference, and the National Council of Federated Church Women.

In 1950 the UCCW joined with eleven other interdenominational agencies to form the National Council of Churches in Christ in the U.S.A (NCCC). As a part of the NCCC, the movement became known as the General Department of United Church Women (UCW). But, in 1966, the group decided to become autonomous and to encourage the participation of Protestant, Eastern Orthodox, Roman Catholic, and other Christian women. At the same time, it changed its name to Church Women United.

The CWU's *Directory and Information Handbook* describes the organization as "a women's movement fundamentally grounded in the biblical principles of the Christian faith and the richness of denomination diversity." Principal goals cited by the CWU are "to grow in our faith and to extend our vision of what it means to be Christian women of faith in society today"; "to strengthen visible ecumenical community"; "to work for a just, peaceful and caring society"; and "to use, responsibly and creatively, the resources God had entrusted to us—our intelligence, our time, our energy, our money—as we carry out the mission of Christ through Church Women United" (pp. 4–6).

Since the 1960s, CWU has worked to combat racism; to appreciate social, ethnic, and racial diversity; and to promote women's participation in the church and the community. Listed among the organization's accomplishments are the work of some of its members in the civil rights movement of the 1960s; a project, known as "The Imperative" and begun in 1986, that was designed to help break the cycle of poverty faced by millions of women and children; and conferences with African-American, Korean, Latino, and Anglo women in Los Angeles following the uprising of 1992. The priorities for the 1996–2000 quadrennial are making the world safer for women and children and enhancing and strengthening Church Women United. In keeping with the former goal, the CWU endorsed the Stand for Children March on Washington, held in June 1996.

As of 1997, the CWU comprised more than 1,400 state and local units, and the organization claimed a total membership of about 500,000 in the United States and Puerto Rico.

References: Church Women United, pamphlet, "Church Women United" (n.d.); Church Women United, pamphlet, "Church Women United Legislative Office, Washington, D.C." (n.d.); Church Women United, *Directory and Information Handbook* (n.d.).

Clarke, James Freeman (1810–1888)

James Freeman Clarke, a leading Unitarian minister and reformer of the mid-nineteenth century, was born April 4, 1810, in Hanover, New Hampshire. The son of Samuel and Rebecca Parker (Hull) Clarke, James was reared primarily by his grandfather, James Freeman, the minister who had led King's Chapel in Boston into Unitarianism in 1785–1787. Young James Clarke attended Boston Latin School beginning in 1821. He then attended Harvard College, graduating in 1829, and Harvard Divinity School, from which he graduated in 1833. After his ordination in Boston on July 21, 1833, he moved to Louisville, Kentucky, where he headed a new Unitarian congregation. While in the slave state of Kentucky, Clarke began to work for the abolition of slavery. He edited the monthly *Western Messenger* there from 1836 to 1839, which spread his views on the subject. Clarke returned to Boston in 1840 and in 1841 he founded and became pastor at the Church of the Disciples. With the exception of a period of about four years when illness kept him from the pulpit (1850–1854), Clarke remained pastor at the church until his death.

The Church of the Disciples caused some anxiety among religious circles because the laity enjoyed what was for the time an unusual amount of power. Clarke brought men and women together with the goal of applying the ideals of Christianity to contemporary social problems. He believed that religion should serve to free all that were oppressed. Clarke was an advocate for temperance and for women's rights and promoted the expansion of "woman's sphere" to include the public arena.

In addition to his pastoring, Clarke served as a professor at Harvard Divinity School (1867–1871) and wrote a number of theological works. Probably his best-known book is his two-volume work on comparative religion, *Ten Great Religions* (1897), which provided a new and more accepting approach to non-Christian religions. Clarke died in Boston on June 8, 1888, at the age of seventy-eight. Shortly after his death, the *Woman Suffrage Leaflet 2, No. 14* (February 15, 1889) published a statement of his views on women's right to vote. Clarke wrote that "[o]ne of the most important of the reforms proposed at the present time is that which shall give the suffrage to women. It is not merely a political question, but a social question, a moral question, and a religious question" (Kimmel and Mosmiller, 1992, p. 234).

See also: Antislavery Movement; Woman Suffrage

References: Henry Warner Bowden, *Dictionary of American Religious Biography*, 2nd ed. (1993); James Freeman Clarke, *Ten Great Religions: An Essay in Comparative Theology* (1897); Elizabeth Frost-Knappman, *Women's Progress in America* (1994); Michael S. Kimmel and Thomas E. Mosmiller, eds., *Against the Tide: Pro-Feminist Men in the United States, 1776–1990: A Documentary History* (1992); J. Gordon Melton, *Religious Leaders of America* (1991); Edward L. Queen II et al., eds., *The Encyclopedia of American Religious History* (1996).

Clergy

Only recently have American women made significant headway in achieving full clergy status. Christian tradition held that ministers evolved from Jesus' twelve disciples, who carried on Christ's ministry following his death. Church authorities have excluded women from the ministry with the argument that since all of Christ's apostles were male, all ministers should be male. During the early nineteenth century, some smaller denominations, including the Quakers, ordained women, but it was not until 1853 that a woman was ordained in a major American denomination. In that year, Antoinette Brown Blackwell was ordained a pastor of the Congregationalist church in the small town of South Butler, New York. But Blackwell's tenure as a minister was short. She was treated with such disdain by other members of the clergy and by many members of her congregation that she asked to be relieved of her post just one year after her ordination. By the late nineteenth century, some congregations that had the power to select their clergy were choosing women. Nevertheless, it was not until the period between the late 1950s and mid-1970s that the larger Protestant denominations in the United States began to officially approve the ordination of women.

In the nineteenth and early twentieth centuries, women were best able to attain leadership roles when religions were in their formative stages and when they legitimized religious authority through the Holy Spirit. Among the most successful of these women were Ann Lee, leader of the Shakers; Mary Baker Eddy, founder of the Church of Christ, Scientist; Ellen Gould White, founder of the Seventh-Day Adventist Church; and Aimee Semple McPherson, who established the International Church of the Foursquare Gospel.

In the United States today, approximately 80 percent of the Protestant denominations ordain women, and more than a third of all theological students are women, compared with 10 percent in the 1970s. But even though increasing numbers of women have entered the clergy, many congregations have found it difficult to visualize a woman as their pastor. Therefore, women have had a difficult time getting work in churches and have often found themselves serving in educational, counseling, or ecumenical roles. However, as the numbers of women entering the clergy continue to rise, they are gradually becoming accepted as congregational leaders.

Although the Vatican has soundly rejected the idea of women priests in the Roman Catholic Church, some Catholic women are preparing for the priesthood, even though they doubt that ordination of women will come in their lifetime. The shortage of priests in the Roman Catholic Church has led to the training of many women for work in parishes. These women do not consecrate the Eucharist or hear confession, but they perform many other duties normally assigned to a member of the clergy.

At about the same time that the major Protestant denominations were accepting women clergy, branches of Judaism were beginning to ordain women rabbis. In 1956, the Central Conference of American (Reform) Rabbis endorsed the ordination of women, and the first woman rabbi was ordained in 1972. Two years later, the smaller Reconstructionist branch of Judaism ordained its first female rabbi, and in 1985 the Conservatives followed suit. The third major branch of Judaism, the Orthodox, has not approved the ordination of women.

Despite the increase in the numbers of women clergy, they still earn less than men. The lack of congregations willing to open their pulpits to women has resulted in women settling for part-time work, specialized ministries, or employment in lower-paying parishes. Nevertheless, women who have found work within the clergy have reported a higher rate of job satisfaction than their male counterparts.

The ordination of women has brought new dimensions to the ministry. Female clergy have frequently focused on issues such as sexual harassment, domestic violence, AIDS, and rape, which church leaders have traditionally ignored. Some clergywomen have developed new liturgies and practices that reach out to the women of their congregations. Clergywomen of the 1990s continue to be pioneers, making way for a future when a woman in the pulpit will not be considered unusual.

See also: Baptists; Blackwell, Antoinette Brown; Eddy, Mary Baker; Eilberg, Amy; Episcopal Church; Lutheran Church;

McPherson, Aimee Semple; Methodists; "Philadelphia 11"; Presbyterian Church; Roman Catholic Church; White, Ellen Gould **References:** Jackson W. Carroll, Barbara Hargrove, and Adair T. Lummis, *Women of the Cloth: A New Opportunity for the Churches* (1981); Kimberly K. Estep, "Amy Eilberg," in Frank Magill, ed., *Great Lives from History: American Women Series* (1995); Betsy Covington Smith, *Breakthrough: Women in Religion* (1978); Barbara Brown Zikmund, "Women in the Clergy," in Sara E. Rix, ed., *The American Woman, 1988–89: A Status Report* (1988).

The Clergy Consultation Service on Abortion

In May 1967, a time when abortion was illegal in the United States, Reverend Howard Moody of the Judson Memorial Church in New York City founded the Clergy Consultation Service on Abortion (CCS). The purpose of the CCS was to counsel women who were experiencing unwanted pregnancies and to help them secure abortions from skilled abortionists if they so desired. Originally comprising twenty-six ministers and one rabbi who volunteered their time to the organization, the referral service began its operation in the basement of the Judson Memorial Church. The CCS grew over the next several years until it had developed a national network that included more than a thousand counselors. Branches opened across the country, though mostly in cities and in college towns. Some of the counselors were arrested for their abortion referral activities, and the others realized that they were in jeopardy of being charged for what was illegal activity in most states until the Supreme Court decision on *Roe v. Wade* legalized abortion in 1973.

Because of the prominence and moral authority of the clergy who were volunteers with the CCS, the organization was an open challenge to the existing laws, and it played an influential role in the abortion movement.

See also: Abortion
References: Kathryn Cullen-DuPont, with Annelise Orleck, *The Encyclopedia of Women's History in America* (1996); Flora Davis, *Moving the Mountain: The Women's Movement in America since 1960* (1991); Marian Faux, *Crusaders: Voices from the Abortion Front* (1990).

Comstock, Elizabeth Leslie Rous (1815–1891)

Elizabeth Leslie Rous Comstock, nineteenth-century Quaker minister and reformer, was born October 30, 1815, in Maidenhead, England. She was the eldest of the seven daughters of William and Mary (Kekwick) Rous, both descended from a long line of Quakers. She received her education in Quaker schools in Islington and Croydon, and after graduation, she taught in two similar schools. She left teaching upon her marriage to Leslie Wright on April 6, 1848. A druggist and market gardener, he died three years later, leaving her with an infant daughter.

For several years after her husband's death, Elizabeth earned her living as a shopkeeper. She continued in this occupation after moving to Belleville, Ontario, Canada, in 1854, but her growing interest in religion led her to devote increasingly more attention to public ministry. She credited the prominent English Quaker minister and reformer Elizabeth Fry for inspiring her to religious and benevolent pursuits. In 1858 Elizabeth Rous Wright married John T. Comstock and moved to his home in Rollin, Michigan, a Quaker settlement that was a station on the Underground Railroad. She adopted the abolitionist cause and participated in the smuggling of escaped slaves to safety.

Meanwhile, Comstock also developed her skills as a speaker and a Christian minister and was soon involved in a variety of reform movements. With the full support of her husband, who was himself a humanitarian, she involved herself in the causes of peace, temperance, women's rights, and prison and asylum reform. During the Civil War, she spent much of her time visiting army camps and hospitals. There, she comforted the sick and wounded with reminders of God's mercy and love. In 1879–1880, as vast numbers of freed blacks made an exodus to Kansas in hopes of escaping persecution and finding true freedom and happiness, Comstock felt a call to assist them and went to Kansas herself. Through the Quaker periodical *Friends' Review,* she encouraged people of her faith to aid the blacks with money, food, and clothing. She also lobbied citizens of Illinois and Nebraska to help black immigrants find housing and employment in those states.

Throughout the 1870s and 1880s, Comstock traveled to the major eastern cities on behalf of social causes. As a result, she became one of the most influential Quaker women of her time. Her avowed purpose in life was "To bear our Father's messages of love and mercy to the largest household on earth—the household of affliction" (Willard, 1972, p. 593). To further her goal, she visited thousands of prisoners on both sides of the Atlantic and carried her preaching to a reported eighty-five thousand inmates of poorhouses. Comstock also led temperance meetings in large cities and towns throughout the United States. By example, she was particularly inspiring to members of the Quaker faith, encouraging them to find individual spiritual regeneration through social welfare work.

In 1885, following the death of her husband, Comstock moved to Union Springs, New York. She died there on August 3, 1891.

See also: Society of Friends (Quakers)
References: Elizabeth Frost-Knappman, *Women's Progress in America* (1994); Edward T. James, ed., *Notable American Women, 1607–1950,* vol. 1 (1971); Rufus M. Jones, *The Later Periods of Quakerism* (1970, reprint); Frances E. Willard, *Woman and Temperance* (1972, reprint).

Comstock Law

In 1873, President Ulysses S. Grant signed the Act for the Suppression of Trade in, and Circulation of, Obscene Literature and Articles of Immoral Use, commonly known as the Comstock Law. Named for Anthony Comstock, a pious young dry-goods clerk and a prominent crusader for moral purity, the law was a product of the conservatism that permeated middle-class America in the late nineteenth and early twentieth centuries. In the years following the Civil War, religious and political leaders had led the way with mounting campaigns to rid the nation's cities of vice, and Comstock's drives to keep so-called obscene materials from the hands of the public received their support.

By today's standards, the Comstock Law's definition of "obscene" was extraordinarily broad. Unless the information was written in euphemistic language, educational materials about male and female sexuality, birth control, and sexually transmitted diseases were considered pornographic under the law. In 1912 the *New York Call* challenged the law when a series of articles by Margaret Sanger, "What Every Girl Should Know," was declared "unmailable" under the Comstock Law. On orders from Washington, the ban was lifted, and the articles were allowed to circulate.

The power of the Comstock Law was further lessened in 1938 following Sanger's involvement in a test case aimed at U.S. Customs officials who tended to enforce bans on "obscene materials" more strictly than the Post Office. Customs seized a shipment of pessaries (devices worn in the uterus to prevent conception) that Sanger had arranged to be shipped from Japan to a doctor in New York. In the court case that followed, Judge August Hand argued that the Comstock Law's position on birth control was obsolete. Judge Hand's decision served to lift all federal bans on birth control.

In addition to limiting women's access to information about birth control, the Comstock Law aimed to halt the practice of abortion, which had been on the increase since the 1840s. The law was a boon to the cause of many middle-class Americans who worried that socially dominant white Anglo-Saxon Protestants were on the verge of being overrun by immigrants who had many children and who did not believe in birth control. Likewise, the Comstock Law served men who wished to gain control of the abortion practice, which then was dominated by women. The law made no distinction between drugs used for abortion and other types of contraceptive materials— all were designated pornographic. It was not until 1973 that the Supreme Court, in *Miller v. California,* was able to agree on a definition of obscenity.

See also: Birth Control
References: Linda Gordon, *Woman's Body, Woman's Right: A Social History of Birth Control in America* (1977, reprint 1986); Winston E. Langley and Vivian C. Fox, *Women's Rights in the United States: A Documentary History* (1994); David J. Pivar, *Purity Crusade: Sexual Morality and Social Control, 1868–1900* (1973).

Concerned Women for America

Founded in January 1979 by religious activist Beverly LaHaye, Concerned Women for America (CWA) is an organization that has become associated with the religious right. LaHaye established CWA out of concern that the United States was leaning in the direction of secular humanism and that God and traditional American values were being ignored. With the slogan, "Putting families first!" the CWA,

LaHaye writes in the CWA information packet, "is committed to fighting for the traditional Judeo-Christian values that build and strengthen families." The organization began with nine members but grew quickly, claiming half a million members in 1984.

The CWA offers women a way to be politically active while remaining in the home and being subservient to their husbands, for it is LaHaye's belief that God intended women to play a servant's role. It was natural, then, that the group opposed the ratification of the Equal Rights Amendment during the early 1980s and that LaHaye urged CWA members to pray for the amendment's defeat. The organization is also against abortion, feminism, legislation for equal pay for comparable work, pornography, condom advertising on television, violence and vulgarity in the mass media, gay rights, and anything that hints of secular humanism. The CWA supports voluntary school prayer, the teaching of creationism in biology classes, educational vouchers, and mandatory HIV testing for marriage licenses. During the 1980s, the CWA endorsed President Ronald Reagan's efforts to aid the Nicaraguan contras.

Headquartered in Washington, D.C., the CWA is organized into over 1,200 local Prayer/Action Chapters with a membership totaling over 600,000 nationwide. The organization publishes a monthly magazine, *Family Voice,* which updates its readers regarding legislation in Congress and activities in the various chapters and includes articles on issues important to the CWA. Concerned Women for America is considered one of the most influential right-wing religious groups in the country.

See also: Fundamentalism; LaHaye, Beverly Jean; Schlafly, Phyllis Stewart
References: Stephen Bates, *Battleground: One Mother's Crusade, the Religious Right, and the Struggle for Control of Our Classrooms* (1993); Concerned Women for

America, information packet (1997); Glenn H. Utter and John W. Storey, *The Religious Right: A Reference Handbook* (1995).

Cramer, Malinda Elliott (1844–1906)

Malinda Elliott Cramer, founder of Divine Science, was born in Greensboro, Indiana, on February 12, 1844. Although little information is available regarding her childhood, it is known that her parents, Obediah and Mary Henshaw, were Quakers. From about age sixteen, Malinda suffered from an illness. Acting on advice from her physician, who thought a warmer climate might improve her health, Malinda moved to San Francisco in 1870. Although her poor health persisted, she remained in California, where she married Charles Lake Cramer, also a Quaker, in 1872.

In the years that followed, Malinda continued to seek medical treatment, yet her physical condition remained poor. Cramer later recalled that one day in 1885, a doctor who was treating her suggested that she see a specialist. She claimed that she refused to do so and, in that refusal, reached a turning point in her life. Instead of seeing another doctor, she spent an hour in meditation and prayer and came to realize that if she were to be healed, it would be through the power of the Holy Spirit. Although she did not recover immediately, the healing process had begun, and soon she considered herself to be completely well. Before long she was providing free treatments to anyone who came to her.

Whether or not Cramer developed her ideas through her own experiences has been questioned, especially since her healing came at about the same time that the Christian Science movement reached San Francisco. A group of metaphysical healers, primarily women, had organized there by 1886. According to one ac-

count, Cramer joined many of these women in April 1887 to study under Emma Curtis Hopkins, the founder of what has come to be called New Thought. Inspired by Hopkins's lectures, Cramer soon became a teacher herself. She incorporated Home College in May 1888 and began offering courses in what she called "Divine Science," distinguishing her work from Christian Science (although Mary Baker Eddy had previously used the term as a synonym for Christian Science). J. Gordon Melton speculates that Cramer may have picked up the term from Wilberforce Juvenal Colville, who had published a book with "Divine Science" in the title in 1888. Late in 1888, with her husband's help, Malinda Cramer began publishing *Harmony*, a metaphysical magazine that became quite influential during the last decade of the nineteenth century.

For the next several years, Cramer traveled and lectured throughout the western United States. She published her first book, *Lessons in the Science of the Infinite Spirit,* in 1890, which reiterated the basic metaphysical lessons that had been published previously in her magazine. She later rewrote the lessons and published them in *Divine Science and Healing* (1902). In 1892 she created the International Divine Science Association, an umbrella organization that encompassed the numerous metaphysical centers that were springing up throughout the country. It was the first of several attempts to establish an ecumenical organization for New Thought, with which Divine Science is affiliated.

On a trip to Denver, Cramer met Fannie James, with whom she had been corresponding, and James's sisters, Nona Lovell Brooks and Alethea Small. Cramer and the sisters developed an understanding that resulted in the sisters opening the Colorado College of Divine Science in 1898 and in Brooks's traveling to San Francisco in the fall of that year. There, on December 1, 1898, Cramer ordained her.

Much of Cramer's work in San Francisco was destroyed in the 1906 earthquake. Cramer died on August 2, 1906, of injuries suffered during the quake. After her death, the center of Cramer's Divine Science movement shifted to Denver. Through the work of its new leaders, Divine Science survived to become an important part of the New Thought movement.

See also: Brooks, Nona Lovell; Eddy, Mary Baker; Hopkins, Emma Curtis
References: Charles S. Braden, *Spirits in Rebellion: The Rise and Development of New Thought* (1984); J. Gordon Melton, *Religious Leaders of America* (1991).

Crawford, Florence Louise (1872–1936)

The founder of the Apostolic Faith Church, an international Pentecostal group, Florence Louise Crawford was born in Coos County, Oregon, on September 1, 1872. Her parents were freethinkers who frequently hosted prominent atheists when they traveled through Oregon on speaking tours. But Florence was curious about the Christian faith, and one day, without her parents' knowledge, she attended a church service with a friend. A number of years passed before she was converted, during which time she married Frank M. Crawford and bore a son, Raymond Robert (1900).

Florence Crawford's conversion came during a dance party. A voice that she believed to be God's said, "Daughter, give me thine heart." Crawford later remembered, "The music died away and I left the ballroom" (Melton, 1986, p. 58). She went home to pray. After taking some time to reflect upon her beliefs and the responsibilities that came with the acceptance of Christ, Crawford joined a Methodist church and became an energetic servant of Christ. She also became actively involved in the social reforms of the early-twentieth-century Progressive movement. She was president of the California Woman's Christian Temperance Union and also visited jails and preached in the slums. At the same time, Crawford longed for a deeper Christian experience. As a Methodist, she had read about the teachings of John Wesley, and she came to believe in the experience of sanctification, in which the Holy Spirit can purify a believer.

In 1906 a friend told Crawford about the Asuza Street Church in Los Angeles, which was holding Pentecostal revivals. Crawford attended the church several times. On one occasion she had her long-sought experience of sanctification. A few days later she felt she was baptized by the Holy Spirit, as evidenced by her speaking in tongues. In addition to her spiritual enlightenment, Crawford underwent changes in her physical condition. She had long been a sickly person, suffering various disabilities, including lung problems and bouts of spinal meningitis, which affected her eyes. Not long after her sanctification experience, her bodily afflictions were healed.

Crawford became an enthusiastic worker for the mission on Asuza Street. The pastor of the church, the Reverend William J. Seymour, appointed her state director. In that capacity she became an itinerant missionary, traveling through California. Then, in December 1906, Crawford journeyed to Salem, Oregon, intending to broaden the scope of her work. There a group of people from Portland heard her speak. They were so impressed with her preaching that they invited her to take charge of a little mission that had been established in a refurbished blacksmith shop in Portland. Crawford agreed and consequently broke with Reverend Seymour. Her ministry was called the Apostolic Faith

Church (a name originally employed by Charles Fox Parham, originator of the modern Pentecostal movement). Crawford's sect stressed the three separate spiritual experiences of justification—a "born again" experience; sanctification (holiness)—by the act of God's grace; and baptism of the Holy Ghost—the "enduement of power from on High upon the clean, sanctified life" (Apostolic Faith Mission, 1965, p. 48).

Because of the rather unusual nature of the Pentecostal religious experience, practitioners were frequently persecuted. Crawford and the Apostolic Faith Church were no exception. As time passed, every window of the church was broken and had to be boarded up. In 1908 the church headquarters was moved to a building near the harbor, on Front and Burnside in downtown Portland. At about the same time, Crawford's son was converted. He was later ordained to the ministry and became his mother's assistant.

During the summer of 1908, Crawford published the first issue of the church's newspaper, *The Apostolic Faith,* and by the end of the year was producing both German and Norwegian editions. Her intent was to launch a worldwide ministry. The first mission outside the United States was established in Sweden in 1911, and another was founded in Norway in 1912. The following year she began to preach to the sailors at Portland's harbor, who in turn began to carry the Apostolic Faith around the world. In 1919 the church purchased an airplane, which her son used to distribute literature and spread the faith throughout the Pacific Northwest.

When Florence Crawford died in Portland on June 20, 1936, she was the leader of a thriving Pentecostal ministry. The church had a solid base in the northwestern United States and Canada and missionary work was ongoing in Scandinavia and elsewhere.

References: Apostolic Faith Mission, *A Historical Account of the Apostolic Faith* (1965); J. Gordon Melton, *Biographical Dictionary of American Cult and Sect Leaders* (1986); J. Gordon Melton, *Religious Leaders of America* (1991); Gloria E. Myers, unpublished paper, "The Apostolic Faith through the Lens of Sociology," Portland State University (1989).

Crosby, Frances Jane (Van Alstyne) (1820–1915)

Popularly known as Fanny Crosby, poet and hymn writer Frances Jane Crosby was born March 24, 1820, in Southeast, New York. The daughter of John and Mercy Crosby, Fanny was blinded when she was six weeks old when an incompetent doctor prescribed hot poultices for her eye infection. Fanny's father died when she was a year old, and Fanny moved with her mother to North Salem, New York, soon after. In 1828 they moved to Ridgefield, Connecticut, where Fanny spent the remainder of her childhood. Fanny received her early education in various forms: from her mother, who read to her; by memorizing passages from the Bible; and by occasional attendance at the neighborhood school.

In 1835 Crosby entered the New York Institution for the Blind in New York City. While there, she was recognized for her ability to compose simple verses, and a well-known visiting phrenologist, George Combe, encouraged her to put greater effort into her writing. Crosby graduated from the school in 1843 and joined the faculty as a teacher of English grammar, rhetoric, and ancient history. A year later she appeared in Washington, D.C., before a joint session of Congress to testify to the abilities of the blind. In 1841 the *New York Herald* printed her eulogistic poem on the death of President William Henry Harrison, and Crosby's first book of poems, *The Blind Girl and Other Poems,* was published in 1844.

Frances Jane Crosby (1906)

life she produced words to accompany melodies and, more frequently, wrote poems that others set to music. Among the hymn writers she collaborated with were Ira D. Sankey, evangelist Dwight L. Moody's song leader, and Howard Doane, who added musical scores to over a thousand of her poems.

Though overly sentimental by today's standards, Crosby's poems were commercial successes in her time and were especially popular among the Methodists. Some of the best known and most enduring of her hymns are "Blessed Assurance," "I Am Thine, O Lord," "Jesus, Keep Me Near the Cross," "Pass Me Not, O Gentle Savior," "Safe in the Arms of Jesus," and "Savior, More Than Life to Me." Altogether she wrote between fifty-five hundred and nine thousand hymns. (Many of her hymns were written under pseudonyms, which makes it impossible to determine an exact number.) In the last years of her life, Crosby wrote two autobiographical volumes: *Fanny Crosby's Life Story* (1903) and *Memories of Eighty Years* (1906). She died in Bridgeport, Connecticut, on February 12, 1915.

References: Henry Warner Bowden, *Dictionary of American Religious Biography*, 2nd ed. (1993); Edward T. James, ed., *Notable American Women, 1607–1950* (1971); J. Gordon Melton, *Religious Leaders of America* (1991); Samuel J. Rogal, *Sisters of Sacred Song* (1981).

In the early 1850s Crosby attended religious revival meetings in New York City, was spiritually awakened, and joined the Methodist Church. At about the same time, she worked with her school's music director, George F. Root, a man who was to become one of the nineteenth century's most renowned hymn writers. Together they composed a cantata and some secular songs, some of which became popular songs of the period. In 1858 Crosby married Alexander Van Alstyne, a teacher at the school who, like her, was blind. Crosby resigned her position at the school and moved with her husband to Maspeth on Long Island. A year later their newborn baby died. The couple returned to Manhattan, but their marriage slowly broke apart. Alexander died in 1902.

In 1864 Crosby met William Bradbury, a prolific hymn writer who was looking for someone who could write words to his music. She worked with him for several years, and for the remainder of her

Cullom Bill

Introduced in Congress by Representative Shelby Cullom of Illinois during the winter of 1869–1870, the Cullom Bill proposed that polygamy, as practiced by the Mormons in the Territory of Utah, should be declared illegal. The bill included provisions that would allow wives to testify against their husbands in court and the confiscation of property of persons who were imprisoned under the law or who attempted to evade prosecution. In response, Mormon women, under the guidance of their patriarchal leaders, gathered by the hundreds to hold "indignation meetings" to protest government interference in their church's plural marriage system. Mormon leaders extended the vote to women in 1870, which non-Mormons interpreted as a calculated move to increase the Mormon electorate. The Cullom Bill passed in the House but not in the Senate. However, antipolygamists did not concede the fight. The bill was reintroduced in 1880 with a revision that included the disfranchisement of women. Again the Cullom Bill was defeated in the Senate. But, in 1887, Congress passed the Edmunds-Tucker Act, which made plural marriages illegal. Striking a blow at women, the act included a clause that revoked woman suffrage in the Utah Territory.

See also: Church of Jesus Christ of Latter-Day Saints (Mormons); Edmunds-Tucker Act
References: Leonard J. Arrington and Davis Bitton, *The Mormon Experience: A History of the Latter-Day Saints* (1979); Eleanor Flexner, *Century of Struggle: The Woman's Rights Movement in the United States* (1970); Marilyn Warenski, *Patriarchs and Politics: The Plight of the Mormon Woman* (1978).

Cults

Although there are varying definitions of cults, they are usually considered to be relatively small groups whose beliefs, practices, and values differ from those of mainline or traditional forms of religion. Members frequently remove themselves from the larger society and devote their lives to serving the cult and its leader. Researchers have found that cults often appeal to people in search of a morally absolute set of definitions and rules to follow concerning gender roles. This was true whether the communes practiced mandatory celibacy, group-controlled marriage, or "free love." Researchers have also found that both males and females in religious communes evidenced a lower tolerance for ambiguity than men and women in secular communes.

A study of women who had voluntarily left religious communes found that they frequently were drawn into religious cults with thoughts of surrendering to a dynamic male leader. They left when they found themselves living under extremely unequal and oppressive circumstances. Such practices as exploitation by leaders, the establishment of harems, and leaders' support of husbands who psychologically or physically abused their wives became intolerable to the women. The role conflict between the pure and passive behavior expected of women within the group and the bold and seductive behavior that was encouraged when women were proselytizing and publicly soliciting for the cult also influenced women's decisions to leave.

In his study of modern cults, Andrew J. Pavlos finds that these groups are only partially open to women. Cults frequently claim egalitarian ideologies, but reality usually differs from their rhetoric, largely due to their traditional view of females. The Hare Krishnas, for example, consider feminism undesirable at best. However, some Wicca or witchcraft groups, which might also be defined as "cults," have adopted radical feminist viewpoints and have limited membership to females only. Most Spiritualist groups in the United States are also friendly to women's authority.

Some young women are willing to accept the submissive roles assigned them within many of the cults. Mary W. Harder, in her study of the Jesus movement in the mid-1970s, found that many young women who joined that fundamentalist sect had previously been living free and easy lives, experimenting with drugs and practicing premarital sex.

Women in the movement were held to submissive roles and were not involved in decisionmaking (except for deaconesses, who had little authority). Viewed as sensuous beings and temptresses, they were expected to dress modestly so as not to arouse males. In an era when publicity surrounded women's rights campaigns, young women of the Jesus movement appeared to be seeking the stability provided within a strict religious and social environment.

Since the end of World War II, there has been an outburst of new religions in America. Currently, there are approximately five to six hundred alternative religions in the United States that can be defined as cults, including those defined in a broader sense such as Christian Science.

See also: Wicca; Witchcraft
References: John Butterworth, *Cults and New Faiths* (1981); Mary W. Harder, "Sex Roles in the Jesus Movement," *Social Compass* 21, no. 3 (1974): 345–353; Carl Haywood, "The Authority and Empowerment of Women among Spiritualist Groups," *Journal for the Scientific Study of Religion* 22, no. 2 (June 3, 1983): 156–166; Richard Kyle, *The Religious Fringe: A History of Alternative Religions in America* (1993); J. Gordon Melton, *Encyclopedic Handbook of Cults in America* (1992); Andrew J. Pavlos, *The Cult Experience* (1982); Thomas Robbins, *Cults, Converts, and Charisma: The Sociology of New Religious Movements* (1988).

Curtiss, Harriette Augusta (1856–1932)

Harriette Augusta Curtiss, cofounder of the Order of Christian Mystics and later the Universal Religious Foundation, was born in Philadelphia, Pennsylvania, in 1856. Her parents were John Horace Brown, organizer of the Pennsylvania State Teachers' Association, and Emma Brightly Brown. Curtiss received a cultured education and developed into a talented musician and actress. After starring in a number of amateur theatrical productions, Curtiss had the opportunity to become a professional, but her mother dissuaded her from doing so. She therefore put her writing talents to use, for many years authoring a column for the *Philadelphia Inquirer* under the pen name "The Bachelor Girl."

As years passed, she found herself to be a gifted clairvoyant and eventually launched a career in the realm of mysticism. In 1907 she married F. Homer Curtiss, and together they began working as occult teachers and writers. In the year of their marriage they founded the Order of the 15, which in 1908 became known as the Order of Christian Mystics. Its purpose was to show relationships between theosophical teachings and orthodox Christianity. Harriette, who became known within the order as Rahmea, assumed the role of teacher, and her husband took the position of secretary. They worked together to prepare material for publication, though Harriette was the primary author. Throughout the rest of her life, she issued monthly lessons for students.

The Curtisses produced a number of books. The first was compiled from Harriette's written responses to questions from students and was entitled *Letters from the Teacher* (1909). Her early lessons were combined in *The Voice of Isis* (1912), which became the order's basic introductory text. Later, a more advanced text was published under the title, *The Message of Aquaria* (1921). The Curtisses wrote several books during World War I, including *The War Crisis* (1914) and *The Key to the Universe* (1915). In the latter volume they contended that all personal experiences are expressions of one great law based upon mathematical principles and that the "unfoldment of the godlike possibilities inherent in each Soul follows, step by step, the same order of events that is followed in the evolution of the Cosmos, and that such steps are symbolized by the first 22 numbers." *Realms of the Living Dead?* appeared in 1917. They published *The Key of Destiny* in 1919, a sequel to *The Key to the Universe,* and other volumes followed in later years.

During the war, the Curtisses founded the Church of the Wisdom Religion, a less exclusive group than their earlier order. In 1929, after the Curtisses moved to Washington, D.C., the church was incorporated as the Universal Religious Foundation. After many years of teaching, writing, and traveling, Harriette Curtiss died in Washington on September 22, 1932.

References: Harriette Augusta Curtiss and F. Homer Curtiss, *The Key of Destiny* (1919); Alberta Lawrence, ed., *Who Was Who among North American Authors, 1921–1939,* vol. 1 (1976); J. Gordon Melton, *Religious Leaders of America* (1991).

Cushman, Vera Charlotte Scott (1876–1946)

Vera Charlotte Scott Cushman, a leader and an organizer of the Young Women's Christian Association (YWCA), was born in Ottawa, Illinois, on September 19, 1876. She was the second of the three children of Samuel Swann and Anna Margaret (Tressler) Scott. Her father was an immigrant from northern Ireland who, with his brothers, founded dry goods stores in Illinois, which eventually grew to become the prominent Chicago wholesale and department store firm of Carson, Pirie, Scott and Company. Vera's early years were spent in Ottawa, except from 1887 to 1891, when her father ran a bank in Salina, Kansas. The Scott family was very religious, with strong feelings for foreign missions. Samuel Scott served as a Presbyterian elder; Anna Scott was active in church-related benevolent work; and Vera's brother, George, eventually became a minister and executive secretary of the Presbyterian Board of Foreign Missions.

As a girl, Vera received instruction in music, elocution, and homemaking in addition to the usual academic studies. She attended the fashionable Ferry Hall in Lake Forest, Illinois, and in 1898 she graduated from Smith College. While at Smith, she was involved in several student organizations; she served as president of the Christian Association, the student affiliate of the YWCA. She remained active with that organization after leaving Smith.

On October 15, 1901, Vera Scott married James Stewart Cushman, a New York businessman engaged in real estate and manufacturing. The Cushmans resided in New York City but also maintained a home in Newport, Rhode Island. They never had children. Vera Cushman became known as a woman of wealth and social prominence, and one who was dedicated to religious and social service. Much of her volunteer efforts were in support of the YWCA. Active with the organization on both the national and international levels, Cushman was a member of the committee that, in 1906, united the two existing YWCA organizations to establish the YWCA of the U.S.A. She served on the National Board for the next three decades and was vice president of the national YWCA for several terms between 1906 and 1936. In 1913 she served as vice chair of the YWCA campaign that raised $4 million for new buildings in just fourteen days.

During World War I, Cushman served as chairman of the War Work Council of the YWCA, one of seven war service organizations created by the government. She traveled throughout the United States and Europe, overseeing the construction and the management of the YWCA Hostess Houses that were being built near training camps, naval stations, and hospital camps. These houses provided food, housing, and recreational facilities for nurses, signal corps workers, and other women in the war zones, as well as places for soldiers to meet with friends and relatives. In the summer of 1919, as a result of her service during the war, Cushman was one of six women to be honored with the Distinguished Service Medal.

After the war, Cushman became increasingly involved in international work. In 1920 she was a delegate to the International Suffrage Convention in Geneva; she was a member of the executive committee of the Presbyterian Women's Board of Missions from 1920 to 1921; she served as vice president of the League of Nations Non-Partisan Association in 1923; and, from 1924 to 1938, Cushman served as a vice presi-

dent of the World's Council of the YWCA. She assisted in the formation of the YWCA's World Service Council, an organization designed to help sister organizations in other countries. Her responsibilities with the council took her to places around the globe, as she attended meetings and surveyed activities in Europe, China, India, South America, and the Near East. Cushman died in Savannah, Georgia, on February 1, 1946, of a coronary occlusion suffered on the way to a vacation in Florida.

See also: Young Women's Christian Association

References: Edward T. James, ed., *Notable American Women, 1607–1950*, vol. 1 (1971); J. Gordon Melton, *Religious Leaders of America* (1991); Marion O. Robinson, *Eight Women of the YWCA* (1966).

Daly, Mary (1928–)

American feminist and theological writer Mary Daly was born in Schenectady, New York, on October 16, 1928. The daughter of Frank X. and Ann Catherine (Morse) Daly, Mary grew up in the Roman Catholic faith. She received her bachelor of arts degree from the College of St. Rose, Albany, New York, in 1950; her master of arts degree from the Catholic University of America, Washington, D.C., in 1952; and her doctorate from St. Mary's College, Notre Dame, Indiana, in 1954. Her major fields of study were philosophy and theology, which she taught at Cardinal Cushing College, Brookline, Massachusetts, from 1954 to 1959. From 1959 to 1966 she participated in the junior year abroad program for American students at the University of Fribourg in Switzerland, again teaching philosophy and theology. While at that university, she earned a second doctorate in 1965. Since 1969 she has been a professor of theology at Boston College.

Since entering her profession, Mary Daly's theology has evolved from mainstream Roman Catholicism to a radical feminist, post-Christian philosophy. Her early writings reveal a woman working from inside Roman Catholicism to inspire reforms within the church. In *The Church and the Second Sex* (1968), Daly argues that the church has promoted the idea of women being inferior and must take much of the responsibility for the oppression of women within society. This work was one of the first major works to be written from the perspective of feminist theology since publication of Elizabeth Cady Stanton's *The Woman's Bible* at the end of the nineteenth century. In 1975 *The Church and the Second Sex* was reissued with a feminist post-Christian introduction by the author, and the book was revised in 1985. Daly's *Beyond God the Father: Toward a Philosophy of Women's Liberation* (1973) reveals her further movement away from the teachings of the Catholic Church. She rejects the doctrine of original sin as sexist and encourages women to rename God, the world, and themselves according to their own experiences as women. In *Gyn/Ecology: The Metaethics of Radical Feminism* (1978), Daly makes a complete break with Christianity and advocates the separation of women into a new religious movement of lesbian radical feminists. She also offers her readers a new feminist vocabulary, taking derogatory terms for women, such as "shrew," "hag," and "spinster," capitalizing them and using them as words of praise. Daly continues to add to her glossary of old words with new definitions in *Pure Lust: Elemental Feminist Philosophy* (1984) and, with coauthor Jane Caputi, *Webster's First New Intergalactic Wickedary of the English Language* (1987).

Daly's writings are controversial, both inside and outside feminist circles. Some critics consider her work important as a challenge to traditional thinking. Some find her language humorous and free from patriarchal patterns. Others feel that the way she uses language makes her books difficult to read and thus obscures her message and dilutes what would otherwise be a significant contribution to feminist theory. Whether or not her readers agree with her work, her writings continue to stimulate thought and discussion, especially among feminists and theologians.

See also: Ecofeminism; Feminist Theology; Ruether, Rosemary Radford; *The Woman's Bible*
References: Mary Daly, *Beyond God the Father: Toward a Philosophy of Women's Liberation* (1973); Mary Daly, *Pure Lust: Elemental Feminist Philosophy* (1984); Mary Daly and Jane Caputi, *Webster's First New Intergalactic Wickedary of the English Language* (1987); David W. Diehl, "Theology and Feminism," in June Steffensen Hagen, ed., *Gender Matters: Women's Studies for the Christian Community* (1990); James G. Lesniak, ed., *Contemporary Authors New Revision Series,* vol. 30 (1990); Jennifer S. Uglow, *The Continuum Dictionary of Women's Biography* (1989); Lindsy Van Gelder, "A Yahoo's Guide to Mary Daly," *Ms.* (February 1979).

Day, Dorothy (1897–1980)

Cofounder of the *Catholic Worker* and a woman who dedicated her life to social justice, Dorothy Day was born in Brooklyn, New York, in 1897. While she was still a child, her family moved to Oakland, California, and then to Chicago, following destruction of their California home in an earthquake. Growing up on Chicago's West Side, Day was disturbed by the many poor people living in the city's slums. She found it difficult to understand why some people lived in luxury while others had to struggle to survive. In later years, she would devote her life to confronting and repairing these abuses.

When she was sixteen, Day began her studies at the University of Illinois at Urbana, where she had received a scholarship. But she was eager to begin her work to help others and dropped out of college after her sophomore year. Day moved to New York, where she obtained a job at the *New York Call,* a socialist newspaper, and became involved in campaigns for workers' rights. Over the next few years, she held various jobs, wrote and traveled, and eventually settled in an artists' colony in Staten Island, New York. There she met Forster Battingham, who became her common-law husband. The union produced a daughter, Tamar, in 1927. Having once considered herself "agnostic," Day had gradually been drawn to religion and, by the time of her daughter's birth, was attending mass regularly. Shortly after her daughter was born, she had Tamar baptized in the Roman Catholic Church, and Day herself joined the church.

When the Great Depression struck the country a few years later, Day became concerned that the church was not doing enough to help the suffering poor. In an attempt to raise the issue, she and a colleague, Peter Maurin, established a newspaper, the *Catholic Worker,* in 1933. The paper advocated social justice. It called for the upholding of the rights of workers, promoted racial equality, opposed anti-Semitism, and denounced lynching. But Day and Maurin went beyond just words in a newspaper and put their commitment to social justice into action. It was not long before a movement developed around them. They established "houses of hospitality," which provided services for the poor by offering food and shelter to those in need. The first house was in New York, but soon more opened across the country. While hundreds of people lined up for help, many others volunteered as workers. Day and Maurin also held conferences in which scholars, workers, priests, and others gathered to share ideas.

Throughout her life, Day continued to be an advocate for justice for all people. Besides aiding the poor, she supported strikers in labor disputes, and in the 1930s she picketed the German embassy to protest the Nazis' persecution of Jews. Day was also a committed pacifist, believing that wars settled nothing. Although most Catholics supported General Francisco Franco during the Spanish Civil War, Day favored total neutrality. After the bombing of Pearl Harbor, Dorothy voiced opposition to the United States' fighting in World War II, urging Americans to turn the other cheek and love their enemy. During the Cold War that followed, Day was arrested five times and jailed four times for defying civil-defense drills. Her commitment to peace led her to help found Pax, an organization of Catholic pacifists that in 1972 became known as Pax Christi.

While she campaigned for peace, Day did not forsake her dedication to social justice. During the 1950s and 1960s, when taking a stand against racists often meant risking one's life, Day was active in the civil rights movement. From 1938 she was an advocate for the rights of migrant workers, protesting unfair wages and unsafe working conditions; during the 1970s, she went to jail for her advocacy of the migrant worker's cause. Despite her radicalism, on most issues Day remained a traditional Catholic, speaking out against abortion, birth control, and the Equal Rights Amendment. After devoting most of her life to the betterment of conditions for humankind, Dorothy Day died in 1980. Since November of 1997 efforts have been underway to gather evidence that might someday result in Day's canonization.

See also: Roman Catholic Church
References: Robert Coles, *Dorothy Day: A Radical Devotion* (1987); Dorothy Day, *The Long Loneliness: The Autobiography of Dorothy Day* (1981, reprint); Rick Hampson, "Movement Builds to Canonize Dorothy Day," *USA Today* (March 12, 1998): 4; James J. Kenneally, *The History of American Catholic Women* (1990); William D. Miller, *A Harsh and Dreadful Love: Dorothy Day and the Catholic Worker Movement* (1973); June O'Connor, *The Moral Vision of Dorothy Day* (1991); Julie F. Parker, *Careers for Women as Clergy* (1993); Mel Piehl, *Breaking Bread: The Catholic Worker and the Origin of Catholic Radicals in America* (1982).

Deaconesses

During the last half of the nineteenth century, a new opportunity opened for Protestant women wishing to hold leadership roles within their churches, the opportunity to become deaconesses. The Lutheran, Episcopal, and Methodist churches had the greatest successes in bringing the office of deaconess to America, although Presbyterians and some smaller denominations made more limited attempts to participate in the movement. Deaconesses performed functions that included nursing, visiting, and offering relief to the poor and sick in their homes and serving in foreign missions.

The first female diaconate in America was established in 1849–1850 by a Lutheran pastor, William Passavant of Pittsburgh, Pennsylvania. Modeled after a thriving Lutheran institution at Kaiserwerth, Germany (which also became a model for diaconates of other Protestant denominations), it included a hospital, a motherhouse, and an organization—the Institution of Protestant Deaconesses. Initially, the Lutheran Church in America showed little interest in the diaconate, few women appeared to be attracted to the organization, and many Lutherans considered it too similar to a Roman Catholic convent. Passavant's diaconate foundered but was restored in Milwaukee, Wisconsin, in 1893, after the deaconess movement had acquired advocates among larger numbers of Lutherans. During the thirty years from 1885 to 1915, various bodies of the Lutheran Church established diaconates in cities in mid-Atlantic and midwestern states. Playing a major role in the organizing of diaconates in Brooklyn, New York, and Minneapolis, Minnesota,

In the late 1800s, many Protestant women were trained as deaconesses to serve their churches; the first seven deaconesses for the African Methodist Church shown here were trained at a school in Cincinatti (1902).

was a Norwegian deaconess, Elizabeth Fedde, who trained deaconesses, founded motherhouses, and helped to establish hospitals in both cities.

"Sisterhoods" in the Episcopal Church performed functions similar to those of deaconesses in other Protestant churches, and some orders preferred the term "deaconess." Anne Ayres, who in 1845 became the first Episcopal sister, founded the Sisterhood of the Holy Communion in New York City in 1852. The Community of St. Mary, a sisterhood with a more monastic tradition, was established in New York City by Harriet Starr Cannon in 1865. By 1880 there were six major sisterhoods within the Episcopal Church, but they were not recognized by the Episcopal General Convention until 1889.

The deaconess program within the Methodist Church was the most successful among American Protestants. Much of

the credit goes to Lucy Jane Rider Meyer, who opened the Chicago Training School for City, Home, and Foreign Missions in Chicago in 1885. The school developed out of what Meyer saw as a need for a school for women entering religious work. A year later she began building a "deaconess home," which became connected to the school. In May 1888, the General Conference of the Methodist Episcopal Church authorized the use of deaconesses and established general rules for them. It was not long before other deaconess groups began to form, though they tended to clash rather than to work together. In 1939 the Methodist Church put all deaconess groups under the authority of one single board.

Although women like Meyer pressed their churches to ordain women and allow them to work on an equal basis with men, the vast majority of male church leaders preferred to earmark the deaconess position as service work, set apart from church leadership. As long as they were convinced that the deaconesses were performing functions associated with the prevailing conception of the female domain, male leaders did not feel the women threatened male authority. Nevertheless, as official representatives of their churches, deaconesses enjoyed a status that few women attained. Most deaconess training schools were relatively inexpensive, allowing the women to receive a degree of professional training in theology, social service, and nursing that they otherwise could not have afforded.

Reaching its height in the early decades of the twentieth century, the deaconess movement began to fade in the 1920s. Although most Protestant diaconates did not require the binding vows found in Roman Catholic orders, many Protestants continued to be uncomfortable with similarities between deaconesses and nuns. By the middle of the century, women had found other opportunities opening for them, both in their churches and in social service professions.

See also: Ayres, Anne; Cannon, Harriet Starr; Episcopal Church; Fedde, Elizabeth; Lutheran Church; Meyer, Lucy Jane Rider **References:** Mary Sudman Donovan, *A Different Call: Women's Ministries in the Episcopal Church, 1850–1920* (1986); Edward T. James, ed., *Notable American Women, 1607–1950* (1971); L. DeAne Lagerquist, *From Our Mothers' Arms: A History of Women in the American Lutheran Church* (1987); Susan Hill Lindley, *"You Have Stept Out of Your Place": A History of Women and Religion in America* (1996); J. Gordon Melton, *Religious Leaders of America* (1991); Cecyle S. Neidle, *America's Immigrant Women* (1975).

Declaration of Rights and Sentiments and Its Resolutions

As they prepared for the first women's rights convention, held in Seneca Falls, New York, July 19–20, 1848, the leaders of the new movement realized that they needed a manifesto that would lay out their grievances and resolutions. The result was a *Declaration of Rights and Sentiments and Its Resolutions,* written primarily by Elizabeth Cady Stanton, that was modeled on the American Declaration of Independence. Written into the document are references to the intent of "God," or the "Creator," regarding women's place in the world as well as grievances concerning women's subordinate position in the church. Religious references include the following:

> We hold these truths to be self-evident: that all men and women are created equal; that they are endowed by their Creator with certain inalienable rights. . . .
>
> He [referring to men] allows her in Church, as well as State, but a subordinate position, claiming Apostolic authority for her exclusion from the ministry, and, with some exceptions, from any public participation in the affairs of the Church. . . .
>
> He has usurped the prerogative of Jehovah himself, claiming it as his right to assign for her a sphere of action, when that belongs to her conscience and to her God. . . .

And the women resolved:

> That woman is man's equal—was intended to be so by the Creator. . . .
>
> That woman has too long rested satisfied in the circumscribed limits which corrupt customs and a perverted application of the Scriptures have marked out for her, and that it is time she should move in the enlarged sphere which her great Creator has assigned her. . . .
>
> That, being invested by the Creator with the same capabilities, and the same consciousness of responsi-

bility for their exercise, it is demonstrably the right and duty of woman, equally with man, to promote every righteous cause by every righteous means; and especially in regard to the great subjects of morals and religion, it is self-evidently her right to participate with her brother in teaching them.

The foregoing resolutions were all readily accepted by the convention. Of the total of twelve resolutions in the document, the only one to create controversy was one that argued that women had a "sacred right to the elective franchise."

See also: Stanton, Elizabeth Cady; Woman Suffrage; *The Woman's Bible*
References: Henry Steele Commager, ed., *Documents of American History,* 7th ed. (1962); Eleanor Flexner, *Century of Struggle: The Woman's Rights Movement in the United States* (1970); Elizabeth Cady Stanton, *Eighty Years and More: Reminiscences, 1815–1897* (1898); Elizabeth Cady Stanton et al., eds., *History of Woman Suffrage,* vol. 1 (1889; reprint 1969).

Dickinson, Frances (1755–1830)

Born in London, England, in 1755, Frances Dickinson cofounded the first Roman Catholic convent in the United States. On May 1, 1772, Dickinson joined a Carmelite convent in Antwerp, Belgium. (The Carmelite order in the Roman Catholic Church is named for Mount Carmel in Israel, where the order originated.) Dickinson assumed the name Clare Joseph of the Sacred Heart of Jesus and made her final vows on June 3, 1773.

Father Charles Neale, an American and a relative of Mother Bernardina Teresa Xavier of St. Joseph (formerly Ann Teresa Matthews), was confessor to the Antwerp convent. He invited Sister Clare Joseph to accompany Mother Bernardina and her two nieces to America and to help them establish a Carmelite mission there. She agreed and emigrated to the United States in 1790, cofounding the Carmel Convent in Port Tobacco, Maryland, on October 15, 1790. It was the nation's first Roman Catholic convent. Sister Clare Joseph immediately became assistant to Mother Bernardina, the convent's first prioress. Following Mother Bernardina's death in 1800, Sister Clare Joseph succeeded her, serving until she died at the convent in 1830.

As prioress, Sister Clare Joseph trained novices and maintained the order's rule in a setting far from sisterly authority or advice. Yet the community prospered, with plentiful crops, until the period 1818 to 1829, when a long costly lawsuit over their land caused financial problems for the convent. After the death of Father Neale in 1823, the income from the plantation was insufficient to support the convent. In 1831, a year after Sister Clare Joseph's death, the convent relocated to Baltimore. Most of the later Carmelite convents in the United States originated with this convent or with its branches.

See also: Matthews, Ann Teresa; Roman Catholic Church; Roman Catholic Women's Orders (Nuns)
References: Edward T. James, ed., *Notable American Women, 1607–1950* (1971); Robert McHenry, ed., *Liberty's Women* (1980); Phyllis J. Read and Bernard L. Witlieb, *The Book of Women's Firsts* (1992).

Dilling, Elizabeth Kirkpatrick (Stokes) (1894–1966)

Author, lecturer, and crusader for the religious and political far right, Elizabeth Kirkpatrick Dilling was born in Chicago, Illinois, on April 19, 1894. Her father, a Scotch-Irish Presbyterian, died when Elizabeth was six weeks old, so she followed the tradition of her mother's side of the family and attended the Episcopal Church throughout her childhood. She received her education in private schools, including the Catholic Academy of Our

Lady in Chicago. People who knew Elizabeth during her childhood remembered her as being an "unusually emotional" girl, and she was similarly described as an adult (H. Moore, 1963, p. 243). As a teenager, she was deeply interested in the Episcopal religion and is said to have sent girlfriends thirty- and forty-page letters on biblical topics.

In 1918 she married Albert Wallwick Dilling, a Lutheran, who joined his wife in the Episcopal Church upon the couple's marriage. The marriage eventually ended in divorce in 1943. Dilling lived quietly as a wife and mother of two children in an affluent North Shore suburb of Chicago until the early 1930s. A vacation trip to the Soviet Union in August 1931 changed her life. In her travels within the Soviet Union, she found a communism that crippled the economy, promoted scarcity, and undermined freedom. She was greatly concerned over what she described as the "government destruction of faith in God, religion, and morality" (Benowitz, 1996, p. 55). Worried that an unwary America might soon find itself under communist control and the people would suffer the same religious, social, economic, and political hardships that the Russians endured, she embarked on a lifelong campaign against communism and anyone or anything that appeared to threaten Christianity.

In 1932 Dilling wrote and published *Red Revolution: Do We Want It Here?* in which she warned that the Communist Party planned "to overthrow our government and establish a Soviet government here as part of a plan for world revolution" (Benowitz, 1996, p. 55). Americans could easily be fooled, she wrote, because friends of the Communist Party "usually pose as 'neutrals,' 'liberals,' 'lovers of mental freedom,' etc., seldom as crude Communists." This notion of a fifth column of anti-American subversives with connections to the Communist Party became the basis of her broad search for communists, a search that soon encompassed the majority of America's intelligentsia, universities, moderate to liberal religious organizations, and the Roosevelt administration—almost everyone whose social and political philosophies were less conservative than hers.

In 1934 she self-published *The Red Network: A "Who's Who" and Handbook of Radicalism for Patriots,* a book that brought her national fame. What made *The Red Network* famous and sold thousands of copies was its listing of hundreds of organizations and prominent people Dilling considered either communists or communist sympathizers—renowned people ranging from Jane Addams to Sigmund Freud, as well as names of rabbis and other clergymen, authors, and professors. *The Roosevelt Red Record* followed in 1936, in which she accused the Roosevelt administration of being riddled with communists. Two years later, Dilling combined her superpatriotism with her religious zeal and established the Patriotic Research Bureau in downtown Chicago. Her letterhead stated the purpose of the organization: "For the Defense of Christianity and Americanism."

During the early years of her campaign, Dilling called upon her audiences to accept Christianity "as an antidote to Communism," but by 1940 her "defense of Christianity" had taken on an anti-Semitic tone that would eventually overtake her anticommunist fervor (Benowitz, 1996, p. 60). Under the pseudonym "Reverend Frank Woodruff Johnson," Dilling wrote and published *The Octopus* (1940), which charged that Jews were conspiring to rob Gentiles of their American constitutional rights. She admired Adolf Hitler and agreed with the führer that Germany's post–World War I economic problems were caused by Jews. In addition to her writings, Dilling spread her messages through speaking engagements—occasionally on the radio, but more often she traveled the country giving evangelical-style lectures at churches and lecture halls and before such patriotic organizations as the American Legion and Daughters of the American Revolution.

After the United States entered World War II, government agencies began to investigate Dilling's alleged subversive activities, and in 1942 she was indicted along with twenty-seven others on charges of conspiring to engage in seditious activity. Despite the indictment, Dilling continued to spread her message of "Christianity and Americanism" and to speak out against all whom she considered her "enemies" and the enemies of the United States. In July 1943, she told a Chicago audience that America's true enemies were not Germany, Italy, or Japan, but the Jews, Negroes (whom she believed were tools of communists and Jews), and the New Deal. For Dilling, the war was part of a communist-Jewish conspiracy to gain global control. She contended that communists and Jews had infiltrated the Roosevelt administration and manipulated the government to pressure the Japanese until they bombed American territory. Now the communists and Jews were profiting by having the United States fight their battles against Hitler and the Third Reich. In early 1945, when news of the full extent of the Holocaust reached the United States, Dilling told her readers that she did not believe that six million Jews had been killed in concentration camps.

Following the war, Dilling's attacks against Jews became increasingly vicious: Pearl Harbor was "a planned and maneuvered butchery to shock the American people into going to war for Jewry" (Benowitz, 1996, p. 94); Franklin Roosevelt and Jews were mass murderers for instigating the war with Japan; and she announced that she was circulating a petition for the United States to tighten immigration laws against alien Jews and that she intended "to campaign for assistance to help the displaced Jews of the world go to their already established Jewish Homeland—Biribidjan" (Benowitz, 1996, p. 94), an isolated area in east Siberia where Stalin had attempted to settle Russian Jews.

In 1948 she married fellow anticommunist and anti-Semite Jeremiah Stokes, who had for the past two years been assisting her at the Patriotic Research Bureau. Her last book, *The Plot Against Christianity* (n.d., ca. 1953), another self-publication, expressed Dilling's fears that Jews were determined to destroy Christianity and "Christian morality" and had been plotting such destruction for centuries. Dilling remained an active campaigner for her causes until her death. During her lifetime, perceptions of Dilling ranged from those of her followers who considered her a brave, Christian woman to accusations from her detractors that she was a dangerous fascist. Others simply dismissed her as a crackpot. Dilling was fanatical in her beliefs, never allowing for other points of view and created for herself a lifelong mission to change the world to meet her specifications. Her diatribes against Jews and communists contributed to the anti-Semitism that spread throughout the United States in the 1930s and 1940s and to the Red Scare hysteria that followed World War II. Dilling died in Chicago on April 29, 1966.

See also: Anti-Semitism; Fundamentalism
References: June Melby Benowitz, "Speaking Out: Right-Wing American Women, 1933 to 1945," (Ph.D. diss., 1996); Glen Jeansonne, *Women of the Far Right* (1996); Harry Thornton Moore, "The Lady Patriot's Book," *The New Republic 85* (January 8, 1936); Richard Gid Powers, *Not without Honor: The History of American Anticommunism* (1995); Leo P. Ribuffo, *The Old Christian Right: The Protestant Far Right from the Great Depression to the Cold War* (1983).

Divorce

Within the Roman Catholic faith, marriage is a sacrament and divorce is prohibited. In the sixteenth century, Protestant reformers, believing only baptism and communion to be essential to salvation, said that marriage was not a sacrament. Soon divorces were being granted in Protestant lands, and grounds for divorce were broadening. The Church of England broke from Roman Catholicism but retained its doctrine on the matter of divorce. The history of divorce in colonial America reflected specific colonial conditions and was usually dependent upon the level of English control. Divorce was most common in Puritan-dominated New England, where leaders disagreed with the Anglican Church over a variety of issues. In the Massachusetts Bay Colony, a divorce could be obtained in civil court on the grounds of a wife's adultery or desertion by either spouse. The double standard on adultery persisted until the middle of the eighteenth century. Historian Nancy F. Cott has found evidence to indicate that during the eighteenth century, it was easier for Massachusetts males to obtain divorces than it was for females. Divorce was less common in New York, Pennsylvania, and New Jersey and was prohibited in Georgia (until 1798), North Carolina (until 1814), and South Carolina (until 1868).

Although New England states passed divorce legislation shortly after the United States gained independence, it was not until the last half of the nineteenth century that there was a rapid increase in American divorce. The early legislation did not pass without controversy. In 1814 prominent Congregational pastor Timothy Dwight denounced Connecticut's liberal divorce law and condemned all but scriptural divorce (for adultery only). The Mormon-dominated Utah Territory passed a divorce law in 1852 that permitted a divorce once the petitioner demonstrated that he or she was a "resident or wish[ed] to become one" (Phillips, 1988, p. 1). As a result, some non-Mormon religious leaders criticized divorce as a forerunner of bigamy or polygamy.

After pressures from conservatives led to a tightening of Connecticut divorce laws, Theodore Woolsey, the president of Yale, and Samuel Duke, a Congregational minister from Vermont, were encouraged that further changes could occur. They founded the New England Divorce Reform League in 1881, the first organized opposition to liberal divorce policies and the increasing rate of divorce. In 1863 the Episcopal Church forbade ministers to perform any marriage involving a divorced person unless he or she was the innocent party in a case of adultery. The rule was tightened in 1907 to require the innocent party to wait at least a year following the divorce before remarrying. Other major Protestant churches followed the lead of the Episcopalians. The Presbyterian, Methodist Episcopal, and Reformed churches all placed restrictions on church marriages for divorced persons. More liberal was the General Synod of the Evangelical Lutheran Church, which in 1907 passed a resolution stating that since the Reformation the church had recognized adultery and willful desertion as grounds for divorce and including other grounds, such as impotence, extreme cruelty, conspiracy against life, and habitual drunkenness.

In 1903, twenty-five American Protestant denominations formed an Inter-Church Conference on Marriage and Divorce in an attempt to formulate a common policy regarding remarriage. Their work together to obtain uniform divorce laws in America led to the formation of a National Congress on Uniform Divorce Laws, with delegates from forty-two states and territories. However, no uniform agreement could be reached among the states.

From the middle of the nineteenth century, women's rights activists joined in the crusade to liberalize divorce laws. Women like Elizabeth Cady Stanton campaigned for divorces for mental and physical cruelty and drunkenness, and for women's right to child custody and property in the event of a divorce. By the end of the century, women were suing for divorce over their husbands' failure to act responsibly or to respect their wives' autonomy.

Despite increased pressure from some religious leaders, the divorce rate in the United States was rapidly increasing. Whereas in 1880, one in every twenty-one marriages ended in divorce, by 1900 the rate was one in twelve. Following World War I, the divorce rate surged again, increasing 40 percent from the period 1914–1918 to 1919–1920. At least part of the rise was due to marital infidelity during the war. With the advent of "no-fault" divorce laws beginning in the 1960s, which recognized that there were circumstances wherein neither spouse need take responsibility for the failure of a marriage, moralistic and fault-based precepts were discarded. Yet although civil laws have been liberalized, a number of churches, most notably the Roman Catholic Church, continue to uphold their restrictions on divorce.

References: Nelson Manfred Blake, *The Road to Reno: A History of Divorce in the United States* (1962); Nancy F. Cott, "Divorce and the Changing Status of Women in Eighteenth-Century Massachusetts," in Kathryn Kish Sklar and Thomas Dublin, *Women and Power in American History: A Reader, Vol. 1 to 1880* (1991); Roderick Phillips, *Putting Asunder: A History of Divorce in Western Society* (1988); Roderick Phillips, *Untying the Knot: A Short History of Divorce* (1991).

Dix, Dorothea Lynde (1802–1887)

Prominent nineteenth-century humanitarian and social reformer Dorothea

Dorothea Lynde Dix (undated photo)

Lynde Dix was born to Joseph and Mary (Bigelow) Dix on April 4, 1802, in Hampden, Maine (then a part of Massachusetts). She grew up in an unstable household, in which her father, an itinerant Methodist minister, failed to sufficiently provide for the family. It seems that neither parent was a positive role model; nor did they offer Dorothea the nurturing that she needed and desired. When she was twelve years of age, Dorothea left home and moved to Boston to live with her grandmother, Dorothy Dix, the widow of a prosperous physician, chemical manufacturer, and land promoter. But Dorothea was a headstrong girl who had difficulty adjusting to the strict disciplinary style of her grandmother, and it was not long before she went to live with her great aunt in Worcester, Massachusetts. She later returned to her grandmother's house to complete her education.

In 1821 Dix founded her own school in Boston and developed a curriculum that emphasized the natural sciences and the responsibilities of ethical living. She wrote and published a science textbook, *Conversations on Common Things,* in 1824, and a year later edited a book of poems entitled *Hymns for Children.* From the beginning of her teaching days, she was convinced that it was a teacher's duty to create a self-critical moral awareness in students, and in 1832 she wrote a book, *American Moral Tales for Young People,* that illustrated her ideas on the subject. She wrote several other books during this period, including *Evening Hours* (1825), *Meditations for Private Hours* (1828), and *The Garland of Flora* (1829). In the meantime, Dix had become acquainted with William Ellery Channing, the charismatic father of Unitarianism, and she became attracted to the faith herself. Dix later put the Unitarians' idealistic commitment to social justice into action.

She abandoned her teaching in 1836, when increasingly serious bouts with tuberculosis forced her to rest, and spent the next two years in England. Upon her return to Boston, she found that she had inherited a large sum of money and would no longer have to work to support herself. Nevertheless, and despite continued poor health, she was adverse to inactivity.

A turning point in her life came in March 1841, when a young clergyman asked her to start a Sunday school class for women at a prison in East Cambridge. There she found women suffering under deplorable conditions, with prisoners and mentally insane women confined together. Many of the insane were naked and filthy and confined to an unheated section of the jail. Some bore evidence of repeated whippings. Dix was so horrified by the conditions that she immediately launched a career aimed at reforming institutions that housed the mentally ill.

In 1843, after a fact-finding mission in which Dix observed conditions in jails throughout Massachusetts, she reported the results of her research to the state legislature and demanded change. As a result of her campaign, an asylum for the mentally ill was expanded and renovated in Worcester, and insane persons were removed from jail. Over the next forty years, Dix continued her crusade throughout the United States and Canada. She has been credited with achieving legislative reforms to help the mentally ill in fifteen states, with personally overseeing the establishment of thirty-two mental health hospitals, and with inspiring the founding of more than one hundred asylums for the mentally ill.

During the years immediately preceding the Civil War, Dix's crusade took her to Europe, Turkey, and Russia. In Italy she had an audience with Pope Pius IX, who pledged his personal support for her work. After the outbreak of the Civil War, Dix was appointed superintendent of nurses for the United States Sanitary Commission. Although she was devoted to her duties, Dix was less successful as an administrator than as a reformer and was frequently criticized for her lack of tact and flexibility. In 1863 her responsibilities were reduced. Soon after the war ended, Dix returned to her crusades on behalf of the mentally ill.

Dorothea Dix died at a hospital in Trenton, New Jersey, that she had founded many years before, on July 18, 1887.

See also: Reform Movements
References: Kathryn Cullen-DuPont, with Annelise Orleck, *The Encyclopedia of Women's History in America* (1996); Eleanor Flexner, *Century of Struggle: The Woman's Rights Movement in the United States* (1970); David Gollaher, *Voice for the Mad: The Life of Dorothea Dix* (1995); Elizabeth Lasch-Quinn, "Dorothea Dix and Mental Health Reform," in Randall M. Miller and Paul A. Cimbala, eds., *American Reform and Reformers: A Biographical Dictionary* (1996); Helen E. Marshall, *Dorothea Dix: Forgotten Samaritan* (1937); Robert McHenry, ed., *Liberty's Women* (1980).

Drexel, Mary Katharine, Mother (1858–1955)

Founder of the Sisters of the Blessed Sacrament for Indians and Colored People, Mary Katharine Drexel was born in Philadelphia, Pennsylvania, on November 26, 1858. Drexel's family was both wealthy and altruistic, distributing aid to the poor and making financial contributions to support mission work among African Americans and Native Americans. Upon their father's death in 1885, Drexel and her two sisters were left an inheritance of $14 million.

Drexel's interest in aiding the less fortunate continued. In 1887, she had an audience with Pope Leo XIII, who suggested she enter missionary work. After many months of suffering great inner turmoil in regard to her future, Drexel chose to follow the pope's advice and to devote her life to mission work. She also decided to use a portion of her inheritance to establish a new religious order.

In 1889, Drexel entered the novitiate of the Sisters of Mercy in Pittsburgh. After she took her vows, she founded the Sisters of the Blessed Sacrament for Indians and Colored People. On February 12, 1891, when she made her vows as the first of the Sisters of the Blessed Sacrament for Indians and Colored People, she added a special vow: "To be the mother and servant of the Indian and Negro races." The following year, the mother house was established at Cornwells Heights, Pennsylvania. The order received official approval in 1913.

For forty years, Mother Mary Katharine directed the order's work, curtailing her strenuous activity only after suffering a heart attack in 1935. By the time of her death, the order had grown to over five hundred sisters living in fifty-one convents. The order had established three houses of social service and sixty-one schools, including a boarding school for Pueblos in Santa Fe, New Mexico, in 1894 and a school for African-American girls in Rock Castle, Virginia, in 1899. In 1915, the order founded Xavier University in New Orleans. The university received its charter in 1925, the only Roman Catholic college for African Americans in the United States.

Mother Mary Katharine died of pneumonia and heart failure in Cornwells Heights, Pennsylvania, on March 3, 1955. By the time of her death, she had contributed over $12 million to the church. The first stage of the beatification procedure began for Mother Mary Katharine in 1964. In the 1990s, the process that may lead to her canonization is still pending.

See also: Roman Catholic Church; Roman Catholic Women's Orders (Nuns)
References: Henry Warner Bowden, *Dictionary of American Religious Biography,* 2nd ed. (1993); Consuela Marie Duffy, *Katharine Drexel: A Biography* (1972); Nancy A. Hewitt, "Drexel, Mother Mary Katharine," in Barbara Sicherman and Carol Hurd Green, eds., *Notable American Women: The Modern Period* (1980); James J. Kenneally, *The History of American Catholic Women* (1990); Phyllis J. Read and Bernard L. Witlieb, *The Book of Women's Firsts* (1992); Ellen Tarry, *Katharine Drexel: Friend of the Oppressed* (1990).

Dunne, Sarah Theresa (1846–1919)

Known by Native Americans as Great Holy White Chief Woman, Sarah Theresa Dunne, or Mother Mary Amadeus of the Heart of Jesus, was a pioneer in the establishment of church institutions in the American Northwest. Born in Akron, Ohio, on July 2, 1846, Sarah Dunne enrolled in a school run by the Ursuline Order of the Roman Catholic Church at Cleveland when she was a young child. According to tradition, she astonished her playmates when she predicted that she would someday be a missionary in Alaska, then a practically unknown outpost of Russian settlement (the United States purchased the territory in 1867). In 1862, at the age of sixteen, Sarah joined the Ursuline community in Toledo, Ohio, taking her vows there on August 23, 1864. Ten years later, though she was the youngest of the nuns in the community, she was selected the superior and became known as Mother Mary Amadeus of the Heart of Jesus. Under her leadership, the Toledo community prospered and a convent at nearby Youngstown was reestablished.

In the early 1880s, Mother Mary responded to the call of Bishop John Baptist Brondel, the first bishop of the new diocese of Helena, Montana, who appealed for nuns to serve in the West. In January 1884 Mother Mary left Ohio for Miles City, Montana, where she founded both a boardinghouse and a parish school. During April of that year, she journeyed for four days to begin work with the Cheyenne Indians at a mission that was deemed so dangerous that the priests fled, leaving it in the hands of Mother Mary and two other nuns. From the time of her arrival, Mother Mary gained the respect of the Cheyenne, and she became known as Make-Makehona Wikona, or Great Holy White Chief Woman. She learned the traditions and the language of the tribe, and she earned their trust. As years passed, she also established and taught at schools for the Blackfoot and Crow tribes and raised money for them when the federal government withdrew funding for their education. Her hard work and austere lifestyle earned her the admiration and respect of the Native Americans.

Mother Mary traveled to Rome in 1900, where her endeavors were discussed at a conference. As a result, the work of the Ursulines was reorganized, and Mother Mary was appointed the superior of the Montana mission and provincial. An injury from a train accident during her return from Rome left her crippled for the remainder of her life. Nevertheless, the Ursulines needed her,

and she remained active. Within a few years of her injury, she was appointed provincial of the North of the United States, headquartered in Middletown, New York. Almost immediately after receiving the new post, she established a novitiate to train new members. Mother Mary sent three Ursulines to Alaska in 1905, and two years later she went to Alaska herself.

In Alaska, Mother Mary performed missionary activity in areas where no white woman had been before. She was caught in blizzards a number of times and once saved a man from drowning. Between 1910 and 1912, she founded a convent that was so deep in the wilderness that it could be reached only by dogsled. She also established two missions, St. Ursula's-by-the-Sea and St. Michael's, and organized ministries to the Inuit. In 1912 she settled in Seattle, Washington, and founded a novitiate for the Alaska mission. The final years of Mother Mary's life were spent between Alaska and Seattle. She died in Seattle on November 10, 1919, and was buried in Montana near the Native Americans she loved. A fire at the Ursuline convent at St. Michael's destroyed her papers, leaving few records available for the study of Mother Mary's life.

See also: Roman Catholic Women's Orders (Nuns)
References: James J. Kenneally, *The History of American Catholic Women* (1990); J. Gordon Melton, *Religious Leaders of America* (1991); Dudley G. Wooten, "A Noble Ursuline," *Catholic World* 111 (August 1920): 580–602.

Dyer, Mary Barrett (c. 1615–1660)

Mary Dyer, who chose death over banishment for her Quaker faith, was born Mary Barrett in London, England. The exact date of her birth is not known, but it is believed she was born in or near the year 1615. She married William Dyer in 1633, and the couple emigrated to Massachusetts two years later. The Dyers eventually had five children who survived infancy. In the months following her arrival in the Massachusetts Bay Colony, Mary became a friend and admirer of Anne Hutchinson, whose unorthodox religious teachings upset the Puritan clergy and government leaders. When Hutchinson was excommunicated in 1637, Dyer was the only person to accompany her out of the church. And when Dyer delivered a stillborn child soon after, Governor John Winthrop was not surprised. He perceived the deformed child to be punishment for Dyer's heresy.

After leaving Boston, the Dyers established themselves in Newport, Rhode Island. Then, in the early 1650s, they spent five years in England, during which time Mary became a follower of George Fox, the founder of the Society of Friends (Quakers). She returned to America in 1656 and went to Boston in 1657, probably for the purpose of confronting authorities over their new, stringent laws against the Quakers. Puritan leaders considered their Quaker neighbors that "accursed sect of heretics" (Lerner, 1977, p. 471). Dyer was imprisoned in Boston but was released when her husband promised to keep her quiet until she had left the colony. Two years later, Mary returned to visit two male Quakers, William Robinson and Marmaduke Stevenson, who had been jailed under a more recent law that banished Quakers from the colony under pain of death. Dyer was herself arrested and banished. She and the two men were threatened with execution should they return. All three returned within a month, purposely defying the law. They were sentenced to death on October 27, 1659, and were led to the gallows.

Dyer was forced to watch the two men die. But she was given a reprieve, prearranged by the intervention of her son William and Governor John Winthrop. Mary refused the reprieve but was deported to Rhode Island. Feeling that she was under the command of God, Mary returned to Boston in May 1660. Despite the pleas of her husband, who was not a Quaker and who declared that he could not understand his wife's "madness," she was hung in Boston on June 1, 1660 (Lerner, 1977, p. 472). Only one Quaker was executed in Massachusetts after Dyer—William Leddra, who was put to death on March 14, 1661. Later that year the King of England ordered that such executions be stopped.

Dyer had considered herself an autonomous human being. She did not believe herself subordinate to anyone, whether they be government officials or her husband.

See also: Hutchinson, Anne Marbury
References: Hugh Barbour and J. William Frost, *The Quakers* (1988); Edith Deen, *Great Women of the Christian Faith* (1959); Gerda Lerner, *The Female Experience: An American Documentary* (1977); Horatio Rogers, *Mary Dyer of Rhode Island: The Quaker Martyr* (1896); Rosemary Radford Ruether and Rosemary Skinner Keller, eds., *Women and Religion in America*, vol. 2 (1986).

Ecofeminism

Since Francoise d'Eaubonne first introduced the term "ecofeminism" (*eco-feminisme*) in 1974, a growing number of feminists have joined the movement to halt what they perceive as the exploitation of both women and nature. Ecofeminism is a distinctive branch of feminism, in that it criticizes humankind's domination of nonhuman nature, called "naturism," as part of its critique of hierarchical social systems. Though they are especially interested in women-nature connections, ecofeminists explore other important "isms" of oppression: sexism, racism, classism, and anti-Semitism. As they see it, these "isms" are all linked, for they all require domination by a patriarchal culture.

There is no one ecofeminism, nor is there one ecofeminist philosophy. One area in which there are a wide variety of opinions is in the realm of religion. For many feminists, Spiritualism is an important aspect of ecofeminism. Some remain within the traditional religions of Judaism, Christianity, Hinduism, and Buddhism with the idea of transforming them. These ecofeminists hope to eliminate patriarchy within the major religions, which they theorize would lead to environmentally responsible, nonsexist practices and otherwise nonoppressive theologies. Other ecofeminists attach themselves to an earth-based spirituality similar to that of Native American cultures. Still others criticize feminists who, by connecting themselves to an earth-based spirituality, might reinforce the stereotype of women being closer to nature than men.

Since it is a relatively new movement, ideas surrounding the meaning and future of ecofeminism continue to be tested among its adherents as the movement continues to develop.

See also: Daly, Mary; Feminist Theology; Ruether, Rosemary Radford
References: Carol J. Adams, ed., *Ecofeminism and the Sacred* (1993); Carol P. Christ and Judith Plaskow, ed., *Womanspirit Rising: A Feminist Reader in Religion* (1979); Rosemary Radford Ruether, *Gaia and God: An Ecofeminist Theology of Earth Healing* (1992); Rosemary Radford Ruether, *Sexism and God-Talk: Toward a Feminist Theology* (1983).

Eddy, Mary Baker (1821–1910)

Mary Baker Eddy, writer, theologian, and founder of the Christian Science Church, was born July 16, 1821, in Bow, New Hampshire. She was the youngest of the six children of Mark and Abigail (Ambrose) Baker. Frequent illness plagued Mary's childhood years. At times she was unable to walk. She was an intellectually bright child who had aspirations of someday becoming a writer, but she also had a particular interest in religion. As an adolescent, she had debates with her father over religion that often were so intense that Mary became ill to the point of having paroxysmal seizures. These frightened her parents, who doted on her.

Mary Baker Eddy (undated photo)

On December 10, 1843, Mary married George Washington Glover, a Charleston, South Carolina, building contractor. Six months later she was a widow, her husband having died of a fever in June 1844; and on September 11, 1844, she became a mother when her only child, a son she named George, was born. Mary's frequent illnesses, which had barely abated since childhood, continued. She was unable to properly care for her child who, at the age of seven, was taken from her to live with the family nurse in northern New Hampshire.

Mary married for a second time in June 1853. Her husband, Daniel Patterson, was a struggling dentist. The couple's financial troubles and mismatched personalities, along with Mary's chronic illnesses, apparently resulted in a rocky marriage, and they were often apart. A long separation began by accident in 1861 when Daniel went to Bull Run to get a close-up view of a Civil War battle. He got a closer look than he had bargained for when he was captured by the Confederate cavalry and imprisoned.

While her husband was in prison, Mary sought healers to help her overcome her illnesses. In 1862 she traveled to Portland, Maine, to become a patient of Phineas Parkhurst Quimby. Within a week of joining his patients, she was much improved. From that time on, her feelings for Quimby and his ideas about healing became the dominating influence on her life. Quimby rejected the idea that a person was healed by medicine. More important, he believed, was the patient's conviction that he or she could be cured. At first, Quimby had experimented with mesmerism, but he found that if he just sat and talked with patients, he could find the causes of their troubles and restore them to health.

Mary was convinced of the effectiveness of Quimby's treatments. When her husband escaped from Confederate prison, he returned home to find his wife transformed. She was no longer dependent upon him and was considering engaging in a little healing herself. Psychobiographer Julius Silberger, Jr., holds that Mary encountered a problem in her practice of healing others, in that she frequently fancied herself afflicted with the ailments of those she cared for. Mary looked at the problem differently, however, believing that the healing practice weakened the healer. When Quimby died in January 1866, she was further convinced of the truth of this theory.

In February 1866, Mary fell on the ice. This event is celebrated in Christian Science as its founding moment because it was a turning point in its founder's life. Descriptions of the extent of her injury vary, but while she was undergoing treatment for her injuries, she underwent a religious conversion. She believed she heard the voice of God proclaim,

"Daughter, arise!" She stood up and walked, fully recovered. Mary was certain that it was her absolute faith in Christ that had healed her, and Christian faith became the core of her theology. From that point onward, she was a stronger woman, ready to create a secure existence for herself. The Pattersons' long-strained marriage broke apart for good by the end of the year. They finally divorced in 1873.

Mary's quest for security was a long struggle. Between 1866 and 1870 she moved from one friend's household to another, staying with them until she wore out her welcome. Then, in 1870, she reached an agreement with a young man, Richard Kennedy. She would teach him her healing methods, and they would split the profits from curing the sick. Soon she had several students who were paying tuition to hear her lectures and agreed to send her portions of their future profits from their practices. Though the partnership between Mary and Richard Kennedy lasted only about two years, it was financially rewarding, for when they divided their assets, her share was $6,000, a significant sum in the 1870s.

During 1875, an important year for Mary, she published her major work, *Science and Health,* in which she expounded her theories. On the subject of illness and healing, she wrote that "sickness is no more the reality of being than is sin." She also found a name for her theology—"Christian Science." Later in the year, Asa Gilbert Eddy, a former patient of one of her pupils, became a student of Christian Science himself. Asa Gilbert and Mary Baker Eddy married on New Year's Day, 1877.

The next several years were filled with tumult. Eddy chartered the Church of Christ, Scientist, in 1879 and the Massachusetts Metaphysical College in Lynn two years later. But lawsuits and resignations instigated by pupils and former and current employees disrupted the growth of the church. Finally, in the winter of 1881–1882, Eddy left Lynn forever. She moved to Boston in April 1882, taking the Metaphysical College with her. By this time, she had become an impressive speaker, and her following was growing.

Asa Gilbert Eddy died in June 1882. It might have been an embarrassment for a woman renowned for her healing abilities, but Mary blamed his death on what she called "malicious mesmerism." She insisted that her enemies, mostly disenchanted former students, had conspired and were directing MAM—malicious animal magnetism—against her.

As she aged, Eddy took a less active role in the church, closed the college, but remained in ultimate control of the church. She published what at least one biographer describes as an "idealized autobiography" in 1891, *Retrospection and Introspection* (Silberger, 1980, p. 201). The Mother Church, the First Church of Christ, Scientist, in Boston was dedicated in 1895, but Eddy was not present. If anything, Eddy's retirement added to her influence, for she was gaining a reputation for saintliness.

Despite her ill health, which prevented her from making public appearances, Eddy established the daily *Christian Science Monitor* in 1908. Two years later, on December 3, 1910, Mary Baker Eddy died in Chestnut Hill, Massachusetts, of pneumonia. At the time of her death, she led a religious organization that numbered nearly 100,000 members. Today, there are about three thousand branches of the church in more than fifty countries.

References: Mary Baker Eddy, *Science and Health with Key to the Scriptures* (1934); Robert Peel, *Mary Baker Eddy,* 3 vols. (1966, 1971, 1977); Lyman P. Powell, *Mary Baker Eddy: A Life Size Portrait* (1930, reprint 1950); Julius Silberger, Jr., *Mary Baker Eddy: An Interpretive Biography of the Founder of Christian Science* (1980).

Edmunds-Tucker Act

The Edmunds-Tucker Act, passed in Congress in 1887, declared plural marriages illegal and disenfranchised Mormon men who practiced polygamy. Also included in the act was a clause that revoked woman suffrage in the Utah Territory. The Edmunds-Tucker Act was the culmination of a long battle between Mormons and non-Mormons over the issue of polygamy. Several times since 1869, Congress had attempted to pass legislation that would pronounce polygamy illegal. In response, Mormon leaders had encouraged women to rally in support of their system, and Mormon women were given the vote in 1870, probably for the purpose of increasing Mormon influence on the issue of plural marriage. Aware that the Edmunds-Tucker Act was pending in Congress, two thousand Mormon women gathered at the Mormon Tabernacle in Salt Lake City in 1886 to display their unity in opposition to the measure. Despite fervent pleas and protests from the Mormon community, Congress passed the act. The Edmunds-Tucker Act was both a blow against Mormonism and against women; women of Utah Territory did not regain suffrage until 1896, when Mormon leaders renounced plural marriages and Utah was admitted to statehood.

See also: Church of Jesus Christ of Latter-Day Saints (Mormons); Cullom Bill
References: Eleanor Flexner, *Century of Struggle: The Woman's Rights Movement in the United States* (1970); Samuel W. Taylor, *Rocky Mountain Empire: The Latter-Day Saints Today* (1978); Marilyn Warenski, *Patriarchs and Politics: The Plight of the Mormon Woman* (1978).

Amy Eilberg (1984)

Eilberg, Amy (1954–)

The first woman to be ordained as a rabbi in the Conservative branch of Judaism, Amy Eilberg was born October 12, 1954, in Philadelphia, Pennsylvania. Her parents, Joshua and Gladys Eilberg, taught her Jewish culture and tradition and involved her in Jewish causes, including their concerns over the plight of Jews in the Soviet Union. As a teenager and a leader of the Conservative youth movement's United Synagogue Youth (USY), Amy traveled to the Soviet Union. There she visited Jews who had been denied permission to emigrate to Israel, seeing firsthand the hardships that many Jews continued to face.

Eilberg's interest in Jews and Judaism continued as she enrolled in Brandeis University in 1972 with a plan to pursue a career in Jewish education. In 1976, she graduated summa cum laude with a degree in Near Eastern and Judaic studies. Eilberg wanted to be a rabbi, but the Conservative branch of Judaism did not ordain women and did not allow them to enroll in rabbinical study. Therefore, she entered the Jewish Theological Seminary in New York in 1976, with the understanding that she would pursue a master's degree in the Talmud. Following receipt of that degree in 1978, she spent a year teaching in Israel.

When in 1979 the Jewish Theological Seminary agreed to suspend all debate on the issue of the ordination of women, Eilberg set aside her ambitions to become a rabbi and enrolled in Smith University, where she received a master's degree in social work in 1984. Just prior to her graduation from Smith, the Jewish Theological Seminary voted to accept women into their program of rabbinical study. By this time, Eilberg had married Rabbi Howard Schwartz, and the couple were living in Providence, Rhode Island. After careful consideration of the adjustments in their married life that would result from a commuting marriage, Eilberg began her studies at the seminary. She received her degree on May 12, 1985, becoming the first woman rabbi to be ordained in the Conservative branch of Judaism. At the time of her ordination, Eilberg told the press, "I feel very excited, very proud, not just for myself but for all women. As of today, Jewish women need never again feel that their gender is a barrier to their full participation in Jewish life" (Cantor, 1995, p. 46).

Meanwhile, Rabbi Schwartz had obtained a position at the University of Indiana, Bloomington. The couple were able to reunite when, following her ordination, Eilberg accepted employment as community rabbi at the Jewish Welfare Federation and chaplain at the Methodist Hospital, both in Indianapolis. Later, she moved to the San Francisco Bay area, where she obtained work in the Jewish Healing Center and then became chaplain at Stanford University Hospital. Since entering the rabbinate, Eilberg, a committed feminist, has fostered discussion of gender-specific language in the Jewish tradition. She is pleased that Jewish women have created new rituals and ceremonies that allow women greater participation within Judaism and encourage them to "open up

the old books and enter into a new relationship with them, with love, but also with the courage to ask hard questions" (Cantor, 1995, p. 46).

As a social worker, Eilberg has prompted Jewish leaders to address controversial issues in medical ethics. Of particular concern to Eilberg are the issues of surrogate motherhood and AIDS and questions surrounding the artificial prolonging of dying. By her continuing efforts to provide service to the community and to raise important issues within Conservative Judaism, Eilberg has set an example for other women aspiring to religious leadership as well as to the social service professions.

See also: Clergy; Jews; Priesand, Sally Jane; Sasso, Sandy Eisenberg
References: Aviva Cantor, "Rabbi Eilberg," *Ms.* 14, no. 6 (December 1985): 45–46; "End of a Vigil," in *Time* 125 (February 25, 1985): 61; Kimberly K. Estep, "Amy Eilberg," in Frank Magill, ed., *Great Lives from History: American Women Series* (1995); Phyllis J. Read and Bernard L. Witlieb, *The Book of Women's Firsts* (1992).

Eisenstadt v. Baird

The case of *Eisenstadt v. Baird* (1972) challenged the constitutionality of the "Crimes against Chastity" law of the state of Massachusetts, a law that made it illegal to provide unmarried people with contraceptives and that required married persons to obtain contraceptives only from doctors or by doctors' prescriptions. Bill Baird, a birth control rights activist, deliberately tested the law when he distributed contraceptive foam to twelve unmarried female students at Boston University. Baird was arrested, convicted, and jailed for his actions. In 1972 the U.S. Supreme Court declared the Crimes against Chastity law unconstitutional on the basis that it violated the equal protection guarantee of the Fourteenth Amendment by discriminating against unmarried persons.

In his opinion on *Eisenstadt*, Justice William Brennan stressed the right of the *individual*, married or unmarried, to privacy in issues relating to childbearing. Many religious groups perceived this decision as one of a series of blows against morality, dating from the early 1960s and culminating in the *Roe v. Wade* decision in 1973.

See also: Birth Control
References: James West Davidson et al., *Nation of Nations: A Narrative History of the American Republic,* vol. 2 (1990); Flora Davis, *Moving the Mountain: The Women's Movement in America since 1960* (1991); Marian Faux, *Roe v. Wade: The Untold Story of the Landmark Supreme Court Decision That Made Abortion Legal* (1988); Elizabeth Frost-Knappman, *Women's Progress in America* (1994).

Emerson, Ralph Waldo (1803–1882)

Ralph Waldo Emerson, philosopher, prominent Transcendentalist, essayist, poet, and women's rights advocate, was born in Boston, Massachusetts, on May 25, 1803. He received a bachelor of arts degree from Harvard College in 1821 and went to teach at a school for girls. After three years, he became dissatisfied with his work and enrolled in Harvard Divinity School, where he prepared for the Unitarian ministry. He graduated in 1826 and in 1829 became a pastor at the Second Church (Unitarian) in Boston. On September 30, 1829, he married Ellen Louisa Tucker and felt a great loss when she died less than seventeen months later. Although he married again (Lidian Jackson in 1835), he never fully recovered from his grief over Ellen's death. Throughout the time he served the Second Church, Emerson continued to seek religious truth. He eventually became dissatisfied with Unitarianism, and he resigned from his pastorate in September 1832.

In December 1832, Emerson embarked on a tour through Europe, where he became acquainted with a number of men in the literary field, including Thomas Carlyle, Samuel Taylor Coleridge, John Stuart Mill, and William Wordsworth. During this hiatus in his career, he formed what became the base of his philosophy of Transcendentalism, the belief that "God is in every man" and that men and women could rely upon their intuition to guide them. He published *Nature* in 1836, which became a strong motivator for the Transcendentalist movement of the mid-nineteenth century. In 1837 he embarked on a career as a lecturer and was soon renowned for his public speaking. Along with feminist Margaret Fuller and other Transcendentalists, he was a contributor to the movement's quarterly journal, *The Dial,* from 1840 to 1844. Although he was no longer associated with any church, he continued to preach until 1847.

Emerson, who advocated freedom in both religion and society to allow individual realization of whatever potential lay in one's soul, was an avid abolitionist who also supported the women's rights movement. Yet he was reluctant to become an active participant in the latter movement. Although he was first invited to attend a women's rights convention in Worcester, Massachusetts, in 1850, it was five years before he accepted such an invitation. It seems that the reason for his reluctance was that he was uneasy over the idea of a woman ever holding public office. He believed that women should be recognized as equals but did not think that a true lady would desire to become a public official. When he finally attended a women's rights convention in Boston on September 20, 1855, he delivered a speech entitled "Woman," in which he called women the "civilizers of mankind." He insisted that women had "an unquestionable right to their own property" and to political equality, and if they desired the vote, they should have it, as well as equal rights in education (Kimmel and Mosmiller, 1992, pp. 217–220).

In addition to his popularity as a lecturer, Emerson was admired both in America and in Europe for his poetry and essays. Among his many publications are *Essays: First Series* (1841), *Essays: Second Series* (1844), *Poems* (1846), *Representative Men* (1850), *English Traits* (1856), *The Conduct of Life* (1860); *May-Day and Other Pieces* (1867), *Society and Solitude* (1870), and *Letters and Social Aims* (1876). Published posthumously were *Natural History of Intellect* (1893) and *Journals of Ralph Waldo Emerson* (1909–1914).

Emerson died in Concord, Massachusetts, on April 27, 1882.

See also: Fuller, Margaret; Transcendentalism
References: Gay Wilson Allen, *Waldo Emerson: A Biography* (1981); Henry Warner Bowden, *Dictionary of American Religious Biography* (1977); Elizabeth Frost-Knappman, *Women's Progress in America* (1994); Michael S. Kimmel and Thomas E. Mosmiller, eds., *Against the Tide: Pro-Feminist Men in the United States, 1776–1990, A Documentary History* (1992); Edward L. Queen II et al., *The Encyclopedia of American Religious History* (1996); Robert D. Richardson, Jr., *Emerson: The Mind on Fire* (1995); Mark Van Doren, ed., *The Portable Emerson* (1946).

Episcopal Church

The Episcopal Church, which formed itself from the remains of the Church of England following the American Revolution, now has a membership of approximately three million. It is governed by the triennial General Convention, which is composed of a House of Bishops and a House of Clerical and Lay Deputies. Of the Protestant churches in America, the Episcopal Church is the most traditional, with a worship service rooted as much in Roman Catholicism as in Protestantism. The Episcopal Church, like the Catholic Church, regards its clergy as sacramentally ordained in the One, Holy, Apostolic Church of God that has been in existence since the time of Christ. But, unlike the Catholic Church and amid much controversy, the General Convention of the Episcopal Church has recently granted women the opportunity to become priests and bishops.

It took many years of struggle before women finally achieved equality within the Episcopal Church. Church rules on the position of women dated back to the sixteenth-century Anglican Church. Women were expected to dress modestly. Considered unclean because of their monthly menstrual flow, women were restricted from approaching within ten feet of the altar. Although their roles within the church were limited, from colonial times Anglican and, later, Episcopalian women were expected to take a major part in the religious education of their children. Within the home, through family prayer and other indirect means, women could have an influence on the religious lives of both their children and their spouses.

The first ordination of an Episcopal woman in America occurred in 1845, when Anne Ayres was consecrated an Episcopal sister without legal sanction by canon law and without precedent. Seven years later, Ayres founded the Sisterhood of the Holy Communion in New York City. By 1880 there were six major sisterhoods within the Episcopal Church. Some of the sisterhoods that provided social service to their communities preferred to use the term "deaconess." In 1889 the Episcopal General Convention accepted the existence of the Order of Deaconesses in the Protestant Episcopal Church of the United States. However, women deaconesses were not only set apart from the men but were virtually ignored. They had no authority within the church and no liturgical functions, as deacons did; unlike deacons, they were not ordained; and the deaconesses had to be unmarried. (The church defined deacons as pastoral ministers. They offered spiritual guidance. Priests were considered sacramental ministers, who absolved, blessed, and consecrated bread and wine at Eucharist. Bishops were defined as overseers.)

In 1920 the Lambeth Conference of Anglican bishops worldwide, of which Episcopal bishops were a part, declared that deaconesses were to be fully ordained clergy within holy orders. But in 1930 the next Lambeth Conference withdrew its statement. Five years later the worldwide Anglican church released a report stating that there was no theological reason why women should not be ordained to the priesthood. The report concluded, however, that for the present, only men should be admitted to the priesthood.

Deaconesses were usually welcome only in remote areas. The church had a similar rule for lay readers, those members of congregations who stand at the pulpit and read from the Bible. Although Episcopal law stated that occasionally a godly and competent woman could be a lay reader, this could only occur in an isolated place, where no man was available. Thus, women's opportunities to serve in such roles were few.

Throughout the middle decades of the twentieth century, women continued to crusade for recognition within the church. In the 1960s, the church began to show some flexibility in its attitude toward women, and Episcopal seminaries began to admit women, though the women received no promises of ordination. Nevertheless, like the male students, the women wanted to be priests. In 1967 the General Convention changed church law so as to allow women to become lay readers on an equal basis with men. Three years later, the General Convention at Houston, Texas, voted to make women full deacons, allowing them the same privileges as male deacons. This was the first time that they were acknowledged as full deacons. But at the same convention, a resolution to ordain women as priests was defeated. A similar resolution was defeated again in 1973.

Before the next General Convention could meet, three retired bishops ordained eleven women as priests at the Church of the Advocate in Philadelphia on July 29, 1974. Although supporters agreed that the ordinations were irregular, opponents denounced them as invalid. The House of Bishops held an emergency meeting two weeks later. When the bishops emerged, they declared the ordinations invalid and censured the ordaining bishops, but women who were desirous of becoming priests were not deterred. In 1975 four more female deacons were ordained in Washington, D.C. Then on September 16, 1976, the General Convention passed a resolution opening both the priesthood and episcopate to women. Nevertheless, opposition and bitterness continued, causing some individuals and parishes to break away from the church rather than accept the changes. Out of the secession came a new body, the Anglican Church of North America. Eventually the Episcopal House of Bishops instituted a "conscience clause" that allowed a bishop to refuse to ordain women within his particular diocese.

Controversy over the ordination of women continued during the decade following the 1976 General Convention, only to intensify when it appeared that a woman might be elected and consecrated to the highest clerical order of bishop. In September 1988, the Diocese of Massachusetts elected Reverend Barbara Clementine Harris suffragan (assisting) bishop, second in charge of a diocese that counted approximately 100,000 members. Opposition heightened when it was learned that she was not only a woman but also divorced, African American, and a political and social liberal. Despite the controversy, women have continued to be ordained as priests and bishops within the Episcopal Church. From 1988 to 1998, the number of female Episcopal bishops grew to four.

See also: Ayres, Anne; Harris, Barbara Clementine; "Philadelphia 11"
References: Alla Bozarth-Campbell, *Womanpriest: A Personal Odyssey* (1978); Susan Hill Lindley, *"You Have Stept Out of Your Place": A History of Women and Religion in America* (1996); Aleathia Dolores Nicholson, "Barbara Harris," in Jessie Carney Smith, ed., *Epic Lives: One Hundred Black Women Who Made a Difference* (1993); Rosemary Radford Ruether and Rosemary Skinner Keller, eds., *Women and Religion in America*, vol. 3 (1986); Betsy Covington Smith, *Breakthrough: Women in Religion* (1978).

Equal Rights Amendment

The Equal Rights Amendment (ERA), which reads: "Equality of rights under the law shall not be denied or abridged by the United States or by any state on account of sex," became a source of controversy within religious groups during the 1970s and early 1980s. Originally introduced by feminist Alice Paul and the National Woman's Party in 1923, it was not until 1970 that the bill received consideration by the full House of Representatives. Having been passed by both the House (voting 354 to 23) and the Senate (voting 84 to 8), in October 1971 and March 1972, respectively, the amendment was put in the hands of the states. Pro-ERA groups and individuals campaigned hard for its ratification by the individual states, and initially it appeared as though the ERA would win approval. By 1973 thirty states had ratified the amendment, with only eight more needed before it would become a part of the U.S. Constitution.

The rapid progress toward the Equal Rights Amendment becoming law led to a conservative backlash. Religious conservatives were concerned that the ERA would alter male and female roles ordained in the Bible and would thereby threaten the family. They contended that it would legitimize homosexuality and would result in numerous other horrors, such as unisex bathrooms and the drafting of women into combat duty; and they voiced fears that women would lose all protective legislation, especially alimony and child support. Concerned Women for America (CWA), an organization associated with the religious right, worked in opposition to the amendment, as did Phyllis Schlafly, a Roman Catholic, and her right-wing Eagle Forum. Leaders within major denominations, including the Roman Catholic Church and the fundamentalist branch of the Southern Baptist Convention, urged that the ERA be defeated. By the late 1970s, thousands of religious conservatives endorsed the New Christian Right's fight to defeat the amendment. The Church of Jesus Christ of Latter-Day Saints took an official stance against the amendment, which led to its defeat in Utah's predominantly Mormon legislature.

There were, however, some women from conservative denominations who broke with their churches and formed or joined pro-ERA associations, including Sonia Johnson, a cofounder of Mormons for ERA. Not all Roman Catholics accepted the anti-ERA position. Although the National Council of Catholic Women voiced its disapproval of the amendment, several Catholic women's organizations gave it their official endorsement. The Rabbinical Alliance of America opposed the ERA, but the American Jewish Congress and the National Council of Jewish Women announced their support. Among other backers of the amendment were the United Presbyterian Church, the Unitarian Universalist Association, and Church Women United.

A survey conducted by the National Opinion Research Center (NORC) in 1982 revealed that nonreligious persons were more likely (88 percent in favor) than their religious neighbors to have supported the ERA in 1982. Sixty-one percent of the fundamentalist Protestants surveyed favored the amendment, as did 72 percent of other Protestants, 77 percent of Catholics, and 81 percent of Jews. The NORC found a reverse correlation between church attendance and one's support of the ERA, with 47 percent of those attending church several times a week expressing their approval of the amendment, whereas 80 percent of those who attended church only rarely said they felt the amendment should be passed.

Despite wide support for the Equal Rights Amendment, the opposition was loud and raised questions over what the future held for America if the ERA became a part of the U.S. Constitution. The controversy over the amendment caused some states to rescind their earlier approval, and the measure foundered. On June 30, 1982, time ran out for the ERA's ratification, and it went down to defeat.

See also: Concerned Women for America; Fundamentalism; Johnson, Sonia Harris; Schlafly, Phyllis Stewart

References: Stephen Bates, *Battleground: One Mother's Crusade, the Religious Right, and the Struggle for Control of Our Classrooms* (1993); Margaret Lamberts Bendroth, *Fundamentalism and Gender: 1875 to the Present* (1993); Janet K. Boles, *The Politics of the Equal Rights Amendment: Conflict and the Decision* (1979); Sonia Johnson, *From Housewife to Heretic* (1981); Michael Lienesch, *Redeeming America: Piety and Politics in the New Christian Right* (1993); Susan Hill Lindley, *"You Have Stept Out of Your Place": A History of Women and Religion in America* (1996); Jane J. Mansbridge, *Why We Lost the ERA* (1986); Glenn H. Utter and John W. Storey, *The Religious Right: A Reference Handbook* (1995).

Evangelicals

The urge to evangelize has existed among American religious groups since the early colonial days, when Quakers and other dissenters embarked on missions to convert others to their faith. In the early years of the United States, the revivals of the Second Great Awakening inspired American men and women to spread the idea of perfectionism. Evangelicals then threw support to such reforms as temperance, abolition, improved conditions for prisoners, and women's rights.

In the late nineteenth and early twentieth centuries, there was a surge of women eager to serve Christ. Some of the women entered mission work, others joined the deaconess movement, and still others participated in interdenominational organizations or in nondenominational agencies like the Woman's Christian Temperance Union or the Young Women's Christian Association. Included in the rush to spread the Gospel were a number of women who were entering the evangelical pulpit. Turn-of-the-century evangelical women found opportunities to preach and pastor because many of their churches promoted an egalitarian concept of women in the ministry. Religious historian Janette Hassey finds that this point of view was greatly influenced by holiness churches and even some Pentecostal groups interacting with other branches of Evangelicalism.

Evangelicals of this era are distinguished from more "liberal" Protestants by their stress on the Bible as the word of God and their belief in premillennialism. During the 1880s, they began opening schools to train laypeople for religious service, and women made up a large portion of the enrollees in these Bible institutes. Since graduates were expected to fill roles secondary to the ordained ministry, such as missionaries, evangelists, Sunday school teachers, and other church work, schools like the famous Moody Bible Institute held less rigorous academic standards than most seminars or colleges. Although few of the schools'

Evangelicals are reknowned for their zeal to convert others to Christianity; here the Evange-listic Committee of New York City holds a convert's rally at Carnegie Hall (September 14, 1908).

leaders believed in the ordination of women, attendance at such institutes provided women with female role models as well as opportunities to take on a measure of religious leadership. When the Moody Bible Institute launched a pastors' program during the late 1920s, women were accepted as students, and the first woman graduated from the course in 1929. However, as Susan Hill Lindley notes, female graduates usually found themselves pastoring in small, poor, or rural congregations (Lindley, 1996, p. 325).

As the century progressed, greater emphasis was placed upon the training of ministers, and the academic standards at the Bible institutes became increasingly stringent. As a result, by mid-century female enrollment in ministerial programs was discouraged, and women were channeled into courses deemed more appropriate to their sex.

There is a great variation among evangelicals as to how their religious convictions are put into practice. Most possess the desire to convert others to Christianity and are actively committed to some sector of the institutional church. They often desire to center their activities around their religious convictions, and overall they tend to be more conservative than the mainstream on most moral issues.

See also: Fundamentalism; Second Great Awakening
References: Margaret Lamberts Bendroth, *Fundamentalism and Gender: 1875 to the Present* (1993); Janette Hassey, *No Time for Silence: Evangelical Women in Public Ministry around the Turn of the Century* (1986); Susan Hill Lindley, *"You Have Stept Out of Your Place": A History of Women and Religion in America* (1996); Edward L. Queen II et al., eds., *The Encyclopedia of American Religious History* (1996); Robert Wuthnow, *The Struggle for America's Soul: Evangelicals, Liberals and Secularism* (1989).

Falwell, Jerry (1933–)

Popular television evangelist, antifeminist, and founder of the Liberty Baptist Fellowship, Jerry Falwell was born in Lynchburg, Virginia, on August 11, 1933. Although his mother was a devout Christian, Jerry had little interest in religion until 1952, when he had a "born again" experience after listening to a broadcast of Charles Fuller's "Old-Fashioned Revival Hour." In 1953 he entered the Baptist Bible College, the school of the Baptist Bible Fellowship in Springfield, Missouri, and completed his study three years later. He returned to Lynchburg, where he became the pastor for a dissenting group, a decision that led to his break with the Baptist Bible Fellowship. Within a year, Falwell's preaching was carried on the radio and on one television station. His Thomas Road Baptist Church grew steadily. A new sanctuary seating one thousand congregants was dedicated in 1964, and his television broadcast, the "Old-Time Gospel Hour," was appearing on three hundred stations by 1971. Under his leadership, the Thomas Road Bible Institute opened its doors in 1972, and the Lynchburg Baptist Theological Seminary was established a year later. In the 1980s, the early graduates of the seminary formed a new Baptist denomination, the Liberty Baptist Fellowship.

During the 1970s, Falwell was one of the organizers of the Moral Majority Foundation and Moral Majority, Inc., two national organizations that promoted the renewal of moral values among the American people. The movement that formed around the two groups appeared to be highly influential among conservative Americans. The Moral Majority worked to elect Ronald Reagan as president in 1980, though the extent of its effectiveness is in dispute. Among the central goals of the Moral Majority was the defeat of the Equal Rights Amendment (ERA). Falwell himself was adamant in his opposition to feminism, concluding that feminists "are prohomosexual and lesbian" (Falwell, 1980, p. 185). Centering his arguments on his notion of what was best for American families, he denounced the ERA as an attack on both religion and the family. Falwell complained that "[m]any women have never accepted their God-given roles" and was of the opinion that feminists "live in disobedience to God's laws and have promoted their godless philosophy throughout our society" (Falwell, 1980, p. 150).

Falwell believed that, in an ideal family, the wife should be submissive to her husband and the husband should wield all authority within the family, including spiritual authority. He felt that married women should not be employed outside the home unless their families were in dire economic need. He objected to government intrusion into family life and argued against federally funded day care centers and shelters for battered women.

In the late 1980s, Falwell became involved in the scandal that brought down the television evangelist Jim Bakker. He took over Bakker's PTL Club and tried to save it, but the scandal had hurt all involved in television ministry, and Falwell returned to focusing on his own organizations. He announced the disbanding of the Moral Majority in 1989, stating that the movement had accomplished its goals.

See also: Bakker, Tammy Faye; Equal Rights Amendment
References: Jerry Falwell, *Listen America!* (1980); Jerry Falwell, *Strength for the Journey: An Autobiography of Jerry Falwell* (1987); Michael Lienesch, *Redeeming America: Piety and Politics in the New Christian Right* (1993); J. Gordon Melton, *Religious Leaders of America* (1991).

Farmer, Sarah Jane (1847–1916)

Founder of Greenacre summer conferences on comparative religion and of the first American Baha'i community, Sarah Jane Farmer was born July 22, 1847, in Dover, New Hampshire. Her father, Moses Farmer, was an admirer of Ralph Waldo Emerson, and he reared Sarah in the Transcendentalist tradition. Her mother, Hannah (Shapleigh) Farmer, was a zealous abolitionist, and the Farmer home became a way station on the Underground Railroad. In the 1860s, Moses acquired a position with the U.S. Department of the Navy in Newport, Rhode Island, where the family remained until 1882.

Sarah was the only surviving child of the Farmer family and was unmarried, so when her father resigned his post in Newport due to illness and moved with his wife to the small community of Eliot, Maine, Sarah accompanied her parents. Once they had settled in their new home, both women became involved in philanthropic work. Hannah Farmer opened a home for unwed mothers, and Sarah began to take steps toward building a community library.

In 1889, Sarah Farmer entered into a partnership with four local businessmen and built Greenacre Inn, a resort that would accommodate one hundred guests. Although it was a popular summer vacation spot for Bostonians, the inn failed to make a financial profit for the investors and by 1892 had to close for part of the summer due to shortage of funds.

Farmer attended the World's Columbian Exposition in Chicago in 1893. There she was inspired by the program at the Parliament of Religions, which brought together people of varying religions throughout the world. Farmer decided that she would try to change Greenacre into a summer conference center where lecturers from various religions could speak. It would be open to all, with the condition that no speaker could argue with other lecturers. She was able to convince her business partners to allow her to organize the conferences at the inn, and the first Greenacre Institute was launched in July 1894. The conferences, which were offered free of charge, drew large numbers of people, including many who could not afford Greenacre Inn's prices for lodging. These people pitched tents on the resort's grounds.

In the beginning, Greenacre was closely connected with the American Transcendentalist movement, and speakers frequently lectured on the lives and works of Ralph Waldo Emerson and Henry David Thoreau. A change occurred in 1896, when the Monsalvat School for Comparative Religions was established as a separate part of Greenacre. The school attracted lecturers from around the world who spoke on a variety of religions, including Christianity, Islam, Buddhism, and Hinduism. Although the institute was a popular success attracting thousands of people, as a profit-making enterprise it was a failure, and it was nearly bankrupt by 1899.

In 1900 friends paid the expenses for an exhausted and ailing Farmer to cruise the Mediterranean in hopes of regaining her health. Among the places she visited was Persia, where she met Abdu'l-Baha, leader of the Baha'i faith, who at the time was in prison as a result of his religious and political teachings. Abdu'l-Baha impressed Farmer because his teachings corresponded to her hopes for religious toleration and spiritual unity. Founded in Persia (modern Iran) in 1844 and based on the teachings of Abdu'l-Baha's father, the prophet Baha'u'llah, the Baha'i faith encourages toleration, peace, and cooperation. The Baha'is believe that their religion, formed most directly out of Judaism, Christianity, and Islam, is the culmination and perfection of a number of religions.

A year after her visit to the Mediterranean, Farmer added the study of Baha'i to the Monsalvat School's program. The Transcendentalists were unhappy over the development, and tension arose at the institute. Then beginning in 1901, a number of members of the Baha'i faith traveled to Greenacre. Over the next several years, the Transcendentalists and Baha'is remained tolerant of each other, even while the Baha'is were gaining influence within the institute.

In 1910 Farmer became gravely ill, suffering from both physical and mental problems, and was placed in an insane asylum in Portsmouth. She was no longer able to prevent further conflict between the Transcendentalists and the Baha'is. Farmer died of pneumonia and heart failure in 1916. In 1913 the Baha'is voted the other trustees out of the institute and transformed Greenacre and the Monsalvat School into forums for the teachings of Baha'u'llah.

There is dispute over whether Farmer approved of the Baha'i takeover of Greenacre. Some historians doubt that Farmer would have fully subscribed to such a plan since she was a believer in religious pluralism and it was for that ideal that she established the Greenacre Institute. There is also speculation that Farmer was so disturbed over the Baha'i takeover of Greenacre that she was driven to insanity. Nevertheless, Farmer did claim herself to be a convert to the Baha'i faith, and its belief in the unity of all religions did correspond to her own religious convictions. Although Farmer's position regarding the conflicts that took place at Greenacre during the final years of her life will likely never be known, most modern followers of the Baha'i faith consider her their American founder.

References: Shoghi Effendi, *God Passes By* (1957); Kimberly K. Estep, "Sarah Jane Farmer," in Frank Magill, ed., *Great Lives from History: American Women Series* (1995); Jessyca Russell Gaver, *The Baha'i Faith: Dawn of a New Day* (1967); William McElwell Miller, *The Baha'i Faith: Its History and Teachings* (1974).

Fedde, Elizabeth (1850–1921)

Elizabeth Fedde, pioneer American Lutheran deaconess and Norwegian-American welfare worker, was born December 25, 1850, at Feda in Flekkefjord, Norway. She was one of the seven children of Andreas Villunsen Feda and Anne Marie Oldsdatta. (Elizabeth later altered her surname from Feda to Fedde.) When she was nineteen years of age, Elizabeth went to Stavanger to become a domestic worker in a private home. While there she learned of the recently established Deaconess Institute in Christiania (now Oslo). Elizabeth had been raised in the atmosphere of the pietistic Haugean movement within the Lutheran Church. Followers of Hans Nielsen Hauge (1771–1824) adopted their leader's devotion to the "living faith" rather than to the formalized doctrine preached by the regular clergy of the Norwegian State Church. It was most likely Fedde's religious faith that inspired her in 1873 to enter the motherhouse of the new Deaconess Institute. Although she disliked the nunlike black bonnets worn by this

Protestant sisterhood, Elizabeth believed in the organization's mission: In addition to its religious aspects, the institute had founded the first training school for nurses in Norway. During her five years of training, Fedde learned rigid discipline while she received instruction in religion and nursing. At the end of her training, Fedde was sent to Tromsø in northern Norway, where she nursed the sick for the next four years.

A letter from her brother-in-law in December 1883 changed the course of Fedde's career by awakening her to the plight of Norwegian immigrants in America. Most of them faced problems both with language and with adjusting to urban life. The Swedish-Norwegian consul and his wife and the pastor of the Norwegian Seaman's Mission in Brooklyn were attempting to make arrangements for the support of a social worker who would be required to assist Norwegian immigrants. Although support was not assured, Fedde chose to accept the challenge. The directors of the motherhouse in Oslo disowned her for her decision and told her that she would not be eligible for any aid from them. Fedde was, however, able to enlist the initial support of several Norwegian Lutheran pastors in New York.

Fedde arrived in New York in April 1883 and immediately set to work to help organize a Voluntary Relief Society for the Sick and Poor (later the Norwegian Relief Society). With no assistance coming from Norway, she began to train sisters herself. In 1885 Fedde not only opened a nine-bed hospital in Brooklyn but also began her training program. Four years later, the Norwegian Relief Society built a much larger hospital. In 1892 the society was reincorporated as the Norwegian Lutheran Deaconesses' Home and Hospital. It is now known as the Lutheran Medical Center. Soon Fedde introduced an ambulance service that was available to people of all national backgrounds.

From 1888 to 1890, Fedde spent time in Minneapolis, where she founded another deaconess home and a hospital. She then returned to New York, where she pleaded with the state legislature for state aid for the hospital. Her lobbying paid off. After funding was granted, Fedde remained in New York long enough to see that her projects to provide food, clothing, and health care to Norwegian immigrants were prospering and that the newcomers were becoming Americanized. During her thirteen years in the United States, Fedde organized the first effective nursing system within the Scandinavian community in America and was the leading force in the founding of two hospitals that have since become major medical centers.

Fedde returned to Norway in 1896 and married Ola A. P. Slettebo, who had been waiting for her while she was in America. The couple made their home on a farm near Egersund, Norway. She died there on February 25, 1921.

See also: Lutheran Church
References: Edward T. James, ed., *Notable American Women, 1607–1950* (1971); J. Gordon Melton, *Religious Leaders of America* (1991); Cecyle S. Neidle, *America's Immigrant Women* (1975).

Female Hebrew Benevolent Society

The Female Hebrew Benevolent Society (FHBS) was founded in Philadelphia on November 24, 1819, and was most likely the idea of a Jewish social worker, Rebecca Gratz. The society's chief purpose was relief. It was influenced by the Female Association for the Relief of Women in Reduced Circumstances, an organization that Gratz had helped to found in 1801. At the time of the founding of the FHBS, the United States was in a depression, and Jews were suffering. Gratz and other Jewish women believed that it was important that Jews help their own. The new society, which marked the beginning of Jewish women organizing for social welfare, centered their work on helping widows and orphans. Women of the FHBS solicited funds from both Jews and Gentiles, but they were particular in regard to whom they helped. The society investigated the backgrounds of the needy to determine that they were of good moral character and offered aid only to those they defined as "respectable poor."

The FHBS was the first of hundreds of Jewish women's societies to be established in the United States. This new organized philanthropy created a new type of woman—the Jewish social worker. Usually women of comfortable financial means, they offered aid to the less fortunate and in so doing hoped to "uplift" the poor, both economically and morally. Although the Jewish woman helped the poor, social work also bolstered her own self-esteem. She felt that she was doing worthwhile work in a field that had traditionally been dominated by men. By the end of the nineteenth century, no Jewish community of any size was without a woman's organization. Some were affiliated with congregations; others were not.

See also: Gratz, Rebecca; Jews; National Council of Jewish Women
References: Charlotte Baum, Paula Hyman, and Sonya Michel, *The Jewish Woman in America* (1976); Aviva Cantor, *Jewish Women/Jewish Men: The Legacy of Patriarchy in Jewish Life* (1995); Jacob R. Marcus, *The American Jewish Woman: A Documentary History* (1981); Jacob R. Marcus, *The American Jewish Woman, 1654–1980* (1981).

Female Moral Reform Society

The Female Moral Reform Society was founded in New York City on May 12, 1834, by a group of pious Christian women. This group had much in common with the Female Benevolent Society, established in New York at about the same time, but the Female Moral Reform Society was more dynamic and soon overshadowed the former organization. The middle- and upper-class women who formed the two groups shared the ambitious goal of converting the city's prostitutes to evangelical Protestantism and closing New York's many brothels, but the Female Moral Reform Society carried its crusade to a broader scale: They hoped to battle the double standard that condemned female sexual transgressions but condoned male sexual freedom. Among the pronouncements at their initial organizational meeting was the resolution that "the licentious man is no less guilty than his victim, and ought therefore, to be excluded from all virtuous female society" (Berg, 1976, p 153). They insisted that it was the duty of all women, whatever their religious denomination, to work together to carry out moral reform.

In the fall of 1834, the society chose Reverend John McDowall as its missionary to New York's prostitutes. McDowall had become an activist against prostitution during the early 1830s, determined to rescue "fallen women." As missionaries for the Female Moral Reform Society, McDowall and his two male assistants distributed Bibles and led prayer meetings at the city's brothels. More effective tactics included early morning visits to the sporting houses, at which time the missionaries would rouse the prostitutes and their customers with loud readings of biblical passages followed by prayers and hymns. On other occasions they would position themselves across the street from the brothels and record the names of the clientele. Society members also visited and kept vigil at brothels, gathered together to pray, and reported the names of establishments and their patrons in the group's weekly journal. All of these methods hurt business for brothel owners and employees. Not only were men deterred from entering the houses when they saw that their identities were being noted, but the sight of groups of Christian men and women gathered for prayer served to inhibit their sexual ardor.

The Female Moral Reform Society's actions met with anger from the public. These women were speaking out on a topic—prostitution—that was not deemed proper for ladies to discuss. Moreover, they were actually entering houses of ill repute. Such activities were considered unwomanly and immodest. But the women of the society felt that, as Christians, they should do all they could for moral reform and went so far as to attack the clergy for failing to endorse their program.

Although they purposely disrupted business at New York City's brothels, the Female Moral Reform Society attempted to assist young women whom they believed had been forced into prostitution and those who wished to reform. Society members helped concerned parents by visiting brothels in search of information about runaway daughters. For those prostitutes who sought to reform, the society opened a House of Reception that was intended to serve as a refuge and a place where former ladies of the night could learn new trades while being instructed in morality and religion. The House of Reception, which never had more than a small number of inhabitants, closed in 1836 within two years of its opening. An employment service the society established to assist women who previously felt that they had only two choices—prostitution or starvation—was more successful.

Despite the failure of its House of Reception, the Female Moral Reform Society continued its campaign to fight the double standard. Its weekly newspaper, *The Advocate of Moral Reform*, founded in January 1835, grew to become one of the nation's most widely read evangelical papers. Almost every issue denounced the depraved nature of the American male and called for the creation of a national union of women to combat male immorality. A huge association of women was needed if the reformers hoped to see morality prevail within a male-dominated society. As the organization began to spread across the country, the society decided to change its name to the American Female Reform Society. By 1839 the group had grown to include 445 auxiliaries, mostly in New York and in greater New England.

Historian Carroll Smith-Rosenberg points out that in many ways the Female Moral Reform Society can be seen as a militant women's organization. Although not overtly a part of the women's rights movement, the society did side with the feminists on a number of issues. Most notably, by the 1840s the American Female Moral Reform Society was emphasizing the idea of advancing conditions for women in the labor force. Society leaders argued that women were capable of fulfilling many more jobs than they were currently given opportunities to perform, and they felt that women should be given decent wages for their work. Early in its history, the society began to hire only women employees, and by 1841 women filled jobs in the organization that had previously been deemed suitable only for men, such as editor of the *Advocate* and financial officer.

The society's executive committee was frequently in close contact with members of the women's rights movement. One of the nation's best-known women's rights activists, Quaker minister Lucretia Mott, was a founder and secretary of the Philadelphia Female Moral Reform Society. But there was a limit to how far the society's members were willing to stretch their traditional roles as women. When the *Advocate* included an article written by feminist and abolitionist Sarah Grimké in which she criticized women's traditional role and attacked the Protestant ministry and orthodox interpretations of the Bible, many members of the society wrote to complain. Grimké's article was the last the *Advocate* ever published by an overt feminist.

Members of the American Female Moral Reform Society were willing to accept the idea that the home was woman's "sphere" and that she should have control of that sphere, especially in the realm of the religious and moral teaching of her family. A woman was justified in playing a role outside the home if she saw that men were disobeying God's commandments, such as involving themselves with prostitutes or drinking alcoholic beverages.

Throughout the society's existence, it lobbied for legislation to dismantle inequities in the legal system that hurt women. Its most significant victory came in 1848, when the New York state legislature passed the Act to Punish Seduction as a Crime, which decreed that any man found guilty of seducing and having sexual relations with an unmarried female would be sent to prison.

The Female Moral Reform Society emerged out of the nation's search for perfection, an idea that was an offshoot of the Second Great Awakening religious movement, which lasted well into the early 1830s. As the society grew, it gave women confidence in their abilities to organize and to carry out responsibilities once considered outside women's sphere. In the 1850s, the organization once again changed its name and its focus, becoming the American Female Guardian Society and Home for the Friendless. Its weekly journal changed its name to the *Advocate and Family Guardian* and adopted a decidedly feminist tone.

See also: Evangelicals; Grimké, Sarah Moore; Mott, Lucretia Coffin; Perfection-ism; Second Great Awakening; Woman Suffrage

References: Barbara Berg, *The Remembered Gate: Origins of American Feminism—The Woman and the City, 1800–1860* (1976); Nancy A. Hewitt, *Women's Activism and Social Change: Rochester, New York, 1822–1872* (1984); Carroll Smith-Rosenberg, "Beauty, the Beast, and the Militant Woman: A Case Study in Sex Roles and Social Stress in Jacksonian America," in *American Quarterly* 23 (1971): 562–584; Carroll Smith-Rosenberg, *Disorderly Conduct: Visions of Gender in Victorian America* (1985).

Feminist Theology

Feminist theology is a theology that is practiced from the point of view of the feminist theory of social equality. Traditional religion, feminists contend, has been practiced from a male perspective and has been unjust to women. Feminist theology began with the publication of Elizabeth Cady Stanton's *The Woman's Bible* in 1895 and 1898 and resurged in the mid-1960s along with the rise of the second women's movement. Feminists argue that the female perspective has much to contribute to religion. Rosemary Radford Ruether, a prominent theologian within mainstream feminism, asserts that the feminist cause is important to human liberation as a whole because it points to a change of values from those of patriarchy. Domination, possession, and conquest are important values within patriarchy, whereas the leading values of feminism are reciprocity and acceptance of mutual limitations.

Although feminists agree that male-dominated traditional religion has oppressed women, they differ in regard to theological position. Within Christianity, some who have been described as "biblical" or "evangelical" feminists contend that the Bible is the infallible word of God but that it does not teach the patriarchy as God's ideal. They argue that teachings of male-female equality can be found in the Bible. The Apostle Paul, they maintain, spoke for the customs of his time, but customs have changed. There is now no reason why women cannot be deacons, ministers, or bishops, and women should not be subordinate to male authority in the church.

Those who, like Ruether, are described as "mainstream" or "reformist feminists" seek to work within traditional religion to reform its position on male-female relationships. They maintain that although the Bible contains the word of God, it is not itself the perfect word of God. Because of its fallibility, the Bible should be ignored in the instances where it supports patriarchy. Mainstream feminists point to the egalitarian life of Jesus and to the women who kept his memory alive following his crucifixion as evidence of God's word.

A third group of feminists, characterized as "radical" or "revolutionary," is itself divided into two subgroups. One, the "radical Christians," finds that patriarchal biases against women so pervade the Bible that God's word cannot be found within the Bible itself or within any tradition within the Bible. Instead, truth can be found in the experiences of the "woman church," a community of women-affirming churches that seek liberation from patriarchal oppression. They contend that the woman-church was present in primitive Christianity and is now resurfacing as evidence of God's work of human liberation. The second subgroup, the "radical post-Christians," argue that biblical authority and Christianity must be rejected if women are to be liberated. They believe that women must rename God and the world in accordance with their own religious experience, one that is independent of males, whom some consider inferior. Lesbianism and witchcraft may be a part of the experience. For them, the Mother Goddess is a better conception of the divine.

Women of other major religions have also sought to adapt feminist theology to their beliefs. Jewish feminist theology fully includes women in tradition. Examples of the effects of feminism within Judaism are the additions of rituals that honor a girl's birth and her coming of age. Hindu and Buddhist feminist theology began after 1970, aroused by Western women's interest in the goddess worship included in these religions and by Hindu and Buddhist women's desire to eliminate oppression of women in their own religions.

See also: Biblical Authority and Women's Rights; Daly, Mary; Ecofeminism; Ruether, Rosemary Radford; *The Woman's Bible*
References: Carol J. Adams, ed., *Ecofeminism and the Sacred* (1993); Carol P. Christ and Judith Plaskow, eds., *Womanspirit Rising: A Feminist Reader in Religion* (1979); David W. Diehl, "Theology and Feminism," in June Steffensen Hagen, ed., *Gender Matters: Women's Studies for the Christian Community* (1990); Jo Ann Kay McNamara, *Sisters in Arms: Catholic Nuns through Two Millennia* (1996); Jonathan Z. Smith, ed., *The HarperCollins Dictionary of Religion* (1995); Elizabeth Cady Stanton, *The Woman's Bible: Parts I and II* (1895, 1898).

The "Feminization" of American Religion

In recent decades, scholars have identified the nineteenth century as an era when American religion became "feminized." During colonial days and at the beginning of the nineteenth century, there was no doubt as to who held the most influence within America's churches and synagogues. Although women usually composed the majority of the congregation, men controlled the pulpit and all of the hierarchical roles within their denominations. Men were the missionaries and the defenders of their faith. They were the elders, deacons, and bishops. There were, of course, some exceptions. Quaker women arrived in America as missionaries in the mid-seventeenth century, and some Quaker women became ministers. But despite the loosely egalitarian ideals of the Society of Friends' faith, men usually made their congregations' business decisions. Some Roman Catholic women arrived in the United States shortly after the American Revolution to found communities of sisters, but these were normally established at the instigation of men and their funding was in male hands.

As the nineteenth century opened, women were flocking into churches and church-related organizations. Women's prayer groups, missionary and education societies, charitable organizations, Sunday school groups, and moral reform associations multiplied at a phenomenal rate. This was especially the case among Protestant women because, as historian Nancy F. Cott points out, Protestants were seeking to "counteract religious indifference, rationalism, and Catholicism and to create an enduring moral social order" (Cott, 1977, p. 133).

Changes in interpretations of Christ developed during the nineteenth century, with the recreated Christ taking on characteristics defined as feminine. The new Christ, seen as a human who was self-sacrificing, dominated by love, and ready to forgive his enemies, was playing a role much like that of the "true woman" of the nineteenth century. At the same time, women were writing hymns, novels, and treatises that depicted a warm and loving Christ.

Although there were still few women preachers in the pulpits of the mainline denominations at the close of the nineteenth century, women had carved out new roles for themselves within their churches, roles that brought them influence. Women's increased prestige apparently instilled fear in the hearts of many of the men who watched as their own power diminished.

References: Anne M. Boylan, *Sunday School: The Formation of an American In-stitution, 1790–1880* (1988); Nancy F. Cott, *The Bonds of Womanhood: "Woman's Sphere" in New England, 1780–1835* (1977); Ann Douglas, *The Feminization of American Culture* (1977); Susan Hill Lindley, *"You Have Stept Out of Your Place": A History of Women and Religion in America* (1996); Barbara Welter, "The Feminization of American Religion, 1800–1860," in Mary S. Hartman and Lois Banner, eds., *Clio's Consciousness Raised: New Perspectives in the History of Women* (1974).

Fillmore, Myrtle Page (1845–1931)

Cofounder of the Unity School of Christianity and creator of the oldest children's magazine in the United States, Myrtle Page Fillmore was born in Pagetown, Ohio, on August 6, 1845. Her birth name was Mary Caroline, but she was called "Myrtle" from childhood. She was the youngest of the nine children of Marcus and Lucy (Wheeler) Page. Both parents were staunch Methodists who raised their children to strictly avoid worldly diversions such as dancing, card playing, and theatergoing. Myrtle's early education was in public schools. She later attended Oberlin College, graduating from the "Literary Course for Ladies" in 1869.

After graduation, Myrtle moved to Clinton, Missouri, where she taught school and lived with her brother David. When she was about thirty years old, she accepted a teaching position in Denison, Texas, and taught there until 1878. While in Denison, she met Charles Fillmore, whom she married in 1881. The Fillmores moved to Colorado following their marriage and then to Kansas City, Missouri, in 1884.

For some time, Myrtle had been suffering from tuberculosis. Soon after she moved to Kansas City, she learned that her prognosis was grim. However, a turning point came in her life in 1886, when she and Charles went to hear the lectures of Eugene B. Weeks, a disciple of Emma Curtis Hopkins, who founded the

New Thought movement in America. Listening to Weeks, Myrtle suddenly realized that, as a child of God, sickness was not a part of her inheritance. Her health slowly but steadily improved until she was completely cured. Myrtle wanted everyone to know about the "beautiful law" of spiritual healing. At first her husband was skeptical, but eventually he too was convinced of this new metaphysical approach to healing. Both Myrtle and Charles went to Chicago to study under Emma Curtis Hopkins.

The Fillmores worked together to spread these new ideas. In 1889 they founded a magazine called successively *Modern Thought, Christian Science Thought, Thought,* and after 1895, *Unity.* They incorporated the Unity School of Practical Christianity in 1903 (renamed Unity School of Christianity in 1914) and launched another magazine, *Weekly Unity,* in 1909. Theirs became the largest of the movements collectively known as New Thought. (In 1922, however, Unity withdrew from the International New Thought Alliance.)

Although in the beginning the Fillmores sought to supplement rather than to replace the established churches, the Unity movement gradually took on the appearance of a separate religious group. The Fillmores had a training school for ministers and teachers and operated a network of Unity centers in cities outside Kansas City. They outgrew several Kansas City buildings, so following World War I, they moved out of the city and established Unity Farm near Lee's Summit, Missouri. Unity Farm later became the organization's headquarters.

Myrtle was especially interested in children and in 1893 launched the oldest children's magazine in the United States, *Wee Wisdom.* She served as the magazine's editor for thirty years. *Wee Wisdom* eventually won a large readership outside New Thought circles. Myrtle also took charge of Unity's Sunday school for the Kansas City center and wrote numerous articles for several periodicals. She died at Unity Farm on October 6, 1931, but the Unity movement continued to prosper under the leadership of her husband and later her sons and various grandchildren.

References: Henry Warner Bowden, *Dictionary of American Religious Biography,* 2nd ed. (1993); Myrtle Fillmore, *How to Let God Help You* (1956); Myrtle Fillmore, *Myrtle Fillmore's Healing Letters,* 14th ed. (1978); Edward T. James, ed., *Notable American Women, 1607–1950* (1971); J. Gordon Melton, *Religious Leaders of America* (1991).

Finney, Charles Grandison (1792–1875)

Charles Grandison Finney, a famous and influential evangelist of the Second Great Awakening who helped further the roles of women in religious endeavors, was born in Warren, Connecticut, on August 29, 1792. He was the son of Sylvester and Rebecca (Rice) Finney. As a young man, Finney looked forward to a college education and was preparing to attend Yale. Then, a schoolmaster convinced him that he could complete the work of a college curriculum by himself in much less time. Finney later regretted that he followed his schoolmaster's advice.

Finney taught school for several years before beginning the study and practice of law (1818–1821). It appeared that this tall man, whose musical talents, personality, and good looks made him popular at social gatherings, was destined for a successful law career. But at the age of twenty-nine, Finney had a religious experience in which he seemed to see Jesus Christ standing before him and received what he described as a "mighty baptism of the Holy Spirit" and a call from the Lord to plead his cause (*Dictionary of American Biography,* p. 394). Finney abandoned his law practice and put all his energy into studying the Scripture and converting others. He applied for a candidacy for the ministry at the St. Lawrence Presbytery but did most of his study independently and drew his own conclusions from his readings of the Bible. Nevertheless, the presbytery licensed him in March 1824, and he was ordained the following July. In October 1824 he married Lydia Andrews of Whitestown, New York.

Despite being ordained a Presbyterian, Finney did not adhere to Calvinistic tenets. He rejected the doctrine of "human depravity," the Calvinist belief that humans had a natural and almost irresistible urge to sin. Finney preached the terrible consequences of disobeying God's law but emphasized an individual's ability to repent and to achieve salvation. Indeed, he was convinced that it was theoretically possible for men and women to live their lives entirely free of all sin—to live perfectly.

Finney began holding his revivals in small towns along the Erie Canal in western New York. Unlike earlier revivalists who had portrayed revivals as the miraculous work of God, Finney considered them human creations and employed various techniques designed to speed conversions. Among these was the "anxious seat," a bench upon which those who were ready for conversion sat and awaited the moment of awakening, while others in the audience prayed for them. Finney's most successful revival was in Rochester, New York, in 1830–1831. He reached his audiences through expressive language, homely illustrations, and direct appeals to people in the audiences. People hearing Finney came away from his revivals convinced that their sins had been washed away and that they were beginning a new life.

Soon Finney had achieved such fame that he was invited to preach in large cities. In 1832 he became pastor of the Second Free Presbyterian Church in New York City. He became dissatisfied with the working of the disciplinary system of the Presbyterian Church. The Broadway Tabernacle was organized for him in about 1834, and he withdrew from the Presbyterian denomination in 1836. He preached at the Broadway Tabernacle from 1836 to 1837.

Along with popularity and fame came controversy, and Finney had a number of detractors. His assertion that people could live in a state of perfection and his belief that revivals were human contrivances drew criticism from traditionalists. Also, Finney encouraged women to pray in public and to give testimonials of their religious experiences in church. He often converted husbands only after first converting their wives and daughters. His attitudes toward women speaking in public shocked many, including another famous preacher of the time, the liberal Lyman Beecher.

In 1835 Finney was invited to establish a theological department at Oberlin College in Ohio, the first college open to all, regardless of sex or race. Although he tried both to work at Oberlin and to retain his pastorate in New York City, the arrangement was detrimental to his health. Consequently, he resigned from the Broadway Tabernacle. He served as president of Oberlin from 1851 to 1866, where he was also the minister at the First Congregational Church from 1835 to 1872. He remained at Oberlin until 1875. Finney died in Oberlin on August 16 of that year.

Probably the most famous of the evangelists of the era of the Second Great Awakening, Finney's influence was great. Although he was not an active abolitionist, his preaching of human perfection helped to stir the abolitionist cause. His liberal ideas about women speaking in public influenced women like feminist Elizabeth Cady Stanton, who early in life was greatly moved during one of Finney's New York revivals. Finney recognized that without the participation of women, who outnumbered male converts two to one, it was doubtful that any revival would be successful.

See also: Perfectionism; Second Great Awakening
References: Henry Warner Bowden, *Dictionary of American Religious Biography*, 2nd ed. (1993); *Dictionary of American Biography*, vol. 6 (1931); Keith J. Hardman, *Charles Grandison Finney, 1792–1875: Revivalist and Reformer* (1987); Susan Hill Lindley, *"You Have Stept Out of Your Place": A History of Women and Religion in America* (1996).

Flappers

The emergence of the "flapper" in the late 1910s and early 1920s fueled concern among traditionalists that American morals were in rapid decline. The typical flapper was a young woman who bobbed her hair and wore skimpy dresses with short skirts over few underclothes. Corsets were loosened or thrown away altogether. Smoking, drinking, gambling, joyriding, close or "wild" dancing, kissing, and petting were also associated with the flapper. Following on the heels of the "virtuous woman" of the Victorian era, the flapper appeared to traditionalists as a threat to the future of womanhood and, therefore, culture and society as a whole.

Christian fundamentalists were among the most outspoken opponents of the flapper. Many agreed with a writer for the *Herald and Presbyter* who in 1919 linked "public morals" directly to women's dress. Between 1920 and 1925, the *Moody Bible Institute Monthly* published a number of articles that denounced the flapper as immodest and careless of her virtue. Not only did the flapper's dress indicate her personal lack of modesty, but it tempted and corrupted the men around her. The 1920s saw a

rise in premarital sex, and flappers received most of the blame.

The flappers were part of an upheaval in manners and morals in the 1920s as the nation made the transition to a modern, industrialized society. But this upheaval was limited to a small segment of society. Millions of Americans of both sexes were faithful to traditional behaviors and standards.

See also: Fundamentalism
References: Betty A. DeBerg, *Ungodly Women: Gender and the First Wave of American Fundamentalism* (1990); Paula S. Fass, *The Damned and the Beautiful: American Youth in the 1920's* (1977); Jean E. Friedman, comp., *Our American Sisters: Women in American Life and Thought* (1973); Nancy Woloch, *Women and the American Experience* (1984).

Flower, Amanda Cameron (1863–1940)

Amanda Cameron Flower, founder of the Independent Spiritualist Association of the United States of America, was born in Owen Sound, Ontario, Canada, on October 15, 1863. Although there is little information available regarding her early life, it is known that she was one of the four children of Abraham and Margaret (Day) Cameron. Amanda moved from Canada to the United States when she was twenty-seven years old, eventually settling in Michigan. She married and had one son with a Mr. Coffman. When Coffman died, she married Frank Flower.

From early adulthood Amanda Flower had been attracted to Spiritualism, and pastored for the first time in Owosso, Michigan. Early in the twentieth century, she invested money from her late husband's life insurance in a church building in Grand Rapids, which she opened as the Church of Truth. She was the pastor of the church from 1904 to 1939. In 1908 she incorporated the Spiritualist Temple Society (Church of Truth) in Grand Rapids. At about the same time,

Flower became affiliated with the Michigan State Spiritualist Association, a unit of the National Spiritualist Association of Churches (NSAC).

For a number of years, Flower was actively involved in establishing new Spiritualist congregations throughout the Midwest. Then, in the 1920s, she began to question some of the regulations governing NSAC churches. She wanted greater freedom of belief and was particularly unhappy with the rule that prohibited ministers from working in nonaffiliated churches. In 1924 she developed a plan for a new association that would emphasize the role of independent associations and be controlled only by their unity. Flower then withdrew from the NSAC and incorporated the Independent Spiritualist Association of the United States of America (ISA). The ISA's general beliefs and its educational standards were similar to those of the NSAC, but it tolerated those who remained faithful to the doctrine of reincarnation and other Theosophical principles.

Although it remained geographically limited to several midwestern states, Flower's association grew quickly. Soon after the organization's founding, she established and edited (until 1935) the association's newsletter. In 1931 she was elected president of the association for life. As its leader, she regularly traveled to visit ISA churches, and in 1933 she was a speaker at the Chicago World's Fair. Flower died on November 20, 1940.

See also: Spiritualism
References: J. Stillson Judah, *The History and Philosophy of the Metaphysical Movements in America* (1967); J. Gordon Melton, *Religious Leaders of America* (1991).

Foote, Julia A. J. (1823–1900)

African-American preacher Julia A. J. Foote was born in Schenectady, New York, in 1823, the daughter of former slaves who had purchased their freedom. Both parents were devout Christians who, despite suffering discrimination from the members, attended a white Methodist Episcopal Church. According to Julia, her parents "were not treated as Christian believers, but as poor lepers" (Foote, 1988, p. 11). Racial segregation in Schenectady prevented Foote from attending local schools. Her parents therefore found her work in a white household, where her employers used their influence to enable her to attend a school outside the city. From the age of eight, Julia was eager to learn to read the Bible, but the opportunity for her to attend school did not come until she was ten. Her strong desire to read the Bible inspired her to study diligently, and she learned to read and to spell quite rapidly. As it turned out, she received more than an academic education from her first schoolteacher, John Van Paten. The teacher shocked his students and the community when he was found guilty of murdering a local woman. Julia witnessed his subsequent hanging, an event that caused her nightmares for many a night. At the age of twelve, she left school to tend her four younger siblings while her mother worked. Soon the family moved to Albany, New York.

Throughout her childhood, Julia worried over her "sinfulness." When she was fifteen, she underwent a conversion experience at a Sunday church meeting, at which time she fell to the floor unconscious and had to be carried home. She subsequently joined an African Methodist Church and continued her quest to learn more about the Bible.

When Julia was eighteen, she married George Foote, a sailor who belonged to the church that she attended. The Footes moved to Boston soon after their wedding. George worked outside the city, returning home only on weekends. But Julia was soon occupied, working to help others find salvation. She joined the local African Methodist Episcopal (AME) Zion Church and began to spread the news of the wonders of sanctification to fellow congregants. Her husband disapproved of her activities and told her that if she did not stop, he would send her "back home or to the crazy-house" (Foote, 1988, p. 59). Julia refused to obey him. As a result, he became increasingly alienated from her. Soon, George went to sea, leaving his wife alone for six months. With no children to tend to and much leisure time, Julia visited neighboring households where she talked about Jesus and salvation. She became convinced that God had called her to a preaching career.

Jehiel Beman, the minister of the AME Zion Church in Boston was disturbed over a movement within the congregation to permit Foote to speak from his pulpit, and he let it be known that he would not allow her to do so. In response, she held meetings in her house. Beman then accused her of being a schismatic, and he set out to have her excommunicated from the church. Foote soon moved to Binghamton, New York, where her parents lived at the time. There she returned to preaching the doctrine of sanctification in informal gatherings of believers. In 1845 Foote began travels that would take her as far west as Cincinnati while she spread her message. She returned to Binghamton in 1849 to nurse her dying father but again set out as an itinerant preacher after his death in May of that year. Her ministry was abruptly curtailed in 1851 when she was stricken with a throat ailment. Over the next few years, Foote's life was upset further by the deaths of her mother, husband, and a close friend and associate, Sister Johnson. Apparently it was not until about 1869 that her throat healed to the point that she was able to resume preaching. Foote's activities over the next twenty-five years are not known.

In 1894 Foote became the first woman in the AME Zion Church to be ordained a deacon. At the end of her life, in 1900, she was ordained an elder of the church, only the second woman of her denomination to hold so high an office. Foote died on November 22, 1900.

See also: African Americans
References: William L. Andrews, ed., *Sisters of the Spirit: Three Black Women's Autobiographies of the Nineteenth Century* (1986); Julia A. Foote, "A Brand Plucked from the Fire," in *Spiritual Narratives* (1988); Susan Hill Lindley, *"You Have Stept Out of Your Place": A History of Women and Religion in America* (1996).

Forbes, Lilian Stevenson (1869–1945)

A pioneer in elementary Sunday school work with the Southern Baptist Convention, Lilian Forbes Stevenson was born in Eminence, Kentucky, on September 5, 1869. She received her education in Louisville public schools. After graduating from high school, Forbes attended a normal school in preparation for a career as a teacher. Inspired by the preaching of Dwight Lyman Moody, she converted to the Baptist faith at the age of twelve or thirteen. At this time she was baptized into the congregation of the East Baptist Church in Louisville. She taught her first Sunday school class there, a group of junior boys.

Forbes taught school for a short while and then entered the business sector. Eventually she turned to religious work, becoming a pastor's assistant and church secretary. Returning to her interest in Sunday school education, she coauthored lessons for the junior level. She moved to Alabama, where she served as secretary of elementary Sunday school work and became the Alabama Sunday school secretary. In 1916 she wrote *The Home Department of the Sunday School*, the first book on extension work to be published by Southern Baptists. Two years later, she became secretary of the Elementary Department of the Sunday School Board, a department then existing in name only. Forbes took on the responsibility of organizing and training workers in several states of the Southern Baptist Convention while promoting the work of the various age levels within Sunday school education.

During the seventeen years of her service with the Sunday School Board, Forbes launched the publication of the periodical *Elementary Messenger* and wrote individual manuals for both primary and junior superintendents. In 1922 she wrote *Program Material for Beginner and Primary Workers.* Meanwhile, and until her retirement in 1935, she fulfilled a heavy schedule of field work, speaking and teaching throughout the South. Lilian Stevenson Forbes died in Jackson, Mississippi, on May 30, 1945.

See also: Sunday School Movement
References: Clifton Judson Allen et al., eds., *Encyclopedia of Southern Baptists,* vol. 1 (1958).

Fox, Margaret (1833–1893)
Fox, Kate (Catherine) (1839–1892)

In 1848 the sisters Margaret and Kate Fox were living with their parents in Hydesville, New York, when they reported unusual rapping sounds in their bedroom. They then began to relate tales of being in contact with the spirit world, the first experience of this type recorded in U.S. history. They identified their spirit connection as Charles B. Rosma, an itinerant peddler. The girls said that Rosma had told them that he had been murdered five years earlier and had been buried under their house.

The next day, the family's cellar was excavated, and human hair and pieces of bone were uncovered. Their anxious parents sent the girls away from the home—Margaret to Rochester and Kate to Auburn, New York. But the strange rappings followed them. In 1849, the girls went professional and began to give public demonstrations of their communications with the spirit world. Their success as touring Spiritualists led hundreds of others to imitate them. Circles of Spiritualists formed across the country. The Fox sisters had many followers, including such well-known personalities as William Cullen Bryant, James Fenimore Cooper, and Horace Greeley. Though he frequently voiced doubts about the significance of the "rappings," Greeley invited the sisters into his home to hold seances.

Skepticism over the veracity of the Fox sisters' claims of communication with the spiritual world followed them throughout their lives. In 1888, Margaret confessed that the "rappings" and alleged contacts with the dead were a hoax. She retracted her statement a short time later, but the damage to the sisters' reputations was complete. In the later years of their lives, Margaret and Kate suffered from alcoholism. Kate died in New York City on July 2, 1892, and Margaret died in Brooklyn, New York, on March 8, 1893. At the time of their deaths, even Spiritualists refused to honor them. Their lives are examples of how women, especially before the twentieth century, found in moral, spiritual, and religious activities a path for development.

See also: Spiritualism
References: William Harlan Hale, *Horace Greeley: Voice of the People* (1950); R. Laurence Moore, "The Spiritualist Medium: A Study of Female Professionalization in Victorian America," in Esther Katz and Anita Rapone, eds., *Women's Experience in America: An Historical Anthology* (1980); Phyllis J. Read and Bernard L. Witlieb, *The Book of Women's Firsts* (1992).

Fox, Selena (1949–)

Leader of the Wiccan-Pagan community and founder of the Circle Sanctuary, Selena Fox was born in Arlington, Virginia, on October 20, 1949. She was raised in a fundamentalist Southern Baptist family. Fox's spiritual experiences, such as out-of-body travel and psychic visions, began during her childhood. As a teenager, she was interested in dreams, the psychic, and parapsychology, and she withdrew from the Southern Baptist Church while still in high school. Among her reasons for leaving the church was the church's disapproval of dancing and its refusal to ordain women into the clergy. Following high school, Fox pursued her interest in psychology at the College of William and Mary. She earned a bachelor of science degree in 1971 and has enrolled in additional studies in clinical and social psychology at such institutions as Rutgers University, the University of Wisconsin, and the Mendota Mental Health Institute.

In addition to her academic and professional studies, Fox has received training in many spiritual disciplines, including alchemy, yoga, Druidism, Taoism, neo-Pagan witchcraft, Christian spiritualism, Buddhism, and Native American shamanism. She led her first Pagan ritual at the age of twenty-one, when she was president of Eta Sigma Phi, the classics honor society at William and Mary. Fox embraced the Wiccan religion after college, eventually becoming a high priestess in several traditions.

Fox founded the Church of Circle Wicca (now known as Circle Sanctuary or simply Circle) at Sun Prairie near Madison, Wisconsin, in 1974. The church began with meetings in the farmhouse that Fox shared with her companion Jim Alan. In 1978 Fox began to devote full time to the Wiccan ministry. She began a newsletter, *Circle Network News,* which quickly became the largest circulating neo-Pagan periodical in North America, and the Circle Sanctuary was incorporated as a Wiccan church. It was one of the first Wiccan churches in

the United States to be officially recognized as a church by state and federal governments.

Fox and Alan were evicted from their home in 1979 by a landlord who did not approve of the Wiccans. After several moves to other farmhouses, they purchased 200 acres of farmland near Barneveld and Mount Horeb, Wisconsin. The site became a nature preserve, organic herb farm, and church headquarters. There Fox established the School for Priestesses, which was the first contemporary ecumenical ministerial program of its type for women involved in goddess-oriented forms of spirituality. Fox practices a form of Wiccan-shamanism, an eclectic form of neo-Pagan Goddess worship. In 1984 Fox and Alan ended their common-law relationship. Two years later, Fox married Dennis Carpenter, a Wiccan priest and former school psychologist.

In the mid-1980s, neighbors of the sanctuary who were upset over the presence of witches attempted to remove the church or at least limit its activities. With help from the Pagan community and from civil rights activists, Fox succeeded in saving the sanctuary. In 1988 local governments recognized the church's right to exist and to use the land. Three years later the Circle began a school for ministers that provides ecumenical leadership training for men and women. The teachers there are priests and priestesses from a variety of Pagan lines of thought and groups connected with the Circle Network (an all-encompassing title for agencies associated with Fox's Circle).

Throughout her career as a Wiccan-Pagan leader, Fox has been an activist for religious freedom. In addition to her campaign to give Pagans the right to worship, she has worked successfully to allow Wiccan priestesses to minister as clergy in prisons and to protect sacred burial grounds of Native Americans. In

1985 she was a leader in the effort to defeat the Helms Amendment, which sought to eliminate tax-exempt status for Wiccan churches.

See also: Wicca; Witchcraft
References: Rosemary Ellen Guiley, *The Encyclopedia of Witches and Witchcraft* (1989); J. Gordon Melton, *Encyclopedia of American Religions,* 4th ed. (1993); J. Gordon Melton, *Religious Leaders of America* (1991).

Frost, Yvonne (1931–)

Yvonne Frost, cofounder of the Church and School of Wicca, is one of the more controversial figures within the neo-Pagan movement. She was born Yvonne Wilson in Los Angeles, California, in 1931. Her parents were conservative Baptists who raised Yvonne in the faith, but from childhood she was dissatisfied with her inherited religion. When she reached adulthood, she began a study of world religions in an attempt to find a more personally meaningful faith. She married in 1950, but the relationship lasted only ten years. Following her divorce, Yvonne returned to school, earning an associate of arts degree in secretarial skills from Fullerton Junior College in Fullerton, California, in 1962. While in college she became intrigued by the study of Spiritualism and psychic development.

Not long after graduation, Yvonne met her future husband at the major aerospace company in Anaheim, California, where they both worked. Gavin Frost, a mathematician and scientist, was involved in witchcraft. Discovering their mutual attraction to the occult, Yvonne and Gavin began to explore witchcraft together. They were initiated into the Celtic tradition of Wicca, and in 1965 they founded the Church and School of Wicca in St. Louis, Missouri. The school began as a correspondence course, advertised as the "School of Wicca" in occult magazines. It soon had a large following, enrolling thousands of students. However, the majority have never completed the course, and the Frosts have accepted only several hundred for initiation into the Craft.

The Frosts were married in 1970, and they have one child. In 1972 Gavin gave up his aerospace career in order to join Yvonne as a full-time worker for the Church and School of Wicca. They moved their home and headquarters to New Bern, North Carolina, in 1974–1975. Gavin is archbishop of the church, and Yvonne serves as bishop. Both have taken vows of poverty, and the fees charged at the school cover only operational and administrative expenses.

The church's philosophy, as presented in the Frosts' first book, *The Witches' Bible* (1972), has been controversial. It argues that the Ultimate Deity is not definable, which is in opposition to the beliefs of most neo-Pagans, who emphasize the power of the Goddess. The church also drew criticism in its early years by holding that homosexuals did not fit into the Craft. The church has gradually changed its position and is now open to people of all sexual orientations.

Among the more than a dozen books authored by the Frosts are *The Magic Power of Witchcraft* (1976); *A Witch's Guide to Life* (1978); *Meta-Psychometry: Key to Power and Abundance* (1978); and *Power Secrets from a Sorcerer's Magnum Arcanum* (1980).

See also: Wicca; Witchcraft
References: Rosemary Ellen Guiley, *The Encyclopedia of Witches and Witchcraft* (1989); J. Gordon Melton, *Encyclopedia of American Religions,* 4th ed. (1993); J. Gordon Melton, *Religious Leaders of America* (1991).

Fuller, Margaret (1810–1850)

Author, critic, Transcendentalist, and feminist Margaret Fuller was an influential woman in the mid-nineteenth century. She

Margaret Fuller (engraving based upon Alonzo Chappel painting)

was born in Cambridgeport, Massachusetts, on May 23, 1810, to Timothy and Margaret (Crane) Fuller. Timothy Fuller was a lawyer and politician who believed in hard work. Margaret Crane Fuller was an avid reader of novels, literature, and history. Both parents were devout Unitarians. As such, they believed that the acquisition of knowledge pleased God, and they worked to instill a love of knowledge in their daughter Margaret, who was naturally bright. Her father began tutoring her at age four, and she knew the basics of both English and Latin grammar by the age of six. By age nine she was reading standard political histories and biographies and many major texts of Latin literature. After her father's tutoring, she went on to attend private schools, including Miss Susan Prescott's Young Ladies Seminary at Groton, Massachusetts.

Although Fuller absorbed her parents' love of knowledge, by the time she entered her twenties she had become concerned that she could not accept the teach-

ings of the Unitarian faith. She questioned Christ's divine attributes and his mission as a savior and teacher. In hopes of resolving her dilemma, she began to study religion, searching for a satisfying intellectual basis for the Christian faith. But the more she read, the more she doubted.

In 1835, at the invitation of her friend James Clarke, a young Unitarian minister, Fuller contributed an article for the first issue of his new Transcendentalist magazine, the *Western Messenger*. Transcendentalism, which favored human intuition over reason, was inspired by German idealists such as Immanuel Kant and by Eastern mystical philosophies. Many of the leaders of the movement in the United States came from the Unitarian faith. At first Fuller was not much of a Transcendentalist. She was drawn to Transcendentalism in 1836–1837 after staying three weeks in the home of Ralph Waldo Emerson, the genius of the movement in the United States.

Fuller's father died in 1835, and she took charge as head of the family. To earn money, she taught school in Boston and then in Providence, Rhode Island, from 1837 to 1838. Fuller returned to Boston in 1839. There she launched "conversation" classes, which continued until 1844. The conversation classes were a series of meetings for a circle of women of Boston. They attracted educated women, women interested in new trends, ardent supporters of the Transcendentalist movement, and the wives of leading Transcendentalists. Conversation was of utmost importance to Transcendentalists, and it was through conversations with Transcendentalists like Emerson and Theodore Parker that Fuller developed the idea for the series. The classes were designed to stimulate thinking and to put ideas into action. Mythology, art, ethics, the ideal, faith, health, great men, and women's rights were among the many topics of discussion. The classes contributed to the growth of organized feminism in America. With her conversation classes, Fuller launched her career as a Transcendentalist leader. In 1841 she opened her classes to both men and women.

Fuller joined Emerson and others to produce the quarterly journal *The Dial*. Beginning operation in 1840, *The Dial* became the major journal of the Transcendentalist movement. Its purpose was to stimulate people into thinking for themselves. Fuller also took part in the founding of the Transcendentalist commune Brook Farm, though she never lived there. She visited often but wanted to live an independent life. In 1844 Fuller published her first book, *Summer on the Lakes*. Soon after, Horace Greeley invited her to New York to become the literary critic for the *New York Tribune*. Her second book, *Woman in the Nineteenth Century* (1845), became a feminist classic and was influential at the 1848 Seneca Falls women's rights convention. In 1846 Greeley appointed Fuller foreign correspondent, and she went to Europe; first to England and France and then to Rome in April 1847. While in Rome she met a young Roman nobleman, Giovanni Angelo, Marchese d'Ossoli. The couple became lovers in the fall of 1847, though they probably did not marry until the summer of 1849. Their son Angelo Eugene was born September 5, 1848. Fuller and Ossoli were active in the revolution of 1848–1849. When the Roman republic was overthrown in July 1849, the couple fled the city. They made their way to Florence, where Fuller began to write a history of the Roman revolution. With hopes of getting the book published in the United States, the Ossoli family set out for the United States aboard the *Elizabeth*. All three family members were lost at sea on July 19, 1850, when their ship ran aground off Fire Island, New York.

See also: Woman Suffrage
References: Charles Capper, *Margaret Fuller, an American Romantic Life: The Private Years* (1992); Bell Gale Chevigny, *The Woman and the Myth: Margaret Fuller's Life and Writings* (1976); Edward T. James, ed., *Notable American Women, 1607–1950* (1971); Mary Kelley, *Margaret Fuller* (1994).

Fundamentalism

The growing prestige and prominence of science in the late nineteenth and early twentieth centuries presented challenges to the high cultural standing of religion. Scholars had closely analyzed the historical origins of the Bible, and psychologists were explaining the religious impulse in terms of human emotional needs. At the same time, Catholic and Jewish immigrants were flocking to America. Although liberal Protestants mostly responded to scientific discoveries and to the influx of new Americans by accepting the findings of science and giving aid to the immigrants, another type of reaction was building among some more conservative Protestants. This other reaction came to be known as "fundamentalism." Margaret Lamberts Bendroth identifies a third factor, anxiety over gender roles, that was present at the birth of fundamentalism and led to fundamentalist leaders placing limits upon women's participation within their churches.

Taking the name of their movement from a series of pamphlets, *The Fundamentals*, published in 1909–1914, fundamentalists adopted four basic principles: belief in the virgin birth of Christ; the death of Christ in payment for the sins of humankind; the bodily resurrection of Christ; and the divine inspiration of every word in the Bible. The latter tenet had a significant effect upon women in the fundamentalist movement because it meant that their roles would be governed largely by the apostle Paul's pronouncements on women. Often cited were Paul's

Letter to the Ephesians 5:22–24, commanding wives to be submissive to their husbands, and I Corinthians 14:34–35, instructing women to be silent in church.

By the 1920s, fundamentalists had adopted the belief that only males had the true aptitude for religion. The Victorian idea that women were the pious sex and the keepers of morality was now reversed. With evangelist Aimee Semple McPherson a notable exception, the 1920s saw a trend toward the male domination of fundamentalist leadership. In 1930 the Independent Fundamental Churches in America explicitly eliminated women as voting members, and Gordon College's trustees limited the proportion of female students to one-third. The 1930s found the World Christian Fundamentals Association (WCFA) having few women officers and paying little attention to feminine issues.

With flappers in mind, male fundamentalist leaders denounced the emerging "new woman" of the 1920s as frivolous, self-indulgent, and immoral. The ideal woman remained at home as a self-sacrificing wife and mother. By neglecting their "natural" duties, these modern women were contributing to the decline of society's morals. Fundamentalist schools like the Moody Bible Institute responded to the advent of the flapper by incorporating dress codes and other rules that would ensure that women maintained a high degree of modesty. As Susan Hill Lindley points out, fundamentalists of the 1920s and 1930s placed even stricter limits on a woman's sphere than had been the case in the nineteenth century, for now women were dissuaded from participating in the reform and religious activities that had been permitted by their fathers and grandfathers. It was not until the new feminism of the 1970s that women again broke into the upper ranks of fundamentalist hierarchies.

Although they placed rigid limits on woman's sphere, fundamentalist leaders realized that their churches could not function without the presence and support of women. They were therefore happy to accept financial backing from women, and women did serve as foreign missionaries. They also found opportunities in education. Henrietta Cornelia Mears found a niche for herself within fundamentalism as a Sunday school teacher and as a writer and publisher of religious literature.

With the revival of feminism in the 1970s, some fundamentalists took a new look at the Bible and the apostle Paul's views on women and concluded that Paul might have been mistaken. However, by the end of the decade most leaders had come to reject feminism. At the same time, many fundamentalist leaders had become a part of the New Christian Right, a movement to impress conservative values upon American society. This new movement was not solely fundamentalist but included other Christians who adhered to the right's positions on issues such as family and the Equal Rights Amendment. Members of the New Christian Right have become involved in a number of issues of concern to women. They stand by the fundamentalist position that women's natural and divinely ordained role is that of wife and mother. Also, they vehemently oppose both abortion and homosexuality, contending that both are forbidden by the Bible and are threats to the traditional family and its values. The New Christian Right claimed a number of successes in the 1980s. Among these were their perceived influence on the election of Ronald Reagan, the defeat of the Equal Rights Amendment, and the defeat of a number of gay rights measures in local jurisdictions. However, the overall effectiveness of the political campaigns of the New Christian Right has not been determined. The movement has quieted down in the 1990s, but it is still alive.

See also: Biblical Authority and Women's Rights; Equal Rights Amendment; Flappers; McPherson, Aimee Semple; Mears, Henrietta Cornelia

References: Margaret Lamberts Bendroth, *Fundamentalism and Gender: 1875 to the Present* (1993); Michael Lienesch, *Redeeming America: Piety and Politics in the New Christian Right* (1993); Susan Hill Lindley, *"You Have Stept Out of Your Place": A History of Women and Religion in America* (1996); Glenn H. Utter and John W. Storey, *The Religious Right: A Reference Handbook* (1995).

Gage, Matilda Joslyn (1826–1898)

Born March 25, 1826, into a wealthy family in upstate New York, Matilda Joslyn Gage was one of the most radical leaders of the nineteenth-century women's movement. She was the only child of Helen Leslie Joslyn and Hezekia Joslyn. Her father, who was an advocate of abolition, temperance, free thought, and women's rights, encouraged his daughter to pursue a much more challenging education than what was typical for young women of her era. He tutored her at home in such nontraditional subjects as Greek, mathematics, and physiology. When she was fifteen, Matilda enrolled in Clinton (New York) Liberal Institute, where she completed her formal education. In 1845 she married Henry H. Gage, with whom she raised four children.

Although her family responsibilities prevented her from taking an active role in the women's movement, Gage was an avid supporter of women's rights. She first entered public life when she spoke at the Third National Woman's Rights Convention held in Syracuse, New York, in September 1952. Once her children were grown, she joined the crusade. Never a strong speaker, she took on the roles of organizer, writer, and editor. When the movement split following the Civil War, Gage joined Elizabeth Cady Stanton and Susan B. Anthony in the new National Woman Suffrage Association (NWSA) to protest the idea that getting the vote for women should be set aside in favor of securing enfranchisement of black males. In

May 1875 she began one year's service as president of the NWSA. During the 1870s and early 1880s, the three women compiled and edited the first three volumes of the *History of Woman Suffrage* (vol. 1, 1881; vol. 2, 1882; vol. 3, 1886). Although she held positions within NWSA that were roughly equivalent to those held by Stanton and Anthony, Gage did not become as famous as the others in the "triumvirate."

Like Stanton, Gage came to view religion, the Christian church in particular, as the greatest obstacle to the uplifting of women. In 1878, at a convention of the NWSA, both women came out in support of controversial resolutions attacking religion. When she was unable to prevent the NWSA from reuniting with the conservative American Woman Suffrage Association in 1890, Gage returned to her efforts to free women "from the bondage of the church" (Wagner, 1990, p. 225). She founded the antichurch National Woman's Liberal Union in 1890 and contributed to Elizabeth Cady Stanton's two-volume *The Woman's Bible* (1895 and 1898). During this period, Gage also wrote her own treatise on the role of church and state in the historical oppression of women, *Woman, Church and State* (1893). In a work that was highly controversial at the time but has since been praised as "one of the most important theoretical documents produced by the nineteenth century woman's movement" (Wagner, 1990, p. 225) Gage took a broad survey of the laws and practices that have historically forced women into subordination and submission. Further, she argued that males have not only labeled women as inherently inferior but hypocritically instituted a double standard of sexual and moral behavior.

Gage looked forward to the day when those who shared her views would rise up against the church in rebellion against "those theological dogmas upon which the very existence of the church is based" (Gage, 1893). She insisted that "no rebellion has been of the importance with that of Woman against the tyranny of Church and State; none has had its far reaching effects" (Gage, 1893). Gage believed that once all existing forms of these institutions were overthrown, what was left would be a "regenerated world" (Gage, 1893, p. 246).

Matilda Joslyn Gage, who was regarded as "one of the most logical, fearless, and scientific writers of her day" (Wagner, 1990, p. 225), died in Chicago of heart disease on March 18, 1898.

See also: Stanton, Elizabeth Cady; *The Woman's Bible*
References: Kathryn Cullen-DuPont, with Annelise Orleck, *The Encyclopedia of Women's History in America* (1996); Matilda Joslyn Gage, *Woman, Church and State* (1893, reprint 1972); Edward T. James, ed., *Notable American Women, 1607–1950*, vol. 2 (1971); Susan Hill Lindley, *"You Have Stept Out of Your Place": A History of Women and Religion in America* (1996); Sally Roesch Wagner, "Gage, Matilda Joslyn," in Angela Howard Zophy with Frances M. Kavenik, eds., *Handbook of American Women's History* (1990).

Gardener, Helen Hamilton (1853–1925)

Helen Hamilton Gardener, feminist, Free Thought writer, and reformer, was born Alice Chenoweth in Winchester, Virginia, on January 21, 1853. Her parents were Katherine A. (Peel) Chenoweth, an or-

thodox Calvinist, and Alfred Griffith Chenoweth, a Methodist circuit rider. Most of Gardener's early years were spent with her family in Greencastle, Indiana, but she attended high school in Cincinnati, Ohio. She continued her education at Cincinnati Normal School, from which she graduated in 1873. After two years of teaching school, she married Charles Seldon Smart in 1875 and moved with him to New York City in 1880. There, she studied biology at Columbia University, lectured in sociology at the Brooklyn Institute of Arts and Science, and began publishing some of her own writings (under masculine pseudonyms) in newspapers.

In New York, Gardener met Robert Green Ingersoll, a famous Free Thought lecturer. She found that her own thought was similar to his. Taking Ingersoll's advice, in 1884 she began a series of lectures on free thinking in which she denounced ministers who denigrated women. She published the lectures the following year, under the title *Men, Women, and Gods, and Other Lectures*, using the pen name Helen Hamilton Gardener. She eventually adopted the name legally.

Feminism was an important theme in Gardener's Free Thought writing. She denounced Christianity for its oppression of women and wrote two novels that expressed her anger. *Is This Your Son, My Lord?* (1890), which dealt with prostitution and attacked the double standard, had popular appeal and sold widely. Works that followed included *A Thoughtless Yes* (1890), a collection of stories; *Pray You, Sir, Whose Daughter?* (1892), a book that dealt with the inferior position of married women; *Pushed by Unseen Hands* (1892), stories; and *An Unofficial Patriot* (1894), a fictionalized biography of her father. In 1894 she published *Facts and Fictions of Life*, which contained a carefully researched and famous essay, "Sex in Brain," that she had written several years earlier. It refuted the theory that women are inferior because they generally possessed smaller brains than men. The essay attracted the attention of feminist Elizabeth Cady Stanton, who subsequently invited Gardener to assist her with the production of *The Woman's Bible* (1895).

Following her husband's death in 1901 and her marriage to Selden Allen Day the following year, she spent five or six years traveling around the world. When she returned, she settled in Washington, D.C., where she gradually began to emerge as a lobbyist for female suffrage. In 1913 she was appointed to the task of reorganizing the Congressional Committee of the National American Woman's Suffrage Association (NAWSA) after radical suffragists and followers of Alice Paul resigned to form the Congressional Union. She was elected a vice president of NAWSA in 1917. Her social contacts with leading political figures, most notably President Woodrow Wilson and Speaker of the House Champ Clark, made her an important lobbyist in the latter stages of the suffrage movement. She soon became known as NAWSA's "diplomatic corps."

In April 1920, Wilson appointed her to the U.S. Civil Service Commission, the highest federal position held by a woman until that time. She remained in her post until her death in Washington, D.C., on July 26, 1925. In keeping with her commitment to Free Thought, no religious observances were held at her funeral.

See also: Stanton, Elizabeth Cady; *The Woman's Bible*
References: Helen H. Gardener, *Men, Women, and Gods, and Other Lectures* (1885); Edward T. James, ed., *Notable American Women, 1607–1950*, vol. 2 (1971); Robert McHenry, ed., *Liberty's Women* (1980); J. Gordon Melton, *Religious Leaders of America* (1991).

Garrison, William Lloyd (1805–1879)

Radical abolitionist, women's rights advocate, and religious reformer William Lloyd Garrison was born December 12, 1805, in Newburyport, Massachusetts. His father, a sailor, abandoned the family in 1808, and William was raised by his mother, a devoted Baptist. As a youth, Garrison was known for his piety, and he even considered becoming a missionary. Although he eventually turned to journalism, the reform spirit that he carried with him throughout his adulthood had its roots in the religious enthusiasm of his youth. A Christian perfectionist who believed in humankind's ability to live with a pure heart, Garrison refused to compromise with sin. In time he would disrupt religious services at pro-slavery churches and attack the clergy for having impure hearts.

In 1829 Garrison joined the abolitionist movement at the invitation of Benjamin Lundy, a Quaker opposed to slavery. Two years later, Garrison established his abolitionist weekly, *The Liberator,* and in 1833, along with brothers Arthur and Lewis Tappan, he cofounded the American Anti-Slavery Society. In a time when politics was considered outside "women's sphere," Garrison invited both men and women to join the movement. The women who joined him were the first avowed feminists in America and included Maria Weston Chapman, Abby Kelley Foster, Lucretia Coffin Mott, and Sarah and Angelina Grimké. Garrison believed in the immediate emancipation of slaves but felt that this could be accomplished through the peaceful means of "moral suasion," by convincing people that slavery was sinful and must therefore be abolished. Although he opposed war, he accepted a rebellion of the oppressed should all peaceful means fail.

Garrison was a strong supporter of the political equality of the sexes and encouraged the full participation of women in all antislavery societies. His stand on women's role in the movement, coupled with his criticisms of religious and governmental institutions for condoning slavery, led to a split in the American Anti-Slavery Society in May 1840. Later that year, when the World Anti-Slavery Convention in London would not permit the participation of women delegates, Garrison refused to take his seat. Throughout his career as a leader of the antislavery movement, Garrison would not be swayed from his insistence that all who considered slavery a sin should be welcomed into the American Anti-Slavery Society.

When the Civil War erupted, Garrison threw his support to the war and to the Republican Party. After the Thirteenth Amendment was ratified in December 1865, he declared the abolitionists' goals fulfilled. Garrison closed down *The Liberator,* resigned from the American Anti-Slavery Society, and called for aid for the freed slaves. He continued to voice support for women's rights and by 1868 was hopeful that women would soon have the vote. When female suffrage failed to come to pass as quickly as he had anticipated, Garrison in 1870 began to speak more forcefully on women's behalf. Although he broke with Susan B. Anthony and Elizabeth Cady Stanton over the women's rights leaders' tactics and some of their choices of allies, he remained an advocate for women's rights until his death. Garrison died in New York on May 24, 1879.

See also: Antislavery Movement; Grimké, Angelina Emily; Grimké, Sarah Moore; Mott, Lucretia Coffin; Stanton, Elizabeth Cady; Woman Suffrage
References: Eleanor Flexner, *Century of Struggle: The Women's Rights Movement in the United States* (1970); George M. Fredrickson, ed., *William Lloyd Garrison* (1968); Elizabeth Frost-Knappman, *Women's Progress in America* (1994); Walter M. Merrill, *Against the Wind and Tide: A Biography of Wm. Lloyd Garrison* (1963); James Brewer Stewart, *Holy Warriors: The Abolitionists and American Slavery* (1976).

Gates, Susa Amelia Young (1856–1933)

Writer, publisher, and a women's leader in the Church of Jesus Christ of Latter-Day Saints, Susa Amelia Young Gates was born in Salt Lake City, Utah, in early 1856. She was the forty-first child of church president Brigham Young. Her mother was Lucy Bigelow, the twenty-second of Young's more than fifty wives. Following a private education, which included music and ballet, Gates entered the University of Deseret when she was thirteen years of age. Her father later forced her to withdraw when he learned that she had played a role in her sister Dora's elopement. She was then sent to Saint George, Utah, where in 1877 she became the first person to be baptized for the dead in the new Saint George Temple. Baptism for the dead is one of the main temple rites in which living Mormons serve as proxies for dead people of earlier generations. When she was sixteen, Susa married Alma Bailey Dunford, a dentist and an alcoholic. She divorced him five years later, in 1877. He raised their two children. On January 5, 1880, she married Jacob F. Gates, with whom she had eleven children. Only four of these children lived to become adults.

In addition to time spent bearing and rearing children, the 1880s and 1890s found Gates focusing her energies on writing, missionary work, education, and matters of concern to women. In the 1880s, Gates began to write articles for several church periodicals, with most of her work appearing under the pseudonym "Homespun." She accompanied her husband on a four-year mission to Hawaii, beginning in 1885. When she returned to Utah, she launched the *Young Woman's Journal,* which became the official magazine of the Young Ladies' Mutual Improvement Association (YLMIA) in 1897, and began editing (until 1922) the *Relief Society Magazine.* She also be-

Susa Amelia Young Gates

she suffered a nervous and physical breakdown. Sidelined for three years, she underwent a period of religious introspection. Once she recovered, she turned to genealogical and temple work. Gates was one of the organizers of the genealogical work for which the Mormon Church has become famous, establishing genealogy departments in two newspapers—the *Inter Mountain Republican* and the *Deseret News* in 1906. She compiled instructional manuals for genealogical researchers, constructed a system for indexing names, and published the *Surname Book and Racial History*. When she was president of the Daughters of the Utah Pioneers, she established their House of Relics, and in 1923 she became head of the Genealogical Society of Utah's Library and Research Department. She personally catalogued more than sixteen thousand names of members of the Young family.

Gates has also written a number of books, including *Lydia Knight's History, John Steven's Courtship, History of the Young Ladies' Mutual Improvement Association,* and *The Prince of Ur.* In collaboration with her daughter Leah Dunford Widtsoe, she wrote *The Life Story of Brigham Young.* Gates died of cancer in Salt Lake City on May 27, 1933.

See also: Church of Jesus Christ of Latter-Day Saints (Mormons)
References: Mary Bywater Cross, *Quilts and Women of the Mormon Migration* (1996); J. Gordon Melton, *Religious Leaders of America* (1991); Louise Plummer, "Susa Young Gates," in Daniel H. Ludlow, ed., *Encyclopedia of Mormonism,* vol. 2 (1992); Richard S. Van Wagoner and Steven C. Walker, *A Book of Mormons* (1982).

came well known as a public speaker. In the years that followed, Gates became one of the most powerful women in the Mormon Church. She joined the board of the YLMIA in 1899, and in 1919 became the corresponding secretary of the General Board of the Relief Society. Gates was the only woman to have an office in the church office building, and she was often referred to as the "thirteenth apostle."

In addition to her work within the church, Gates became active with the National Council of Women in the United States and represented the YLMIA at seven of its meetings. Twice the council appointed her to speak at International Council of Women meetings, in London in 1899 and in Copenhagen in 1901. In London she joined other council women for tea with Queen Victoria.

Gates's work came to a temporary halt at the beginning of the new century when

Gaylor, Anne Nicol (1926–)

Atheist and feminist Anne Nicol Gaylor founded the Freedom from Religion Foundation in Madison, Wisconsin, in 1976. She was born in Tomah, Wisconsin, in 1926. Her father was a farmer and her mother a schoolteacher. Both parents were freethinkers who did not consider anyone who believed in the Bible a true intellectual. Anne graduated from the University of Wisconsin at Madison in 1949 and began a career in journalism. In the 1960s Anne and her husband, Paul Gaylor, purchased a small newspaper, the *Middleton Times,* which served the Madison suburbs.

Gaylor's career as an activist began in the early 1970s when she joined in both atheist and feminist causes. She perceived religion as a major cause of the oppression of women and felt that the elimination of religion would greatly aid women's goal of liberation. Gaylor joined Madalyn O'Hair's American Atheists, but it was not long before she became involved with a group that was dissatisfied with O'Hair's undemocratic management of her organization. In 1976 Gaylor and others who had voiced disillusionment with O'Hair's running of American Atheists were expelled from the group. With the help of her supporters, Gaylor founded the Freedom from Religion Foundation and was elected the foundation's first president. Within a year of its creation, two hundred people had joined the organization. Although the foundation is atheistic in its belief and practice, its members maintain a variety of Free Thought or nontheistic points of view. In addition to atheism, they hold philosophies of humanism, secularism, and agnosticism. Gaylor has been a leader in establishing the Freethinkers Anti-Defamation League, whose purpose is to protect the rights and reputations of atheists, agnostics, and secular humanists. In 1983 she published a collection of her writings, *Lead Us Not into Penn Station.* She has filed a number of lawsuits in connection with atheists' strong belief in the separation of church and state. In 1982 she sued to prevent President Ronald Reagan from naming

1983 as the Year of the Bible, and in 1988 she protested the use of churches as polling places. She has also campaigned to remove Bibles from hotel and motel rooms.

To advance the feminist cause, Gaylor founded the Women's Medical Fund, which has assisted women who could not otherwise afford to pay for abortions. She has been an officer in Protect Abortion Rights and in 1975 published her book on abortion rights, *Abortion Is a Blessing.*

See also: O'Hair, Madalyn Mays Murray
References: J. Gordon Melton, *Encyclopedia of American Religions,* 4th ed. (1993); J. Gordon Melton, *Religious Leaders of America* (1991); Gordon Stein, ed., *The Encyclopedia of Unbelief* (1985).

Gratz, Rebecca (1781–1869)

Rebecca Gratz, social worker and founder of the first Hebrew Sunday School Society, was born into a wealthy merchant's family in Philadelphia, Pennsylvania, on March 4, 1781. From her youth, Gratz had been interested in both charity work and religion. In 1801, at the age of twenty, she helped to establish the Female Association for the Relief of Women in Reduced Circumstances and served for a time as secretary of that organization. She was a founder of the Philadelphia Orphan Asylum, which opened in 1815, and served as secretary of the institution from 1819 to 1859. In 1819, Gratz played a leading role in the formation of the Female Hebrew Benevolent Society in Philadelphia, which marked the beginning of Jewish women organizing for social welfare.

An Orthodox Jew, Gratz was devoted to the Jewish tradition and was determined to foster it. She was especially interested in religious education for Jewish children and, for a short while in 1818, held a religious school in her home. In 1838, she founded the Hebrew Sunday School Society in Philadelphia. Modeled

Rebecca Gratz (undated portrait by Edward Greene Malbone)

stantly searching for new ways to help those in need, and out of concern that young people without supportive families would encounter more than the usual problems in life, Gratz played a major role in the establishment of the Jewish Foster Home and Orphan Asylum, which opened in 1855.

Gratz, who is remembered for her charm, beauty, and dignity in addition to her contributions to the fields of education and social work, died in Philadelphia on August 27, 1869.

See also: Female Hebrew Benevolent Society; Jews
References: Henry Warner Bowden, *Dictionary of American Religious Biography,* 2nd ed. (1993); Jacob R. Marcus, *The American Jewish Woman: A Documentary History* (1981); Jacob R. Marcus, *The American Jewish Woman, 1654–1980* (1981); Phyllis J. Read and Bernard L. Witlieb, *The Book of Women's Firsts* (1992).

on the Christian nondenominational American Sunday School, established in 1812, the Hebrew Sunday school was the first Sunday school for Jewish children in the United States and served as a prototype for all others to follow for decades to come. There, Jewish children, most of whom were recently arrived immigrants from central and, later, eastern Europe, were taught religion, culture, and morality. Gratz and other school officials hoped that religious indoctrination would guarantee the survival of Jewish tradition in the next generation of Jews. The school charged no tuition and was open to both girls and boys. Jewish historian Jacob R. Marcus, in *The American Jewish Woman: A Documentary History,* considers the school to have been the "most important Jewish children's educational innovation in the nineteenth century" (Marcus, 1981, p. 135). Gratz served as president of the school, which was staffed mostly by women, for twenty-six years. Con-

Great Awakening

The period of religious revivals and religious excitement that came to be known as the Great Awakening began in the 1720s and reached its peak in the 1740s. Early stirrings of religious enthusiasm began with a small number of evangelical Calvinists who urged the necessity of conversion. Among them were William Tennent and his four sons, all ministers, who kindled religious fervor among their fellow Presbyterians throughout the Middle Colonies. In the 1730s the Tennents established the "Log College" (later Princeton) for the purpose of training other preachers. In New England, Congregational clergymen like Yale-educated Jonathan Edwards sought to awaken "backsliders" to consciously strive for salvation, and he also promoted revivals. However, it was not until the arrival from England of preacher George Whitefield that the Great Awakening took its full-fledged and widespread form. Although his message was not new—like other Calvinist clergymen he preached that salvation was totally dependent upon the mercy of a pure, all-powerful God—Whitefield's presentation was significantly different. He had a theatrical preaching style that attracted large audiences as well as many enthusiastic imitators. Whitefield toured America from the fall of 1739 to January 1741. By the time he returned to England, he had inspired thousands to join churches or to form new ones.

Besides revitalizing participants' religious lives, the Great Awakening resulted in the founding of colleges, ignited humanitarian and missionary fervor, and fomented broad social and cultural changes. The revivals, often led by itinerant clergy, were not always welcomed by established ministers. Not only did some of the traveling preachers fail to observe expected proprieties, but some criticized the more traditional church leaders. Such occurrences infuriated many of the established clergy and led to bitter controversies. Also, the revivalists often invited the laity to assume greater personal responsibility for their religious lives and to take on more power within their churches. This was a challenge to the clerical hierarchy and to the established social order of clergy over laity. The result was an undermining of clerical authority in American society. The upper classes also came to oppose the revivals, partly because of their distaste for the emotional and physical excesses displayed by the participants, but also because they perceived that the challenge to hierarchical authority extended to society at large, and they felt threatened.

On the surface, the experience of the Great Awakening was essentially the same for both men and women. Overall the proportion of male converts during the period was greater than that of females. Nevertheless, women continued to outnumber men in American churches.

Some scholars have viewed the Great Awakening as an important event in women's history because of its emphasis on a religious style that came to be associated with women. This is the idea of conversion experience coming from the "heart" rather than from the "head." Although colonial Americans did not make a head-heart distinction along gender lines, some scholars see in the Great Awakening the roots of what came to be called the "feminization" of American religion in the nineteenth century.

The Great Awakening also helped to expand the roles of women by offering the idea that authority came through the experience of grace and not from formal theological training. Although few Christian denominations of the eighteenth century approved of women preaching in public, many churches came to accept women's participation in various other religious activities. Women offered religious instruction within their homes and prayed or offered encouragement in religious meetings, and a few participated in the business meetings of their churches. For women, perhaps the most important aspect of the Great Awakening was that it opened the way for them to build upon their accepted religious roles within their families, so that by the third quarter of the nineteenth century their influence had grown to include the public domain.

See also: Second Great Awakening
References: Francis J. Bremer, *The Puritan Experiment: New England Society from Bradford to Edwards* (1977); Jon Butler, *Awash in a Sea of Faith: Christianizing the American People* (1990); Merle Curti, *The Growth of American Thought*, 2nd ed. (1951); James West Davidson et al., *Nation of Nations: A Narrative History of the American Republic*, vol. 1 (1990); Susan Hill Lindley, *"You Have Stept Out of Your Place": A History of Women and Religion in America* (1996); Angela Howard Zophy with Frances M. Kavenik, eds., *Handbook of American Women's History* (1990).

Grimké, Angelina Emily
(1805–1879)

Angelina Grimké, together with her sister Sarah Grimké, became an outspoken abolitionist and crusader for women's rights. She was born February 20, 1805, in Charleston, South Carolina, the youngest child of John Faucheraud and Mary (Smith) Grimké. Her father, Judge John Grimké, was a planter, slaveholder, politician, and member of South Carolina's ruling elite. He was the master of his family, which enjoyed the social amenities associated with the southern upper class. They lived in an elegant home on a plantation near Beaufort during the cooler months and resided in Charleston between mid-May and November. They attended musical events, balls, carnivals, and races. Every Sunday the entire family, including their many servants, attended the local Episcopal Church. Religion was very important to the Grimké family. The children attended Sabbath school and were only excused from the household's daily prayers if they were ill.

All of her life, Angelina cared little about society's proprieties. When she was thirteen, she shocked the clergyman at her church when she said she could not go through with the confirmation ceremony because she did not agree with the pledge in her prayer book. She converted from the Episcopal to the Presbyterian Church and was formally admitted into the latter church in 1826. Angelina was attracted to the Presbyterian Church because it was much more liberal than the Episcopal Church, allowing her to establish a prayer meeting with Baptist, Methodist, Congregationalist, and Presbyterian women. Yet she could not understand how the Presbyterian Church, like other Christian churches, was able to stand by and do nothing while white Christians enslaved African-American Christians. Once she appeared at a meeting of the elders of her church, all slaveholders, and dared to suggest that they speak out against slavery. They, of course, demurred.

Angelina's membership among the Presbyterians lasted only a year. In 1827 she left the Presbyterian Church to become a Quaker, believing the Society of Friends offered the liberalism she was looking for. Two years later, she left Charleston to join her sister Sarah in Philadelphia. Sarah had converted to Quakerism in the early 1820s. Angelina was admitted as a member of the Society of Friends in 1831. Soon she fell in love with a fellow Quaker, Edward Bettle, and was grief-stricken when the young man died of cholera in 1832.

Never one to abide by rules that she considered unjust, in 1835 Grimké disobeyed Quaker directives that forbade members from enlisting in organizations outside their sect and joined the Philadelphia Female Anti-Slavery Society. The same year, she drew ire from her Quaker friends when they read in *The Liberator* a pro-abolitionist letter she had written the paper's editor, William Lloyd Garrison. Soon, Grimké was gaining a reputation for her antislavery point of view. Her influential pamphlet, *Appeal to the Christian Women of the South* (1836), argued for black equality and for the slave's natural right to freedom. The American Anti-Slavery Society, which printed her pamphlet, held her work in such regard that she was invited to become an agent for the organization and give talks throughout New England. Sarah Grimké joined her sister's campaign against slavery, and the two women became the first American female agents for the abolitionist cause.

Their lectures began as "parlor talks," but soon their large audiences demanded larger accommodations, and the women spoke in churches. The thought of women lecturing in churches shocked most ministers, but the crowds gathering to listen to the Grimké sisters continued to grow until their audiences numbered in the hundreds. Although initially their talks were directed at women, an increasing number of men appeared among the throngs. Most came to hear Angelina, for of the two sisters she was the better speaker.

Although a few ministers willingly offered their churches to the abolitionists for use as lecture halls, a number of New England clergymen objected. They not only opposed many of the ideas of the radical abolitionists but also felt that God had created women the inferior sex and that females thus had no right to speak in public. In a Pastoral Letter issued in behalf of the General Association of Massachusetts Congregational Churches on July 28, 1837, the Reverend Nehemiah Adams denounced the Garrisonian abolitionists. The letter also berated the Grimké sisters for lecturing in public, which made it difficult for them to find churches willing to open for their talks. Nevertheless, the sisters continued to draw large audiences to their meetings and stopped only in late 1837, when both sisters were overcome by illness.

Angelina began lecturing once again early in 1838 and on February 21, 1838, became the first woman in history to address an American legislative body when she spoke before the Massachusetts state legislature in Boston. Her speaking tour was cut short when she married Theodore Dwight Weld, an abolitionist and supporter of women's rights, on May 14, 1838. Two days later she spoke before the Anti-Slavery Convention of American Women in Pennsylvania Hall and gave one of her finest speeches for the abolitionist cause while an angry mob was poised to riot outside. This was her last speech before her retirement from the lecture circuit to become a wife and mother. Meanwhile, the Society of Friends disowned her for marrying Weld, a non-Quaker. But by this time Angelina had become disillusioned by the Quakers' and other established churches' resistance to the crusade for the immediate emancipation of slaves and joined other abolitionists in rejecting formal theology for a "more Christian" humanitarian creed.

Although she refrained from making further public appearances, throughout her life Angelina remained a supporter of equality for African Americans and for women. In 1839, she and Sarah assisted Weld in the research and writing of his influential book *American Slavery as It Is: Testimony of a Thousand Witnesses.* Angelina died in Hyde Park, Massachusetts, on October 26, 1879.

See also: Antislavery Movement; Grimké, Sarah Moore; Perfectionism; Reform Movements; Woman Suffrage
References: Blanche Glassman Hersh, *The Slavery of Sex: Feminist Abolitionists in America* (1978); Gerda Lerner, *The Grimké Sisters from South Carolina: Rebels against Slavery* (1967); James Brewer Stewart, *Holy Warriors: The Abolitionists and American Slavery* (1976).

Grimké, Sarah Moore (1792–1873)

Although she was not as vocal nor as radical as her younger sister, Angelina Grimké, Sarah Moore Grimké was one of the first women to speak out publicly for abolition and women's rights. Born in Charleston, South Carolina, on November 26, 1792, she was the second daughter and sixth child of John and Mary Smith Grimké. Sarah was raised in a privileged household, ruled by her father, Judge John Faucheraud Grimké, a plantation owner, slaveholder, lawyer, and politician. The judge saw that his children were well-educated in the Episcopal faith as well as in useful secular subjects. The boys were educated in the professions, and the girls were sent to "schools for ladies," where they were expected to learn skills that would make them proper wives and matrons in South Carolina society. They were taught such skills as needlework, drawing,

Sarah Moore Grimké (undated portrait)

singing, and music as well as enough reading, writing, and arithmetic to allow them to manage a household.

Sarah's interests far exceeded those of most young women of her era. She was interested in all that her older brother Thomas was learning, and studied mathematics, geography, history, Greek, and the natural sciences. However, when Sarah asked her father to allow her to study Latin, Judge Grimké said "no." Although Sarah became frustrated over the limits set upon her education, she also could not understand why slave children, who were anxious to learn all they could about messages of the Gospel, were forbidden by law to learn to read the Bible. At one point, she knowingly disobeyed the South Carolina statute and gave her waiting-maid private reading lessons. After the two girls were caught in their act of defiance, Sarah realized that as a female in a male-dominated society, she was as helpless as a slave.

Limits placed upon her sex prevented Grimké from fulfilling her dream of be-coming a lawyer. Yet she felt that she needed a purpose in life—she wanted to do something useful. In about 1816, she attended a revival meeting and decided to give up her lively social life. To reinforce her intent, she engaged in a series of private consultations with a Presbyterian minister. Though she could not at that time hold to the strict path she had set out for herself, later years would find her filled with religious zeal and leading an austere lifestyle.

In the early 1820s, Grimké became interested in joining the Quakers. Always saddened by the institution of slavery, Grimké was impressed when she learned that a number of Quakers had decided to stop the practice of buying, selling, and keeping slaves. The Society of Friends' plain dress as well as the opportunity for women to become Quaker ministers also appealed to Grimké. She moved to Philadelphia, where there was a large Quaker community, and in May 1823 she was formally accepted as a member of the Fourth and Arch Street Meeting of the Society of Friends.

Despite her eagerness to join the Quakers, Grimké soon became discouraged. Quakers stressed spontaneous inspiration as the basis of any remarks made in meeting. This was especially important for anyone desiring to become a minister. Since she did not have a natural ability to speak before large audiences, meetings became stressful for her. Grimké also became frustrated when she was unable to motivate the Friends to work actively to abolish slavery. Though she continued to perform her religious and social duties, by 1835 she had become disenchanted with orthodox Quakerism.

Although Sarah was slower than her sister to become an outspoken abolitionist, in 1835 she joined Angelina in protesting the Friends' discrimination against African Americans, who were required to sit on "colored benches" in Quaker meeting.

In 1836, following a rebuke from an elder when she attempted to speak in meeting, Sarah finally felt able to break away from the orthodox Quakers and allow her conscience to guide her future. She decided to join her sister in her antislavery crusade, and together the women became the nation's first female agents for the abolitionist movement.

Amid controversy over women speaking in public as well as over the issue of slavery, Sarah and her sister drew large crowds. Sarah was still not confident of her ability to lecture before large audiences and allowed Angelina to lead the talks. Late in 1836, Sarah published an antislavery pamphlet, *Epistle to the Clergy of the Southern States,* pointing out contradictions between the teachings of Christianity and the institution of slavery. The indifference toward, or often even the defense of, slavery by people who professed to be Christians caused Sarah to consider rejecting all churches. Her animosity toward the clergy was reinforced when, on July 28, 1837, the General Association of Massachusetts Congregational Churches issued a Pastoral Letter that, without naming names, castigated abolitionist William Lloyd Garrison and the Grimkés for using churches for lecture halls for their talks on "agitating subjects." Further, the Pastoral Letter berated the women for allowing themselves to become public lecturers.

As they defended themselves against those who criticized them, as women, for speaking in public on the slavery issue, the Grimké sisters became advocates for women's rights. Both women began linking the causes of slaves with those of women. In 1838 Sarah published *Letters on the Equality of the Sexes,* which attacked the biblical argument so often used to support theories of women's inferiority. Sarah argued that the Scriptures reflected the male-dominated society that prevailed at the time they were written and that God in fact had intended that men and women be equal. Her *Letters* were well-received by women, and they helped to ignite the women's rights movement.

The Society of Friends finally disowned Sarah Grimké, not for her outspokenness, but for attending Angelina's wedding on May 14, 1838, to a man outside the faith. Sarah had an opportunity to air her grievances against the Friends when Elizabeth Pease, a British Quaker, asked the sisters for information about discrimination within the Society of Friends in America. Sarah obliged by recounting her own and Angelina's experiences with the Quakers of Philadelphia and gathered statements from others who had suffered discrimination as Quakers.

Following Angelina's marriage, both sisters retired from the lecture circuit. Sarah lived with the Welds and helped her sister with domestic duties. Both sisters aided Theodore Dwight Weld as he prepared his most famous work, *American Slavery as It Is: Testimony of a Thousand Witnesses,* published in 1839.

Throughout the balance of her life, Sarah remained interested in the women's rights movement. In 1867, at the age of seventy-five, she completed a book-length translation of French poet Alphonse Lamartine's *Joan of Arc.* In 1870 she joined Angelina and forty other women in a voting demonstration at a Hyde Park, Massachusetts, polling place. The following year she traveled the countryside distributing John Stuart Mill's *The Subjection of Women.* Sarah died December 23, 1873, in Hyde Park.

See also: Antislavery Movement; Female Moral Reform Society; Grimké, Angelina Emily; Pastoral Letter of 1837; Perfectionism; Reform Movements; Woman Suffrage
References: Blanche Glassman Hersh, *The Slavery of Sex: Feminist Abolitionists in America* (1978); Gerda Lerner, *The Grimké Sisters from South Carolina: Rebels against Slavery* (1967); James Brewer Stewart, *Holy Warriors: The Abolitionists and American Slavery* (1976).

Hadassah

Hadassah, the Women's Zionist Organization of America (HWZDA), is the largest Jewish women's organization in the world. Its founder was Henrietta Szold, a Jewish scholar and a convert to the cause of women's rights. She visited Palestine in 1909 and witnessed conditions there that made her an advocate for the ideals of Zionism (a movement for the cause of reestablishing a Jewish national state) for the rest of her life. On February 24, 1912, Szold and a group of women gathered in New York City to form an organization that they called the "Hadassah Chapter of Daughters of Zion." Two years later the name was shortened to Hadassah, the Hebrew name for Queen Esther. The purpose of the organization was to promote Jewish religious and social ideals through education in America and to establish public health facilities and nurses' training in Palestine.

A year after its founding, Hadassah received funding to send two nurses to Palestine and to open a training center for nurses. Unfortunately, the outbreak of World War I prevented the plan for the training center from reaching fruition. At the end of the war, in 1918, the Henrietta Szold Hadassah School of Nursing opened with an enrollment of thirty students. Since then, the organization has built and maintained the Hadassah Medical Organization, which encompasses the Hadassah University Hospital on Mount Scopus, Israel, as well as the Hadassah University Medical Center at Ein Karem, Israel. These and other Hadassah medical facilities serve Muslims, Christians, and Jews.

When Jewish refugees began to arrive in Palestine from Germany in 1933, Szold was approached by Recha Freier, the wife of a German rabbi, who suggested that she help make arrangements for the settlement of German Jewish children in Palestine. Although funds were lacking and no facilities were available for the children, Szold was soon convinced of the necessity for action and became a zealous leader of what became known as Youth Aliyah, Hadassah's relief movement for refugee children. The first group of children arrived in Haifa in 1937, with a total of thirteen thousand escaping Nazi Germany by 1945. Since that time, Hadassah has helped relocate other groups of children, including some from Ethiopia in the 1980s.

Throughout the organization's existence, education has been an important component of Hadassah's program. It currently maintains the Hadassah College of Technology in Jerusalem and operates Hadassah Career Counseling Institute for high school students, young adults, and new immigrants. Hadassah's educational department, long committed to the dissemination of Jewish values and the strengthening of ties between the Jewish communities in the United States and in Israel, produces guides that can be used by beginning or advanced students in such areas as history, literature, Hebrew, and current events. Among Hadassah's publications are *The American Scene,* a magazine issued three times a year; *Hadassah Associates Medbriefs* and *Hadassah Headlines,* quarterly newsletters containing medical news; and the monthly *Hadassah Magazine* that is sent to every member and has the largest circulation of any Jewish publication in the United States. The magazine contains articles on art, medicine, parenting, current affairs, and Hadassah-related people and projects in Israel and the United States.

Headquartered in New York City, Hadassah employs a staff of about 150, serving an organization that has grown to include nearly 400,000 members.

See also: Jews; Szold, Henrietta
References: Jacqueline K. Barrett, ed., *Encyclopedia of Women's Associations Worldwide* (1993); Susan Hill Lindley, *"You Have Stept Out of Your Place": A History of Women and Religion in America* (1996); Simon Noveck, ed., *Great Jewish Personalities in Modern Times* (1960); Abby Schmelling, "Hadassah," in Angela Howard Zophy with Frances M. Kavenik, eds., *Handbook of American Women's History* (1990); Elinor Slater and Robert Slater, *Great Jewish Women* (1994).

Hanaford, Phebe Ann Coffin
(1829–1921)

Universalist minister, feminist, and author Phebe Ann Coffin Hanaford was born in Siasconset on the island of Nantucket, Massachusetts, on May 6, 1829. Her parents, George W. Coffin and Phebe Ann (Barnard) Coffin, were descended from old New England families. Their daughter received a solid education in public and private schools on Nantucket, studied Latin and mathematics with an Episcopal clergyman, and began to teach school herself when she was sixteen. Although she was reared a Quaker, Phebe converted to the Baptist faith following her marriage on December 2, 1849, to Joseph Hibbard Hanaford.

Phebe Hanaford devoted most of her time during the first few years of her married life to raising her two children. At the same time, Hanaford was drawn to the temperance and antislavery causes, and to religious evangelism. She had long been interested in writing and after her marriage began to put her talents to use in support of her crusades. In 1852 she published her first book, *My Brother,* a collection of poetry and prose. It was soon followed by an antislavery work, *Lucretia, the Quakeress* (1853), and *The Best of Books and Its History* (1860), a collection of her lectures on the Bible. Of her fourteen major works, her *Abraham Lincoln* (1865), which sold twenty thousand copies, was probably the most successful. Also popular was her *Life of George Peabody* (1870), a biography of the noted philanthropist.

In the 1860s, Hanaford left the Baptist faith and joined the Universalists. She preached her first sermon while visiting her hometown on Nantucket in 1865, and a year later she substituted for Reverend Olympia Brown at the Universalist Church at South Canton, Massachusetts. Brown encouraged Hanaford to enter the ministry, and in 1867 Hanaford became the pastor at the Universalist Church in Hingham, Massachusetts. A year later, she was ordained as a minister with the American Universalist Association and was formally installed as the pastor at Hingham. She also became the minister of the Universalist parish at Waltham, Massachusetts.

Meanwhile Hanaford had become caught up in the women's rights movement, and in 1869 she helped to organize the American Woman Suffrage Association. Although this was the more conservative of the leading woman suffrage organizations, it seems that she remained on good terms with members of both groups. In later years, she was one of the ministers to lead services at the International Council of Women (1888), and she assisted in the funeral services of both Elizabeth Cady Stanton (1902) and Susan B. Anthony (1906).

Hanaford moved to New Haven, Connecticut, in 1870 to accept a call to the First Universalist Church. While there, she became the first woman to serve as chaplain in a state legislative body in the United States when both the Connecticut house and senate invited her to officiate on several occasions. Later in the 1870s, Hanaford moved to the Church of the Good Shepherd in Jersey City, New Jersey. After three years, she left when the congregation split over the issue of women in the ministry. For several years she preached to her supporters in a public hall. Then in 1884 she returned to New Haven to become pastor of the Second Church (Universalist). In addition to her work in New Haven, Hanaford lectured throughout New England and the mid-Atlantic states. She retired from active preaching in 1891 and settled in New York City. Hanaford died in Rochester, New York, on June 2, 1921.

See also: Woman Suffrage
References: Phebe A. Hanaford, *Life of George Peabody* (1870); Edward T. James, ed., *Notable American Women, 1607–1950,* vol. 2 (1971); *Dictionary of American Biography,* vol. 8; J. Gordon Melton, *Religious Leaders of America* (1991).

Handfasting

Handfasting is the rite of marriage in neo-Paganism and neo-Pagan witchcraft. The ceremony is performed within a magic circle with a high priestess or high priest officiating. A handfasting is intended to last only as long as the couple remains in love, not until death. There may be an exchange of silver or gold rings with the couple's Craft names engraved in runes, a "magical" alphabet of symbols. In some ceremonies the couple jumps over a broomstick for good luck.

The high priestess uses the broom symbolically to sweep away all evil. The great rite of sexual intercourse may also be performed symbolically or in actuality. Great feasting and celebration follow the ceremony.

Since the high priestess or high priest is usually not a legally ordained minister, handfasting ceremonies are normally preceded or followed by a legal marriage ceremony.

See also: Adler, Margot; Wicca; Witchcraft
References: Rosemary Ellen Guiley, *The Encyclopedia of Witches and Witchcraft* (1989); J. Gordon Melton, ed., *Religious Leaders of America* (1991).

Harkness, Georgia Elma (1891–1974)

Prominent Methodist theologian Georgia Elma Harkness was born April 21, 1891, in Harkness, New York. The daughter of J. Warren and Lillie (Merrill) Harkness, she grew up on the family farm near the town that had been named for her grandfather. Georgia had her first religious experience at the age of nine, when she attended a revival meeting led by a traveling evangelist. Five years later, she joined the local Methodist Episcopal Church to which her parents belonged. She maintained her membership in this church for the rest of her life.

After her graduation from high school, Harkness entered Cornell University on a scholarship. While there, she was inspired by the Student Volunteer Movement to commit her life to foreign missions. She was also a member of the Student Christian Association. In 1912 Harkness graduated from Cornell and began teaching school. Six years later, she enrolled in Methodist-affiliated Boston University, from which she earned two master's degrees (M.R.E. and M.A.) in religious education and completed her doctorate in philosophy in 1923.

During her final year of graduate school, Harkness taught religious education at Elmira College in Elmira, New York, and then joined the faculty of the school's philosophy department in 1923. She held that position until 1937. In 1926 Harkness was ordained a local deacon and in 1938 a local elder. (Until 1956, local ordination was the only form of ordination open to Methodist women. The local ordination allowed her to perform most ministerial roles but denied her membership in the Church's Annual Conference.) Harkness readily accepted invitations to preach and was an advocate of women's rights within the church. She published her first book, *Conflicts in Religious Thought*, in 1929.

Harkness's intellectual interests slowly shifted from philosophy to religion. She spent one and a half years at the Union Theological Seminary in New York City (1935–1937) and left Elmira College in 1937 to teach religion at Mount Holyoke College. She was unhappy at the latter college and left in 1939 to teach applied theology at Garrett Biblical Institute (now Garrett-Evangelical Theological Seminary) in Evanston, Illinois. In 1950 Harkness joined the faculty at the Pacific School of Religion in Berkeley, California, again teaching applied theology.

From the early 1940s, Harkness was interested in making theology meaningful to laypeople. In pursuing this goal, she wrote a number of articles and books in a very readable style. Although the simplicity of her language brought her some criticism from academics who accused her of being a popularizer, her work was in keeping with her commitment to bring theology to the laity. Among her many books were *The Dark Night of the Soul* (1945), a discussion of suffering and its religious meaning; *Understanding the Christian Faith* (1947); *Prayer and the Common Life* (1948); *Toward Understanding the Bible* (1954); and *Christian Ethics* (1957).

By the 1950s, Harkness was recognized as an ecclesiastical leader. She worked for Methodism on a national level, beginning in 1944 when she was elected to the church's Board of World Peace, and was a delegate to the general conferences in 1948, 1952, and 1956. In 1948 she was chosen a delegate to the first gathering of the World Council of Churches in Amsterdam and attended later council meetings in Lund, Sweden (1952), and Evanston, Illinois (1956).

Harkness retired from the Pacific School of Religion in 1961 but continued to write and to speak around the country. She supported the "second wave" of the women's movement that began in the late 1960s. By the early 1970s, she was disturbed because women's gains in wages in all areas of employment continued to be small, women were still not well represented in government, and women held few positions in the church hierarchy. Her dissatisfaction with women's progress inspired her to write *Women in Church and Society: A Historical and Theological Inquiry* (1972), hoping that it would arouse her readers into righting injustices toward women. She was one of the first to link history with theology in an attempt to take a broad look at woman's historical place in church and society. When Harkness's career ended, she was the best-known female theologian of her time. Garrett-Evangelical Theological Seminary later named a chair in applied theology in her honor. Harkness died in Claremont, California, on August 21, 1974.

See also: Methodists
References: Henry Warner Bowden, *Dictionary of American Religious Biography*, 2nd ed. (1993); Georgia Harkness, *Women in Church and Society: A Historical and Theological Inquiry* (1972); J. Gordon Melton, *Religious Leaders of America* (1991); Barbara Sicherman and Carol Hurd Green,

eds., *Notable American Women: The Modern Period* (1980).

Harris, Barbara Clementine (1930–)

Born in Philadelphia on June 12, 1930, Barbara Clementine Harris was to become the first female bishop of the Episcopal Church. She was raised an Episcopalian, baptized and confirmed at St. Barnabas Church in Germantown, Pennsylvania. From an early age, she was active within the church. While in her teens, Harris played piano for the church school and also founded the church's Young Adults Group, the largest organization of its type in the city, with fifty to seventy members.

After graduating from high school in 1948, Harris, herself an African American, went to work for Joe Baker Associates, a public relations firm owned by a black man. She excelled in her work there, soon becoming the editor of a publication that endorsed African-American colleges and later attaining the position of president of Baker Associates. In 1968 she joined Sun Oil Company, where she became a top public relations executive.

Outside her paid employment, Harris was active with the racially mixed St. Dismas Society. The St. Dismas Society held religious services in prisons and counseled and visited with inmates. Harris also became a board member of the Pennsylvania Prison Society. Altogether, she was a volunteer in the prisons for fifteen years.

In the early 1960s, Harris joined the civil rights movement and spent her summer vacations helping to educate and register black voters in the South. Harris married in 1962, but the marriage ended in divorce three years later. She participated in the Martin Luther King, Jr.–led march from Selma to Montgomery, Alabama, in 1965.

During these years, Harris increasingly returned to her spiritual roots. In 1968 she transferred to the North Philadelphia Church of the Advocate. When in 1976 the Episcopal Church opened the priesthood to women, Harris was interested, and she began to study for the ministry. In 1979 Harris was ordained a deacon and served as a deacon-in-training in the Church of the Advocate until she was ordained a priest in 1980. Between 1980 and 1984, she was priest-in-charge at St. Augustine-of-Hippo in Norristown and then became interim rector at the Church of the Advocate until 1988. From 1984 to 1988, she served as executive director of the Episcopal Church Publishing Company. On September 24, 1988, Reverend Harris was elected suffragan (assisting) bishop, second in charge of the approximately 100,000-member diocese of Massachusetts. Harris was the first woman and twenty-ninth black to be elected to the bishopric.

There was some controversy over her election to the bishopric: She was divorced (although her predecessor and a male competitor were also); traditionalists believed that since Christ's apostles were male, present-day bishops should also be male; her educational, theological, and ministerial background did not follow the usual path to the episcopate (she had attended the Metropolitan Collegiate Center in Philadelphia in 1976, Villanova from 1977 to 1979, and William Smith College in 1981; had completed seminary requirements; and had eight years of parish experience); and she was viewed by some as too liberal.

Bishop Harris works to see that the church does not ignore such issues as racism, sexism, class discrimination, and the rise of the AIDS epidemic among teenagers. She crusades for the civil rights of AIDS sufferers. She speaks out in favor of women's rights and has long been a supporter of the Union of Black

Episcopalians (UBE), an organization that advocates black participation throughout the church and the eradication of racism among the clergy and in society.

See also: African Americans; Clergy; Episcopal Church; Kelly, Leontine Turpeau Current

References: Aleathia Dolores Nicholson, "Barbara Harris," in Jessie Carney Smith, ed., *Epic Lives: One Hundred Black Women Who Made a Difference* (1993); Beth Schneider, "Harris, Barbara C.," in Dorothy C. Salem, ed., *African American Women: A Biographical Dictionary* (1993); Michael Williams, *The African American Encyclopedia*, vol. 3 (1993).

Healy, Eliza (1846–1918)

Nun, teacher, and the first African American to hold a position of leadership in a religious order in North America, Eliza Healy (later Sister Mary Magdalen) was born in Macon, Georgia, on December 23, 1846. Her father, Michael Morris Healy, was an Irish immigrant plantation owner and her mother, Eliza Clark (Healy), was his slave and wife. Mixed-race marriages were illegal in Georgia, so they were married in a ceremony held in another state. Five of their children— Eliza, her brothers, James Augustine Healy, Patrick Francis Healy, and Alexander Sherwood Healy, and her sister Amanda Josephine—would become active within the Roman Catholic Church in America. When Eliza was a toddler, her father made plans to sell his plantation and move to the North, where he could legally free his family from slavery, but both he and his common-law wife died in 1850. Nevertheless, the executors of his estate sent the younger of the ten Healy children to New York to reside with an older brother. The elder children had previously been sent north to be educated.

Eliza's older brother Hugh assumed responsibility for the children, and Eliza, her brother Eugene, and sister Amanda Josephine were baptized as Catholics in the Church of St. Francis Xavier in New York on June 13, 1851. In September of that year, the children were placed in the care of the Notre Dame sisters in Quebec. Healy received her elementary education with the nuns at St. Johns, Quebec, and her secondary schooling at Villa Maria in Montreal. After graduation, she moved to Boston, where she lived with her brother Eugene and sister Amanda Josephine at the home of their foster parents Mr. and Mrs. Thomas Hodges. Their brother James, whose career in the church was flourishing, purchased a home in West Newton, Massachusetts, for his siblings in 1864. Eliza lived there for ten years. In January 1868, Eliza, Amanda Josephine, and her brother James traveled to Europe and Asia with Mrs. Hodges.

Eventually, Healy made the decision to embark on a religious career, and she entered the novitiate of the Congregation of Notre Dame in Montreal in 1874 to prepare for a career as a nun and teacher. She took her basic vows in 1876, becoming known as Sister Mary Magdalen, and her final vows in 1882. She was assigned as a teacher, first at St. Patrick's School in Montreal and then at various other locations in Ontario and Quebec. Sister Mary Magdalen is credited with restoring a financially faltering school at Huntington, Quebec, to solvency before moving on, in 1898, to the congregation's Mother House in Montreal. There she became director of English studies. After two years she was assigned to the congregation's normal school, also in Montreal.

In 1903 Sister Mary Magdalen was appointed superior of Villa Barlow at St. Albans, Vermont. This was a finishing school with an affiliated convent. Again, she faced the task of returning the school to financial stability, which she accomplished to such an extent that it became one of the most prosperous houses in the

United States. She won the respect of the sisters at the convent for her wisdom, kindness, and pious life, as well as her eagerness for hard work and willingness to observe the same strict rules of discipline that she imposed upon them.

Late in her life, Sister Mary Magdalen was assigned to the post of superior to the Academy of Our Lady of the Blessed Sacrament at Staten Island, New York. She died there on September 13, 1918, as a result of advanced heart problems.

See also: African Americans; Roman Catholic Women's Orders (Nuns)
References: Rayford W. Logan and Michael R. Winston, *Dictionary of Negro Biography* (1982); J. Gordon Melton, *Religious Leaders of America* (1991); Jessie Carney Smith, ed., *Notable Black American Women* (1992).

Heck, Barbara Ruckle (1734–1804)

Known as "the mother of American Methodism," Barbara Ruckle Heck has been credited by many as the cofounder of the Methodist Church in the United States. Born in Ballingrane, Ireland, in 1734, she joined a society of Methodists when she was eighteen years old. Barbara Ruckle married Paul Heck in 1760 and immigrated to New York soon after. There were no Methodist churches in New York when she arrived, so she joined the Trinity Lutheran Church in New York City. Her daughter was baptized in that church and her cousin Phillip Embury, a Methodist preacher, also belonged to the Lutheran Church.

In 1766 Heck was shocked when she came across a group of acquaintances playing cards in her brother's home. Worried about the spiritual welfare of her family, friends, and acquaintances, she persuaded Phillip Embury to open his home and to return to preaching. A congregation of five heard the first Methodist sermon in New York City in 1766, but soon the gatherings outgrew the Embury home. Embury proposed

they build a small wooden structure on leased land, but Heck envisioned a larger, permanent church. Heck's wishes prevailed, and a large stone chapel was built on a site on St. John Street. The first service in the new church was held October 30, 1768. There is some debate over whether Heck or Robert Strawbridge, an early Methodist preacher in the Baltimore, Maryland, area, should receive credit for founding American Methodism. Both worked to found Methodist societies at about the same time, she in New York and he in Maryland. But it was Heck's society that achieved permanent status and constructed the first Methodist church building in the United States. The church became the center of early Methodism in America and was the headquarters of Joseph Pilmore, an officially authorized Methodist missionary who arrived in New York City in 1769.

Soon after Pilmore's arrival, the Hecks moved to the Lake Champlain area, where Barbara organized another Methodist society. With the American Revolution threatening, the Hecks, who were Loyalists, moved to Sorel near Montreal, Canada, in 1774, and Paul Heck enlisted in the British army. Barbara Heck established a Methodist society there. She died in Ontario, Canada, on August 17, 1804.

See also: Methodists
References: Henry Warner Bowden, *Dictionary of American Religious Biography*, 2nd ed. (1993); Edith Deen, *Great Women of the Christian Faith* (1959); Phyllis J. Read and Bernard L. Witlieb, *The Book of Women's Firsts* (1992); Rosemary Radford Ruether and Rosemary Skinner Keller, *Women and Religion in America*, vol. 2 (1986); William Warren Sweet, *Methodism in American History* (1933).

Henderlite, Rachel (1905–1991)

Born in Henderson, North Carolina, on December 30, 1905, Rachel Henderlite became the first woman to be ordained a minister of the Southern Presbyterian Church in the United States. She earned a bachelor of arts degree in English from Agnes Scott College in Decatur, Georgia, in 1930 and then taught high school for a year before returning to college to pursue a degree in biblical education. In 1936 she received a master of arts degree from the Biblical Seminary at New York University and then began teaching—first at Mississippi Synodical College in Holly Springs and then at Montreat College near Black Mountain, North Carolina. In 1944 she began a sixteen-year professorship at the Presbyterian School of Christian Education in Richmond, Virginia, while completing a doctorate at Yale Divinity School (1949). While in Richmond, Henderlite helped found the city's first African-American Presbyterian Church, and in 1963 she participated in the Reverend Martin Luther King, Jr.'s historic March on Washington. During the 1950s, she was a visiting professor at Kinjo College in Nagoya, Japan (1950–1951), and was director of educational research on the Board of Education of the Presbyterian Church, U.S. (1957–1959). From 1959 to 1965, she was the board's director of curriculum development.

Henderlite did not actively seek ordination to the ministry until colleagues urged her to do so. In 1965, upon receiving the unanimous approval of the 125 commissioners in the Richmond, Virginia, presbytery, Henderlite became minister of the All Souls Presbyterian Church in Richmond. The following year, she became the first woman professor of Christian education at the Austin Presbyterian Theological Seminary in Texas. She retired from the seminary in 1972 as a professor emerita. In 1976 Henderlite became the first woman president of the Presbyterial Council of Church Union. She was president of the Consultation of Church Union in 1980,

at which time ten leading Protestant denominations gathered together to work toward ecumenical unity.

Henderlite published a number of theological works during her career. Among them are *Exploring the Old Testament* (1945); *Exploring the New Testament* (1946); *A Call to Faith* (1955); *Paul, Christian and World Traveler* (1957); *Forgiveness and Hope* (1961); and *The Holy Spirit in Christian Education* (1964). In keeping with her commitment to education, all of her books were written principally for the lay reader.

In 1984 Henderlite was honored with the prestigious Union Medal from Union Theological Seminary, and in 1990 a scholarship was established in her name at the Presbyterian School of Christian Education in Richmond. Rachel Henderlite died of a heart attack in Austin, Texas, on November 6, 1991.

References: Lois A. Boyd and R. Douglas Brackenridge, *Presbyterian Women in America: Two Centuries of a Quest for Status*, 2nd ed. (1996); "Rachel Henderlite: First Woman Ordained by Presbyterian Church, U.S. Taught Six Years at Austin Seminary," obituary (c. November 19, 1991); "Rachel Henderlite: 1905–1991," *The Presbyterian Outlook* (December 2–9, 1991); "Rachel Henderlite Dies at Her Austin Home," *Windows* (November 1991); Phyllis J. Read and Bernard L. Witlieb, *The Book of Women's Firsts* (1992).

Higginson, Thomas Wentworth (1823–1911)

Radical minister, politician, soldier, and author Thomas Wentworth Storrow Higginson was one of the leading male advocates of women's rights of the nineteenth century. He was born December 22, 1823, in Cambridge, Massachusetts, the youngest of the ten children of Stephen and Louisa (Storrow) Higginson. Although he dropped "Storrow" from his name prior to entering college, historians believe that his mother had considerable influence upon his life, especially in the realm of religion. Living in the shadow of Harvard College, Thomas entered the school when he was thirteen years old and graduated second in his class in 1841, when he was seventeen. Following graduation, he began teaching but was unhappy in that profession. After two years, he returned to Harvard as a graduate student. He then spent three years during which he could not decide on the direction of his advanced study. Then in 1846 he entered the senior class of Harvard's Divinity School, graduating in 1847.

During the six years from 1841 to 1847, Higginson became drawn to what would become his two favorite causes, woman suffrage and abolitionism. He was so opposed to slavery that at the age of twenty-two he declared that he would do everything in his power to promote the dissolution of the Union. Despite his radical positions, Higginson was able to obtain a position as pastor of the Unitarian First Religious Society of Newburyport, Massachusetts. He both began his career as a clergyman and married his fiancée, Mary Elizabeth Channing, in September 1847. An outspoken pastor, Higginson soon sought a broader audience and unsuccessfully ran for Congress as a Free Soil candidate in 1850. He left the First Religious Society but remained in Newburyport until he accepted a call at a Free Church at Worcester, Massachusetts, where he remained until the outbreak of the Civil War in 1861.

During the 1850s, the cause of abolition took precedence over other reforms with which Higginson was concerned. On May 25, 1854, he led hundreds of men in the storming of the courthouse in Boston in a failed attempt to free a well-educated fugitive slave named Anthony Burns. Following the passage of the Kansas-Nebraska Act in 1854, Higginson worked to see Kansas admitted into the Union as a free state. In 1856 he published an antislavery tract, *A Ride through Kansas*. During the Civil War, he was captain of the 51st Massachusetts Volunteers until he accepted and retained command as colonel of the 1st South Carolina Volunteers, the first black regiment in the Union army (November 1862 to May 1864). Complications from a slight wound caused him to leave the army. Later Higginson recounted his experiences with the South Carolina Volunteers in *Army Life in a Black Regiment* (1870).

When he left the army, Higginson joined his wife in Newport, Rhode Island, and began a career as a writer. His only novel, *Malbone* (1869), and collected sketches, *Oldport Days* (1873), were among the works he produced there. In 1877 his wife died. He then spent several months traveling abroad before settling again in Cambridge, Massachusetts. Higginson married Mary Potter Thacher in February 1879. From the time of his return to Cambridge and throughout the rest of his life, Higginson devoted his energies to writing and to reforms, especially women's rights.

Among Higginson's writings in support of women's rights are *Women and the Alphabet: A Series of Essays* (1859), which argues that women's equality was primarily dependent on education; and *Women and Men* (1888), which again pleads the case for equal opportunity for women. From 1870 to 1884, he edited the *Woman's Journal* with suffragist leader Lucy Stone and her husband, Henry Blackwell. Higginson died in Cambridge at the age of 87 on May 9, 1911.

See also: Antislavery Movement
References: *Dictionary of American Biography,* vol. 5 (1932, 1933); Elizabeth Frost-Knappman, *Women's Progress in America* (1994); James Brewer Stewart, *Holy Warriors: The Abolitionists and American Slavery* (1976).

Hispanic Americans

Hispanic Americans, or Latino/Latina people, are of a variety of national origins: Approximately 61 percent are Mexican; 12 percent are Puerto Rican; 5 percent are Cuban; 13 percent come from the Caribbean, Central America, and South America; and 9 percent are described as "other," mostly descendants of very early, and often Spanish, settlers in the southwestern United States. There is also considerable racial diversity among Hispanics. For example, in the 1990 census, 55 percent of Mexican Americans considered themselves to be "white" and 38 percent described themselves as "mestizo" or "Chicano." Only 48 percent of Puerto Ricans on the mainland listed themselves as "white," but 84 percent of Cubans described themselves as "white" (Dolan and Deck, 1994, pp. 6–7).

Until recently, religion played a compelling role in the lives of Hispanic women. Roman Catholicism, which teaches that women must be subordinate to their husbands, is the predominant religion in Hispanic cultures. Women, however, have long been the primary carriers of the religious belief system, tending to the religious education of their children. Scholars of Mexican American culture have found that gender divisions are very much in evidence during religious celebrations, particularly postbaptismal and funeral celebrations. Men visit and talk outside the home while women prepare food, and then women serve the men before they themselves eat. At funerals women have traditionally done most of the praying.

Since the 1960s, Hispanic women's roles have expanded both within the Roman Catholic Church and outside it. The institutional church is dominated by non-Hispanics, but old, wise, and pious women in Hispanic communities play important religious roles outside of the church. Home altars are important to Hispanic cultures, and these older women play leading roles in fostering them. Before Vatican II (1962–1964), Latinas' roles were mainly through confraternities and sodalities, which were lay bodies of women doing work useful to their parishes. Some organizations, like the Legion of Mary, included both women and men. But Ana María Díaz-Stevens found in her study of Hispanic women that even before Vatican II, Latinas' lay organizations had more numbers, resources, and dynamism than organizations of Hispanic men or non-Hispanics (Díaz-Stevens and Stevens-Arroyo, 1998, pp. 254–259).

The strength of the influence of the Roman Catholic Church in the everyday lives of Hispanics has waned in recent decades. This may be partly due to the fact that Hispanic men (as well as women) have long had to struggle for recognition in religion in the United States. The first Hispanic Roman Catholic bishop, the Mexican-American Patricio Flores, was ordained in San Antonio in 1970, almost a century after the first African-American bishop (James Augustine Healy, 1875). Some Hispanic women have joined Roman Catholic sisterhoods, but they have frequently been disappointed to find that their training separated them from the Hispanic culture.

The first Latina to achieve leadership within the Roman Catholic Church in America was Encarnacin Padilla de Armas (d. 1992). Born into a wealthy Puerto Rican family, she married a Cuban. Upon his death, she had to seek employment to survive. Puerto Rican independence and the Church were her passions. She helped Msgr. Ivan Illich set up the Institution for Intercultural Communication in Ponce, Puerto Rico, and she challenged Francis Cardinal Spellman on his responsibilities to New York Puerto Ricans.

Since Vatican II the Hispanic woman's role in religion has grown much more rapidly than previously, and the women themselves have sought to work within their own cultural groups. A survey in the early 1970s found that among Hispanic sisters only 25 of 961 were in ministry to their own people. Then, in April 1971, fifty nuns from eight states gathered in Houston, Texas, to address the problem. The result was the founding of *Las Hermanas* for the purpose of providing more active service to the Hispanic people. *Las Hermanas,* a Catholic organization for women and women's ministry, did for all Hispanic women in religious orders what the organization of Mexican-American priests, PADRES (formed a year earlier), did for Hispanic men. They gained national influence.

Studies have found that through the present, Mexican-American women in the southwestern United States have long been more dependable than men as volunteers for church fundraisers. As was the case for hundreds of thousands of American women during the nineteenth century, church work has offered Mexican-American women an opportunity to learn leadership and organizational skills under circumstances acceptable to their society and culture. Yolanda Tarango, and theologian Ada María Isasi-Díaz, represent a feminist element within the Hispanic population who are attempting to reform the Catholic Church by removing the sexism ingrained in its structure and some of its tenets. They feel that the patriarchy of the Roman Catholic Church has hurt women deeply, and they call upon the Church to repent. They subscribe to "Hispanic Women's Liberation Theology," in which liberation, not equality, is the goal, for they contend that equality within a patriarchal church and cultural framework would not be sufficient (Isasi-Díaz and Tarango, 1996, pp. x–xii, 3).

While Roman Catholicism remains the predominant religion within the Hispanic community, Protestant denominations have long been experiencing growth. In 1990 it was estimated that approximately 20 percent of the 20 million Hispanics in the United States are Protestant. Among the traditional Protestant churches, the Southern Baptists probably have the largest population of Hispanics. Pentecostal churches have also attracted large numbers of Latinos and Latinas. Some are now serving as pastors within Pentecostal and other denominations. Among the Hispanic women who are preachers in Pentecostal churches are Leonicia Rosado and Consuelo Urquiza. Overall, the Protestant churches have offered Hispanic women a greater range of choices for religious service.

References: Ana María Díaz-Stevens, "Latinas and the Church," and Joan Moore, "The Social Fabric of the Hispanic Community since 1965," in Jay P. Dolan and Allan Figueroa Deck, eds., *Hispanic Catholic Culture in the U.S.: Issues and Concerns* (1994); Ana María Díaz-Stevens and Anthony M. Stevens-Arroyo, *Recognizing the Latino Resurgence in U.S. Religion: The Emmaus Paradigm* (1998); Ada María Isasi-Díaz and Fernando F. Segovia, eds., *Hispanic/Latino Theology: Challenge and Promise* (1996); Ada María Isasi-Díaz and Yolanda Tarango, *Hispanic Women—Prophetic Voice in the Church: Toward a Hispanic Women's Liberation Theology* (1988); Vicki L. Ruiz, *From out of the Shadows: Mexican Women in Twentieth-Century America* (1998); Moises Sandoval, *On the Move: A History of the Hispanic Church in the United States* (1990); Norma Williams, *The Mexican American Family: Tradition and Change* (1990).

Holiness Movement

The Holiness movement, which emerged in the middle of the nineteenth century, had its origins in Methodism, emphasizing the second blessing of sanctification, or holiness. For several reasons, the movement was open to women preachers and leaders. Believers viewed sanctification by the Holy Spirit as a more important qualification for preaching than formal education, and many women who were sanctified felt that they were called to preach. Also, there were those who felt that since women helped to bring sin into the world, they should help to remove it.

Among the most influential of the early Holiness preachers was Phoebe Worrall Palmer, a Methodist woman whose famous "Tuesday Meetings for the Promotion of Holiness" began in 1835 (though she herself did not experience sanctification until 1837) and continued for thirty-seven years. Among the many prominent people who had attended Palmer's meetings was temperance leader Frances Willard, who as a young woman was involved in the movement. From the 1860s to the early 1910s, African-American evangelist Amanda Berry Smith led Holiness revivals in both black and white camp meetings in the United States and participated in Holiness conferences and evangelistic speaking engagements throughout the world. Hannah Whitall Smith, who is noted for her 1875 book, the *Christian's Secret of a Happy Life,* was a well-known leader of the Holiness movement by the time she became the first superintendent of the Woman's Christian Temperance Union's Evangelical Department.

Although Holiness advocates initially preferred to remain within the Methodist Church, their strong emphasis on the second blessing of sanctification combined with the emotionalism of their revivals eventually led to a split from the church and the formation of separate denominations. In a time when women were barred from most pulpits, they were allowed to preach in a number of the Holiness congregations. For example, Albert B. Simpson, founder of the Christian and Missionary Alliance (CMA) in 1885, gave women a prominent place in church ministry and also included them on the executive board committee and as professors of Bible study. In 1887, one-half of all the CMA's vice presidents were women. The Church of God (organized in 1881) hired several female evangelists, and by 1902 approximately one-fourth of its two hundred leaders were women. From the time of its founding in 1894, the Church of the Nazarene accepted the idea of female clergy and ordained women by 1908. In 1930 approximately 30 percent of the preachers in the Pilgrim Holiness Church were women. Alma Bridwell White, who broke with traditional Methodists over her exuberant preaching style, formed her own Holiness denomination, the Pillar of Fire Church, in 1901 and proclaimed herself the first female bishop in church history. But as in the Salvation Army, which from the late nineteenth century was aligned with the Holiness movement, the percentage of women in prominent roles in Holiness churches began to decline in the middle of the twentieth century while the proportion of women leaders in mainline churches grew. Nevertheless, the participants in the Holiness movement played an important part in bolstering the cause of women's rights in the late nineteenth century and the early decades of the twentieth century, especially in the realm of religious leadership.

See also: Palmer, Phoebe Worrall; Salvation Army; Smith, Amanda Berry; Smith, Hannah Whitall; White, Alma Bridwell
References: Sherry Sherrod DuPree, ed., *Biographical Dictionary of African-American Holiness-Pentecostals, 1880–1990* (1989); Nancy Hardesty, Lucille Sider Dayton, and Donald W. Dayton, "Women in the Holiness Movement: Feminism in the Evangelical Tradition," in Rosemary Radford Ruether and Eleanor McLaughlin, eds., *Women of Spirit: Female Leadership in the Jewish and Christian Traditions* (1979); Janette Hassey, *No Time for Silence* (1986); Edward T. James, ed., *Notable American Women: 1607–1950,* vol. 3 (1971); Susan Hill Lindley, *"You Have Stept Out of Your Place": A History of Women and Religion in America* (1996); Vinson Synan, *The Holiness-Pentecostal Tradition: Charismatic Movements in the Twentieth Century,* 2nd ed. (1997).

Hopkins, Emma Curtis (1853–1925)

Emma Curtis Hopkins, the founder of the New Thought movement, was born to Lydia (Phillips) and Rufus Curtis at Killingly, Connecticut, on September 2, 1853. Both parents were well educated and enjoyed reading. Their daughter Emma attended Woodstock Academy in Connecticut and, after graduation, remained for a while as an instructor. In July 1874, she married George Irving Hopkins, an English teacher. The marriage was not happy and eventually ended in divorce. Their only child, John, died in 1905.

Hopkins had a healing experience through Christian Science in 1881, and in 1883 she moved to Boston to learn more about that religion by enrolling in Mary Baker Eddy's course. Three months later, Hopkins was made a practitioner of Christian Science. Eddy was so impressed with her student's abilities that in 1884 she appointed her editor of the *Christian Science Journal.* But the relationship between the two women quickly deteriorated as Hopkins sought spiritual truth by consulting sources beyond the writings of Eddy. By 1886 Hopkins had moved with her husband to Chicago, where in the spring of that year she established an office as an independent practitioner of Christian Science. A year later, Hopkins founded in her home what was to become the Christian Science Theological Seminary, and soon her students created the Hopkins Metaphysical Association. Hopkins was president of the seminary and chief writer for the magazine *Christian Metaphysical* (1887–1897). A permanent headquarters was established in Chicago in 1888 for what would become known as the New Thought movement.

Hopkins developed a large following of people who were interested in pursuing independent spiritual freedom, in finding cures through the mind, and in understanding God's existence in all living things. Hopkins emphasized mysticism in her teaching and writing, drawing ideas from the Bible and from non-Christian scripture as well as from great philosophers. Her theology was markedly different from Eddy's in its development of a strong feminist position. Hopkins believed that throughout history God had been revealed in three distinct parts: the Father (during the period of the patriarchs); the Son (in whose time the lower classes had begun to rise from servitude); and the Mother Spirit (evidenced by the elevation of women during the nineteenth century). As J. Gordon Melton points out in *Religious Leaders of America* (1991), Hopkins thus was the first woman in modern times to link the idea of a feminine deity with the rise in the status of women. Although Eddy denounced her as an upstart and her instruction as incorrect or misleading, Hopkins's followers praised her as an effective and persuasive teacher.

The first class graduated from her seminary in January 1889. At that time Hopkins assumed the role of a Christian bishop and ordained the graduates to the ministry. In the seminary's first four years, most of the 111 students to complete the program and to be ordained by Hopkins were women.

Hopkins retired from her work in Chicago in 1895 and moved to New York City. She taught some courses, but for most of the remaining thirty years of her life she limited her teaching to several select students whom she taught privately. Among her private pupils were author Ella Wheeler Wilcox, essayist John Jay Chapman, and literary hostess Mabel Dodge Luhan. Between 1920 and 1922 she wrote her most famous work, *High Mysticism.* Hopkins's writings, together with her classes at the seminary, combined to influence religious thought from coast to coast. Her teachings had tremendous impact upon men and women who founded their own independent metaphysical groups. Among Hopkins's students were Charles and Myrtle Fillmore (cofounders of the Unity School of Christianity), Malinda Cramer (founder of Divine Science), and Annie Rix Militz (founder of the Homes of Truth). J. Gordon Melton notes that every major contemporary New Thought organization is rooted in Hopkins's teaching.

Emma Curtis Hopkins died of a heart attack in New York City on April 8, 1925.

See also: Eddy, Mary Baker; Fillmore, Myrtle Page; Militz, Annie Rix
References: Henry Warner Bowden, *Dictionary of American Religious Biography,* 2nd ed., (1993); James T. Edwards, ed., *Notable American Women: 1607–1950,* vol. 2 (1971); Stephen Gottschalk, *The Emergence of Christian Science in American Religious Life* (1973); J. Gordon Melton, *Encyclopedic Handbook of Cults in America* (1986, 1992); J. Gordon Melton, *Religious Leaders of America* (1991).

Howe, Julia Ward (1819–1910)

Fervent abolitionist, author, and social reformer Julia Ward Howe was born in New York City on May 27, 1819, the daughter of Samuel Ward, a wealthy Episcopal banker, and Julia (Cutler) Ward. Until she was nine years old, she received her education from nurses and governesses. She then continued her studies at private schools for young ladies. Julia loved music and both sang and played the piano. Her mother died when Julia was five years old, and in the years that followed she received a strict upbringing. Kept at home and prohibited from socializing in the manner of other young women, she spent her enforced isolation reading and writing. During the brief time span of 1839 to 1840, Julia lost both her father and a brother, Henry. She turned to religion for consolation, but instead of experiencing the joy of conversion, she became overcome with feelings of guilt for not having appreciated her father's solicitude. Soon she was pouring out her misery in poems. Eventually she turned toward a more liberal Christianity that believed that although humankind was by no means perfect, people could reform themselves. In April 1843 she married Samuel Gridley Howe ("Chev"), a doctor, reformer, and head of the Perkins Institution and Massachusetts Asylum for the Blind in Boston. Throughout their marriage Chev, who was about twenty years her senior, sought to restrict his wife's activities outside their home.

Following her marriage, Howe grew attracted to Unitarianism. Her first child, a baby girl born March 12, 1844, was christened by Unitarian and social reformer Theodore Parker. By the winter of 1846, she was regularly attending Parker's rather unorthodox services. But at her husband's urging, she began attending services at the Church of the Disciples. James Freeman Clarke, who was noted for his theological and social radicalism, was the church pastor. Though she preferred Parker and sometimes sneaked to the Melodeon to hear him preach, she was never quite able to accept his denial of the divinity of Jesus Christ. Both Clarke and Parker preached against the institution of slavery, and Howe soon joined the abolitionist movement.

Howe, who read Greek, Latin, and the philosophical works of Immanuel Kant, began writing and publishing her own works in the mid-1850s. She published her first volume of poetry, *Passion Flowers,* in 1854. This book had little success, nor did her subsequent pre–Civil War works, which included *Words for the Hour* (1857), her second book of poems; *Leonora, or the World's Own* (1857), a melodrama that shocked Bostonians; and *A Trip to Cuba* (1860), a travelogue in a style popular at the time. Meanwhile, she assisted her husband with the publication of the *Commonwealth,* an antislavery newspaper, although he preferred to keep her out of his business affairs and vehemently objected to her participating in any type of public activity.

Not long after the outbreak of the Civil War in 1861, Howe visited an army camp outside Washington, D.C. The military scene inspired her to write a new poem, "Battle Hymn of the Republic," set to the music of an old folk tune that had also been used for "John Brown's Body." Published in the February 1862 issue of *Atlantic Monthly,* the song quickly became the semiofficial song of the Union army. Howe received $5 for it. The "hymn" was religious in tone, with much of its inspiration coming from the Bible. Howe's biographer, Deborah Pickman Clifford, observes that the verses reflect Howe's return to the stern evangelical creed of her childhood. Howe envisioned the Union cause as part of the ongoing conflict between the forces of God and the powers of evil.

From the time that she began involvement in antislavery work, Howe found herself working more and more with women. She discovered that they had interests in common outside the home, and by 1868 she had converted to the suffrage cause. Howe became a wholehearted participant in the woman suffrage movement. She was a leader of both the New England Woman Suffrage Association and the American Woman Suffrage Association for many years. A proponent of the ordination of women, Howe herself frequently preached in Unitarian pulpits. She also became an advocate for temperance and for the cause of peace and, in 1871, became the first president of the American branch of the Woman's International Peace Association. In 1872 she blamed the failure of the movement to organize a women's international peace congress on the fact that too many women interpreted literally Saint Paul's strictures against women preachers. Howe's husband, Chev, who had long opposed her speaking in public, died in January 1876.

Throughout her long life, Howe continued to write, publishing travel books, poetry, collections of essays, and biographies. None of these works was particularly popular, however, and her celebrity as a writer continued to be based primarily upon the "Battle Hymn of the Republic." In 1908 she became the first woman to be elected to the American Academy of Arts and Letters. After her death in Newport, Rhode Island, on October 17, 1910, more than four thousand people attended her funeral at Boston's Symphony Hall.

See also: Antislavery Movement; Clarke, James Freeman; Parker, Theodore; Unitarians/Universalists
References: Deborah Pickman Clifford, *Mine Eyes Have Seen the Glory: A Biography of Julia Ward Howe* (1979); Eleanor Flexner, *Century of Struggle: The Woman's Rights Movement in the United States* (1970); Mary H. Grant, *Private Woman, Public Person: An Account of the Life of Julia Ward Howe from 1819 to 1868* (1994); Robert McHenry, ed., *Liberty's Women* (1980); Edward L. Queen II et al., *The Encyclopedia of American Religious History* (1996).

Hutchinson, Anne Marbury (1591–1643)

Anne Marbury Hutchinson, the first woman in America to challenge the orthodox teachings of Puritans and to create her own religious sect, was born in Alford, Lincolnshire, England, to Francis and Bridget (Dryden) Marbury. The exact date of her birth is not known, but she was baptized in the Anglican Church on July 20, 1591, a ceremony that usually occurred three days after a child's birth. Anne received her schooling from her father and, it seems, inherited from him a rebellious spirit and an eagerness

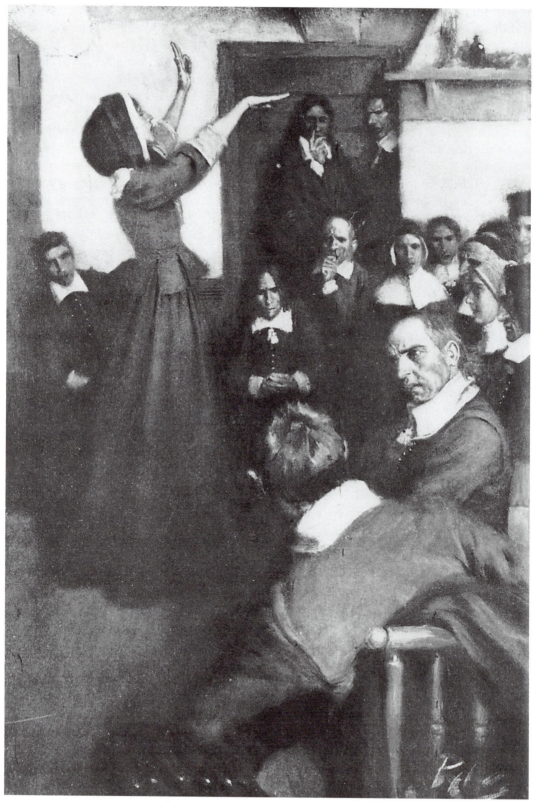

Anne Marbury Hutchinson was the first woman in America to challenge the orthodox teachings of her Puritan church (engraving from Harper's Monthly, February 1901).

to question authority. Francis Marbury was a schoolmaster and an Anglican minister who as a young preacher had twice been censured and imprisoned by his clerical superiors when he had demanded stricter training and better education of those aspiring to the ministry. Such criticism of church policy was tantamount to criticizing the queen, for Elizabeth I headed the Church of England. Shortly before Anne's birth, Francis Marbury was again censured by his superiors and removed from the pulpit when he began denouncing aspects of policies and ritual associated with the Church of England. He was unable to return to his profession for three years.

In 1605 the family moved to London, where Anne remained until her marriage to William Hutchinson, a wealthy businessman, on August 9, 1612. The marriage was a happy one and, unlike most unions at the time, was a partnership of equals. The couple lived in Alford for twenty-two years, during which time Anne gave birth to fourteen of her fifteen children.

At about the time the Hutchinsons settled in Alford and began their family, female preachers were beginning to practice throughout England. Although the established church was hostile to the idea of women ministers, Anne was supportive of women in the clergy. She was especially fond of one, the "Woman of Ely," who made a lasting impression upon her. Both Anne and William became intrigued when they learned of a young male minister, John Cotton, vicar of St. Botolph's in Boston, Lincolnshire. Cotton was an Anglican minister with Puritan leanings, known as a brilliant preacher and an excellent orator. Part of his appeal was his softening of the concept that humans were born into sin, telling his followers that people fell out of grace as a result of their own sinful actions, not through original sin. It was not through good works but by the grace of God that one might enjoy salvation. This doctrine likely comforted Anne, who lost three children, including two daughters who died within weeks of each other in 1630.

William and Anne Hutchinson often traveled to Boston to listen to Cotton's sermons, and soon Anne held meetings at her home in Alford, where she discussed Cotton's sermons and presented her reinterpretations of those sermons and the Bible. Most of those attending her meetings were women.

In 1633 John Cotton was denounced by Anglican authorities and banished to the Massachusetts Bay Colony, where he became a well-respected clergyman. The Hutchinsons, who had for several years been considering a move to New England to escape crackdowns on religious dissenters and restrictions on business enterprises under King Charles I, decided to follow their minister to the colony.

The Hutchinsons arrived in Boston, Massachusetts Bay Colony, in September 1634. Both William and Anne quickly made friends, prospered, and were admitted to the highest level of colonial society. Anne, a skilled nurse and midwife, was greatly admired by the women but was held in suspicion by male leaders like her neighbor, former governor John Winthrop, who feared she was using her midwifery skills to advance plots against them.

It was not long before Anne again was holding meetings in her home to discuss her interpretations of the Scriptures and of John Cotton's sermons. She accepted the doctrine of the covenant of grace, which assured that faith alone would lead to salvation, and rejected the covenant of works, which was based on original sin and required individual "good works." Anne reinterpreted Cotton's sermons well beyond his intended messages. Although Cotton insisted that those among the elect must be entirely free of religious or political control by anyone who had not undergone a conversion experience, Anne expanded his ideas into a broad attack on clerical authority.

She eventually contended that the only clergymen in the colony who had undergone a conversion experience were Cotton and her brother-in-law John Wheelwright. All others lacked authority over those who, like her, had been saved. And she disagreed with many of the laws that the Puritan leaders had imposed upon the colonists. The requirement that the Sabbath be strictly observed particularly irked her, for it did not take into account circumstances such as sickness and childbirth that might cause people, especially women, to occasionally remain at home.

The crowds gathering at Anne Hutchinson's meetings grew. Soon men as well as women were in her audiences. Among the attendees were some of Boston's most prominent citizens, including the new young governor, Henry Vane. Her doctrine challenged authority and was more permissive than that of orthodox Puritanism, allowing the affluent Massachusetts Bay merchants and craftsmen to use their own consciences to guide them in their business affairs.

Anne's following grew to the point that by 1636 Hutchinsonianism was being argued throughout the community and beyond, and the town of Boston was split between Hutchinsonians and orthodox Puritans. Her detractors called Anne and her followers "Antinomians," a sixteenth and seventeenth-century pejorative term meaning "against the law," or "Familists," linking Hutchinsonians with a radical European sect. The only clergyman to side with Anne was her brother-in-law John Wheelwright. Historian Selma R. Williams, in *Divine Rebel: The Life of Anne Marbury Hutchinson,* found that John Cotton was deeply intent on his studies of theology at the time and mostly avoided involvement in the controversy.

The conflict between the Hutchinsonians and the establishment came to a head in 1637, when Anne's followers refused to supply soldiers, supplies, or money to the military for their expedition against the Pequot Indians. Newly elected governor John Winthrop found their response unforgivable.

Winthrop called for a religious synod, the first to be held in New England. Lasting nine days, from August 30 to September 7, 1637, it dealt a powerful blow to the Hutchinsonians and to Anne herself. The synod found scores of the opinions of Anne and her followers to be erroneous or blasphemous and denounced her, as a woman, for holding large religious meetings in her home.

In November Anne was called to trial before the General Court (legislature) on charges of heresy. Her knowledge of Scripture proved superior to that of her interrogators. However, she made a slip that sealed her fate when she claimed that she had received direct revelation from the Holy Spirit, for Puritans believed that such revelations had ended in biblical times.

Anne, forty-six years old and pregnant with her sixteenth child, was banished from Massachusetts Bay Colony. In the spring of 1638, she joined her family and friends in a new settlement on the island of Aquidneck in Narragansett Bay in present-day Rhode Island. Shortly after her arrival, she suffered a painful miscarriage, delivering a noticeably deformed baby. In the seventeenth century, such a birth was considered a sign that the child's parents had sinned. When reports of this "monstrous birth" reached Massachusetts Bay, authorities accepted the event as confirmation that they had been right in their actions against Anne Hutchinson.

In 1642 William Hutchinson died, and Anne and her six youngest children moved to the Pelham Bay area of Long Island, a part of the Dutch colony of

New Netherland. The following year Anne and five of her children were massacred by Indians. Only her youngest daughter was spared.

See also: Calvinism; Puritans

References: Emery Battis, *Saints and Sectaries: Anne Hutchinson and the Antinomian Controversy in the Massachusetts Bay Colony* (1962); Lyle Koehler, *A Search for Power: The "Weaker Sex" in Seventeenth-Century New England* (1980); Winnifred King Rugg, *Unafraid: A Life of Anne Hutchinson* (1930); Selma R. Williams, *Divine Rebel: The Life of Anne Marbury Hutchinson* (1981).

International Association of Women Ministers

The International Association of Women Ministers (IAWM) was organized in the Young Men's Christian Association (YMCA) building in St. Louis, Missouri, on November 21, 1919. M. Madeline Southard was both the founder and the first president of the association. Although most major Christian denominations did not ordain women clergy at that time, when the first issue of the IAWM's quarterly journal, *The Woman's Pulpit,* was released in 1922, it listed 150 members. Since its founding, the organization has grown to include members from North America, Europe, Asia, Africa, South America, and Australia, and it is open to ordained, licensed, certified, and rostered ministers and to women who meet the requirements for ordination but whose denominations do not permit women to serve as ministers. The IAWM also offers membership to retired ministers, to female college or theological school students intending to enter the Christian ministry, and to male clergy and others who subscribe to the purposes and goals of the association.

The IAWM promotes the development of an international and ecumenical fellowship among women ministers and equal ecclesiastical rights for women. It also encourages women in their study for the Christian ministry and in its brochures urges women to grow as women in ministry and to "participate in continuing education for efficiency in Christian ministry." Stated among its goals is the desire to "create a closer relationship among peoples of different ages, races, sexes, economic groups, faiths, and cultures," and to "continue to work for meaningful relationships with member churches of the National and World Council of Churches to further the ministry of Christ."

See also: Clergy
References: Jacqueline K. Barrett, ed., *Encyclopedia of Women's Associations Worldwide* (1993); International Association of Women Ministers brochure (n.d., c. 1996); Julie F. Parker, *Careers for Women as Clergy* (1993).

Jackson, Mahalia (1911–1972)

Considered by many to be the greatest name in twentieth-century gospel music, Mahalia Jackson was born in New Orleans, Louisiana, on October 26, 1911. Her father was a longshoreman and a barber who preached at a neighborhood church on Sundays. Her mother died when she was five years old, and her father took her and her older brother to live with her Aunt Duke. She lived there until she was sixteen, though she made nightly visits to her father's barbershop. Jackson was the product of a strict religious upbringing. She was not allowed to sing secular music but was to limit her musical activities to singing in her father's church choir. Secretly, she listened to musical recordings of popular artists Bessie Smith, Ida Cox, and Enrico Caruso.

When Jackson was sixteen, she went to Chicago to live with her Aunt Hannah. She joined the Greater Salem Baptist Church choir and became a member of the Johnson Singers, a group that sang in neighborhood churches for a small fee. Her outstanding contralto voice was soon recognized, and she became a soloist. Although her popularity spread and she was invited to sing at storefront and tent churches, the more formal African-American congregations did not find the syncopated rhythms of her songs acceptable; nor did they approve of her body movements—her tendency to shake and twist as she sang. Nevertheless, her fame continued to grow.

Mahalia Jackson (April 16, 1961)

Jackson made her first recording, "God Gonna Separate the Wheat from the Tares," in 1934. The record became popular and was soon followed by others. It was another decade before she recorded her first big hit, "Move On Up a Little Higher" (1945). Altogether, eight of her recordings sold more than a million copies. Among them are "I Believe," "He's Got the Whole World in His Hands," "I Can Put My Trust in Jesus," "Just over the Hill," "When I Wake Up in Glory," and "Just a Little While to Stay Here."

Despite possessing a voice that held great potential for blues singing, Mahalia Jackson sang only religious songs and refused to perform in any environment that she did not consider appropriate. Therefore, she never sang in nightclubs or anywhere that liquor was served. Jackson sang on radio and television, including on the half-hour "Mahalia Jackson Show" that ran from September 26, 1954, to February 6, 1955. Beginning in 1950, she performed each year before a packed Carnegie Hall in New York City. She sang in churches, prisons, hospitals, and concert halls; in command performances before heads of state; and at the Newport Jazz Festival in a program devoted entirely to gospel music. In January 1961 she sang at the inauguration of President John F. Kennedy.

In the 1960s Jackson became active in the civil rights movement. Despite her fragile health and warnings from her doctors to reduce her demanding schedule, she was determined, she said, to do all she could to lessen the divisions between blacks and whites. Jackson died in Evergreen Park, Illinois, on January 27, 1972.

References: Robert Anderson and Gail North, *Gospel Music Encyclopedia* (1979); Laurraine Goreau, *Just Mahalia, Baby* (1975); Robert McHenry, ed., *Liberty's Women* (1980); Jules Schwerin, *Got to Tell It: Mahalia Jackson, Queen of Gospel* (1992).

Jehovah's Witnesses

Originating in the 1870s, the Jehovah's Witness movement grew from a handful in the 1880s to almost six million adherents a hundred years later. Over the years, the Witnesses have been called by a variety of names, including Zion's Watch Tower Society, Watch Tower Bible and Tract Society, Millenial Dawnists, and Russellites. They adopted their pres-

ent title in 1931. Strict limits have been placed on women's roles within the movement's structure since the 1890s, and its hierarchy is all male. Women of the faith are expected to be subservient to males within the congregation as well as to their husbands. Nevertheless, female Jehovah's Witnesses do have roles to fill within the society.

Each congregation has a theocratic service school, which in forty-five minute meetings teaches witnesses to speak before an audience and indoctrinates them in history, theology, and other matters. The schools cover biblical material in the manner of the mainline theological seminaries but in much less depth. Female witnesses give talks in the school, but women are not allowed to use the podium to address the congregation. They are forbidden to teach the congregation directly, so they can stand behind the podium only when relating their individual experiences. Only if no qualified male is available can a woman officiate at congregational meetings, and then she must wear head coverings in deference to the males who are present.

Joseph Franklin Rutherford, who was president of the society from 1917 to 1942, regarded women as inferiors who should keep their proper place. He felt that if women were in power in religion and state the sacredness of the home would be destroyed and men would turn away from God. Because women were inferiors, Rutherford did not believe that they should be objects of romantic love. During the 1930s and 1940s, young witnesses were told by their leaders that they should refrain from marriage for the sake of preaching work. Couples who did marry were frequently pressured to avoid having children, and sexual relationships were discouraged.

Following Rutherford as president of the society was Nathan Homer Knorr, who had a considerably different view of marriage. By the late 1950s, the antimarriage stance of the Jehovah's Witnesses had ended, and the society began teaching that the family was the basic unit of the theocratic society of Jehovah's Witnesses. Romantic love, too, was gradually rehabilitated, though a single life is still encouraged in order for witnesses to have considerable time to serve the society. Young couples are discouraged from starting families too early so that child care does not prevent them from evangelizing for the community.

Husbands are expected to provide for their wives in both the physical and spiritual sense. Wives are to care for the home and obey their husbands as "unto the Lord." Women are also expected to dress modestly. Married women usually perform most of the preaching work done by congregation service workers (known as "publishers"), which consists of passing out literature door-to-door, and often visit the sick and care for the poor. Women are generally told to remain with their husbands even if their spouses abuse them mentally or physically. If a woman is a witness and her husband is not, she is still expected to obey him.

References: James J. Beckford, *The Trumpet of Prophecy: A Sociological Study of Jehovah's Witnesses* (1975); Jerry Bergman, *Jehovah's Witnesses and Kindred Groups: A Historical Compendium and Bibliography* (1984); Anthony A. Hoekema, *The Four Major Cults: Christian Science, Jehovah's Witnesses, Mormonism, Seventh-day Adventism* (1963); M. James Penton, *Apocalypse Delayed: The Story of Jehovah's Witnesses* (1986).

Jews

The first Jewish settlers arrived in the United States in the mid-seventeenth century. But by 1860, with a total population of thirty-one million, there were only 150,000 Jews. The population of Jews was growing, however. Between 1840 and 1880, approximately 250,000 German Jews settled in the United States. In their homelands, Jews were frequently segregated into closed communities called *shtetls*. They came to America in search of greater economic opportunity than that available to them in Germany and also because of the turmoil created by the revolutions of 1848. Yet it was not until the late nineteenth century that persecution in eastern Europe caused Jews to emigrate to America in large numbers. The German Jews had been more middle class and Western-educated and tended to Americanize quite easily, but when the eastern European Jews arrived in the United States, they sought to maintain their culture and traditions in the midst of peoples of other customs and religions.

As strangers in a new land, women played an important role in preserving Jewish tradition. Often young women were sent by their families before the men, since the women could find work in the garment and other trades. It was the role of a married woman to dress the children, maintain the home, and prepare the meal for *Shabbat,* the Sabbath. They raised their daughters to become good Jewish wives and mothers and taught them their obligations for the survival of the faith. However, the roles of Jewish women were limited compared to those of men. Throughout Jewish history, the scholar was held in highest esteem, and the scholar was always a man. A woman's intellect was deemed inferior to that of a man, and academies of learning were closed to women. It was men who delved into religious study, men who read the Torah. Jewish women were not considered full members of the congregation. They were not allowed to vote, nor were they counted in a *minyan,* the required number of at least ten people needed for public prayer. And they were required to sit apart from men during worship, usually in balconies.

German Jews brought Reform Judaism to America. In the mid-nineteenth century, these Reform Jews were looking to raise the status of Jewish women. In the 1850s, women began to push for the right to sit with men on the main floor of synagogues. Temple Emanuel in New York City abolished the women's gallery in 1854, and others soon followed. Rabbi Isaac Wise, a dynamic leader of American Reform Judaism in the mid-nineteenth century, favored female suffrage, the establishment of a special religious academy for girls, the inclusion of women on temple school boards, and the ordination of women as rabbis. (One hundred years would pass before the ordination of the first female rabbi in the United States.) Under Rabbi Wise's direction, the Philadelphia Rabbinical Conference of 1869 replaced the traditional marriage ceremony, in which the bride is a silent partner, with a reciprocal declaration and a double-ring ceremony. Religious divorces, which could be instituted only by the husband, were eliminated in favor of civil divorce.

Just as in the Gentile world of nineteenth-century Victorian America, for the Jew the home still remained the married woman's place. But the synagogue had now become a part of "woman's sphere" as well. Jewish women also began to venture into previously male-dominated fields of social reform. Women joined organizations like the Female Hebrew Benevolent Society, founded in 1819, and aided organizations like the Philadelphia Jewish Foster Home, established in 1855. Still, though elevated for their spiritual qualities, Jewish women continued to be considered intellectually inferior to their male counterparts.

As more and more Jewish immigrants arrived in the United States, Jewish women's organizations stepped in to assist the newcomers. Also during the late nineteenth century, Reform congregations had begun to found sisterhoods. These women performed a variety of duties connected with their temples, including fund-raising to care for and beautify their religious buildings and charitable work. The National Federation of Temple Sisterhoods was founded in 1913, and five years later Conservative women established the National Women's League of the United Synagogues of America. Meanwhile, Hannah Greenebaum Solomon, a prominent Jewish woman from Chicago, had established the National Council of Jewish Women in 1893 for the purpose of furthering the cause of religious education and philanthropy. In 1912 Henrietta Szold founded Hadassah, a Zionist organization for women. Through their organizations, Jewish women, like their Christian sisters, were playing increasingly active roles within their communities.

Other changes were occurring in the lives of Jewish girls and women who arrived with the wave of eastern European immigrants during the late nineteenth and early twentieth centuries. Young Jewish women frequently found themselves earning meager pay as factory workers, helping to support their families. But some, especially the younger daughters, were able to benefit from the educational opportunities that were available in the United States and rise from the poverty that had been the lot of their parents and older siblings. As they adapted to the American culture, they frequently became distanced from their traditional, Orthodox parents.

Despite Jewish women's increasing visibility within the community and their expanded presence within their temples and synagogues, it was not until Sally Jane Priesand was ordained on June 3, 1972, that the United States had its first female rabbi. Several women before her had attempted to become rabbis, including Martha Neumark in the early 1920s and

Helen Hadassah Levinthal in 1939. Paula Ackerman had performed the functions of a rabbi for a Reform congregation in Meridian, Mississippi, for approximately three years after her rabbi husband's death in 1951 and until a "regular" rabbi was selected to replace him. But it was not until 1956 that a committee of the Central Conference of American Rabbis in the Reform branch of Judaism granted its approval for the ordination of women. The Reconstructionist branch ordained its first female rabbi, Sandy Eisenberg Sasso, in 1974, and Amy Eilberg became the first woman rabbi in the Conservative branch in 1985. The Orthodox branch of Judaism does not ordain women.

Women rabbis have brought new outlooks into the practice of Judaism. Many have worked to uplift the status of women within their religion. Some, like Rabbis Sasso and Eilberg, have endeavored to establish new rituals and ceremonies that allow females greater participation within Judaism. They have also raised controversial issues, such as surrogate motherhood and the problem of AIDS, which male leaders had largely overlooked. Although initially female rabbis had difficulty finding congregations that would offer them work, they are now gaining acceptance within American temples and synagogues.

See also: Ackerman, Paula; Eilberg, Amy; Hadassah; National Council of Jewish Women; Priesand, Sally Jane; Sasso, Sandy Eisenberg; Solomon, Hannah Greenebaum; Szold, Henrietta
References: Charlotte Baum, Paula Hyman, and Sonya Michel, *The Jewish Woman in America* (1976); Susan Hill Lindley, *"You Have Stept Out of Your Place": A History of Women and Religion in America* (1996); Julie F. Parker, *Careers for Women as Clergy* (1993); Sally Priesand, *Judaism and the New Woman* (1975).

Johnson, Sonia Harris (1936–)

Sonia Harris Johnson, a feminist who defied the Mormon Church to support the Equal Rights Amendment, was born in Malad, Idaho. She was the third of five children in a Mormon family, living in Washakie, Utah. The family moved to Logan, Utah, when Sonia was about twelve years old. She met her future husband, Rick Johnson, while both were attending Utah State University. Sonia received a bachelor of arts degree from that university in June 1959 and married Rick on August 21. Later she wrote that she had been determined to be the ideal Mormon wife, prepared to sacrifice her education for the benefit of her husband. She worked outside the home while Rick completed graduate school, but she managed to complete the requirements for a master of arts degree at Rutgers University and was awarded a doctorate there in 1965.

During the next decade, the Johnsons lived in various locations within the United States and in Southeast Asia where Sonia taught and performed missionary work for the Mormon Church. When she was in her early thirties, she began suffering from arthritis. Hoping to be cured of this debilitating disease, she fasted, prayed, and finally went to a bishop for a blessing. Within days after he anointed her head with oil, laid his hands on her head, and prayed that she be healed, she found that she was practically pain-free.

In 1976 the Johnsons moved to Sterling Park, Virginia, near Washington, D.C. Not long after her move, Sonia became drawn to the women's rights movement and to the campaign for the Equal Rights Amendment (ERA). She was disturbed that the Mormon Church denounced the amendment, and she soon came to the conclusion that the church was wrong in its emphasis on patriarchal traditions. She began calling herself a "radical feminist" (Johnson, 1981, p. 111), and for a while was angry with God for permitting women to be oppressed. After some reflection on the issue, she came to believe that "men had made God in their own image to keep control of women" (Johnson, 1981, p. 118). Soon she was asking why women could not themselves remake God into an image that would not disempower or disenfranchise half the human race. In 1978 she became one of four women to found the organization Mormons for ERA. She became a participant in marches in support of the ERA and gave testimony in Congress on behalf of Mormons for ERA.

Although Rick Johnson had been sympathetic to his wife's feminism, at his instigation the Johnsons divorced after approximately twenty years of marriage. Although devastated, Sonia continued with her crusade for the ERA. Mormon leaders denounced her political activities and excommunicated her in December 1979. The following year, she was arrested as one of the "Bellevue 21," women who chained themselves to the gates of the Mormon Temple in Bellevue, Washington, to protest what they saw as the church's oppression of women.

Johnson has written several books. In *From Housewife to Heretic* (1981), she described events leading to her feminism and eventual excommunication from the Mormon Church. Later books by Johnson include *Going Out of Our Minds: The Metaphysics of Liberation* (1987) and *The Ship That Sailed into the Living Room: Sex and Intimacy Reconsidered* (1991). In 1984 she campaigned for president on the Citizens Party ticket, winning 1 percent of the vote.

See also: Church of Jesus Christ of Latter-Day Saints (Mormons); Equal Rights Amendment
References: Elizabeth Frost-Knappman, *Women's Progress in America* (1994); Sonia Johnson, *From Housewife to Heretic* (1981); Sonia Johnson, *Going Out of Our Minds: The Metaphysics of Liberation* (1987); Sonia Johnson, *The Ship That Sailed into the Living Room: Sex and Intimacy Reconsidered* (1991).

Judson, Ann Hasseltine (1789–1826)

Ann (often called Nancy) Hasseltine Judson, born in Bradford, Massachusetts, in 1789, was the first American woman to become a foreign missionary. As a child, Ann was fond of learning. Apparently she was also devoutly religious, reportedly spending much of her time reading religious books and praying, and she was a lively girl who was fond of parties. At some point, when she was sixteen or seventeen years old, Ann underwent a conversion experience and became convinced that her life up to that point had been sinful. Her conversion experience likely was the result of her participation in the New England religious revival of 1806. She was so inspired by the revival that she made up her mind to devote her life to religious work. Ann studied at Bradford Academy and became a teacher at the age of eighteen.

Ann met her future husband, Adoniram Judson, at a meeting held in her father's home, of the first American Board of Commissioners for Foreign Missions. Judson, a Congregational minister, was interested in becoming a missionary, and Ann realized that if she married him she would lead the life of a missionary's wife. The couple married in Bradford on February 5, 1812, and left for India the following day. They arrived in Calcutta on June 18, 1812. While voyaging to Calcutta, the Judsons had read *Lives of Martyrs and Saints* as well as several books on baptism. Upon their arrival in India, they converted to the Baptist faith and became Baptist missionaries. But missionaries were unwelcome in India, so the Judsons decided to establish a mission in Rangoon, Burma. They arrived in Rangoon in July 1813, where they worked to convert the local people to Christianity. In September 1815 Ann gave birth to a son, Roger Williams, the first child born to white parents in Burma. He died just eight months later.

on October 24, 1826. Ann, who had helped her husband translate biblical texts into Burmese, did not live to see the fulfillment of her dreams of establishing the Christian faith in Burma. When Adoniram's translation of the Bible was completed following Ann's death, it became the foundation of Christian teaching in Burma. By the time of Adoniram's death in 1850, there were sixty-three Christian missions in Burma, and 163 missionaries.

See also: Missionaries
References: Edith Deen, *Great Women of the Christian Faith* (1959); Ethel Daniels Hubbard, *Ann of Ava* (1941, reprint 1971); Edward T. James, ed., *Notable American Women, 1607–1950*, vol. 2 (1971); James Davis Knowles, *Life of Mrs. Ann H. Judson, Late Missionary to Burma*, microfilm (1830); Caroline Zilboorg, ed., *Women's Firsts* (1997).

Ann Hasseltine Judson (undated portrait)

A tropical illness forced Ann to leave Burma for America in 1822. When she returned to Burma in the late summer of 1823, she and Adoniram traveled to Ava, the capital of Burma, to form a mission there. But upon their arrival in February 1824, war was threatening between the British and Burmese. Within months they were surrounded by battle. The Burmese emperor suspected that the Judsons were spying for the British, and Adoniram was thrown into prison. Ann became a virtual prisoner in her house. She did manage to follow her husband as he was moved from prison to prison. Adoniram became ill and emaciated while in prison, and Ann was herself stricken with smallpox and later another tropical disease.

At war's end, Adoniram was released from prison, and the Judsons came under British protection. The couple set up a mission in Amherst in lower Burma in the spring of 1826, but soon Ann was again ill with fever. She died in Amherst

Judson, Emily Chubbuck (1817–1854)

Writer and missionary Emily Chubbuck Judson was born in Eaton, New York, on August 22, 1817. She was the fifth child of Charles and Lavinia (Richards) Chubbuck. Emily was a frail child, and the conditions she faced as a girl did not improve her chances for health. Her family was poor, and Emily not only performed a number of strenuous household tasks but at the age of eleven began working twelve hours a day in a woolen factory. Although she was unable to attend the local district schools on a regular basis, she received sufficient education to develop a talent for writing and to become a teacher for the local schools.

The Chubbuck family were devout Baptists, and Emily had a deep interest in religion. Upon reading of the work of missionary Adoniram Judson in Burma, she decided that she too would become a missionary. From 1832 to 1840, she worked as a teacher while continuing her own education. In 1840 she entered the Utica Female Seminary for advanced study and a year later became a teacher of English there. Meanwhile, she wrote various verses and sketches for a local paper to earn money to help support her parents. Over the next few years, Emily published several books: a Sunday school book, *Charles Linn, or How to Observe the Golden Rule* (1841); *The Great Secret, or How to Be Happy* (1842); *Allen Lucas, or the Self-Made Man* (1842), and *John Frink* (1843). Though her earnings were small, she managed to save $400 to buy a home for her ill parents. In 1844 she became a regular contributor to the *New York Mirror,* writing under the name "Fanny Forester." Many of her sketches were later published in two volumes: *Trippings in Author-Land* (1846) and *Alderbrook: A Collection of Fanny Forester's Village Sketches, Poems, &c* (1847).

During the winter of 1845–1846, Chubbuck met the Reverend Adoniram Judson, who approached her about writing a biography of his second wife, Sarah Hall Boardman Judson, who had recently died. During their collaboration on the book, Emily and Adoniram fell in love. They married on June 2, 1846. A month later, they sailed for Burma and arrived in Moulmein in November.

Despite her frailty, Emily adapted to the hardships of missionary life. In the months after her arrival in Burma, Emily completed the biography of Sarah, *The Memoir of Sarah B. Judson, Member of the Mission to Burma,* which was published in 1848. On December 24, 1847, she gave birth to her first child, Emily Frances. The next two years found continuous illness in the Judson family. In 1850 Adoniram's doctor encouraged him to take a sea voyage to help recover his health. While his wife, expecting their second child, waited for him in Burma, Adoniram began the sea journey, but he died aboard ship on April 12, 1850, and was buried at sea. On April 22, unaware

that she was a widow, Emily gave birth to Charles Judson. The infant died the same day. She was left to care for four fatherless children, three of Sarah's and one of her own. Emily returned to America in October 1851 and purchased a home in Hamilton, New York, in May 1852. Two years later, she died there of tuberculosis on June 1, 1854.

See also: Judson, Ann Hasseltine; Judson, Sarah Hall Boardman; Missionaries
References: Edith Deen, *Great Women of the Christian Faith* (1959); *Dictionary of American Biography,* vol. 5 (1930); Edward T. James, ed., *Notable American Women, 1607–1950,* vol. 2 (1971).

Judson, Sarah Hall Boardman (1803–1845)

Missionary to Burma, hymn writer, and translator of religious tracts, Sarah Hall Boardman Judson was born in Alstead, New Hampshire, on November 4, 1803. Most of her early years were spent in Danvers and then in Salem, Massachusetts. The eldest of the thirteen children of Ralph and Abiah O. Hall, she spent much of her girlhood tending to household chores. Her busy schedule in the home, coupled with a lack of financial resources, hindered her education. But she was eager to learn and found various means of self-education. Sarah developed an interest in religion and in mission work at an early age, as well as an interest in poetry. When she was thirteen, she wrote a poem eulogizing the death of the son of missionaries Adoniram and Ann Hasseltine Judson. She joined the First Baptist Church in Salem in 1820 and wrote poems that appeared in Christian periodicals. Sarah wrote a poem to honor Ann Judson upon the missionary's visit to New England in 1823. A poem she wrote upon the death of missionary James Coleman drew the attention of George Dana Boardman, a Baptist missionary who had volunteered to replace

Coleman in Burma. Sarah married George Boardman in July 1825.

Within two weeks of their wedding, the Boardmans sailed from Philadelphia to Calcutta, intending to work with Adoniram Judson in lower Burma. But war had erupted in Burma, forcing the couple to remain in Calcutta for a year. While there, they studied the Burmese language under native teachers, and Sarah gave birth to their first child. They arrived in lower Burma in the spring of 1827, soon settling in the new city of Moulmein. They later moved to Tavoy on the Bay of Bengal, about 150 miles to the south. Four years of hardship and tragedy followed, including the robbery of all of their valuables; recurring tropical sickness; the deaths of two of their three children; and finally, on February 11, 1831, the death of George Boardman himself.

Despite her travails, Sarah chose to remain a missionary in Burma. Over the next three years, she established small village schools and made missionary journeys into the Burmese hills to continue the Boardmans' evangelizing work with the Karens, a jungle people despised by the Burmese. On April 10, 1834, she became the second wife of Adoniram Judson, whose first wife, Ann, had died in 1826. Like Ann, Sarah helped her husband translate religious materials into Burmese. She herself translated the first part of *Pilgrim's Progress* into Burmese and also wrote twenty hymns in Burmese. In the ten years that followed her marriage, Sarah bore eight children, five of whom survived infancy. As time passed, she necessarily devoted much of her time to caring for her family. In June 1845, ill with dysentery and exhausted from many years of childbearing, Sarah set sail for America, along with Adoniram and three of their children. En route, their ship developed a leak that forced them to stop at Port Louis, Isle of France, on July 5. While in port, Sarah suffered a relapse. The Judsons left on a second ship for Boston, but Sarah died while the ship was anchored in the harbor at the island of St. Helena on September 1, 1845 (sources differ). After her burial on St. Helena, Adoniram continued on to the United States. Two of Sarah's sons later became prominent ministers. George Dana Boardman, Jr., became an eminent clergyman in Philadelphia, and Edward Judson served as pastor of the Judson Memorial Church in New York City. Edward also wrote a biography of his father.

See also: Judson, Ann Hasseltine; Judson, Emily Chubbuck; Missionaries
References: Edith Deen, *Great Women of the Christian Faith* (1959); *Dictionary of American Biography*, vol. 5 (1930); Edward T. James, ed., *Notable American Women: 1607–1950*, vol. 2 (1971).

Kelly, Leontine Turpeau Current (1920–)

The first African-American woman to be elected bishop of a major religious denomination, Leontine Turpeau Current Kelly was born March 5, 1920, in Washington, D.C. She was the seventh of the eight children of Reverend David DeWitt Turpeau, Sr., a Methodist minister, and Ila (Marshall) Turpeau. During the 1920s, the family moved to Cincinnati, Ohio, where Leontine attended public schools. An early influence upon her life was her elementary school principal, Jennie D. Porter, who was Cincinnati's first black principal and the first African American to earn a doctoral degree at the University of Cincinnati.

Growing up in a parsonage with a father who was a Methodist minister gave Leontine a solid religious background. Like most other American churches during the first half of the twentieth century, the Methodist Church was racially segregated, a circumstance that displeased Reverend Turpeau. He, along with his wife who was active within the black community, therefore encouraged the Turpeau children to work to alter the perspectives of white Christians in regard to racial issues as a step toward improving American society as a whole.

Between 1938 and 1941, Leontine attended West Virginia State College (later West Virginia State University). She left school following her junior year, when she married fellow student Gloster Current. When the couple divorced in the

1950s after fifteen years of marriage, she felt devastated and turned to her religious study and prayer to help her through this turbulent period of her life.

In 1956, Leontine married James David Kelly, a Methodist minister, who inspired her to return to college to complete her degree and who encouraged her to advance her credentials within the Methodist Church. Leontine followed her husband's advice and completed her bachelor's degree at Virginia Union University in Richmond in 1960. At about the same time, she became a lay speaker in the Methodist Church. She remained active in church affairs throughout the 1960s, even while she worked as a social studies teacher in local public schools. When her husband died in 1969, the Congregation of Galilee Church in Edwardsville, Virginia, asked her to succeed him. At first she served as a layperson in charge of the church, but soon she felt that God wanted her to become an ordained minister. She enrolled in theological studies and received a master of divinity degree from Union Theological Seminary in Richmond in 1976.

During the 1970s and into the 1980s, Kelly's positions and responsibilities within the Methodist Church advanced. She began as a deacon in 1972, went on to pastor two churches, and was evangelism executive for the church's Board of Discipleship in Nashville, Tennessee. In 1984, of the forty-six bishops in the Methodist Church, only one, Marjorie Swank Matthews, was female, and she was retiring. The church was looking for another woman to replace her. Kelly was a ministerial member of the white male–dominated southeastern jurisdiction of the United Methodist Church. Although she had the support of other clergywomen, Kelly tried but failed to win election in her jurisdiction. She was, however, elected by the Western jurisdiction and became the first African-American woman to be elected bishop in any major religious denomination in the United States. At the time of Kelly's consecration on July 20, 1984, a white woman, Reverend Judith Craig, also entered the United Methodist bishopric.

Kelly's area of responsibility encompassed northern California and Nevada and included 386 churches with approximately 100,000 members. She retired as bishop in 1988, at the age of 68, due to the requirement that bishops who reach the age of 66 must retire at the end of their terms. Nevertheless, she continues to be active in community service work, believing that the church and politics can join together to effect change.

See also: African Americans; Harris, Barbara Clementine; Methodists
References: Kenneth A. Briggs, "Methodists Elect 19 to Leadership," *New York Times* (July 29, 1984): 19; DeWitt C. Dykes, Jr., "Leontine Kelly," in Jessie Carney Smith, ed., *Epic Lives: One Hundred Black Women Who Made a Difference* (1993); Marilyn Marshall, "Leontine T. C. Kelly: First Black Woman Bishop," in *Ebony* 40, no. 6 (November 1984): 164; "Words of the Week" in *Jet* 75, no. 15 (January 16, 1989): 40.

King, Coretta Scott (1927–)

First known for her role as the wife of the Reverend Martin Luther King, Jr., Coretta Scott King later became famous herself as a writer and lecturer for civil rights. She was born Coretta Scott near Marion, Alabama, on April 27, 1927, to Obadiah and Bernice (McMurry) Scott. She attended a black public school until

seventh grade and then enrolled in Lincoln High School, a semiprivate school. Lincoln was a school for blacks only, but it boasted modern facilities and employed both African-American and white teachers. Coretta later recalled that the brave and dedicated faculty who fought discrimination while they educated their young African-American students, along with the school's concern for humanity, helped prepare her for her future life with Martin Luther King, Jr. Following her high school graduation, she attended Antioch College in Yellow Springs, Ohio, an institution that had just recently opened its doors to black students. There she was active in the local branch of the National Association for the Advancement of Colored People (NAACP) and joined Quaker peace groups while studying music and elementary education. While a student at Antioch, she sang at her first of many public concerts. She received a bachelor's degree in music and elementary education in 1951. Upon her graduation from Antioch, Coretta was determined to develop her voice to its full potential and began advanced study at the New England Conservatory of Music in Boston. While in Boston, she met Martin Luther King, Jr., a graduate student at Boston University. The couple married June 18, 1953, and Coretta received another bachelor's degree in music education, with a voice major, in June 1954.

Three months after her graduation, Coretta moved with her husband to Montgomery, Alabama, where he had accepted the position of pastor of the Dexter Avenue Baptist Church. In December 1955, she supported Reverend King in his leadership of the Montgomery bus boycott. While raising four children, she remained at her husband's side throughout his crusade for civil rights and nonviolent social change. She endured telephone threats against her and King's lives and a bomb attack on their home. Coretta also received reports, leaked by the Federal Bureau of Investigation, of her husband's romantic indiscretions with other women. In fact, Coretta was so committed to movements for civil rights and for nonviolence that she often ignored her husband's requests that she spend less time in the public world as an activist and more time in the home attending to duties as a wife and mother.

Following Martin Luther King, Jr.'s death from an assassin's bullet on April 4, 1968, Coretta Scott King continued to campaign for nonviolence and for civil rights for minorities. In June 1969, she traveled to Washington, D.C., to participate in what was known as the "Poor-Man's March," which was associated with the Poor People's Campaign launched by Martin Luther King and other activists of the Southern Christian Leadership Conference in 1967. Coretta Scott King was the keynote speaker at a program held at the Lincoln Memorial on June 19, 1969.

It was Coretta King's desire to establish a living memorial to her husband that would maintain his legacy and encourage the completion of his unfinished work. She founded the Martin Luther King, Jr., Center for Nonviolent Social Change in Atlanta, Georgia, which was declared a National Historic Site by the National Park Service in 1980. When Congress established the Martin Luther King Holiday Commission in 1984 to make plans for the first official celebration of the civil rights leader's birthday, Coretta Scott King was elected chairperson of the commission. In the 1990s, however, Reverend King's family, including Coretta, have been criticized for their handling of the civil rights leader's legacy. The 1997 celebration of the Martin Luther King, Jr. holiday was marred by charges that the family was more concerned with monetary profit than with creating a living memorial to their husband and father.

Coretta Scott King has received numerous honors for her own work. Among the many tributes she has received over the past three decades are more than one hundred honorary doctoral degrees. In 1969, she became the first woman to preach at a regular service at St. Paul's Cathedral in London, England. She was also the first woman to deliver the Class Day address at Harvard University. In the late 1970s, President Jimmy Carter appointed her as one of three public delegates to the thirty-second General Assembly of the United Nations. Her honors have come as a result of her indefatigable efforts as a speaker and writer in support of minorities in the United States and throughout the world.

See also: African Americans
References: A. B. Assensoh, "Coretta Scott King," in Jessie Carney Smith, ed., *Epic Lives: One Hundred Black Women Who Made a Difference* (1993); Sondra Henry and Emily Taitz, *Coretta Scott King: Keeper of the Dream* (1992); Coretta Scott King, *My Life with Martin Luther King, Jr.* (1969).

Kohler, Rose (1873–1947)

Rose Kohler, a painter, a sculptor, and an activist for reforms within Judaism, was born into a prominent Jewish family in 1873. Both her father, Kaufman Kohler, and her mother's father, David Einhorn, were prominent rabbis of the more radical wing of the Reform movement in America. She also became absorbed in the Reform movement and was national chairperson of the National Council of Jewish Women's Committee on Religious Schools.

Kohler advocated changes in Reform Judaism that would put Jewish women on an equal level with Jewish men. For example, women were not counted in the *minyan,* the required minimum of ten people necessary for public prayer. They were not considered full members of their

Rose Kohler (undated photo)

See also: Eilberg, Amy; Jews; Priesand, Sally Jane; Sasso, Sandy Eisenberg
References: Susan Hill Lindley, *"You Have Stept Out of Your Place": A History of Women and Religion in America* (1996); Julie F. Parker, *Careers for Women as Clergy* (1993); Rosemary Radford Ruether and Rosemary Skinner Keller, eds., *Women and Religion in America*, vol. 1 (1986).

Kohut, Rebekah Bettelheim (1864–1951)

Educator, social worker, and founder of the Kohut College Preparatory School for Girls, Rebekah Bettelheim Kohut was born in Kaschau, Hungary, on September 9, 1864. She was the third child and youngest daughter of Albert Siegfried and Henrietta (Wientraub) Bettelheim. Her father, who held lifelong interests in theology and the natural sciences, was both a rabbi and a doctor. Henrietta Bettelheim was a teacher, an occupation normally reserved for men in Hungarian Jewish communities. Though Rebekah held great admiration for her father, she later stated that it was her mother who inspired her "to seek out all kinds of less sheltered activities" (Sicherman and Green, 1980, p. 403).

The Bettelheim family emigrated to the United States in 1867, where Albert became rabbi of a synagogue in Philadelphia and then in Richmond, Virginia. His wife died in 1870, and he remarried. The Bettelheims moved to San Francisco in 1875, where Rebekah completed high school and normal school and attended the University of California at Berkeley. For a while during this period, she experienced some religious doubts. But soon she came to believe that it was her mission in life to become "a worker in the front ranks of American Jewish womanhood," and she began involving herself in community service (Sicherman and Green, 1980, p. 403). On February 14, 1887, she married Alexander Kohut, a famous Hungarian rabbinical scholar. Kohut was a widower,

congregations and had no voting privileges. Although both Jewish boys and girls received instruction in their Jewish heritage, girls were prevented from going beyond a certain point in their education. As a young woman, Kohler began to speak out against these inequities.

In 1895 Kohler voiced her concerns over the education of Jewish children in a speech before the National Council of Jewish Women. She questioned the tradition that treated boys and girls as equals as children but then allowed them to have different Jewish obligations as teenagers and adults. Rose was not alone in her concerns. Many other Jewish men and women raised serious questions and considered making changes in the traditions within Judaism. Kohler and women like her helped to bring about reforms that eventually led to the ordination of the first woman rabbi in the United States in 1972, twenty-five years after Kohler's death.

twenty-two years her senior, who had eight children. Before her wedding, Rebekah wrote her sister, "I go to New York to be the wife of a great man and to become a mother to the motherless" (Sicherman and Green, 1980, p. 403).

For the next several years, Rebekah Kohut cared for the children and helped her husband translate his sermons from German into English for publication. As the wife of a rabbi, she played a prominent role in the organization of women's groups within the Reform synagogues. She also returned to volunteer work, participating in the New York Women's Health Protective Association. At times she taught classes at the Education Alliance, a school founded by wealthy German Jewish Americans who desired to Americanize the poor Jewish immigrants from eastern Europe. In 1893, Kohut was invited to speak before the first Congress of Jewish Women at the World's Fair in Chicago but was unable to do so because she was caring for her ailing husband. He died in May 1894, leaving her with a number of stepchildren to raise.

At about the same time, Kohut learned that her sisters and stepmother were suffering financial troubles and that with her father and brother no longer living, the responsibility of helping them rested upon her shoulders. There was an estate, but soon that was also lost. Then, in 1899, with financial help from banker and philanthropist Jacob H. Schiff, Kohut opened the Kohut College Preparatory School for Girls, a day and boarding institute. Although she hired other teachers for general education, Kohut made the girls' religious instruction her special responsibility. The school was highly successful, but she closed it in 1906, believing that her children continued to need her at home.

In the years that followed, Kohut made special endowments to Yale University to subsidize research and publication of Jewish scholarship. In 1912 she created the Alexander Kohut Memorial Collection, giving the university several thousand volumes of Near Eastern literature from her late husband's library, and in 1919 the family established the Alexander Kohut Research Fellowship in Semitics for graduate students.

During the mid-1910s, Kohut became involved in efforts to help women find gainful employment, and in 1914 she established the Employment Bureau of the Young Women's Hebrew Association. After the United States entered World War I, she chaired the Employment Committee of the Women's Committee for National Defense, which attempted to act as a clearinghouse for the working women of New York. By August 1917, she was doing similar work on a national level.

When the war ended, Kohut sought to aid Jews in eastern Europe who had been impoverished by the war. She was a leader of the National Council of Jewish Women's organization for relief work and made a number of trips to Europe during the 1920s for purposes of gathering information to determine the types of aid that would be needed. At its meeting in Vienna in 1923, Kohut was elected president of the World Congress of Jewish Women.

Back in the United States, in 1931 Governor Franklin D. Roosevelt appointed Kohut to the New York State Advisory Council on Employment and to the Joint Legislative Commission on Unemployment. In 1934 she returned to the field of education, becoming an administrator at the Columbia Grammar School, a private school for boys. Kohut left this position after several years but continued to be active in philanthropic, governmental, religious, and women's organizations until her death in New York City in 1951.

See also: National Council of Jewish Women
References: Charlotte Baum, Paula Hyman, and Sonya Michel, *The Jewish Woman in America* (1976); Jacob R. Marcus, *The American Jewish Woman: A Documentary*

History (1981); Marcus, *The American Jewish Woman, 1654–1980* (1981); Rosemary Radford Ruether and Rosemary Skinner Keller, eds., *Women and Religion in America*, vol. 3 (1986); Barbara Sicherman and Carol Hurd Green, eds., *Notable American Women: The Modern Period* (1980).

Kugler, Anna Sarah (1856–1930)

Anna Sarah Kugler, a pioneer medical missionary, was born in Ardmore, Pennsylvania, on April 18, 1856. Her father was an influential Lutheran lay leader and public official. Her early education was in public and private schools. An interest in medicine and missionary work led her to attend the Woman's Medical College of Pennsylvania. Founded in 1850, the college's female graduates were, in the 1870s, only beginning to gain recognition from state and county medical societies. Kugler graduated from the college in 1879. For the next three years, she worked as an assistant physician in the State Hospital for the Insane in Norristown. Then, in August 1883, she left the United States to become a missionary in India. Kugler worked under the sponsorship of the Woman's Home and Foreign Mission Society of the General Synod of the Evangelical Lutheran Church in the U.S.A. Initially, she was sent to India as a teacher because the society was hesitant to embark on the new field of medical missionary work. Nevertheless, once she arrived at Guntur Mission in Madras State, she added medical work to her teaching and evangelical responsibilities. Two years later, Kugler was officially designated a medical missionary, becoming the first Lutheran woman to hold that position, and was granted a small amount of funds for supplies.

In August 1886 Kugler opened the first dispensary among the Telegu people, but because of a lack of funding, it was another seven years before a separate dispensary building was constructed. With the arrival of an assistant and a nurse in the mission came the need for living facilities, and a residence for medical missionaries was completed in 1895. A fifty-bed hospital was erected three years later.

Although most of her adult life after 1883 was spent in India, Kugler returned to the United States in 1889 for additional training, and again in 1893 to participate in the Lutheran Women's Congress that was held in connection with the World's Columbian Exposition in Chicago. After her return to India, the medical compound at Guntur continued to expand. Included at the site was a maternity and surgical building, a children's ward, a nurses' home, and a nurses' training school, which graduated its first class in 1901. In addition to her duties at Guntur, Kugler played an active role in the founding of the Union Mission Tuberculosis Sanitarium in Arogyavarun, where she was for a while the supervising physician. She also aided in the establishment of the Medical College for Women in Vellore, which opened in 1917. In recognition of her medical service, the British government decorated Kugler in 1905 and in 1917 added a bar to the medal to honor her continued outstanding work.

In 1928, following an illness that caused her to make one last trip to the United States, Kugler wrote and published her memoir, *Guntur Mission Hospital*. She later returned to India and died at Guntur Mission on July 26, 1930.

See also: Missionaries
References: Mary L. Hammack, *Dictionary of Women in Church History* (1984); Erwin L. Lueker, ed., *Lutheran Cyclopedia* (1975); Robert McHenry, ed., *Liberty's Women* (1980); Regina Markell Morantz-Sanchez, *Sympathy and Science: Women Physicians in American Medicine* (1985); E. Clifford Nelson, ed., *The Lutherans in North America* (1975).

Kuhlman, Kathryn (1907–1976)

Itinerant evangelist Kathryn Kuhlman was one of the best-known spiritual healers of the mid-twentieth century. Born in

Concordia, Missouri, on May 7, 1907, to Emma (Walkenhorst) and Joseph Adolph Kuhlman, Kathryn was descended from a long line of Lutherans. However, during her youth she attended both the Methodist and Baptist churches, which her parents preferred. At the age of fourteen, Kuhlman had a religious experience that increased her interest in religion and led her to join the Baptist church that her father attended. Within two years, she left school, joined her sister Myrtle Parrott, and enlisted in the evangelistic troupe led by her brother-in-law Everett B. Parrott. Kuhlman traveled to the West with the Parrott Tent Revival, preaching primarily to Baptist audiences because the Methodists did not yet permit women to preach.

By 1928 Kuhlman was conducting independent services. While preaching in Denver, Colorado, during the early 1930s, she was approached by leaders of the Denver Revival Tabernacle, who asked that she be the church's pastor. Persuaded by their promise to build her a tabernacle, Kuhlman accepted their proposal, and though she had never attended a seminary, she was ordained by the Evangelical Church Alliance. (Some women, like Kuhlman, were recognized as possessing such talents as religious evangelists that they were able to take alternate paths to ordination.) In 1934 the Kuhlman Revival Tabernacle opened in Denver and soon became one of the fastest-growing churches in the West. But scandal erupted within the church after evangelist Burroughs A. Waltrip appeared as a guest speaker in 1937. Waltrip fell in love with Kuhlman and divorced his wife and left their two children to marry her. The scandal destroyed the congregation. Kuhlman and Waltrip left Denver and traveled the sawdust circuit for several years before settling in Los Angeles.

Early in 1944, Kuhlman had a religious experience in which she made a promise to the Holy Spirit. She chose her relationship with the Holy Spirit over that with her husband. Three days later she left Waltrip. Kuhlman then moved to Franklin, Pennsylvania, where she established a successful ministry at the Gospel Revival Tabernacle.

Soon after her arrival in Franklin, Kuhlman began to hear testimonies from people who claimed to have experienced God moving through them and to have been cured by the Holy Spirit of various ailments, including tumors and blindness. Kuhlman began to include this healing feature in her sermons. She never claimed to personally heal anyone and disliked the term "faith healer," insisting that it was through the power of God that people experienced cures from their illnesses.

In 1947 Kuhlman began making half-hour radio broadcasts and at about the same time moved her services to Pittsburgh, Pennsylvania, where she rented the Carnegie Auditorium. Her preaching was so popular that soon she was also giving services in Youngstown, Ohio, and preaching monthly sermons in Los Angeles, California. During 1951 Pittsburgh ministers picketed her services, complaining that Kuhlman took congregants away from their churches. Her radio messages were soon heard across the country. In 1962 Kuhlman's book, *I Believe in Miracles,* became a best-seller and brought her nationwide name recognition. She moved to Los Angeles in 1966 and launched a weekly television program that continued until her death. Altogether, she taped five hundred half-hour programs. Also during the 1960s, she established the Kathryn Kuhlman Foundation, which set up foreign missions; started two radio stations; organized food assistance; and created ministries, including Teen Challenge led by Pentecostal minister David Wilkerson.

Kuhlman was known for her exceptional speaking ability, energy, flamboyant style, and personal integrity. Her outreach extended to many middle-class Protestants and Catholics, groups that in the past had paid little attention to spiritual healers. Although she believed in the ordination of women, Kuhlman rejected feminism and agreed with those who believed that women should serve as ministers only when no man was available. She believed that the Bible favored female subjection and once told an interviewer that "the husband should be the head of the family" (Ruether and Keller, 1986, p. 243). But she viewed Christianity as a religion that had raised the status of women in the ancient world by freeing them from male oppression. "I could never see how women could reject Christ," she said, "because he gave dignity to women" (Ruether and Keller, 1986, p. 243). Kuhlman died in Tulsa, Oklahoma, on February 20, 1976. Although her foundation floundered and died soon after, her work has been carried on by Florida Pentecostal minister Benny Hinn.

References: Henry Warner Bowden, *Dictionary of American Religious Biography*, 2nd ed. (1993); Charles H. Lippy, ed., *Twentieth-Century Shapers of American Popular Religion* (1989); J. Gordon Melton, *Religious Leaders of America* (1991); Rosemary Radford Ruether and Rosemary Skinner Keller, eds., *Women and Religion in America*, vol. 3 (1986).

LaHaye, Beverly Jean (1929–)

Beverly Jean LaHaye, writer, lecturer, and founder of Concerned Women for America, was born in 1929 Beverly Jean Ratcliffe in Detroit, Michigan. She attended Bob Jones College in Cleveland, Tennessee, where she met young Baptist minister Tim LaHaye. She was eighteen years old when the couple married. After college, the LaHayes moved to various locations across the country, from South Carolina to San Diego, California, wherever Tim LaHaye's church assignments took him. Until the early 1970s, Beverly was content to keep house, care for the couple's four children, and perform volunteer work for her husband's church.

Beverly LaHaye's life reached a turning point when she attended a conference for Sunday school teachers. After listening to a speech by Christian psychologist Henry Brandt, she approached him, hoping for some sympathy for her melancholy state of mind. Instead, he told her that she was a selfish woman and that God wanted people to focus on others. Beverly realized that Brandt's assessment of her situation was correct, and she suddenly became filled with a new spirit. Soon, she entered public life, joining her husband, who had become well known on the lecture circuit as a defender of biblical morality. Tim and Beverly LaHaye became a team and began giving family life seminars, aimed at showing Christian couples how to enjoy happy marriages.

The couple's seminars proved very successful. They sold tapes of the seminars

Beverly Jean LaHaye (1997)

by mail and earned up to a million dollars a year. For a while they hosted a half-hour television program, "The LaHayes on Family Life," that played on Christian stations. The couple collaborated on several books designed to help Christians achieve successful marital relationships and to raise virtuous children. Beverly also wrote some books on her own.

During the late 1970s, LaHaye became concerned that the United States was heading in the direction of humanism, which emphasizes people working out their own solutions to life's problems, leaving God out (though others disagree with this definition of humanism). She decided to devote her life to the defeat of humanism. To help carry out her plan, in January 1979, she founded Concerned Women for America (CWA). The organization grew quickly, from twenty-four members in March 1979 to a claimed one-half million in 1984. In 1985 the LaHayes moved to Washington, D.C., where she established a new national headquarters. The CWA boasted more than 600,000 members in 1997.

During the 1980s, LaHaye and the CWA received the respect of right-wing fundamentalists across the country. The Reagan White House named Beverly LaHaye to its Family Policy Board, and Paul Weyrich, a conservative activist, considered the CWA the most influential group among the religious right in the late 1980s. In 1992, Liberty University awarded LaHaye an honorary doctorate of humanities for her achievements in protecting the rights of the family. A year later, the National Religious Broadcasters named her radio talk show, "Beverly LaHaye Live," the best talk show of the year for 1993. LaHaye currently serves on the board of Liberty University, on the advisory committee of the Child Protection Fund, and on the board of directors for the National Republican Coalition for Life. Journalist Stephen Bates, in *Battleground,* a book describing a fight LaHaye and the CWA joined over "secular humanist" textbooks in Hawkins County, Tennessee, believes that LaHaye challenges Phyllis Schlafly as the religious right's leading woman.

See also: Concerned Women for America; Fundamentalism; Schlafly, Phyllis Stewart
References: Stephen Bates, *Battleground: One Mother's Crusade, the Religious Right, and the Struggle for Control of Our Classrooms* (1993); Concerned Women for America, information packet (March 7, 1997); Tim LaHaye and Beverly LaHaye, *Against the Tide: How to Raise Sexually Pure Kids in an "Anything-Goes" World* (1993); Glenn H. Utter and John W. Storey, *The Religious Right: A Reference Handbook* (1995).

Lathrop, Rose Hawthorne (1851–1926)

Writer and cofounder of the Dominican Congregation of St. Rose of Lima, Rose Hawthorne Lathrop, who later took vows as Sister Mary Alphonsa, was born in Lenox, Massachusetts, on May 20, 1851. Her parents, author Nathaniel Hawthorne and Sophia (Peabody) Hawthorne, were Unitarians but, except for family prayers, neglected their children's religious education. When Rose was two, she moved with her parents to Liverpool, England, where her father was U.S. consul. After Nathaniel Hawthorne resigned his post four years later, the family spent time in France and Italy and a final year in England before returning to Massachusetts in 1860. In Italy Rose became acquainted with the Roman Catholic Church, the denomination she would convert to later in her life.

Rose received her education from her parents, from governesses, and at various Massachusetts schools. Nathaniel Hawthorne died in 1864, and in 1868 Rose moved with her mother, brother, and sister to Dresden, Germany. Two years later she joined her mother in London, England, where she enrolled in the school of the South Kensington Museum. Sophia Hawthorne died in March 1871. Six months later, Rose married George Parsons Lathrop, whom she had met in Dresden.

The Lathrops settled in the vicinity of Boston, Massachusetts, where George worked for the *Atlantic Monthly* and later as an assistant editor. In 1877 he became editor of the Boston *Sunday Courier.* During this time Rose wrote poetry and short stories, which appeared in a variety of magazines, including *Harper's Bazaar* and *St. Nicholas.* She published a book of her poems, *Along the Shore,* in 1888. The Lathrops' only child, Francis Hawthorne, was born in November 1876. Although George and Rose were not received into the Roman Catholic Church until 1891, they baptized their son in that faith shortly after his birth.

Francis Hawthorne Lathrop died of diphtheria in 1881. Unable to remain in a home filled with memories of their son, his parents first traveled to Europe and then relocated to New York City. George Lathrop took a job as literary editor for the New York *Sunday Star,* and Rose resumed her writing. Though the couple collaborated on a book, *A Story of Courage* (1894), which told the story of the founding of the Visitation order of nuns of the Roman Catholic Church in Washington, D.C., the Lathrops' marriage was disintegrating. Frequent quarrels and George's problems with alcohol led to their permanent separation in 1895. George died three years later.

In the year following the breakup of her marriage, Rose embarked on a new vocation. Inspired by others who had tended the poor and sick and influenced by her father's concern for the sufferings of humankind, Rose chose to devote the remainder of her life to caring for cancer victims. She spent three months in training at the New York Cancer Hospital and then began hospice work in the slums of Manhattan's Lower East Side. Lathrop's work was supported by friends and others who learned of her program and from royalties earned from her book *Memories of Hawthorne* (1897), which she published under her maiden name.

In 1898 Lathrop was joined by an early associate, Alice Huber, and they began calling themselves Servants for Relief of Incurable Cancer. The following year Archbishop Michael A. Corrigan gave the women permission to become lay sisters of the Dominican third order. On December 8, 1900, Lathrop and Huber took vows as Sister Mary Alphonsa and Sister Mary Rose, respectively. Their community, known as the Dominican Congrega-

tion of St. Rose of Lima, established a motherhouse, a novitiate, and a cancer hospital at Rosary Hill Home in Westchester County, New York. Now Mother Alphonsa, Lathrop moved there in June 1901, while Sister Mary Rose remained in New York City. The two women made their final vows in 1909.

From its humble beginnings, the sisters' work to help the terminally ill rapidly expanded. In 1912 their hospice in Manhattan, St. Rose's Free Home, moved from its fifteen-bed quarters to a new building that housed seventy-five patients. The home at Rosary Hill had forty beds. Mother Alphonsa received patients of all races and faiths. Her order was devoted entirely to nursing and relieving the sufferings of those facing the final days of their lives. Mother Mary Alphonsa died at Rosary Hill Home in Hawthorne, New York, on July 9, 1926.

See also: Roman Catholic Women's Orders (Nuns)
References: Henry Warner Bowden, *Dictionary of American Religious Biography,* 2nd ed. (1993); Edward T. James, ed., *Notable American Women, 1607–1950* (1971); Theodore Maynard, *A Fire Was Lighted: The Life of Rose Hawthorne Lathrop* (1948); *New Catholic Encyclopedia* (1967).

Lazarus, Emma (1849–1887)

Poet, author, and defender of the Jewish people, Emma Lazarus was born in New York City on July 22, 1849. Her parents, Esther (Nathan) Lazarus and Moses Lazarus, were affluent Sephardic Jews, and they saw that their daughter received an excellent private education. Her religious education, however, was minimal, and she ceased attending services, although she did display some interest in Jewish literature and history. When she was eighteen, Lazarus published her first book of poetry, *Poems and Translations, Written between the Ages of Fourteen and Sixteen* (1867).

Emma Lazarus (undated portrait)

A turning point came in Lazarus's life in 1881. Pogroms against Jews in Russia, which erupted following the assassination of Czar Alexander II, caused thousands of Jews to flee to the United States. Observing the plight of the Russian Jews, Lazarus developed a passionate concern for these people while identifying as never before with her Jewish heritage. Lazarus, whose cultured manners, refined intelligence, and lack of adherence to Jewish traditions had led to her acceptance in Gentile society, now witnessed the growing anti-Semitism that was being directed at the hordes of eastern European immigrants. Through her poetry and prose she denounced Christianity's history of anti-Semitism, praised the heroes of Jewish history, and defended eastern European Jews. Writing in Jewish magazines, Lazarus urged those American Jews who were well-to-do and established in the United States to come to the aid of their less fortunate brethren. More

than a decade ahead of the modern Zionist movement, she called for a national Jewish homeland in Palestine. Lazarus herself helped to establish the Hebrew Technical Institute in New York for the purpose of providing education and job training to recent immigrants.

The last, and most popular lines of her famous poem, "The New Colossus" (1883), which was eventually inscribed on the pedestal of the Statue of Liberty in New York's harbor, reflect her sympathy for the immigrants:

> Give me your tired, your poor,
> Your huddled masses yearning to
>   breathe free,
> The wretched refuse of your teeming
>   shore.
> Send these, the homeless, the tem-
>   pest-tost to me,
> I lift my lamp beside the golden
>   door!

Lazarus's activities were cut short when she became ill during the summer of 1884. The following year, she began a tour of Europe with her sisters that was to last eighteen months, but she became critically ill in Paris and was bedridden there until July 1887. She then returned to New York City, where she died of cancer on November 19, 1887, at age thirty-eight.

References: Kathryn Cullen-DuPont, with Annelise Orleck, *The Encyclopedia of Women's History in America* (1996); Edward T. James, ed., *Notable American Women, 1607–1950*, vol. 2 (1971); Susan Hill Lindley, *"You Have Stept Out of Your Place": A History of Women and Religion in America* (1996); Dan Vogel, *Emma Lazarus* (1980); Bette Roth Young, *Emma Lazarus in Her World: Life and Letters* (1995).

Lee, Ann (1736–1784)

Founder in America of the United Society of Believers in Christ's Second Coming, a religious sect commonly known as the

Shakers, Ann Lee was born February 29, 1736, in Manchester, England. Her father, John Lee, was a blacksmith. The name of her mother is unknown, but she apparently was a devout member of the Anglican Church. Like most daughters of working-class English families in the eighteenth century, Ann received no formal education. From the time she was a young girl, she worked in textile mills. At first she was a velvet cutter, and later she worked twelve-hour days preparing cotton for looms. When she was twenty, she put millwork behind her and became a cook in a public infirmary.

Unlike her mother, Ann had little interest in the Anglican religion. She did, however, join the crowds of people who went to listen to the famous revivalist preacher, the Reverend George Whitefield, when he was in Manchester. In 1758 Ann joined an association of dissenters, the United Society of Believers in Christ's Second Coming, led by former Quakers James and Jane Wardley, and this proved to be a turning point in her life. The group exhorted people to repent and to prepare themselves for the imminent coming of Christ, who would this time appear in the form of a woman. Upon arrival, Christ would establish a millennial kingdom on earth. Worship within the Wardley group has been described as lively and informal. Services began with quiet meditation, but soon worshippers became caught up in emotional expression. Prophesies concerning the end of the world, individual testimonies of manifestation and revelation, and physical expression such as falling and jerking, dancing and shaking were all included in the service. The group's Quaker roots, combined with its mode of worship, led to its being called "Shaking Quakers."

At the urging of her parents, in 1762 Ann married Abraham Standerin, an illiterate blacksmith. Historians have conjectured that her parents were attempting to distract her from her attachment with the Wardley group. If that was their intent, they failed, for soon Standerin too joined the sect. Later Ann's father also became a member. During the course of her marriage, Ann delivered four children, all of whom died in infancy. The fourth birth was her most difficult, and Ann almost died herself. Upon the baby's death in October 1766, Ann turned to God for consolation. Ann became convinced that the source of her pain and, in fact, the source of all evil lay in the practice of sexual cohabitation. It became her belief that one could achieve salvation only through publicly confessing one's sins and through celibate living as Jesus had done.

Ann became increasingly vocal within the Wardley sect and participated in the group's efforts to attract attention to its message by disrupting the religious services in local churches. Members of the group, including Ann, were arrested, prosecuted, fined, and imprisoned for assault, destruction of property, and breaking the Sabbath. While confined in prison in 1770, Ann had a vision in which Christ appeared and told her that she was to become his special instrument—"Mother of the New Creation." Also in her vision God revealed to her that the original sin of Adam and Eve was sexual intercourse and she witnessed their expulsion from the Garden of Eden. Mother Ann was even more convinced that celibacy was the only way to salvation. After another arrest, Mother Ann was placed in an insane asylum. While there, she had another vision. She claimed that this time Jesus had revealed to her that she was his anointed successor.

The Wardleys, who were convinced that God was both male and female, accepted Mother Ann as Jesus' successor and spread the word among the members of their sect. Shakers did not worship

Mother Ann or Jesus but held them in profound reverence as the first elders of the church.

In the spring of 1774, Mother Ann received a vision that urged her to minister in America. It was not difficult to leave England for, like other dissenting religious groups, the Shakers experienced a number of arrests as well as verbal and sometimes physical abuse from their non-Shaker neighbors. And despite their rowdy evangelizing, the Shakers had won few converts. Mother Ann left England with her husband and eight members of the sect in May 1774. Upon arriving in New York City, the group was forced to separate in order to earn money. But these—the early stages of the American Revolution—were dangerous times for British pacifists like Mother Ann and the Shakers, and they became anxious to leave the city. In 1776 the Shakers found land that they were able to lease for as long as they wanted in Niskeyuna, near Albany. By this time, Mother Ann and her husband had separated because Abraham could no longer accept the Shakers' commitment to celibacy.

On May 19, 1780, the Shakers for the first time opened their religious service to the general public. Several visitors underwent conversion experiences, and news of the event quickly spread. Soon the small community was swarming with curiosity seekers and people truly thirsting for religion. At one point, the Shakers came under suspicion of the American authorities, who were engaged in war with Britain. The Americans suspected that the sect was a front organization for the British, and Mother Ann Lee was arrested. She was only freed when her brother William and other elders convinced the governor to release her.

News of the arrest and release of a religious pacifist drew sympathy from many New Yorkers. Encouraged by the public response, in 1781 Mother Ann and several elders launched a missionary tour into the neighboring states of Massachusetts and Connecticut. But Shakerism proved to be just as controversial in America as it had been in England. Sometimes the controversy led to violence. On one occasion Mother Ann was attacked by a mob in Petersham, Massachusetts. The rioters dragged her down a flight of stairs and tore off her clothes. Nevertheless, the missionary tour, which lasted from May 1781 to September 1783, drew a number of converts and eventually led to the founding of future Shaker communities in New England.

When the missionaries returned to New York, the elders began to experiment with the practice of joint ownership for which Shaker communities would become well known. Communal living under Shakerism was based upon the understanding that whatever was attained by one individual's efforts would be used for the benefit of all.

In July 1784, William Lee died. Mother Ann, who was unwell herself, was greatly saddened by her brother's death and wished to join him. Two months later, on September 8, 1784, Mother Ann Lee cried out that she saw her brother William coming, in a gold chariot, to take her home and then she died. Her passing led to a crisis within the Shaker faith, but elder James Whitaker held the United Society of Believers together, and the movement survived into the twentieth century. Besides founding a religious movement of her own, Ann Lee's actions and ideas helped to inspire future generations both inside and outside her movement. The Shakers were the first organized group in America to speak out as conscientious objectors against all wars. Their practices of celibate living and the sharing of their possessions among themselves influenced people to aspire to human perfection, and Ann's understanding of God as both a masculine and a feminine deity gave Shakers a theological basis for promoting equal rights for women.

See also: Clergy; Perfectionism
References: Edward Deming Andrews and Faith Andrews, *Work and Worship: The Economic Order of the Shakers* (1974); Terry D. Bilhartz, "Ann Lee," in Frank Magill, ed., *Great Lives from History: American Women Series* (1995); Nardi Reeder Campion, *Ann the Word: The Life of Mother Ann Lee, Founder of the Shakers* (1976); Lawrence Foster, *Women, Family and Utopia: Communal Experiments of the Shakers, the Oneida Community, and the Mormons* (1990).

Lee, Gloria (Byrd) (1926–1962)

Founder of the Cosmon Research Foundation, Gloria Lee, who claimed to have contact with flying saucers, was born in Los Angeles, California, on March 22, 1926. When she was a child, she acted in Hollywood movies and for a time was a model and a singer. A longtime interest in flying influenced her to become a flight attendant when she was an adult. Following her marriage to aircraft designer William Byrd in 1952, she took a position as ground hostess at Los Angeles International Airport and remained in that job for several years.

In 1952 George Adamski became the first person to achieve fame by claiming to have had contact with aliens from outer space. These extraterrestrials, he maintained, operated flying saucers. Gloria Lee reported her first contact with aliens in September of the following year. She said that they were connecting with her at the airport where she worked by means of automatic writing. The contacts increased her interest in flying saucers, and she soon joined several psychic and Theosophical groups, hoping to learn more about them.

Lee claimed that she regularly received messages from a being from a saucer who identified himself as J. W., a resident of the planet Jupiter. He told Lee that she was a reincarnated Venusian. At first they communicated through automatic writing, but before long they were contacting each other via telepathy. Several psychics reported seeing J. W. around Lee. On one occasion, J. W. contacted her to tell her to look at the sky. She did and saw an unidentified flying object (UFO) traveling overhead. The UFO event was reported independently by various people in the Los Angeles area. Impressed by Lee's communications with nonearthly beings, several small quasi-religious telepathic contact groups holding lectures in New York City considered her their absentee high priestess.

Lee's contacts motivated her to found the Cosmon Research Foundation in 1959. She also published her first book, *Why We Are Here!* (1959), which describes the nature of the theosophical spiritual hierarchy as an interstellar command. (The spiritual hierarchy comprises mahatmas, or spiritual masters, who theosophists believe live on through the centuries in various incarnations. They guard their knowledge, teaching it only to worthy students.) Lee argued that the instructors were aliens from outer space. Her book stressed vegetarianism and a positive attitude toward sexuality. A second book, *The Changing Conditions of Your World*, was published in 1962.

Her first book and her foundation gave Lee prominence within the contactee community. She worked with Mark (whose public name was Charles Boyd Gentzel), a founder of the Mark-Age Meta Center in Florida, and found that they were twin souls. She later learned that J. W. had been incarnated in human form as Jim Speed, a man she met at the center.

In September 1962 Lee traveled to Washington, D.C., to speak with government officials. J. W. had telepathically given her plans for a spaceship, and she was to present them to scientists. Lee and her companion, foundation member Hedy Hood, took a room at the Hotel Claridge, and following J. W.'s instructions, Lee began a fruit juice fast. There are two versions of the end of the story. One is that she was to continue until she was visited by government officials. A second reports that she was to fast until a "light elevator" arrived to carry her away to Jupiter. In any event, no one came. On November 29, 1962, she went into a coma, and she died on December 2.

In death Lee was said to have communicated with others of the contactee community, including Yolanda, another founder of the Mark-Age Meta Center. Yolanda's alleged conversations with Lee resulted in the booklet, *Gloria Lee Lives!* (1963). Verity, a medium with the Heralds of the New Age in New Zealand, produced a book that was supposedly dictated by Lee. It claimed that Lee had become a member of the Ashtar Command, "an Etheric Band of Beings whose commander-in-chief is Jesus of Nazareth" (Melton, 1986, p. 156). For several years, Lee was remembered as a martyr of the contactee movement, but she was forgotten after leadership changes in the 1970s.

References: Paris Flammonde, *The Age of Flying Saucers* (1971); J. Gordon Melton, *Biographical Dictionary of American Cult and Sect Leaders* (1986); J. Gordon Melton, *Religious Leaders of America* (1991).

Lee, Jarena (1783–?)

Jarena Lee, perhaps the first female preacher of the First African Methodist Episcopal Church, was born in Cape May, New Jersey, on February 11, 1783. An African American who was probably born free, Jarena became separated from her parents at the age of seven when they hired her out as a servant in a household about 60 miles from her home. Little else is known of her youth, except that she did return to Cape May to visit her parents when she was about fourteen years old.

Her parents were not religious, but it is likely that Jarena received some religious schooling in her new home. She later recounted that her first religious experience occurred shortly after she began her service. Jarena lied to her employer regarding a task she was to have attended to but had not performed. Jarena recalled that "the Spirit of God moved in power through my conscience, and told me I was a wretched sinner" (Lee, 1988, p. 3). Although she promised God that she would never again lie, she found it difficult to refrain from sinning. But, she remembered, "the Spirit of the Lord . . . continued mercifully striving with me, until his gracious power converted my soul" (Lee, 1988, p. 3). Her conversion experience occurred in about 1804, when Jarena was twenty-one years of age.

Reverend Richard Allen, the minister at her local church in Philadelphia whose preaching she found uplifting, helped to inspire Jarena's conversion experience. She later recalled that while in church, three weeks after she first heard Allen preach, she felt overwhelmed by the spirit of the Lord and realized that she had been granted salvation. Four or five years passed, during which time she had many doubts about her conversion and on several occasions had been in such despair that she contemplated committing suicide. A Methodist man, William Scott, helped her when he described the doctrine of "sanctification," as interpreted by the founder of Methodism, John Wesley. Jarena asked God for sanctification of her soul and, about three months after her conversations with Scott, was finally convinced that she had received it. Then she heard a voice tell her to "go preach the Gospel!" (Lee, 1988, p. 10).

Jarena approached Reverend Allen and told him that she wished to preach among the Methodists. Allen advised her that it was acceptable for women to hold prayer meetings but not to become preachers. She accepted his decision and set aside her aspirations to preach. In 1811, shortly after her meeting with Allen, she married Joseph Lee, pastor of a church outside Philadelphia.

Joseph Lee died in about 1818, leaving Jarena with a two-year-old child and an infant. She began to preach, and Richard Allen, who by then had become bishop of the African Methodist Episcopal Church, finally approved her desire to preach. From then on preaching became the center of her life. Although she was never licensed by the church as a preacher, she traveled thousands of miles preaching the Gospel.

Lee kept a journal of her experiences as a preacher, and in 1833 she hired an editor to arrange a portion of her religious journal into narrative so that it would be appropriate for publication. She thought that others might be more easily led to Christ by reading how God worked in and through her. In 1836, one thousand copies of her *Life* were printed. Lee distributed the books herself, at camp meetings, in churches, and on the streets. Three years later, she had another thousand copies printed. She published her *Religious Experience and Journal* in 1849, which told the story of her life up to the age of fifty. There is no record of Lee's life beyond 1849, and her date of death is unknown.

Lee was a groundbreaker for further preaching among African-American women. In 1850 a group of African Methodist Episcopal women who, like Lee, felt called to preach but were unlicensed, joined together in an attempt to help women preach in local churches. Although the organization fell apart within two years, it was an indication of the women's eagerness to preach and their awareness of the limitations placed upon women.

See also: African Americans; Second Great Awakening

References: Andrews, William L., ed., *Sisters of the Spirit: Three Black Women's Autobiographies of the Nineteenth Century* (1986); Jarena Lee, "Religious Experience and Journal of Mrs. Jarena Lee," in *Spiritual Narratives* (1988); Bert James Loewenberg and Ruth Bogin, eds., *Black Women in Nineteenth-Century American Life: Their Words, Their Thoughts, Their Feelings* (1976); Marla J. Selvidge, *Notorious Voices: Feminist Biblical Interpretation, 1500–1920* (1996).

Lincoln (Mowry), Salome (1807–1841)

A pioneer among women preachers, Salome Lincoln was born in Raynham, Massachusetts, on September 13, 1807. When she was fifteen years old, she had a religious conversion while sitting under a tree in a grove near her home. Lincoln later recalled that she was meditating upon her life, which she considered so sinful that she would never receive God's grace. Then suddenly she thought, "Has not Christ died for the very worst of sinners? I cannot be worse than the worst—perhaps there is yet mercy for *me!*" Lincoln dropped on her knees and prayed. Then, "O, what glory filled my soul at that moment!" (Davis, 1843, p. 31). She remembered that when she stood up, everything around her appeared to be fresh and new, and everything seemed to be praising the Lord. Lincoln wanted to tell the entire world about Jesus Christ, for she was overcome with the sense of having been saved.

Lincoln was baptized on April 8, 1823, but for a while after her conversion she felt that her religious devotion was backsliding. "The church," she said, "began to decline, and I with the rest" (Davis, 1843, p. 32). Her religious fervor was revitalized sometime in 1825 when religious revivals reached Raynham and the vicinity where she was working in a textile mill. The idea of a woman becoming a preacher was practically unheard of in early nineteenth-century America, so

Lincoln struggled with the thought for some time. Although she realized that society would likely oppose her preaching in public, she felt that she had God's approval.

Lincoln preached her first sermon on October 17, 1827, at a meeting about 2 miles from the Lincoln family home. She was not scheduled to preach, but when she realized that the minister who had been expected was not going to appear, she stood up and spoke to a group of mostly young people. In 1830 Lincoln became a full-time itinerant minister, touring New England and holding revival meetings (usually in private homes) over the next five years. In December 1835 she married a minister of her church, Elder Junia S. Mowry. As a wife, she continued to preach on various occasions until 1840. The Mowrys' first child, Mary Elizabeth, was born in November 1837, but she died when she was a year old. A second daughter was born in early 1841, but Salome was ill with consumption at the time of the baby's birth. Salome Lincoln Mowry died at her home in Tiverton, Massachusetts, on July 21, 1841.

References: Almond H. Davis, *The Female Preacher, or Memoir of Salome Lincoln* (1843, reprint 1972); Gerda Lerner, *The Female Experience: An American Documentary* (1977); Susan Hill Lindley, *"You Have Stept Out of Your Place": A History of Women and Religion in America* (1996).

Livermore, Mary Ashton Rice (1820–1905)

Suffragist, temperance leader, and author Mary Ashton Rice Livermore was born December 19, 1820, in Boston, Massachusetts. She was the fourth child and the first to survive infancy of the six children of Timothy and Zebiah Vose Glover (Ashton) Rice. Timothy Rice was a Baptist of uncompromising Calvinistic faith and high ethical standards. Although his

wife was more lenient, the Rice children were raised in a strict religious environment in which the family held religious services twice a day, and the children were expected to read the entire Bible every year. As a result of her rigorous Calvinistic upbringing, Mary lived much of her life fearing that she was destined for eternal damnation.

Most of Mary's childhood was spent in Boston, interrupted only once when her father moved the family to western New York, where he tried farming for two years. Mary received her education at local public and private schools. After graduating from the Hancock Grammar School at age fourteen, she attended the Female Seminary of Charlestown and within a year of her enrollment had become a part-time teacher in addition to being a pupil. After graduation in 1836, she remained for two more years as an instructor of French, Latin, and Italian. In 1839 she accepted a position as tutor for a family on a Virginia plantation, where she remained for three years. Mary returned to Massachusetts in 1842 to teach at a private coeducational school at Duxbury. While teaching in Duxbury, she met the Reverend Daniel Parker Livermore, a minister of the Universalist Church. In addition to the man himself, Mary was attracted to Daniel's Universalist faith of love, hope, and salvation. Married on May 6, 1845, they lived together happily until Daniel's death in 1899.

For the first sixteen years of their marriage, Mary aided her husband in his work as a clergyman, cared for their three daughters, and supplemented the family income by writing stories and poems for religious periodicals. In 1857, while working as a pastor at the Second Universalist Church in Chicago, Daniel purchased the *New Covenant*, a Universalist monthly that he had been editing. Mary was associate editor of the journal, which remained in the family until 1869.

Throughout her marriage Mary Livermore had engaged in occasional charitable work, but with the outbreak of the Civil War in 1861 she threw her full energy into humanitarian work. She volunteered her services to the Northwestern Branch of the United States Sanitary Commission, a government agency that provided relief for the sick and wounded of the Union army. Together with her close friend and fellow worker in Chicago charities, Jane C. Hoge, Livermore made frequent speaking tours; wrote thousands of letters; strove to obtain funds, surgical supplies, and food supplements for the army; and campaigned for the establishment of over three thousand local aid societies in five states. She traveled to the front with supplies, toured Union hospitals, offered comfort to soldiers, and provided reports to government officials that helped them improve conditions for their men. Livermore also accompanied large numbers of invalid soldiers after they were discharged from the army to go home to die.

Livermore's wartime experiences convinced her of the need for woman suffrage. Previously she had believed that social reforms could be effected without granting women the vote. In 1868 she delivered the opening address at Illinois's first woman suffrage convention, was elected president of the Illinois Woman Suffrage Association that emerged from it, and served as president of the American Woman Suffrage Association from 1875 to 1878. In 1869 she established *The Agitator,* a paper devoted to the suffrage cause. When *The Agitator* merged with the Boston-based *Woman's Journal,* Livermore, who had recently moved with her family to Melrose, Massachusetts, became editor of the new periodical. She resigned from the journal in 1872 to devote more time to the lecture circuit. Over the next quarter-century, Livermore was a popular platform speaker, discussing issues of education and temperance as well as topics in history and politics. Between 1875 and 1885, as president of the Massachusetts branch of the Woman's Christian Temperance Union, Livermore delivered temperance sermons in churches and in other gatherings throughout the state. She retired from the lecture circuit in 1895.

After her husband died in 1899, Livermore was drawn to Spiritualism and reported having conversations with the deceased clergyman. During her last years, she suffered from severe pain in her eyes and happily awaited the day that she would be reunited with Daniel. Livermore died in Boston of bronchopneumonia and heart disease on May 23, 1905.

See also: Woman Suffrage; Woman's Christian Temperance Union

References: Henry Warner Bowden, *Dictionary of American Religious Biography,* 2nd ed. (1993); *Dictionary of American Biography,* vol. 11 (1933); Edward T. James, ed., *Notable American Women, 1607–1950,* vol. 2 (1971); Mary A. Livermore, *The Story of My Life* (1897).

Lowry, Edith Elizabeth (1897–1970)

Edith Elizabeth Lowry, who directed an interdenominational ministry for migrant workers for several decades and was an executive within various church councils, including the National Council of Churches, was born in Plainfield, New Jersey, on March 23, 1897. She was raised by her parents, Elizabeth Darling and Robert Hanson Lowry, in the Baptist faith. Attending local public elementary and high schools, Lowry continued her education at Wellesley College, where she studied languages and graduated with a bachelor of arts degree in 1920. Two years later, she began her lifelong career in mission work, joining the staff of the Department of Education and Publicity of the Board of Missions of the Presbyterian Church in the U.S.A. (However, she remained a Baptist throughout her life.) In 1926 she became executive secretary of the Council of Women for Home Missions, one of the country's early national ecumenical agencies.

Lowry's major responsibility with the Council of Women was to work among migrant workers, and in 1929 she became the director of the migrant ministries program. She held this position throughout the Great Depression. Lowry made frequent visits to migrant camps, where she observed the difficult living conditions and then made speeches and wrote articles to bring the workers' plight to public attention. In the three decades that she directed the program, the staff of professionals hired to work among the migrants grew from three to thirty-five. These included social workers, nurses, ministers, and schoolteachers.

In 1936 Lowry was appointed to the post of executive secretary of the Council of Women. Three years later she became the first woman to be invited to speak on the National Radio Pulpit, and she spoke on the theme "Women in a Changing World." She led the Council of Women when it merged with a like agency, the Home Missions Council of North America, in 1940 and was named coexecutive secretary of the unified agency. In 1938 Lowry compiled and published a widely read book, *They Starve That We May Eat,* which described the difficult life faced by migrant workers and offered suggestions for solutions to the problem. Among her ideas was the proposal that federal, state, and local government agencies work together to provide adequate health services and housing for workers and school facilities for their children. She urged that these agencies also see that the migrants and their children be protected from exploitation in labor. In 1940, she and two associates compiled a second book, *Tales of Americans on Trek.*

Meanwhile, her work among the migrants themselves continued. During the 1940s she created new services among them, including day care centers for the children of working parents. In 1950 the Home Missions Council combined with other agencies to form the National Council of Churches, and Lowry became the first secretary of the council's Board of Home Missions. Again, she was able to use her position to help the migrants. She developed a program that could reach people in the more remote migrant camps, carrying recreational, health, and religious supplies to the workers by station wagon.

Lowry retired from the council in 1962 but consulted for two years with the National Council on Agricultural Life and Labor in Washington, D.C., a clearinghouse for thirty-five private national organizations concerned with farm labor problems. The final years of her life were spent on a farm in Vermont. She died in Claremont, New Hampshire, on March 11, 1970.

References: Edith E. Lowry, ed., *They Starve That We May Eat* (1938); J. Gordon Melton, *Religious Leaders of America* (1991); Barbara Sicherman and Carol Hurd Green, eds., *Notable American Women: The Modern Period* (1980).

Lutheran Church

The Lutheran Church in the United States seems to have been slower than other mainline denominations to grant women responsible roles in the service of their church. With the exception of the work of their deaconesses, Lutheran women took longer than most other Protestant women to organize missionary societies, study groups, or other activities within their churches.

The Lutheran faith has existed in America since colonial times, arriving with the early German and Scandinavian immigrants in the seventeenth and early eighteenth centuries. A second wave of German immigrants arrived in the early nineteenth century, and more Scandinavians followed after the Civil War. Although women were active in helping to organize their new American congregations, usually two to three decades passed before they were able to establish separate societies within their local churches. Women in some Lutheran congregations formed charitable societies early in the nineteenth century, but it was not until the 1870s and 1880s that they organized in earnest. Historian L. DeAne Lagerquist finds that there was opposition in some churches when women began holding meetings separately, with some opponents fearing that the women's time would be devoted to gossip, although others were afraid that the women might form cliques that would divide the congregation.

Of all Lutheran women's activity in the nineteenth and early twentieth centuries, it appears that the deaconess movement was the most successful. It eventually became one of the three most productive deaconess movements among Protestant churches in this country. The first female diaconate in America was established in 1849–1850 by a Lutheran pastor, William Passavant of Pittsburgh, Pennsylvania. Modeled after a thriving Lutheran institution at Kaiserwerth, Germany (which also became a model for diaconates of other Protestant denominations), it included a hospital that would become known as the Pittsburgh Infirmary (later the Passavant Hospital), a motherhouse, and an organization called the Institute of Protestant Deaconesses. Although four German deaconesses came to the United States in 1849 to staff the infirmary and the first American deaconess was consecrated the following year, the institution received little support from the Lutheran Church, and few American women were attracted to the organization. Many Lutherans thought the diaconate to be too much like Roman Catholic communities. When interest in deaconesses revived in the 1880s and 1890s, Passavant's diaconate re-emerged in Milwaukee, Wisconsin, in 1893, with a motherhouse, a hospital, and a training program.

As historian Susan Hill Lindley points out, the late nineteenth century found American Lutherans divided by ethnic and theological differences. Thus, the various bodies of the church established separate diaconates, which likely contributed to the initial sluggishness of the deaconess movement among Lutherans. Largely due to the work of Elizabeth Fedde, a Norwegian deaconess who came to the United States in 1883, the centers of deaconess work among Norwegian-American Lutherans were in Brooklyn, Chicago, and Minneapolis. In addition to the Passavant diaconate in Milwaukee, much of the German-American deaconess work was concentrated in Philadelphia; Danish-Americans were established in Brush, Colorado; and Swedish-American Lutherans managed institutions in Omaha and Axtell, Nebraska, and St. Paul, Minnesota. Despite their varying backgrounds, several of the diaconal groups united to form the Lutheran Deaconess Conference in North America in 1894. This became the first inter-Lutheran agency in the United States.

Although most Lutheran deaconesses became involved in hospital work, some performed social work or were active in foreign missions. Lutherans were careful to classify the women's work as a "ministry of mercy"; women were not ordained to preach God's word (Lindley, 1996, p. 130). Lindley finds that because of the centrality of the motherhouse ideal, Lutherans considered their deaconesses distinctive and foremost among diaconates in America. They saw their diaconate as a school, church, home, family, and religious congregation that was superior to others because its members were totally committed to their work and to Christ. The deaconess movement within the Lutheran Church achieved its highest numbers of participants during the first third of the twentieth century.

The Lutheran Church was somewhat slower than many other Protestant denominations to send female missionaries overseas, but by the end of the nineteenth century Lutheran women had become active in the missionary movement. Since they were unable to become ordained pastors, mission work was one of the few ministerial careers open to women. Lagerquist reports that there were usually three types of female missionaries: deaconesses, other single women, and wives of male missionaries. They served as teachers, dormitory matrons, nurses, doctors, and in various other positions. As in other Protestant denominations, female missionaries in the Lutheran Church usually worked among women and children. Women working in the mission field could usually count on the financial and moral support of women in their churches in America.

The purpose of most Lutheran women's groups was to support foreign missions, though they eventually broadened their understanding of "mission" to include support of home missions, the church's educational and charitable programs, and social action projects. Although the women appear to have been more active and more dedicated to mission work than Lutheran men, their missions associations were unable to develop autonomy in terms of organization or financial control until well into the twentieth century. Lindley finds this to be the case even in their prayer or study groups and especially so among Lutheran women living in the Midwest.

Given women's lack of organizational power, it is perhaps not surprising that the ordination of women to the ministry was not seriously debated within the Lutheran Church in the United States until the late 1950s and 1960s. American Lutherans were behind the Lutheran churches in Norway and Sweden, in which female ordination was approved in 1938 and 1958, respectively. However, once the ordination issue was brought up for discussion, the debate was not as bitter as in other Protestant denominations. Both the Lutheran Church in America and the American Lutheran Church (now united as the Evangelical Lutheran Church in America) approved the ordination of women at their 1970 conventions, and each of these bodies had ordained one woman by 1972. The third major body of the church, the Missouri Synod, voted 674 to 194 to not permit women to hold pastoral office, basing the decision on the Pauline injunction that women "keep silence in the churches" (I Corinthians 14:34) and that women were not to teach or to have "authority over men" (I Timothy 2:12). Today both the Missouri Synod and the smaller Wisconsin Synod disapprove of the ordination of women to the ministry.

See also: Andrews, Barbara; Fedde, Elizabeth; Kugler, Anna Sarah
References: Gracia Grindal, "How Lutheran Women Came to Be Ordained," in Gloria E. Bengtson, ed., *Lutheran Women in Ordained Ministry: 1970–1995* (1995); L. DeAne Lagerquist, *From Our Mothers' Arms: A History of Women in the American Lutheran Church* (1987); Susan Hill Lindley, *"You Have Stept Out of Your Place": A History of Women and Religion in America* (1996); E. Clifford Nelson, *Lutheranism in North America, 1914–1970* (1972).

Lyman, Mary Reddington Ely (1887–1975)

One of the first female theologians in American Protestantism, Mary Reddington Ely Lyman was born in St. Johnsbury, Vermont, on November 24, 1887. The youngest of the four daughters of Henry Guy and Adelaide (Newell) Ely, Mary was raised in the Congregational Church, where her father was a deacon. She attended local schools, graduating from St. Johnsbury Academy in 1906. In 1911 Mary graduated from Mount Holyoke College in South Hadley, Massachusetts. She then taught high school in Connecticut for two years before returning to Mount Holyoke to serve as general secretary of the Young Women's Christian Association (YWCA) from 1913 to 1916. In that position she taught evening Bible classes. She so enjoyed the classes that she enrolled in Union Theological Seminary in New York City in 1916 as the only woman in her class. Mary graduated at the top of her class in 1919. Because she was a woman she was not allowed to attend the commencement luncheon and was required to sit in the balcony, away from her class, during the graduation ceremony. She continued her education at Cambridge University in England for two years, but the university refused to grant her a theological degree because she was a woman and would not issue her transcript for the same reason. Returning to the United States, Mary taught at Vassar College while pursuing her doctorate at the University of Chicago. She earned her doctorate with her dissertation "The Knowledge of God in the Fourth Gospel," graduating magna cum laude in 1924. The dissertation was published under the title *Knowledge of God in Johanine Thought* the following year.

In 1926 Mary Ely married Eugene N. Lyman, Marcellus Hartley Professor of the Philosophy of Religion at Union Seminary. Mary began teaching religion at Barnard College in New York in 1929, remaining in that post until 1940. She also taught part-time at Union Theological Seminary. During the 1930s, Lyman wrote several theological works, including *The Fourth Gospel and the Life*

of Today (1931), *The Christian Epic* (1936), and *Jesus* (1937). When Eugene Lyman retired in 1940, the couple moved to Virginia. There Mary became dean and professor of religion at Sweet Briar College. Her husband died in 1948, and the following year Mary was ordained a Congregational minister in Cummington, Massachusetts, a town where Eugene Lyman had grown up and where the couple had spent their summers during their marriage. In 1950 Lyman returned to Union Theological Seminary as Morris K. Jessup Professor of English Bible and dean of women students. She was the first woman to hold a faculty chair at Union and one of the first women to be a full professor in any American seminary. As time passed, she began to recognize her unique role as a woman in the higher echelons of the church. She overcame her dislike of crusading and became an advocate for women desiring professions in churches and theological schools.

Lyman retired from her professorship in 1955 but remained busy as a lecturer and was active with the World Council of Churches. She also continued writing, publishing two books in 1960, *Death and the Christian Answer* and *In Him Was Life: A Study Guide on the Gospel of St. John*. In 1961 Mary Lyman moved to Claremont, California. She died there on January 9, 1975.

References: J. Gordon Melton, *Religious Leaders of America* (1991); Melanie Parry, ed., *Larousse Dictionary of Women* (1996); Barbara Sicherman and Carol Hurd Green, eds., *Notable American Women: The Modern Period* (1980).

Lyon, Mary (1797–1849)

Mary Lyon, a pioneer in women's education and founder of Mount Holyoke Seminary, was born February 28, 1797, in Buckland, Massachusetts, to Aaron and Jemima (Shepard) Lyon. Her ancestors,

Mary Lyon (undated photo)

mostly farmers and craftsmen, included ministers, deacons, and selectmen. Aaron Lyon, a veteran of the American Revolution, was a farmer. He died before Mary reached her sixth birthday. When Mary's mother remarried in 1810 and moved with her new husband, Jonathan Taylor, to Ashfield, Massachusetts, she left her twenty-one-year-old son Aaron to manage the family farm. Mary, who was then age thirteen, remained with him to perform the many domestic chores at the homestead. Her brother paid her $1 a week for her efforts.

For many years Lyon attended a Baptist church where her grandmother's brother, Elder Enos Smith, preached. It was during one of his sermons in 1816 that Lyon first experienced the assurance of God's presence. But when she was baptized six years later, it was as a member of the Congregational Church. As a young woman, Lyon's interest was drawn to missionary work. She was a generous contributor to the cause, giving to the American Board of Commissioners for Foreign Missions all her adult life.

Little is known of Lyon's early education, but in the summer of 1814 she began to teach at a school in the village of Shelburne Falls, launching her career as an educator. She found the experience unpleasant. Her pay was seventy-five cents a week plus room and board, but she "boarded round," living an equal number of days with each pupil. Young and inexperienced, Lyon had problems maintaining discipline in the classroom. She later recalled that after the term ended she had resolved never to teach again, but she returned the following summer. With the exception of the years 1835 to 1837, when she was struggling to organize Mount Holyoke Seminary, she taught at least part of every year for the rest of her life.

While she was teaching others, Lyon strove to enhance her own education. In the fall of 1817, she enrolled at Sanderson Academy in Ashfield, Massachusetts. While there, she became a legend in the area by learning the entire Latin grammar text in three days and reciting it before her class. She also developed a friendship with a girl named Amanda White. White's father, who was a strong believer in education, helped Lyon, who could not afford to pay for a second term at the academy. He arranged for a tuition waiver, and she boarded with the White family. Both Thomas White and his wife gave Lyon practical assistance and encouragement for the next twenty-five years.

Lyon spent a term at Amherst Academy in 1818, studying Latin, science, and history. There she watched as the academy and townspeople made plans to build a college and saw that citizens were ready to provide funding for the project. In 1821 Lyon attended a seminary in Byfield, Massachusetts. There she encountered the teaching that would influence her the rest of her life. The Reverend Joseph Emerson, the founder of the seminary, had what Lyon considered an unusually high estimate of the intellectual powers of women. He treated them as he treated men. Lyon also admired Emerson's assistant, Zilpah Polly Grant. The two women developed a friendship that would help Lyon during the years 1824–1834 as she made her way toward her ultimate goal of furthering the education of young women.

After her term at Byfield, Lyon returned to Sanderson Academy as a teacher. She left in 1824 to work with Grant at the new Adams Academy in Londonderry, New Hampshire, earning $5 a week plus board. Lyon taught a seven-month summer term there and, in between, independently conducted three-month winter terms at a girls' school in Buckland for six years. A stimulating and innovative teacher, Lyon explored new ways of instruction, including involving her students in discussions of current events.

In 1828 the Adams trustees forced Grant out of the academy because they disagreed with her on academic and religious matters. Grant then established Ipswich (Massachusetts) Female Seminary and was the school's first principal. Her friend Mary Lyon left Adams to become a teacher at Ipswich. While Lyon taught, she continued to attend classes, studying at both Amherst College and the Rensselaer School (later Rensselaer Polytechnic Institute). A bout with typhoid in 1828 led Lyon to decide to leave Buckland Seminary and devote her time and energies to her work at Ipswich.

Both Grant and Lyon endeavored to acquire strong financial backing for the Ipswich Female Seminary. When their efforts failed, they attempted to raise funds for a new institution, a New England Female Seminary for Teachers. But they

drew only modest support, and that soon disappeared.

During the summer of 1833, Lyon traveled through the northern United States, visiting schools and colleges and observing their management. Her tour inspired her to work harder for a means to improve female education. In 1834 she presented a plan for a residential seminary to be founded and maintained by the Christian public. Tuition and board would be as low as possible to draw bright young women whose only obstacle to higher education was the lack of sufficient funds to meet expenses.

The first $1,000 toward the funding of the seminary came from women living in the Ipswich area. As her plans began to take shape, Lyon resigned from the Ipswich Seminary in 1834. She ignored critics who argued that higher education for women would prevent them from performing their true function as wives, mothers, and homemakers. Despite the naysayers, several towns invited her to establish her institution in their communities, anticipating that it would serve to help their local economies. Lyon chose the town of South Hadley, Massachusetts, which contributed $8,000 toward the construction of the school. Mount Holyoke Seminary (now College) was chartered in 1836, and opened in 1837 with an enrollment of eighty young women.

Lyon headed the school and served as its principal for almost twelve years. She worked tirelessly for the school as long as she was able. During her years at Mount Holyoke, Lyon's interest in missionary work was strengthened. In 1843 she wrote A Missionary Offering, in which she pleaded for the missionary cause that had attracted her during her youth. She contributed almost half her salary to mission work and inspired teachers and students to donate to the cause as well. Many eagerly enlisted in mission work themselves. Others married missionaries and aided their husbands as they sought to educate and spread Christianity in foreign lands.

Early in 1849, as she was beginning to recover from a bout with erysipelas, Lyon, who was close to her family, learned that a nephew had committed suicide. The shock and agony she suffered upon learning the news likely contributed to a relapse of her illness. She died in her rooms at Mount Holyoke on March 5, 1849.

See also: Mount Holyoke College
References: Eleanor Flexner, *Century of Struggle: The Woman's Rights Movement in the United States* (1970); Willystine Goodsell, *Pioneers of Women's Education in America* (1931); Elizabeth Alden Green, *Mary Lyon and Mount Holyoke: Opening the Gates* (1979); Edward T. James, ed., *Notable American Women, 1607–1950,* vol. 2 (1971).

MacLaine, Shirley (1934–)

Although best known as an actress and movie star, Shirley MacLaine emerged in the 1980s as a leading spokesperson for the New Age movement. She was born Shirley MacLean Beatty in Richmond, Virginia, on April 24, 1934. Her family was Southern Baptist, but she and her brother, Warren, were raised in a relatively liberal environment. Ballet was central to her world from the time she was three years old, and she began taking dance lessons in her preschool years. By the time she was in high school, she was dancing professionally.

After graduating from high school, MacLaine moved to New York. She was eighteen years old and working in the chorus of a Broadway musical when she met Steve Parker. They married in 1954. MacLaine's first big break in show business came that same year, when she was selected to replace Carol Haney in the Broadway production of *The Pajama Game.* Before long she was a well-known and respected actress.

Inspired by Marlon Brando, who encouraged her to join a protest against capital punishment, in the 1960s MacLaine became one of many Hollywood celebrities who were politically active. She was outspoken in her opposition to American involvement in Vietnam, was a delegate to both the 1968 and 1972 Democratic Party conventions, and campaigned for George McGovern in 1972. MacLaine also became known for her statements in support of environmental protection, women's rights, and civil rights.

MacLaine was at the height of her acting career when she wrote her first book, *Don't Fall Off the Mountain* (1970). Her second book, *You Can Get There from Here,* appeared five years later. Her marriage, however, was coming to an end, and she and Parker divorced in 1977. At about the same time, she began to explore the spiritual aspect of her nature and of others and became convinced of the existence of a spirit world. She visited a number of Spiritualist mediums, or channels as they are called within the New Age movement, and told the story of her early psychic/spiritual experiences in *Out on a Limb* (1983).

MacLaine continued her exploration of the occult throughout the 1980s, including participating in sessions with J. Z. Knight, who is reputed to be the channel for an entity named Ramtha. MacLaine's book *Dancing in the Light* (1985) discusses this experience and also tells of sessions with San Francisco medium Kevin Ryerson. After the book was adapted into a television movie in 1987, MacLaine emerged as a leader of the New Age movement. She began to give lectures and workshops, teaching what she had learned during her years of experience within the movement. She has also raised money to open New Age centers. Initially, MacLaine relished giving the seminars, enjoying the people and the constant ebb and flow of energy within her audiences. In addition, she felt more like a student who was sharing her experiences with others than like a teacher. Eventually, however, she put an end to the seminars. They had grown to become too large and she began to feel uncomfortable when others in the New Age movement began to take her words too seriously. She found that she could not accept the responsibility of that kind of power. MacLaine has since written a book on meditation, *Going Within: A Guide for Inner Transformation* (1989), in which she stresses the importance of knowing and loving oneself in order to understand and love the world in which one lives. Also in 1989, she produced a home video, *Shirley MacLaine's Inner Workout,* which quickly became popular. In 1995 she published *My Lucky Stars,* a memoir of the four decades that she has worked in Hollywood.

References: Shirley MacLaine, *Dancing in the Light* (1985); Shirley MacLaine, *Going Within: A Guide for Inner Transformation* (1989); Shirley MacLaine, *My Lucky Stars: A Hollywood Memoir* (1995); Shirley MacLaine, *Out on a Limb* (1983); Shirley MacLaine, *You Can Get There from Here* (1975); J. Gordon Melton, *New Age Encyclopedia* (1990); J. Gordon Melton, *Religious Leaders of America* (1991).

Mallory, Kathleen Moore
(1879–1954)

Kathleen Moore Mallory, longtime leader of the Woman's Missionary Union (WMU) of the Southern Baptist Convention, was born January 24, 1879, in Summerfield, Alabama. She was the third of the six children of a prominent southern family. As a girl, she was an excellent student, and she later attended the Woman's College of Baltimore (now Goucher College), graduating in 1902. During her senior year, she became engaged to a young medical student, Janney Lupton. The couple postponed marriage while Lupton completed his studies and established his practice. Meanwhile, Mallory worked as a teacher. Mallory

and Lupton never married because the young man died of tuberculosis in 1907.

After the death of her fiancé, Mallory decided that she did not have the personality to be a schoolteacher and sought another career. She found solace in her local church, the First Baptist Church of Selma, and was soon actively involved in church work. It was not long before she was the leader of the Woman's Missionary Union for her area, and in 1909 she became the secretary of the state WMU organization. Her energetic work for missions came to the attention of national WMU leaders, and when the position of corresponding secretary became vacant in 1912, Mallory was elected to the post. Mallory moved to Baltimore, where the organization had its headquarters, in September of that year. There she rented a small apartment and threw herself into the work of the WMU. She became known for her spartan existence and the systematic manner in which she carried out her responsibilities with the WMU. Mallory made two extended trips to the mission field, visiting Asia in 1923–1924 and South America in 1930, but otherwise remained close to her office. On each of these occasions, she paid her own way and would not accept a salary for those months away from headquarters.

Throughout her many years in office, Mallory wrote and edited much of the annual *WMU Yearbook.* She wrote her only book, the *Manual of WMU Methods,* in 1917, and from 1920 to 1948 she edited the Baptist monthly *Royal Service.* In 1921 she directed the move of the WMU to its new headquarters in Birmingham, Alabama. Under her leadership, the WMU was organized into an efficient fund-raising vehicle for the Baptist convention and its missionary programs. Mallory was a devoutly religious woman who frequently turned to prayer to help meet her many challenges. She is credited with keeping the WMU financially solvent during the decade of the Great Depression and with making the WMU the influential organization within the Baptist convention that it is today.

After leading the WMU for thirty-six years, Mallory retired in 1948. She spent several more years in Birmingham before moving to Selma, where she lived out her final years. Following her retirement, the WMU honored Mallory by naming a number of buildings for her. Kathleen Mallory died in Selma on June 17, 1954.

See also: Armstrong, Annie Walker; McIntosh, Martha E.; Woman's Missionary Union

References: Catherine B. Allen, *Laborers Together with God: 22 Great Women in Baptist Life* (1987); J. Gordon Melton, *Religious Leaders of America* (1991); Annie Wright Ussery, *The Story of Kathleen Mallory* (1956).

Marshall (LeSourd), Sarah Catherine Wood (1914–1983)

Best-selling writer of religious books, Sarah Catherine Wood Marshall was born in Johnson City, Tennessee, on September 27, 1914. Her early years were spent in Mississippi and West Virginia, where her father, a Presbyterian clergyman, pastored congregations. As a child, she developed a love for reading and writing and dreamed of becoming a professional writer. After graduation from high school, she settled in Atlanta, Georgia, while she attended school at Agnes Scott College in nearby Decatur. While in college, she heard about a young Scottish minister, Peter Marshall, who preached at Westminster Presbyterian Church, and she began attending church services there. She was anxious to meet him, and she finally did so when they were both speaking at a prohibition rally outside Atlanta. Sarah Wood and Peter Marshall were married in 1936. A year later Peter answered a call to become pastor of the historic New York Avenue Presbyterian Church in Washington, D.C., and the couple moved to the nation's capital.

Sarah Marshall became ill with tuberculosis in 1943 and was bedridden for two years. She spent much of this time "soul searching" and began to think seriously about becoming a writer "who will make [a] real contribution to my generation and to the world." Later she wrote that during her illness, she sent two petitions to God, one concerning her desire to become a writer, and the other asking that He send into her life "the right persons at the right time for the implementation of these dreams." After sending her messages to God, she felt well enough to leave her sickbed. From that point on, she steadily began to recover from the disease. In 1947, not long after her recovery, Peter was struck by his first heart attack. He survived and was named chaplain for the U.S. Senate the same year. But on January 25, 1949, he suffered a second heart attack and died. Sarah, who had always been dependent upon a man (first her father and then her husband) for support, was left to raise her nine-year-old son and to create a career of her own.

An opportunity arrived for Marshall almost immediately, when she was approached by the Fleming H. Revell Company to prepare an edited edition of Peter's sermons. As the editing work progressed, she began to feel what she described as a "deep satisfaction and inner contentment known only to those who have found the right vocational spot for them." The resulting *Mr. Jones, Meet the Master* (1949) became a best-seller. It was followed by *A Man Called Peter* (1951), the story of Peter Marshall's life. Highly successful, the book was on the *New York Times* best-seller list for a record-breaking fifty consecutive weeks. It sold over three million copies and in 1955 was made into a successful movie by 20th Century Fox. Her work led to her being named "Woman of the Year" in 1953 by the Women's National Press Club. Marshall continued to write about her husband, but she was also becoming famous herself. In 1957 she published her autobiography, titled *To Live Again,* which also sold well.

In 1959, after a period of soul-searching to decide if remarriage might be an act of betrayal of her first husband, Sarah Marshall married Leonard LeSourd, the executive editor of *Guideposts.* She continued her successful writing career with books that included *Beyond Ourselves* (1961); an inspirational novel, *Christy* (1967); and *Something More: In Search of a Deeper Faith* (1974). The LeSourds united with popular writers Elizabeth Sherrill and John Sherrill during the mid-1970s to establish Chosen Books, a publishing firm with a focus on religious books. *Adventures in Prayer* (1975) was the first of Marshall's contributions to the new publishing venture, followed by *The Helper* (1978), *Meeting God at Every Turn* (1980), and *Catherine Marshall's Story Bible* (1983).

Weakened by her bout with tuberculosis in the 1940s, Marshall grappled with lung problems again in the 1980s. She died on March 18, 1983. Shortly before she died, she compiled and edited some of her late husband's writings, published in *The Best of Peter Marshall* (1983). A second inspirational novel, *Julie* (1984), was published posthumously.

References: Catherine Marshall, *Christy* (1967); Catherine Marshall, *Julie* (1984); Catherine Marshall, *A Man Called Peter* (1951); Catherine Marshall, *Mr. Jones, Meet the Master: Sermons and Prayers of Peter Marshall* (1949, reprint 1982); Catherine Marshall, *To Live Again* (1957); Peter Marshall, *The Best of Peter Marshall* (1983); J. Gordon Melton, *Religious Leaders of America* (1991).

Matthews, Ann Teresa (1732–1800)

Ann Teresa Matthews, as Mother Bernardina Teresa Xavier of St. Joseph, helped to found the first monastery of a religious order in the United States. She was born in Charles County, Maryland, in 1732 to parents who raised her in a religious environment during a time when Roman Catholics faced legal and social discrimination in Maryland. Matthews left Maryland in 1754, traveling to Hoogstraeten, Belgium, where she entered an English contemplative order of Discalced Carmelites. In September of that year, she entered the order as Sister Bernardina Teresa Xavier of St. Joseph and made her profession in November 1755. For the next thirty-five years, Sister Bernardina remained at the monastery. She rose in rank, progressing to the position of mistress of novices in the monastery, and in 1774 was elected prioress.

Following the colonists' victory in the American Revolution, discriminatory laws against Roman Catholics were eliminated. At about the same time, Holy Roman Emperor Joseph II had begun to dissolve monasteries in the Netherlands, and Bernardina's brother, Father Ignatius Matthews, urged the nuns to move to the United States. These factors opened the way for the establishment of the order of Discalced Carmelites in America.

After many months of raising funds and gaining permission to found an order in the United States, Mother Bernardina and four companions set sail for America in the spring of 1790. She traveled with Father Charles Neale and Sister Clare Joseph Dickinson, as well as two nieces, Sister Eleanora and Sister Aloysia. The group settled at Port Tobacco River, Maryland. There they established the Carmel convent on October 15, 1790, first monastery of any religious order in the United States. (The Ursuline convent in New Orleans was founded in 1727, but in 1790 this city was still in French territory.)

The order drew novices from the local region and added ten nuns by 1800. They accepted their first postulant, Elizabeth Carberry, only one week after settling in

America. Mother Bernardina remained prioress until her death on June 12, 1800.

See also: Oblate Sisters of Providence; Roman Catholic Church
References: James J. Kenneally, *The History of American Catholic Women* (1990); Robert McHenry, ed., *Liberty's Women* (1980); Caroline Zilboorg, ed., *Women's Firsts* (1997).

Matthews, Marjorie Swank (1916–1986)

Marjorie Swank Matthews, the first woman to be elected bishop of a major American denomination, was born in Onawa, Michigan, on July 11, 1916. From childhood she had the desire to someday become a missionary teacher in Asia, but because of the Great Depression in the 1930s, Matthews could not afford to attend college. Instead, she enrolled in a secretarial school. In 1938 she married and bore a son. Since her husband was in the military, the family moved frequently. The marriage ended in divorce in 1946, leaving her with the responsibility of supporting herself and her son. Matthews obtained a position as a secretary to the president of a manufacturing company and to the treasurer of the company.

Matthews had been an active laywoman within the United Methodist Church when, at age forty-seven, she felt called to the ministry. She had no seminary training when she entered the profession as a part-time local pastor. The "local pastor" is often considered a kind of third-class citizen among the clergy, or as Matthews once described the position, "There is no lower form of life on the ecclesiastical totem pole" (Lyles, 1980, p. 779). Her desire to climb the ecclesiastical ladder led her to enroll in college. In 1968 she graduated with a bachelor of arts degree and highest honors from Central Michigan University. She next attended Colgate Rochester Divinity School, receiving a bachelor of divinity degree in 1972, before completing her education at Florida State University, earning her master's degree in 1974 and her doctorate in 1976.

Meanwhile, Matthews was pastoring at a number of rural parishes in New York, Florida, and Michigan. While she was serving small churches in Michigan, Bishop Dwight Loder took notice of her exceptional abilities, and after she completed her schooling, she received an appointment as district superintendent of West Michigan's Grand Traverse District Conference. She was soon elected as a delegate to the church's General Conference. In the years immediately following her graduation from Florida State University (1976–1980), Matthews battled breast cancer and survived.

Matthews was elected to head the delegation from West Michigan to the 1980 General Conference. At the North Central Jurisdictional Conference on July 17, 1980, and after a long struggle, she was elected on the twenty-ninth ballot to the episcopacy and was assigned to the Wisconsin area. She also received an assignment to work with the General Conference Commission to Study the Episcopacy and District Superintendency. Because she was sixty-four years old when elected, she was limited to one four-year term of service as an active bishop. She presided over an area that included 522 churches with 399 ministers and approximately 135,000 Methodist congregants. Matthews succumbed to cancer and died in Grand Rapids, Michigan, on July 2, 1986, just two years after her retirement.

See also: Methodist Church
References: James E. Kirby, *The Methodists* (1996); Jean Caffey Lyles, "An Improbable Episcopal Choice," *Christian Century* (August 13–20, 1980): 779–780; J. Gordon Melton, *Religious Leaders of America* (1991).

McBeth, Sue (1830–1893)

Presbyterian missionary Sue McBeth was born in Scotland in 1830. She emigrated to Ohio with her parents, Alexander and Mary (Henderson) McBeth in 1832. After completing her education at the Steubenville Female Seminary in 1854, Sue McBeth became a teacher and was soon employed at Fairfield University, a branch of the State University of Iowa. In 1858 she received an invitation from the Presbyterian Board of Foreign Missions to apply for work with the Choctaw Indians. Two years later she began teaching Native American girls, only to have her work interrupted by the Civil War. In 1863 she became one of the first female agents of the United States Christian Commission, a Protestant-sponsored relief organization that cared for the sick and wounded in northern military hospitals. She served at the Jefferson Barracks in St. Louis, Missouri. When the war was over, she remained in St. Louis as an urban missionary.

In 1873 the Presbyterian Board of Foreign Missions recommended McBeth for work among the Nez Percé Indians. The next twenty years of her life were spent mostly at the Lapwai agency in Idaho, where she became devoted to her work. Although she was not ordained, she conducted a school for the training of Native American ministers. Like most late nineteenth-century white Protestant ministers, McBeth was convinced that the conversion of Native Americans must be total, that they needed to adopt both Christianity and white culture. Her position was unusual, however, in that she was given the responsibility of training adult males to the ministry at a time when females were expected to focus their mission work on women and children. McBeth also spent considerable time compiling a dictionary of the Nez Percé language. In 1879 her sister Kate joined her at the Lapwai agency. Sue Mc-Beth died of Brights' disease on May 26, 1893, at Mount Idaho, Idaho.

See also: Missionaries
References: Edward T. James, ed. *Notable American Women, 1607–1950*, vol. 2. (1971); Susan Hill Lindley, *"You Have Stept Out of Your Place": A History of Women and Religion in America* (1996); James H. Smylie, *A Brief History of the Presbyterians* (1996).

McFague, Sallie (TeSelle) (1933–)

Sallie McFague (TeSelle), a prominent feminist theologian of the latter half of the twentieth century, was born in Quincy, Massachusetts, on May 25, 1933. She was the daughter of Maurice Graeme and Jessie (Reid) McFague. Sallie received her advanced education at Smith College, earning a bachelor of arts degree there in 1955. Pursuing an interest in theology, she then attended Yale University, from which she received a bachelor of divinity degree in 1959. On September 12 of that year she married Eugene A. TeSelle, Jr., a professor. The couple had two children. After her marriage, McFague completed her formal education, graduating with a doctorate from Yale in 1964.

From 1963 to 1965, McFague, who is of the Methodist faith, was a lecturer at Yale Divinity School. She then moved to Nashville, Tennessee, where she joined the faculty at Vanderbilt University. During the course of her long career there, she served for a while as dean of the Divinity School and most recently as Carpenter Professor of Theology. During the period from 1967 to 1975 she was editor of *Soundings: A Journal of Interdisciplinary Studies* and also edited two volumes, *The Family, Communes, and Utopian Societies* (1971) and *The Rediscovery of Ethnicity* (1973). McFague, who describes herself as a Christian, feminist, ecological theologian, has authored a number of theological works, including *Literature and the Christian Life* (1966); *Speaking in*

*Parables: A Study in Metaphor and The-
ology* (1975); *Metaphorical Theology:
Models of God in Religious Language*
(1982); *Models of God* (1987), which develops three heuristic models of God—
God as mother, God as lover, and God as
friend; and *The Body of God: An Ecological Theology* (1993). Through her work,
McFague has attempted to expand the
study of the relationship between God
and the world to uncover dimensions that
have yet been unexplored and to resurrect
models that have long been neglected, including the organic model of God and the
world.

See also: Ecofeminism; Theologians
References: Ann Evory and Linda Metger,
eds., *Contemporary Authors* (1984); Susan
Hill Lindley, *"You Have Stept Out of Your
Place": A History of Women and Religion
in America* (1996); Sallie McFague, *The
Body of God: An Ecological Theology*
(1993); Christine Nasso, ed., *Contemporary
Authors*, vols. 21–24, first revision (1977).

McIntosh, Martha E. (Bell)
(1848–1922)

Martha E. McIntosh, the founding president of the Woman's Missionary Union
of the Southern Baptist Convention, was
born in Society Hill, South Carolina, on
September 29, 1848. Her father, James
H. McIntosh, was a wealthy planter and
slaveowner. She was given the name of
her mother, Martha (Gregg) McIntosh,
but friends and family called her Mattie.
The family regularly attended the Welsh
Neck Baptist Church, and Mattie's religious education was supplemented with
frequent Bible readings in the room of
her paternal grandmother. She received
her secular education first at St. David's
Academy, one of the South's few coeducational schools, and later attended a
boarding school in Charleston. Four of
Mattie's brothers fought in the Civil War.
Although their home was ransacked during the conflict, all family members and

most of the family's fortune survived.
While her brothers went on to become
prominent in their professions, Mattie
and her sister Louisa became involved in
foreign missions.

McIntosh's interest in missions was
sparked in 1872 when Ellen C. Edwards,
a member of the Welsh Neck Baptist
Church, returned from a trip to Baltimore with news of the new Woman's
Mission to Woman organization. This
was the first influential women's missionary society among Southern Baptists.
When a local women's missionary group
was organized two years later, both
McIntosh sisters joined. Soon Louisa
began encouraging a friend to found a
society in another town. Upon hearing of
the activity at Welsh Neck, J. A. Chambliss, the vice president of the Foreign
Mission Board, wrote directly to Mattie
McIntosh under the mistaken belief that
she was the organizer. Chambliss was
seeking to create a central committee for
the promotion of women's missionary
societies in South Carolina and invited
her to serve on the committee. After
some consideration, McIntosh accepted,
and she became secretary of the new
committee.

Thinking that she needed a middle initial to make her signature appear more
businesslike, McIntosh added an "E." to
her signature. Over the next two decades,
she was an energetic promoter of foreign
missions, serving as chairwoman or corresponding secretary of the South Carolina
Central Women's Committee until 1894.
Under her leadership, the women of South
Carolina led all other states in providing
financial support for foreign missions.
McIntosh regularly attended the Southern
Baptist Conventions, where women held
informal meetings to discuss missions. In
1887 she and Annie Walker Armstrong of
Baltimore began planning the founding of
a Baptist women's organization but delayed formal establishment until the fol-

lowing year. When the Woman's Missionary Union (WMU) was created in 1888, McIntosh became the group's first president. Independently wealthy, she gave the fledgling organization a significant share of her fortune. One of her first acts as president was to persuade the WMU to sponsor an annual Christmas offering for foreign missions, as suggested by pioneer missionary Lottie Moon.

McIntosh served as president of the WMU for four years but then declined reelection. She agreed to serve as vice president from South Carolina but would not run for office in 1895. This decision appears to have come as a result of her engagement to Theodore Percy "T. P." Bell, who headed the Southern Baptist Convention's Sunday School Board. They married in January 1895, and McIntosh moved to her husband's home in Nashville. The Bells moved to Atlanta a year later, where T. P. owned a prominent Baptist newspaper, *The Christian Index*. McIntosh went to work as editor of the newspaper's home department, and she also served on the executive board of the Woman's Missionary Union of Georgia.

In 1914 McIntosh's stepdaughter, Ada, went to China as a missionary. T. P. died in 1916, and two years later McIntosh accepted Ada's invitation to join her in China. She assisted Ada at her station in Tengchow until ill health and political instability in China prompted their return to the United States in 1921. At home in Ridgecrest, North Carolina, McIntosh and her stepdaughter involved themselves in welfare work among women of the area. McIntosh died unexpectedly at her home in Ridgecrest on October 14, 1922.

See also: Armstrong, Annie Walker; Woman's Missionary Union
References: Catherine B. Allen, *Laborers Together with God: 22 Great Women in Baptist Life* (1987); J. Gordon Melton, *Religious Leaders of America* (1991).

McPherson, Aimee Semple (1890–1944)

Aimee Semple McPherson, evangelist and founder of the Church of the Foursquare Gospel, was born in a farmhouse near Salford, Ontario, Canada, on October 9, 1890. Her father, James Kennedy, was a staunch Methodist, and her mother, Minnie Kennedy, was a crusader for the Salvation Army. Their daughter, therefore, grew up in a religious environment, attending both the Methodist Church and Salvation Army Sunday school meetings.

Aimee's religious faith was first tested in 1905 when she read Charles Darwin's theories on evolution in her high school textbook. Her fundamentalist background taught her that the true story of the beginning of mankind was in Genesis, yet she found that Darwin's theories seemed logical. She began to question all she had learned in church and Sunday school. "If the Scriptures tell one lie," she reasoned, "they must leak like a sieve." (Epstein, 1993, p. 30). The more research she did, the more she sided with Darwin. Then, suddenly, she changed her mind. The textbook, she decided, had been a test of faith, and just in time, her eyes had been opened "to the awful position one must be in who accepts the teachings of this book" (Epstein, 1993, p. 33).

At the age of seventeen, Aimee underwent a religious conversion and joined the Pentecostal faith. At the same time, she fell in love with Robert Semple, the Pentecostal evangelist who helped to inspire that conversion, and married him on August 12, 1908. She was accepted as a regular preacher for the Full Gospel Assembly in 1909 and traveled with her husband to China in the spring of the following year, where the couple engaged in missionary work. Both Semples soon contracted malaria and dysentery. Aimee recovered, but Robert Semple died on August 17, 1910. A month later she

Aimee Semple McPherson (undated portrait)

gave birth to a daughter, Roberta Semple. When she returned to the United States later in the year, she arrived with the intention of continuing her late husband's Pentecostal work but was soon distracted from that purpose.

Aimee married Harold McPherson, a young accountant, in February 1912. Their son Rolf was born in March of the following year. After the birth, Aimee became extremely depressed. During these difficult months, she began to hear what she described as the voice of God. "Preach the Word! Preach the Word!" the voice told her (Epstein, 1993, p. 73). She tried to comply by teaching Bible study classes at Pentecostal churches in and near Providence, Rhode Island. But this did not satisfy the voice, which exhorted her to become an evangelist, even though

a woman evangelist was not accepted in middle-class American society in 1914. Aimee became deathly ill with neurasthenia, heart trouble, and internal bleeding. Doctors treated her with multiple surgeries, including an appendectomy and a hysterectomy, and she felt that God was punishing her with these tortures. She begged God to let her die. She was on the verge of death and heard a nurse say, "She's going." Then she heard the other voice ask, "NOW WILL YOU GO?" She whispered that she would (Epstein, 1993, p. 75). All at once the pain was gone, and soon McPherson was up and well. So, in an age when for many people the sight of a woman preaching was a horror, Aimee Semple McPherson left her husband to become evangelist "Sister" Aimee. The couple divorced in 1921.

The young evangelist soon developed a reputation as a dynamic speaker, and the crowds attending her tent revivals grew. Between 1916 and 1923, she crossed the United States, coast to coast, six times, and traveled round-trip between New England and Florida twice. In 1918 she was probably the first woman, along with her mother and children, to travel across the country in an automobile without a man's help. Sister Aimee spoke in tents, churches, concert halls, and speakeasies, attracting Protestants and Catholics, blacks and whites to her services. In Denver, she was kidnapped by the Ku Klux Klan, who wanted her to speak at one of their secret meetings. She complied but spoke in favor of tolerance and love for all mankind. Some Klansmen responded by discarding their white robes.

Few people accepted all the Pentecostal charismata, or gifts of the spirit, the four major charismata being glossolalia (speaking in tongues), prophecy, interpretation of tongues, and the power of healing. It is therefore likely that Sister Aimee's revival meetings attracted audiences through a combination of desire and faith, prayer and oratory. People were curious to see this popular female evangelist and then were captivated by her voice. Some came under religious trances while listening to her.

Sister Aimee's first experience as a healer came in 1920, when a young Catholic woman who was suffering from rheumatoid arthritis went to one of the revivals. Sister Aimee followed her instincts as she prayed for the woman and laid her hands upon the woman's head. When the service ended, the woman walked out without her crutches and free of pain.

In 1917 Sister Aimee began writing and editing a newsletter that would become *The Bridal Call,* a publication that heralded the imminent arrival of Christ, the bridegroom of the church. At about the same time, she began to use drama, or "illustrated sermons" in her services when she directed a play depicting the story of the wise and foolish virgins. These illustrated sermons became more elaborate as time passed and helped to draw crowds to her revivals. In 1918 she told a Philadelphia reporter that experience, not doctrine, was what her revivals were all about. It was the experience of her performance that appealed to and stirred the crowds.

In Los Angeles, on New Year's Day, 1923, Sister Aimee dedicated her long-desired Angelus Temple "to the cause of interdenominational and worldwide evangelism" (Epstein, 1993, p. 247). There she would house her International Church of the Foursquare Gospel, based on the doctrine of (1) Jesus, the only savior; (2) Jesus, the great physician; (3) Jesus, the baptizer with the Holy Spirit; and (4) Jesus, the coming bridegroom, lord, and king. She did not intend the temple to be a parish church but a learning center, with the hope that people who found salvation at her meetings would become evangelists themselves. Instead,

most remained at the temple, attaching themselves to Sister Aimee. Biographer Daniel Mark Epstein notes that by the time the temple opened, Sister Aimee was preaching a mainstream fundamentalism. Though the practices of speaking in tongues, divine healing, and baptism in the spirit remained a significant part of the experience at the temple, Sister Aimee avoided the term "Pentecostal" because that religion remained controversial.

Aimee Semple McPherson was one of the first radio evangelists, finding that her voice over the air waves was just as effective as it was in person. In February 1924 she gave her first broadcast over her own station, Radio KFSG—Kall Four Square Gospel—the first religious broadcasting station. Her license to operate the station was the first granted to a woman by the Federal Communications Commission.

Sister Aimee was an advocate for women in ministry, maintaining that those who had a clear "call" should fill any ministry functions to which they felt called, regardless of gender. Yet many offices and duties at Angelus Temple were gender-specific: The ushers and elders were men; women could serve as deaconesses but not as elders.

By 1925 several hundred thousand people looked to Aimee Semple McPherson as their religious leader and expected exemplary morals on her part. Yet scandal dogged Sister Aimee in the late 1920s, including an alleged love affair. In 1926, when she failed to return from a swim in the Pacific, the world thought she had drowned. Five weeks after her disappearance, she showed up in Arizona with a tale of having been kidnapped. Everyone was surprised she was alive, and many were suspicious, thinking she had perhaps been with her "lover," because her story seemed so far-fetched.

In 1927 Sister Aimee broke with her mother, who had competently handled most of the church's financial affairs. Sister Aimee took control and made some unwise decisions, which nearly bankrupted the church. Mother and daughter temporarily reconciled in early 1930, and Minnie Kennedy straightened out the church's financial affairs. But the two argued later that year over Aimee's morals (she had bobbed her hair and had begun to dress stylishly, not modestly in white virginal clothes as before); her lifestyle (close associates now included people in show business); and her theology, which had become less fundamentalist. In August 1930, she suffered a mental and physical breakdown and was absent from the pulpit for ten months.

The final years of Sister Aimee's life were not happy. In September 1931, she defied the church prohibition against remarrying while a spouse was still alive and married actor David Hutton. He was a fortune hunter, and the marriage was short-lived. They divorced in 1934. Throughout the 1930s and early 1940s, Sister Aimee battled a number of illnesses, continued rumors, debt, and lawsuits over control of the church. She feared that others were plotting to take over the temple. In 1936, she broke with her daughter, who was widely assumed to be her chosen successor.

Despite the turmoil among church officials, the International Church of the Foursquare Gospel continued to grow. At the time of her death in 1944, there were more than four hundred branch churches with approximately twenty-two thousand members, and the organization was poised for future growth. When Aimee Semple McPherson died in Oakland, California, of an accidental overdose of barbiturates on September 27, 1944, her son, Rolf McPherson, was named president of the International Church of the Foursquare Gospel. There are now over 25,500 Foursquare churches in seventy-four countries.

See also: Evangelicals; Salvation Army
References: Edith W. Blumhofer, *Aimee Semple McPherson: Everybody's Sister* (1993); Daniel Mark Epstein, *Sister Aimee: The Life of Aimee Semple McPherson* (1993); Robert V. P. Steele, *Storming Heaven: The Lives and Turmoils of Minnie Kennedy and Aimee Semple McPherson* (1970).

Mears, Henrietta Cornelia (1890–1963)

Christian educator and founder of Gospel Light Publishers, Henrietta Cornelia Mears was born in Fargo, North Dakota, on October 23, 1890. When she was a child, her family moved to Minneapolis, where they joined the First Baptist Church. The pastor of the church was William Bell Riley, one of America's leading fundamentalist pastors. Mears had a natural talent for teaching and began to teach Sunday school at the age of twelve. Her interest in education continued through her college years at the University of Minnesota. After graduation, she embarked on a career as a schoolteacher, teaching in Beardsley and North Branch, Minnesota, before returning to Minneapolis to join the faculty at Central High School. Upon her return to Minneapolis, she again taught Sunday school at First Baptist Church.

During the 1920s, Mears met the pastor of the First Presbyterian Church in Hollywood, California. He was impressed with the manner in which she had helped to build the Sunday school program in Minneapolis and offered her a position at his church. Mears became director of Christian education at the church, a position she held from 1928 until her death in 1963. Enrollment in the Sunday school program grew rapidly under Mears's guidance, increasing from 1,450 pupils at the time she began her work to four thousand pupils by 1930.

Not long after becoming director of Christian education at the church, Mears began a thorough survey of church school literature. She found it to be inadequate. Not only was the material difficult for children to read and understand, it failed to meet Mears's doctrinal expectations. She insisted that Christian education be Christian. Every lesson, she believed, must honor Christ and be faithful to the words of the Bible. Mears began to write her own lessons, never intending that her literature be sold. But after some urging from others interested in her work, in 1933 Mears founded Gospel Light Press (later Publishers) and put twelve of her courses into print. By the end of the year, thirteen Sunday schools were using her materials, and sales continued to grow until by 1940, Gospel Light had become the fourth largest independent publisher of Sunday school literature in the United States.

In addition to her writing, teaching, and publishing, Mears was a leader in the founding of the National Sunday School Association in the 1930s and has been given much of the credit for the revival of the Sunday school concept. Mears did not believe that religious education should stop upon a youth's graduation from high school, so in the 1930s and 1940s she worked to develop college-level programs. She established the Forest Home Camp Grounds near San Bernardino, California, which became a retreat center aimed at college-age youth. During a trip to Europe shortly after World War II, Mears began to envision a program that would reach out to college campuses across the United States. Together with some young people in her congregation, she formed the Fellowship of the Burning Heart to pursue her vision. One man, William Bright, who participated in the fellowship's 1947 meeting, developed Campus Crusades for Christ. Another organization to emerge from the fellowship was the Hollywood Christian Group, an association that in-

cluded many famous people whose celebrity made it difficult for them to attend church as ordinary worshippers.

Despite her successes in the realm of religious education, Mears considered men to be the spiritual leaders and women to be the followers. For this reason, she turned down all offers to preach in churches and focused most of her attention on her male students. Reverend Billy Graham gave Mears credit for having the deepest influence on his life outside of his wife and mother. Henrietta Mears died in Los Angeles on March 18, 1963.

See also: Fundamentalism
References: Margaret Lamberts Bendroth, *Fundamentalism and Gender: 1875 to the Present* (1993); J. Gordon Melton, *Religious Leaders of America* (1991); Rosemary Radford Ruether and Rosemary Skinner Keller, eds., *Women and Religion in America,* vol. 3 (1986).

Mennonites

The first Mennonites to arrive in America came from Switzerland and Germany during the first half of the eighteenth century, coming initially to Pennsylvania in search of religious freedom and fertile farmland. Later-arriving Mennonites came to America from Russia during the late nineteenth and early twentieth centuries. Although they were also seeking to escape religious persecution, these Mennonites were more likely to settle in urban areas. Their history of persecution and escape and their strong devotion to God, their families, and each other combined to cause Mennonites to create tightly knit communities.

Mennonites have traditionally maintained a simple, humble, and peaceful lifestyle, based upon their interpretation of the Bible and early Christian practices. Women were expected to be nurturing, submissive, and godly, whereas men were the leaders and providers. But among present-day Mennonites, the roles of women vary according to which of the dozens of Mennonite groups they belong to. The Mennonite experience covers a broad spectrum, ranging from the Old Order Mennonites, in which the only acceptable role for a woman is homemaker and mother and in which segregation of the sexes in church is common, to the more progressive Mennonites like those in the General Conference, whose women frequently pursue a college education and professional careers.

The dress of Mennonite women also varies. Long, dark dresses and bonnets are worn by members of the Old Order. Women among the Conservative Mennonites wear modest pastel dresses with a double layer of cloth across the bosom and three-quarter to full-length sleeves. Hairstyles are simple, usually pulled back in a bun or a simple knot, and the head is covered by a sheer piece of netting or tulle, known as a "prayer veil." Women of the liberal groups, although they still dress simply, wear mainstream clothing.

Mennonites have traditionally adhered to the religious principle of "headship" that defines a hierarchical order of God-Christ-man-woman, clearly placing men above women. Members of the faith contend, however, that headship does not imply that men are superior to women but that each sex has God-given roles to play. Though women are to be submissive to their husbands, the husband is expected to love his wife as he loves God. More liberal Mennonite couples strive toward an egalitarian marriage, view headship in terms of working together as a team, and frequently define the hierarchical order as God-Christ-man/woman.

Although some Mennonite women now serve their churches as deacons and ministers, the Mennonite Church was relatively late in creating distinctive roles for women. During the nineteenth and early twentieth centuries, some women, like teacher Annie C. Funk (1874–1912)

and physician Caroline Banwar (1901–1952), worked in foreign missions, and ministers' wives often helped their husbands in their work for the church. Mennonite women's sewing circles began to form during the 1890s, but it was not until 1915 that these circles were organized by Clara Eby Steiner into the churchwide Mennonite Woman's Missionary Society. Male leaders found the women's attempts at autonomy unacceptable, and by 1928 the Mission Board took control of the women's work and renamed the society the General Sewing Circle Committee of the Mennonite Board of Missions and Charities. It was not until the 1970s that Mennonite women made significant gains in acquiring influential positions within the church. Even so, in the more traditional conferences men are the church leaders, and the woman's role is confined to domestic duties. These women do not see themselves as oppressed but perceive their power as coming from their role as mothers, shaping the beliefs and values of the next generation.

See also: Women's Missionary and Service Commission of the Mennonite Church
References: Janet Mancini Billson, *Keepers of the Culture: The Power of Tradition in Women's Lives* (1995); Leo Driedger, *Mennonite Identity in Conflict* (1988); Susan Hill Lindley, *"You Have Stept Out of Your Place": A History of Women and Religion in America* (1996); Harry Loewen and Steven Nolt, *Through Fire and Water: An Overview of Mennonite History* (1996); Eve MacMaster, "The Story of Clara Eby Steiner and the Beginnings of WMSC," *WMSC Voice* (January–April 1990); Dorothy McCammon and Beulah Kauffman, as told to Saralyn Yoder, "Cautious Progress in a Time of Change: WMSC in the '60s and '70s," *WMSC Voice* (July–August 1990).

Methodists

When Methodism arrived in America amid the mid-eighteenth-century revivals of the Great Awakening, women had a greater religious voice than in most denominations. Influenced by his remarkable mother, Susanna, who by example had shown him that women were indeed capable of leading prayer and providing religious instruction, Methodism's founder, John Wesley, was open to women playing a more active role. A woman, Barbara Ruckle Heck, known as "the Mother of American Methodism," has been credited with founding, in 1768, the first Methodist society in America to achieve permanent status. Although Methodist women were not given full religious equality as clergy, they were permitted to exhort in public, and some, such as Lydia Hawes of Indiana in the 1830s, became well known in their communities for their eloquent speaking.

By the middle of the nineteenth century, with the Methodist Episcopal Church becoming well established and affluent, it also became more conventional in its attitudes toward women in religion. Women were discouraged from preaching and were guided into more decorous occupations, especially Sunday school teaching. If they desired to do more, they could take advantage of opportunities offered in foreign missions. This was especially appealing once the Women's Foreign Missionary Society organized in 1869 as an independent agency of the church.

Throughout the nineteenth century, some Methodist women challenged the limits set for them by male church leaders. Among them were women like Phoebe Palmer, a founder of the famous "Tuesday Meetings for the Promotion of Holiness" and a leader of the Holiness movement. Evangelist Margaret "Maggie" Newton Van Cott's outstanding speaking voice led to her being granted a "local preacher's license" by her community church. Anna Howard Shaw first sought ordination in 1878, but the New England Conference of the Methodist Episcopal Church,

North, refused to grant full ordination to women. Two years later she was ordained as the first female minister of the Methodist Protestant Church.

There soon developed another option for women wishing to serve the church. More than in any other Protestant denomination, the deaconess movement of the late nineteenth century had its greatest success in Methodism. Much of the credit goes to Lucy Rider Meyer, who in 1885 founded the Chicago Training School for City, Home, and Foreign Missions for Methodist women desirous of serving their church. The school experienced rapid growth and built a home for deaconesses the following year. There were soon large numbers of graduating students who were eager to become missionaries in foreign lands or to establish more deaconess training institutions in other areas of the country. In 1888 the General Conference of the Methodist Episcopal Church authorized the use of deaconesses and imposed general rules upon them. Soon deaconess centers were found in cities like New York, Boston, Cincinnati, Detroit, and Minneapolis. It is estimated that Meyer's school alone, during her thirty-four years of leadership, graduated at least five thousand deaconesses and that she and her graduates founded at least forty major Methodist institutions.

In the twentieth century, Methodist women gradually worked their way into leadership positions within the church. After more than two decades of controversy, women were allowed to be seated and were granted minority status at the church's General Conference. By this time some of the smaller bodies within Methodism, including the African Methodist Episcopal Zion Church, several of the Holiness churches, and the New York Conference of the Methodist Protestant Church, had ordained women. The New England Conference of the Methodist Episcopal Church,

North, which had declined Anna Howard Shaw's petition for ordination, finally recognized the ordination of women in 1924. Prominent Methodist theologian Georgia Harkness, who in 1942 told a gathering of Methodists that the church was the last stronghold of male dominance, was one of many Methodist women to campaign for equality in religion. The African Methodist Episcopal Church finally gave women full ordination rights in 1948, and the Colored Methodist Episcopal Church did the same six years later, but it was not until 1956 that the United Methodist Church granted women full ordination. In 1980 women made another important breakthrough within religious hierarchies with the election of Marjorie Swank Matthews as a Methodist bishop. She was the first woman to be elevated to such a post in a mainline denomination. By 1992 eight women had been elected to the Methodist bishopric.

See also: Foote, Julia A. J.; Harkness, Georgia Elma; Heck, Barbara Ruckle; Matthews, Marjorie Swank; Meyer, Lucy Jane Rider; Palmer, Phoebe Worrall; Van Cott, Margaret Newton

References: Margaret Lamberts Bendroth, *Fundamentalism and Gender: 1875 to the Present* (1993); Rosemary Skinner Keller, Louise L. Queen, and Hilah F. Thomas, *Women in New Worlds: Historical Perspectives on the Wesleyan Tradition*, 2 vols. (1981, 1982); James E. Kirby, *The Methodists* (1996); Susan Hill Lindley, *"You Have Stept Out of Your Place": A History of Women and Religion in America* (1996); Donald B. Marti, "Methodist Women in the Nineteenth Century," in Angela Howard Zophy with Frances M. Kavenik, eds., *Handbook of American Women's History* (1990); World Methodist Council and the Commission on Archives and History, *The Encyclopedia of World Methodism* (1974).

Meyer, Lucy Jane Rider
(1849–1922)

A pioneer in the field of social work and in the Methodist deaconess movement,

Lucy Jane Rider Meyer was born in New Haven, Vermont, on September 9, 1849. Her parents, Richard Dunning Rider and Jane (Child) Rider, were devout Christians who led their children in their daily Bible readings and prayer. Lucy had a "conversion experience" at age thirteen while attending a Methodist revival with her family.

Throughout her life, Lucy sought to further her education. She graduated from the New Hampton Literary Institution in Fairfax, Vermont, in 1867 and spent three years as a tutor and teacher before enrolling in Oberlin College in 1870. After graduating from Oberlin in 1872, she studied at the Woman's Medical College of Pennsylvania between 1873 and 1875 and then spent the next two years employed as principal of Troy Conference Academy in Poultney, Vermont. In 1877 and 1878, Lucy studied chemistry for a year at Massachusetts Institute of Technology. She then accepted an appointment as professor of chemistry at McKendree College in Lebanon, Illinois. In 1881, she resigned from the college to become field secretary of the Illinois State Sunday School Association. While she held that position, she came into contact with leaders in the fields of education, social work, and religion, in all of which she held an interest.

On May 23, 1885, Lucy married Josiah Shelly Meyer, a Chicago businessman. Their son, Shelly Rider, was born in 1887, the same year that she completed her medical degree at the Woman's Medical College of Chicago. In 1885, shortly after their marriage, the Meyers opened the Chicago Training School for City, Home, and Foreign Missions. The school developed out of what Lucy saw as a need for a school for women entering religious work, such as those becoming missionaries. During the two-year program, the trainees spent time doing social work among Chicago's poor.

Several of Lucy Meyer's trainees helped her establish the first American "deaconess home," which became connected to the school. (The Methodist Church in Germany had been working with deaconesses since 1836.) In May 1888, the General Conference of the Methodist Episcopal Church authorized the use of deaconesses and prescribed general rules for them. Deaconesses in the Methodist Church did not take vows. They earned no salary but did receive room and board, plus a small allowance. Their primary function was to perform social work in urban areas. Meyer wrote a history, *Deaconesses: Biblical, Early Church, European, American . . .*, which was published in 1889.

As editor of the *Deaconess Advocate*, the journal of the Chicago Training School, Meyer maintained a policy of tirelessly working to broaden the vision of readers to imagine opportunities for women that stretched beyond their traditional sphere. She saw deaconess work as a means of giving women more choices of professions and pressed the church to help the women's movement by ordaining women to work on an equal level with men. In 1905 Meyer published a social protest novel, *Mary North*, which reflected her interest in charitable work.

Not long after Meyer founded the first deaconess association, other deaconess groups began to form. Struggles between the various organizations caused unhappiness for Meyer. In 1908, Meyer founded the Methodist Deaconess Association, which was one of the more liberal houses. The Methodist Church failed to put the deaconess groups under the authority of one single board until 1939.

At its peak in 1910, the Chicago Training School had an enrollment of two hundred. When Meyer and her husband resigned from their posts as principal and business manager of the school in 1917, records showed that approxi-

mately five thousand students had been trained for missionary and social work. After years of working to educate others, providing help to the poor, and broadening opportunities for women both inside and outside the Methodist Church, Lucy Jane Rider Meyer died in Chicago, Illinois, on March 16, 1922.

See also: Methodists; Missionaries
References: Edward T. James, ed., *Notable American Women, 1607–1950* (1971); Phyllis J. Read and Bernard L. Witlieb, *The Book of Women's Firsts* (1992); Rosemary Radford Ruether, "Lay Women in the Protestant Tradition," in Ruether and Rosemary Skinner Keller, eds., *Women and Religion in America*, vol. 1 (1986).

Militz, Annie Rix (1856–1924)

Annie Rix Militz, a leader in the early New Thought movement and a founder of Homes of Truth, was born in California in March 1856. Little is known of the early years of her life, but she had been teaching in San Francisco for about ten years when, in 1887, she became a student of Emma Curtis Hopkins, the originator of the New Thought movement. In her classes with Hopkins, Annie found her life's work. After her third lesson, she gave up her job in the public schools and went to work in a classmate's small metaphysical bookstore. She, her sister Harriet Rix, and Sadie Gorey (or Gorie), the bookshop's owner, soon began to conduct classes of their own in the store, though their teachings were in line with those of Hopkins. Meanwhile, Annie continued to read books in the metaphysical field. Although she was never bound by any one strict creed, she remained true to one basic belief—the "Allness of God" (Braden, 1984, p. 313).

Soon Annie and Gorey outgrew the bookshop. They found larger quarters in rooms above a store, but before long their work had grown to the extent that they purchased the store and built a hall for their meetings. At first their center was called the "Christian Science Home," but the name was later changed to Home of Truth. Annie worked in the home for three years before leaving to accept an invitation in 1890 to pursue advanced studies at the Christian Science Theological Seminary in Chicago, where Hopkins was president. Annie graduated and was ordained by Hopkins in June 1891. She then joined the staff as a professor of Scripture revelation. During the winter of 1892, she married Paul Militz, whom she had met at the seminary. She returned with her husband to San Francisco in 1893, to find the Homes of Truth (there were now two in the Bay Area) so prosperous that she decided to open one in Los Angeles. The home there also flourished, and the movement soon spread to other cities. Before long there were Homes of Truth in cities along the entire west coast, from Victoria, British Columbia, to San Diego, California.

During her stay in Chicago, Militz had formed close ties with Charles and Myrtle Fillmore, founders of the Unity movement within New Thought. At Charles's request, beginning in 1898 Militz wrote a series of twelve lessons that outlined her basic teachings. Published the following year as *Primary Lessons in Christian Living and Healing,* the book was used as a Unity text for about ten years and as the basic text for Homes of Truth for many years more. In later years, she published two additional books, *Spiritual Housekeeping* (1910) and *Prosperity through Knowledge and Power of the Mind* (1913).

In Los Angeles in 1911, Militz began publishing the *Master Mind,* one of the major New Thought magazines. The periodical had a wide circulation, reaching many outside the Homes of Truth movement. At the same time, Militz was in demand as a lecturer and teacher, both in the United States and abroad. She was an active member of the International New Thought Alliance and was present at the organization's first international congress in London in 1914. Now at the height of her success, in 1916 Militz established the University of Christ in Los Angeles to train New Thought leaders.

The Homes of Truth was a loosely knit organization, with each home being completely autonomous and no formal membership required. Historian Charles S. Braden, in *Spirits in Rebellion,* suggests that people affiliated with it because they appreciated the practical Christianity they found in the teachings and writings of Militz and her associates as well as the types of activities that were pursued in the homes. Militz continued her involvement with the movement and remained the editor and publisher of *Master Mind* until her death in 1924. The magazine carried on under the direction of Militz's sister, Harriet Rix, and with a new name, *The Christ Mind,* for some time after Militz's death. At least one Home of Truth still exists, although the lack of a formal organization makes it difficult to determine the number of homes still functioning.

See also: Fillmore, Myrtle Page; Hopkins, Emma Curtis
References: Charles S. Braden, *Spirits in Rebellion: The Rise and Development of New Thought* (1984); J. Gordon Melton, *Religious Leaders of America* (1991).

Ministers' Wives
Seen as selfless, pure, and the perfect wife, mother, and church member, the minister's wife has become a stereotype in the minds of large portions of the general population. Few occupations bring such close scrutiny of one's entire family as the ministry. And for the wife of a minister, such attention often leads to the creation of a public image that is not always consistent with her real personality. Thus the wives themselves frequently reinforce the "minister's wife" stereotype.

Yet despite the stereotype, historically the role of minister's wife has offered many women opportunities to broaden their spheres of influence.

In his study of ministers' wives in the nineteenth century, Leonard I. Sweet finds that young women were eager to marry ministers. Marriage to a clergyman allowed a woman the chance to become an assistant or even a partner in her husband's ministry. Women like Narcissa Prentiss Whitman and Eliza Hart Spalding welcomed the opportunity to serve alongside their husbands as they proselytized among the Native Americans, and others like Maud Booth became partners with their husbands in religious evangelism and in leading reform movements. On a local level, it was often the minister's wife who made the effort to organize and run women's groups, whether they were prayer groups, Bible study classes, or missionary societies.

Being the wife of a minister also had its disadvantages. Not only was she expected to fit the stereotype of the perfect wife, mother, and congregant, she was also expected to perform the traditional "duties" of a minister's wife like superintending the Sunday school, maintaining the church library, and organizing women's groups without financial compensation. Considering that the personalities of ministers' wives were as varied as those among the general population, it is unlikely that all wives welcomed the relatively public role that they were supposed to play. In 1898 Margaret Blackburn wrote *Things a Pastor's Wife Can Do, by One of Them,* in which she suggested that when a minister's wife is overwhelmed by her duties, she should pray. Beyond that, she advised, "It sometimes occurs that the very best thing a pastor's wife can do is to say 'No'" (Douglas, 1965, p. 5).

Although in the twentieth century, ministers' wives have increasingly developed careers of their own both inside and outside of the ministry, pressures to remain true to the stereotype have continued. Liz Greenbacker and the Reverend Sherry Taylor surveyed more than two hundred ministers' wives for *Private Lives of Ministers' Wives* (1991). Sixty-eight percent of the respondents had their own careers. When they were asked for their definition of the traditional role of a minister's wife, they all described the traditional, stereotypical wife. But when asked if their own lives matched that of their definition, almost all gave a negative response. Yet they also gave long lists of jobs and responsibilities that they had taken on within their husbands' congregations, duties that were also included in the list of duties performed by the stereotypical minister's wife. Some said they did so because they wanted to, not because they were required to.

The women reported advantages to being the wife of a minister: Over half (51 percent) cited "the ready-made community of friends and church family" as making them happy, and a quarter were especially pleased when they saw that people were touched by their husband's ministry (Greenbacker and Taylor, 1991, p. 322). Other advantages included sharing in the joys and sorrows of the laity, pride in their husbands' work, the opportunity to meet all kinds of people, and the chance to serve with their husbands.

Yet the pressures placed upon a minister and his wife take their toll. One negative aspect of marriage to a minister is loneliness: In the Greenbacker-Taylor survey, wives of clergymen reported that loneliness or the lack of close friends was one of the greatest disadvantages of their role. They also noted that sharing the hurts of the members of their congregations, experiencing a lack of privacy, moving, being paid substandard salaries, watching family needs being put second to the church, and having no weekends off in the usual sense were problems associated with their positions.

Despite the burden of the myth of the "perfect wife and church member," many ministers' wives believed that in order to survive in the role, the best advice they could offer to another wife of a clergyman was to "be yourself" (Greenbacker and Taylor, 1991, p. 326).

References: William Douglas, *Ministers' Wives* (1965); Liz Greenbacker and Sherry Taylor, *Private Lives of Ministers' Wives* (1991); Susan Hill Lindley, *"You Have Stept Out of Your Place": A History of Women and Religion in America* (1996); Leonard I. Sweet, *The Minister's Wife: Her Role in Nineteenth-Century American Evangelicalism* (1983).

Missionaries

Prior to the American Civil War, women's involvement in foreign missions was principally as wives of males who had answered the calling or as members of church-based societies involved in activities designed for the support of foreign missions. There were some exceptions, but until the later decades of the nineteenth century, most mission board leaders did not consider it appropriate for women to perform the role of a missionary. Single women accepted for foreign mission work were usually young, in their twenties, and were attached to a mission family for purposes of protection and propriety. Married or single, the women who worked in foreign missions faced the same hardships, performed similar duties, and were equally as devoted to proselytizing non-Christians as were men who answered the call. But constraints against women going beyond their "sphere" prevented them from being ordained to the ministry. Therefore, they were not considered "full" missionaries, allowing male missionaries and mission agency officials to devalue their work and keep their salaries low.

Many of these women were well prepared for their work in the field. For example, Mary Lyon founded Mount Holyoke College in 1837 for the purpose of training women to become missionaries and teachers because of her own interest as well as the growing desire of women to become religious workers. Some of her most gifted students went on to become the wives of foreign missionaries and missionaries themselves. Soon other institutions were training women for mission work as well.

In 1812 Ann Hasseltine Judson and her husband, Adoniram Judson, became one of the first missionary couples to travel to foreign lands, and Ann was probably the most famous female missionary of the nineteenth century. Although they set out in the service of the Congregationalist faith, they had hardly begun their work before they converted to the Baptist denomination. As a missionary in India and Burma, Ann suffered considerable adversities while she served the church as a teacher, an evangelizer, and an assistant to her husband in his translations of the Scripture into Burmese. After Ann died in 1826, Sarah Hall Boardman married Judson and aided him with his work. Upon Sarah's death, Emily Chubbuck became Judson's third wife and assistant. All three of the Judson women had decided early in life that they wanted to devote their lives to religious work. Marriage to a missionary had provided them that opportunity.

With the opening of the West, Christians felt compelled to convert the Native Americans. In the 1830s churches began to establish missions in the far West. Narcissa Prentiss Whitman (who when single had been rejected by the Presbyterian mission board because she was unmarried) and Eliza Hart Spalding accompanied their husbands to the Pacific Northwest. In 1847 the Whitmans were murdered by some of the Native Americans they had

Women have been active in missionary work for more than a century; these missionaries in Asia appeared in Helen Barrett Montgomery's Western Women in Eastern Lands *(1910).*

sought to proselytize. Narcissa was only one of many missionary wives to be extolled as martyrs in the Christian cause. By 1873, when Sue McBeth and her sister Kate journeyed to Idaho to convert the Nez Percé to Christianity, women had become accepted as missionaries in their own right, though they were expected to work among women and children only. Single women such as Baptist missionary Charlotte (Lottie) Diggs Moon had begun serving alone in foreign lands by the final third of the nineteenth century, though they too usually focused their proselytizing on women and children.

As women's missions societies grew and as their work in foreign missions gained acceptance, greater opportunities opened for women in foreign missions. They performed a variety of roles, including those of evangelist, teacher, and health care worker. By the end of the nineteenth century, women like physicians Clara Swain and Anna Sarah Kugler were holding positions as medical missionaries. Scholars have found that despite their push for greater responsibilities in their work, most women who were active in foreign missions either ignored the women's movement at home or denounced it. Nor did they attempt to attain positions within the upper ranks of the church hierarchy. Some scholars theorize that missionary women did not want to be connected with the "radical" image associated with nineteenth- and early-twentieth-century feminism. Indeed, the women in missions considered their work an extension of the "feminine" role of nurturer and guardian of family morals. Others conclude that female missionaries devoted so much energy to their missions that they had little time to consider involving themselves in the women's movement. Regardless of their stand on the issue of equal rights, these women helped broaden the female experience by proving to themselves and

the world that they could effectively perform the duties of a missionary.

See also: Judson, Ann Hasseltine; Judson, Emily Chubbuck; Judson, Sarah Hall Boardman; Kugler, Anna Sarah; McBeth, Sue; Missionary Societies; Mount Holyoke College; Spalding, Eliza Hart; Whitman, Narcissa Prentiss

References: Opal Sweazea Allen, *Narcissa Whitman: An Historical Biography* (1959); Edith Deen, *Great Women of the Christian Faith* (1959); Elizabeth Alden Green, *Mary Lyon and Mount Holyoke: Opening the Gates* (1979); Patricia R. Hill, *The World Their Household: The American Women's Foreign Mission Movement and Cultural Transformation, 1870–1920* (1985); Rosemary Skinner Keller, "Lay Women in the Protestant Tradition," in Rosemary Radford Ruether and Rosemary Skinner Keller, eds., *Women and Religion in America*, vol. 1 (1986); James Davis Knowles, *Life of Mrs. Ann H. Judson, Late Missionary to Burma* (1830); Susan Hill Lindley, *"You Have Stept Out of Your Place": A History of Women and Religion in America* (1996); Robert McHenry, ed., *Liberty's Women* (1980); Ann White, "Counting the Cost of Faith: America's Early Female Missionaries," *Church History* 57, no. 2 (March 1988): 19–30.

Missionary Societies

The earliest women's missionary society of record was the Boston Female Society for Missionary Purposes. Founded in 1800 by a group of Congregational and Baptist women, it was most likely a product of the evangelical spirit that was rising during the early years of the Second Great Awakening. In the decades that followed, other small groups of Protestant women organized to create societies that offered them opportunities to contribute to both home and foreign missions. Until the 1860s, most of the women's groups were local, interdenominational, and under the authority of male boards. However, during the last four decades of the nineteenth century, women's interest in missions was burgeoning. More women were becoming foreign missionaries, and thousands were beginning to band together to offer their services in aid of converting the "heathens" overseas. The first national interdenominational women's society, the Woman's Union Missionary Society, was established in 1860, but soon various groups began to break away as new women's societies began to be founded in individual denominations.

Prior to the Civil War, the women's missionary societies became known for their small but regular financial contributions to foreign missions. These groups were often known as "cent" or "mite" societies. Such offerings were welcomed by male religious leaders, and they were in keeping with the nineteenth-century image of women as pious and self-sacrificing. But as with other women's religious societies of the era, these groups provided women with opportunities to broaden their outlook and taught them how to raise money, maintain records, and organize for a cause. The women's enthusiasm led them to seek greater responsibility within mission work, so that by the early 1860s their roles had greatly expanded.

Because most religious denominations of the nineteenth century denied women ordination to the ministry and prevented them from taking on leadership roles within the church structure, women sought other means to put their religious fervor into action. Education and missions were virtually the only areas open to women where they felt they could wield some influence. In the later decades of the century, more and more women were flocking to these fields. As historian Rosemary Skinner Keller finds, there were more females "involved in women's missionary society work after the Civil War than in all areas of the social reform and women's rights movements combined. Between 1861 and 1894, foreign missionary societies were organized by and for women in thirty-three denominations, and home missionary societies in

seventeen" (Keller, 1986, p. 242). Although some of the women's groups were independent, others operated as auxiliaries or in association with a male-led general mission board.

High on the list of goals for most of the women's missionary societies was the desire to educate and "uplift" the heathen women of foreign lands or America's urban ghettos. First of all, they sought to bring Christianity into women's lives in order to save their souls. Providing a basic education to women was a second priority, and mission societies supported schools that would teach native women basic literacy and domestic skills in addition to religious study. Health care was a third focus of women's activity. They sent female medical missionaries to foreign lands and helped fund clinics and hospitals.

Women's missionary societies of the twentieth century continue to support both home and foreign missions, seeking to spread the Gospel, enrich the spiritual lives of Christians, and render humanitarian assistance to the needy. Many of these organizations are now celebrating more than a hundred years of service.

See also: Missionaries; Woman's Home and Foreign Mission Society; Woman's Missionary Union; Women's Missionary and Service Commission of the Mennonite Church; Women's Missionary Society of the African Methodist Episcopal Church

References: Patricia R. Hill, *The World Their Household: The American Women's Foreign Mission Movement and Cultural Transformation, 1870–1920* (1985); Rosemary Skinner Keller, "Lay Women in the Protestant Tradition," in Rosemary Radford Ruether and Rosemary Skinner Keller, eds., *Women and Religion in America*, vol. 1 (1986); Susan Hill Lindley, *"You Have Stept Out of Your Place": A History of Women and Religion in America* (1996); Woman's Missionary Union, *Annual Report 1996* (n.d., c. 1997).

Modesto, Ruby E. (1913–1980)

Medicine woman Ruby Modesto was born in 1913 on the Martinez Reservation in the Coachella Valley of southern California. Her father was of the Cahuilla people of the area, and her mother was a Serrano woman from the Morongo Reservation. Until she was ten years old, Ruby spoke no English, learning only the language of her father's people. As a child, Modesto attended the Moravian church on the reservation with her mother and considered herself a Christian. But as she grew older, she felt a need to pursue the religion of her ancestors. Modesto's relatives were members of the Dog Clan, and her father, grandfather, great-grandfather, and many uncles and granduncles were shamans, or *puls*. From them she learned shamanistic teachings and traditions.

One aspect that distinguishes a *pul* is a dream helper. When she was about ten years old, Modesto received her dream helper, Ahswit, the eagle, but she remained a Christian and did not become a shaman until later in life. She eventually found her ties to the ancient Cahuilla religion too strong to resist, and she chose to be a *pul* rather than to continue as a Christian. In addition to her responsibilities as a shaman, which included her specializing in the treatment of persons possessed by demons, Modesto taught Cahuilla language classes and was a guest lecturer on native culture and tradition at local colleges. She worked with anthropologists to preserve information about her people and her personal spiritual beliefs. In 1977 she and Richard Lando cowrote an article, "Temal Wakish: A Desert Cahuilla Village," in *The Journal of California Anthropology*. She also collaborated on a book designed for the study of Native American traditions, *Not for Innocent Ears* (1980), with Guy Mount. Modesto died in California on April 7, 1980.

See also: Native Americans
References: Gretchen M. Bataille, *Native American Women: A Biographical Dictio-nary* (1993); Arlene Hirschfelder and Paulette Molin, *The Encyclopedia of Native American Religions* (1992); Ruby Modesto and Guy Mount, *Not for Innocent Ears: Spiritual Traditions of a Desert Cahuilla Medicine Woman* (1980).

Moise, Mary (1850–1930)

A pioneer in Pentecostal social work and the founder of the Moise Faith Home in St. Louis, Missouri, Mary Moise (née Maria Christina Gill) was born into a prominent family in Richmond, Virginia, in 1850. She married a Confederate army veteran, Albert Welborne Moise, and moved with him to St. Louis in 1880. A lifelong Episcopalian, at the urging of Bishop Daniel S. Tuttle, she opened her home as an Episcopal "faith home" and welcomed women in trouble. Women in poor financial circumstances, prostitutes, and those in other unfortunate situations found their way to her home. The Moise Faith Home was also used for the training of future ministers. Mary found her work exciting and satisfying, but her husband was not so enthusiastic. In 1905 he arranged for an amicable separation.

By this time, Moise's work had brought her some renown, and she was honored at the 1904 St. Louis World's Fair. In 1905 she established a second center, the Door of Hope Rescue Mission, and became its director. Two years later, she united with the Pentecostals in the area and became a Pentecostal herself at about the same time. Moise moved her house of mercy into larger quarters in 1909 and was soon joined by Leonore O. (Mother Mary) Barnes, a skillful evangelist, and her husband, Victor Barnes.

Although Moise initially was friendly toward all Pentecostals, in the 1920s she adopted two beliefs that were outside the Pentecostal mainstream. First, she became one of the early converts to what was called "oneness teaching," which disavowed the doctrine of the Trinity and advocated baptism in the name of Jesus only. Next, she adopted the belief that if Christians had faith, they could live until the return of Jesus.

Moise died in St. Louis on September 12, 1930. Due to her many years of work with the more unfortunate women of the city, she had become a well-known and respected citizen. She received generous financial support from the community, which enabled her to open more missions, though by the time of her death only the original center remained. It closed about ten years later.

See also: Pentecostalism
References: Stanley M. Burgess, *Dictionary of Pentecostal and Charismatic Movements* (1988); J. Gordon Melton, *Religious Leaders of America* (1991).

Montgomery, Carrie Judd
(1858–c. 1946)

Preacher, writer, editor, and social worker Carrie Judd Montgomery was born in Buffalo, New York, on April 8, 1858. The daughter of devout Episcopalian parents, Carrie made a spiritual commitment to and was confirmed in that faith herself when she was eleven years old. She was studying at Buffalo Normal School, preparing for a career as a teacher, when she suffered a fall that made her an invalid. Through the ministrations of an African-American woman, Mrs. Edward Mix, she was healed. Carrie wrote of the experience in a book, *The Prayer of Peace* (1880), in which she also encouraged her readers to pray for physical healing. Writing was not a new experience for her; she had been publishing poems since she was a teen. A Presbyterian minister, Albert Benjamin Simpson, who would later establish the Christian and Missionary Alliance (CMA) as a result of his own healing experience, read Carrie's book and put her in contact with other early promoters of the healing ideal. When the CMA was founded in 1885, Carrie was appointed recording secretary of the board.

Meanwhile, in 1881 Carrie publicly entered the ministry by establishing a periodical, *Triumphs of Faith,* which she edited for sixty-five years. The magazine bridged the Holiness and Pentecostal movements and provided a nonsectarian forum for other denominations to communicate their concerns and teachings on common themes that had significant influence upon the healing movement, social service activities, and worldwide missions. Also in the early 1880s, Carrie began to give testimony on healing in public and spoke at conventions that Simpson sponsored. At about the same time, she turned the room in which she had been healed into a faith sanctuary, where people could go to pray. Soon afterward, she opened Faith Rest Cottage in Buffalo, where the sick could go for comfort, prayer, encouragement, and teaching. It was one of several homes that were established during the late nineteenth century by people who had faith in divine healing.

Early in 1890 Carrie moved to Oakland, California. In the spring of that year, she married George S. Montgomery, a wealthy businessman who owned property in Beulah (later Beulah Heights), an area near Oakland. There the Montgomerys founded the Home of Peace in 1893, an establishment similar to Faith Rest Cottage, but one that would serve as a center for a variety of ministries. The Montgomerys launched the Shalom Training School in 1894 to train future missionaries and opened an orphanage in 1895. They operated the orphanage until 1908, when they turned its administration over to the Salvation Army. They also donated property to the Salvation Army to build a rescue home for girls. The Montgomerys themselves had one child, a daughter they named Faith.

During her first year in Oakland, Carrie Montgomery organized a CMA church. She and her husband also joined the Salvation Army and were active with that organization for several years. Another project of the Montgomerys was the launching of a campground called "Elim Groves" at Cazadera, where prominent Pentecostals and leaders of other denominations ministered.

In about 1906, both Carrie and George Montgomery became involved in the Pentecostal movement. She prayed for the baptism in the Holy Spirit, finally receiving the experience of speaking in tongues while at the home of a friend in Chicago in 1908. Despite her conversion, she continued to maintain favorable relations with the non-Pentecostal CMA and continued to speak at their conventions. In 1914 she became a charter member of the Assemblies of God Church, now one of the largest Pentecostal denominations in the United States.

During her lifetime, Montgomery wrote several books, including *Lilies from the Veil of Thought* (1878), *Heart Whisperings* (1897), *Secrets of Victory* (1921), *Heart Melody* (1922), and *Under His Wings* (1936). Conflicting dates have been given for her death, but it is likely she died in Oakland, California, in 1945 or 1946.

See also: Pentecostalism
References: Stanley M. Burgess, *Dictionary of Pentecostal and Charismatic Movements* (1988); Mary L. Hammack, *Dictionary of Women in Church History* (1984); J. Gordon Melton, *Religious Leaders of America* (1991).

Helen Barrett Montgomery (Missions, *June 1922*)

Montgomery, Helen Barrett (1861–1934)

Helen Barrett Montgomery was the first woman to be elected president of a major religious denomination, the Northern Baptist Convention, in the United States. Nellie, as she was originally called, was born into a Baptist family in Kingsville, Ohio, on July 31, 1861, the eldest of the three children of Emily (Barrows) and Adoniram Judson Barrett. As her mother had been prior to her marriage, Helen's father was a teacher at the time of his daughter's birth. In 1870 Adoniram Barrett obtained a position as principal of the Collegiate Institute in Rochester, New York. While there, he enrolled in Rochester Theological Seminary, graduating from that institution in 1876. He then became pastor of Lake Avenue Baptist Church in Rochester, retaining this post until his death in 1889. The Barrett children inherited their father's passion for education. Helen attended Livingston Park Seminary before entering Wellesley College in 1880. She studied Latin in high school and Greek in college. Her major at Wellesley was in education, and after graduation in 1884, she taught at the Rochester Free Academy and Wellesley Preparatory School. Her teaching career ended upon her marriage in 1887 to businessman and fellow Baptist William A. Montgomery, though throughout their marriage William lent his support to his wife's projects outside the home and seemed proud of her accomplishments.

Following her marriage, Helen Montgomery organized a large and influential women's Bible class at her father's church, a class she taught for forty-four years. Although she was never ordained, in 1892 the congregation gave her a license to preach. A year later, she became the first woman president of the Women's Educational and Industrial Union of Rochester. With Montgomery at the helm, the union launched various campaigns for civic reform and social welfare, and it became one of the city's most dynamic organizations. The union introduced art classes and manual training into the public schools, made legal aid available to the poor, sponsored the city's first public playground, operated milk stations for needy mothers that eventually evolved into child welfare clinics, and built a settlement house in Rochester's Italian district. When a "good government" movement began in the mid-1890s, the union gave the campaign its full support. One result was a reorganization of the school board, with Montgomery elected its first female member in 1899.

Over the next few decades, Montgomery involved herself in numerous projects. She lectured on educational topics, served as president of the Women's American Baptist Foreign Mission Society from 1913 to 1924, and in 1915 cofounded the World Wide Guild, an organization that recruited women for Baptist missionary service. Her interest in mission work led her to serve as president of the National Federation of Women's Boards of Foreign Missions for the year 1917–1918 and to contribute two volumes to a series of study books on mission work: *Christus*

Redemptor (1906), on missions in the Pacific islands; and *Western Women in Eastern Lands* (1910).

In 1913 Montgomery toured the world with Lucy Peabody, a close associate in many of her campaigns, to acquire a firsthand impression of missions in the field. Montgomery's travels resulted in the book *The King's Highway* (1915), which sold more than 160,000 copies. In 1921 she was elected president of the Northern Baptist Convention, the first woman to head a major American religious denomination. In addition to continuing to write about missionary work, she translated the Greek New Testament into modern English, as *The Centenary Translation of the New Testament* (1924).

Helen Barrett Montgomery died in the home of her daughter in Summit, New Jersey, on October 19, 1934. In her will, she bequeathed $450,000 to more than eighty selected churches (in addition to the thousands of dollars she and William had contributed during their lifetimes).

See also: Baptists; Peabody, Lucy Whitehead McGill Waterbury
References: Edith Deen, *Great Women of the Christian Faith* (1959); Edward T. James, ed., *Notable American Women, 1607–1950* (1971); J. Gordon Melton, *Religious Leaders of America* (1991); Phyllis J. Read and Bernard L. Witlieb, *The Book of Women's Firsts* (1992); Rosemary Radford Ruether and Rosemary Skinner Keller, eds., *Women and Religion in America,* vol. 3 (1986).

Moon, Charlotte (Lottie) Diggs (1840–1912)

Charlotte Diggs Moon, a missionary to China for nearly four decades, was born in Albermarle County, Virginia, on December 12, 1840. Christened Charlotte Diggs, her name was later shortened to Lottie. Her father, Edward Harris Moon, was master of a "Viewmont," a fine plantation home near the Blue Ridge Mountains. He had been reared a Presbyterian but was indifferent to the faith. Anna Maria (Barclay) Moon, Lottie's mother, was a devout Baptist who read religious texts to her children. For many years, there was no church near the Moon home so Anna Moon held services in her parlor on Sunday mornings. Her children attended, as did the Moons' servants and neighbors. When Lottie was about two years old, a Baptist church was organized in Scottsville, about 10 miles from Viewmont. Edward Moon converted to the Baptist faith, became the largest contributor to the new building, and joined the congregation with his family.

Lottie received her early education from a governess in her home. In 1854 she enrolled in the Virginia Female Seminary (known as Hollins College after 1855), where she excelled in her studies. She entered the Baptist-supported Albermarle Female Institute at Charlottesville in 1857. Two years into her studies, Lottie, who had previously been disinterested in religion, was converted at a revival held at the college. In 1861 she became one of the first southern women to receive a master's degree from the college. Since the Civil War erupted at about the time of her graduation, Lottie returned home to help her mother. When the war ended, she began a career as a teacher, first tutoring in Alabama, then teaching in a school for girls in Kentucky, and finally working with a friend to establish a small school in Cartersville, Georgia.

In 1872 Lottie's sister Edmonia became a missionary in China. Lottie joined her in September of the following year. She learned Chinese quickly and was soon working with her sister. Based in Tengchow, they traveled from village to village, teaching, counseling, comforting, and evangelizing among the Chinese women. Edmonia became ill in 1876, and Lottie accompanied her back to Virginia. But by Christmas of the following year, Lottie was again in Tengchow. She worked in the

mission school there but eventually came to believe that she could better reach young Chinese women and girls by visiting them in their own communities. In 1885 she journeyed to Pingtu, an area where no woman missionary had gone before. There she rented a small house that became a sanctuary for missionaries traveling in the area. Remaining true to her conservative southern upbringing and to rigid interpretations of the Gospel in regard to limits placed upon women, Moon taught women and girls only. But when Chinese men begged to learn more of the Gospel from her, she agreed to allow them to study alongside the women. Except for a furlough to Virginia in 1892–1893, Moon divided her time between Pingtu and Tengchow until 1894, when she made a permanent move back to Tengchow.

According to her biographers, Moon's patience and calm demeanor helped to break down initial animosities against her on the part of the Chinese. Often faced with a lack of funds, she dressed in simple Chinese clothes, slept on a brick bed, and ate food purchased in the village market. She persevered through revolutions as well as smallpox and other epidemics. During the Boxer Rebellion of 1900, Moon evacuated to Japan briefly but soon returned to China.

Throughout her time in China, Moon sent letters urging denomination leaders to send more missionaries and supplies to China. In 1888 the Lottie Moon Christmas Offering was established, providing three additional missionaries the first year. After the Boxer Rebellion, she used her entire personal savings and pleaded for money and food from America to alleviate the famine conditions in China. When her own health began to fail, fellow missionaries sent a doctor to examine her. The doctor found that she was undernourished and starving to death. In December 1912, upon her doctor's orders, she set sail for home, accompanied by Cynthia Miller, a missionary nurse. Four days into the journey, on December 24, 1912, Moon died in the harbor at Kobe, Japan.

The Lottie Moon Christmas Offering has continued as a memorial to Moon. In the fund's first seventy-five-year period, more than $50 million was raised. The money has gone toward the building of churches, hospitals, and homes for missionaries; has paid missionaries' salaries; and has financed other needs of Southern Baptist missions.

See also: Missionaries
References: Edith Deen, *Great Women of the Christian Faith* (1959); Mary L. Hammack, *Dictionary of Women in Church History* (1984); Una Roberts Lawrence, *Lottie Moon* (1927); Anna Seward Pruitt, *Up from Zero* (1938); Walter Sinclair Stewart, *Later Baptist Missionaries and Pioneers,* vol. 2 (1929).

Joanna Patterson Moore (from her book The Power and Work of the Holy Spirit)

Moore, Joanna Patterson (1832–1916)

A pioneer in Baptist home mission work and a leader in taking Sunday school instruction to African Americans, Joanna Patterson Moore was born in Clarion County, Pennsylvania, on September 26, 1832. She was raised in the Episcopal Church of her father's faith, though she was also influenced by her Presbyterian mother. Moore later claimed that she had backslid from her faith. In 1852, after attending a Baptist revival meeting, she converted and joined the Baptist church. Nevertheless, she appreciated that she had a background in the Episcopal and Presbyterian faiths and, in later years, observed that "all our evangelical churches agree on all but a very few subjects and these few have been so largely discussed that they have grown to be mountains and separated God's children, and made them forget the ten thousand subjects upon which they agree" (Moore, 1903).

Although she had only limited schooling, Moore had been a teacher since she was sixteen years old. After her conversion, she felt compelled to become a missionary. In 1862 she entered Rockford (Illinois) Seminary, graduating a year later. She immediately began her mission career, working in refugee camps for former slaves who had recently been freed as a result of the Emancipation Proclamation. The American Baptist Home Mission Society gave her their backing but no salary. With moral and some financial support from her home church in Belvidere, Illinois, in November 1863 she began giving Bible lessons to black women and children on an island in the Mississippi River. The following year she moved to Helena, Arkansas, and began work at an orphanage that had recently been established by the Quakers. She was there approximately four years before transferring to another Quaker orphanage in Lauderdale, Mississippi, in

1868, but she returned to Illinois in 1869 to be with her mother, who had fallen ill.

Although the American Baptists had initially been reluctant to commission women, they changed their policy during the 1860s and began to actively recruit them. In the 1870s the Baptists established three regional women's missionary organizations, including the Woman's Baptist Home Missionary Society. Moore served this society, which supported her with financial help and missionary assistance, moving to New Orleans, Louisiana, in 1873 to work among blacks. The Woman's Foreign Mission Society (organized in 1871) attempted to influence her to travel to foreign lands, but she remained on the home mission field, continuing her involvement with blacks. When the Woman's American Baptist Home Missionary Society was established in 1877, Moore was the first person to be commissioned. With the help of four assistants, she expanded her work throughout Louisiana and into neighboring states. She also opened a home for elderly women in New Orleans. Her endeavors earned her a reputation as a major figure in Baptist home missionary work. Moore established Sunday schools and missions throughout the South, helped organize African-American Baptist churches, organized training schools, and enlisted both black and white teachers and evangelists to help her in her labors, broadening the mission society's vision and scope.

Over the next decade, Moore continued her work in the black community. Among her contributions to the cause were her establishment of the Bible Band in 1884, a program that distributed Bibles to African Americans; her launching of *Hope* magazine in 1885, which she edited for the next twenty-six years and for which she wrote Bible lessons the rest of her life; and her organization of a training school for black women in 1887. The latter project came to an abrupt halt in 1890 when the White League, a white supremacist group that opposed the school, ran Moore out of town.

Moore settled in Little Rock, Arkansas, in 1891, where she began a new program, the Sunshine Bands, a plan to establish Sunday schools in people's homes and thus reach children who did not attend church. What is usually regarded as her greatest contribution to the evangelism of southern blacks, the Fireside School, was begun in 1892. Through her *Hope* magazine, Moore promoted a time of daily prayer and study in individual family homes. Each month the family would report their progress to their church, and the church would then give a report to Moore. In addition to the material printed in her magazine, Moore constructed a three-year curriculum.

Moore moved again, to Nashville, Tennessee, in 1894. She lived there for the next twenty-two years, devoting much of her time to writing and editing. She wrote an autobiography detailing her mission work, *"In Christ's Stead,"* in 1903. Some of Moore's time was spent traveling, encouraging others to perform mission work, and raising money. During one such trip in 1916, she caught bronchitis while in Selma, Alabama, and died there on April 15, 1916.

See also: Baptists; Missionaries; Missionary Societies
References: Eleanor Hull, *Women Who Carried the Good News* (1975); Bill J. Leonard, ed., *Dictionary of Baptists in America* (1994); J. Gordon Melton, *Religious Leaders of America* (1991); Joanna P. Moore, *"In Christ's Stead": Autobiographical Sketches* (1903); Walter Sinclair Stewart, *Later Baptist Missionaries and Pioneers*, vol. 1 (1928); James D. Tyms, *The Rise of Religious Education among Negro Baptists* (1979).

Mormons (See Church of Jesus Christ of Latter-Day Saints)

Mott, Lucretia Coffin (1793–1880)

Lucretia Coffin Mott, Quaker minister, abolitionist, and pioneer activist for women's rights, was born on January 3, 1793, on Nantucket Island, Massachusetts. Her father was captain of a whaling ship and was often away from home for lengthy periods of time. His wife was left in charge of the care and maintenance of the family and the household economy. Such responsibilities were greater than those experienced by most women of the era, but the frequent absences of male heads of households in whaling communities like Nantucket made it necessary to place more than usual trust in the communities' women. With her mother and Nantucket women as role models, Lucretia was able to build confidence in her own abilities as a girl and, later, as a woman.

Most of Lucretia's education was in schools managed by the Society of Friends. When the family moved to Boston in 1804, she briefly attended a non-Quaker private school and then a public school for a year, but in 1806 she enrolled in Nine Partners Boarding School, a Quaker academy near Poughkeepsie, New York. Lucretia excelled at her studies and after two years was made an assistant teacher and offered a permanent position on the staff. In 1811, she married James Mott, Jr., an assistant principal at the school. Following their marriage, the couple left teaching and moved to Philadelphia.

Tragedy struck the family when the Motts' three-year-old son died in 1817. Lucretia Mott sought relief from her grief through religious readings and reflection. On one occasion she felt moved to express herself in a Friends' Meeting and offered a simple prayer. The sympathy and support she received as a result of her public expression encouraged her to speak often, and in 1821 she was officially recognized as a Quaker minister.

Seldom did a woman as young as Mott receive such an honor, but she was gifted with a pleasant, clear speaking voice as well as the ability to present her messages with sincerity and in logical, simple language.

The 1820s found conflicts within the Society of Friends. The growing power of the wealthy Philadelphia Quaker elders disturbed many members, including Mott. The problem reached a climax in the late 1820s, when the elders decided to discipline aged Quaker minister Elias Hicks, whom they accused of preaching heresy. Hicks was a controversial figure, but he had a large following. He preached fiery sermons critical of slavery and the new evangelicalism that was becoming popular among Friends. He felt they were losing the true spirit of Quakerism. In 1827, the Society of Friends split over the controversy between the elders and Hicks, those taking Hicks's side being referred to as "Hicksites." The Motts chose to back Hicks, although Lucretia encountered persecution and feuds within her own family as a result of her choice. The new Hicksite branch of the Society of Friends needed Mott's ministering talents. She helped where she could, but her role as a mother of five surviving children kept her in the Philadelphia area. In the early 1830s, she was able to begin traveling to outlying areas of Pennsylvania and New Jersey, where conflict between the two branches of Quakers was especially fierce.

A national issue that was becoming increasingly controversial as the nineteenth century progressed was that of slavery. Lucretia Mott had opposed the institution of slavery all of her life, so when she and her husband became acquainted with abolitionist William Lloyd Garrison, they did all they could to help him spread his message of immediate emancipation for all slaves. The Motts arranged for Garrison to give talks in the area, offered their home for meetings, and invited the participation of both men and women. Although the mixing of the sexes in gatherings for political discussion seemed natural for Mott, it was not a commonly accepted practice within nineteenth-century American society.

In December 1833, Mott organized the Philadelphia Female Anti-Slavery Society, one of the first women's political groups. Most of the women in the organization were Quakers, but there were also some Presbyterians and Unitarians among the group. Several middle-class black women were also members of this pioneer organization, a fact that shocked the majority of the citizens of Philadelphia. By the mid-1830s, public opposition to the antislavery movements, particularly toward those who advocated immediate emancipation, had grown violent. Mobs attacked and destroyed businesses and homes of both blacks and abolitionists in several northern states, including Pennsylvania. On a visit to Delaware, Mott had stones thrown at her carriage.

The Society of Friends attempted to bar the subject of slavery from its meetings because the majority feared discord among the members, but Mott refused to avoid the topic. In 1837 she was among the women who created the Anti-Slavery Convention of American Women in New York City and led the organizing of a second convention in Philadelphia the following year. Following the fourth day of the convention, a mob burst open the locked doors of Philadelphia's Pennsylvania Hall and set the building aflame. Not satisfied with the destruction of the hall, the rioters looked for new targets. The Motts' home was saved by a quick-witted friend, who yelled out, "On to the Motts!" and pointed in the wrong direction.

In 1840 Mott was one of the delegates to the World Anti-Slavery Convention in London. But when the convention opened, female delegates were excluded from active participation in the proceedings. For Mott, this was not the only disappointment of her trip to Great Britain. As a minister for the Hicksites, she faced rude treatment from British Quakers who had sided with the Orthodox Friends during the time of the schism and continued to believe that those who sided with Elias Hicks were heretics. Despite the problems she encountered in Britain, Mott considered her trip worthwhile. She made new friends, including Elizabeth Cady Stanton, with whom she had long discussions concerning women's rights. This began a chain of events that would lead to the 1848 Woman's Rights Convention in Seneca Falls, New York.

Over the next several years, Mott became more deeply involved in an ongoing fight with the Society of Friends over her continued antislavery activities. The elders were also angered over her occasional sermons in Unitarian churches and questioned whether her theology was not more Unitarian than Quaker. The belief she shared with early Quakers, that every day should be equally a day of worship and that a special day of Sabbath should be eliminated, led to charges of heresy both from inside and outside the Society of Friends.

Although she joined with other Quakers in deploring war and violence, once the Civil War began, Mott felt it should be fought to the finish, to end slavery once and for all. Following the war, in 1866 she was named president of the newly formed American Equal Rights Association. When in 1867 the organization divided over the Fourteenth Amendment and the issue of whether it should support black male suffrage or hold out for votes for women, Mott sided with the feminists who believed it necessary to oppose the amendment unless the word *male* was eliminated. Mott continued her crusades for peace, religious freedom, and women's rights until her death. Throughout her life she forged the way for later women reformers and served as an inspiration for generations to come. Mott died in her home near Philadelphia on November 11, 1880.

> See also: Antislavery Movement; Female Moral Reform Society; Peace Movements; Society of Friends (Quakers); Woman Suffrage
> References: Margaret Hope Bacon, *Valiant Friend: The Life of Lucretia Mott* (1980); Otelia Cromwell, *Lucretia Mott* (1958); Lloyd C. M. Hare, *The Greatest American Woman: Lucretia Mott* (1937, republished 1972).

Mount Holyoke College

Chartered as Mount Holyoke Female Seminary in 1836, Mount Holyoke in South Hadley, Massachusetts, was the first women's seminary in the United States. It opened its doors in November 1837, the first institution to offer American women an education at the postsecondary level. The school developed out of female reformers' recognition that if women were ever to gain a social status on a level equal to men, they needed to be well educated. Mary Lyon (1797–1849), the founder of Mount Holyoke, was one of the first reformers to advance female education. In 1834 she wrote of her vision for a seminary for young women that would be affordable even for those of ordinary financial means, and she circulated a plan that described the school as a "residential seminary to be founded and sustained by the Christian public," with board and tuition as inexpensive as possible (James, 1971, p. 445). Young women attending the school would be trained as teachers and missionaries. As she struggled to establish her institution of higher learning for women, ministers of churches that led in the founding of men's colleges of the era

opposed Lyon's plans as impractical, unwise, and even un-Christian. Nevertheless, her dreams reached fruition.

When Mount Holyoke Female Seminary opened in November 1837, eighty women ages seventeen and older were enrolled in the school's three-year program (which extended to four years in 1861). They received academic training in a Christian environment, attending prayer meetings and listening to Mary Lyon's commentary on the Scriptures. The curriculum included courses in English grammar, ancient geography, ancient and modern history, political science, botany, rhetoric, math, chemistry, astronomy, geology, ecclesiastical history, evidences of Christianity, logic, moral philosophy, natural theology, and natural philosophy (preparation for child rearing). Lyon sought female teachers who held high literary qualifications and who were filled with benevolent, self-denying zeal. Aspiring students were required to pass difficult entrance exams, which became increasingly demanding from one year to the next. Lyon's high admission standards led to improved quality of education at both the elementary and secondary levels as teachers sought to prepare their brightest students for the seminary.

In addition to improving educational standards in the lower grades, Mount Holyoke Seminary's early graduates left a significant imprint on American society. Many of Lyon's graduates went on to become teachers or to found new colleges for women. These women helped to further improve education in the United States for both males and females. Some of Lyon's most gifted graduates helped extend the school's influence around the world as they traveled to foreign lands as missionaries or missionaries' wives.

In 1888 the name of the school was changed to Mount Holyoke Seminary and College. A year later the school awarded its first baccalaureate degree. It adopted its present name, Mount Holyoke College, in 1893. In the mid-1990s, the college continues to be a women-only institution. An independent college of liberal arts and sciences, it enrolls just under two thousand students. For the academic year 1994–1995, there were 1,957 students from forty-nine states and fifty-two countries. Although Mount Holyoke offers graduate education at the master's level, of the 1,957 students noted above, 1,946 were undergraduates. The college seeks women of outstanding intellectual ability, and admission requirements remain stringent.

See also: Lyon, Mary
References: *American Colleges and Universities,* 13th ed. (1987); Eleanor Flexner, *Century of Struggle: The Woman's Rights Movement in the United States* (1970); Elizabeth Alden Green, *Mary Lyon and Mount Holyoke: Opening the Gates* (1979); Edward T. James, ed., *Notable American Women, 1607–1950,* vol. 2 (1971); *Peterson's Guide to Four-Year Colleges, 1997,* 27th ed. (1996).

Mountain Wolf Woman
(1884–1960)

Winnebago healer and peyotist Mountain Wolf Woman was born in April 1884 into the Thunder Clan at East Fork River, Wisconsin. When she was about two years old, she became very ill, and her mother took her to an old woman named Wolf Woman for healing. In the Winnebago tradition, the mother was in a sense giving her child away to the healer, though the child continued to live with her parents. In addition to carrying out the usual healing procedures, the old woman offered her life and longevity to the child. This was in accordance with the Winnebago belief that if a person failed to live an entire life of one hundred years, the person could share the good things from his or her remaining years as well as the forces of his or her personal power. Wolf Woman gave the child the name Xehaciwinga, or Mountain Wolf Woman, which bestowed upon her the protection of the Wolf Clan spirit in addition to that of the Thunder Clan into which she was born.

From the time she was a little girl, Mountain Wolf Woman sought knowledge of medicines. She learned Native American medical practices and spent much of her life working to heal people. Until the 1930s, when Winnebago women began going to hospitals to give birth, Mountain Wolf Woman served as a midwife. In the mid-1940s, she served as "health officer" at the Black River Falls, Wisconsin, mission, reporting illnesses to the county public health nurse.

Mountain Wolf Woman married twice. The first marriage was arranged by her brother against her wishes and was an unhappy experience for her. It ended in divorce after the birth of her second child. She later married Bad Soldier, with whom she had nine additional children. Mountain Wolf Woman had her first experience with peyote at the time she was about to deliver her third child. From then on, she and her family regularly attended Saturday peyote meetings. One of her sons became a leader of Half Moon meetings, which is a branch of the peyote church. Mountain Wolf Woman once had a vision while taking peyote and felt a sensation of happiness and contentment. The vision convinced her that the peyote religion was holy and directed toward the Christian God. She also came to believe in the curative powers of peyote. In 1958 she financed a peyote meeting that commemorated the fiftieth anniversary of the introduction of peyote into Wisconsin.

Although Mountain Wolf Woman believed that peyote was more effective than traditional ways, she continued to practice Winnebago customs. She sang Winnebago songs and danced the tribe's traditional dances, including the Scalp Dance and the Medicine Dance. Her adherence to the customs and social behaviors of the Winnebago people helped to preserve a culture that was on the verge of extinction. In 1958 Mountain Wolf Woman began work on her autobiography with Nancy Oestreich Lurie, who audiotaped her story. First she dictated an account of her life in the Winnebago language, then repeated it in English. Mountain Wolf Woman, who in addition to her adherence to Winnebago ways and to the practice of peyote was a devout Christian, was able to merge the three traditions. Following her death in Black River Falls, Wisconsin, on November 9, 1960, her Winnebago friends conducted a wake for her, the peyotists held a meeting in her house on the evening of her funeral, and she received a Christian burial at the local mission church and cemetery.

See also: Native Americans
References: Gretchen M. Bataille, *Native American Women: A Biographical Dictionary* (1993); J. Gordon Melton, *Religious Leaders of America* (1991); Mountain Wolf Woman, with Nancy Oestreich Lurie, ed., *Mountain Wolf Woman: Sister of Crashing Thunder* (1966).

Muslims

The majority of Muslims in America are immigrants or descendants of immigrants from Arab and Eastern European countries and from Muslim countries such as Pakistan. Islamic history in America dates back to the colonial and early republic eras, when large numbers of Muslims came to America as slaves from West Africa prior to 1850; however, little of their Islamic beliefs and culture survived. Arab immigrants began arriving in noticeable numbers during the last quarter of the nineteenth century, when there was an influx of Syrian men (many of whom were Christian) coming to the United States in search of employment. By 1900, one-third of the Arab immigrants were women, though very few were Muslim. It was not until the early twentieth century, when Muslims began arriving from countries of the disintegrating Ottoman Empire, that the Islamic faith began to take hold in the United States. And it was only in the 1940s, when families arrived to join their husbands and fathers, that significant numbers of Muslim women began arriving in the United States.

Although the Islamic faith considers men and women equal in terms of basic religious responsibilities, including the requirement to fulfill the five "Pillars of Islam," portions of the Koran portray women as subordinate to men in other matters. Defenders (both male and female) of the tradition of female subordination argue that men are given authority over women because it is the man's duty to financially support and protect his family. Because of their domestic responsibilities, women usually pray within their homes rather than attend communal prayer services in mosques. Some mosques discourage women's attendance, though Muslim women in America are more likely to be seen in mosques than are women in Islamic nations. A woman's physical condition will occasionally affect her participation in religious observances. For instance, if a woman is menstruating, pregnant, or nursing, she is normally relieved of the most severe requirements of the Ramadan fast.

Muslims in the United States practice their faith in varying degrees. Some strictly adhere to Islamic tradition, whereas others appear more secularized. The same is true regarding the wearing of the traditional Islamic dress. Muslim women's dress ranges from full veiling, to the choice to wear the traditional garb of *hijab* (head scarf), longish skirt, and the three-quarter to full-length sleeves, to wearing modest Western-style street clothes. Some Muslim women have experimented with modern American dress but have reverted to the Islamic dress after finding that they feel more "protected" under the covering of the traditional garb.

More than in culturally Muslim countries, in America mosques serve as cultural centers for the relatively small Muslim communities. Women have found mosque offices to be places where they could gather for conversation. As Susan Hill Lindley points out, Muslim women have engaged in activities in connection with their mosques that are similar to those of Christian and Jewish women in their churches and synagogues. Women cannot, however, become *imams,* the traditional leaders of worship.

As a small minority within the United States, Muslim immigrants and their descendants have had to make decisions regarding what aspects of American culture they should adopt. In general, the patriarchal extended family of the Islamic world has given way to the smaller nuclear family. This change, studies have found, has created a rise in the status of American Muslim wives. Most Muslims in this country have set aside the tradition of arranged marriages and have adopted the American form of courtship and marriage. Although Islamic law forbids women to marry non-Muslims, male Muslims may marry a Christian or a Jew. Nevertheless, marriage outside the faith is strongly discouraged for both sexes. As in marriage, Muslims in the United States follow American procedures for divorce. But, especially among first-generation Muslim couples, the wife will not use her American right to divorce her husband. This is because in traditional Islam, unless specifically stated otherwise in the marriage contract, only the husband has the right to divorce. In America, however, husbands rarely use their religious right of oral divorce.

Since the end of World War II, there has been a rapid increase in the numbers of Muslims in the United States. Many have arrived as immigrants, but there have also been a number of native-born Americans who have converted to Islam. Most of the converts have been African Americans, but a small number of white Americans have also adopted the Islamic faith. Scholars have recently estimated that early in the twenty-first century, the population of Muslims will overtake Jews to become the second-largest religious group in America.

References: Abdo A. Elkholy, *The Arab Moslems in the United States* (1966); Eric J. Hooglund, ed., *Crossing the Waters: Arabic-Speaking Immigrants to the United States before 1945* (1987); Susan Hill Lindley, *"You Have Stept Out of Your Place": A History of Women and Religion in America* (1996); Edward L. Queen II et al., eds., *The Encyclopedia of American Religious History* (1996); Evelyn Shakir, *Bint Arab: Arab and Arab American Women in the United States* (1997).

Nathan, Maud (1862–1946)

A leader in the women's rights movement, Maud Nathan was probably the first woman to play a major role in an American Jewish worship service. She was born in New York City on October 20, 1862, to Robert Weeks Nathan and Annie Augusta (Florance) Nathan. Both parents were descendants of Sephardic Jews, who had come to the United States from England in the seventeenth century, and Maud was raised in strict observance of Jewish tradition. With some reservations, she accepted the tenets of that very conservative branch of Judaism. "Loyalty to the traditions of my faith," she wrote, "has always remained firm, but my life has not been bounded by the walls of the synagogue" (Nathan, 1933, p. 49). When she was seventeen, Maud married her first cousin, Frederick Nathan, a prosperous banker in his midthirties, on April 7, 1880.

Throughout her adulthood, Nathan was an active participant in the Jewish community. She served on the board of Mount Sinai Training School for Nurses, was president of the first sisterhood of Congregation Shearith Israel, and played an important role in the New York section of the National Council of Jewish Women. Her community activism, coupled with her exceptional speaking ability, brought her an invitation in 1897 to read a paper in lieu of the sermon at Temple Beth-El in New York City. Her paper, entitled "The Heart of Judaism," argued that Judaism basically was a love of righteousness and urged Jews to devote themselves to social justice.

Nathan also involved herself in reforms outside the Jewish community. In 1890, she helped to found the Consumers' League of New York, an organization that called upon consumers to work for reforms within industry. Nathan, who became president of the league in 1897, was particularly eager to improve working conditions in factories and shops. She was also an active participant in the movement for women's rights and held leadership positions in a number of woman suffrage and labor organizations, including the Equal Suffrage League of New York. She wrote *The Story of an Epoch-Making Movement* (1926) and her autobiography, *Once Upon a Time and Today* (1933). Nathan, who was unique in her ability to combine her devotion to religious orthodoxy with her determination to work for reforms in the secular community, died December 15, 1946, in New York City.

See also: Jews; Woman Suffrage
References: Elizabeth Frost-Knappman, *Women's Progress in America* (1994); Edward T. James, ed., *Notable American Women, 1607–1950* (1971); Jacob R. Marcus, *The American Jewish Woman: A Documentary History* (1981); Maud Nathan, *Once Upon a Time and Today* (1933); Caroline Zilboorg, ed., *Women's Firsts* (1997).

Nation, Carry Amelia Moore (1846–1911)

Religious zealot and temperance agitator Carry Amelia Moore Nation was born

Religious zealot and temperance agitator Carry Amelia Moore Nation reads her Bible in Wichita's Sedgwick County Jail after vandalizing a local saloon.

November 25, 1848, in Garrard County, Kentucky. She was the eldest of the six children of George and Mary (Campbell) Moore. George Moore was a prosperous planter and stock trader until the outbreak of the Civil War. During the war, the family moved to other areas of Kentucky, to Missouri and Texas, and then back to Missouri, where George eked out a living from real estate transactions. Mary Moore suffered mental disorders (apparently manic-depressive), and her treatment of Carry ranged from intense affection to violent antipathy. She was eventually committed to a mental institution.

Carry's childhood was not happy. In addition to her father's financial troubles and her mother's mental illness, Carry suffered digestive disorders during these years and was herself a semi-invalid throughout much of her youth. She had only a few years of formal education in both public and private schools, along with infrequent private tutoring. The Moore family belonged to the Christian Church (Disciples of Christ), and Carry was ten when she had her first conversion experience. Many of her early religious influences came from her association with her father's black slaves. As a child, Carry was impressed with their methods of praising God, especially their songs and shouting. Carry also adopted many of their religious beliefs, particularly their animism. Throughout her life, Carry experienced periods of extreme spiritual distress that alternated with times of joyous excitement. She claimed that God directed all her major decisions.

Despite warnings from her parents that her fiancé was addicted to liquor, on November 21, 1867, Carry married Charles Gloyd, a young physician. They settled in Holden, Missouri. Within a week of the wedding, Carry realized that she should have heeded her parents' advice, for Gloyd's drunkenness terrified her. The marriage was miserable but of short duration. Although she was pregnant, Carry soon left Charles, and he died, apparently of alcoholism, in 1869. After her husband's death, Carry and her baby daughter moved into the home of her mother-in-law. Carry earned a teaching certificate from the State Normal School at Warrensburg, Missouri, and then taught in Holden for four years. In 1877 she married David Nation, a lawyer, newspaper editor, and part-time Christian minister. Carry was unhappy in the marriage and later said that she came to believe that God had denied her a loving marriage so that she could work to defend the homes of others.

In 1879 the Nations moved to Texas and, about ten years later, to Medicine Lodge, Kansas. During her time in Texas, Carry Nation reported having a number of mystic experiences. In Medicine Lodge, Nation became known for her kindness to the poor, but she also appointed herself the primary guardian of local morals. Among those she criticized were the minister and others in the Christian church that she attended. She was expelled from the church, so she joined the Baptists before finally adopting a faith of her own that incorporated the doctrines of several religions. Nation believed that she had a role to play in Christ's second coming, that she was to lead the fight against liquor trafficking.

Although Kansas had been legally "dry" since 1880, most counties tolerated false pharmacies and loosely disguised "joints." Nation founded the local branch of the Woman's Christian Temperance Union (WCTU) in 1892 and, with the help of a few militant women, led a campaign to close the joints of Medicine Lodge. During the summer of 1899, she entered one of the joints and stood in tears while singing a temperance song. A crowd gathered, and the place was shut down. She repeated her performance in joints throughout the town, and soon Medicine Lodge was completely dry. Believing that she was di-

vinely ordained to do so, over the next few years Nation traveled throughout Kansas and into other states, determined to close all liquor-distributing establishments. Nation would enter a joint; sing hymns; alternately read passages from the Bible and curse the establishment; and then proceed to smash mirrors, bar furniture, immodest paintings on the walls, and thousands of dollars worth of liquor stocks. Nation was a large, muscular woman, standing almost 6 feet tall and weighing about 175 pounds. In the spring of 1900, she began using a hatchet to render greater destruction during her forays of "smashing." After wrecking the barroom of the Hotel Carey and other expensive saloons in Wichita, Kansas, that spring, she was arrested and sentenced to the Sedgwick County Jail for seven weeks.

With her Bible in one hand and her hatchet in the other, it was not long before Nation had destroyed saloons from coast to coast and had become a nationally known figure. She was arrested approximately thirty times, usually on charges of disturbing the peace. Although the WCTU did not endorse her methods, other temperance groups donated funds to support Nation's crusade. Dozens of Kansas's saloons closed as a result of her campaign (though it seems that many later reopened). In 1901 David Nation, who disapproved of Carry's extremism in reform and in religion, divorced his wife on charges of desertion. She was left penniless but began earning money by lecturing. Nation began by speaking to large audiences in auditoriums and concert halls and briefly earned as much as $300 per week. But as her popularity waned, she resorted to the vaudeville circuit. For a while Nation appeared as a sideshow attraction at Coney Island and in 1903 debuted at the Lyceum Theatre in Elizabeth, New Jersey, as a barroom smasher in *Hatchet-*

ation. Though criticized for these commercial activities, Nation apparently truly believed that her performances were a special style of missionary activity. In 1909 she published her autobiography, *The Use and Need of the Life of Carry A. Nation,* in which she tells of her life as one of God's messengers.

Although most people found Nation's actions laughable, she did have supporters who believed that she was the nation's savior and sent thousands of small donations. Most of the money went to pay her fines and court costs; to support her home for the wives and mothers of drunkards in Kansas City, Kansas; and to finance a series of short-lived prohibition magazines.

In 1908 Nation went to Great Britain to lecture on liquor, tobacco, and women's fashions but was greeted with antagonism. A year later she settled in Boone County, Arkansas, where she rested from her crusades. After a female owner of a Montana saloon beat her in January 1910, Nation never used her hatchet again. She died in Leavenworth, Kansas, on June 9, 1911. By drawing the public's attention to the "evils" of alcohol, Nation's attacks on saloons contributed to the eventual passage of the Eighteenth Amendment to the Constitution, which started Prohibition.

See also: Temperance Movement; Woman's Christian Temperance Union
References: Herbert Asbury, *Carry Nation* (1929); Edward T. James, ed., *Notable American Women, 1607–1950,* vol. 2 (1971); *Dictionary of American Biography,* vol. 13 (1934); Carry A. Nation, *The Use and Need of the Life of Carry A. Nation,* rev. ed. (1909); Robert Lewis Taylor, *Vessel of Wrath: The Life and Times of Carry Nation* (1966).

National Black Sisters' Conference

Founded in 1968, the National Black Sisters' Conference (NBSC) is headquartered in Washington, D.C., and represents approximately fifteen hundred black Catholic women religious in the United States. Its stated purpose is "to strive to provide ongoing communication and dialogue that focus on the education and support of African-American women religious" (National Black Sisters' Conference pamphlet). The NBSC promotes networking to provide mutual support through prayer, study, solidarity, and programs. It seeks to encourage a positive self-image among its members and the African-American people. The NBSC sees itself as a "strong voice supporting women and confronting individual racism found in society and in the Church," and as "a group of women with vision who work increasingly for the liberation of our people" (National Black Sisters' Conference pamphlet). Projects include educational programs for black children; programs designed to facilitate change and community involvement in inner-city parochial schools and parishes; a Black Women's Project designed "to develop a collective sense of heritage, identity, purpose and vision relative to Black Catholic Women"; (National Black Sisters' Conference pamphlet) and the Sojourner Truth House, which provides spiritual affirmation for black religious and laywomen. Publications include a newsletter, *Signs of Soul,* and "Tell It Like It Is: Catechetics from the Black Perspective."

See also: African Americans
References: Jacqueline K. Barrett, ed., *Encyclopedia of Women's Associations Worldwide* (1993); "National Black Sisters' Conference," pamphlet (n.d., c. 1997); "National Black Sisters' Conference," statement (n.d., c. 1997); Sister Patricia J. Chappell, letter to author (July 21, 1997).

National Council of Catholic Women

The National Council of Catholic Women (NCCW) was founded in 1920 under the direction of Catholic bishops.

The stimulus behind the organization's founding was the growing concern among both male clerics and a large number of Catholic women that changes were taking place in American society that jeopardized female purity and traditional family values. The growing popularity of birth control, the rising divorce rate, and the recently introduced Equal Rights Amendment were of particular concern to the women who joined the NCCW. But although the NCCW has held to relatively traditional views in regard to the family and women's roles, throughout its history the NCCW has taken some progressive stances in other areas of social welfare and on national and international issues. For example, following World War II, the NCCW allied with Catholic Relief Services (CRS) to provide food and clothing for the people of war-torn Europe. This project led to the formation of the Works of Peace, through which the NCCW and CRS have worked together in seventy-six countries for more than fifty years. Also, in 1981, prior to the bishops' pastoral letter on the subject, the NCCW dispensed a strong resolution in support of disarmament and the abolition of nuclear weapons.

Currently, the NCCW serves as a forum for Catholic women to discuss issues in church and society and to develop leadership and management skills. The organization also continues to initiate and advance programs in religious, educational, social, and service areas. Recent projects include a wellness fair, during which participants learned about important health issues for women, and the Clothesline Project, which is a visual display that bears witness to violence against women.

Headquartered in Washington, D.C., the NCCW has approximately six thousand affiliates in 113 dioceses in the United States. The organization publishes a bimonthly magazine, *Catholic Woman,* as well as various planning and program materials.

See also: Roman Catholic Church
References: Jacqueline K. Barrett, ed., *Encyclopedia of Women's Associations Worldwide* (1993); Annette Kane, letter to author (July 16, 1997); Susan Hill Lindley, *"You Have Stept Out of Your Place": A History of Women and Religion in America* (1996); National Council of Catholic Women, *Catholic Woman* (May/June 1997 and July/August 1997).

National Council of Jewish Women

When the National Council of Jewish Women (NCJW) was founded by Hannah Greenebaum Solomon in 1893, its purpose was to further the cause of religious education and philanthropy. Soon, however, the NCJW was involved in numerous causes affecting humanity. Among its many projects was the development of the Port and Dock Department, which helped prevent the exploitation of penniless Jewish women who arrived with the hordes of immigrants at the beginning of the twentieth century. Members of the NCJW greeted incoming boats and then aided immigrants with clothing, food, and help in locating relatives. The NCJW was especially concerned over the vulnerability of unescorted women, fearing they might become caught in the white slavery trade that was prevalent at the turn of the century. Their anxiety over immigrant Jewish girls entering prostitution led to the NCJW quietly taking over the management of a Home for Wayward Girls on Staten Island. These actions by the NCJW were important because they helped to quell the accusations of some anti-Semites that white slave trafficking was rampant in the Jewish community.

In the early years of the twentieth century, the NCJW crusaded for the elimination of child labor and campaigned for adequate housing for low-income groups.

It lobbied for mothers' pensions, slum clearance, food and drug regulations, wage and hour laws for women, movie censorship, uniform marriage and divorce laws, and the enactment of federal anti-lynching laws. After World War I, the NCJW, in continuation of its efforts to aid newcomers to America, published a monthly newsletter, *The Immigrant,* and a pamphlet entitled *What Every Emigrant Should Know.* During the 1930s, the NCJW strove to combat anti-Semitism with education and organized a Committee of One Thousand to strengthen Jewish women's knowledge of their history, tradition, and culture. The group also gave aid to Jewish refugee children from Germany. After World War II, the NCJW continued to help people in need, whether they were refugees, immigrants, orphans, or soldiers. In the 1990s, the NCJW sponsors programs on education, social action, and community services for women, children, and the elderly. It aims to improve the quality of life for people of all ages, races, religions, and socioeconomic levels. The group's principal publication, the *NCJW Journal,* which focuses on constitutional rights, aging, the family, child welfare, Israel, and Jewish life, is published quarterly. Approximately 100,000 members form the NCJW of the mid-1990s, with two hundred local branches in thirty-nine states.

See also: Jews; Nathan, Maud
References: Charlotte Baum, Paula Hyman, and Sonya Michel, *The Jewish Woman in America* (1976); Shawn Brennan, ed., *Women's Information Directory* (1993); Sally Priesand, *Judaism and the New Woman* (1975).

Native Americans

Practices differ from tribe to tribe but, overall, Native American culture has historically provided women with more prominent and powerful roles in the realm of religion than enjoyed by their Euro-American counterparts. Among American Indians of the Columbia River Plateau, for example, both males and females could become shamans, and they were considered equal in ability for that role. Shamans, who were believed to have close connections to the spirit world, were the tribe healers. In addition to using herbal medicines, they often called upon spirits to help them cure the ill. On the plateau, native children of both sexes went on quests for guardian spirits. However, the Blackfoot on the Great Plains have long believed that the vision quest is unnecessary for women because of their innate spiritual powers.

In some tribes wherein women participate in vision quests, the search for a spiritual guardian occurrs as part of the rituals surrounding the onset of menstruation. Nearly all American Indian groups mark this important social and religious rite of passage in some manner, for most consider the menstrual period to be a time when women might be in especially close contact with spirits. Amid fears that a menstruating woman might pose spiritual dangers to others in the tribe, she is sometimes kept away from community activities during her menses.

Religion is central to all aspects of Native American life. The division of labor among the sexes has often been influenced by religion. Some tribes believe that men draw upon spiritual powers associated with the necessary taking of life, while women were linked to spiritual powers connected with creating and nurturing life. These powers likely contribute to the acceptance of women as shamans in many tribes. Overall, however, women have found themselves in the powerful leadership role of shaman less frequently than men.

Scholars have found that the arrival of Europeans and the growth of white American culture introduced a variety of ideas that had significant influence upon

Edward Curtis photograph of an Athapaskan Hupa female shaman of northwestern California (1923). Among the Athapaskan tribes, most of the shamans are women.

gender ideology among Native Americans, including Christian redefinitions of gender complementarity and gender hierarchy. In matrilineal societies such as Iroquois and Navajo, Euro-American definitions of male heads of households increased male power at the expense of women as matrilineal kin groups gave way to nuclear families. Euro-American missionaries sometimes found Native American women to be too independent. In the mid-nineteenth century Father Joseph Joset, a Jesuit missionary to the Columbia River Plateau, complained that women did not learn Christian subordination and were so independent that they could drive their husbands away if they were unhappy with them. Many Native American women resisted the changes that missionaries were attempting to make to their society. For example, Seneca women opposed Quaker pressures to adopt individual land ownership and modified other Quaker innovations such as weaving, which was introduced to them as an individual activity, but which they adapted to allow them to continue their traditional practice of working collectively.

Like the Quakers, most missionaries and other Christians had hopes of assimilating the Native Americans into white American religion, culture, and society. Almost all were insensitive to the American Indians' potential loss of their own traditions and identity. Even the most sympathetic missionaries believed that the Native Americans would benefit by adopting Christianity and white culture. In 1869 the American government became directly involved with the churches and their efforts to assimilate the natives. The government established the Board of Indian Commissioners, whose members were wealthy churchmen, and Christian churches were given control over reservations. Rivalries among the various denominations involved caused the pro-

gram to fail, and in 1887 it was replaced by forced acculturation through the Dawes Act.

Central to Protestant efforts to convert and "civilize" Native Americans was education. In order to read the Bible, a person needed to be literate. And missionaries felt that Native American students could better learn the culture and values of white society if they were apart from tribal life. Thus, boarding schools became integral to missionary work among American Indians. To counter the actions of the government and Christian missionaries, a few native women, including Polingaysi Qoyawayma of the Hopi people, Maria Solares of the Chumash tribe, Buffalo Bird Woman of the Hidatsas, Mountain Wolf Woman of the Winnebagos, and Ruby Modesto of the Cahuilla people, sought to record and pass on traditions that would otherwise have been lost. Today there are young people within some Native American groups who are far more defiant of Euro-American institutions, including the religious ones, than were their parents and grandparents. The practice of taking Native American children from their families and placing them in boarding schools without parental consent gradually declined, and ended with the Indian Child Welfare Act of 1978.

Also in 1978 Congress passed the American Indian Religious Freedom Act (AIRFA) in an attempt to direct policy toward promoting the free exercise of Native American religions. The act recognized the need for American Indians to have access to unspoiled sacred sites, to have use of natural resources normally protected by conservation and other laws, and to participate in traditional Native American ceremonies. However, many people believe that the act has not been successful. American Indian rights to ritual peyote ingestion and to their burial grounds are still restricted. An example is the U. S. Supreme Court's ruling in *Lyng v. Northwest Indian Cemetery Protective Association* (1988), which allowed for the exploitation of the burial grounds of the Yurok, Karok, and Tolowa Indians of northern California. The ruling was a severe blow to both these tribes and to Native Americans as a whole.

Most non-Indians do not understand Native American religion. For Native Americans, religion embraces their entire understanding of the cosmic order and their place within it. It is their belief that there is a spiritual realm upon which life depends, and this realm is one with nature and humanity. Thus, Native American culture as a whole is entwined with their religious beliefs.

See also: Buffalo Bird Woman; Modesto, Ruby E.; Mountain Wolf Woman; Qoyawayma, Polingaysi; Solares, Maria; Tekakwitha, Kateri
References: Gretchen M. Bataille, *Native American Women: A Biographical Dictionary* (1993); Gretchen M. Bataille and Kathleen Mullen Sands, *American Indian Women: Telling Their Lives* (1984); Thomas C. Blackburn, ed., *December's Child: A Book of Chumash Oral Narratives* (1975); Laura F. Klein and Lillian A. Ackerman, eds., *Women and Power in Native North America* (1995); Susan Hill Lindley, *"You Have Stept Out of Your Place": A History of Women and Religion in America* (1996); Mountain Wolf Woman, with Nancy Oestreich Lurie, ed., *Mountain Wolf Woman: Sister of Crashing Thunder* (1966); Polingaysi Qoyawayma (Elizabeth Q. White), *No Turning Back* (1964); Christopher Vecsey, ed., *Handbook of American Indian Religious Freedom* (1991).

Nerinckx, Charles (1761–1824)

Father Charles Nerinckx, a Belgian priest of the Roman Catholic Church, was exiled from Belgium during the French Revolution and arrived in the United States in 1804. He began service in Kentucky missions the following year. There were colonies of Catholics in Kentucky at the time, composed of immigrants from Maryland. Many of these people had brought slaves.

Nerinckx established a religious community of women in 1812, the Friends of Mary at the Foot of the Cross, soon to be known as the Sisters of Loretto. Shortly after its founding, the sisters organized a school for girls, and at Nerinckx's prompting, they enrolled several African-American girls. In 1824, Nerinckx urged three of the black girls to become candidates for admission to a special religious order that would bear resemblance to the Sisters of Loretto but would admit only black women. He wanted them to administer a refuge for elderly and useless slaves. This would have been the first foundation of African-American sisters in the United States.

Nerinckx's plans failed to come to fruition because he had critics who accused him of being too strict in his governance of the missions and others who disapproved of his ideas of forming an order of black sisters. He was forced to leave Kentucky. Once Nerinckx left, Bishop Guy Chabrat (1787–1868) of the Bardstown diocese released the African-American women from their vows and sent them home. Nerinckx died in 1824, soon after leaving Kentucky.

See also: African Americans; Oblate Sisters of Providence; Roman Catholic Church; Sisters of Loretto at the Foot of the Cross
References: Cyprian Davis, *The History of Black Catholics in the United States* (1992); James J. Kenneally, *The History of American Catholic Women* (1990); J. H. Schauinger, "Nerinckx, Charles," *New Catholic Encyclopedia*, vol. 10 (1967).

New Thought Movement

Although some religious historians trace the roots of New Thought back to sixteenth-century Spanish scholar and theologian Michael Servetus, typically the term "New Thought" represents a movement that began in late-nineteenth-century America. It was part of an idealist revival that included the ethical culture movement, Christian Science, and other groups. New Thought covered a broad range of theological, philosophical, and practical approaches to God, to the world, and to life and its problems, including matters of health. It was neither a church, nor a cult, nor a sect and asked for no adherence to creeds.

As defined by the Metaphysical Club of Boston (founded in 1896), among the followers' beliefs was faith in a divine humanity—that God was an in-dwelling spirit, "All-wisdom, All-goodness, ever present in the universe as a warm and tender Father" (Braden, 1984, pp. 9–10). Regarding the issue of health, advocates of New Thought believed that the remedy for curing most bodily disease was metaphysical, that sickness was a negative condition caused by uneasiness of mind and that faith in one's own God-given power would lead one back to health. New Thought emphasized individuals' roles in playing out their lives; that there was no punishment in the afterlife but that human beings punished themselves as they adhered to or broke the eternal law of life. People were responsible for living their lives according to the dictates of their conscience.

New Thought has evolved during its one hundred years of history. It now teaches that the mind is continually advancing and that New Thought itself can never be a completed product. Throughout its history, New Thought has been a positive religion, emphasizing the goodness in life and humankind's closeness to God.

From its beginning, women have had considerable influence within the New Thought movement. Emma Curtis Hopkins is often credited with founding the movement in the late 1880s, after separating from Mary Baker Eddy and certain tenets of the Church of Christ, Scientist. Hopkins emphasized mysticism in her teachings and writings, and she developed a strong feminist position that linked the idea of a feminine deity with the rise in the status of women. Other women who became well known within the movement as they carried on Hopkins's teachings, wrote New Thought literature, or founded independent organizations of their own included Harriet Emilie Cady, Malinda Elliott Cramer, Myrtle Page Fillmore, and Nona Lovell Brooks. Loosely organized and treating both sexes as equals, New Thought offered women opportunities to hold positions in leadership that were not usually open to them in the mainstream religions of the late nineteenth and early twentieth centuries.

See also: Brooks, Nona Lovell; Cady, Harriet Emilie; Cramer, Malinda Elliott; Fillmore, Myrtle Page; Hopkins, Emma Curtis
References: Charles S. Braden, *Spirits in Rebellion: The Rise and Development of New Thought* (1984); Horatio W. Dresser, *A History of the New Thought Movement* (1919); Martin A. Larson, *New Thought Religion: A Philosophy for Health, Happiness and Prosperity* (1987).

Nichols, Mary Sargeant Neal Gove (1810–1884)

Health, education, and moral reformer Mary Sargeant Neal Gove Nichols was born in Goffstown, New Hampshire, on August 10, 1810. As a child, she was sickly and shy and had little formal education. She was, however, an avid reader. By the age of eighteen, she was teaching and publishing stories and poems in local newspapers. At the same time, she was secretly studying medical texts. When she was twenty years old, she married Hiram Gove, a Quaker and an unsuccessful milliner. Their marriage was not happy. Hiram Gove has been described as a boorish, brutal, and greedy husband. He initially burned his wife's books, but once he found that they were making money, he exerted his legal right to keep all her earnings. The couple eventually divorced.

In 1832 Mary launched her career in health reform when she began providing cold-water treatments to overworked local women. About five years later, Hiram and Mary moved to Lynn, Massachusetts, where Mary opened a girls' school. It is likely that the school was the first school in the United States to teach scientific topics to girls, and Mary was one of the country's first female lecturers on anatomy, physiology, and health. She was a "Grahamite," an admirer of Sylvester Graham, a temperance reformer and popular health advocate. In keeping with his ideas on diet and regimen, she lectured on the values of eating healthful foods; exercising regularly; taking daily cold-water baths; and abstaining from alcoholic beverages, coffee, and tea.

Long separated from her husband, whom she divorced in 1847 or 1848, Mary had an affair with fellow writer and reformer Thomas Low Nichols in 1847. Together they published the *Water-Cure Journal* and opened a water-cure business in New York City as well as a girls' summer school in Port Chester, New York. The Nicholses (Mary took his name, even though she did not marry him), who believed in free love and the right of every woman to choose the father of her child, were too radical for most reformers of their time. Both Thomas and Mary opposed marriage as the source of all evil, and they wrote several works criticizing the institution. Mary contended that a truly emancipated woman was in good health in both body and spirit and believed in God, and reverently obeyed his laws, and therefore had no need for laws to protect her chastity. In the mid-1850s the Nicholses moved to Yellow Springs, Ohio, to found Memnomia, a utopia for those willing to adhere to the Nichols' strict dietary regimen in the free-love community. In 1857,

after Mary had a vision in which a number of church fathers appeared and spoke with her, the commune broke up and the couple adopted Catholicism. They no longer advocated free love but traveled throughout the Midwest giving lectures on Catholicism. When the Civil War broke out in 1861, the Nicholses moved to England, where they created a water-cure establishment near the spa town of Malvern. Mary Nichols died in England on May 30, 1884.

During her lifetime, Nichols wrote a number of short stories for *Godey's Lady's Book* (under the pseudonym Mary Orme) as well as several novels. Her novels include *Uncle John: or, "It Is Too Much Trouble"* (1846); *Agnes Morris: or, the Heroine of Domestic Life* (1849); *The Two Loves: or, Eros and Anteros* (1849); *Uncle Agnes* (1864); and *Jerry: A Novel of Yankee American Life* (1872). In addition, she wrote a fictionalized autobiography, *Mary Lyndon: or, Revelations of a Life* (1855).

See also: Utopian Communities
References: Grace Adams and Edward Hutter, *The Mad Forties* (1942); Elizabeth Frost-Knappman, *Women's Progress in America* (1994); Mary (Sargeant) Nichols, *Mary Lyndon, or, Revelations of a Life* (1855); William G. Shade, "Nichols, Mary Gove," in Angela Howard Zophy with Frances M. Kavenik, eds., *Handbook of American Women's History* (1990); Taylor Stoehr, *Free Love in America: A Documentary History* (1979).

Noyes, John Humphrey (1811–1886)

Religious reformer and founder of the Oneida Community, John Humphrey Noyes was born in Brattleboro, Vermont, on September 3, 1811. His father, John Noyes, had for a short time been a minister, and his mother, Polly (Hayes) Noyes, was a strong-minded and deeply religious woman who prayed that John Humphrey would grow up to be a preacher as well.

But although he was given a strict religious upbringing, during his college years at Dartmouth he was more interested in other subjects. After graduating from Dartmouth College and commencing to study law, in 1831 he was converted in a religious revival conducted by ex-lawyer Charles Grandison Finney. Noyes turned from law to religion, studying theology at Andover and then Yale. At the end of the 1832 school year, he received a license to preach. In the meantime, Noyes had become attracted to Christian perfectionism and, in February 1834, publicly announced that he was free of sin. Although he asserted that this did not mean that he was not in need of improvement, he claimed that he had a pure heart and was free of sin. Although Yale tended toward the doctrine of perfectionism, the school could not tolerate Noyes's bluntness, so his license to preach was revoked only two years after it was issued.

Noyes spent the next several years traveling and exploring his own religious convictions while attempting to convert others. He finally settled in Putney, Vermont, where, in 1838, he married Harriet Holton. During the first six years of their marriage, Noyes began to form new ideas on wedded life and sexuality as he watched his wife suffer through five deliveries, with only one surviving child. To spare Harriet further suffering, Noyes began practicing what he called "male continence," intercourse without ejaculation.

Meanwhile, Noyes had continued to draw converts to his ideas on perfectionism, and in 1845 he established the Putney Corporation, or Association of Perfectionists. They began to practice "biblical communism" of property and in 1846 introduced "complex marriage," a system in which each person was married to every other member of the opposite sex. It was Noyes's belief that such a practice by purified Christians would

eliminate jealousy and possessiveness. His conversion to this idea was likely connected with his attraction to Mary Cragin, a married friend of both John and Harriet Noyes. Eventually both John and Mary sought and received permission from their spouses to consummate their mutual sexual need for each other. The citizens of Putney did not share Noyes's views on marital freedom, however, and Noyes was arrested for adultery. He left Vermont in 1847 and went to Oneida, New York. There in 1848 Noyes, his family, the Cragins, and a group of others who shared his outlook began the Oneida Community. Noyes retained the role of the community's divinely inspired leader for more than thirty years.

For a male of the mid-nineteenth century, Noyes held some unusually egalitarian views regarding women. He believed that monogamous marriage, obligatory sex, and too many pregnancies and children made women into slaves. Noyes saw the solution as a combination of complex marriage (which included women's right to refuse to have intercourse) and male continence. He also promoted comfortable clothing for women, in contrast with the confining clothing of the time. The usual dress of the women at Oneida was short skirts with ankle-length trousers or pantalets underneath. But though Noyes considered women's intelligence almost as great as men's and was determined to liberate women from the bonds of femininity, he was still of the belief that women were generally inferior to men.

Although the Oneida Community prospered, the community's unconventional sexual practices drew anger and harassment from the public. There was also dissension within Oneida itself, including tensions between Noyes and his son, Theodore. In 1879 Noyes was pressured to leave New York. He settled in

Canada with a few of his followers and died there on April 13, 1886.

See also: Oneida Community; Perfectionism; Utopian Communities

References: Elizabeth Frost-Knappman, *Women's Progress in America* (1994); Karen Gillenwater, "The Oneida Community," in Angela Howard Zophy with Frances M. Kavenik, eds., *Handbook of American Women's History* (1990); Spencer Klaw, *Without Sin: The Life and Death of the Oneida Community* (1993); Susan Hill Lindley, *"You Have Stept Out of Your Place": A History of Women and Religion in America* (1996); Charles Nordhoff, *American Utopias* (1993).

Oblate Sisters of Providence

Established in 1829 by a white French priest and four black women refugees from Haiti, the Oblate Sisters of Providence was the first successful foundation of African-American sisters in America.

In 1827, a Sulpician priest named Jacques Hector Nicholas Joubert de la Muraille (1777–1843) became pastor of St. Mary's Chapel on Paca Street, in Baltimore, where Haitian refugees gathered for worship. Joubert soon realized that Haitian children were having difficulty learning their catechism because they could not read. His concern over the problem likely led to his acquaintance with two young Haitian women who had opened a free school in their home. When the women voiced their willingness to lead a life devoted to God, Joubert began to think about forming a religious community. Soon, a third young woman, and then a fourth, allied with the group. By the summer of 1828, they were boarding eleven girls and had nine additional girls as day students. Meanwhile, they began their religious life.

The leader of the group was Elizabeth Lange, who became the first superior. Marie Madeline Balas, Rosine Boegue, and Almeide Duchemin Maxis were the other founding members. The mothers of both Lange and Maxis later joined the community. Initially, the formation of an African-American order was controversial, but Joubert received the support of Archbishop James Whitfield, the ordinary of Baltimore.

The four women made their profession of faith on July 2, 1829, and their congregation was called the Oblate Sisters of Providence. The Virgin Mary became the principal patron of their order. A secondary patron was St. Frances of Rome (1384–1440), chosen in part because she, like the four women, had founded a community of women who were not cloistered. Also, the women in St. Frances's community had renewed their vows every year, a tradition that the Oblate Sisters of Providence were to follow. Another secondary patron was St. Benedict, the Moor. The African Benedict, who had died in 1589, was canonized in 1807 as a statement against the slave trade. By choosing him as a secondary patron, the sisters brought some African spiritualism into their community. Pope Gregory XVI gave his approval to the community in 1831.

The habit of the early sisters was a black dress with a white collar and a large white bonnet. Later, a black bonnet was substituted for the white, and a black cape was worn when the women were outside the convent. In 1906 the sisters began to wear a veil and white linen guimpe.

Their school for girls was successful from the beginning, and their order grew. Although their principal function was as a devout religious community and as operators of the school, when cholera struck Baltimore in 1832, the sisters volunteered to help nurse the sick. One of the sisters died of cholera after nursing the archbishop and his housekeeper.

On November 5, 1843, Father Joubert died. From that point until 1847, when a young Bavarian Redemptionist priest, Thaddeus Anwander (1823–1893), became chaplain for the Oblate Sisters of Providence, they were virtually ignored by church authorities. Samuel Eccleston, who was archbishop of Baltimore at the time, is said to have suggested that there was no need for the African-American religious order. He reportedly recommended that they disband and enter domestic service, believing that there was a greater need for house servants than there was for black nuns.

The community survived and, with the help of Father Anwander, added some activities to their agenda. In 1857, the order opened a school for boys in Baltimore. During the Civil War, in 1863, the sisters established a school for black children and a night school for women in Philadelphia. The Philadelphia school prospered in the beginning but closed in 1867. The order established a free school for African-American girls and women in Baltimore in 1864. Many of the students were children of freed slaves. In 1865, the sisters opened an orphanage in Baltimore and two years later established an orphanage in New Orleans. Such institutions were sorely needed in the aftermath of the Civil War because abandoned black children made up a large proportion of the orphans in America.

The contributions of the Oblate Sisters of Providence showed church authorities that African-American women were just as capable as white women in carrying out the functions of a religious community. They opened doors for future black orders and set a strict example for them to follow. In the early 1990s, there were more than 150 sisters serving in seven states, the District of Columbia, and Costa Rica. Wearing a chain around their necks that symbolizes the slavery from which many of their early members came, the sisters direct schools and day care centers.

See also: African Americans; Nerinckx, Charles

References: M. A. Chineworth, "Oblate Sisters of Providence," in *New Catholic Encyclopedia,* vol. 10 (1967); Cyprian Davis, *The History of Black Catholics in the United States* (1992); Christopher Kauffman, *Tradition and Transformation in Catholic Culture: The Priests of Saint Sulpice in the United States from 1791 to the Present* (1988); James J. Kenneally, *The History of American Catholic Women* (1990).

O'Connor, Flannery (1925–1964)

Widely acclaimed Catholic novelist Flannery O'Connor, whose birth name was Mary Flannery O'Connor, was born March 25, 1925, in Savannah, Georgia, into one of the state's oldest Catholic families. She received her schooling in parochial schools in Savannah until she moved with her parents, Edward Francis and Regina (Cline) O'Connor, to Milledgeville, Georgia. There she attended Peabody High School, from which she graduated in 1942. In 1945 she graduated from Georgia State College for Women (now Georgia College) with a degree in social science. During her college years, O'Connor was an avid writer and cartoonist and frequently contributed to the college's literary magazine. Next she attended the Graduate School of Fine Arts at the University of Iowa, where she participated in the school's famous writer's workshop. She graduated from the university with a master of fine arts degree in 1947.

While at the University of Iowa, O'Connor published her first story, "Geranium," in *Accent* magazine (summer 1946). The following year she received the Rinehart-Iowa Prize for *Wise Blood,* which would become her first novel. Following graduation from the University of Iowa, O'Connor embarked on a career as a writer. Although she was a devout Catholic, she did not use Catholic characters or settings in her writings. Nevertheless, her faith was central to her work. Her plots were often bizarre tragedies and her characters grotesque misfits who fell to increasingly miserable levels as they, wittingly or not, sought salvation. For O'Connor, a Catholic novel was based on the truths of fall, redemption, and judgment. Her novels also represented reality in a world (not necessarily Catholic) of things and human relationships. O'Connor believed that if a novelist tried to see through the eyes of the church, the result would be pious trash.

In 1950 O'Connor came close to dying before she was diagnosed as having lupus erythematosus, the disease that had taken the life of her father. She returned to Milledgeville to live with her mother on the family farm. While her mother cared for her, O'Connor continued to write. In 1955 she published a well-received collection of short stories, *A Good Man Is Hard to Find,* and produced her second novel, *The Violent Bear It Away,* in 1960.

Flannery O'Connor died in Milledgeville on August 3, 1964. At the time of her death she had completed the stories for *Everything That Rises Must Converge* (1965), which was published posthumously. During her short career, O'Connor received several O. Henry Awards, and the posthumous collection, *The Complete Stories of Flannery O'Connor* (1971), received the National Book Award in 1972. A collection of her letters, *The Habit of Being* (1979), offered a look into the depth of O'Connor's religious faith as well as an understanding of other aspects of the novelist's life.

Although O'Connor was not a feminist, historian James J. Kenneally credits her with making a significant contribution "to the growing independence of Catholic women and to a restlessness with the constraints imposed by society and church"

and asserts further that "[w]ithout her the radicalism of the 1960s would have been stillborn" (1990, p. 160).

See also: Roman Catholic Church
References: Frederick Asals, *Flannery O'Connor: The Imagination of Extremity* (1982); Kathryn Cullen-DuPont, with Annelise Orleck, *The Encyclopedia of Women's History in America* (1996); Sarah Gordon, "Flannery O'Connor," in Angela Howard Zophy with Frances M. Kavenik, eds., *Handbook of American Women's History* (1990); James J. Kenneally, *The History of American Catholic Women* (1990); Carter W. Martin, *The True Country: Themes in the Fiction of Flannery O'Connor* (1969); Flannery O'Connor, *The Habit of Being: Letters of Flannery O'Connor,* Sally Fitzgerald, ed. (1979).

O'Hair, Madalyn Mays Murray (1919–)

The founder of American Atheists, Madalyn Mays Murray O'Hair was born in Pittsburgh, Pennsylvania, on April 14, 1919. Her parents were Lena (Scholle) and John Irwin Mays. It is unclear exactly when Madalyn became an atheist. She claimed that she became an atheist when she was in the sixth grade, after reading the Bible from cover to cover. Yet at the time of her high school graduation, she listed serving God for the betterment of humanity as her life's goal.

Madalyn attended both the University of Toledo and the University of Pittsburgh but left college in 1941 when she eloped with J. Roths. While her husband served in the Pacific during World War II, Madalyn worked for the government as a cryptographer in both North Africa and Italy. Near the end of the war she had an affair with William J. Murray Jr., and gave birth to his son, William J. Murray III. The Rothses divorced soon after the war, and Madalyn took Murray as her last name. There is some dispute over whether she and William ever married. Madalyn returned to college and in 1948 received a bachelor of arts degree from Ashland College, in Ashland, Ohio. After graduation she found work as a psychiatric social worker for government agencies in Baltimore, Maryland. She again returned to college and received a law degree from South Texas College of Law in 1953.

While in Baltimore, Madalyn sued the public schools, claiming that they discriminated against her son William because he had asked to be excused from morning prayers and Bible readings. In her lawsuit she asked that Bible readings and recitations of the Lord's Prayer be banned from public schools. The case was appealed through the court system. Finally, in October 1962, after it had been joined with another similar case, *Schempp v. School District of Abington Township* (Pennsylvania), the Supreme Court ruled that Bible reading and the Lord's Prayer were religious exercises. Thus Bible readings and the recitation of the Lord's Prayer in public schools were unconstitutional under the First and Fourteenth Amendments. Although O'Hair has taken credit for banning Bible readings and *all* prayer from public schools, she was only partly responsible for the decision. In addition, not all prayer has been banned from the schools; voluntary prayer is still allowed.

Because of the publicity surrounding the case and the unpopularity of Madalyn Murray's lawsuit, the family felt pressured to move from Baltimore. They moved to Hawaii and then to Mexico. While in Mexico, Madalyn met Richard O'Hair, whom she married in 1965. The couple settled in Austin, Texas. Over the next few years, Madalyn worked to establish a national atheist movement. She organized an American Atheist Radio Series in 1968 and launched *American Atheists Magazine* the same year. In 1969 she published the first edition of *What on Earth Is an Atheist?* The first book from the American Atheist Press and basically a transcript of some of her radio

broadcasts from 1968 to 1969, its purpose was to defend atheism against American intolerance of nonbelievers. A year later she published an account of the court case, *An Atheist Epic: Bill Murray, the Bible and the Baltimore Board of Education.* Also in 1970, she founded the Society of Separationists (later renamed American Atheists) and opened the Charles E. Stevens American Atheist Library and Archives. As she had hoped, American Atheists developed into a national organization.

Over the next twenty years, O'Hair became the most well-known atheist in America. She actively sought media attention, debating well-known clergymen over the existence of God and initiating lawsuits that would attract the public's eye. She sued to have "In God We Trust" removed from United States currency, sued to stop American astronauts from reading the Bible in space, and sued to end tax exemptions for churches. O'Hair lost most of her lawsuits but did win one that overturned the Texas requirement that all officeholders believe in God. Although O'Hair was not the only spokesperson for atheism in America, she was the most outspoken.

In the mid-1970s, members of American Atheists complained of O'Hair's authoritarian style of leadership, and many left to form the Freedom from Religion Foundation under Anne Nicol Gaylor. O'Hair's son William split with his mother in 1977. He later converted to Christianity, and in the mid-1990s leads Government Is Not God, a conservative political action committee, and speaks at fund-raisers for Christian schools. In 1986 O'Hair resigned from the presidency of American Atheists in favor of her son Jon Murray. She made an unsuccessful attempt to take over the American Association for the Advancement of Atheism in 1990, following the death in 1988 of its leader James Hervey Johnson.

William J. Murray III filed a missing-persons report in Austin, Texas, on September 24, 1996, asking that the police department investigate the disappearance of his mother, Madalyn Mays Murray O'Hair, his brother Jon Garth Murray, and Jon's daughter Robin. The trio had dropped out of sight more than a year before the missing-persons report was filed. O'Hair had planned to travel to New York City to picket Pope John Paul II's visit in 1995 but was never seen in that city. In 1997 O'Hair's whereabouts were still not known.

See also: Gaylor, Anne Nicol
References: Cox News Service, "Atheist O'Hair's Son Files Missing-Person Report," *Sarasota Herald Tribune* (October 6, 1996); J. Gordon Melton, *Religious Leaders of America* (1991); Madalyn M. O'Hair, *What on Earth Is an Atheist?* (1969, 1972); Gordon Stein, ed., *The Encyclopedia of Unbelief* (1985).

Oneida Community (1848–1881)

Founded in 1848 by religious leader John Humphrey Noyes, the Oneida Community was one of the first "utopian" communities to grant women roles equal to those of men. Noyes was a believer in perfectionism, the idea that humans could reach a state whereby they would be free of sin. This belief, combined with Noyes's own experiences in marriage, led to a unique social structure and unconventional sexual practices within the Oneida Community.

Noyes believed that for a society to be perfect, it must be free of private ownership, for private ownership bred selfishness and jealousy. He maintained that conventional marriage led to similar problems and sought an alternative form of matrimony. For more than thirty years, members of the Oneida Community practiced "complex marriage," a system in which each person was married to every other member of the opposite sex. Exclusive attachments between a man and woman were not allowed, but a woman could refuse to have sexual intercourse with any man who approached her. Noyes considered this practice beneficial to women because, in contrast to traditional marriage, they were not considered the property of men. Women were, in fact, encouraged to take the initiative in sexual relationships. The choice of partners was frequently made according to one's level of spiritual progress, wherein those lower on the scale were urged to seek out persons who were above them. This often meant that older women introduced young men to sexual intercourse and older men initiated young women. An essential component of the system was what Noyes referred to as "male continence." This was the practice of withdrawal prior to ejaculation, which was expected to be performed unless conception was desired. In 1869 the community instituted a new practice, one they called "stirpiculture," or selective breeding. Through stirpiculture they hoped to replace random procreation with planned propagation that would produce "superior" offspring. Noyes and other male leaders were disproportionately represented among the fathers in this program.

The Oneida Community held a number of benefits for women. Besides offering them sexual freedom without fears of frequent pregnancies, they were encouraged to develop interests outside women's traditional sphere. Women labored alongside men in agriculture and industry, participated in sports like baseball and swimming, and were encouraged to attain a broad education. Nevertheless, women did not advance to become top leaders of the community, and they rarely spoke during Oneida's planning meetings. Although they were urged to broaden their activities, they were almost solely responsible for domestic duties, including child care. And although Noyes and other males in the community sympathized with

This woodcut from Frank Leslie's Illustrated Newspaper *shows female bookkeepers at work in the busy office of the Oneida Community of free lovers in New York (1870).*

the plight of the average nineteenth-century woman and believed that women were *almost* as intelligent as men, they continued to assume that men were superior to women.

The Oneida Community prospered and enjoyed a mostly peaceful coexistence with neighboring communities for three decades. But although local people seemed accepting of the group, other Americans, especially the clergy, found their untraditional practices immoral. By the late 1870s, dissension had developed within Oneida itself as younger men grew resentful over stirpiculture and as some who had left to attend Yale or Harvard returned with questions concerning the community's theology. In 1879 Noyes moved to Canada with a few of his followers, and the remaining Oneidans formally abandoned the practice of complex marriage. On January 1, 1881, the community was disbanded and was replaced by a joint stock company.

See also: Noyes, John Humphrey; Utopian Communities
References: Karen Gillenwater, "The Oneida Community," in Angela Howard Zophy with Frances M. Kavenik, eds., *Handbook of American Women's History* (1990); Spencer Klaw, *Without Sin: The Life and Death of the Oneida Community* (1993); Susan Hill Lindley, *"You Have Stept Out of Your Place": A History of Women and Religion in America* (1996); Charles Nordhoff, *American Utopias* (1993).

Osborn, Sarah Haggar Wheaten (1714–1796)

Sarah Osborn, an eighteenth-century religious leader and author, was born in London, England, on February 22, 1714. She emigrated with her parents to Boston in 1722, later moving to Freetown, Rhode Island, and finally to Newport, Rhode Island, in 1729. Married at age eighteen to sailor Samuel Wheaten and widowed less than two years later, she became a schoolteacher in order to earn a living for herself and her one-year-old son. In 1737, while she was still a young widow, Sarah underwent an emotional religious experience that led to her converting to Puritanism and joining the First Church of Newport. Several years later, influenced by the preaching of famous Great Awakening revivalists George Whitefield and Gilbert Tennent, who visited Newport in the early 1740s, she consented to lead a young women's religious group. Known as the Female Society, the group met in her home for the next fifty years. The society was at the center of the next great revival in Newport in 1766–1767.

Meanwhile, Sarah married again, becoming the wife of Henry Osborn in 1742. Unfortunately, her second husband's poor health and failures in his business left him unable to support the family, so Sarah soon returned to teaching. When she was not teaching school, she was busy writing in her journals, writing spiritual autobiography, or composing book-length devotional commentaries. It is estimated that she wrote approximately fifty volumes, all reflecting her religious zeal. She also spent many of her waking hours in prayer and self-examination in an effort to determine where she stood in the eyes of God.

With some reluctance, Osborn emerged as a religious leader in the 1760s. In 1765 she became concerned about some blacks who were looking for a place to worship. A year later, a group of blacks was meeting in her home on Tuesday evenings, and three to four dozen slaves regularly attended her Sunday night sessions. It was not long before there were groups of people, black and white, women and children and young men, meeting in separate gatherings in her home almost every night of the week. She led all but the young men's group. When a local minister questioned the appropriateness of her religious activities in light of the limits society had placed on the roles of women, she de-fended her behavior by insisting that she had no desire to become a religious leader and had no intentions of infringing upon the role of male clergy. Osborn also maintained that she had not overlooked her domestic duties. Moreover, she believed that God had called her to her work and that she was fulfilling a role that others had overlooked. Although the revivalist spirit diminished by 1768, and white attendance at her meetings dropped off, blacks continued to gather at her home on Sunday evenings.

Sarah Osborn died in Newport in 1796. In 1799 her minister, the Reverend Samuel Hopkins, compiled a biography of her life, *Memoirs of the Life of Mrs. Sarah Osborn,* to publicize her piety and unflinching devotion to Christianity.

See also: Great Awakening
References: Charles E. Hambrick-Stowe, "The Spiritual Pilgrimage of Sarah Osborn (1714–1796)," *Church History* 61 (December 1992): 408–421; Susan Hill Lindley, *"You Have Stept Out of Your Place": A History of Women and Religion in America* (1996); Mary Beth Norton, "'My Resting Reaping Times': Sarah Osborn's Defense of Her 'Unfeminine' Activities, 1767," *Signs* 2 (winter 1976): 516–529.

Owen, Robert Dale (1801–1877)

Antebellum reformer, freethinker, and advocate of women's rights, Robert Dale Owen was born in Glasgow, Scotland, on November 7, 1801. His mother, Ann Caroline (Dale) Owen, was a devout Presbyterian, but his father, Robert Owen, was an agnostic (though he did not interfere with his wife's religious instruction to their children). The elder Owen was a prosperous textile manufacturer as well as a pioneer socialist and an influential advocate of communitarian experiments. In 1825 Robert Dale came to the United States with his father and settled at New Harmony, Indiana, where his father sought to put his socialist and perfectionist theories into practice. Like his father, Robert Dale

Owen embraced the life of a reformer. He assisted his father with the operation of the community, and in 1826 he became editor of the community's *New Harmony Gazette*. Under the younger Owen, news was a secondary matter in the *Gazette*. He focused instead on problems in society. Having received an excellent and progressive education himself, he came to consider the lack of adequate education as the major cause of poverty and began promoting a state-supported school system. He also questioned the wisdom of Christianity and denounced both strict Sabbatarianism and indissoluble marriage.

In 1827 Robert Dale Owen met Scottish-born reformer Frances Wright, and together they critiqued the sectarian school system, traditional Christianity, and the oppression of women. He accompanied Wright to the modest experimental community that she had established in Nashoba, Tennessee, for liberated African Americans, but he was disappointed when he saw how small and crude the commune was. In 1829 he became editor of her newly launched magazine, the *Free Enquirer,* which advocated a number of reforms, including more liberal divorce. Two years later, he published *Moral Physiology; or, A Brief and Plain Treatise on the Population Question,* which called for birth control and denounced the sexual irresponsibility of the lower classes. He promoted the equality of the sexes and condemned the moral double standard with the argument that men seduce trusting women, then abandon them to the "scorn of a cold, a self-righteous, and a wicked world" (Kimmel and Mosmiller, 1992, p. 336).

Although he criticized traditional religion as well as religious leaders and institutions of his day, by the mid-1850s Owen was revealing a burning interest in Spiritualism, and he wrote at least two books with a Spiritualist theme. *Footfalls on the Boundary* (1860) defended the Spiritualist movement that had become popular in the mid-nineteenth century, and *The Debatable Land between This World and the Next* (1871), written after ten years of psychic research, provided a further analysis of spiritual investigation into life after death. He conceived of Spiritualism as an ally of Christianity. Although he frequently quoted from the Bible, throughout much of his life Owen independently sought religious truth.

Owen married Mary Jane Robinson in 1832, at which time he made it clear that he did not accept laws that gave him control over his wife. He became a lawmaker himself during the 1840s and 1850s, serving in the Indiana house of representatives (1836–1839). From 1843 to 1847 he spent two terms as a member of the U.S. House of Representatives, where he drafted the bill for the founding of the Smithsonian Institution. In 1850, as a member of the Indiana constitutional convention, Owen played a prominent role in securing property rights for married women and widows. Although in his later years he looked back upon his association with Frances Wright with regret and considered his reforming activities of the late 1820s to have been immature and extravagant, he remained an avid supporter of women's equality until he died on June 24, 1877.

See also: Utopian Communities; Wright, Frances
References: Elizabeth Frost-Knappman, *Women's Progress in America* (1994); Carol A. Kolmerten, *Women in Utopia: The Ideology of Gender in the American Owenite Communities* (1990); Richard William Leopold, *Robert Dale Owen: A Biography* (1940, reprint 1969); Robert Dale Owen, "Moral Physiology" (excerpt) (1831), in Michael S. Kimmel and Thomas E. Mosmiller, eds., *Against the Tide: Pro-Feminist Men in the United States* (1992); Edward L. Queen II et al., eds., *The Encyclopedia of American Religious History* (1996); Anne Taylor, *Visions of Harmony: A Study in Nineteenth-Century Millenarianism* (1987).

Packard, Sophia B. (1824–1891)

Sophia B. Packard, teacher, religious worker, and founder of Spelman College, was born on January 3, 1824, in New Salem, Massachusetts. She was the third daughter and fifth child of Winslow and Rachel (Freeman) Packard. Betsey Sophia, as she was called throughout her childhood, received a solid education, but only as a result of her own persistence. Beginning at age fourteen, she alternately taught school and attended school herself from year to year. She graduated from the Charlestown (Massachusetts) Female Seminary in 1850 and became an assistant teacher there a year later. She taught for a time on Cape Cod and in 1855 took a position at the New Salem Academy, where she had once been a student.

In New Salem, Packard met Harriet E. Giles (1833–1909), and the two became lifelong friends and associates. Over the next several years, the two women taught together in schools in Massachusetts and Connecticut and briefly opened a school of their own in Fitchburg, Massachusetts. Packard accepted a position as coprincipal at the Oread Collegiate Institute in Worcester, Massachusetts, in 1864, and Giles began teaching there as well. The women left the school in 1867 and moved to Boston. There Packard worked for an insurance firm until 1870, when she was hired as an assistant to the Reverend George C. Lorimer of the Shawmut Avenue Baptist Church.

Despite it being uncommon for a woman to hold such a position, Lorimer had confidence in Packard's abilities. When he became pastor of Tremont Temple in Boston in 1873, Packard went with him. Her principal duties were to conduct women's prayer meetings, teach in the Sunday school, and visit the sick. During her years at the Tremont Temple, Packard developed an interest in the plight of the former slaves still residing in the South. She helped organize the Woman's American Baptist Home Mission Society, an auxiliary to the American Baptist Home Mission Society. The latter group had been building mission schools since 1832. Packard presided at the auxiliary's first meeting and became its first treasurer. A year later, she was appointed to the executive post of corresponding secretary. She traveled to the South in 1880 and returned filled with determination to establish a school for African-American women and girls in Georgia. After almost a year of consideration, the society reluctantly gave its support for the plan. Both Packard and Harriet Giles immediately left for Atlanta.

On April 11, 1881, with the aid of the Reverend Frank Quarles, a leader in the black community, the women opened their school in the basement of the Friendship Baptist Church, which Quarles pastored. Beginning with eleven students, enrollment grew rapidly, reaching eighty by midsummer. The school suffered a setback when the society withdrew its financial support, but Packard persisted until the society made a firm commitment to the school and recommenced paying Packard's and Giles's salaries in January 1882. By February there were 150 pupils, and the school employed a third teacher.

Packard then involved herself in a fund-raising campaign to earn money for suitable facilities for the school. The American Baptist Home Mission Society made a down payment on a parcel of land and some existing buildings, and John D. Rockefeller donated money to complete the purchase. The school moved to its new location in February 1883, and in 1884 the school was named Spelman Seminary in honor of Mrs. Rockefeller and her parents, who had been passionate abolitionists. Fund-raising continued as the school expanded. When fire destroyed one building, it was rebuilt in 1888 and named Packard Hall. Spelman Seminary was granted a charter that same year, and Packard was named treasurer of the board of trustees.

While recovering from an illness, Packard took a vacation to Egypt and the Holy Land in 1890. She returned to the seminary, but on June 21 of the following year, she suffered a cerebral hemorrhage while en route to New England for the summer and died at a hotel in Washington, D.C. Giles succeeded her as president of the seminary. Spelman Seminary, which in 1924 became Spelman College, grew to become a highly respected institution. In 1929 it affiliated with Morehouse College and Atlanta University to become part of a major learning center for southern blacks.

References: J. Gordon Melton, *Religious Leaders of America* (1991); Edward T. James, ed., *Notable American Women, 1607–1950,* vol. 3 (1971).

Palmer, Phoebe Worrall (1807–1874)

Evangelist, religious author, and a leader of the perfectionist, or Holiness, movement in the United States, Phoebe Worrall Palmer was born December 18, 1807, in New York, New York. Her parents, Henry Worrall and Dorothea (Wade) Worrall, were devout Methodists and raised their ten children on a strict regimen of daily family worship. When she was nineteen, Phoebe married Walter C. Palmer, a New York physician. Tragedy struck the couple early in their marriage when two of their sons died. Phoebe and Walter viewed the boys' deaths as a sign from God to devote more of their time to religious activities. In 1832, while attending a religious revival in New York's Allen Street Methodist Episcopal Church, where they were members, the Palmers dedicated themselves to the work of spiritual holiness.

Phoebe Palmer's career as an evangelist began in 1835, when she and her sister Sarah Lankford directed small gatherings of women at what they called "Tuesday Meetings for the Promotion of Holiness." These were religious services that included readings from the Scriptures, prayer, and personal testimonies. Soon, Sarah turned the leadership of the meetings over to her sister. Drawing on the ideas of John Wesley, the founder of Methodism, as well as on her own experiences, Palmer preached the Holiness, or perfectionist, doctrine of "entire sanctification." She believed that people, if they had the desire and dedication, could be assured of sanctification. Unlike Wesley, who saw the process of sanctification as the goal toward which the Christian life led, Palmer contended that such holiness could *immediately* become available if one had complete faith in Christ.

Phoebe Palmer's Tuesday meetings continued for thirty-seven years. In 1839 men joined, many of whom later became leaders of the perfectionist movement, including John Dempster, founder of Concord (later Boston) and Garrett seminaries, and Bishop Leonidas L. Hamline. By 1858, Palmer's meetings had become broadly evangelical, attracting laymen and ministers from a variety of denominations.

In addition to the Tuesday meetings, Phoebe, along with her husband, began to spend approximately six months of each year attending Methodist camp meetings and leading Holiness revivals in the eastern United States and Canada. The couple spent four years in Britain, from 1859 to 1863, leading revivals there. Phoebe also spread her ideas on religion through her writing. Her works included *The Way of Holiness* (1845); *Present to My Christian Friend: Entire Devotion to God* (1845); *Faith and Its Effects* (1846); *Incidental Illustrations of the Economy of Salvation: Its Doctrines and Duties* (1855); *Promise of the Father* (1859); and *Pioneer Experiences: The Gift of Power Received by Faith* (1867). In *Promise of the Father* she cited biblical authority for women's right to participate in church work. Palmer edited *Guide to Holiness,* the principal journal of the perfectionist movement, from 1862 until her death in 1874.

Although she essentially avoided two of the most controversial issues of her day—abolition and women's rights—Palmer became a hardworking pioneer for social reform. She worked to aid the poor, especially those in prisons and in orphanages. Her most important contribution was a mission built in one of New York City's most squalid neighborhoods, the Five Points district. Established in 1850, the mission became a model for the settlement houses of the late nineteenth and early twentieth centuries. It included a chapel, schoolrooms, baths, and rent-free apartments for indigent families. Palmer also played an important role in forming the Ladies Christian Association (later Union), an organization that conducted prayer meetings, Bible study, and boarding houses in city slums and founded rescue homes for delinquents and asylums for the deaf.

Phoebe Palmer died in New York City on November 2, 1874, but not without a legacy. She was one of the leading revivalists of the Second Great Awakening. During her lifetime, Palmer's writings and lectures inspired Methodist clergy and laymen and had great influence on religious and social thought. Among her many followers was General William Booth, founder of the Salvation Army.

See also: Perfectionism; Second Great Awakening
References: Edward T. James, ed., *Notable American Women, 1607–1950* (1971); J. Gordon Melton, *Encyclopedia of American Religions* (1993); J. Gordon Melton, *Religious Leaders of America* (1991); Norman H. Murdoch, *Origins of the Salvation Army* (1994).

Parker, Theodore (1810–1860)

Theodore Parker, an influential theologian, clergyman, abolitionist, and supporter of woman suffrage, was born on a farm near Lexington, Massachusetts, on August 24, 1810. The eleventh and youngest child of John and Hannah (Stearns) Parker, Theodore was among the sixth generation of Parkers born in Massachusetts. A precocious child, he developed an interest in theology even before he entered primary school. The demands of farmwork allowed little time for formal education, so he supplemented his schooling by teaching himself from borrowed books during his leisure hours. Teachers taught him Greek and Latin, but he learned modern languages, botany, astronomy, and metaphysics by himself. When he was seventeen, Parker began four years of teaching in local school districts before opening a school of his own in Watertown in 1832.

In April 1834 Parker entered Harvard Divinity School and graduated in July 1836. He accepted an offer to become pastor at the Unitarian Church in West Roxbury, a suburb of Boston. There he married Lydia Cabot on April 20 and was ordained on June 21, 1837. Although in his sermons Parker avoided controversial topics, he privately came to discard reliance on miraculous revelations and to depend upon the direct, intuitive functioning of the human spirit. At this time there were divisions within the Unitarian Church over the issue, and when Parker's position became known, he was cut off from other Boston clergymen. In January 1845 he resigned from his post at West Roxbury and became minister for the new Twenty-Eighth Congregational Society of Boston. In November 1852 the congregation moved its quarters to the large Boston Music Hall.

From the pulpit of his own congregation, on lecture tours, and in publications, Parker discussed a variety of contemporary issues, including human rights, war, temperance, divorce, education, women's rights, and slavery. He was a perfectionist, believing that social injustices would be righted once humanity realized the infinite perfection of God and people came to live holy lives. His inspirational message won him thousands of followers, but his outspoken opposition to slavery also brought him bitter enemies. During the late 1840s and 1850s, Parker wrote a number of articles on the slavery issue, and in 1848 he published *A Letter to the People of the United States Touching the Matter of Slavery*. He was an outspoken opponent of the Fugitive Slave Law (1850) and actively participated in aiding the escape of fugitive slaves. He was also a member of a secret committee that supported John Brown's raid at Harpers Ferry.

Parker was a supporter of women's rights and believed that women should have the opportunity to participate in public affairs. One of Parker's admirers was women's rights activist Elizabeth Cady Stanton, who attended his sermons during the mid-1840s. She found his liberal theology soul-satisfying, and he was influential in her search for religious independence. On March 27, 1853, Parker preached "A Sermon of the Public Function of Women" at the Music Hall, in which he laid out his position on women's rights. He argued that women should have equal rights and responsibilities with men, stating, "If woman is a human being . . . she has the Nature of a human being . . . she has the Right of a human being . . . [and] she has the duty of a human being." (Kimmel and Mosmiller, 1992, p. 214).

Illness plagued Parker beginning in the spring of 1857. His health worsened considerably in January 1859, and he was forced to end all public activity. He traveled to Mexico in February and then to Europe in June 1959. Parker died in Florence, Italy, on May 10, 1860.

See also: Antislavery Movement; Perfectionism; Stanton, Elizabeth Cady
References: Henry Steele Commager, ed., *Theodore Parker* (1947, 1960); *Dictionary of American Biography*, vol. 14 (1934); Elizabeth Frost-Knappman, *Women's Progress in America* (1994); Theodore Parker, "A Sermon of the Public Function of Women" (1853), in Michael S. Kimmel and Thomas E. Mosmiller, eds., *Against the Tide: Pro-Feminist Men in the United States* (1992); Elizabeth Cady Stanton, *Eighty Years and More: Reminiscences, 1815–1897* (1898, republished 1993).

Pastoral Letter of 1837

On July 28, 1837, a group of Congregational ministers of the General Association in Massachusetts issued a Pastoral Letter that berated abolitionists for speaking on "agitating subjects" in churches. The letter, drafted by the Reverend Nehemiah Adams, was particularly critical of female abolitionists, in effect condemning Angelina and Sarah Grimké (though it did not mention them by name) for venturing outside their "natural" spheres to speak in public before "mixed" audiences of men and women. To reinforce the theories of the pastors of the General Association, the letter cited the New Testament as to women's "appropriate duties and influence." Reverend Adams argued that woman's strength lay in her weakness and compared her to a vine "whose strength and beauty it is to lean upon the trellis-work." If the vine were to "assume the independence and overshadowing nature of the elm, it [would] not only cease to bear fruit, but fall in shame and dishonor to the dust" (Lerner, 1967, p. 189). The letter sparked the first controversy in America over women's rights and set the tone for the antifeminist rhetoric heard throughout the nineteenth century. The letter also served to prompt clergymen to refuse the Grimké sisters the use of their churches for their antislavery lectures.

Many women rushed to the support of the Grimkés and responded favorably to any references the sisters made to the rights of women. In 1838 Sarah Grimké replied to the Pastoral Letter with a pamphlet, *Letters on the Equality of the Sexes,* which is considered the first document written by an American woman that seriously addresses the issue of women's rights. She argued that the Scriptures cited in the Pastoral Letter reflected the patriarchal society that had produced them. Grimké contended that God had created woman as man's companion and his equal. Thus, she had just as much right to address mixed audiences as a man.

See also: Antislavery Movement; Grimké, Angelina Emily; Grimké, Sarah Moore; Woman Suffrage
References: Elizabeth Frost-Knappman, *Women's Progress in America* (1994); Blanche Glassman Hersh, *The Slavery of Sex: Feminist Abolitionists in America* (1978); Gerda Lerner, *The Grimké Sisters from South Carolina: Rebels against Slavery* (1967).

Pastoral Plan for Pro-Life Activities
In 1975 the National Conference of Catholic Bishops (NCCB) initiated the Pastoral Plan for Pro-Life Activities, a strategy designed to enlist the aid of American Roman Catholics in putting an end to legalized abortion. Among their stated goals was the passage of a constitutional amendment that would provide "protection for the unborn child to the maximum degree possible" and the passage of "federal and state laws and adoption of administrative policies that [would] restrict the practice of abortion as much as possible" (Rubin, 1994, p. 20). They also called for ongoing research into and refinement and precise interpretation of court decisions relating to the abortion issue, and "support for legislation that provides alternatives to abortion" (Rubin, 1994, p. 20). The bishops' plan was to garner the support of Catholics (and non-Catholics who shared their goals) to work within their churches, local organizations, dioceses, and states for pro-life activities.

Basic to the plan was the goal to elect "pro-life" candidates to Congress in order to obtain the passage of a constitutional amendment that would prohibit abortion. The NCCB also sought to develop education and public information programs that would disseminate its pro-life views and to promote and sponsor pregnancy counseling units and other alternatives to abortion. The NCCB saw the abortion issue as a challenge to the church and to American society to restore "respect for human life at every stage of existence," a challenge that called forth Christian "faith and courage" (Rubin, 1994, p. 24).

See also: Abortion; The Clergy Consultation Service on Abortion; Roman Catholic Church
References: Kathryn Cullen-DuPont, with Annelise Orleck, *The Encyclopedia of Women's History in America* (1996); Flora Davis, *Moving the Mountain: The Women's Movement in America since 1960* (1991); National Conference of Catholic Bishops, "Pastoral Plan for Pro-Life Activities" (1975), in Eva R. Rubin, ed., *The Abortion Controversy: A Documentary History* (1994).

Peabody, Lucy Whitehead McGill Waterbury (1861–1949)

Lucy Whitehead McGill Waterbury Peabody, Baptist lay leader and pioneer in ecumenical foreign missions programs, was born March 2, 1861, in Belmont, Kansas. She was the second child and eldest daughter of merchant John McGill and Sarah Jane (Hart) McGill. When the town of Belmont was destroyed during the Civil War, the family moved to Pittsford, New York, where they resided for several years. In 1873 they relocated to Rochester, New York, where John McGill worked as a produce dealer. Lucy attended Rochester Academy, graduating in 1878 as valedictorian of her class. For the next few years she taught at the local State School for the Deaf while taking some courses at the University of Rochester.

In August 1881 Lucy McGill married Norman Mather Waterbury, a Baptist minister. Soon after their marriage, the couple sailed to India to begin mission work among the Telegu people. Reverend Waterbury died in November 1886, leaving Lucy with their three small children. One of the children died on the journey home to the United States. Upon her return to Rochester, Waterbury returned to teaching. Then, in 1890 she moved to Boston to accept a position as corresponding secretary with the home department of the Woman's Baptist Foreign Missionary Society. She served that agency until her marriage to Henry W. Peabody in 1908. Peabody was a prominent and wealthy Baptist who owned a Boston import and export firm. When he died later in the year, his wife was left a woman of independent means, able to devote her energies to religious and philanthropic work.

As early as 1890, Peabody had begun to advocate an ecumenical approach to foreign missions. Together with Helen Barrett Montgomery, she had called for an interdenominational day of prayer for missions. That observance has since become known as the World Day of Prayer. In 1900 Peabody helped to organize the Committee on the United Study of Foreign Missions, and in 1902 she was appointed its chairperson. In that role, a position she filled for twenty-seven years, she helped produce numerous materials for women's study groups, organized and promoted conferences and summer schools, and represented American women at international mission conferences. The most important of these conferences was the ecumenical conference in Edinburgh, Scotland, in 1910. In 1906 Peabody launched a children's mission magazine, *Everyland,* which she edited for twelve years.

When in 1913 the American Baptists merged several mission associations to form the Woman's Baptist Foreign Mission Society, Montgomery became the society's president and Peabody its vice president for the foreign department. Montgomery and Peabody toured Asia in 1913–1914, financing the journey themselves and carrying credentials from the interdenominational Federation of Women's Boards of Foreign Missions. After returning to the United States, Peabody made it her goal to see interdenominational Christian women's colleges established in India, China, and Japan. In 1920 John D. Rockefeller offered a gift of $1,000,000 under the provision that Peabody raise an additional $2,000,000 by January 1, 1923. A one-month extension of the deadline allowed her to raise the required money to establish seven women's colleges.

Meanwhile, Peabody became caught up in the modernist-fundamentalist controversy that was dividing the Northern Baptists during the 1920s. Peabody was a confirmed fundamentalist who promoted evangelism over education and joined others in advocating the recall of all modernists from foreign missions. In

1927, when she perceived that modernists were putting limits on the mission work of her own family members, Peabody resigned all of her denominational offices and organized the autonomous and fundamentalist Association of Baptists for Evangelism in the Orient. Peabody was president of the organization until she retired in 1935. When in 1939 the association began mission work in Brazil, it adopted its present name, the Association of Baptists for World Evangelism. It also aligned with Regular Baptist Churches.

In addition to her mission work, Peabody was an advocate of prohibition. In 1934 she published *Kidnapping the Constitution,* which denounced the repeal of the Eighteenth Amendment. She wrote several other books during her career, including a memorial of her husband, *Henry Wayland Peabody, Merchant* (1909). Lucy Peabody died February 26, 1949, in Danvers, Massachusetts.

See also: Baptists; Fundamentalism; Montgomery, Helen Barrett
References: Edward T. James, ed., *Notable American Women, 1607–1950,* vol. 3 (1971); J. Gordon Melton, *Religious Leaders of America* (1991); Lucy Peabody, *Henry Wayland Peabody, Merchant* (1909); Rosemary Radford Ruether and Rosemary Skinner Keller, eds., *Women and Religion in America,* vol. 3 (1986).

Peace Movements

Women have long made up a large proportion of the participants in America's peace movements. Although motherhood, with the associated fear that sons or husbands would be lost in war, has been a strong motivation behind women's campaigns for peace, religion too has played an important role. Some religious groups, including Quakers, Mennonites, and Jehovah's Witnesses, adopted pacifism, renouncing the use of violence in any form. Under some circumstances, religious women have found it difficult to adhere to the pacifist traditions of their faith. For example, although she deplored war and violence, once the Civil War was underway, Quaker minister and strong abolitionist Lucretia Mott believed the war should be fought to the finish so that slavery could be ended once and for all.

From the late nineteenth century to World War I, peace was an important cause for female reformers. Although the groups through which they advocated peace were overwhelmingly white and Protestant, the National Council of Negro Women and the National Council of Jewish Women also became involved in the movement. They were united in the belief that wars were the product of a male-dominated world and that certain gender traits associated with males, including competitiveness and violence, were leading causes of wars. During the 1899 Hague Conference on international disarmament and arbitration, women initiated a Peace Day that was celebrated throughout the United States.

Some of the leading female reformers were advocates for peace. As president of the Woman's Christian Temperance Union (WCTU), Frances Willard traveled to Paris to attend the first Universal Peace Conference in 1889. Later, under the leadership of Hannah Bailey, the WCTU organized a peace department that published the *Banner of Peace.* The outbreak of World War I led to the founding of the first autonomous women's peace organization, the Women's Peace Party (WPP). With the sense that it was up to women to return peace and moral order to the world, a number of prominent female reformers joined together to form the WPP. In the decade immediately following the war, several more women's peace groups were established, including the National Committee on the Causes and Cure of War, the largest of the women's peace organizations; the Women's International League for Peace and Freedom (WILPF), which grew out of the WPP and the International Congress of Women at the Hague; and the absolutely pacifist Women's Peace Society. Despite its maintaining a pacifist stance even after the bombing of Pearl Harbor, the WILPF was the only one of these groups to survive World War II.

In the eyes of strong pacifists like Roman Catholic Dorothy Day, there was nothing that justified war. During the Spanish Civil War of the late 1930s, she favored total neutrality even while most Catholics supported General Francisco Franco. After the bombing of Pearl Harbor, Day continued to retain her pacifist stance, arguing that Americans should turn the other cheek and love their enemy. During the Cold War, she helped to found the organization of Catholic pacifists that came to be known as Pax Christi.

During World War II, there were some women on the extreme far right whose anti-Semitism caused them to condemn American participation in the war. They placed much of the blame for the war upon "international Jews," whom they claimed had manipulated the United States into the conflict. A leader of these women was Episcopalian Elizabeth Kirkpatrick Dilling, who spread propaganda alleging that there was a more important war in progress, a battle between Christians and Jews. Jews and communists, she said, were profiting by having the United States fight their battles against Adolf Hitler and the Third Reich.

Antiwar groups with politics ranging across the political spectrum came under investigation by the U.S. government both during and after World War II. Whether the motivations behind their activism were political or religious seemed to make no difference, for charges of communism were frequently being aimed at peace advocates. Throughout the history of the peace movement, reasons for participating in the peace organizations have differed from one woman to another. For example, membership in the WILPF is mixed, including both activists and academics and the religious and nonreligious. Quakerism has, however, proven to be a significant force within several sections of the WILPF, including in the United States, revealing that the religious aspect of women's peace movements continues. In fact, some scholars of feminism have given the peace movement a portion of the credit for the birth of a new religion—ecofeminism. Evolving from the peace activism within radical and socialist feminism, ecofeminism focuses upon the protection of the earth. This includes defending the planet from the ravages of male-inspired wars.

See also: Day, Dorothy; Dilling, Elizabeth Kirkpatrick
References: Harriet Hyman Alonso, *Peace as a Woman's Issue: A History of the U.S. Movement for World Peace and Women's Rights* (1993); Margaret Hope Bacon, *Valiant Friend: The Life of Lucretia Mott* (1980); Robert Coles, *Dorothy Day: A Radical Devotion* (1987); Catherine Foster, *Women for All Seasons: The Story of the Women's International League for Peace and Freedom* (1989); Erika A. Kuhlman, *Petticoats and White Feathers: Gender Conformity, Race, the Progressive Peace Movement, and the Debate over War, 1895–1919* (1997); June O'Connor, *The Moral Vision of Dorothy Day* (1991).

Penrose, Romania Pratt (1839–1932)

Pioneer female physician and champion of women's causes within the Church of Jesus Christ of Latter-Day Saints, Romania Pratt Penrose was born Romania Brunnell on a farm in Indiana on August 8, 1839. Her parents, Esther and Luther Brunnell, converted to Mormonism when Romania was a young girl, and she moved with them to the Mormon community at Nauvoo, Illinois. The family arrived in Nauvoo in 1846, just when the

Mormons were abandoning the town to move to Salt Lake City, Utah. Unable to afford the westward journey, the Brunnells returned to Indiana. Not long after, Romania's father left to join the California Gold Rush, hoping to raise enough money for the family to afford the journey to Utah. Meanwhile, Romania and her mother remained on their Indiana farm. Unfortunately, her father contracted typhoid fever in a mining camp and died.

Despite the family's hardships, Romania was able to attend school, including the Female Seminary in Crawfordsville, Indiana. While at the seminary, she developed an interest in studying medicine, believing that such knowledge might have saved the life of a friend.

Still desirous of joining the Mormon community in Salt Lake City, in 1855 Romania, her mother, and three siblings traveled to Omaha, Nebraska, where they attached themselves to a wagon train bound for Utah. The Brunnells arrived in Salt Lake City in September 1855. There, in 1859 Romania became the first wife of Parley P. Pratt, Jr., the eldest son of a prominent first-generation Mormon family. Although Parley was on missions to the East Coast and to England during the first decade of their marriage, the couple had seven children, five of whom survived infancy. Meanwhile, Romania assisted her husband with the editing of his father's papers, which they published as *The Autobiography of Parley P. Pratt* (c. 1874).

In 1873 Mormon president Brigham Young rekindled Romania's interest in medicine when he urged women to study the subject. It was his idea that women focus on the fields of pediatrics and obstetrics in order to care for women in childbirth and their babies. Romania sold her piano and other possessions, left her children with her mother, and went to New York to study medicine at

Women's Medical College. Young helped finance her education. Women of the Relief Society also aided her with moral and financial support because there was a lack of doctors in the Mormon community, especially in the fields of obstetrics and pediatrics. Her final two years of study were at Women's Medical College in Philadelphia, from which she graduated in 1877. Her thesis was "Puerperal Hemorrhage, Its Cause and Cure." She remained in Philadelphia for an additional two years while she concentrated on learning more about treatment of diseases of the eye and ear.

When she returned to Salt Lake City in 1879, Romania received a warm welcomed from Mormon leaders. She soon established her medical practice and began teaching classes in basic anatomy, obstetrics, and physiology. She also wrote a number of articles on hygiene and related topics for the church's women's magazines. To her surprise, her husband in the meantime had taken a second wife. She was not terribly upset since she had always accepted plural marriage as a basic doctrine of the church, but their lengthy separation had caused them to grow apart, and for that and other reasons, she eventually decided to end her marriage to Pratt. They were divorced in 1881.

Apparently, the divorce caused her little problem within the Mormon community. She traveled to New York City to attend the 1882 Woman's Suffrage Convention and became an active participant in the cause. A year later she became a visiting physician and later a resident physician at Deseret Hospital. In 1886 she married again, becoming the third plural wife of Charles Penrose. Also that year, she wrote an article in defense of plural marriage, in light of efforts by Congress to make the practice illegal. (Polygamy became illegal as a result of the Edmunds-Tucker Act of 1887, which also revoked woman suffrage in Utah). Her husband would soon be a prominent member of the church, becoming an apostle in 1904. In 1907 he was made leader of the European Mission. Meanwhile, Romania was busy organizing branches of the church's Relief Society and involving herself in activities in support of woman suffrage. She represented Utah and was a speaker at the 1908 Woman's International Suffrage Alliance meeting in Amsterdam. In 1911 she took on the role of counselor to the church president.

Romania retired from medicine in 1912 but continued her work with the church's relief societies. She died in Salt Lake City on November 9, 1932.

See also: Church of Jesus Christ of Latter-Day Saints (Mormons)
References: Vicky Burgess-Olson, *Sister Saints* (1978); J. Gordon Melton, *Religious Leaders of America* (1991); Richard S. Van Wagoner and Steven C. Walker, *A Book of Mormons* (1982).

Pentecostalism

Pentecostalism takes its name from the biblical day of Pentecost, when the Holy Spirit is said to have descended on Christ's disciples and presented them with the gift of tongues, enabling them to spread the message of the Gospel in other languages. Growing out of the Wesleyan/Holiness tradition that emphasized the second blessing of sanctification, Pentecostals believe that evidence of sanctification comes with the charismata, or gifts of the spirit. These gifts include glossolalia (speaking in tongues), prophecy, interpretation of tongues, and the power of healing. The gift of tongues was usually the most important indicator of sanctification. Tradition places the beginning of Pentecostalism in the Asuza Street revival of 1906, which was under the direction of William J. Seymour, a black clergyman. He had briefly been the

student of Charles H. Parham, a white man who launched the Apostolic Faith movement and led a Bible school in Topeka, Kansas. According to Pentecostalist tradition, it was at the Bible school that a woman, Agnes N. Ozman, became the first student to speak in tongues. This event reportedly occurred on January 1, 1901.

Early in its history, Pentecostalism was open to both female and black leaders, though not all Pentecostal churches ordained women. Like those in the Holiness movement, Pentecostals believed that if people, whether male or female, were moved by the spirit to preach the Gospel to others, they should do so. Often cited was Joel 2:28, "your sons and your daughters shall prophesy." Among women who became Pentecostal leaders were Florence Louise Crawford, a worker for the Asuza Street mission and later founder of the Apostolic Faith Church, and Maria Beulah Underwood Woodworth-Etter, an evangelist and founder of the Woodworth-Etter Tabernacle. Woodworth-Etter, the first woman to become famous for her preaching, helped blaze the trail for other female evangelists, including Pentecostal preacher Aimee Semple McPherson.

By the 1920s, as the Pentecostal denominations became better organized, its clergy better educated, and its hierarchies more structured, women found it increasingly difficult to gain access to the higher levels of leadership. African American Ida Bell Robinson was one woman who was affected by these changes. Robinson, who had been ordained earlier, became upset when in 1924, her denomination, the United Holy Church, put restrictions on women's ordination. She responded by forming her own denomination, the Mount Sinai Holy Church of America, which gave women prominent roles in church leadership. Another African

American, Lizzie Woods Roberson, seems to have accepted the limits placed upon women. Early in the 1910s, she founded the Woman's Department within the Church of God in Christ (COGIC). COGIC was the largest black Pentecostal denomination in America and one that did not ordain women. Under Roberson's guidance, the church's Woman's Department became one of the most powerful organizations of its type in the country.

From the beginning of the Pentecostal movement, female attendance and participation far outnumbered that of males. Although women's opportunities to preach did not correspond to their numbers, they frequently led the singing and often led the testimony services. But despite their relatively high ranks within their congregations, Pentecostals felt that within their homes, women should be subservient to their husbands. For according to church doctrine, males were second in command after God and Jesus Christ.

See also: Crawford, Florence Louise; McPherson, Aimee Semple; Roberson, Lizzie Woods; Robinson, Ida Bell; Woodworth-Etter, Maria Beulah Underwood References: Elaine J. Lawless, *Handmaidens of the Lord: Pentecostal Women Preachers and Traditional Religion* (1988); Susan Hill Lindley, *"You Have Stept Out of Your Place": A History of Women and Religion in America* (1996); Vinson Synan, *The Holiness-Pentecostal Tradition: Charismatic Movements in the Twentieth Century*, 2nd ed. (1997).

Perfectionism

Although the idea of "perfectionism" can be traced to the seventeenth-century Puritans' quest for a pure Christian society and to John Wesley's search for Christian perfection in the eighteenth century, it did not become a movement until the nineteenth century. Then, evangelists like Charles Grandison Finney and Phoebe Worrall Palmer raised perfectionism to a popular, though controversial, theology in the 1830s and 1840s. Finney, probably the most influential clergyman of the Second Great Awakening and the most famous of the perfectionist movement, asserted that a benevolent God was little by little revealing his will to a rational humankind. God's intentions were indeed so clear that even the common people would eventually understand the ultimate truths and could effectively maintain holy lives. Finney insisted that Christians should not be satisfied until they were as perfect as God. Similar to the Puritans before him, Finney viewed Americans as the people who could lead the world to holiness and to salvation. In a sermon in Rochester, New York, in 1830, Finney told his audience that if Christians joined together and dedicated themselves to their task, they could convert the entire world and bring about the millennium in three months. Although Finney's preaching inspired thousands of people to aspire to an evangelistic and sin-free life, some clergymen considered his preaching radical and heretical. Lyman Beecher, a respected minister of the time, denounced Finney for suggesting that man could emulate God.

Despite the controversy, the quest for perfection strengthened the American people's interest in improving society and prompted the establishment of a variety of organizations for reform. Perfectionist groups were more radical than the benevolent societies of the era, for they sought to eliminate rather than alleviate the nation's social problems. Moral reform was a major priority for perfectionists, the Female Moral Reform Society being a direct product of Finney's revivals. The temperance and abolitionist movements, as well as education and asylum reforms, were all enhanced as a result of Americans' desire for perfection.

Perfectionism also stimulated the founding of utopian communities and the formation of new philosophies. John Humphrey Noyes accepted completely Finney's preaching of the concept of perfectionism and in 1848 established the Oneida Community, where he would place his own ideas of human perfection into action. Transcendentalism, which flourished between 1835 and 1860, was a perfectionist philosophy, holding to a belief in the unity and divinity of human beings and nature.

Perfectionists accepted the basic institutions of their society, but they desired to effect changes in churches, government, and community that would conform to the impulses of evangelical and constitutional precepts. For women, who made up a majority of perfectionist reformers in many communities, such activism helped to broaden their roles within society. Although they remained subordinate to men in civil affairs, they now had a legitimate place as guardians of morality.

See also: Antislavery Movement; Female Moral Reform Society; Finney, Charles Grandison; Palmer, Phoebe Worrall; Puritans; Second Great Awakening; Temperance Movement
References: Irving H. Bartlett, *The American Mind in the Mid-Nineteenth Century*, 2nd ed. (1982); Merle Curti, *The Growth of American Thought*, 2nd ed. (1951); Nancy A. Hewitt, *Women's Activism and Social Change: Rochester, New York, 1822–1872* (1984); J. Gordon Melton, *Encyclopedia of American Religions*, 4th ed., (1993).

"Philadelphia 11"

The General Convention of the Episcopal Church in America had, in 1970, granted women the opportunity to become ordained to the diaconate but stalled on the issue of female priests. In 1974, a group of eleven female deacons of the Episcopal Church who sought ordination to the priesthood became known as the "Philadelphia 11." Three retired bishops agreed to ordain the women at the Church of the Advocate in Philadelphia. On July 29,

1974, the eleven women—Merrill Bittner, Alla Bozarth-Campbell, Allison Cheek, Emily Hewitt, Carter Heyward, Suzanne Hiatt, Marie Moorefield, Jeannette Piccard, Betty Schiess, Katrina Swanson, and Nancy Wittig—were ordained Episcopal priests. At an emergency meeting two weeks later, the House of Bishops declared the ordinations invalid and censured the ordaining bishops.

The decision of the House of Bishops did not deter female deacons' ambitions to become priests. In 1975, four more female deacons were ordained at the Church of St. Stephen and the Incarnation in Washington, D.C. The following year, the General Convention opened ordination as priests and bishops to women, and in 1977 the fifteen women were officially ordained to the priesthood.

See also: Episcopal Church; Harris, Barbara Clementine
References: Alla Bozarth-Campbell, *Womanpriest: A Personal Odyssey* (1978); Aleathia Dolores Nicholson, "Barbara Harris," in Jessie Carney Smith, ed., *Epic Lives: One Hundred Black Women Who Made a Difference* (1993); Priscilla Proctor and William Proctor, *Women in the Pulpit: Is God an Equal Opportunity Employer?* (1976); Betsy Covington Smith, *Breakthrough: Women in Religion* (1978).

Piccard, Jeannette Ridlon (1895–1981)

Born in Chicago, Illinois, on January 5, 1895, Jeannette Ridlon Piccard acquired fame, first as a record-setting balloonist and later as one of the first women to be ordained a priest in the Episcopal Church. Jeannette, the daughter of John R. Ridlon, an orthopedic surgeon, and Emily Caroline (Robinson) Ridlon, knew from the time she was eleven years old that she wanted to be a priest. But it would be many years before the Episcopal Church would ordain women priests. In the early twentieth century, most middle-class Americans like the Ridlons considered it a

Jeannette Ridlon Piccard and husband (1934)

woman's place to raise a family and care for her husband. So when Jeannette told her mother of her career goals, Emily Ridlon burst into tears.

Although clinging to the hope of someday entering a seminary, Jeannette attended Bryn Mawr, where she majored in philosophy and psychology and received a bachelor of arts degree in 1918. She then entered the University of Chicago, where she received a master's degree in organic chemistry in 1919. There she met Swiss scientist Jean Felix Piccard, a professor at the university, whom she married in August 1919.

For the next fifteen years, Jeannette was a mother and homemaker, living in both Switzerland and in various cities in the United States. Each time the family moved, Jeannette would immediately seek out and join a new Episcopal church. At this stage in her life, Jeannette strictly adhered to the traditions in the church, never questioning the church's position on women.

Jeannette's life reached a turning point in 1934. Jean's brother Auguste Piccard had become famous as the inventor of the stratospheric balloon, and Jean was as knowledgeable about ballooning as his brother. After Auguste's death in 1933, Jean made plans to lead an expedition into the stratosphere, where he would study the effect of cosmic rays and other stratospheric phenomena. But he was short of funds, and he needed a pilot. Jeannette, who had become a skilled balloonist in her own right, volunteered to be his pilot. On October 23, 1934, she piloted the balloon that took her and Jean 57,579 feet into the stratosphere, a record-breaking height above the earth.

In 1938, Jeannette took a step toward her future career as a priest when she agreed to preach a sermon at a small Episcopal mission in Provo, Utah. Of course, preaching to a tiny gathering at an Episcopal outpost in Utah was a far cry from entering the priesthood. Yet by the mid-1930s there were signs that the Episcopal Church was becoming more liberal in regard to the position of women in the church.

Jeannette received a doctorate in education from the University of Minnesota in 1942. Not able to find a teaching job due to American involvement in World War II, she worked for the Office of Civil Defense and as a volunteer for the Red Cross and for her church. Over the next two decades, she designed aeronautical experiments and acted as a consultant for the Office of Naval Research. Shortly after her husband's death in 1963, Jeannette became a consultant to the director of the National Aeronautics and Space Administration's Johnson Manned Spacecraft Center in Houston.

In 1965 she became acquainted with Denzil Carty, an African-American Episcopal priest. To him, she confided her long-held desire of becoming a priest.

Having suffered discrimination himself, Carty understood Jeannette's circumstances. He introduced her to Suzanne Hiatt, a young woman who shared Piccard's desire to become a priest. Jeannette was excited. For the first time in her life, she had met another woman who felt the way she did.

In 1967 Jeannette wrote a motion that would allow men and women to be selected as lay readers for the Episcopal Church on an equal basis. As the rules stood at the time, only men could stand at the pulpit and read from the Bible unless the congregation was in an isolated place where no man was available. Piccard's motion was passed at the General Convention in Seattle, Washington, in 1967 and became church law.

In 1970 the General Convention of the Episcopal Church granted women the opportunity to become deacons with the same rights and privileges as male deacons. Piccard was thrilled. After a period of study, she became a deacon on June 29, 1971. In the fall of 1972, she joined the General Theological School in New York City, intent upon qualifying for the priesthood. As a woman of seventy-seven, she found studying difficult. Nevertheless, she passed the general ordination exam the following year. Disappointment followed when the General Convention voted down a proposal for the ordination of women priests. When Suzanne Hiatt telephoned her in July 1974 to ask Jeannette if she wanted to join the group that would be ordained in Philadelphia on July 29, Piccard eagerly assented. The ordination was led by three retired bishops and was in defiance of the General Convention's ruling of the previous year. Piccard was the first of the eleven women ordained that day.

Two weeks after the ordination of the "Philadelphia 11," the House of Bishops held an emergency meeting to determine what to do about the ordination. They decided to consider the ordinations "invalid," and the new women priests were stripped of their priestly duties. Piccard remained a deacon at St. Philip's Episcopal Church in St. Paul, though she firmly believed that she was a priest. In September 1976 the General Convention voted to approve the ordination of women priests. Piccard was officially ordained a priest of the Episcopal Church on January 6, 1977. She became associate director of St. Philip's Episcopal Church. Shortly before her death from cancer on May 17, 1981, she was made an honorary canon of the Cathedral of St. Mark in Minneapolis.

See also: Episcopal Church; Harris, Barbara Clementine; "Philadelphia 11"
References: Alla Bozarth-Campbell, *Womanpriest: A Personal Odyssey* (1978); Janet Podell, ed., *The Annual Obituary, 1981* (1982); Betsy Covington Smith, *Breakthrough: Women in Religion* (1978).

Presbyterian Church

Although excluded from the pulpit and prohibited from ordination throughout much of their history, women in the Presbyterian Church were active members. Informal accounts acknowledge that their services date from the time of the formation of the General Assembly in 1789, but it is not until 1811 that official documents mention the contributions of the women of the church. Women's activities included volunteering in mission work and in benevolent and reform organizations. In the early nineteenth century, they began to break away from the male-led organizations. Not only had Presbyterian women no decisionmaking powers in the regular church organizations, but they were not allowed to speak at church gatherings attended by both men and women. Therefore, they began forming independent benevolent societies to support foreign and domestic missionaries, teachers, doctors, orphans, and widows.

In 1811 the General Assembly of the Presbyterian Church in the U.S.A. (PCUSA; later, United Presbyterian Church in the U.S.A.) announced its support for the women's work. But clergymen suggested that the women provide services only to women and children because of the commonly held belief that women should not speak in public. This limitation was also in concurrence with the ideas of John Calvin, upon whose teachings the Presbyterian Church is based. Calvin had specified women's subordination to men. Most pastors approved of the women's societies because they proved to be effective fund-raisers for missions, and they contributed beneficial services to their congregations. One project that was popular for a time during the mid-nineteenth century was to support young men while they attended seminaries. However, women were frequently disappointed when the young men returned and preached on the inferiority of women.

Presbyterian women made indirect contributions to worship by writing conversion novels and verses that occasionally became popular hymns. Susan and Anna Warner and Elizabeth Prentiss, all from New York state, wrote preaching novels that were read by thousands.

In the years following the Civil War, the missionary societies focused on organizing foreign and home missions and working with freed slaves. The first denominational woman's board, the Woman's Executive Committee of Home Missions (WEC), was established in 1878 to benefit and cooperate with the Board of Home Missions of the PCUSA. Under the leadership of its president, Katherine Bennett, the WEC was highly successful in raising both money and enthusiasm. The WEC won incorporation in 1915, allowing it to receive legacies in its own right. Distinct from the Board of Home Missions, it was the first women's organization to report directly to the General Assembly. The regional foreign missionary societies, which had heretofore been independent of one another, united in 1885 to form the Committee of Presbyterian Women for Foreign Missions. In 1920 it joined the Board of Foreign Missions.

Women in other Presbyterian denominations also were organizing missions during the 1870s and 1880s. The Women's General Missionary Society (WGMS) of the United Presbyterian Church of North America (UPNA) became known as one of the most efficient women's groups of the nineteenth and twentieth centuries. Its policy was to only perform work that was related to women and children.

Like most major religious denominations, the Presbyterian Church was reluctant to ordain women as deacons, elders, or ministers. Because of women's identification as "nurturers," the office of deacon was the first to open to women. In the late nineteenth century, most women working for the church were volunteers, but some earned wages, especially those in religious education and missions. Yet the clergy continued to oppose women in the pulpit. Later, beginning with UPNA in 1906, the Cumberland Presbyterian Church (CPC) in 1921, and PCUSA in 1929, women began to be ordained to ruling elder status. In 1889 a presbytery in the more liberal CPC ordained Louisa Woolsey as a minister. The General Assembly declared the ordination invalid in 1894, but the CPC refused to back down.

The 1920s saw a push for ordination among Presbyterian women. Women had recently won national suffrage and were seeking to gain equality in other areas of their lives. Also, Presbyterian women were angered over a recent reorganization initiated by PCUSA that resulted in the takeover of the WEC by 1923. After twice rejecting amendments to its constitution that would open the way for the ordination of women ministers, an amendment was finally passed in 1955–1956, and in 1956 Margaret Towner became the first Presbyterian woman to be ordained. The more conservative UPNA made no efforts to allow the ordination of women as ministers until it united with the PCUSA in 1958. Then only reluctantly did it accept women's full access to the ordained ministry.

The Southern Presbyterian Church (PCUS), which had formed when southern presbyteries split from the PCUSA in 1862 over theological differences stemming from the Civil War, was slower to allow women prominent roles within the church. Although women could participate in fund-raising for foreign and home missions, conservative ministers resisted their attempts to organize regional groups like their PCUSA counterparts. It was not until 1888 that southern Presbyterian women began to organize. In 1912, ignoring loud opposition from some men, the General Assembly gave its approval for a superintendent of women's work at the denominational level to coordinate the women's efforts and promote to women the church's educational, spiritual, and mission programs. Hallie Paxson Winsborough, superintendent from 1912 to 1929, named the organization the Women's Auxiliary. At first advised by male secretaries of the executive committees of PCUS, the advisory council was composed of women beginning in 1927.

The auxiliary and other Presbyterian women's organizations that developed in later years presented women with a variety of experiences and responsibilities within the church. They developed programs of Bible and mission studies, created committees on community and race relations, planned churchwide conferences, and learned leadership skills. In the 1950s, two of the women's organizations, the Board of Women's Work and the Women of the Church, began a campaign to have women equally represented on all boards, agencies, and committees in the PCUS. After the defeat of an ordination amendment in 1955 and most likely spurred on by the ordination of Margaret Towner in the PCUSA in 1956, the ordination of women became a priority among the women of the PCUS. In 1963 the committee rewriting the church's constitution deleted references to gender in the qualifications for ordination, and the change was approved the following year. In May 1965 Rachel Henderlite became the first female to be ordained to the ministry within the PCUS.

In 1983 the United Presbyterian Church in the U.S.A. reunited with the PCUS. Five years later the women's groups united under the title Presbyterian Women.

See also: Henderlite, Rachel
References: Lois A. Boyd and R. Douglas Brackenridge, *Presbyterian Women in America: Two Centuries of a Quest for Status*, 2nd ed. (1996); Susan Hill Lindley, *"You Have Stept Out of Your Place": A History of Women and Religion in America* (1996); Diana Ruby Sandersen, "Presbyterian Women's Groups," in Angela Howard Zophy with Frances M. Kavenik, eds., *Handbook of American Women's History* (1990); James H. Smylie, *A Brief History of the Presbyterians* (1996).

Priesand, Sally Jane (1946–)

The first American rabbi, Sally Jane Priesand was born June 27, 1946, in Cleveland, Ohio. From high school on, she had dreamed of becoming a rabbi, even though at that time there were no female rabbis. Several women before her had attempted to become rabbis, including Martha Neumark in the early 1920s and Helen Hadassah Levinthal in 1939, but they were never admitted to the rabbinate. In 1956 a committee of the Central Conference of American Rabbis, in the Reform branch of Judaism, was established to examine the issue of women rabbis and in the same year granted its

Sally Jane Priesand (1972)

approval. So when Priesand entered the Cincinnati branch of the Hebrew Union College—Jewish Institute of Religion, the way was open for her to enter the rabbinate. Nevertheless, she had been in the program for four years before people realized that she was really serious about becoming a rabbi. By her sixth year, she began to receive mounting publicity as a "first."

On June 3, 1972, after eight years of study and graduating with a master's degree in Hebrew letters, Priesand was ordained the first woman rabbi in the United States. But once she had accepted the ancient rite of *s'micha* (ordination), she found it difficult to find work. Some Reform synagogues refused to interview her because of her sex. Others interviewed her, but then told her that their congregations were not ready for a woman rabbi. But soon she found a temporary job at a synagogue in Illinois and later became an assistant rabbi at Stephen Wise Free Synagogue in New York. From 1979 to 1981, she was rabbi at Temple Beth El in Elizabeth, New Jersey, and chaplain at Lenox Hill Hospital in New York City before becoming rabbi at Monmouth Reform Temple in Tinton Falls, New Jersey.

Rabbi Priesand continues to fulfill the duties of a rabbi and to educate others about the richness of Jewish tradition. She has also been concerned with issues of human relations and with women's issues and has written a book, *Judaism and the New Woman* (1975), that explores the limitations placed on women within Judaism. Although she has faced prejudice as a result of her being a woman in a traditionally male occupation, she also has received a number of awards in honor of her work, both as a rabbi and as a representative of women.

See also: Clergy; Eilberg, Amy; Jews; Sasso, Sandy Eisenberg
References: Kathleen Litzenberg, ed., *Who's Who of American Women 1997–1998* (1996); Julie F. Parker, *Careers for Women as Clergy* (1993); Sally Priesand, *Judaism and the New Woman* (1975); Priscilla Proctor and William Proctor, *Women in the Pulpit: Is God an Equal Opportunity Employer?* (1976).

Promise Keepers/Praise Keepers

Promise Keepers, a Christian men's religious movement, was founded in 1990 by Bill McCartney, a University of Colorado at Boulder football coach. The women's group, Praise Keepers, cofounded by Donna Henley and Ann Adler, was established in 1996 for the purpose of carving a path similar to that begun by the men. The two organizations share the goal of using their devotion to God to return men and women to their traditional family roles and responsibilities. Starting small, with only seventy-two men at its first convention, Promise Keepers has enjoyed rapid growth with an estimated 500,000 attending the organization's conventions in 1996 and hundreds of thousands participating in the group's gathering in Washington, D.C., in October 1997. Its annual budget for 1997 was $107 million. The women's group is still in its initial stages, but nearly three hundred women were present at the first convention of the Praise Keepers in Lake Ozark, Missouri, on November 15, 1996.

To be admitted into the Promise Keepers, a man must make seven commitments: to honor Christ through prayer, worship, and obedience to God's word; to pursue vital relationships with a few other men, with the understanding that he needs brothers to help keep his promises; to practice spiritual, moral, ethical, and sexual purity; to build a strong marriage and family; to support pastors and churches; to reach out to those of other races and religious denominations; and to love the Lord and one's neighbor and teach all nations about Christianity. Like the men, women in the Praise Keepers must make seven similar commitments, first to God and, second, to their husbands. They believe that a wife should be under the authority of her husband and that the role of a woman is to be a homemaker and a "prayer warrior" and to be supportive of her husband.

From the outset, Praise Keepers realized that their point of view might not be popular with feminists or with those who considered that work outside of the home was a necessity. In this they were correct, for the Promise Keepers (likely because of the large size of the organization and its male-only membership policy) have aroused considerable protest from feminist groups. The National Organization for Women (NOW) has launched an anti–Promise Keepers campaign, arguing that the men's movement is a covert attempt to take back the rights for which women have fought for more than 150 years. The Religious News Service reported that Patricia Ireland, presi-

dent of NOW, said, "The Promise Keepers speak about 'taking back America' for Christ, but they also mean to take back the rights of women." Other women disagree, arguing that the Promise Keepers has had a positive effect on men and has helped to strengthen family ties.

Although the Promise Keepers are drawing criticism from feminists and from others who believe the Promise Keepers have connections to right-wing politics, the movement continues to gather strength. On October 4, 1997, well over 100,000 men gathered in Washington, D.C. for a Promise Keepers rally. Because they had stopped charging admission for convention goers, the Promise Keepers encountered financial difficulties in 1997. But publicity concerning their plight and a call for funds soon brought forth an announcement of their return to financial solvency.

See also: Fundamentalism
References: Ken Abraham, *Who Are the Promise Keepers? Understanding the Christian Men's Movement* (1997); Associated Press, "Promise Keepers Ready to Atone," *Sarasota Herald-Tribune* (October 4, 1997): 3A; Margaret Lamberts Bendroth, *Fundamentalism and Gender: 1875 to the Present* (1993); "Feminists to Protest Promise Keepers," *Fort Worth Star-Telegram,* reprinted in *Sarasota Herald-Tribune* (September 21, 1997): 4A; Karen Testa, "Christian Women Form Praise Keepers Group," in *Sarasota Herald-Tribune* (December 7, 1996): 4E.

Prophet, Elizabeth Clare (1940–)

Born Elizabeth Clare Wulf in Red Bank, New Jersey, on April 8, 1940, Prophet is the leader of the Church Universal and Triumphant, a New Age group in the Theosophical tradition. Although she was raised in the Christian Science faith, she began reading Theosophical material produced by the "I AM" Movement at an early age. She met her future husband, Mark L. Prophet, in 1961 while attending Boston University. He had been involved with several groups influenced by the "I AM" Movement and had formed one of his own, Summit Lighthouse in Washington, D.C., in 1958. They were a compatible couple with common interests, and they married within a year of their first meeting. Together they wrote Summit Lighthouse's basic text, *Climb the Highest Mountain* (1972).

Over the years, Summit Lighthouse has moved several times, first to Colorado Springs, then to Pasadena and Malibu, and later to a 33,000-acre area in Montana known as Paradise Valley. Following Mark Prophet's death in 1973, Elizabeth Prophet became the group's leader. She also adopted her late husband's function as the messenger, or spokesperson, for the ascended masters of the Great White Brotherhood, which she believed he had joined. (The Great White Brotherhood is the name most commonly given to the spiritual hierarchy that was first presented to the occult world by Helena Petrovna Blavatsky in the 1880s.) After taking control of the Summit Lighthouse, she changed its name to the Church Universal and Triumphant. The Summit Lighthouse remains as the educational arm of the church. Not long after her husband's death, Prophet married Randall King.

Prophet, who serves as spiritual leader of the church, is known by her followers by several titles, including Vicar of Christ, Mother of the Flame, and the more affectionate name of Guru Ma. Outside her duties as teacher and liturgical leader, her major task is to publicly spread what are believed to be the messages of the Great White Brotherhood. These messages are published in the church's periodical, the *Pearls of Wisdom.* Any special messages that she receives she publishes in her many volumes. Among these are *The Great White Brotherhood in the Culture, History, and Destiny of America* (1976); *The*

Chela and the Path (1976); *Quietly Comes the Buddha* (1977); and *Mysteries of the Holy Grail* (1984).

Prophet claims to be the reincarnation of the biblical Martha and maintains that Jesus once spoke directly to her in her past life. He allegedly told her that she would continue to be reborn until the dawn of the Age of Aquarius. Now that it has arrived, she claims she was given the responsibility to herald it. In the 1980s Prophet began to refer to herself and the church as gnostic Christians and wrote three volumes on what she considered the lost aspects of Jesus' ministry. These were *The Lost Years of Jesus* (1984) and *The Lost Teachings of Jesus* (two volumes, 1986, 1988).

Prophet and her church have been under frequent attack from local residents, former church members, and from the anticult movement. She has been criticized as a charismatic demagogue who controls the lives of the church members. In the late 1980s, she was denounced for her apocalyptic predictions, which resulted in the church constructing a number of bomb shelters on its Montana property. Randall King, whom she had divorced, was one of her most severe critics. She later married Edward Francis. Francis was arrested in 1989 when he devised and pursued a plan to obtain weapons illegally and to store them on the church's property. He served a short term in jail for his activity.

In 1990, after a warning from Prophet that nuclear war was imminent, members of her Church Universal and Triumphant sold their homes, closed their bank accounts, and moved to the valley, where they proceeded to stockpile food and survival goods in underground concrete and steel bunkers that had been built by the church. When Prophet's prediction failed to come to pass, her followers maintained that their prayers had helped prevent a cataclysm.

References: George A. Mather and Larry A. Nichols, *Dictionary of Cults, Sects, Religions and the Occult* (1993); J. Gordon Melton, *Religious Leaders of America* (1991); J. Gordon Melton, *New Age Encyclopedia* (1990); J. Gordon Melton et al., *New Age Almanac* (1991); Peter Occhiogrosso, *The Joy of Sects: A Spirited Guide to the World's Religious Traditions* (1994).

Pugh, Sarah (1800–1884)

Educator, abolitionist, and women's rights activist Sarah Pugh was born in Alexandria, Virginia, on October 6, 1800. She was the second child and only daughter of Jesse and Catharine (Jackson) Pugh. Her father died when she was three years old, and she moved with her mother to Philadelphia. Reared a Quaker, Sarah's education included two years at a Quaker boarding school in Westtown, Pennsylvania. In 1821 she began a teaching career at the Friends' School of the Twelfth Street Meeting House in Pennsylvania. She remained at the school until a split between the Orthodox Quakers and the more liberal Hicksite Quakers in 1827 led to her resignation in 1828. The disagreements among the Quakers brought about Pugh's own religious questioning, which eventually led to her adopting a Unitarian faith that put a stress on good deeds. In 1829 she founded an elementary school, where she taught until 1840.

In the mid-1830s, Pugh became caught up in the abolitionist movement. She supported William Lloyd Garrison and his ideas for immediate and unconditional emancipation, and she joined the Philadelphia Female Anti-Slavery Society. One of Pugh's best friends, Quaker minister and abolitionist Lucretia Mott, was the principal organizer of the group. When in 1838 a mob burned Philadelphia's Pennsylvania Hall, where the second Anti-Slavery Convention of American Women was meeting, Pugh opened her schoolhouse so that the women could complete their discussions. In 1840 she traveled with Mott and others as a delegate to the World Anti-Slavery Convention in London, England. When the women were denied permission to participate, Pugh wrote the letter of protest on behalf of the Pennsylvania delegates. She spent the next ten years caring for her elderly mother. After her mother's death in 1851, Pugh campaigned for the abolitionist cause in both the United States and in Britain.

Although welcoming the emancipation of slaves that came with the Civil War, the conflict awakened Pugh to the peace attestations of her Quaker ancestors and reinforced her commitment to peace. Following the war, she worked to improve the circumstances of the freed slaves and became involved in the women's rights movement. In later years, she was active with the Philadelphia Moral Education Society (established in 1873); her work included circulating petitions in opposition to a proposed law to license prostitution in Pennsylvania.

On August 1, 1884, Pugh died in Germantown, Pennsylvania, where she had lived for the past twenty years with her brother and sister-in-law. Although she never became as famous as other reform leaders, Pugh's religious commitment to the performance of good deeds inspired her to quietly carry out the necessary duties that kept the movements going.

See also: Antislavery Movement; Mott, Lucretia Coffin; Society of Friends (Quakers); Woman Suffrage
References: Otelia Cromwell, *Lucretia Mott* (1958); Elizabeth Frost-Knappman, *Women's Progress in America* (1994); Edward T. James, ed., *Notable American Women, 1607–1950*, vol. 2 (1971).

Puritans

The reforming Protestants who became known as "Puritans" first appeared in England during the 1560s. They were adherents of John Calvin and were given the title "Puritans" as a result of their desire to "purify" the Anglican Church. Unable to reform the church and society in England and suffering persecution from church and government authorities, many emigrated to New England between the 1620s and 1640s. It was their intention to build a society, based upon a religious foundation, that the entire world would wish to emulate as a "city on a hill." Except for the Separatists who settled in Plymouth or Rhode Island, the Puritans who emigrated to New England continued to consider themselves spiritual members of the Church of England but established a system of self-governing congregations that ignored the authority of the Anglican bishops. The Puritans arrived in the New World as families, resulting in a much closer male/female ratio than in other American colonies.

Almost from the beginning of the colony, many of the practices of the Massachusetts Bay Puritans diverged from those of the Puritans remaining in England. The New England Puritans set higher standards for determining who was among those elected to salvation and who could thus become members of the church. Although English Puritans normally accepted anyone who had repented their sins, professed their faith, and were upstanding members of society, the Puritans in Massachusetts Bay insisted upon a much more stringent examination. Potential members were required to stand before the congregation, undergo questioning, and describe their spiritual life and conversion experience. But, for the male saints of Massachusetts Bay, the rewards for acquiring membership in the church went beyond the religious. Every adult male accepted as a saint was granted full citizenship, including the right to vote in civil elections.

Women were attracted to Puritanism in the religion's early days, for its attitude toward women appeared more liberal than that of the Anglican Church. Calvinism taught that, like Adam, Eve was created in God's image and, thus, spiritual equality was ordained by God. There were even hints that, with proper education, women might be capable of entering the ministry. Such an occasion never came to pass, but a few congregations did allow women to vote for candidates for the ministry and to register their opinions in cases of admissions of new members or disciplinary action.

Divorce laws under the Puritan authorities in America gave some women opportunities they would have never had in England. Unlike the Anglican Church, Puritans did not consider marriage a sacrament but a civil contract. They therefore accepted the idea of divorce, but only in extreme cases such as adultery, cruelty, desertion, or male impotence. Divorces were rare, but they did give women a means to escape an intolerable marriage. Studies of divorce records indicate that more women in seventeenth-century New England sued for divorce than men and that more women succeeded in having divorces granted.

Puritan doctrine taught that the love of a man and his wife compared to the bond between Christ and the church. Such precepts idealized the marital relationship, giving it a oneness of spirit, yet it also placed the husband at the head of the household, just as Christ was head of the church. Wives were expected to obey their husbands, who, in turn, were required to be kind to their wives. But, regardless of the extent of a couple's love for one another, they were constantly reminded to love Christ more.

Although Puritanism perceived women as spiritual equals, they were not viewed as civil equals, and among Puritans in America there was some debate over their value to society. Clergyman John Cotton defended the female sex, describing women as "creatures without which there is no comfortable [l]iving for man," and contended that only blasphemers "call them a necessary Evil, for they are a necessary Good; such as it was not good that man should be without" (Ulrich, 1987, p. 106). At least part of a woman's role, according to Cotton, was to make life comfortable for men.

Most Puritans viewed women as intellectually inferior to men. Women were also considered morally vulnerable, making them more easily influenced by Satan. This attitude helped to inspire accusations of witchcraft against women. During the Salem Witch Trials of 1692, most of the accused were women.

In the mid-1630s, Anne Hutchinson challenged the perception of women's intellectual inferiority when she began holding religious meetings outside the church. Although she had followed John Cotton, one of the most respected Puritan clergymen, to America, she caused a split in the community when she rejected portions of Puritan ideology and gained a large following of both men and women. When brought to trial in 1637–1638, she proved that her knowledge and understanding of biblical texts was at least as good as that of her male inquisitors. Yet in the eyes of the authorities, her disruption of the Puritan community had proven that women were indeed vulnerable to the powers of the devil. Mary Dyer, a follower of Anne Hutchinson, was further proof to them of the inferiority of women. Dyer converted to Quakerism but would not leave the Massachusetts Bay Colony. She was hanged in 1660 for preaching "heresy" and for refusing to leave the colony. Although women had earlier been eager to adopt Puritanism, many became outspoken dissenters as the religion failed to meet their needs.

Puritanism was in decline by the end of the seventeenth century. Immigrants who were of other religions began to arrive and settle in New England, and Puritans lost their dominant majority. At the same time, the second generation of Puritans was largely apathetic about the founders' mission to America. Second-generation women were more likely than men to go through the conversion process that would place them among the elect, or "saints," and in the eighteenth century they outnumbered men as full members of the churches. However, they had no voting rights, so the church continued to be dominated by men.

See also: Calvinism; Captivity Sermons; Dyer, Mary Barrett; Hutchinson, Anne Marbury; Salem Witch Trials
References: John Putnam Demos, *A Little Commonwealth: Family Life in Plymouth Colony* (1970); John Putnam Demos, *Past, Present and Personal: The Family and the Life Course in American History* (1986); Perry Miller, *The New England Mind: From Colony to Province* (1953); Edmund S. Morgan, *The Puritan Dilemma: The Story of John Winthrop* (1958); Laurel Thatcher Ulrich, *Good Wives: Image and Reality in the Lives of Women in Northern New England, 1650–1750* (1982); Selma R. Williams, *Divine Rebel: The Life of Anne Marbury Hutchinson* (1981).

Qoyawayma, Polingaysi (1892–?)

Polingaysi Qoyawayma, an educational reformer who sought to preserve Native American culture and tradition, was born in 1892 in the Hopi village of Oraibi in Arizona. When she was a child, Qoyawayma's father worked for a Mennonite missionary. Qoyawayma was impressed by the kindness of the missionaries, and she enjoyed learning Christian hymns. She later recalled that she was too young to realize that the missionaries were on the Hopi reservation for purposes of teaching the Native Americans the sinfulness of their ways and leading them away from their ancient beliefs and toward Christianity. Although her father assisted the missionaries, he was a conservative among the Hopi, intent upon retaining tribal tradition.

When Qoyawayma was about age twelve, she went to California to attend one of the government-run boarding schools that had been established following the military defeat and subordination of the American Indians. Schools like the one that Qoyawayma attended were under the jurisdiction of the U.S. Bureau of Indian Affairs and were usually operated by Christian missionaries. With the stated goal of "Americanizing" the Native American children, the missionaries took the youngsters from their homes (often by force and without the consent of their parents) and taught them the English language, the Christian religion, and Western dress and manners. As a result, when the children returned home after many years of instruction, they were alienated from their tribal heritage.

Although as a child she had willingly attended the government-run school, as an adult Qoyawayma refuted her education. In 1924 she became a teacher of Native American children herself and developed a curriculum that included American Indian culture. Although she gave her students lessons in English, she also instructed them in the Hopi and Navajo languages. She eventually succeeded in persuading John Collier, the commissioner of the Bureau of Indian Affairs, to support this type of education for the children of any Native American families who wished it. Qoyawayma did not oppose assimilation into the white world, but she wished to preserve the various American Indian cultures. She retired from teaching in 1954, but she continued to communicate her concerns about Native American education. In 1964 she published her autobiography, *No Turning Back,* in which she describes Hopi tradition and the problems that haunted her life as a result of being removed from her culture.

The practice of taking Native American children from their homes gradually became less common. In 1975, for example, Congress enacted the Indian Self-Determination and Education Assistance Act, which acknowledged the autonomy of the tribes and returned the power to deliver educational services themselves. The Indian Child Welfare Act of 1978 ended the government's practice of taking Native

American children from their families without their parents' consent by requiring that cases involving child foster care and adoption be heard in tribal rather than state courts if a child has a permanent home on the reservation.

Sources give no date for Qoyawayma's death.

See also: Native Americans
References: Duane Champagne, ed., *The Native North American Almanac* (1994); Kathryn Cullen-DuPont, with Annelise Orleck, *The Encyclopedia of Women's History in America* (1996); Polingaysi Qoyawayma (Elizabeth Q. White), *No Turning Back* (1964); John Snider, "Qoyawayma, Polingaysi," in Angela Howard Zophy with Frances M. Kavenik, eds., *Handbook of American Women's History* (1990).

Quakers
See **Society of Friends (Quakers)**

Reform Movements

During the nineteenth century, American men and women became involved in numerous social, welfare, and political reform movements. At the base of almost all of these reforms was religion. The revivals of the Second Great Awakening (c. 1795–1835), which brought the idea that the country's ills could be cured and that society could be perfected, inspired citizens to embark on crusades to reform America. For women, the religious aspect of the reform movements allowed them much greater opportunities than ever before to participate in causes that affected the common good.

In nineteenth-century America, a time during which a woman's role was deemed to be that of homemaker, caregiver, wife, and mother, women were expected to remain apart from public life. Part of a mother's responsibility was to direct the moral education of her children and to wield some influence upon the morals of her spouse. Early in the century, there were signs that women's field of influence was beginning to broaden as women began joining together to uplift the morals of society at large. Initially, women became involved in church-based associations, participating in Bible study, prayer groups, Sunday schools, and charitable works. Soon, however, they began to participate in organizations that were not necessarily attached to their churches but that still considered religion to be at the base of their reform activities. Women joined temperance societies, moral reform groups, and abolitionist associations, all of which had close connections to the belief in the perfectibility of humankind.

Historians have come to see a progression by which women's participation in religious organizations eventually led to the Seneca Falls Convention of 1848 and the campaign for women's rights. Their church-associated groups taught them leadership and fund-raising skills and the effectiveness of organization. Those who moved on to become involved in the major reforms of the era, particularly the temperance and abolitionist causes, were able to further hone their leadership and organizational skills. The male-dominated abolitionist cause was important to the development of the women's movement because it allowed women to realize the strict limits that most men were placing upon their participation in the antislavery movement. Also, their extensive work within abolitionist organizations gave them the self-confidence to embark on a crusade of their own.

Religion became less dominant in the lives of reformers by the end of the nineteenth century, though some, such as Frances Willard, brought the Protestant missionary zeal into the campaign for women's rights. Also, the missions movement remained in force at the turn of the century, with city women working through religious organizations to provide social services to immigrants and the poor. The twentieth century has seen fewer religious-based reform movements, though in recent years both women and men, especially those connected with Christian fundamentalist denominations, have attempted to reform America by crusading to "restore family values."

See also: Antislavery Movement; Dix, Dorothea Lynde; Female Moral Reform Society; Peace Movements; Second Great Awakening; Settlement House Movement; Sunday School Movement; Temperance Movement

References: Harriet Hyman Alonso, *Peace as a Woman's Issue: A History of the U.S. Movement for World Peace and Women's Rights* (1993); Nancy F. Cott, *The Bonds of Womanhood: "Woman's Sphere" in New England, 1780–1835* (1977); Eleanor Flexner, *Century of Struggle: The Woman's Rights Movement in the United States* (1970); Noralee Frankel and Nancy S. Dye, eds., *Gender, Class, Race, and Reform in the Progressive Era* (1991); Blanche Glassman Hersh, *The Slavery of Sex: Feminist Abolitionists in America* (1978); Nancy A. Hewitt, *Women's Activism and Social Change: Rochester, New York, 1822–1872* (1984); Sheila Rowbotham, *Women in Movement: Feminism and Social Action* (1991); Mary P. Ryan, *Cradle of the Middle Class: The Family in Oneida County, New York, 1790–1865* (1981).

Regan, Agnes Gertrude (1869–1943)

Social worker and Catholic educator Agnes Gertrude Regan was born in San Francisco, California, on March 26, 1869. She was the fourth child of Mary Ann (Morrison) Regan and James Regan. Agnes received her early education in Catholic schools and in 1887 graduated from San Francisco Normal School. For the next thirty-two years she worked in the field of education in San Francisco's public schools, serving as an elementary school teacher from 1887 to 1900, as a principal from 1900 to 1914, and then as a member of the board of education from 1914 to 1919. She also played an active role in securing California's first teachers' pension law.

In 1920 Regan represented the San Francisco diocese at the founding meeting of the National Council of Catholic Women (NCCW) in Washington, D.C. She moved to the nation's capital a few months later to begin a twenty-year career as executive secretary of the organization. An important component of the NCCW's program was attention to social concerns. As executive secretary, Regan initiated a variety of programs to offer services to working women, immigrants, and the poor. Regan championed world peace and modest dress and argued against birth control and the Equal Rights Amendment. She frequently testified in congressional hearings on matters of importance to herself and to the NCCW. She also played an important role in the education of social workers. In 1921 she assisted in the founding of the National Catholic School of Social Service, a two-year program that offered a master's degree. In 1940 the program was incorporated into the curriculum of Catholic University. From 1922 she served as an instructor at the school, until she was appointed assistant director in 1925. With the exception of two years when she served as acting director (1935 to 1937), Regan held the position of assistant director until her death.

In addition to her employment at the school, Regan continued to work for the NCCW. From 1939 to 1940, she was a member of the White House Conference on Children in Democracy. Regan also took time to serve on the board of directors of the National Travelers' Aid Society and on the advisory committee of the Federal Women's Bureau, and she participated in the Catholic Association for International Peace. She received a number of honors during her years of social service, including the papal decoration Pro Ecclesia et Pontifice (1933). Regan died in Washington, D.C., on September 30, 1943.

See also: National Council of Catholic Women; Roman Catholic Church

References: James J. Kenneally, *The History of American Catholic Women* (1990); Karen Kennelly, ed., *American Catholic Women: A Historical Exploration* (1989); J. Gordon Melton, *Religious Leaders of America* (1991).

Richmond, Cora Lodencia Veronica Scott (1840–1923)

Cora Lodencia Veronica Scott Richmond, one of the best-known American Spiritualist mediums of the nineteenth century, was born in Cuba, New York, on April 21, 1840. It is said that she was born with a "veil," which according to popular lore is a sign that a person is blessed with supernatural gifts. Her mother, Lodencia Veronica Butterfield, a Presbyterian, and her father, David W. Scott, who has been described as being independent in his religious views, developed an interest in Spiritualism during the 1840s. When Cora was about age eleven, her family moved briefly to Hopedale, Massachusetts, where a Universalist clergyman, Adin Ballou, had established a Spiritualist-influenced colony, and then to Waterloo, Wisconsin, where a midwestern branch had been organized.

In the fall of 1851, signs that Cora was indeed gifted as a medium began to appear. According to Spiritualist tradition, she soon came under the control of several spirits, including a German physician who guided her in treatment of the ill. Her mother and several of her aunts also became mediums. Cora was still only eleven when she began to demonstrate her gifts in public. David Scott accompanied his daughter on lecture tours that took them from Wisconsin to western New York. When she was about age fourteen, Cora moved to Buffalo, New York, after receiving an invitation to become a medium for a small church. In 1856 she moved to New York City, where she married a hypnotist named Benjamin Hatch. Hatch lived off her earnings and physically abused his young bride, and she soon divorced him. In her successive marriages (the precise number of which is unknown) she controlled her own earnings. Now sixteen years old, she moved to Baltimore, where she remained until 1873. While there, she published a 250-page poem titled *Hesperia.*

In 1873 Cora traveled to England, with intentions of staying six months. The months stretched into two years as her exceptional speaking ability and demonstrations of trance phenomena proved popular with her English audiences. While in England, she became acquainted with many of the most prominent British Spiritualists, including Wilberforce J. Colville, a medium with whom she would appear when he later visited the United States. Reformer Robert Dale Owen, who held a deep interest in Spiritualism, became an admirer of Cora's work, describing her as an "enlightened . . . judicious . . . [and] eloquent exponent of the principles of what, in modern phrase, is termed Spiritualism" (Barrett, 1895).

Cora returned to the United States in 1875, lecturing before audiences from New York to San Francisco. In 1878 she married businessman William Richmond, and the couple settled in Chicago, where Cora pastored a church. For the rest of her life, she served as a minister in Chicago and was active within the Spiritualist community. She helped organize the National Spiritualist Association and was elected the group's first vice president. Her husband published the two works that she wrote during her years in Chicago, *The Soul in Human Embodiments* (1887) and the two-volume *Psychosophy* (1888, 1915).

Cora Richmond died in Chicago on January 3, 1923.

See also: Owen, Robert Dale; Spiritualism
References: Harrison D. Barrett, *Life Work of Mrs. Cora L. V. Richmond* (1895);

J. Gordon Melton, *Religious Leaders of America* (1991); R. Laurence Moore, *In Search of White Crows: Spiritualism, Parapsychology, and American Culture* (1977).

Roberson, Lizzie Woods
(1860–1945)

Lizzie Woods Roberson, founder of the Woman's Department of the Church of God in Christ, the largest Pentecostal denomination in North America, was born a slave in Philips County, Arkansas, on April 5, 1860. Her father died during the Civil War, and Lizzie was reared in poverty. Though her mother could neither read nor write, she saw that her children were well educated. Lizzie married Henry Holt in 1881, but he died soon after. She was not affiliated with any religion until 1892, when she joined the Baptist Church.

In 1901, after reading a paper called "Hope" by pioneer home missionary Joanna Patterson Moore, Lizzie had a saving experience of Christianity. Lizzie met Moore, and Moore, who was a member of the white American Baptist Home Mission Society, arranged for Lizzie to receive two years of schooling at Baptist Academy in Dermott, Arkansas. After she finished her schooling, Lizzie became matron of the academy. In 1911 Charles Harrison Mason, the founder, in 1906, of the Pentecostal Church of God in Christ (COGIC), spoke at the Baptist Academy. Lizzie was so impressed that she left the Baptists and joined COGIC. Under Mason's ministry, she received the baptism of the Holy Spirit, with the initial evidence of speaking in tongues, the definitive Pentecostal religious experience. Soon she went to work for Elder R. L. Hart in Trenton and Jackson, Tennessee.

Mason was impressed with Lizzie's piety and conscientiousness, and he appointed her overseer of women's work within the church. Although COGIC did not recognize the ordination of women, Mason considered women essential to the functioning of the church and felt they needed to be led by other spiritually mature women. Drawing upon her experiences with the Baptists, Mother Roberson, as she became known, created a powerful Woman's Department, one of the most commanding of any denomination. She organized women into prayer, Bible, and home and foreign mission bands. Once a woman had achieved salvation and holiness, Roberson urged her to seek general literacy, biblical literacy, professional achievement, and other skills. Mother Roberson admonished women to dress modestly; to wear skirts hemmed below the knee; and to avoid open-toed shoes, jewelry, and feathers.

Not long after joining COGIC, Lizzie met an Elder Roberson, whom she later married. For some time the couple traveled together as evangelists. In their later years, they moved to Omaha, Nebraska, where they established a church. Elder Roberson became pastor, but his wife continued to travel on behalf of her women's work. She also campaigned to raise funds for the building of a national headquarters of COGIC in Memphis, and a hall of the building was named for her. Roberson died in Memphis in November 1945, shortly after the building's convocation ceremony.

References: Sherry Sherrod DuPree, ed., *Biographical Dictionary of African-American Holiness-Pentecostals, 1880–1990* (1989); J. Gordon Melton, *Religious Leaders of America* (1991); Rosemary Radford Ruether and Rosemary Skinner Keller, eds., *Women and Religion in America*, vol. 3 (1986); Dorothy C. Salem, ed., *African American Women: A Biographical Dictionary* (1993).

Robertson, Ann Eliza Worcester
(1826–1905)

Missionary and Bible translator Ann Eliza Worcester Robertson was born at

Brainerd Mission, Cherokee Nation, Tennessee. At the time of Ann Eliza's birth, on November 7, 1826, her parents, Congregational minister Samuel Austin Worcester and Ann (Orr) Worcester, had been missionaries to the Cherokees for approximately one year. The family moved to the capital of the Cherokee Nation, New Echota, Georgia, while Ann Eliza was still an infant. In 1831 Samuel Worcester was imprisoned in the Georgia State Penitentiary for his refusal to recognize the state's authority over the Cherokees' land. He won his appeal to the Supreme Court in the famous decision *Worcester v. Georgia* (1832), but President Andrew Jackson ignored the court ruling and removed the Cherokees to Oklahoma. The Worcesters also went to Oklahoma, where they established Park Hill Mission in 1836. Ann Eliza, who until this time had received most of her education at home and at the mission, enrolled in the St. Johnsbury (Vermont) Academy in 1843. She excelled in her studies of the Greek and Latin languages. After her graduation in 1847, she returned to Park Hill to assist her parents as a teacher.

In 1849 Ann Eliza was appointed a teacher at the new Tullahassee Manual Labor Boarding School, which was sponsored jointly by the Creek Nation and the Presbyterian Board of Foreign Missions. The school opened in January 1850, and on April 16, 1850, she married its principal, Presbyterian minister William Schenck Robertson. She also joined her husband's denomination. In addition to her responsibilities as a wife and mother (she eventually bore seven children, three of whom died in infancy), Robertson taught at the school, supervised school housekeeping, and helped her husband produce texts in the Creek language.

The outbreak of the Civil War brought disruption to the mission. The Creeks made a treaty with the Confederacy, closed the school, and expelled the missionaries. The Robertsons moved to the North. Reverend Robertson supported his family first by teaching in Illinois and later, from 1864 to 1866, by supervising an orphan institute in Highland, Kansas. At the Creeks' request, the family returned to Tullahassee in December 1866. There they found that only the brick walls of the school were left standing. The school reopened in 1868, and the Robertsons continued their missionary, teaching, translating, and publishing work. The school burned down in 1880, and Reverend Robertson died a few months later.

After her husband's death, Ann Eliza went to live with her daughter Alice (who would later become the second woman ever elected to the U.S. Congress) in Muskogee, Oklahoma. Ann Eliza continued to perform her translating work, and in 1887 she completed the Creek New Testament, a work that she had begun with her husband years before. She continued to revise it up until her death but also published translations of Genesis and Psalms and produced a new Creek hymnal. She translated the New Testament directly from the Greek but had the help of another missionary in translating the Old Testament Hebrew. Her accomplishments brought her an honorary doctorate in 1892 from the University of Wooster in Ohio. Ann Eliza Robertson died in Muskogee on November 19, 1905.

See also: Missionaries
References: Edward T. James, ed., *Notable American Women, 1607–1950,* vol. 3 (1971); J. Gordon Melton, *Religious Leaders of America* (1991); "William Schenk Robertson," in *Dictionary of American Biography,* vol. 16 (1935).

Robinson, Ida Bell (1891–1946)

The founder of the largest African-American Pentecostal denomination headed by a woman, Ida Bell Robinson was born

August 3, 1891, in Hazelhurst, Georgia. She was the seventh child of Annie and Robert Bell. Most of her childhood was spent in Florida. From the time she was a young girl, Ida was known for her religious enthusiasm. She began her ministry while still a teenager, leading prayer services in various homes in Pensacola, Florida. In 1909 Ida married Oliver Robinson and moved with him to Philadelphia, Pennsylvania, in 1917. Marriage did not quell Ida's passion for the ministry. She became pastor of Mount Olive Holy Church, an affiliate of the United Holy Church, in 1919.

Word of her talents for ministering spread, and her small congregation grew. Women were especially drawn to her services. By the early 1920s, they outnumbered male congregants two to one and were demanding a more active role in the church. Women's demands apparently caused male leaders to feel threatened, and they ended public ordinations for women. Upset over male oppression in general and particularly over their stand on the ordination of women, Robinson spent ten days fasting and praying for guidance. When the ten days were over, Robinson made the decision to leave the United Holy Church to found a denomination that would be free of male domination. This new church, the Mount Sinai Holy Church of America, received its charter in Philadelphia in 1924 and was to become the largest African-American Pentecostal denomination led by a woman. From its beginning, women played prominent roles in the church's leadership.

Robinson, who stressed spiritual healing, is said to have been a great preacher. People packed the church to listen to her two- to three-hour sermons. She believed that God brought to the world four types of people: the elect or chosen of God; the compelled, who had no choice but to be saved; those who are not predestined for salvation but who are capable of being saved; and the damned, who are destined for hell. She had strict rules governing the moral behavior of church members and frowned upon short dresses, neckties, and worldly amusements. In the twenty-two years from the founding of Mount Sinai Holy Church to Robinson's death in 1946, the church grew to include eighty-four affiliate churches, stretching along the east coast from New England to Florida. Robinson ordained 163 ministers, of whom 125 were women. She also established missions in Cuba and Guyana. Ida Bell Robinson died on April 20, 1946, while visiting in Florida.

References: Sherry Sherrod DuPree, ed., *Biographical Dictionary of African-American Holiness-Pentecostals, 1880–1990* (1989); J. Gordon Melton, *Encyclopedia of American Religions*, 4th ed. (1993); Rosemary Radford Ruether and Rosemary Skinner Keller, eds., *Women and Religion in America*, vol. 3 (1986); Dorothy C. Salem, ed., *African American Women: A Biographical Dictionary* (1993).

Rogers, Aurelia Spencer (1834–1922)

Prominent children's worker in the Church of Jesus Christ of Latter-Day Saints, Aurelia Spencer Rogers was born in Deep River, Connecticut, on October 4, 1834. She was the daughter of Catherine (Curtis) Spencer and Orson Spencer, a former Protestant minister. When Aurelia was seven years old, her parents converted to Mormonism and moved with their children to the Mormon community at Nauvoo, Illinois. Catherine Spencer died in the mid-1840s, at about the time that the Mormons were abandoning Nauvoo and journeying to Salt Lake City, Utah. Her husband was on a mission to England when she died, so Aurelia and her older sister Ellen cared for their four younger siblings. They lived for a while in Nebraska before making the difficult journey to the Salt Lake City area. In 1851, three years after her arrival in Utah, Aurelia married Thomas Rogers and settled near Salt Lake City, in Farmington, Utah. Aurelia gave birth to twelve children, seven of whom survived infancy. After the death of one of her children, she came close to losing faith in God. Her faith was restored when she remembered a letter from her father in which he wrote that she should keep her trust in God even when life was difficult. She then prayed to God, asking his forgiveness for doubting him.

In the spring of 1878, Aurelia Rogers had a conversation with Eliza Snow over the problem of rowdy boys in Farmington and other Mormon communities, fearing that they would not become proper husbands for the girls of the community. Snow, who was president of the Relief Society and one of the plural wives of the late Mormon president Brigham Young, agreed that something had to be done to alleviate the problem. She suggested that an organization be established to help train them for manhood. With Snow's support, acting Mormon president John Taylor authorized the new association and appointed Rogers as its first president. In 1878, with the help of her counselors Louisa Haight and Helen M. Miller, she formed the first Primary Association. There were 224 children present at the first Primary Association meeting on August 25, 1878. Organized according to age groups, the children received lessons in the benefits of obedience, faith in God, prayer, and proper etiquette. It was not long before the idea of the Primary Association had spread throughout the church.

By 1893, when she was called to the Primary General Board, Rogers was leading a churchwide program. She had by this time expanded her interests to include the women's rights movement. She was Utah's delegate to the 1893 Woman's Suffrage Convention in Atlanta and to the National Council of Women meeting in Washington, D.C., in 1895.

Rogers died at her home in Farmington, Utah, on August 19, 1922.

See also: Church of Jesus Christ of Latter-Day Saints (Mormons); Snow, Eliza Roxey (Smith)
References: Shirley A. Cazier, "Aurelia Spencer Rogers," in Daniel H. Ludlow, ed., *Encyclopedia of Mormonism*, vol. 3 (1992); J. Gordon Melton, *Religious Leaders of America* (1991); Richard S. Van Wagoner and Steven C. Walker, *A Book of Mormons* (1982).

Rogers, Mary Josephine (1882–1955)

Mary Josephine Rogers, who as Mother Mary Joseph founded the Maryknoll Sisters of St. Dominic, was born October 27, 1882, in Roxbury, near Boston, Massachusetts. She was the fourth of the eight children of Abraham and Mary Josephine (Plummer) Rogers. Young Mary attended public school near her home in Massachusetts before enrolling in Smith College. She received a bachelor's degree from Smith in 1905 and then returned to the college as an assistant in the biology department for two years before becoming a teacher in the Boston public school system from 1908 to 1912. While a student at Smith College, Mary had observed the enthusiasm of Protestant mission study groups on campus and regretted that her own denomination, Roman Catholic, did not have similar organizations. When she returned to Smith in 1906, she was encouraged to form a religious group for Catholics. With the help of the Reverend James Anthony Walsh, director of the Society for the Propagation of the Faith, Mary established a mission study club for Smith's undergraduates. In turn, she assisted Walsh with his work to promote mission activity. While teaching in Boston, Mary volunteered as a worker for the

Catholic Foreign Mission Society of America, better known as the Maryknoll Missionaries, which Walsh had organized the previous year.

Soon Mary was recognized as the leader of the group of women who had volunteered to assist Walsh with his project. As more women joined, they began to feel the need to become a religious community. Beginning in July 1916, they sent several petitions to the Vatican for canonical status as a diocesan religious community of the Third Order of St. Dominic. Mary was able to persuade male Catholic leaders that, contrary to their assumptions, women were capable of becoming foreign missionaries, and in February 1920 the women's requests for official recognition were finally granted. The Maryknoll sisters opened an orphanage and school for Japanese Americans that same year, and in 1921 they began mission work in China.

Mary, known as Mother Mary Joseph since 1920, was elected superior general of the order in 1925. She believed that the worship of God was best expressed through one's service to humankind, and she encouraged members of her community to prepare themselves professionally. In 1932, at the motherhouse in Maryknoll, New York, she founded a college (now named for her) to train the sisters for missionary work. In addition to training them to be useful, she taught potential missionaries to respect the cultures of the people with whom they worked. Under Mother Mary Joseph's guidance, Maryknoll sisters worked to help indigenous women to serve their own communities. The sisters taught, nursed, and engaged in various types of social service. Mother Mary Joseph also established a cloistered branch of her community designed to support the work of the congregation through constant prayer.

Initially the work of the Maryknoll sisters was in Asia, but soon it expanded to other mission areas, including Africa, the Middle East, Micronesia, and parts of Latin America. By the time of Mother Mary Joseph's retirement in 1947, there were more than a thousand missionary sisters in more than eighty missions in almost twenty countries. In addition, more than three hundred women were working with cultural minorities within the United States. Mother Mary Joseph's Foreign Mission Sisters of St. Dominic (after 1954 Maryknoll Sisters of St. Dominic) became the largest congregation of Catholic women devoted to mission work in the United States.

Mother Mary Joseph retired in 1947 and died eight years later on October 9, 1955, in New York City.

See also: Roman Catholic Women's Orders (Nuns)
References: Henry Warner Bowden, *Dictionary of American Religious Biography,* 2nd ed. (1993); Susan Hill Lindley, *"You Have Stept Out of Your Place": A History of Women and Religion in America* (1996); *New Catholic Encyclopedia* (1967); Barbara Sicherman and Carol Hurd Green, eds., *Notable American Women: The Modern Period* (1980).

Roman Catholic Church

Although Roman Catholics have been in America since the early colonial period, it was not until the 1820s that they began to make up a sizable proportion of the country's population. From 1820 to 1850, there was a tremendous growth in the presence of the Roman Catholic Church in America, as Catholic immigrants from Ireland and Germany poured into the United States. As in Protestant culture, Catholics subscribed to the idea that a woman's place was in the home: she should be self-sacrificing, the family's caregiver, pious, and subservient to males. For Catholics in the nineteenth century, it was a sin for a wife to disobey her husband.

Women made up the majority of the membership of the Roman Catholic Church in the nineteenth century. As the century progressed and the issue of female suffrage became increasingly prominent, Catholic leaders were forced to speak out on the matter. The majority of Catholic priests and bishops considered female suffrage to be a rejection of divine law and a threat to the family and society. In addition, it was a reform that was associated with Protestantism. Some of the arguments for votes for women revolved around the idea that immigrant males (who were disproportionately Catholic) were voting, whereas white, Anglo-Saxon, Protestant (WASP) women of the middle class could not. There were several Catholic women among the leadership of antisuffrage campaigns, including two socially prominent Washington, D.C., women, Ellen Ewing Sherman and Madeline Vinton Dahlgren, who in the late nineteenth century founded the first antisuffrage organization. Boston author and Roman Catholic Katherine Conway was a leader of antisuffrage forces early in the twentieth century.

Other Catholic women embraced the suffrage cause. Among them were labor leaders Leonora Barry and Mary K. O'Sullivan, who considered the vote a means of improving working conditions for women. In the twentieth century, Catholic clergy gradually became more sympathetic to the need for female suffrage. After it was won, opponents accepted it but insisted that women maintain traditional feminine values and virtues.

As the twentieth century progressed and Protestant women began to convince church leaders to allow them to fill increasingly higher positions within church hierarchies, some Catholic women too began to push for greater power. Through the 1960s, Catholic seminaries had no women as students or teachers, but the situation began to change as a feminist movement started growing within the Catholic Church. From 1962 to 1964, a series of meetings known as the Second Vatican Council, or Vatican II, were held in Rome. Thousands of bishops from around the world attended the sessions. Out of the meetings came changes and repercussions within the Roman Catholic Church that continue to be felt today. Lay Catholic men and women were not only encouraged to participate in the church but were told that they were valued members with valuable ideas and jobs to do. But the speed of the changes depended largely on the local bishop or parish priest. Some of the more liberal priests, who were anxious to implement changes, met with resistance in their parishes from more conservative laity.

In 1968, Pope Paul VI, in his encyclical *Humanae Vitae,* reaffirmed the church's condemnation of artificial birth control. Despite the pope's position on the matter, more and more American Catholic women were using contraceptives. Also in 1968, Roman Catholic theologian Mary Daly published *The Church and the Second Sex,* in which she argued that the church had long promoted the idea of women being inferior to men and must therefore accept much of the responsibility for the oppression of women in society. Daly's radical feminism led to her eventual break from the Roman Catholic Church and from Christianity. Another prominent feminist theologian is Roman Catholic Rosemary Radford Ruether. Unlike Daly, Ruether has chosen to remain a member of the church while attempting to change the system from within.

Interest in female ordination among some Catholics led to the founding in 1975 of the Women's Ordination Conference. Two years later, the Vatican declared that no ordained ministry can be open to women. In 1979, during a visit to the United States by Pope John Paul II, Sister Theresa Kane, as president of both the Sisters of Mercy and the Leadership Conference of Women Religious, publicly asked the pope to consider dialogue about the question of women's ordination. Although some Catholics were upset with her for making the issue public, others praised her courage and her vision. At that time, more jobs had been opening for women within the church. Some parishes were allowing women to distribute communion and to read during mass. By the 1980s more than one-quarter of students enrolled in Roman Catholic theological schools in the United States were women. At the same time, feminist theology was gaining momentum.

When Geraldine Ferraro, a Roman Catholic, ran for vice president of the United States in 1980, her pro-choice position was attacked by some conservative bishops. Ferraro said that although she personally accepted the church's doctrine on abortion, she did not wish to impose her views upon others. Other Catholics came to her support. Twenty-six nuns, four priests, and sixty-nine Catholic laypeople signed an advertisement in the *New York Times* on her behalf, which acknowledged that among Catholics there was a diversity of opinions regarding abortion. Several months later, the Vatican wrote the nuns' religious orders to say that the nuns who signed the advertisement had to either retract their signatures or leave their convents. Eventually a compromise was worked out. In 1987 the Vatican took an official stand against such current medical practices relating to conception as in vitro fertilization, artificial insemination, and surrogate motherhood.

No generalizations can be made about Catholic women. Women within the church come from a variety of back-grounds and come to the church with many points of view. Although religion and spirituality might be at the center of the lives of some, for others church attendance is only a habit or a weekly social occasion. Some Catholic women are political, but many are not. In her study *The Catholic Woman: Difficult Choices in a Modern World* (1993), Jeanne Pieper finds that moderate feminists make up a very large group within the Roman Catholic Church of today and that their numbers are rising. And for many of these women, there are two churches—the Vatican and the real church. Others continue to consider the institutional church necessary for organizational structure and moral direction, as long as the word coming from the Vatican is not too reactionary. Almost all the moderate feminists believe that there is hope for continued reform in the church. Although some of the small group of radical feminists continue to push for change, others have left the church.

At the opposite end of the spectrum from the radical feminists are fundamentalist Catholic women. Many of these women are in the Women for Faith and the Family (WFF) organization, which was founded in September 1984. The purpose of this group is to combat feminism and to show support for the most conservative teachings of the church. Then there are others among Catholic women, those Pieper describes as traditionalists, who believe in the formal teachings of the Catholic Church and hold fast to as many as they can. Their relationship to the church is spiritual rather than political, and they find their religion to be a source of comfort rather than conflict. Many have long been active in their parishes. Some support the ordination of women, whereas others oppose it, finding the idea discomfiting.

In 1994, in a pastoral message on family life, bishops of the Roman Catholic

Church in the United States said that while marital roles differ according to gender, they should be characterized by mutual submission of a husband and wife to each other. This pronouncement was in line with the thinking of many mainline Protestant denominations.

See also: Daly, Mary; Roman Catholic Women's Orders (Nuns); Ruether, Rosemary Radford
References: James J. Kenneally, *The History of American Catholic Women* (1990); Karen Kennelly, ed., *American Catholic Women: A Historical Exploration* (1989); Susan Hill Lindley, *"You Have Stept Out of Your Place": A History of Women and Religion in America* (1996); Gustav Niebuhr, "Wives Urged to Follow Lead of Husbands," New York Times News Service, *Sarasota-Herald Tribune* (June 10, 1998): 15A; Jeanne Pieper, *The Catholic Woman: Difficult Choices in a Modern World* (1993).

Roman Catholic Women's Orders (Nuns)

Religious orders of women have been present within the Roman Catholic Church for more than fifteen hundred years. In America, however, from the colonial period through the eighteenth century, few young Catholic women joined religious orders. Those who did usually went to Europe to do so. The first order to become established in the United States was the Carmelites, who founded the Carmel Convent in Port Tobacco, Maryland, on October 15, 1790. Most of the early orders opened schools for middle- and upper-class girls. Because nuns have historically had difficulty obtaining funding from the male-dominated church, the operation of schools for people who could afford to pay allowed the sisters to support themselves. Orphanages and free schools for the poor followed, as did the establishment of hospitals and social services, the latter of which came to include aid to blacks and Native Americans. In 1809 Elizabeth

Seton founded the Sisters of Charity, the first indigenous American sisterhood.

The nativist climate in America combined with the influx of Roman Catholic immigrants during the period 1830 to 1860 led to the harassment of Catholic nuns. Sensational exposés, supposedly written by "escaped nuns," accused the sisterhoods of luring innocent girls into convents and holding them against their will. Anti-Catholics sometimes accused nuns of bearing babies fathered by priests and then murdering the infants in hopes of hiding their indiscretions.

After the Civil War, Roman Catholic women's orders, like their Protestant sisters, became active in mission work. The most venturesome, including women like Sister Blandina (Rosa Maria Segale) and Mother Mary Amadeus of the Heart of Jesus (Sarah Theresa Dunne) traveled to the Western frontier to work among the Native Americans. There, along with other activities, they established schools, taught in the classrooms, and helped found hospitals and orphanages.

By the middle of the twentieth century, nuns' teaching credentials began to come into question. In the early 1950s, Pope Pius XII became concerned that the nuns employed in Catholic educational institutions were poorly trained. A result of his fear that an injustice was being done to students who were taught by teachers without the necessary credentials was the establishment of the Sisters Formation Conference in 1954. Soon the conference began a program of college education for nuns *before* they entered the classroom as teachers, and Roman Catholic nuns came to be among the most highly educated women in the world. These newly educated women were also among the first women to embrace the social and philosophical changes of the 1960s, particularly the ideas of feminists. But they met with resistance from other Catholic women who were willing to fight to retain the traditions of convent living and government.

Vatican II, or the Second Vatican Council, a series of meetings of the bishops of the world held in Rome between 1962 and 1964, brought changes and continued repercussions within the Catholic Church. Religious orders of both women and men were asked to examine their constitutions and to update them. Most American nuns were enthusiastic about the changes brought about by Vatican II. In 1964 nuns began modifying their dress and examining old rules that governed their orders. They felt that the religious habit, as their dress was called, inhibited their ability to establish rapport with people in the community. Housing practices changed as well. Convent walls no longer isolate the nuns from visitors, and most female communities no longer have a local mother superior.

Female orders within the Roman Catholic Church experienced dramatic growth from 1950, when there were 147,310 American nuns, to 1965, when the number of nuns reached a height of 179,954. In the years that followed, the population of American nuns declined until by 1990 there were only 103,269 nuns, of which half were sixty-six years old or older. In the 1990s there are about four thousand contemplative nuns in the United States, women who take solemn vows of poverty, celibacy, and obedience, promises lived out primarily through a life of prayer and meditation within the cloister. At the same time, there are approximately 100,000 women, in about five hundred active religious orders, who take simple vows, which they carry out in active ministry in the church. (These women are technically called *sisters,* whereas the first group are considered nuns, though the words are often used interchangeably, as they are in this entry.)

Beginning with the civil rights movement in the 1960s, nuns have partici-

pated in almost every social movement in the United States. Hundreds participated in civil rights marches and sit-ins in the South, and when Mexican-American immigrant grape pickers demonstrated for higher wages, convents throughout the country joined in the boycott of grapes. Nuns also became involved in the peace movement protesting the war in Vietnam. In the 1980s groups of nuns, especially the Sisters of Mercy of the Union, were censored by the Vatican for challenging the pope over the issue of ordination of women and for making other challenges to church structure.

Becoming a nun is no longer the only option available to Catholic women desiring to serve the church in a special way. Women now can become principals and administrators of parochial schools as well as administrators within their local parishes. Also, noncanonical communities of women are forming. These women take vows of celibacy, poverty, and obedience and devote themselves to ministry in the church. Because of their noncanonical role, they are not recognized by the Vatican as religious orders, but neither are they under the surveillance and control of authorities in Rome. Thus they are much more independent than traditional orders as they minister within their local communities.

See also: Cabrini, Frances Xavier; Dickinson, Frances; Drexel, Mary Katharine; Dunne, Sarah Theresa; Matthews, Ann Teresa; National Black Sisters' Conference; Nerinckx, Charles; Oblate Sisters of Providence; Roman Catholic Church; Segale, Rosa Maria; Seton, Elizabeth Ann Bayley; Sisters of Loretto at the Foot of the Cross; Tekakwitha, Kateri

References: Helen Rose Fuchs Ebaugh, *Women in the Vanishing Cloister: Organizational Decline in Catholic Religious Orders in the United States* (1993); James J. Kenneally, *The History of American Catholic Women* (1990); Karen Kennelly, ed., *American Catholic Women: A Historical Exploration* (1989); Susan Hill Lindley, *"You Have Stept Out of Your Place": A History of Women and Religion in America* (1996);

Jo Ann Kay McNamara, *Sisters in Arms: Catholic Nuns through Two Millennia* (1996); Jeanne Pieper, *The Catholic Woman: Difficult Choices in the Modern World* (1993).

Rose, Ernestine Louise Sismondi Potowski (1810–1892)

Best known for her outstanding oratory in her campaigns for women's rights and the abolition of slavery, Ernestine Louise Sismondi Potowski Rose also received recognition within the Jewish community for a vigorous defense of Jews and Judaism in the 1860s. Born in Poland in 1810, Rose was the daughter of a rabbi. More interested in books than in learning household tasks, Ernestine convinced her father to hire a private tutor. When she was sixteen, she refused to marry the man her father had chosen. Then she sued her father for her inheritance and won. Shortly thereafter she left Poland and traveled through Europe. Ernestine also gave up Judaism, becoming an atheist. In England, she became a disciple of Utopian socialist Robert Owen and married fellow Owenite William Rose.

The Roses emigrated to the United States in 1836. Ernestine was dismayed to find that women there had no more rights than they did in Europe, but she observed that women were not the only group deprived of rights. Black slaves were suffering too. Soon she became a public orator for the abolitionist cause as well as for women's rights. In a time when few women dared to speak in public, crowds gathered to see and hear her, and Rose became known as the Queen of the Platform.

It is unlikely that the atheistic and outspoken Ernestine Rose would have been looked upon favorably by many Jews in the mid-nineteenth century. As historians have shown, few American Jews (most of them recent immigrants) appear to have been abolitionists or crusaders for women's rights. For the most part, they were concerned with establishing themselves in a new country. Rose displayed little interest in Jews, except as fellow human beings. But she won a place in American Jewish history when, in 1863–1864, she zealously defended Jews against an anti-Semitic attack in the Boston *Investigator*. The author of the article and editor of the paper, Horace Seaver, was a former friend who was apparently unaware of Rose's Jewish origins. When he charged that Judaism was inferior to Christianity and that Jews were inherently corrupt, Rose fired back. Unattached to any theology, she argued that Judaism was no worse than any other religion. Likewise, she contended that Jews were governed by the same laws as other human beings and that all in all, Jews were as good as any other religious group. Seaver replied with further anti-Semitic attacks, and again Rose responded. The debate in the paper lasted three months and, as Rabbi Sally Priesand points out, at the very least it allowed the *Investigator*'s readers to gain a basic knowledge of Jews and of Jewish history.

Throughout the balance of her life, Rose continued to battle for women's rights and for other reforms, both in the United States and in England. She died in Brighton, England, on August 4, 1892.

See also: Jews; Woman Suffrage
References: Charlotte Baum, Paula Hyman, and Sonya Michel, *The Jewish Woman in America* (1976); Elizabeth Frost-Knappman, *Women's Progress in America* (1994); Jacob R. Marcus, *The American Jewish Woman: A Documentary History* (1981); Jacob R. Marcus, *The American Jewish Woman, 1654–1980* (1981); Sally Priesand, *Judaism and the New Woman* (1975).

Ruether, Rosemary Radford (1936–)

Feminist theologian and pioneer in the ecofeminist movement, Rosemary Radford Ruether was born in St. Paul, Minnesota, November 2, 1936, and is the daughter of Robert Armstrong and Rebecca Cresap (Ord) Radford. She is a member of the Roman Catholic Church. Her educational background includes Scripps College, where she completed a bachelor of arts degree in philosophy and religion in 1958, and Claremont Graduate School, where she received a master of arts degree in ancient history in 1960 and a doctorate in classics and patristics in 1965. While a junior at Scripps College, she married Herman J. Ruether, who at the time was a graduate student in political science. Following graduation from Claremont, Ruether accepted an appointment as assistant professor at Howard University in Washington, D.C., a position she held from 1966 to 1974, until she was promoted to associate professor of historical theology at that university. She remained at Howard University until 1976, at which time she became Georgia Harkness Professor of Theology at Garrett-Evangelical Theological Seminary in Evanston, Illinois. Ruether has also lectured at various universities, including Harvard (1972 to 1973) and Yale (1973 to 1974).

When she was in her mid-twenties, Ruether became a social activist. She was in the hospital following the birth of her third child when she decided that despite the Catholic Church's opposition to birth control, she would have no more children. Moved by a Hispanic Catholic woman next to her, who was about to give birth to her ninth child and who was pleading with the doctors to prevent any more from coming, Ruether became an activist for birth control. Following her hospital stay, she published several articles regarding birth control and the Catholic Church. Since then, Ruether has devoted her life to eliminating social injustices by creating dialogue between opposing forces.

Ruether has combined her social activism with religious scholarship and has written numerous articles and books. Much of her work has focused on Western religions and feminist theology, and she has been an important contributor to ecofeminist thought. Her *New Woman/New Earth* (1975) is considered a classic. It was the first ecofeminist book, written before the concept had a name. Ruether has examined and analyzed the organization and structure of Christianity and Judaism and argues that male domination has become deeply imbedded within both religions, as have biases against women. In the case of Christianity, which she believes is more systematic than Jewish thought, Ruether theorizes that Christians inherited a hierarchical and dualistic mentality from the classical world. The dualistic mentality separates God and the world, spirit and nature. In this sense, God and spirit are considered "positive," or superior, and the world and nature "negative," or inferior. Humans are viewed as in between God and the world and as instruments designed to subdue the natural, such as desires of the flesh. Women, who traditionally have been considered closer to nature than men, are perceived as inferior and something to be subdued. Ruether's critique has become a part of ecofeminism.

Although Ruether has long fought against the oppression of women in traditional religions, she criticizes feminists who have constructed religions around Goddess worship, the cult of the Great Mother, or witchcraft. Looking back into history, she points out that the Great Mother grew out of a patriarchal culture that had no thought of liberating women or freeing slaves. Ruether reproaches other radical groups for reversing domination by assigning goodness to females and evil to males.

Throughout her books and articles, Ruether challenges her readers to think for themselves and then perhaps revise their ways of interpreting and understanding religion. Her scholarship and writing, along with her work for a number of boards and organizations that promote peace and human rights, have earned her the respect of her peers. She has received many awards, including honorary doctorates, a Fulbright scholarship to the Universities of Lund and Uppsala in Sweden, and U.S. Catholic of the Year for 1983, given by *U.S. Catholic Magazine.*

See also: Birth Control; Ecofeminism; Feminist Theology; Roman Catholic Church
References: Carol J. Adams, ed., *Ecofeminism and the Sacred* (1993); Anne E. Carr, *Transforming Grace: Christian Tradition and Women's Experience* (1988); Carol P. Christ and Judith Plaskow, eds., *Womanspirit Rising: A Feminist Reader in Religion* (1979); Su A. Cutler, "Rosemary Radford Ruether," in Frank Magill, ed., *Great Lives from History: American Women Series* (1995); June Steffensen Hagen, ed., *Gender Matters: Women's Studies for the Christian Community* (1990); Rosemary Radford Ruether, *Gaia and God: An Ecofeminist Theology of Earth Healing* (1992); Ruether, *Sexism and God-Talk: Toward a Feminist Theology* (1983); Susan M. Trotsky, ed., *Contemporary Authors,* vol. 39 (1992).

Salem Witch Trials

In 1692, jealousies, superstitions, and social, religious, and economic conflicts combined to lead to a hysteria that resulted in the deaths of fourteen women and six men on charges of witchcraft. The episode, which took place in Salem Village (now Danvers, Massachusetts), is an extreme example of the breakdown of the Puritan dream of creating a perfect society in the New World.

The incident began in late 1691, when several Salem Village adolescent girls encouraged a West Indian slave woman, Tituba, to tell their fortunes. When soon after the girls began acting strangely, villagers assumed the girls were "possessed" victims of witchcraft and began questioning them. When pressed to identify their tormentors, the girls named Tituba and two local white women whom the community considered outcasts.

Up to this point, the episode was not unusual. Like most Europeans, seventeenth-century New Englanders held strong beliefs in witchcraft. They accepted the idea that witches were usually women who out of discontent or greed had been coerced into signing a pact with the devil and would thereafter use Satan's evil powers to inflict misery upon others. The crime of witchcraft lay in the initial compact by which the person allowed the devil to use his or her form to perform mischief. There was usually only one defendant in trials for witchcraft. Most of the accused witches in seven-teenth-century New England were women whose circumstances allowed them an unusual amount of independence, such as widows who were left with more than the usual third of a husband's property. Fear of being charged with being in connivance with Satan prevented many a woman with means from venturing beyond the limits that society placed upon women.

Not satisfied with the three named "witches," the adults in Salem Village continued to urge the girls to name more. The village minister, Samuel Parris, opened the door for further accusations when, in his March 27, 1692, sermon, he announced that there were devils within the church. By April 1692 the girls had denounced two prominent, respected, churchgoing women and the village's former minister. With Parris's blessing, accusations multiplied until the jails overflowed with innocent citizens. When the cases went to court, judges ignored the law that banned "spectral evidence"—evidence based on testimony that a spirit resembling the defendant had been seen tormenting the victims. Altogether, 141 people were indicted on charges of witchcraft. Fifty saved themselves from the gallows by confessing. Many of those found guilty clamored to save themselves by implicating others. Twenty who refused to disgrace their names by offering false confessions or by charging the guiltless were put to death.

Although no single cause seems to have triggered the events in Salem Village, the trials reflected tensions within the whole of New England society. The late seventeenth century found New Englanders in the process of change from a relatively closed religious society to one that reached out to embrace the commercial opportunities that were offered through a linkup with the marketplace of the world. Historians' analysis of the situation in Salem Village at the end of the century finds connections between the witch hunt and the evolving world in which the villagers lived. Those who were accused of witchcraft were mostly members of families who were becoming prosperous and who lived closer to the commercial center of Salem Village, whereas their accusers held less wealth and lived nearer the hinterland. Religion also played a role in the trials. The majority of the "witches" were from families who had been dissatisfied with Reverend Samuel Parris and wished to see him replaced. Others were Quakers or Baptists or were friendly with members of these or other faiths, considered heretical among traditional Puritans.

Age and gender also influenced who was among the "possessed" and who became a victim of false accusations. Two-thirds of the accusers were girls aged eleven to twenty, most of whom had lost one or both parents and were forced to support themselves as servants. They most frequently named as witches women of middle age—wives and widows—who had avoided the poverty and uncertain futures that the girls faced.

By the end of 1692, most clergymen in Massachusetts Bay Colony were expressing doubt that justice was being served in Salem Village. Uncomfortable about allegations based upon "spectral evidence," they backed Governor William Phip's decision in October 1692 (following an accusation against his own wife) that forbade further imprisonment for witchcraft. Early in 1693, he pardoned all those who were convicted or suspected of being witches.

After the witch hunt hysteria died down in Salem Village, those on the side of the prosecution, including Samuel Parris, admitted they had made grievous mistakes. Such admissions were unprecedented in a time when the community readily accepted the convictions of persons charged with witchcraft. Only after Parris resigned his post as village minister in 1696 did wounds in Salem Village begin to heal.

See also: Calvinism; Hutchinson, Anne Marbury; Puritans; Witchcraft
References: Paul Boyer and Stephen Nissenbaum, *Salem Possessed: The Social Origins of Witchcraft* (1976); John Putnam Demos, *Entertaining Satan: Witchcraft and the Culture of Early New England* (1982); James J. Lorence, *Enduring Voices,* 2nd ed. (1993).

Salvation Army

The Salvation Army was one of few religious groups of the nineteenth century to offer women opportunities to hold prominent positions in the organization's hierarchy. This nonsectarian group that ministered to all regardless of race, creed, or social status was founded in London, England, by William Booth and his wife, Catherine, in 1865. It arrived in the United States in 1880. General William Booth decided to expand to America after he learned of the success of a new mission in Philadelphia that was modeled after his organization.

On Sunday, October 5, 1879, seventeen-year-old Eliza Shirley, a recent immigrant to the United States and one who had experienced the sensation of finding fulfillment in Christ while at a Salvation Army meeting in England in 1878, had opened a mission designed to serve the poor of Philadelphia. Assisting her were her parents, Annie and Amos Shirley. The two Shirley women, who at the first meeting led a congregation of

The Salvation Army was one of the first religious organizations to offer women opportunities to hold prominent positions (wood engraving from Harper's Weekly, *1880).*

only twelve, were later in the day pelted with mud, sticks, stones, rotten eggs, vegetables, and garbage. But they were not deterred and, within a month after the initial meeting, had gained a following that included one convert. By the end of the year, the family had established a second corps in the city, with Eliza heading one corps and her parents the other.

The Shirleys' successes caused William Booth to send an official group of Salvation Army pioneers to New York in March 1880. The only male in the group, George Scott Railton, led seven women down the gangplank of their ship *Australia,* which had docked at New York's harbor. They sang hymns as they marched from the ship and, upon reaching shore, gathered in a circle for prayer. Soon after their arrival, the group opened a mission in a former brothel in the slums at Five Points. However, they

soon found that city authorities would not allow the army to hold open-air meetings, which stymied their activities in New York. Consequently, Railton left for Philadelphia, placing two women, Captain Emma Westbrook and Lieutenant Alice Coleman, in charge of carrying on the work in New York.

Despite frequent attacks by mobs throwing stones, rotten eggs, and other garbage, the Salvation Army's presence was soon felt in the northeastern United States, and by the 1890s the organization was holding meetings throughout the country. The top post of commander of the army in the United States passed through the hands of several men during the 1880s, and Captain Annie Shirley became the first female divisional officer of the Salvation Army in America when she was appointed to lead the Massachusetts and Maine divisions. She and her sister,

Mary Hartelius, were the first Salvation Army missionaries to leave America when they began conducting army meetings in Sweden in 1883. In 1887 they opened the first official American Scandinavian corps in New York City.

In addition to appointing women to responsible roles within the organization's hierarchy, the Salvation Army actively sought female converts. After General Booth's son Ballington took command in the United States in 1887, his wife, Maud, made work with "fallen women" one of her principal concerns. The Salvation Army offered young women training in domestic activities, including sewing and cooking, and found those women they considered "reformed" positions as domestic helpers or maids in Christian homes. The army made constant efforts to convert the women to Christianity because they believed that the women would not otherwise become truly reformed.

In January 1896 the Ballington Booths broke with the general and relinquished their command. Replacing them as temporary commander was Ballington's sister Evangeline Cory Booth, age thirty-one. In the spring of 1896 her sister Emma Booth-Tucker and brother-in-law Frederick St. George de Lautour Booth-Tucker began command. After Emma's death in 1903, Frederick returned to England, and Evangeline replaced him in 1904. Until that time, Evangeline had been serving in Canada and was used as a troubleshooter, to be sent wherever a critical battle was in progress.

In keeping with Salvation Army tradition of supporting the right of women to preach and to hold positions of leadership, in 1934, after thirty years as leader of the army in the United States, Evangeline Booth was elected to the generalship of the International Salvation Army. However, as the twentieth century progressed, the percentage of women in leadership positions within the Salvation Army declined. This occurred during a time when mainline denominations were opening more opportunities for women. Nevertheless, throughout its history the Salvation Army has received credit for its support of women as preachers and leaders within its organizational hierarchy.

See also: Booth, Evangeline Cory; Booth, Maud Elizabeth Ballington
References: Sigmund A. Lavine, *Evangeline Booth, Daughter of Salvation* (1970); Norman H. Murdock, *Origins of the Salvation Army* (1994); Philip Whitwell Wilson, *General Evangeline Booth of the Salvation Army* (1948); Herbert A. Wisbey, Jr., *Soldiers without Swords: A History of the Salvation Army in the United States* (1955).

Sampson, Deborah (1760–1827)

The experiences of Revolutionary War heroine Deborah Sampson provide an example of the strictness of Christian religious denominations regarding the issue of gender roles. Born December 17, 1760, in Plympton, Massachusetts, Sampson became a member of the First Baptist Church of Middleborough, Massachusetts, in November 1780. After walking to Boston and then on to Bellingham, Massachusetts, on May 20, 1782, she disguised herself as a man and enlisted in the Continental army as Robert Shurtleff (the first and middle names of a brother who died the year she was born). Sampson fought in several skirmishes and was wounded in one near Tarrytown, New York, all the while managing to conceal her identity. It was not until she became ill and was hospitalized with a fever in Philadelphia that her sex was discovered. Sampson was discharged at West Point on October 25, 1783.

Meanwhile, on September 3, 1782, the First Baptist Church of Middleborough excommunicated Sampson. The excommunication was based on strong suspicions that she had been "dressing in men's clothes, and enlisting as a Soldier in the Army," along with unspecified behavior that the church considered "loose and unchristianlike" (James, 1971, p. 227). By the time of her dismissal from the First Baptist Church, however, the adventurous Sampson was far from Middleborough, fighting a war and doing her best to prove that women could hold their own in battle.

Sampson married Benjamin Gannett in 1785 and had three children. In the last decade of the eighteenth century, reports of her military adventures began to attract public attention. In 1797 Herman Mann, to whom she had told her story, wrote and published a romanticized biography, entitled *The Female Review*. In 1802 Sampson herself began to present public lectures on her experiences in the military. She died on April 29, 1827, in Sharon, Massachusetts.

See also: Woman's Sphere
References: Elizabeth Frost-Knappman, *Women's Progress in America* (1994); Kendall Haven, *Amazing American Women* (1995); Edward T. James, ed., *Notable American Women: 1607–1950*, vol. 3 (1971).

Sanapia (1895–1979?)

Sanapia, who was also known by her Christian name, Mary Poafpybitty, and as Memory Woman and Sticky Mother, was a Comanche medicine woman and one of the most powerful Native American women on the Great Plains. She was born into the Yapai band of the Comanche tribe near Ft. Sill, Oklahoma, on May 20, 1895. Her father, Poafpybitty, was a convert to Christianity and was devoted to his adopted religion, whereas her mother, Chapty, was equally devout in her traditional Comanche-Arapaho faith. Sanapia chose her mother's religion over that of her father.

In accordance with tribal tradition, Sanapia was raised by her maternal grandparents, especially her grandmother, who taught her the ways of Comanche life. Her grandmother stressed the importance of learning tribal customs and urged Sanapia to follow in the footsteps of her mother and become an eagle doctor. Also, a maternal uncle who treated her for influenza when she was a young girl extracted a promise from Sanapia that she would become an eagle doctor if she recovered. He gave her the name Memory Woman so that she would not forget her vow.

When she was seven, Sanapia began her formal education at the Cache Creek Mission School, a boarding school. Her training as an eagle doctor began when she was thirteen, during the summer break. Sanapia spent one more year at the mission before returning home to begin three more years of instruction from her mother and her maternal relatives. In those years, she acquired all the skills and knowledge she would need as an eagle doctor. Included in her training was Comanche "doctoring," which combined earthly herbal medicines with spiritual medicines. When Sanapia was seventeen, Chapty transferred her healing power to her daughter in a formal ceremony. Sanapia's knowledge of the eagle power elevated her to a status within Comanche society that was equivalent to that of a man. But though she had the power, Sanapia was not allowed to practice as an eagle doctor until she had reached menopause.

During her lifetime, Sanapia married three times. Her first marriage occurred when she was seventeen and ended shortly after her first son was born. She remarried within a year and had two more children before her second husband died during the 1930s. Emotionally devastated by the loss of her spouse, she dealt with her grief by living a fast life. She drank and gambled excessively and engaged in promiscuous sexual behavior. After several years of hard living, Sanapia's life changed again when her sister asked her to cure her sick child. Her success in this healing led Sanapia to pursue her calling. She remarried and continued her practice. Sanapia's medicine included the treatment of "ghost sickness," an illness that was believed to have been caused by a person's contact with ghosts. She believed that the whirlwinds, or "dust devils," of the Great Plains were the only form that ghosts took in daylight hours. Although she never saw a ghost at night, she thought that its form was probably like that of a human. Sanapia regretted missing the experience but believed that ghosts feared her and avoided her because of her powers. In addition to herbal medicines, her healing methods included elements of psychiatry, the use of peyote, and songs and prayers to call upon the spirits and the medicine eagle for help.

When she reached old age in the 1960s, Sanapia was the only surviving eagle doctor. Afraid that she would not live long enough to find and train a person worthy of and agreeable to accepting the responsibilities of an eagle doctor, Sanapia turned to anthropologist David E. Jones of the University of Oklahoma to record her life and preserve her medicinal ways. Jones's *Sanapia: Comanche Medicine Woman* was published in 1972. It is not known if she ever found a worthy successor to instruct in the ways of an eagle doctor. Conflicting dates are given for her death, ranging from 1968 to 1984. A photograph reveals her to be alive in 1969. The only specific date given for her death is January 23, 1979, in Oklahoma.

See also: Native Americans
References: Gretchen M. Bataille, *Native American Women: A Biographical Dictionary* (1993); Arlene Hirschfelder and Paulette Molin, *The Encyclopedia of Native American Religions* (1992); David E. Jones, *Sanapia: Comanche Medicine Woman* (1972); Sharon Malinowski, ed., *Notable Native Americans* (1995); J. Gordon Melton, *Religious Leaders of America* (1991).

Sasaki, Ruth Fuller Everett (1893–1967)

A major popularizer of Buddhism in America, Ruth Fuller Everett Sasaki was born Ruth Fuller in 1893. She was raised in a strict Presbyterian family but converted to Buddhism when she was in her twenties. During the early years of her marriage to Charles Everett, a prominent Chicago attorney, she spent some time at the yoga ashram in Nyack, New York. It may have been at this ashram that she first learned about Zen. She also studied both the Sanskrit and Pali languages on her own. The Everetts were in Japan in 1930 as part of a world tour. There they met Daisetz Teitaro Suzuki, who taught Ruth the basics of meditation and gave her a copy of his second series of *Essays*. Two years later, she returned to Japan, where she studied and practiced under Nanshinken-roshi, a Rinzai Zen master, for three and a half months. She was among the first Americans to travel to Japan for Zen instruction.

After moving to New York in 1938, Ruth Everett became acquainted with Shigetsu Sasaki-roshi's Buddhist Society of America (later the First Zen Institute of America) and began editing *Cat's Yawn*, the society's journal. She also gave instruction in zazen, which she has described as the preliminary practice in Rinzai Zen "by which mind and body are forged into a single instrument for realization" (Sasaki, 1959). The outlook for the institute and for its founder appeared promising in November 1941, when the First Zen Institute of America soon moved into newer and finer quarters provided by Ruth Everett. Her husband had died in 1940, and by the fall of 1941, she and Sasaki-roshi (who was also known as Sokei-an) were seeing each other socially. The Japanese attack on Pearl Harbor in December 1941 led to the group coming under government observation, and both Everett and Sokei-an underwent extensive questioning by the Federal Bureau of Investigation (FBI). On July 15, 1942, Sokei-an was removed to an internment camp. Everett took steps to secure his release. He was eventually released, and the couple married in 1944. But Sokei-an's incarceration had aggravated his already poor health, and he died in May of the following year.

Prior to his death, Sokei-an had placed the responsibility of finding a successor for the institute in his wife's hands, as well as the task of completing his translation of the recorded sayings of Rinzai, a Chinese master of Zen Buddhism. Since the latter task could only be accomplished by one who had completed a formal study of Zen, Sasaki realized that if she were to comply with the latter request, she would have to move to Japan and live there for the remainder of her life. Upon her move to Japan in 1949, she pursued studies in the Japanese language and in classical Chinese. She also practiced zazen meditation under a Rinzai master. To aid other Americans wishing to study Zen in Japan, in 1956 she established the First Zen Institute of America in Japan. That same year she turned down an opportunity to become a Zen missionary in the United States because she felt that her proper role was that of translator, not proselytizer.

Sasaki renovated a deserted temple on the grounds of Daitoku-ji, Kyoto, that had fallen into disrepair and in 1958 was appointed its priest and abbess. She published several works on Zen, including *Zen: A Method for Religious Awakening* (1959), a short introductory text based on a lecture she delivered at Massachusetts Institute of Technology in 1958, and *The Zen Koan* (1965), which was recognized as the first scholarly examination of the Koan practice. The book includes a history of Koan by Sasaki and her translation of Isshu Miura's Koan study of Rinzai Zen. Sasaki died in Kyoto, Japan, in 1967.

See also: Buddhists
References: Rick Fields, *How the Swans Came to the Lake: A Narrative History of Buddhism in America* (1992); J. Gordon Melton, *Religious Leaders of America* (1991); Isshu Miura and Ruth Fuller Sasaki, *The Koan Zen* (1965); Ruth Fuller Sasaki, *Zen: A Method for Religious Awakening* (1959).

Sasso, Sandy Eisenberg (1947–)

Sandy Eisenberg Sasso, who was to become the first female rabbi in the Reconstructionist branch of Judaism, was born in Philadelphia, Pennsylvania, on January 29, 1947, to Irving and Freeda Eisenberg. Her parents were not particularly religious, but they were proud of their Jewish heritage. As junior high school approached, Sandy's parents enrolled her in a religious school run by the Conservative branch of Judaism, and then they switched her to a Reform religious school. Of the three major branches of Judaism in America, Reform is the most liberal.

As time passed, Sandy spent an increasing amount of time at the synagogue Keneseth Israel, where both boys and girls were urged to participate in the many recreational and educational activities. Sandy was inspired to become confirmed and began to study for a Bat Mitzvah by learning Hebrew and other aspects of Judaism. She became so excited by her studies that she enrolled in the synagogue high school.

In the tenth grade, Sandy won an essay contest at the synagogue. The prize was a three-month-long summer stay in Israel. Upon returning from Israel, she told her rabbi that she wished to enter his profession. Her rabbi was enthusiastic and guided her as she worked with younger children at the synagogue as a teacher and a leader of their services. Occasionally she was asked to repeat her sermons before the entire congregation.

After completing high school, Sandy attended Temple University. While at

Temple, she began to have doubts about becoming a rabbi, since at that time there were no women rabbis. She thought of becoming a writer but soon lost confidence in her writing talents and again focused on religious study. Near the end of her senior year, Rabbi Korn asked Sandy to prepare a special Sabbath service for the synagogue. She was to do the planning, writing, and staging of the service. After weeks of preparation, she gave the service on June 6, 1969. The congregation was impressed. Now Sandy decided to at least try to become a rabbi.

Sandy entered the new Reconstructionist rabbinical college in Philadelphia as the only woman among twenty male seminary students. While at the seminary, she met and married her husband, Dennis Sasso. Upon graduation in 1974, she became the first woman Reconstructionist rabbi in history, and she and Dennis became the first rabbinical couple. Both went job hunting in New York. Dennis was hired almost immediately by the Reconstructionist Synagogue of the North Shore in Great Neck, New York. But soon, Sandy too was hired, becoming a part-time rabbi for a small congregation, the Manhattan Reconstructionist Havurah.

Since her ordination in 1974, Sandy has frequently been invited to lecture in communities outside her congregation. Often when Rabbi Sandy Sasso was asked to speak before other Jewish audiences, she used the opportunity to call for an uplifting of the status of women in Judaism. Although she met with some resistance, most people were pleased with her efforts on behalf of women. Her congregation gave its approval when she and Dennis endeavored to establish a new tradition for female babies that would welcome them into the Jewish community, something similar to the *bris*, the rite of circumcision for baby boys. Sandy introduced the idea of a "covenantal cer-

emony" to be held in the home of the baby girl and her parents on the Sabbath. Much the same as during a *bris*, the rabbi blesses the baby girl, she is given her English and her Hebrew name, and she is welcomed into the covenant. In 1976, Sandy gave birth to a boy, becoming the first rabbi in history to give birth.

In the fall of 1977, a long-sought goal of working with her husband was finally achieved. Both Sandy and Dennis became rabbis for Beth-El Zedeck, a 950-family synagogue in Indianapolis, Indiana. Since her move to Indiana, Sandy has returned to writing. She published *Call Them Builders: A Resource Booklet about Jewish Attitudes and Practices on Birth and Family Life* in 1977 and, with Sue Levi Elwell, wrote *Jewish Women* (1983, rev. ed. 1986). These books were written for adults, but in the 1990s, she has addressed children's curiosity about religious matters in books directed at children: *God's Paintbrush* (1992), *In God's Name* (1994), and *But God Remembered: Stories of Women from Creation to the Promised Land* (1995).

See also: Clergy; Eilberg, Amy; Jews; Priesand, Sally Jane
References: Kathleen J. Edgar, Terrie M. Rooney, and Jennifer Gariepy, eds., *Contemporary Authors*, vol. 151 (1996); Susan Weidner Schneider, *Jewish and Female: Choices and Changes in Our Lives Today* (1985); Betsy Covington Smith, *Breakthrough: Women in Religion* (1978).

Schechter, Mathilde Roth (1859–1924)

Mathilde Roth Schechter, a dedicated proponent of women's rights and founder of the Women's League for Conservative Judaism, was born in Breslau, Germany, on December 16, 1859. Her parents died when she was a young child, and she received much of her education at Breslau's Jewish Orphan House. She excelled in her studies and was sent to a school for advanced students where she was encouraged to enroll in a teachers' seminary.

Mathilde's teaching career began in Hungary, but she moved to London in 1885, where she took further study in English literature. While there she tutored Lucy Friedlander, the daughter of Michael Friedlander, the principal of Jews' College and a sponsor and friend of Jewish writers and intellectuals of the late nineteenth century. One day while she was in the Jews' College Library, Mathilde met Solomon Schechter, a young rabbinical scholar, whom she married in June 1887. The Schechters moved to Cambridge in 1890 when Solomon joined the faculty there. Caring for her husband, her home, and her growing family (the Schechters eventually had three children) became the focus of Mathilde's life.

In 1902 the family moved to New York City, where Solomon became a faculty member at the Jewish Theological Seminary of America. Mathilde returned to teaching when she founded the Columbia Religious and Industrial School for Jewish Girls. An advocate of Zionism, she worked closely with Henrietta Szold in the founding of Hadassah (1912). At the same time, her home had become a gathering place for leaders of the Jewish community.

Solomon, recognizing that laypeople needed to play an essential part in the Conservative movement in order for this fledgling branch of American Judaism to flourish, was a founder of the Conference of the United Synagogue of America in 1913. He died two years later, but his wife strove to fulfill his vision of women's active participation in the movement. Gathering a group of faculty wives and leading women from representative Jewish communities, Mathilde Schechter established the Women's League for Conservative Judaism in 1918. Schechter was the organization's first president, and she developed the league's agenda. The initial purpose of the league was to perpetuate traditional Judaism in America through the home, synagogue, and community, and Schechter laid the foundation for the organization's broad education and publishing programs.

Schechter directed the establishment of the first Student House at Columbia University in New York, a cultural center that served kosher meals to Jewish students. During World War I, she invited the Student Army Training Corps to the center for lectures and refreshments. Despite a severe illness, Schechter continued her involvement with the league until her death in August 1924. Since its founding, the league has grown to a membership of 150,000, with affiliated sisterhoods in Conservative synagogues in the United States, Canada, Puerto Rico, Mexico, Israel, and other parts of the world.

See also: Hadassah; Jews; Szold, Henrietta; Women's League for Conservative Judaism References: Shuly Rubin Schwartz, "Women's League for Conservative Judaism," in Paula Hyman and Deborah Dash Moore, eds., *Jewish Women in America* (1997); Women's League for Conservative Judaism, "Mathilde Schechter: Founder of Women's League for Conservative Judaism" (n.d., c. 1997); Women's League for Conservative Judaism, "Women's League for Conservative Judaism: What it is . . . What it does!" (n.d., c. 1997).

Schlafly, Phyllis Stewart (1924–)

Phyllis Stewart Schlafly, author, speaker, and a leader in the crusade against the ratification of the Equal Rights Amendment and other conservative causes, was born in St. Louis, Missouri, on August 15, 1924. She was the daughter of Odile Dodge Stewart and John B. Stewart. With the exception of the third grade, when she attended a Catholic school, Schlafly's education until grade seven was in public schools. She received the balance of her elementary and her high school education at City House, a prestigious Catholic school known for its rigid and rigorous curriculum. Schlafly was class valedictorian at her graduation in June 1941. She earned a bachelor's degree from Washington University in 1944 while working nights at an arms factory to pay her tuition and living expenses and to save money for graduate school. In June 1945, she graduated from Radcliffe College with a master of arts degree in government. Later, when Schlafly was age fifty-four, she received a law degree from Washington University. Until her marriage to John Fred Schlafly, Jr., on October 20, 1949, she worked as a researcher in Washington, D.C.; managed a successful campaign for a Republican congressional candidate; and edited a newsletter for a financial institution. After marrying Schlafly, a wealthy attorney, she left the workforce to become a homemaker.

Schlafly, who has since raised six children, has asserted that caring for one's family is the most important career for a woman. But Schlafly managed to remain involved in community causes and in Republican politics while fulfilling her homemaker role. In 1952 and again in 1970, she made unsuccessful attempts to win a seat in Congress and served as a delegate or alternate to Republican conventions in 1956, 1960, and 1964. She earned a national reputation during the 1960s when she spoke out and wrote books and articles on behalf of conservative causes. Between 1964 and 1978 she collaborated on five books with Rear Admiral Chester Ward, including *Kissinger on the Couch* and *Ambush at Vladivostok,* and wrote her own *The Power of the Positive Woman.*

When Congress passed the Equal Rights Amendment (ERA) in 1972, Schlafly launched a Stop ERA crusade. Within six years, she had established branches of the organization in forty-five states. As a device to counter the women's liberation movement, Schlafly also founded the Eagle Forum (1975). She succeeded in gaining a following with claims that the amendment would weaken the family, cause homemakers to lose their right to the financial support of their husbands, lead to abortion and lesbianism, subject young women to the draft, and cause men and women to be forced to share public toilets. A devout Catholic, Schlafly claimed further that the ERA would likely force parochial schools to dissolve single-sex schools and require the Catholic Church to ordain women. Her position on this issue drew support from conservative Catholics, fundamentalists, and Orthodox Jews. During the course of the ERA debate, Schlafly requested that leaders of the Eagle Forum pray for the amendment's defeat.

Following the failure of the ERA, Schlafly turned her attention to the campaign against legalized abortion. As president of the Eagle Forum, she has been dedicated to overturning *Roe v. Wade.* She has also crusaded in recent years against pornography, homosexuality, and sex and violence on television.

See also: Abortion; Woman Suffrage
References: Kathryn Cullen-DuPont, with Annelise Orleck, *The Encyclopedia of Women's History in America* (1996); Flora Davis, *Moving the Mountain: The Women's Movement in America since 1960* (1991); Carol Felsenthal, *The Sweetheart of the Silent Majority: The Biography of Phyllis Schlafly* (1981); Glen Jeansonne, "Phyllis MacAlpin (Stewart) Schlafly," in Angela Howard Zophy, ed., with Frances M. Kavenik, *Handbook of American Women's History* (1990); James J. Kenneally, *The History of American Catholic Women* (1990); Karen Kennelly, ed., *American Catholic Women: A Historical Exploration* (1989); Phyllis Schlafly, *The Power of the Positive Woman* (1977).

Scudder, Vida Dutton (1861–1954)

Writer, reformer, professor, and Christian Socialist Vida Dutton Scudder was born

Julia Davida in Madura, India, on December 15, 1861. She was the only child of David Colt Scudder, a Congregationalist missionary, and Harriet Louisa (Dutton) Scudder. David Scudder accidentally drowned less than a year after his daughter's birth, and Harriet returned with their child to the Dutton homestead in Auburndale, Massachusetts. Vida attended private schools in Boston, but much of her youth was spent traveling in Europe with her mother and aunt. During this time, she formed a devotion to beauty and an appreciation of the human past that influenced the way she conducted her life thereafter. When Vida was a teenager, she and her mother were confirmed in the Episcopal Church.

In 1878 Vida enrolled in the first class of the Boston Girls' Latin School, graduating in 1880. She then attended Smith College, where she received a bachelor of arts degree in 1884. During the academic year 1884–1885, she engaged in graduate work at Oxford University as one of the first American women to be admitted to the program. While at Oxford she attended the last lectures of English art critic, writer, and social reformer John Ruskin. Ruskin's talks brought her to realize what a privileged life she had led and made her think about those who were less fortunate. She began researching socialism, reading George Bernard Shaw's *The Fabian Essays* and works by Charles Kingsley, J. F. D. Maurice, and Leo Tolstoy. Scudder returned to Massachusetts in 1885, and in 1887 she began a career as professor of English at Wellesley College that would continue until her retirement in 1928.

Although she was busy with her new teaching career and completing requirements for a master of arts degree at Smith (1889), Scudder's concerns over the unshared wealth of the privileged classes persisted. Her concerns led her to become active in the social gospel movemnt of the era. In 1888 she became a member of the Companions of the Holy Cross, a semimonastic group of women who were devoted to intercessional prayer and social reconciliation. A year later she led in the founding of the College Settlement Association, which was organized with the idea of inspiring fellowship among college women, the laboring classes, and immigrants. Scudder was joined by other women who had seen settlement houses in operation in England. The first settlement opened in 1889 in Rivington Street in the slums of New York City, and the second, the Denison House in Boston's South End, in 1893. Also in 1889, Scudder joined the Society of Christian Socialists, which was sponsored by William D. P. Bliss, and she became a charter member of Bliss's Brotherhood of the Carpenter.

Scudder's socialism and her reformist concerns frequently put her in conflict with the administration at Wellesley. Guilt over not doing enough to help the underprivileged, combined with pressures from college officials to quash her radicalism, led to Scudder's suffering a mental breakdown in 1901. She spent time traveling in Europe (1901–1902) and returned to Boston refreshed and filled with new ideas. Shortly after her return, she established an Italian Circle at Denison House to aid recent immigrants, and in 1903 she was a leader in the founding of the Women's Trade Union League.

Wellesley promoted Scudder to full professor in 1910, but two years later she was again embroiled in controversy. In 1912 she gave a speech in support of striking textile workers at Lawrence, Massachusetts. Despite calls from the opposition demanding Scudder's resignation, Wellesley officials resisted outside pressure and retained Scudder on the college faculty. Realizing that her radicalism hindered her effectiveness at Denison

House, Scudder curtailed her activities there to devote most of her time to teaching and writing. An enthusiastic Episcopalian as well as a socialist, Scudder maintained that Christianity and socialism were compatible. Over the next ten years, she wrote several works on Christian thought and social reform, including *Socialism and Character* (1912), in which she attempted to reconcile for her readers the apparent differences between socialism and Christianity; *The Church and the Hour: Reflections of a Socialist Churchwoman* (1917); and *The Social Teachings of the Christian Year* (1921).

In 1917 Scudder broke with many of her pacifist friends when she chose to support President Woodrow Wilson's decision to enter World War I. However, by 1923 she had moved toward pacifism herself and in that year joined the Fellowship of Reconciliation and gave a series of lectures at a meeting of the Women's International League for Peace and Freedom at Podebrady, near Prague.

Scudder retired from Wellesley in 1928 but continued writing. Her major work, based upon many years of research on the history of the Franciscans, *The Franciscan Adventure,* was published in 1931, and she became known as a scholar of early Franciscan history. During her lifetime, she published sixteen books on literary, religious, and political subjects and edited the works of Percy Shelley, Ruskin, the Venerable Bede, and others. Scudder published her autobiography, *On Journey,* in 1937 and a sequel, *My Quest for Reality,* in 1954. Of all her activities, her writings on social and Christian thought are considered her most important contributions to American culture and society.

After her retirement, Scudder held courses on Christian ethics at Wellesley and at age eighty-five addressed the annual Conference on Christian Social Thinking at the Episcopal Theological School in Cambridge, Massachusetts. She died at her home in Wellesley, Massachusetts, on October 9, 1954, when she choked on a piece of food.

See also: Settlement House Movement; Social Gospel Movement

References: Henry Warner Bowden, *Dictionary of American Religious Biography,* 2nd ed. (1993); Allen F. Davis, *Spearheads for Reform: The Social Settlements and the Progressive Movement* (1967, reprint 1984); *Dictionary of American Biography,* supplement 5 (1977); William L. O'Neill, *Everyone Was Brave* (1969); Barbara Sicherman and Carol Hurd Green, eds., *Notable American Women: The Modern Period* (1980).

Second Great Awakening

The series of revivals known as the Second Great Awakening cut across Protestant denominational lines and occurred in various places throughout the United States from about 1795 to 1835. Revivalists spread the word that not only did God desire to save those who repented of their sins but also that individuals had the ability to reform both themselves and their society. These tenets inspired many of the great social reform movements of the nineteenth century, including temperance and abolition, as well as the organization of missionary societies and biblical study groups.

The Second Great Awakening had a significant impact on women. Since colonial times, women had outnumbered men as churchgoers and converts. Even more women were drawn into religious activities by the new revivals. With evangelical preachers urging all Christians to apply their physical and moral resources to cure the ills of society, women found doors of opportunity opening for them to have an influence on the nation's religious and moral character. Studies have found that wives and mothers were frequently converted before their spouses and children were, and it was through the women's influence that other members of their families joined religious communities. Although it was rare to find women preachers at revivals, women were frequently called upon to give public testimonials of their conversion experiences and sometimes prayed aloud in mixed gatherings. Charles Grandison Finney, one of the most prominent revivalists of the Second Great Awakening, encouraged women to pray in public, although such a practice was discouraged by famous evangelist Lyman Beecher and other, more traditional, religious leaders.

In her study of the women of Oneida County, New York, Mary P. Ryan finds that women of the area played important roles in the revivals of the late 1810s and the 1820s. They created the organizational underpinnings of revivals in Oneida County that would eventually grow beyond their county and into the frontier. Other scholars have found similar evidence of women's contributions to revivals. Historian Susan Hill Lindley believes that women's behind-the-scenes efforts to aid the revivals were at least as important as their public activities in contributing to the success of the awakening and to the growth of women's religious roles. Both as individuals and in groups they prayed that the revivals would be successful. Large numbers of women formed associations that worked to encourage conversions and to assist converts in achieving spiritual lives. Their financial aid and other types of support to missionaries and traveling ministers helped spread Protestant Christianity throughout America.

A direct result of the Second Great Awakening was the growth of women's Bible study groups, missionary societies, and church-related benevolent associations. By the middle of the nineteenth century, the presence of women in local churches and in religious-associated organizations led to what some historians have called the feminization of American religion.

See also: The "Feminization" of American Religion; Finney, Charles Grandison; Great Awakening
References: Nancy A. Hewitt, *Women's Activism and Social Change: Rochester, New York, 1822–1872* (1984); Susan Hill Lindley, *"You Have Stept Out of Your Place": A History of Women and Religion in America* (1996); Edward L. Queen II et al., eds., *The Encyclopedia of American Religious History* (1996); Mary P. Ryan, *Cradle of the Middle Class: The Family in Oneida County, New York, 1790–1865* (1981).

Second Vatican Council

The Second Vatican Council, or Vatican II (1962–1965), marked a turning point in the way the Roman Catholic Church viewed women's roles in the church and in society. Pope John XXIII called bishops of the world to Rome to attend a series of meetings in which nearly every aspect of church policy and practice was open for examination and discussion. Although the voting members were all male, including 2,540 bishops and several heads of men's religious orders, feminists found the documents that came out of Vatican II to be quite encouraging. The council made few outright statements in support of women's liberation but presented some strong pronouncements on the equality of men and women.

In his 1963 encyclical, "Pacem in Terris," Pope John XXIII acknowledged that women would not accept being treated as mere material instruments but demanded equal rights as human beings in both their homes and public lives. And "Gaudium et Spes," the final official document presented by Vatican II, included a statement that argued that social or cultural discrimination based upon "sex, race, color, social condition, language, or religion, is to be overcome and eradicated as contrary to God's interest" (Abbott, 1966, p. 238). The statement continued with the regret that "fundamental personal rights are not yet being universally honored" and gave the example of "a woman who is denied the right and freedom to choose a husband, to embrace a state of life, or to acquire an education or cultural benefits equal to those recognized for men" (Abbott, 1966, p. 238).

But along with these statements of equality, there were qualifications. In "Pacem in Terris," John XXIII maintained that women had the right to working conditions that would meet their needs and responsibilities as wives and mothers, and in "Gaudium et Spes" and other documents, the bishops argued that a person's role in society must be in accordance with his or her nature and that the woman's domestic role must be preserved. As Susan Hill Lindley points out in *"You Have Stept Out of Your Place"* (1996), the council's qualifications on female equality were reinforced by its actions. Not until 1964 were a few women allowed to be present at the council's formal deliberations, and no women were given the opportunity to speak or to vote.

Although the Second Vatican Council was vague on two important issues of concern to women—birth control and the ordination of women—it created a new, enlightened spirit among Roman Catholic men and women. There were changes in the way mass was being said; the altar was turned around so that the priest could face the people; time was set aside for congregants to greet one another; and new songs, written in English, were in Catholic hymnals. People were pleased that the church was reaching out to the community and came to believe that a freer, democratic, and more personal faith was emerging.

See also: Roman Catholic Church; Roman Catholic Women's Orders (Nuns)
References: Walter M. Abbott, *Documents of Vatican II* (1966); Denise Lardner Carmody, *Women and World Religions,* 2nd ed. (1989); Susan Hill Lindley, *"You Have Stept Out of Your Place": A History of Women*

and Religion in America (1996); Jeanne Pieper, *The Catholic Woman: Difficult Choices in a Modern World* (1993).

Segale, Rosa Maria (1850–1941)

Rosa Maria Segale, who later became Sister Blandina, was known for her adventurous spirit, her religious devoutness, and her career as a social worker. Segale was born in Italy in 1850 but emigrated to the United States as a girl. She joined the Sisters of Charity in Cincinnati, taking the name Sister Blandina. In 1872, she traveled alone to the frontier town of Trinidad, Colorado. There, she ran a public school under primitive conditions. On one occasion she intervened with the sheriff to prevent a lynching, and once she tended a member of Billy the Kid's gang. The story goes that, from then on, Billy the Kid was kind toward the Sisters of Charity. When Billy voiced his intention to kill a Trinidad physician who had refused to remove a bullet from a gang member, Sister Blandina stepped in and dissuaded the outlaw from committing the murder.

Sister Blandina moved to Santa Fe in 1876, where she taught school, raised funds for a hospital and an orphanage, and built an industrial school for Indian girls. She helped to expand the town's economy when she inspired Santa Fe's citizens to open a quarry, install a lime kiln, start a brickyard, and establish a lumber mill. She was recalled to Cincinnati in 1894 and went to work caring for Italian immigrants. Although she played a prominent role in the establishment of three schools and four settlement houses for the Italian community, Sister Blandina also worked as a probation officer for the juvenile court and initiated legal action against white slavers who kidnapped young women and forced them into prostitution. After a full life of serving the church and the community, Sister Blandina died in 1941.

See also: Roman Catholic Church; Roman Catholic Women's Orders (Nuns)
References: James J. Kenneally, *The History of American Catholic Women* (1990); Jo Ann Kay McNamara: *Sisters in Arms: Catholic Nuns through Two Millennia* (1996); Julie F. Parker, *Careers for Women as Clergy* (1993).

Seton, Elizabeth Ann Bayley (1774–1821)

Elizabeth Ann Bayley Seton, or Mother Seton, was founder of the American Sisters of Charity and the first American-born saint of the Roman Catholic Church. She was born in New York City on August 28, 1774, the daughter of Richard and Catherine (Charlton) Bayley. Her father was a physician who briefly served the British Army in the American Revolution, conducted medical research, and devoted much of his practice to caring for poor immigrants. In 1777 Elizabeth's mother died from complications of childbirth, and her father remarried the following year. It appears that neither Elizabeth's father nor her stepmother showed her much affection, though Elizabeth remained devoted to her father throughout his life. During her adolescence, problems in the home resulted in Elizabeth and her older sister Mary leaving their father's house to live for a while with relatives in New Rochelle, New York. Elizabeth was a lonely girl and often turned to the Bible for solace.

In 1794, Elizabeth married William Magee Seton, a wealthy New York merchant. The first few years of their marriage were happy, loving, and prosperous. Elizabeth enjoyed a lively social life and raised a growing family. She also devoted some of her time to charity work. In 1797, together with Isabella Marshall Graham, Elizabeth founded a society to help destitute unwed mothers. Then financial setbacks caused the Seton family financial stress, as did the deaths of Eliz-

Elizabeth Ann Bayley Seton (undated lithograph)

abeth's father-in-law in 1798 and her own father in 1801. Also during this period, William Seton became ill with tuberculosis. Thinking that a change of climate might help him fight the disease, William traveled to Italy with Elizabeth and their eldest daughter. He died there in 1803, and Elizabeth was left with five young children.

For some time, Elizabeth Seton had been seeking to lead a more devout religious life. She had grown up in the Episcopal faith, but her family was not devoutly religious. In 1800 she had sought spiritual guidance from Reverend John Henry Hobart, an assistant at Trinity (Episcopal) Church in New York City. While in Italy, she was introduced to the Roman Catholic faith and was soon torn between the two churches. Upon her return to the United States, Elizabeth suffered severe depression. Symptoms of tuberculosis also surfaced at this time. She had been left a poor widow, and only through the financial help of friends and by running a boarding house was she able to keep her family together. When she recovered from her depression in 1805, she announced that she intended to convert to Roman Catholicism.

With the financial support of an Italian friend, Antonio Filicchi, and the moral support of Bishop (later Archbishop) John Carroll of Baltimore, Seton went to Baltimore in 1808 and established the Pace Street School, a small religious school for girls. Three of her initial seven pupils were her own daughters. She enrolled her sons in Georgetown Academy, a Jesuit school for boys. The following year, she moved her school to Emmitsburg, Maryland, and formed a sisterhood, the Sisters of Charity of St. Joseph, later known as the American Sisters of Charity. Seton pronounced her vows before Archbishop Carroll on March 25, 1809. Many difficulties surrounded the early days of the order. When Seton took her vows, she became bound to obey the male leaders of the Catholic Church. Soon she found herself in arguments over the management of her community. Seton also had to fight to remain guardian of her children, a battle she eventually won.

Initially, the primary mission of the Sisters of Charity was the education of girls and young women. The sisters needed financial support to keep their community running; therefore, most of their students were daughters of wealthy families who came from outlying areas and boarded at the school. The order did seek to help the poor and provided free instruction for local children, both white and black. Mother Seton believed that the lives of the girls in her school should be closely regulated. Their days began with prayer in the chapel, followed by lessons that included religious study. Seton's philosophy of education is generally considered the model for the American parochial school system.

As the Sisters of Charity grew, the order expanded its mission. They founded the first Catholic orphanage in the United States in Philadelphia in 1814 and a second orphanage in New York City in 1817. They also established the first Catholic hospital in the country in 1823.

Throughout the time that Mother Seton supervised the Sisters of Charity, she was suffering from tuberculosis. Seton was faced with personal tragedies as well. Two daughters died between 1812 and 1816, one of tuberculosis and the other of a spinal tumor. Tuberculosis spread throughout the order, and many of the sisters died during the early years of the order. Yet despite personal hardships and problems connected with running the Sisters of Charity on an austere budget, Mother Seton remained devoutly religious and intent upon doing her best for the community. In addition to her work as educator and as leader of the sisterhood, she wrote textbooks and spiritual works and translated religious documents from French into English.

Mother Seton died in Emmitsburg, Maryland, on January 4, 1821. In recognition of her spiritual leadership and contributions to the Roman Catholic Church and upon the validation of miraculous cures that resulted from Mother Seton's intervention, she was canonized Saint Elizabeth Ann Seton on September 14, 1975.

See also: Roman Catholic Church; Roman Catholic Women's Orders (Nuns)
References: Joseph I. Dirvin, *Mrs. Seton: Foundress of the American Sisters of Charity* (1975); Leonard Feeney, *Mother Seton: Saint Elizabeth of New York*, rev. ed. (1991); Edward T. James, ed., *Notable American Women, 1607–1950*, vol. 3 (1971); Annabelle M. Melville, *Elizabeth Bayley Seton, 1774–1821* (1976); Marjorie J. Podolsky, "Elizabeth Ann Seton," in Frank Magill, ed., *Great Lives from History: American Women Series* (1995).

Settlement House Movement

Launched in London in 1884 by Anglican clergyman Samuel Barnett and a group of young Oxford students, the settlement house movement quickly crossed the Atlantic. The first settlement house, Toynbee Hall, located in the midst of the poverty of London's East End, was dedicated to alleviating the human suffering that had resulted from rapid industrialization and urbanization. Concerned with the problems faced by the poor, these students and others from the more fortunate classes chose to reside in the settlement and to become neighbors to the needy. Toynbee Hall became a model for similar institutions in both England and the United States. A significant number of the settlement houses in America were under the management of women.

Among the most famous of the American settlement houses were Hull House in Chicago, cofounded by Jane Addams and Ellen Gates Starr (1889); Denison House in Boston's South End, cofounded and headed by Helena Stuart Dudley (1893); and the Henry Street settlement in New York City, founded by public health nurse Lillian Wald (1893). Dudley and Vida Dutton Scudder were among the organizers of the College Settlement Association, which recruited college students to reside in and work in the settlements. Most often the recruits remained only for a short time, but some chose to turn the experience into a career.

Although the programs offered differed from one settlement to another, they usually covered a broad range. They frequently brought cultural activities into the lives of those who normally would not have been able to experience the enjoyments of art, music, and literature. Settlements like Hull House offered a social center for recent immigrants, offering classes in English, civics, cooking, and dressmaking while encouraging them to preserve their traditional crafts. Kinder-gartens, day nurseries, employment bureaus, and laundry facilities could all be found in settlement houses, as could recreational activities, athletic projects, legal assistance, and health care. Settlement house leaders were reformers who involved themselves in campaigns to improve the health, safety, and working conditions faced by the urban poor.

The larger settlements, like Denison House and Hull House, considered themselves nondenominational. However, a number of the smaller houses were operated under the auspices of churches. They often proselytized for their own denominations, making it difficult to draw a line between a mission and a settlement house. By definition, settlement houses differed from missions in that they were more concerned with reforms than with reviving religious faith. Historians have questioned the effects of the Social Gospel movement, which originated in the 1870s, on the launching of settlement houses. Like the settlement house movement, the Social Gospel movement was concerned with the growing poverty in urban areas. Washington Gladden, the originator of the Social Gospel movement, was a Protestant minister who urged fellow church leaders to fight social injustice.

Whether the settlement house movement was a product of the Social Gospel movement remains open to question, but large numbers of men and women who had participated in the latter movement became active in settlement work as well. It was often their religious convictions that motivated them to establish and to manage or reside in a settlement house. Historian Allen F. Davis maintains that religion was a great motivating factor behind the settlement movement. He cites a 1905 poll by William D. P. Bliss that shows that of 339 settlement workers, 88 percent were active members of their churches and that "nearly all admitted that religion had been a dominant influence in their lives" (Davis, 1967, p. 27). For middle-class women who desired a religious vocation, settlement work was one of the few careers open to them.

See also: Scudder, Vida Dutton; Social Gospel Movement
References: Mina Carson, *Settlement Folk: Social Thought and the American Settlement Movement, 1885–1930* (1990); Allen F. Davis, *Spearheads for Reform: The Social Settlements and the Progressive Movement* (1967, reprint 1984); Susan Hill Lindley, *"You Have Stept Out of Your Place": A History of Women and Religion in America* (1996); Herbert Stroup, *Social Welfare Pioneers* (1986); Angela Howard Zophy with Frances M. Kavenik, eds., *Handbook of American Women's History* (1990).

Shakers (United Society of Believers in Christ's Second Coming)

Among the longest-lived and most influential religious utopian communities in the United States, the Shakers originated in Manchester, England, in 1747. Under the leadership of James and Jane Wardley, they broke away from the Quakers. It is possible that the Shakers were influenced by Camisard millenarians, who had escaped to England from France during the persecution that followed the revocation of the Edict of Nantes in 1685. The Shakers, who believed that the second coming of Christ was imminent, acquired their name as a result of their highly emotional and demonstrative worship services. Following a short period of meditation, members shouted, sang, spoke in tongues, danced, and shook with emotion.

Believing that God was both male and female in nature, Shakers accepted member Ann Lee as a female Christ when she related a vision in which Jesus informed her that she was to be his successor. Through her person, a spiritual second coming would be realized. Lee also believed strongly that sexual cohabitation was a great evil and once had a vision

that Adam and Eve were expelled from the Garden of Eden as a result of engaging in sexual intercourse. Those who followed her heeded her words and led celibate lives. As a result of their unorthodox beliefs and behavior, Shakers were persecuted in England and were occasionally imprisoned. During the last of several prison terms in England, Lee had a vision that inspired her to take her message to America. Soon after, in May 1774, Lee and a small group of followers set sail for what was soon to become the United States.

They had not been long in New York City before the pacifist Shakers began to draw suspicion from American patriots who suspected the newly arrived English group were British Loyalists. The tensions in the city that permeated the initial stages of the American Revolution led the Shakers to remove themselves to the countryside as soon as possible. In 1776 they found land in Niskeyuna, near Albany, New York, that they could lease as long as they desired.

In May 1780 the Shakers opened their services to the public for the first time. Some of the people from surrounding areas who went to see the strange community for themselves were converted. Encouraged by their success at Niskeyuna, Lee and several elders traveled into New England, where they faced opposition but gained more converts. Ann Lee died in 1784, shortly after she and the other missionaries returned to Niskeyuna, but Shakerism continued.

In the years that followed Lee's death, Shakerism changed from a charismatic movement into a more structured organization. The elders began to experiment with the practice of joint ownership for which the Shakers would become well known. Property was owned communally and was under the control of the church hierarchy. Men and women remained committed to celibacy, and the sexes were separated as much as possible. They were housed in separate lodgings, usually worked apart, ate at separate tables, and walked through separate doorways. The sexes were normally treated as equals. Duties were usually assigned according to sex, with women performing domestic chores and men working in the fields, but women shared leadership within the church equally with men.

By 1800 there were eleven settlements with about sixteen hundred members in New York and New England. Shakerism achieved its greatest growth during the Second Great Awakening of the early nineteenth century. Shakers traveled to the large revivals, including the great camp meeting at Cane Ridge, Kentucky, where they made many new converts. They proselytized many more during the late 1830s and early 1840s. This was a time of spiritual manifestation, when the spirit of Mother Ann is said to have revealed itself with the purpose of showing Lee's continued concern for her followers. During the mid-1840s, the Shakers gained more converts. When the world failed to come to an end in 1843 or 1844 as religious enthusiast William Miller had predicted, many of his disillusioned followers joined the Shakers. At the height of their proselytizing in the late 1840s, Shakers numbered about six thousand.

Shakers believed that work was a form of worship, and their communities prospered from agriculture and crafts. They became known for the clean, simple lines of their furniture and architecture. The Shakers led modest lives and impressed outsiders with their cleanliness and order.

Membership among the Shakers began to decline after 1850. Their celibate lifestyle prevented natural increase, and by 1900 there were only about one thousand Shakers in the United States. Today, there are virtually no members. Nevertheless, Shakers will be remembered in history for their attempts at perfection through communal living, their uniqueness in granting women equality in leadership, and their simple styles of furniture and architecture.

See also: Lee, Ann; Perfectionism
References: Edward Deming Andrews and Faith Andrews, *Work and Worship: The Economic Order of the Shakers* (1974); Deborah E. Burns, *Shaker Cities of Peace, Love, and Union: A History of the Hancock Bishopric* (1992); Nardi Reeder Campion, *Ann the Word: The Life of Mother Ann Lee, Founder of the Shakers* (1976); Lawrence Foster, *Women, Family and Utopia: Communal Experiments of the Shakers, the Oneida Community, and the Mormons* (1990); John McKelvie Whitworth, *God's Blueprints: A Sociological Study of Three Utopian Sects* (1993).

Shaw, Anna Howard (1847–1919)

Anna Howard Shaw, a Methodist minister, a leader in the woman suffrage movement, and the first American woman to hold divinity and medical degrees simultaneously, was born in Newcastle upon Tyne, England, on February 14, 1847. When she was four years of age, she moved with her family to Massachusetts, finally settling on the Michigan frontier shortly before the outbreak of the Civil War. Shaw spent her teenage years caring for her sickly mother and therefore had little formal education. In her early twenties, she left home to attend high school in Big Rapids. While there, she became interested in becoming one of the Methodist Church's first female ministers. At age twenty-six, she entered Albion College (Michigan), where she spent two years before entering the Theological School at Boston University. There she was the only female in her class of forty-three students. After her graduation in 1878, she pastored at a church in East Dennis, Massachusetts, but the New England Conference of the

Anna Howard Shaw (from The Story of a Pioneer, *1915)*

Methodist Episcopal Church, North, refused to allow her to administer the sacraments. Finally, in 1880, Shaw was ordained as the first female minister of another body of the Methodist church, the Methodist Protestant Church. (The Methodist Episcopal Church, North, did not ordain women until 1924.) Three years later, she returned to Boston University, enrolling in the medical school on a part-time basis. She received her medical degree in 1886.

While in medical school, Shaw became involved in the woman suffrage movement, becoming a lecturer for the Massachusetts Woman Suffrage Association in 1885. From 1888 to 1892, she served as superintendent of the Franchise Department of the Woman's Christian Temperance Union. She was also active in both the American Woman Suffrage Association and the National Woman Suffrage Association prior to their merger in

1890. After the two organizations joined to become the National American Woman Suffrage Association (NAWSA), Shaw became a lecturer for the group and was its vice president from 1892 to 1904. She served as president of the organization from 1904 until 1915. NAWSA floundered under Shaw's leadership, apparently due to her lack of organizational skills.

After the United States entered World War I, in May 1917, President Woodrow Wilson appointed Shaw to chair the Woman's Committee of the U.S. Council of National Defense. She held that post for two years. In appreciation, President Wilson awarded her the Distinguished Service Medal. The final months of her life were spent on the lecture circuit, promoting American participation in the League of Nations. Shaw died in Moylan, Pennsylvania, on July 2, 1919.

See also: Clergy; Methodists; Woman Suffrage
References: Terry D. Bilhartz, "Anna Howard Shaw," in Angela Zophy with Frances M. Kavenik, eds., *Handbook of American Women's History* (1990); Kathryn Cullen-DuPont, with Annelise Orleck, *The Encyclopedia of Women's History in America* (1996); Eleanor Flexner, *Century of Struggle: The Woman's Rights Movement in the United States* (1970); Elizabeth Frost-Knappman, *Women's Progress in America* (1994); Wil A. Linkugel and Martha Solomon, *Anna Howard Shaw: Suffrage Orator and Social Reformer* (1991); Anna Howard Shaw, *The Story of a Pioneer* (1915, reprint 1970).

Sisters of Loretto at the Foot of the Cross

The Sisters of Loretto at the Foot of the Cross was the first American sisterhood without foreign affiliation. The order, a teaching community, was founded in Kentucky in 1812 by Mary Rhodes (1782?–1853) under the guidance of Father Charles Nerinckx, a Roman Catholic priest who had emigrated from Belgium. Nerinckx carried the strict traditions of European monasteries to the United States and required the nuns to begin their day's work at 4:00 A.M. during the summer and at 4:30 A.M. in the winter. The sisters were expected to go barefoot and to sleep on the floor or on straw. In addition to their teaching duties, they labored in the fields and cut and hauled wood. They were allowed to speak for only one hour each day, following dinner. During Lent, they were forbidden to speak at all. Life was so harsh in the community that in one year fifteen of sixteen sisters died of tuberculosis. In 1824, church authorities intervened and modified the rules. Nerinckx left the community. Just prior to his being pressured to leave the community, Nerinckx had attempted to create an affiliate sisterhood of black nuns, but his plan was never realized.

Following Nerinckx's departure, the community expanded. In 1831, Mary Rhodes added an orphanage to the Lorettan school and, the following year, a hospital. The Sisters of Loretto established schools and missions farther to the west and later staffed religious missions around the world. Albanian Agnes Bojaxhiu, who later won the Nobel Peace Prize as Mother Teresa, joined the Lorettans in Ireland and served in their convent in Calcutta for twenty years before establishing the Missionaries of Charity in 1946.

See also: Nerinckx, Charles; Roman Catholic Church; Roman Catholic Women's Orders (Nuns)
References: Cyprian Davis, *The History of Black Catholics in the United States* (1992); James J. Kenneally, *The History of American Catholic Women* (1990); Jo Ann Kay McNamara, *Sisters in Arms: Catholic Nuns through Two Millennia* (1996).

Smith, Amanda Berry (1837–1915)

Amanda Berry Smith was born a slave in Long Green, Maryland, on January 23, 1837, there was little in her early life that foretold of her later career as an internationally famous African-American evangelist. She most likely inherited the fortitude of her father, Samuel Berry, who through industry and determination was able to purchase his freedom as well as that of his wife, Miriam Matthews, and their thirteen children. The family's new home in York, Pennsylvania, became a station on the Underground Railroad during the decade prior to the Civil War. Amanda, who received only a few months of formal education, went to work as a washerwoman. In 1854 she married Calvin Devine. The marriage was not a happy one, but after her religious conversion in March 1856, Amanda was better able to tolerate it as well as the hard work and racial discrimination that she was to face in the years ahead.

Calvin Devine enlisted in the Union army in 1862 and was killed soon after. His widow and the couple's only surviving child (the first died in infancy) moved to Philadelphia the following year. There she met and married James Smith, an ordained deacon in the Old Bethel African Methodist Episcopal Church. The couple had three children, all of whom died in infancy or early childhood. They moved to New York City soon after their marriage, but James, who was a coachman by occupation, was often away. In New York Amanda began attending the "Tuesday Meetings for the Promotion of Holiness" led by Phoebe Palmer, a leader of the perfectionist, or Holiness, movement. Amanda was impressed with the doctrine of sanctification, the belief that Christians can be cleansed of sin and, by an act of the Holy Spirit, become entirely sanctified. In 1868 Amanda experienced this spiritual renewal that she had long been praying for and felt a call to spread the message to others.

The following year both her husband and the last of her five children died, leaving Smith free to devote much of her time and energy to evangelical work. She began by preaching in black churches in New York and New Jersey, earning their respect as an effective speaker. In 1870 she spoke at a white Holiness camp meeting, where she also won the respect of whites who sought to spread the doctrine of Christian perfection. Between 1870 and 1878, Smith became a popular figure within the Holiness movement, participating in camp meetings from Maine to Tennessee.

In 1878 Smith went to England, where she participated in Holiness conferences and took a number of evangelistic speaking engagements. She spent the next two years as a missionary in India and then worked with Methodist missionaries in West Africa, making her headquarters in Liberia. During her eight years in Africa, she organized temperance societies in addition to her missionary work. She left Africa in November 1889 to perform several months of evangelical work in England, Scotland, and Ireland before returning to the United States in September 1890.

After preaching for two years in churches in the East, Smith moved to the suburbs of Chicago and, through her friendship with Frances Willard, became active in the temperance movement. In 1893 Smith published her memoirs, *An Autobiography: The Story of the Lord's Dealings with Mrs. Amanda Smith, the Colored Evangelist*, which has come to be regarded as a classic in Holiness literature. At about the same time she began a newspaper, *The Helper*. Beginning in 1895, Smith began acquiring land in Harvey, Illinois, where in 1899 she opened an orphanage for African-American children. When she retired in 1912 to move to Florida, the state granted the home a charter as the Amanda Smith Industrial School for Girls. Government support kept the institution operating until it was destroyed by fire in 1918.

Amanda Smith died February 24, 1915, in Sebring, Florida, where wealthy real estate man George Sebring had provided a home for her retirement. Her body was taken by train for an elaborate funeral in Chicago and burial in Harvey.

See also: Palmer, Phoebe Worrall; Woman's Christian Temperance Union
References: Henry Warner Bowden, *Dictionary of American Religious Biography*, 2nd ed. (1993); Sherry Sherrod DuPree, ed., *Biographical Dictionary of African-American Holiness-Pentecostals, 1880–1990* (1989); Edward T. James, ed., *Notable American Women, 1607–1950* (1971); J. Gordon Melton, *Religious Leaders of America* (1991); Dorothy C. Salem, ed., *African American Women: A Biographical Dictionary* (1993).

Smith, Hannah Whitall (1832–1911)

Hannah Whitall Smith, a popular preacher and religious writer of the late nineteenth century, was born February 7, 1832, in Philadelphia, Pennsylvania. The daughter of wealthy Quaker parents, John Mickle and Mary (Tatum) Whitall, Hannah received a strict Quaker upbringing, and she was educated in a Society of Friends' school. In June 1851 she married Robert Pearsall Smith, who was also a Quaker, and the couple moved to Germantown. Over the next several years, Robert and Hannah had three children. During the early years of their marriage, the Smiths went through a period of religious questioning. They became dissatisfied with what they considered the spiritual deadness of Quaker doctrine, and at one time Hannah felt that she was completely cut off from God. However, as time passed, both Robert and Hannah became caught up in the new outburst of American revivalism. By the end of the 1850s they had absorbed much of the evangelical spirit of the Holiness movement that had sprung up within Methodism, which taught that sanctification comes through faith and the experience of salvation. In 1859 they resigned from the Quaker meeting. Robert became a Presbyterian, and Hannah joined the Plymouth Brethren.

The Smiths moved to Millville, New Jersey, in 1864. There Hannah grew even more attached to the Holiness movement and, in 1869, Robert began preaching at Holiness camp meetings and publishing the periodical, the *Christian's Pathway to Power*. Hannah contributed to the periodical, and she too began to preach. In about 1872, Robert suffered a nervous breakdown. Believing that a change of scenery would be beneficial, he took a steamer to Europe the following year. In 1874 Hannah and the children joined him in England. There the Smiths became celebrated preachers within the interdenominational Higher Life movement, and Hannah's eloquent speaking style brought her the title "angel of the churches" (James, 1971, p. 314). The Smiths' popularity waned, however, when a sexual indiscretion of Robert's became public. At about the same time as the scandal broke, Hannah's major work, *The Christian's Secret of a Happy Life* (1875), was published. This book, in which Smith called on people to dedicate their lives to God, was successful at the time and has since become a classic among Protestant Christians, selling approximately two million copies worldwide.

In ensuing years, Smith became an advocate for women's rights, frequently speaking in public on issues of suffrage and higher education for women, and was active in the temperance movement. She was a founder of the Woman's Christian Temperance Union (WCTU) and in 1883 became superintendent of the WCTU's Evangelistic Department. The Smiths made a permanent move to England in 1888, and Hannah immediately became involved in the temperance cause there. She also preached whenever the opportunity arose and continued writing. Among her works are *John W. Whitall: The Story of His Life* (1879); *Every-day Religion; or, the Common-Sense Teaching of the Bible* (1893); and

The Unselfishness of God and How I Discovered It: My Spiritual Autobiography (1903). Hannah Smith died on May 1, 1911, in Iffley, England.

See also: Holiness Movement; Temperance Movement; Woman's Christian Temperance Union
References: Elizabeth Frost-Knappman, *Women's Progress in America* (1994); Marie Henry, *The Secret Life of Hannah Whitall Smith* (1984); Edward T. James, ed., *Notable American Women, 1607–1950*, vol. 3 (1971); Robert McHenry, ed., *Liberty's Women* (1980); J. Gordon Melton, *Religious Leaders of America* (1991); Hannah Whitall Smith, *The Christian's Secret of a Happy Life* (1875); Logan Pearsall Smith, ed., *Philadelphia Quaker: The Letters of Hannah Whitall Smith* (1950); Logan Pearsall Smith, *Unforgotten Years* (1939).

Snow, Eliza Roxey (Smith) (1804–1887)

One of the most powerful women in the Mormon Church during the late nineteenth century, Eliza Roxey (sometimes spelled Roxcy or Roxcey) Snow was born on January 21, 1804, in Becket, Massachusetts. In 1806 she moved with her parents, Oliver and Rosetta Leonora (Pettibone) Snow to Mantua, Ohio, where her father prospered as a farmer. It was important to Eliza's parents that their children be well educated. In addition to her formal education, Eliza learned domestic duties, wrote poetry, and began a systematic study of the Bible. Although both Oliver and Rosetta had been devout Baptists throughout most of their lives, they joined the Church of Jesus Christ of Latter-Day Saints shortly after Mormon missionaries arrived in Ohio, around 1830. Eliza was baptized by Mormon prophet Joseph Smith on April 5, 1835. A year later, her brother Lorenzo joined the church. He soon became a leader and served as president from 1898 to 1901.

After 1835, Eliza's poetry was usually religious in theme and spirit. Although it has since been described as "sentimental, didactic, sometimes turgid, and often stilted," her poems were apparently appropriate for her audience and the times (James, 1971, p. 307). Several of her poems were set to music and became Mormon hymns.

Late in 1836, Snow left her parental home to live among the Mormons in Kirtland, Ohio. She boarded with the family of Joseph Smith and became a teacher for his children and a companion to his wife Emma Hale Smith. Later she moved with Smith and other Mormons to the new Mormon town of Nauvoo, Illinois, and she taught school there. In 1842 Snow suggested that a benevolent society be organized for women. Joseph Smith made some changes to her proposal and created the Female (later Women's) Relief Society, naming his wife Emma president. Snow became the society's first secretary. At about this time, polygamy was being introduced into the Mormon Church, and in a secret ceremony, Snow became one of Joseph Smith's wives. By this time, she had achieved some influence on the church through her poetry and hymns, and Smith encouraged her in her work.

Joseph Smith was killed in 1844, and Brigham Young succeeded him as Mormon leader. According to tradition, Snow was carrying Smith's child in 1844 but miscarried after being attacked by a jealous Emma Smith. Snow later became one of Young's plural wives, but she bore him no children. Just prior to the Mormons' departure for Utah in 1845, Young chose Snow to take charge of the records at the Nauvoo Mormon Temple, thus creating a role for women in temple work. In the fall of 1847, she traveled with one of the earliest companies to Salt Lake City. There, in 1855, Young appointed her president of the women's section of the new Endowment House. Among her tasks was ministering to the needs of sick women and children and to women about to give birth. In the mid-1860s, Young put Snow in charge of reactivating the Female Relief Society and named her the organization's second president. Under her leadership, the society established local and regional branches throughout the church. While continuing to perform charitable work, the group also adopted more institutionalized forms of care. It offered classes in hygiene, organized a women's hospital (the first Mormon hospital, in 1882), promoted the education of nurses, and sponsored early women physicians. Snow led in the establishment a women's newspaper, the *Women's Exponent* (1872), which became the organ of the association.

In 1869 Young placed Snow in charge of what would become (in 1878) the Young Ladies' Mutual Improvement Association. Originally founded for the purpose of bringing about a "retrenchment" in the dress and overall manner of young women, it became a highly influential Mormon organization for women. In 1878 Snow presided over a gathering of fifteen thousand women who had come together in defense of polygamy. Two years later she was ordained as president of Latter-Day Saints women's organizations worldwide.

Active with the church until the final years of her life, Snow traveled to Palestine with her brother Lorenzo in 1872–1873, sending back reports in both poetry and prose. In 1876 she helped to organize Utah's exhibit at the Philadelphia Centennial celebration. Snow played a major role in the establishment of the Primary Association (1878) for the purpose of training young boys in disciplined conduct, and in 1881 she was named president of the board of directors of the Deseret Hospital Association.

Eliza Roxey Snow died in Salt Lake City on December 5, 1887, and was buried in Brigham Young's private cemetery.

See also: Church of Jesus Christ of Latter-Day Saints (Mormons)
References: Maureen Ursenbach Beecher, ed., *The Personal Writings of Eliza Roxcy Snow* (1995); Edward T. James, ed., *Notable American Women, 1607–1950*, vol. 3 (1971); Susan Hill Lindley, *"You Have Stept Out of Your Place": A History of Women and Religion in America* (1996); J. Gordon Melton, *Religious Leaders of America* (1991).

Social Gospel Movement

The Social Gospel movement, which arose in the United States during the last quarter of the nineteenth century, was a crusade to involve Christians in social reforms that would make the world more like God's kingdom. It differed from earlier humanitarian and reform work in that it challenged traditional ideas that poverty was a sin or that people were placed in the social strata that God intended. Religious leaders like Walter Rauschenbusch, a young Baptist minister, began to expound on the responsibility of organized religion to work for social justice. Although leaders like Rauschenbusch encouraged male participation in the movement while believing that a woman's place was in the home, recent historians have begun to show that women too were involved in Social Gospel.

Like their male counterparts, women in Social Gospel were concerned with problems associated with urbanization, industrialization, and the tremendous influx of immigrants occurring during the late nineteenth century. As did the men, these women felt the need to put their religious faith into action and to be useful. Women's participation in the movement was hampered to the extent that most male leaders accepted the Victorian notion of a woman's role. At the same time, some men worried about what they perceived as the "feminization of religion," as women, who had long outnumbered men in church membership, appeared to be gaining significant influence within their churches. Thus, male Social Gospel writers appealed directly to men in attempts to achieve greater male involvement in the movement as well as to draw them into churches. Nevertheless, women did become a force within the movement, and a few, most notably Vida Dutton Scudder, became theorists of the Social Gospel.

Included among the Social Gospel organizations with which women became associated were home missions like the Methodist Women's Home Mission Board and the Episcopal Society of the Companions of the Holy Cross. Many deaconesses adopted the Social Gospelers' sentiments; allied with urban reformers; and considered that in order to improve the circumstances of the poor, structural changes needed to be made within American political and economic systems. Although not directly associated with the Social Gospel movement and usually considered more reform-oriented than religious-based, the settlement house movement is often regarded as a product of Social Gospel. Many of the women participating in settlement work were also active within their individual churches, and for many it was their own religious convictions that motivated them to give assistance to immigrants and the poor.

Although women in the Social Gospel movement, like their male counterparts, had a tendency to push their own middle-class, Protestant values upon those they considered less fortunate, their work within the movement gave them an opportunity to expand their understanding of the poor and their environment and to do something to help them.

See also: Scudder, Vida Dutton; Settlement House Movement; Society of the Companions of the Holy Cross
References: Mina Carson, *Settlement Folk: Social Thought and the American Settle-*

ment Movement, 1885–1930 (1990); Allen
F. Davis, Spearheads for Reform: The Social
Settlements and the Progressive Movement
(1967, reprint 1984); Janet Forsythe Fishburn, The Fatherhood of God and the Victorian Family: The Social Gospel in America (1981); Susan Hill Lindley, "You Have
Stept Out of Your Place": A History of
Women and Religion in America (1996).

Society of Friends (Quakers)

Founded in England by George Fox in 1652, the Society of Friends, or Quakers, has traditionally been among the more liberal religions in its attitudes toward the roles of women within the church. Fox and his followers believed that there was an "inner light" of Christ in every person. Quakers revered the scriptures as inspired revelation but were convinced that inspiration and revelation were on-going. Because of this belief in an inner light, Quakers developed an egalitarianism that eventually spanned class and gender. Women numbered among Fox's first converts and Quaker missionaries in a time when women preachers were practically unheard of. Another factor in the Quaker faith that helped to encourage women as preachers was its rejection of formal priestly authority and its focus on lay ministry.

The proselytizing urge brought Quakers to America as early as 1656. Two Quaker women, Ann Austin and Mary Fisher, arrived in Puritan Massachusetts in July 1656 from Barbados. Fearing invasion by this "radical" group, by October 1656 Puritans had passed a law that imposed imprisonment, fines, whipping, and banishment on those they consider a cursed sect of heretics. Yet between 1656 and 1659 thirty-three more Quakers arrived in New England. Meanwhile, laws became more severe, and two men, Marmaduke Stevenson and William Robinson, were hanged in 1659. Mary Dyer became a martyr to her religion a year later, and William Leddra was hanged in 1661. Pu-

ritans, who believed that any woman who deviated from her "natural" role was a "bad woman," sometimes considered Quaker women preachers to be witches. Other colonies passed laws against Quakers, until they were safe only in outlying areas such as Rhode Island, Cape Cod, and Maine. They continued to arrive, however, including fifty-nine missionaries between 1656 and 1663, of which twenty-six were women. It was also a woman, Elizabeth Harris, who introduced Quakerism to the South. She went on a mission to Maryland, and perhaps to Virginia, in 1655 or 1656. By 1657 there were some converts in Maryland.

In the 1670s and 1680s, Quaker proprietors acquired lands in West Jersey and in Pennsylvania, which gave the Society of Friends the opportunity to establish a religious utopia similar to that of the Puritans in New England. They became known for their plain living, dependable work habits, and inventiveness, which enabled many of them to prosper.

The local meeting for worship, the first-day meeting, was the center of Quakerism. Men and women sat separately in a room where silence usually prevailed. Worshippers spoke only when moved by the spirit. In most instances, the speakers were formally recognized as ministers and increasingly included a large minority of women. Quakers held business meetings in addition to those for worship. Men's and women's business meetings were separate but, theoretically, equal. In actuality, men's meetings normally carried more weight, and sometimes women's meetings did not exist.

Whether they were equal to those of Quaker men, Quaker women's meetings provided them with opportunities to learn organizational and administrative skills and provided them with a forum in which they could present their views on social issues. Quaker women eventually adopted the causes of human rights—

A meeting of the Society of Friends, where each member is empowered to speak as a minister (woodcut from Ernest von Hess-Wartburg's Nord Amerika, *1888).*

Native American, African American, and women's rights.

In the mid-nineteenth century, when Quakers represented only a tiny percentage of the American population, Quaker women were extremely influential in reform movements. Most of the Quaker women who ventured into the traditionally male public forum came from the Hicksite branch of the Society of Friends, as the Orthodox were more inclined to remain in their accustomed roles. Of the five women who planned the first women's rights convention at Seneca Falls, New York, in 1848, four were members of the Society of Friends. Approximately 30 percent of the pioneers in prison reform were Quaker women; they comprised about 40 percent of female abolitionists and 15 percent of suffragists born prior to 1830. Three of the best-known leaders of the women's move-

ment in the nineteenth century and the first half of the twentieth century—Lucretia Mott, Susan B. Anthony, and Alice Paul—were all Quakers.

Historians have speculated that the prominent role of Quaker women in the early women's movement led to the adoption of many Quaker values in its ideology and practice: advocating nonviolence in protecting early conventions against angry mobs; including women of all races and walks of life in meetings; working for a consensus rather than making decisions hierarchically; and linking the women's movement with the peace movement.

As with other religious denominations, Quaker women's missionary societies began forming during the last third of the nineteenth century. The Friends Women's Foreign Missionary Union, which after 1948 called itself United Society of

Friends Women, began triennial meetings in 1888.

The Society of Friends remains a small denomination in the United States. The approximately 115,000 Quakers in the nation continue to be committed to the concept of equality. However, many resisted the new feminism that emerged in the 1970s, fearing that it posed a threat to conventional marriages. Others see the new feminism as a logical extension of their history of egalitarianism and welcome institutional changes that allow women the opportunity to hold positions in Quaker-run organizations on an equal basis with men. Some branches of the church have begun to eliminate all sexist terminology, like the all-inclusive "man," from their language.

See also: Antislavery Movement; Ashbridge, Elizabeth Sampson Sullivan; Dyer, Mary Barrett; Mott, Lucretia Coffin; Woman Suffrage; Woman's Christian Temperance Union

References: Margaret Hope Bacon, *Mothers of Feminism: The Story of Quaker Women in America* (1986); Hugh Barbour and J. William Frost, *The Quakers* (1988); Melvin B. Endy, Jr., "The Society of Friends," in Charles H. Lippy and Peter W. Williams, eds., *Encyclopedia of the American Religious Experience: Studies of Traditions and Movements*, vol. 1 of 3 (1988); Thomas D. Hamm, *The Transformation of American Quakerism: Orthodox Friends, 1800–1907* (1988); Susan Hill Lindley, *"You Have Stept Out of Your Place": A History of Women and Religion in America* (1996); Daniel B. Shea, *Spiritual Autobiography in Early America* (1968).

Society of the Companions of the Holy Cross

Founded in 1884 by Emily Malbone Morgan and Harriet Hastings, the Society of the Companions of the Holy Cross (SCHC) became one of the most effective advocates for social justice and reform in the United States. Its members were Episcopal laywomen who were dedicated to developing their own spiritual lives and reaching out to others. The SCHC combined spirituality with social action and served as an outlet for women caught up in the Social Gospel movement of the late nineteenth century. Women gathered to pray and share ideas, and with special concerns over the plight of working women, they campaigned for humanitarian reforms and for interdenominational cooperation. Most women in the SCHC were well-educated professionals. The membership included social workers, doctors, professors, Episcopal deaconesses, and several Episcopal nuns. Originating in New England, the society had chapters in Hartford, Boston, Philadelphia, and San Francisco by 1897, with a membership of 143. By 1908 there were 252 members, including several African-American women, and missionaries had begun to spread word of the SCHC to other lands, including England, India, the Philippines, China, and Puerto Rico.

Emily Morgan was companion-in-charge of the SCHC from the time the organization was established until her death in 1933. Another active member was Vida Dutton Scudder, a writer, professor, and Christian Socialist who joined the SCHC in 1889. She served as director of probationers from 1909 to 1942, unofficially led its radical wing, and urged women to join who, like her, were involved in the settlement movement. In addition to its work within the community, the SCHC had some success in its crusades to persuade the Episcopal Church to become more involved in social reforms. In fact, Mary Sudman Donovan, in *A Different Call: Women's Ministries in the Episcopal Church, 1850–1920* (1986), places the accomplishments of the SCHC women alongside those of prominent Social Gospel reformers Walter Rauschenbusch and Richard T. Ely.

See also: Scudder, Vida Dutton; Settlement House Movement; Social Gospel Movement

References: Allen F. Davis, *Spearheads for Reform: The Social Settlements and the Progressive Movement* (1967, reprint 1984); Mary Sudman Donovan, *A Different Call: Women's Ministries in the Episcopal Church, 1850–1920* (1986); Susan Hill Lindley, *"You Have Stept Out of Your Place": A History of Women and Religion in America* (1996).

Solares, Maria (1842–1923)

Maria Solares, who has played an important role in the preservation of the traditional religion of the Chumash Indians of southern California, was born in 1842. Also known as Maria Isidore del Refugio, she was born and raised in the Chumash Indian village of Alaxulapu, located near the Santa Ynez (Roman Catholic Church) Mission at Santa Ynez, California. At the time of her birth, the Mexican and American cultures were competing for control of California, while the Chumash people were barely holding onto their ancestral way of life. Once Americans began flocking into California in the late 1840s and 1850s, the Spanish/Mexican culture became secondary, and the culture of the Chumash people was pushed down even farther.

Both Maria's father, Bienvenuto, and her mother, Shiguashayum, were descendants of Chumash chiefs, and Maria was instructed in the culture and traditions of her people. She also learned about other cultures when, after her mother's death, she went to live with relatives in a village that housed people of diverse origins. Maria married several times. Her fourth marriage was to Manuel Solares, whose father, Rafael, was one of the last members of a secret society of Chumash known as the *antap*. An *antap* was one who was permitted to enter sacred enclosures during religious ceremonies. From Rafael and his family, Maria gathered considerable knowledge about the *antap* religion.

In the 1850s, the Santa Ynez group of Chumash were moved to the east, to Zanja de Cota (later called the Santa Ynez Indian Reservation). There Maria Solares became known among Native Americans, Mexicans, and whites as a Native American doctor and midwife. When white doctors refused to see Native Americans or Mexicans, Solares cared for them with herbs. She was also frequently called upon to serve as godmother to local children when they were baptized into the Roman Catholic Church, indicating her ability to be at ease with more than one religion. In her later years, she collaborated with John Peabody Harrington of the Smithsonian Institution's Bureau of American Ethnology to study Chumash culture and religion.

Solares died at the reservation on March 6, 1923, but her contributions to the maintenance of Chumash culture did not come to light until 1975. At this time Thomas Blackburn published *December's Child*, a collection of Chumash narratives gathered by Harrington years before. Almost half of the narratives were based upon material that Solares had provided. Among them were the book's most detailed description of the Chumash religion. Today, many of the Native Americans on the Santa Ynez Indian Reservation trace their ancestry to Solares and recognize her as one who has helped to preserve vital cultural and religious information about the Chumash people.

See also: Native Americans
References: Thomas C. Blackburn, ed., *December's Child: A Book of Chumash Oral Narratives* (1975); Travis Hudson, *Breath of the Sun: Life in Early California as Told by a Chumash Indian, Fernando Librado to John P. Harrington* (1979); J. Gordon Melton, *Religious Leaders of America* (1991).

Solomon, Hannah Greenebaum (1858–1942)

Reformer, club woman, and founder of the National Council of Jewish Women, Hannah Greenebaum Solomon was born in Chicago, Illinois, on January 14, 1858. She was the fourth of the ten children of German Jewish immigrants, Michael and Sarah (Spiegel) Greenebaum. Her father was a prosperous businessman and a prominent figure in Chicago's Jewish community. Both of Hannah's parents were active in the city's first Reform congregation. Hannah received a portion of her education at the congregation's Zion Temple school and the balance in public schools. She was enrolled in Chicago's West Division High School for two years before leaving to study piano with Carl Wolfsohn, a well-known Chicago music teacher. Hannah married Henry Solomon, a young merchant who shared her interest in music and the arts, on May 14, 1879. The couple had three children.

For a number of years, Hannah Solomon had been a member of a variety of Jewish social and cultural clubs. In 1877 she and her sister Henriette Frank became the first Jewish members of the prestigious Chicago Women's Club (founded in 1876), and Henriette was the club's president in 1884–1885. Although she considered herself a confirmed feminist, during the early years of her marriage, Solomon's first priority was her family.

In 1890 Solomon was asked to establish a nationwide Congress of Jewish Women as a part of the World Parliament of Religions at the World's Columbian Exposition in Chicago. Through her personal efforts, she gathered together many prominent Jewish women from across the United States, and the Jewish Women's Congress was a success. With her encouragement, in 1893 the congress resolved to become a permanent organization, the National Council of Jewish Women

Hannah Greenebaum Solomon (undated portrait)

(NCJW). The purpose of the NCJW, as Solomon envisioned it, was to further the causes of religious, educational, and philanthropic work among Jewish women. Solomon was elected the first president of the NCJW and held that office until 1905, when she was elected honorary president for life.

Solomon's interests extended to other women's organizations as well as to a variety of philanthropic and reform projects. She was a founding member of the Illinois Federation of Women's Clubs (1896) and the treasurer of the Council of Women of the United States (1899). In 1904 she represented the latter organization at the 1904 International Council of Women in Berlin, and because she was fluent in German and French as well as English, Solomon acted as translator for the other representatives, Susan B. Anthony and May Wright Sewall. During one of her visits to Europe, Solomon helped establish an association of English Jewish women that later became the Union of Jewish Women of England. In conjunction with her work with Russian-Jewish immigrants in Chicago during the 1890s, in 1896 she made a statistical survey of the immigrants in the Jewish section, making note of schools and agencies available in the area to assist the newcomers. A year later she founded the NCJW's Bureau of Personal Service, an organization designed to give aid to immigrants. Solomon frequently worked closely with social worker Jane Addams of Hull House, both in connection with the Bureau of Personal Service and in regard to other issues, especially child welfare. In conjunction with Chicago Women's Club, she played a major role in the establishment of Cook County's juvenile court in 1899 and the Illinois Industrial School for Girls in 1905. She helped relocate the school to a healthier environment, and in 1907 the revived institution became the Park Ridge School for Girls. As a founding member of Chicago's Women's City Club (1910), Solomon worked for a variety of civic reforms.

Solomon, whose life combined a devotion to family, religion, and social reform, died at her home in Chicago on December 7, 1942.

See also: Jews; National Council of Jewish Women
References: Greta Fink, *Great Jewish Women: Profiles of Courageous Women from the Maccabean Period to the Present* (1978); Edward T. James, ed., *Notable American Women: 1607–1950,* vol. 3 (1971); Rosemary Radford Ruether and Rosemary Skinner Keller, eds., *Women and Religion in America,* vol. 1 (1981); Angela Howard Zophy with Frances M. Kavenik, eds., *Handbook of American Women's History* (1990).

Spalding, Eliza Hart (1807–1851)

Pioneer missionary Eliza Hart Spalding, who with Narcissa Prentiss Whitman was one of the first women to cross the Rocky Mountains, was born in Kensington (now Berlin), Connecticut, on August 11, 1807. Little is known of her early life. Most of her youth was spent on a farm in upstate New York. Besides learning the usual farm and household crafts, Eliza received her education at a local female academy. After graduation she taught for a few years, until she married Henry Harmon Spalding (a rejected suitor of Whitman) in 1833.

A devout Christian, Eliza converted to the Presbyterian faith when she was nineteen. Henry Spalding was also a religious man and was intent upon becoming a missionary. During the year prior to their marriage, Henry completed his education at Western Reserve College in Hudson, Ohio. Eliza too moved to Ohio and supplemented her education there as well. Consequently, Eliza was to become the best educated of the women in the Oregon missions. Following their marriage, Henry attended Lane Theological Seminary, a Presbyterian institution located in Cincinnati, as he prepared for missionary work. Again, Eliza too continued her education. In 1834 she wrote to her sister that she was now pursuing Greek and Hebrew studies and taking the same lessons that Henry was taking in the Greek Testament, and in the Hebrew Bible.

With expectations of receiving a government appointment to a teaching post with the Choctaw Indians, Henry chose to leave the seminary in May 1835, at the end of his second year and one year prior to completion of the course. In August 1835, he received word that he would be appointed to a Native American mission if he were an ordained clergyman. Later that month, he was ordained to the Presbyterian ministry. Meanwhile, Eliza had become pregnant, and in the fall of 1835 she gave birth to a stillborn baby.

Henry Spalding was under consideration of the Board of Missions to go with Marcus Whitman and his bride, Narcissa Prentiss Whitman, to the Oregon country to establish missions there. But Spalding was hesitant to accept. On one occasion he publicly announced the he did not want to go into the same mission as Narcissa Prentiss because he questioned her judgment, reflecting his continued resentment over her rejection of his marriage proposal. But Marcus eventually convinced the Spaldings to accompany the Whitmans to Oregon.

In July 1836 Eliza Hart Spalding and Narcissa Prentiss Whitman became the first white women to cross the Continental Divide and the Rocky Mountains. When the missionaries reached Oregon, they split to establish separate missions. The Spaldings settled in Lapwai, among the Nez Percé, in present-day Idaho, and the Whitmans established a mission at Waiilatpu, near the Columbia River in present-day Washington state. The Spaldings were in the midst of a large tribe, well away from the increasingly popular routes of the white people—the Columbia River or Oregon Trail. Their location helped Henry Spalding become the most successful Protestant missionary in the Oregon country. And, according to historian Clifford M. Drury, Eliza was the most loved of all the missionary women.

Within a few months of their arrival at Lapwai, the Spaldings opened a school. While Henry preached and taught farming skills to the Nez Percé, Eliza took charge of the school. There were lessons in English, spinning, knitting, weaving, and sewing, as well as Bible study. On November 15, 1837, Eliza gave birth to a daughter, who was named Eliza after her mother. She was the first white child born in what is now the state of Idaho and was the first of the Spaldings' five children.

On November 29, 1847, the Cayuse in the vicinity of the Whitmans' mission at Waiilatpu initiated an uprising and massacred the Whitmans and twelve others at the mission. Upon hearing the news, the Nez Percé at Lapwai came to the aid of the Spaldings and protected them from the Cayuse who had plotted to kill Reverend Spalding. The events forced the Spaldings to close their mission. On January 8, 1848, Henry, Eliza, and other whites from Lapwai were escorted safely into Portland. The Spaldings eventually settled on a farm near Brownsville, Oregon. Eliza died there of tuberculosis on January 7, 1851.

See also: Missionaries; Whitman, Narcissa Prentiss
References: Opal Sweazea Allen, *Narcissa Whitman: An Historical Biography* (1959); Deborah Dawson Bonde, "Spalding, Eliza Hart," in Angela Howard Zophy with Frances M. Kavenik, eds., *Handbook of American Women's History* (1990); Clifford M. Drury, *Marcus and Narcissa Whitman and the Opening of Old Oregon* (1986).

Spiritualism

Beginning in 1848, when sisters Margaret and Kate Fox of Hydesville, New York, reported "rappings" and contacts with the spirit world, Spiritualism became a popular movement during the second half of the nineteenth century. The Fox sisters demonstrated that people would pay money to witness spiritual manifestations, and a new profession, that of Spiritualist medium, emerged during the 1850s. The occupation was generally identified with women, but men too were mediums. A census of Spiritualist mediums taken in 1859 showed 121 women and 110 men in the profession. Although earnings for both male and female spiritual mediums were modest, it was one of the few occupations open to women during the era.

Females took advantage of the idea that successful mediums were blessed with specific traits that in the nineteenth century were defined as feminine. Characteristics such as intuition, nervousness, impressionability, and extreme sensitivity were deemed valuable for one desiring to become a successful medium. Most important, women were considered to be passive, a trait that better allowed a spirit to manifest anything through the medium. Mediums were believed to be giving up their own identity to become the instrument of others. In this regard, a self-sacrificing, passive woman was considered to be better qualified as a medium than a strong, independent man. Critics of Spiritualism, however, viewed female Spiritualists as persons whose feminine characteristics had been corrupted.

Female mediums like Emma Hardinge and Cora Richmond exhibited joy upon conquering male adversaries. Sometimes male ruffians would attempt to disrupt their lectures. The women would declare victory if they managed to subdue the men and convince them of their spiritual powers. Both Hardinge and Richmond were "trance lecturers," who would enter into a trance and then begin talking.

One critic of Spiritualism was novelist Henry James, who in *The Bostonians* linked Spiritualism to feminism and denounced them both. His attitude was quite typical. Critics, and there were many, charged that Spiritualism promoted immorality by tolerating, and even encouraging, divorce and remarriage. Also, some critics considered women who worked independently from men to be "free lovers." Possibly critics' charges were based upon the fact that a number of feminists, including Elizabeth Cady Stanton, Susan B. Anthony, and Frances Willard, were interested in Spiritualism. However, none of these women ever publicly identified themselves with the movement, nor did they stress any connection between the women's movement and Spiritualism. Victoria Wood-

hull was the only prominent feminist to closely associate herself with Spiritualism. A medium herself, she was elected president of a national Spiritualist association three times during the 1870s. Nevertheless, she was too radical for many in the organization and caused a rift that led to the group's destruction.

Spiritualism helped those who believed in it to function, especially those who had experienced personal tragedy. Loss of a loved one often drew people to Spiritualists in hopes of making contacts with the deceased. Although the movement died down by the turn of the century, Spiritualism has become a part of new movements in the twentieth century, such as the recent New Age movement.

See also: Blavatsky, Helena Petrovna; MacLaine, Shirley; Richmond, Cora Lodencia Veronica Scott; Woodhull, Victoria Claflin

References: Harrison D. Barrett, *Life Work of Mrs. Cora L. V. Richmond* (1895); R. Laurence Moore, *In Search of White Crows: Spiritualism, Parapsychology, and American Culture* (1977); Laurence Moore, "The Spiritualist Medium: A Study of Female Professionalization in Victorian America," in Esther Katz and Anita Rapone, eds., *Women's Experience in America: An Historical Anthology* (1980); Geoffrey K. Nelson, *Spiritualism and Society* (1969).

Stanton, Elizabeth Cady (1815–1902)

Known for her radical ideas, author, lecturer, and pioneer feminist Elizabeth Cady Stanton created an uproar in her later years with the publication of *The Woman's Bible* (1895 and 1898). She was born November 12, 1815, into one of the wealthiest families in Johnstown, New York. Elizabeth's parents, Daniel and Margaret Cady, were Presbyterians, and they raised their family in that faith. Throughout most of her youth, Elizabeth had a gloomy view of a punitive God. But when she was fifteen, she attended revival meetings in Troy, New York, and

Elizabeth Cady Stanton (undated lithograph)

listened to the preaching of the famous evangelist Charles Grandison Finney. Elizabeth became spellbound. Revival theology emphasized an individual's choice to behave in such a manner that he or she would be rewarded with conversion and salvation. Finney's God was just and benevolent, and unlike most clergymen of the era, Finney believed that women should be given the opportunity to pray in public.

The revivals marked a turning point in Elizabeth's religious beliefs. At one of the revivals, she confessed her sins and underwent a conversion experience. However, her self-esteem was snapped almost immediately after her conversion. Elizabeth became ill, grew fearful of judgment, and went home to Johnstown. Nevertheless, the revivals had caused her to start thinking about religion and the role it would play in her life. She began to study and analyze religions and to investigate theological issues. Elizabeth listened to her friend, Quaker minister Lucretia Mott, who encouraged her religious inquiry. She had met Mott while on her honeymoon with her husband, Henry Brewster Stanton, in May 1840. The women had attempted to attend an anti-slavery conference in London but, because of their sex, were not allowed to be seated. Their mutual outrage over the treatment of women at the convention drew Lucretia Mott and Elizabeth Cady Stanton together. Their many discussions regarding the oppression of women led to the first women's rights convention ever held in the United States. It was held at the Wesleyan Methodist chapel in Seneca Falls, New York, July 19–20, 1848.

During the mid-1840s, the Stantons spent several years in Boston. While there, Elizabeth became an admirer of Theodore Parker, a theologian who combined Unitarianism, Transcendentalism, and Christian perfection. He refused to accept the Scriptures literally and suggested that God was an androgynous figure. Parker's liberal theology helped Stanton, who found his lectures soul-satisfying, along her way toward religious independence.

Stanton was among the most radical of nineteenth-century feminists, at times shocking even ardent feminists like Lucretia Mott. Stanton composed the *Declaration of Rights and Sentiments and its Resolutions*, the principal document of the Seneca Falls convention of 1848. The document articulated men's unjust oppression of women and demanded equal rights for women, including the right to vote. Stanton became the first person to publicly demand suffrage for women. She later would stun both men and women with her calls for liberalized divorce laws that would allow women to divorce their husbands on such grounds as drunkenness, insanity, adultery, abuse, or mere incompatibility.

In March 1851, Stanton met Susan B. Anthony, the woman who would be her ally in the cause for women's rights for the next fifty years. Both Stanton and Anthony opposed the Fourteenth (1868) and Fifteenth Amendments (1870) to the U.S. Constitution because they failed to include women as persons with rights of citizenship and suffrage. Stanton and Anthony founded the National Woman Suffrage Association in 1869, and Stanton was its president until the organization merged with its rival, the American Woman Suffrage Association, to form the National American Woman Suffrage Association (NAWSA) in 1890. Stanton served as president of NAWSA from 1890 to 1892.

Between 1881 and 1886, Stanton, Anthony, and Matilda Joslyn Gage compiled three volumes of the six-volume *History of Woman Suffrage*. Stanton's next work, *The Woman's Bible,* proved to be very controversial. She had become a religious skeptic and had also decided that religion was at the base of society's long history of oppressing women. She did not believe that the Bible was the direct word of God, and she wrote *The Woman's Bible* to point to contradictions within the Scriptures and to motivate women to question theological doctrine that disparaged them. Stanton had hoped to involve other women in her research, but few answered her appeals. When the first volume was released in 1895, it met with controversy from both the clergy, who denounced the book as the work of Satan, and from feminists, who considered the work sacrilegious and detrimental to their cause. But *The Woman's Bible* was a best-seller, and Stanton's goal of getting women to think about theological doctrine was achieved. In 1898 Stanton published her memoirs, *Eighty Years and More.* She died in New York City on October 26, 1902. Throughout her life, Stanton worked to free women from the psychological barriers that held them in. She urged them to reject numerous tradi-

tions and to question both church and state whenever they had rules that were detrimental to women.

See also: Mott, Lucretia Coffin; Woman Suffrage; *The Woman's Bible*
References: Lois W. Banner, *Elizabeth Cady Stanton: A Radical for Woman's Rights* (1980); Elisabeth Griffith, *In Her Own Right: The Life of Elizabeth Cady Stanton* (1984); Alma Lutz, *Created Equal: A Biography of Elizabeth Cady Stanton, 1815–1902* (1974); Elizabeth Cady Stanton, *Eighty Years and More: Reminiscences, 1815–1897* (1898, republished 1993); Stanton, *The Woman's Bible: Parts I and II* (1895, 1898, reprint 1972).

Starhawk (Simos, Miriam) (1951–)

Starhawk is the public name of Miriam Simos, a well-known American neo-Pagan witch, feminist, author, and peace activist. She was born in St. Paul, Minnesota, on June 17, 1951, to Jack and Bertha (Goldfarb) Simos. Her father was a social worker, and her mother was a clinical social worker and author. Starhawk was raised in the Jewish tradition and received a strong Hebrew education during her youth. In 1972 she graduated from the University of California at Los Angeles with a bachelor of arts degree in art, and in 1982 she received a master's degree in the feminist therapy program at Antioch West University.

During her years in Los Angeles, Starhawk learned witchcraft from Sara Cunningham, who for several years was head of the Temple of Tipareth in Pasadena, California. Another of her teachers was Zsuzsanna E. Budapest, a witch from Hungary and a founder of feminist Dianic witchcraft. After a move to the San Francisco Bay area in 1973, Starhawk studied faery tradition witchcraft, a tradition based upon the legendary "little people" of Stone Age Britain, with Victor H. Anderson. In 1975 Starhawk was one of the first signers of the Covenant of the Goddess (COG), a national association of Wiccan groups. She served as the organization's first officer for the 1976–1977 term. Starhawk was also a founder of Reclaiming: A Center for Feminist Spirituality and Counseling in Berkeley, California, in 1980. Reclaiming is a feminist collective that offers classes, workshops, public rituals, and private counseling in witchcraft. Starhawk has served the association as director, teacher, and counselor. She has also joined other members of Reclaiming in demonstrations against nuclear power plants and military bases.

Based on the faery tradition, Starhawk's first published book, *The Spiral Dance: A Rebirth of the Ancient Religion of the Great Goddess* (1979), became the most popular introduction to Wicca and neo-Paganism of the 1980s. Over 100,000 copies of the original edition were sold, leading to a tenth anniversary edition in 1989. Other books by Starhawk include *Dreaming in the Dark* (1982) and *Truth or Dare: Encounters of Power, Authority and Mystery* (1987). Although she is a feminist, her rituals include men. She has thus been influential in the increasing contact between feminist women and men in witchcraft and neo-Paganism. One of the core principles of her "thealogy" is that the earth is sacred. Starhawk has also introduced themes of social activism, ideas that were previously absent from much of occult thought.

In addition to her writings and work within the Wiccan and neo-Pagan community, Starhawk has lectured at a number of colleges and universities, including Union Theological Seminary in New York City; the University of California at San Francisco; and California State University at San Francisco, San Jose, and Chico.

See also: Wicca; Witchcraft
References: Rosemary Ellen Guiley, *The Encyclopedia of Witches and Witchcraft* (1989); "Simos, Miriam," in Frances C. Locher, ed., *Contemporary Authors,* vol. 104 (1982); J. Gordon Melton, *Religious Leaders of America* (1991); Starhawk, *The Spiral Dance: A Rebirth of the Ancient Religion of the Great Goddess,* 10th anniversary edition (1989).

Starr, Eliza Allen (1824–1901)

Eminent Roman Catholic writer and artist Eliza Allen Starr was born in Deerfield, Massachusetts, on August 29, 1824. Her birth name was Eliza Ann, but she took Allen as her middle name as an adult. She was the second of the four children of Oliver and Lovina (Allen) Starr. Oliver Starr was a descendant of Comfort Starr, an early settler of the Massachusetts Bay Colony. Eliza's parents encouraged her early interests in art and literature and urged her to go beyond a basic education. In 1845 she went to Boston to study art and painting, and she opened a studio of her own the following year.

At about the time she moved to Boston, Starr began a religious search that led to her eventual adoption of Roman Catholicism. She had been raised a Unitarian but had become dissatisfied with Unitarian theology. After many years of research and contemplation, she finally converted to Catholicism, receiving the rite of baptism in December 1854. For several years she considered the possibility of a religious vocation but abandoned that idea in 1860. Starr's conversion had great influence on her art, which thereafter reflected religious themes.

Starr settled in Chicago in 1856. There she established a studio and became one of the city's first full-time art teachers and the first to teach from nature and casts, insisting that her students never copy the works of others. In addition to her teaching, beginning in 1871 Starr gave an annual series of lectures that continued for two decades. She advocated the advancement of women's education and gave freely of her time and talent to the development of the art department at St. Mary's Academy, Notre Dame, Indiana. Starr also published poems and articles on Christian art in such periodicals as *Catholic World, Catholic Mirror, Ave Maria, London Monthly,* and *Freeman's Journal,* becoming well known within Catholic circles as a lecturer and writer.

Starr's best known work, *Pilgrims and Shrines* (2 vols., 1885), was inspired by her extended visit to Europe from 1875 to 1877. A number of devotional books, most of which were self-illustrated, followed. Among them were *Isabella of Castille* (1889), *Christian Art in Our Own Age* (1891), *Three Keys to the Camera Della Segnatura of the Vatican* (1895), *The Seven Dolors of the Blessed Virgin Mary* (1898), and *The Three Archangels and the Guardian Angels in Art* (1899). In recognition of the latter work, Starr received a medallion from Pope Leo XIII. Earlier she had been awarded Notre Dame University's Laetare Medal (1885) and a special gold medal from the Catholic Congress at Chicago's World's Columbian Exposition (1893).

Eliza Allen Starr died at the home of her brother Caleb Allen Starr in Durand, Illinois, on September 7, 1901.

See also: Roman Catholic Church
References: *Dictionary of American Biography,* vol. 17 (1935); Edward T. James, ed., *Notable American Women, 1607–1950,* vol. 3 (1971); J. Gordon Melton, *Religious Leaders of America* (1991); Mary J. Oates, "Catholic Laywomen in the Labor Force, 1850–1950," in Karen Kennelly, ed., *American Catholic Women: A Historical Exploration* (1989).

Stetson, Augusta Emma Simmons (1842–1928)

Christian Science leader Augusta Emma Simmons Stetson was born October 12, 1842, in Waldoboro, Maine. Her parents, Peabody and Salome (Sprague) Simmons, were devout Methodists. In her in-

Augusta Emma Simmons Stetson (undated portrait)

fancy, Augusta moved with her family to Damariscotta, Maine, where her father worked as a carpenter and an architect. Augusta received her education at Damariscotta High School and Lincoln Academy in New Castle, Maine. She was talented, both as a musician and as a public speaker.

In 1864 Augusta married Captain Frederick J. Stetson, a veteran of the Civil War and a shipbuilder associated with Baring Brothers of London, England. The newlyweds moved to London and then spent some years in Bombay, India, and Akyab, British Burma. But at the age of thirty-one, long plagued by ill health since his incarceration in Libby Prison during the Civil War, Stetson was physically unable to continue in his business, and he retired. The Stetsons returned to the United States, settling in

Boston. Augusta enrolled in the Blish School of Oratory in 1882, hoping to support herself and her husband by giving public lectures.

A turning point in Augusta Stetson's career came in 1884, when she attended a talk on Christian Science by founder Mary Baker Eddy. Eddy, who recognized Stetson's speaking talents and possibilities as a leader in her church, persuaded her to attend classes. Immediately upon completion of Eddy's three-week course, Stetson began to practice as a Christian Science healer. After excursions practicing in Maine and in Boston, Eddy sent her to New York City in November 1886 to organize Christian Science work there. In February 1888 a church of seventeen members was officially incorporated, and in October 1890 Stetson was ordained pastor of First Church of Christ, Scientist, New York City. A year later she organized the New York City Christian Science Institute, which was designed to spread the faith and train more practitioners. Captain Stetson, who was now suffering from rheumatism, joined his wife in New York in 1899. He died two years later from cerebral apoplexy.

Membership in First Church grew steadily, until by 1903 it built a million-dollar structure that was the most opulent of all Christian Science churches and larger than the Mother Church in Boston. A year later an adjoining home was built and furnished for Stetson at a cost of $100,000. Stetson lived on a lavish scale, which, combined with her successful career, caused envy among others. In turn, jealousy incited rumors that Stetson had plans to replace Eddy as leader of the church. In 1902, in a ruling believed to have been at least partially directed at Stetson, Eddy required that all ministers (called "readers") resign after three-year terms. Although Stetson complied with Eddy's demands, she retained her dominant role at First Church.

At Eddy's request, early in 1909 the Christian Science board of directors began an investigation into Stetson's alleged unorthodox views. Prominent among the charges against Stetson were claims that she taught that sex and procreation were sinful and that she was endeavoring by means of mental suggestion (malicious animal magnetism) to bring illness and even death upon her enemies. At the base of these accusations was a struggle for power. Later that year Stetson's license as a Christian Science teacher and practitioner was revoked, and she was excommunicated. But Stetson remained in her home next to First Church and kept her title as principal of the New York City Christian Science Institute.

Despite her excommunication, Stetson remained loyal to Eddy, believing that the founder of Christian Science was merely testing her and that Eddy would eventually reinstate her. When Eddy died in 1910, Stetson did not attempt to replace her but predicted that just as Christ had arisen, Eddy would return to life. Meanwhile, Stetson campaigned to spread her own views. Between 1912 and 1917, she and her students held receptions in New York City. Sometimes as many as eight hundred people gathered to hear readings from the Bible, works by Eddy, and addresses from Stetson. Stetson published a series of pamphlets in which she presented her interpretation of the true Christian Science and attacked what she considered the spiritual decline of the Mother Church in Boston. She published *Reminiscences, Sermons, and Correspondence* (1913) and *Vital Issues in Christian Science* (1914), which reviewed the controversy within the church. Hundreds of her students spread Stetson's influence across the United States.

In 1918 Stetson founded the Choral Society of the New York Christian Institute, a group of three hundred voices that specialized in spiritual music. During World War I, Stetson became a violent American jingoist and a strong believer in the superiority of the Aryan race. In the 1920s she launched a huge advertising campaign, spreading her views in newspapers and magazines and over the radio. Her major work, *Sermons Which Spiritually Interpret the Scriptures and Other Writings on Christian Science,* was published in 1924. Also in that year, she supported the short-lived *American Standard,* a magazine written mostly by her students with the stated purpose of guarding and fostering Nordic supremacy in America.

Shortly before her death, Stetson announced that she would never die. Despite her prediction, she died of edema at the home of her nephew in Rochester, New York, on October 12, 1928. After her death, a diminishing group of friends and students sought to carry on her work.

See also: Eddy, Mary Baker
References: Henry Warner Bowden, *Dictionary of American Religious Biography,* 2nd ed. (1993); *Dictionary of American Biography,* vol. 17 (1935); Stephen Gottschalk, *The Emergence of Christian Science in American Religious Life* (1973); Edward T. James, ed., *Notable American Women, 1607–1950,* vol. 3 (1971).

Stewart, Maria W. (1803–1879)

Lecturer, writer, abolitionist, champion of women's rights, and religious revolutionary Maria W. Stewart, sometimes called Frances Maria Stewart or Steward, was born to free black parents in Hartford, Connecticut, in 1803. She was orphaned at age five and was bound out to a white minister and his family. It seems that during the ten years she lived in the clergyman's home, Stewart absorbed his religious teachings, for by early adulthood she was a devout Christian and possessed considerable knowledge of the Bible. She had little formal education yet became a skilled writer and orator.

Stewart married at age twenty-three, but she was widowed three years later, in 1829. Not long after her husband's death, Stewart began her career as an abolitionist. A zealous opponent of slavery, Stewart gave her first lecture for the abolitionist cause in 1832 and was likely the first American-born woman to speak before a "promiscuous" audience of both men and women, predating the Grimké sisters by approximately five years. Her lectures and articles were published in William Lloyd Garrison's abolitionist journal, *The Liberator,* in the early 1830s. But while speaking out against slavery, Stewart contended that many free blacks in the North fared little better than their brothers and sisters in the South. While bound out as a child, she had learned firsthand of the toil and drudgery suffered by northern blacks.

Stewart advocated independent black institutions and self-help organizations and demanded that Christian educational opportunities become available for all African-American children. If all other means of achieving rights for blacks failed, Stewart believed that racial violence was justified. She viewed the American Revolution as an event from which African Americans should draw inspiration and felt that a just God would punish a nation that allowed such oppression as could be found in the United States in the mid-nineteenth century. Stewart also admonished blacks to plan wisely for their future, to become self-sufficient through education and economy. She opposed the American Colonization Society's plan to relocate blacks on the west coast of Africa, insisting that she would rather be dead than be driven to a foreign land.

Responding to those who criticized her, as a woman, for lecturing in public, Stewart maintained that God supported her right to speak. In a speech she gave in Boston in 1833, Stewart cited biblical examples of Deborah as one who served as both a mother and a judge, Queen Esther as a savior of the Jews, and Mary Magdalene as the first to report on the resurrection of Christ, arguing that if those women could speak out on important issues, so could she.

Stewart's public career lasted only about three years. She left Boston in about 1833 and thereafter supported herself as a teacher in New York City, Baltimore, and soon after the Civil War, in Washington, D.C. Later, she accepted a position as matron of the Freedman's Hospital in Washington (now Howard University Hospital). Little is known of the last years of this woman who set a precedent for women, both black and white, who desired to voice publicly their views on religion and politics. Maria W. Stewart died in 1879.

> **See also:** African Americans; Antislavery Movement; Grimké, Angelina Emily; Grimké, Sarah Moore
> **References:** Ernest G. Bormann, ed., *Forerunners of Black Power: The Rhetoric of Abolition* (1971); Bernard Quarles, *Black Abolitionists* (1969); Marilyn Richardson, *Black Women and Religion: A Bibliography* (1980); Maria W. Stewart, *Maria W. Stewart: America's First Black Woman Political Writer* (1987).

Sunday School Movement

The development of Sunday schools coincided with the era of institution building in the early years of the American republic. Reformers of the period encouraged the establishment of prisons, orphanages, asylums, hospitals, and other facilities. The Sunday school movement was a part of this drive to improve American society. Along with biblical topics, Sunday schools taught their students moral values associated with their religions.

Inspired by British examples from the early 1780s, American Sunday schools actually began as early as 1786, when Francis Asbury (who is usually credited with bringing the first such school to this country) opened a Sunday school in Hanover County, Virginia. In 1790 the Methodists became the first denomination to adopt the Sunday school as official policy, though throughout the early decades of the 1800s, the movement was largely interdenominational. Early schools hired teachers who taught basic reading and writing using the Bible as their text. Americans worried that their children, especially those of the poor, were not receiving the literacy training or the religious knowledge necessary for future citizens of the new republic. They saw the gatherings of noisy children on Sundays, under no visible control and behaving in a manner deemed inappropriate for the "Lord's day," as a social problem. Some saw Sunday schools as a solution to the problem. But by the end of the first quarter of the nineteenth century, these schools had almost disappeared. Replacing them was a new type of Sunday school, with volunteer teachers, that offered a strictly religious curriculum. And although British Sunday schools continued to be aimed at the poor, their American counterparts had become more inclusive. This style of Sunday school began to flourish by the 1830s. The switch from hired teachers to volunteers came in the period from 1800 to 1830, a time when numerous Protestant voluntary associations were emerging. These organizations ranged from denominational missionary societies to interdenominational Bible and tract societies. Many combined evangelizing efforts with charitable activities.

Most early Sunday school founders, such as those who established the First Day Society in Philadelphia in 1791, were men. But despite their limited public roles in nineteenth-century America, women were also pioneers in the movement. Joanna Graham Bethune and her mother, Isabella Graham, opened a Sunday school in New York City in 1803 that was based on the British model. They employed teachers for instruction in reading and writing but presented the religious education themselves, as volunteers.

Sunday schools gave girls, who were frequently discouraged from enrolling in or even denied admission to public schools in the 1810s and 1820s, an opportunity to learn reading and writing. Of the adults attending Sunday schools for the purpose of learning to read, a majority were women. Memorization and recitation of biblical verses were the usual pedagogical techniques, with the idea that these methods would teach the students self-discipline and concentration and would instill information that might reform their behavior.

By the 1820s, most of the Sunday school teachers were female, reflecting the movement toward volunteer teachers. These women found rewards in their work in the form of respect from the public, spiritual enrichment, a broadening of social experiences, and increased responsibility. Restricted from performing most other work within their churches, the women felt that by volunteering as Sunday school teachers they were being "useful." For some, the opportunity to meet men in the ministry and perhaps marry and become a missionary was also an attraction. The majority of the female Sunday school teachers were young, ages eighteen to twenty-five, and were often themselves recruited from the Sunday schools.

Anne M. Boylan, in her study of the Sunday school movement, *Sunday School: The Formation of an American Institution, 1790–1880* (1988), speculates that one reason that more women than men were drawn into Sunday school teaching was that women were apparently more comfortable with emotional displays that often accompanied teaching, that is, weeping, praying, and embracing. Also,

girls were more likely to remain in Bible study than boys, there were more classes for girls than for boys, and the girls had female role models in their teachers. When classes were coeducational, girls usually outnumbered boys.

Despite their smaller numbers, men were usually the leaders of the schools. Women had the opportunity to lead only when they founded their own schools, and they founded many. They also established a number of organizations, such as the Female Union Society for the Promotion of Sabbath Schools in 1816 in New York, and Baltimore's Female (later McKendrean Female) Sabbath School Society (1816), for the purpose of combining several schools. But when women's schools merged with men's, or if a man and a woman founded a school together, the woman usually took a subordinate role. However, women eventually found ways to acquire influence and power. Temperance work was one road to power, and many Woman's Christian Temperance Union organizers, including Frances Willard, had Sunday school experience.

Feminine domination in nineteenth-century Sunday school teaching is a part of what scholars of recent decades have seen as the broader "feminization" of American religion during the era. Although they were prevented from holding power within churches, women were able to influence change in these institutions through their numbers.

Although contemporary Sunday schools remain important to American religious life, they have a more limited role in a child's life than those of the nineteenth century. Teachers, still mostly women and volunteers, essentially provide biblical instruction to the children of their congregations.

References: Anne M. Boylan, *Sunday School: The Formation of an American Institution, 1790–1880* (1988); Robert W. Lynn and Elliott Wright, *The Big Little*

School: The Hundred Years of the Sunday School, 2nd ed. (1980); Edward L. Queen II et al., eds., *The Encyclopedia of American Religious History* (1996); Edwin Wilbur Rice, *The Sunday School Movement, 1780–1917 and the American Sunday-School Union, 1817–1917* (1971).

Szold, Henrietta (1860–1945)

Writer, educator, humanitarian, and founder of Hadassah, Henrietta Szold was born December 21, 1860, in Baltimore, Maryland. She was the eldest of the eight daughters of Rabbi Benjamin Szold and Sophie Szold. Rabbi Szold, a respected Jewish scholar and humanitarian, recognized his daughter's extraordinary intelligence and took it upon himself to ensure that Henrietta had a broad education.

Henrietta Szold began her schooling in the basement of the local synagogue, where she studied the basics of Judaism as well as German, French, and Hebrew. From age eleven she attended public schools, until she graduated from high school at the top of her class at the age of sixteen. While in school, Henrietta had been working as her father's secretary, and he had been supplementing her public education with instruction in the German classics and with reading assignments in general history and philosophy. Together they discussed Rabbi Szold's sermons as well as his research. Later, Henrietta attended lectures at nearby Johns Hopkins University and the Peabody Institute.

Following high school, Henrietta began teaching at a private school for impoverished southern ladies. There she taught English, French, German, algebra, botany, and other subjects. At the same time, she taught Bible classes at her father's congregational school. When she was twenty, Szold began writing articles for Anglo-Jewish weeklies. The articles included news of activities within the

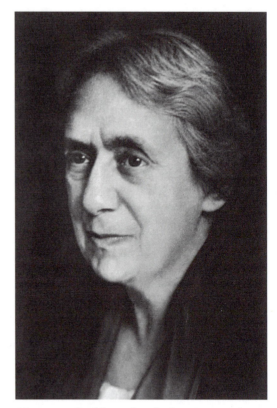

Henrietta Szold (undated photo)

Jewish community, commentaries on current events, and biographies of notable Jews. Her experiences as a teacher and a journalist led her into public speaking, and soon she was addressing literary clubs and young men's Hebrew associations.

In the 1880s Szold became greatly disturbed by news of pogroms against Jews in czarist Russia. The sad plight of Jews escaping Russia and Poland became readily apparent when some began arriving in Baltimore. Szold became determined to do something to help them. With the assistance of the Baltimore Hebrew Literary Society, she opened a night school for immigrant adults in 1889. Designed to help them assimilate into American society and culture, immigrants were taught English, American history, bookkeeping, and other subjects. The school was a success. Starting with only thirty pupils, by 1898, when it became a part of the public school system, more than five thousand immigrants had received training there. It became a model for other night schools for immigrants across the country.

As she became acquainted with the immigrants, Henrietta developed a passion for the idea of Zionism. She believed that the only way Jews could be safe from persecution would be in a country of their own. Szold began to join in the call for a Jewish homeland in Palestine.

In 1893 Szold gave up her career in teaching. She devoted more time to writing and was made secretary of the board of the Jewish Publishing Society of America. It was a paid post, which she held from 1893 to 1915. Szold did most of the publishing work for the first *American Jewish Yearbook,* published in 1899, and was editor of the book from 1904 to 1908. She also wrote fifteen articles for *The Jewish Encyclopedia.*

After her father died in 1902, Szold took it upon herself to prepare his unfinished manuscripts for publication. Once she started, she realized that she needed further study of Judaism if she were to accomplish this task successfully. Therefore, she moved to New York City and enrolled in the Jewish Theological Seminary. In order to receive permission to attend, Szold had to promise school officials that she had no intention of becoming a rabbi.

While at the seminary, she met and fell in love with Louis Ginzberg, more than ten years her junior and a member of the faculty. Szold became a devoted student, spending hours helping him to prepare his lectures, speeches, and articles. She also assisted him with the research and organization of his scholarly work, including his major literary effort, *The Legends of the Jews.* When Ginzberg married in 1909, Szold's heart was broken, contributing to her nervous and physical breakdown soon after.

Upon the advice of her mother, Szold took a leave of absence from the Jewish Publishing Society and traveled to Europe and Palestine. Seeing the Holy Land for herself increased her dedication to the Zionist cause. When she returned home in 1910, she began speaking to a variety of Jewish groups, especially to Jewish women, about both Zionism and women's rights.

In 1912 she played a leading role in the founding of a Zionist women's organization in the United States. Leaders of the Federation of American Zionists criticized Szold for not affiliating with them. But Szold had recently become a convert for women's rights and believed that women could better avoid male dominance by forming separate organizations. At its founding, the group of about forty women was known as the Hadassah Chapter of Daughters of Zion, but two years later the name was shortened to Hadassah, the Hebrew name for Queen Esther. By 1918, Hadassah had more than fifty chapters and five thousand members in the United States. Almost eighty years later the organization has grown to include about sixteen hundred chapters with more than 400,000 members.

Under Szold's leadership, in 1913 Hadassah received funding to send two nurses to Palestine to treat children for trachoma, an eye disease that causes blindness if not treated early. With the help of philanthropist Nathan Strauss and his wife, Hadassah was soon planning to open a training center for nurses in Palestine, but the outbreak of World War I prevented this idea from reaching fruition.

In 1916 Supreme Court Justice Louis Brandeis and federal judge Julian W. Mack instituted a fund to enable Szold to leave her job at the Jewish Publishing Society and devote all her time and energy to the Zionist cause. The money was well spent because until her death Szold worked untiringly to help Jews in Palestine.

Late in World War I, Hadassah sent a medical unit to Palestine, which was designed to provide health care to both Arabs and Jews, and set up hospitals in Tiberias, Jerusalem, Jaffa, Haifa, and Safed. Szold traveled to Palestine herself in 1920 to observe the operation of the medical unit and to acquire a better understanding of the medical needs of the people. She returned to the United States in 1923 but continued to make trips to Palestine.

In 1927, at the Zionist convention in Basel, the World Zionist Organization elected Szold the first female member of the Palestine Zionist Executive Board. At that point she resigned the presidency of Hadassah. Two years later, at the age of sixty-eight, she was reelected to the board. But in 1930, Labor Zionists, who in 1927 had objected to Szold's becoming a member of the executive board, succeeded in engineering her resignation.

For a while, Szold thought her years of work for the Zionist cause had come to an end, but in 1931, she was elected to the *Vaad Leumi*, the executive committee of the newly created Jewish Community Organization of Palestine (Keneseth Israel). She was to be responsible for the group's health and education services. Despite her advanced years, Szold worked energetically for the organization, giving lectures and establishing a bureau for the rehabilitation of juvenile delinquents as well as a training school for social workers. She headed the Central Social Service Bureau until 1939 and chaired the Jerusalem bureau until her death.

Beginning in 1933, as Nazis rose to power, German Jews began arriving in Palestine in great numbers. Szold worked to acquire funding to help settle the immigrants. When Recha Freier, the wife of a German rabbi, suggested that arrangements be made for the settlement in Palestine of groups of German Jewish children, Szold at first thought it was a bad idea. Funds were lacking, and there were no facilities for the children. But soon Freier convinced her of the necessity of this solution, and Szold became an enthusiastic leader of the project known as Youth Aliyah. The first group of children arrived in Haifa in 1937. By 1945, thirteen thousand children were able to escape Nazi atrocities and settle in Palestine as a result of this program.

Henrietta Szold, one of the most influential women in modern Jewish history, died on February 12, 1945.

See also: Hadassah; Jews
References: Greta Fink, *Great Jewish Women: Profiles of Courageous Women from the Maccabean Period to the Present* (1978); Alexandra Lee Levin, *The Szolds of Lombard Street: A Baltimore Family, 1859–1909* (1960); Marvin Lowenthal, *Henrietta Szold: Life and Letters* (1942, reprint 1975); Simon Noveck, ed., *Great Jewish Personalities in Modern Times* (1960); Elinor Slater and Robert Slater, *Great Jewish Women* (1994).

Tate, Mary Magdalena Lewis (1871–1930)

Little is known of the early life of Mary Magdalena Lewis Tate, a leader in the Holiness-Pentecostal movement among African Americans and the founder of the Church of the Living God, the Pillar and Ground of the Truth. It is believed that she was born in Tennessee on January 3, 1871. Admirers have maintained that her pureness of character as a youth brought her the title "Miss Do Right," which led to her followers becoming known as "The Do Righters." She married David Lewis in the 1880s and bore her first child, Walter Curtis Lewis, in 1890 in Vanlier, Tennessee. A second son, Felix Earl Lewis, was born in 1892. Sometime around the turn of the century, she settled with her family in Clinton, Tennessee. There, according to tradition, she experienced a lengthy period of religious turmoil that culminated in her decision to enter public life by preaching the Gospel.

Tate's evangelizing began in 1903 in Steele Springs, Tennessee, and then moved on to Paducah, Kentucky, and Brooklyn, Illinois, where she preached her first sermon. Later, she traveled throughout the South, and by 1907 she had begun to organize Holiness bands, groups of people who taught the Gospel to others. It appears that sometime in the early 1900s Tate terminated contact with her husband. She eventually became known as Mary Magdalena Tate and was affectionately called "Mother Tate"

by her followers. Her early work coincided with the beginnings of the Pentecostal movement that was spreading across the nation. Tate became ill in 1908 but came to believe herself cured, or "sealed and healed," when she was baptized in the Holy Spirit (as evidenced by her speaking in tongues) on Pentecost Sunday (Smith, 1996, p. 626). Weeks later, she began holding revival services in Greenville, Alabama. When the gatherings ended, she led in the formal establishment of the Church of the Living God, the Pillar and Ground of the Truth, which took its title from the Bible (I Timothy 3:15), and she became its chief apostle, elder, president, and first chief overseer. The church was one of the earliest predominantly black Pentecostal denominations in the United States. The board of trustees ordained Tate to the bishopric, and she in turn ordained the first ministers of the church.

Although the early congregations of Tate's church were in the South, she began establishing churches in the North soon after World War I. Her two sons, who had been her helpers and constant companions in her journeys, were among the first four state bishops ordained at the church's general assembly in Tennessee in 1914. At the same conference, the church rules and bylaws were presented in book format, *Constitution, Government and General Degree Book*, of which Tate had written a large portion. In 1923 she opened a publishing house in Nashville. From 1916 to 1924, the church grew rapidly, with congregations organized in more than twenty states; Washington, D.C.; and several foreign countries.

On her last missionary journey to the North in 1930, Tate developed a case of frostbite that required surgery. Gangrene set in, and she died in December 1930. The church became divided into three areas of sixteen states each, with each area placed under a bishop. One of these bishops was Tate's son Felix and another was M. F. L. Keith, the widow of her eldest son. Bruce L. McLeod was the third. Eventually, each of these areas became a separate denomination. The Church of the Living God had approximately two thousand members and about one hundred ministers in 1988 and reported charters in forty-three states and Jamaica in 1992.

References: Sherry Sherrod DuPree, ed., *Biographical Dictionary of African-American Holiness-Pentecostals, 1880–1990* (1989); J. Gordon Melton, *Religious Leaders of America* (1991); Jessie Carney Smith, ed., *Notable Black American Women, Book II* (1996).

Tekakwitha, Kateri (c. 1656–1680)

Also known as Catherine Tekakwitha (Tegakouita, Tegakwitha, or Tagaskouita), Lily of the Mohawks, and La Sainte Sauvagesse, Kateri Tekakwitha is the first Native American convert to Roman Catholicism to be venerated by the church. The precise date of Tekakwitha's birth is not known, but it is believed that she was born in 1656 near present-day Auriesville, New York. She was the daughter of a Mohawk warrior and a Christianized Algonquin mother who had been captured by Mohawks about three years before Kateri's birth. When Kateri was four, smallpox struck her village, killing her parents, impairing Kateri's eyesight, and causing disfigure-

ment to her face. Her uncle, who was a village chief, took Kateri to live with him.

In 1667 the French government sent three Jesuit missionaries to the village. Kateri's uncle was bitterly opposed to Christianity but was forced, by an agreement with the French, to take them in. Kateri was given the task of looking after them during their brief stay. The eleven-year-old girl was apparently much impressed with the quiet, courteous behavior of the Jesuits. When two of the Jesuits returned to continue their missionary work, Kateri was moved to learn all she could about Roman Catholic Christianity. Soon she was rejecting her Native American upbringing. She refused to marry, vowing to forever remain a virgin, and would not work on Sundays. Kateri met secretly with Father Jacques de Lamberville, who was so impressed with her rapidly expanding knowledge of religious doctrine that he baptized her sooner than the usual converts, on Easter Day, 1676. Because of her conversion to Christianity and her nonconformity to tribal ways, Kateri had to face the contempt of her family and others in the village. Food was withheld from her when she refused to work on Sundays, and threats were made against her life. Lamberville counseled her to leave the village, and in 1677, when three Native American converts arrived at the village looking for new recruits, Kateri left with them. Upon learning of her escape, Kateri's uncle vowed to capture and kill both her and her three companions, but he was unable to catch them.

Kateri was taken to the Jesuit mission of Saint Francis Xavier du Sault at Kanawake, Quebec, by the straits of Sault St. Louis. There, she was put under the spiritual care of Anastasie Tegonhatsiongo, a former friend of her mother. Within months of her arrival, Kateri was deemed eligible to take communion. Kateri was determined to lead a religious life, but when she and two other Native American women indicated an interest in forming their own cloister, Catholic authorities told them it was too early to form a Native American cloister. Nevertheless, Kateri was permitted to take a vow of chastity on the Feast of the Annunciation in 1679.

During her short time at the mission, people took note of Kateri's great personal sacrifices and strict penances. She fasted two days a week and, when she did eat, mixed her food with ashes. She stood or walked barefoot for hours on ice and snow, suffered through regular flagellations, and spent three nights rolling back and forth on a bed of thorns. All of this suffering likely contributed to her early death. Kateri Tekakwitha died at the mission during Holy Week, on April 17, 1680. Since her death, numerous miracles have been attributed to her intervention. Because of the miracles and because her life is viewed as one of extraordinary devotion and piety, in 1884 the Jesuits submitted a petition for her canonization. Her name was formally nominated at the Vatican in 1932; she was venerated in 1943; and in 1980 she was beatified, or pronounced blessed.

See also: Native Americans; Roman Catholic Women's Orders (Nuns)
References: Christine Allen, "Women in Colonial French America," in Rosemary Radford Ruether and Rosemary Skinner Keller, Women and Religion in America, vol. 2 (1986); Henry Warner Bowden, Dictionary of American Religious Biography, 2nd ed. (1993); Edward T. James, ed., Notable American Women: 1607–1950, vol. 3 (1971); Sharon Malinowski, ed., Notable Native Americans (1995).

Temperance Movement

The temperance movement, which began in the 1790s and lasted until the passage of the Eighteenth Amendment (Prohibition) in 1919, was one of many reforms of interest to women. Although the movement itself was nondenominational, most supporters of temperance were churchgoers. For although organized religion subscribed to the concept of the cult of domesticity, which placed women in the home, it also perceived women as carrying the responsibility of teaching their children to be sober citizens and influencing their husbands to hold to similar standards. This perception of women's duties would lead to their eventual active involvement in the public crusade for temperance.

The temperance movement emerged following the American Revolution, with leaders advocating a sober citizenry who could govern the new republic in a moral and responsible manner. With the dawn of the new century came the Second Great Awakening, which spawned the idea of perfectionism and the possibility that men and women could achieve sin-free lives. In their quest for perfection, many Americans sought to eliminate the country's social problems, including the problem of alcohol abuse. Most who became involved in the temperance movement hoped to use moral suasion to convince people to drink in moderation. They were not seeking legislation to regulate alcohol consumption, nor were they advocating total abstinence.

As Susan Hill Lindley points out in *"You Have Stept Out of Your Place"* (1996), the temperance movement began to change tactics during the mid-1840s and 1850s, shifting from its primary reliance on persuasion to more political and legislative solutions. When this shift occurred, women, whose influence was limited to the domestic sphere, felt increasingly powerless. It was not until the "Woman's Crusade" of 1873–1874 that women began to play an influential role in public temperance campaigns.

Nevertheless, in the 1840s women's participation in the temperance move-

Women in the temperance movement often demonstrated outside of saloons their husbands frequented (woodcut from The Daily Graphic, *1874, from a pen and ink drawing by Weldon).*

ment was rising, just as their involvement in other social activities, such as benevolent societies and Sunday schools, was expanding. Female Martha Washingtonian societies sprang up beside the all-male Washingtonian associations. These middle-class societies worked with mostly working-class alcohol abusers to convince them to renounce the bottle. By 1842 there were six thousand members of Martha Washingtonian societies in New York City alone. Some of the women joined as a result of personal experiences with drunken husbands.

The "Woman's Crusade" that was launched approximately three decades later was a religious crusade. Many women feared (with some justification) that alcohol abuse was breaking up even middle-class Christian homes, and a significant number of the women who became involved in the movement were of evangelical Protestant backgrounds. They saw themselves as warriors battling sin (Carry Nation being an extreme example) and entered saloons to pray for the redemption of the saloon owners and their patrons. From a small group of women meeting in a Presbyterian church in Hillsboro, Ohio, in December of 1873, the movement grew, until by the summer of 1874 more than nine hundred cities and towns had been visited by the crusaders. Like the original group, most of the branches were organized in churches, and the crusaders frequently drew upon existing church and missionary women's networks. Yet although most ministers supported the women's cause, many opposed their "unwomanly" tactics.

The Woman's Christian Temperance Union (WCTU), founded in November 1874, was a product of the Woman's Crusade. Much better organized than the latter group, by 1900 the WCTU was the largest women's organization in the United States and had added numerous other reforms to its list of causes. Its decision to exclude men from membership helped the organization become one of the most important outlets for the women's movement in the late nineteenth century. Predominantly white, Protestant, and middle class, the WCTU initially attempted to limit alcohol consumption through moral suasion. But realizing that moral suasion was not bringing about the desired results, the organization changed tactics and began advocating legislation to prohibit the consumption of alcohol. It supported the Prohibition Party during the late nineteenth century and, in the early twentieth century, worked alongside the Anti-Saloon League for passage of the Eighteenth Amendment.

Although the amendment was repealed in 1933 and the sale of liquor was once again legal, the temperance movement was an important event in women's history. It served as a vehicle for women to expand their influence in the public sphere while providing them with experience in organizing for their causes. The WCTU was particularly important in giving women a sense of their own power as they worked for a variety of reforms.

See also: Nation, Carry; Perfectionism; Woman's Christian Temperance Union
References: Ruth Bordin, *Frances Willard: A Biography* (1986); Ruth Bordin, *Women and Temperance: The Quest for Power and Liberty, 1873–1900* (1981); Barbara Leslie Epstein, *The Politics of Domesticity: Women, Evangelism, and Temperance in Nineteenth Century America* (1981); Susan Hill Lindley, *"You Have Stept Out of Your Place": A History of Women and Religion in America* (1996); Ian Tyrell, *Sobering Up: From Temperance to Prohibition in Antebellum America* (1979).

ten Boom, Corrie (1892–1983)

Evangelist and author of popular Christian books, Corrie ten Boom was born in Haarlem, the Netherlands, on April 15, 1892, to Casper and Cor ten Boom. Her family was poor, but they took pleasure in music and art. Casper ten Boom, Corrie's father, was a clockmaker and a devout member of the Dutch Reformed Church. He held an unwavering position on the truth of the Bible, and he sent Corrie to a Christian school that he had helped establish. When she was in her teens, Corrie began to meet people in mission work from all over the world and from various Christian denominations, giving her an outlook beyond that of the Dutch Reformed Church. During her youth, she learned the clockmaking trade, which supported her later in life.

Corrie was forty-eight years old when German occupation of Holland began in April 1940. Her father befriended Jews whenever he could, and the ten Booms became active in underground activities. They hid anyone fearing arrest by the Nazis, and they helped Jews find refuge. A panel behind Corrie's bedroom closet led to a secret room for hiding Jews. On February 28, 1944, the ten Boom family was arrested, and Corrie was imprisoned in the concentration camp at Ravensbruck, Germany. Released in early January 1945, she soon began assisting displaced persons and other former prisoners. She also worked with Youth for Christ and traveled. In 1947 she felt called by God to seek a new beginning as a missionary in America. From New York City, she began a world tour that lasted three years. Her speaking ministry took her to Germany in 1948, where she spoke to German Christians.

Ten Boom completed her first book, *A Prisoner and Yet . . .* , in 1954 and wrote several more books during the 1960s. The book that was to bring her fame, *The Hiding Place,* was published in 1971. An autobiographical account of her experiences as an underground worker during World War II, *The Hiding Place* was released as a movie in 1975. Her earnings from her many books, which include *Tramp for the Lord,* with Jamie Bucking-

ham (1974), *In My Father's House: The Years before "The Hiding Place"* (1976), and *He Cares, He Comforts* (1977), allowed her to found Christians, Incorporated, a missionary association, and to expand her ministries throughout the world.

Ten Boom loved the United States and made use of her access to the country's mass media to spread religious messages. When she was not traveling, she spent the final years of her life in California. Following a stroke in August 1978, she remained in poor health until her death in Placentia, California, on April 15, 1983.

References: Carole C. Carlson, *Corrie ten Boom: Her Life, Her Faith* (1983); J. Gordon Melton, *Religious Leaders of America* (1991); Corrie ten Boom, with C. C. Carlson, *In My Father's House: The Years before "The Hiding Place"* (1976); Corrie ten Boom, with John Sherrill and Elizabeth Sherrill, *The Hiding Place* (1971).

Theologians

Although most of the well-known theologians in the United States have been male, women have distinguished themselves in the realm of religious theory since colonial times. In the mid-1630s, Anne Hutchinson, of the Puritan colony at Massachusetts Bay, stepped beyond her prescribed role as a woman when she expounded her personal interpretations of the Scriptures at weekly religious gatherings in her home. Since that time, women have overcome the barriers preventing them from access to religious and academic institutions and have succeeded in acquiring the knowledge necessary to draw their own conclusions regarding biblical texts.

In the nineteenth century, an increasing number of women began to challenge traditional interpretations of the Bible, particularly in regard to the position of women. Although they lacked formal theological training, women like Angelina and Sarah Grimké, Maria W. Stewart, Matilda Joslyn Gage, and Elizabeth Cady Stanton drew conclusions from their readings of the Scriptures that disputed what had heretofore been accepted religious dogma. Their works, including Sarah Grimké's *Letters on the Equality of the Sexes* (1838), Gage's *Woman, Church and State* (1893), and Stanton's *The Woman's Bible* (1895–1898), contributed a new and broader perspective of the Scriptures.

Women intent upon becoming professional theologians found opportunities gradually opening for them in the twentieth century. One of the earliest women to formally enter the field of religious theology as a career was Mary Reddington Ely Lyman (1887–1975), who studied religion at Union Theological Seminary in New York City and at the University of Chicago. She earned her doctorate from the latter institution in 1924 and went on to become a professor of the philosophy of religion at both Barnard College and Union Theological Seminary. Lyman was the first woman to be a full professor in any American seminary. In addition to teaching, Lyman wrote a number of theological works, including *The Fourth Gospel and the Life of Today* (1931), *The Christian Epic* (1936), and *Death and the Christian Answer* (1960).

Both Lyman and her contemporary, Georgia Elma Harkness (1891–1974), were advocates for furthering women's rights within the church. Nevertheless, the breaking down of barriers that obstructed women's rise within religious institutions continued to be slow. For example, it was not until 1966 that the Austin Presbyterian Theological Seminary (established in 1902) in Texas appointed Rachel Henderlite its first female professor of Christian education.

Along with the advent of the second women's rights movement in the late 1960s came a revival of theological thinking on the part of women. Again, women began challenging the male-centered theological tradition by bringing to light the oppression endured by women as a result of patriarchal structures, exclusive language, and misogynist interpretations of religious texts. Unlike Stanton, Gage, and other women who questioned the male-centered tradition in religion, this revival was led by professional theologians such as Mary Daly, Rosemary Radford Ruether, and Sallie McFague. These challenges have resulted in reconstructions of religious history that include new interpretations of events, redefinitions of and replacements of words, and reassessments of assigned male and female roles within religious hierarchies.

See also: Daly, Mary; Feminist Theology; Gage, Matilda Joslyn; Grimké, Angelina Emily; Grimké, Sarah Moore; Harkness, Georgia Elma; Henderlite, Rachel; Hutchinson, Anne Marbury; Lyman, Mary Reddington Ely; Ruether, Rosemary Radford; Stanton, Elizabeth Cady; Stewart, Maria W.; Truth, Sojourner; *Woman, Church and State; The Woman's Bible*

References: Emery Battis, *Saints and Sectaries: Anne Hutchinson and the Antinomian Controversy in the Massachusetts Bay Colony* (1962); Caroline Walken Bynum, *Jesus as Mother: Studies in the Spirituality of the High Middle Ages* (1982); Carol P. Christ and Judith Plaskow, eds., *Womanspirit Rising: A Feminist Reader in Religion* (1979); Mary Daly, *Beyond God the Father: Toward a Philosophy of Women's Liberation* (1973); Mary Daly, *Pure Lust: Elemental Feminist Philosophy* (1984); Matilda Joslyn Gage, *Woman, Church and State* (1900, reprint 1972); Georgia Harkness, *Women in Church and Society: A Historical and Theological Inquiry* (1972); Gerda Lerner, *The Grimké Sisters from South Carolina: Rebels against Slavery* (1967); Susan Hill Lindley, *"You Have Stept Out of Your Place": A History of Women and Religion in America* (1996); Bernard Quarles, *Black Abolitionists* (1969); Rosemary Radford Ruether, *Gaia and God: An Ecofeminist Theology of Earth Healing* (1992); Rosemary Radford Ruether and Eleanor McLaughlin, eds., *Women of Spirit: Female Leadership in the Jewish and Christian Traditions* (1979); Ruether, *Sexism and God-Talk: Toward a Feminist Theology* (1983); Elizabeth Cady Stanton, *The Woman's Bible: Parts I and II* (1895 and 1898, reprint 1972); Maria W. Stewart, *Maria W. Stewart: America's First Black Woman Political Writer* (1987).

Towne, Elizabeth Lois Jones (1865–1961)

Elizabeth Lois Jones Towne, a major figure and publisher in the New Thought movement, was born in Portland, Oregon, on May 11, 1865. She spent her early years in Oregon, raised by her Methodist parents. After leaving school at age fourteen, Elizabeth married when she was fifteen. The marriage was not happy, and Elizabeth did not enjoy the role of a dependent housewife. During this period, she was drawn to the New Thought movement and eventually left Methodism. With financial help from her father, in 1898 Elizabeth launched a New Thought magazine, *Nautilus*. Although it never became an official publication of the New Thought movement, the magazine was an immediate and lasting success.

Elizabeth moved to Holyoke, Massachusetts, in 1900. She divorced her husband and married William Towne. She incorporated her publishing enterprise as the Elizabeth Towne Company, becoming the president and treasurer. Her new husband was named associate editor, and her ex-husband and children were hired as staff. Over the next few years, Towne's career as a lecturer, author, and publisher soared. She wrote many books, including *Joy Philosophy* (1903), *Meals without Meat* (1903), *Practical Methods for Self-Development* (1904), *How to Concentrate* (1904), *How to Grow Success* (1904), *Happiness and Marriage* (1904), *How to Wake the Solar Plexus* (1904), *How to Train Children and Parents* (1904), *You and Your Forces* (1905), *Experiences in Self-Healing* (1905), *The Life Power* (1906), and *Lessons in Living* (1910). Her firm also published the works of many well-known New Thought writers, such as W. W. Atkinson, Browne Landone, and Annie Rix Militz.

As the New Thought movement became more visible by establishing a number of churches, Towne became active in several cooperative groups that worked for a declaration of principles on which the diverse groups could agree. Although she did not believe that New Thought could be organized into a single institution, she considered New Thought a soul "which could form as many bodies or organizations as it wills" (Braden, 1984, p. 193). When the New England Federation of New Thought Centers was created in 1918, Towne was a charter member. In 1924 she was elected president of the International New Thought Alliance. She was ordained the same year in a small New Thought church, the Church of Truth. In 1925 Towne visited England, speaking in many New Thought centers in London and Birmingham.

In addition to her work within the New Thought movement, Towne became involved in social and political issues of the time. She was not only a member but served as president of several organizations: the Business and Professional Women's Club, the Holyoke Women's Club, and the Holyoke League of Women Voters. Towne was a charter member of the Holyoke Council on World Relations and was a delegate to the National Federation on the Cause and Cure of War. She remained active into her eighties and died in Holyoke on June 1, 1961, at the age of ninety-six.

See also: Brooks, Nona Lovell; Hopkins, Emma Curtis; Militz, Annie Rix; New Thought Movement
References: Charles S. Braden, *Spirits in Rebellion: The Rise and Development of New Thought* (1984); J. Gordon Melton, *Biographical Dictionary of American Cult and Sect Leaders* (1986); J. Gordon Melton, *Religious Leaders of America* (1991).

Transcendentalism

Transcendentalism was an idealistic philosophy and literary movement that was popular among New England's middle-class intellectuals from about 1835 to

1860. Its leaders were predominantly Unitarians or former Unitarians who rejected the rationalist theories of the Enlightenment in favor of a belief in a divinity within humans, the unity of human beings and nature, and the supremacy of intuition over reason. Much of their inspiration came from German philosopher Immanuel Kant and English poet, critic, and essayist Samuel Taylor Coleridge. This inspiration was combined with some Eastern mysticism. Major figures in Transcendentalism included Ralph Waldo Emerson, Henry David Thoreau, Theodore Parker, Bronson Alcott, and Margaret Fuller. Some members experimented with communal living on George Ripley's Brook Farm (1841–1847) and at Bronson Alcott's Fruitlands (1844), but these communities were short-lived. The Transcendentalists became better known for their contributions to the reform movements of the mid-nineteenth century, especially abolition and the emerging woman's movement.

Teaching the liberation and fulfillment of the highest potential in *all* human beings, Transcendentalism offered women an ideological base upon which they could argue for equal rights. There were some attempts within Transcendentalism to reform families so as to improve domestic relations. They did not attempt to restructure families but gave wives greater involvement in planning and decision-making. However, at Brook Farm, which was more than 60 percent male throughout most of its existence, women were hardly liberated, for they were saddled with abundant domestic duties. At Fruitlands, founder Bronson Alcott dreamed of a society that would be as harmonious as a family. His community, which was an experiment in practical anarchy and required, among other things, the renunciation of marriage, was short lived.

Despite their theories on equality, most male Transcendentalists, including Emerson, had difficulty envisioning individuality in a woman. Married Transcendentalist women usually took on the traditional role, sacrificing their freedom to dedicate their lives to the care of their families. But Transcendentalism brought women into circles of friends and activities outside the family that offered them social and intellectual contacts not enjoyed by most women of the era.

Although she was not an active Transcendentalist herself, women's rights leader Elizabeth Cady Stanton was influenced by the movement, most particularly by Theodore Parker, a theologian who suggested that God was an androgynous figure. And although she never consciously set out to become involved in a women's rights campaign, Margaret Fuller, who was an editor of the Transcendentalist journal *The Dial* from 1840 to 1842, significantly contributed to the movement for female equality. Between 1839 and 1844 she conducted a series of "conversations" in Boston, where educated women gathered to discuss a variety of topics ranging from religion to art to women's rights. In 1845 Fuller invigorated the fledgling women's movement with the publication of *Woman in the Nineteenth Century*. She argued that women were answerable to God, not to men, and that they should therefore have the opportunity to develop their highest potential and to take on any role that they desired. The book helped to motivate the women at the first woman's rights convention at Seneca Falls, New York, in 1848, and has since become a feminist classic.

See also: Emerson, Ralph Waldo; Fuller, Margaret; Parker, Theodore; Stanton, Elizabeth Cady

References: Bell Gale Chevigny, *The Woman and the Myth: Margaret Fuller's Life and Writings* (1976); Ann Douglas, *The Feminization of American Culture* (1977); Maureen Fitzgerald, "Transcendentalism," in Angela Howard Zophy with Frances M. Kavenik, eds., *Handbook of American*

Women's History (1990); Anne C. Rose, *Transcendentalism as a Social Movement, 1830–1850* (1981).

Truth, Sojourner (c. 1797–1883)

Born into slavery on a plantation in Ulster County, New York, Sojourner Truth became famous as a gifted preacher, abolitionist, and feminist. The exact date of Truth's birth is not known but was probably in 1797. Her birth name was Isabella Baumfree (or Bomefree), and her parents called her Belle. Later in life she adopted the name "Sojourner Truth," a name that described her role as an itinerant preacher spreading God's word.

Truth had several owners, including the cruel John Neely, before being purchased by her long-time master, John Dumont, in 1810. In about 1814 she married another black slave, Thomas, with whom she had five children. Long anxious for freedom, Truth left her husband and the plantation in 1826, one year before she would have been emancipated by New York state law. Her master caught up with her, but a Quaker couple, Isaac and Maria Van Wagenen, offered to employ the escaped slave. At about the same time, Truth became the first African-American woman to successfully sue a white man. With the help of local Quakers, she won the release of her son Peter, who had been sold and illegally taken to Alabama.

It was during this period that religion became an important part of Truth's life. She underwent a conversion experience in about 1827 and joined a Methodist church in Kingston, New York. At the urging of her son Peter's schoolteacher, she moved to New York City, where the boy could enroll in school. In New York City, Truth attended both the predominantly white John Street Methodist Church and the black African Methodist Episcopal Zion Church.

Truth felt close to God and spoke with him constantly. In 1843, she said, God commanded her to leave the city and travel eastward to fulfill her mission to help the needy and the oppressed. It was at this time that she chose to adopt the name "Sojourner Truth." By following God's direction and becoming an itinerant minister, Truth was joining an established tradition of traveling Quaker and Methodist preachers. Some, like herself, were women.

Truth's preaching became popular among the Millerites, a group of followers of William Miller, a New York farmer, who more than a decade earlier had begun to preach of the coming end of the world, expected in 1843 or 1844. Though she was not a Millerite, Truth attracted large audiences at the Millerite camps. Millerites found her to be a talented and inspired preacher and enjoyed listening to her sing.

In 1843 some of her Millerite friends introduced her to a utopian community, the Northampton Association of Education and Industry in Florence, Massachusetts. The community had been founded by a group of well-educated and wealthy people whose purpose was to pursue truth, justice, and equal rights for all. Well-known abolitionist and supporter of women's rights William Lloyd Garrison was a frequent visitor to the Northampton Association, and Truth too developed an interest in both abolitionism and the rights of women. By the time she left the commune, she had embraced both issues. Furthermore, she found that she could earn a living by giving lectures and selling materials on abolitionism to reform-minded audiences.

Since Truth could neither read nor write, Olive Gilbert, an abolitionist she met at Northampton, offered to help Truth publish her memoirs. *Narrative of Sojourner Truth* was published in 1850. Though bookstores refused to carry the

President Abraham Lincoln shows Sojourner Truth the Bible given him by the African-American people of Baltimore (1893).

book, Truth was able to earn enough to support herself by selling her autobiography at abolitionist meetings.

Truth attended her first women's rights conference in Worcester, Massachusetts, in 1850. The following year, she spoke, uninvited, at the women's rights conference in Akron, Ohio. It was at that conference that she spoke her most famous lines. Although white women organizers were too timid to respond publicly to ministers' criticism of them on the basis of women's intellectual, physical, and moral weaknesses, Truth stood up and defended all women. She reminded the men in the audience of all the toils she had suffered as a black woman, especially as a black slave, and asked, "And a'nt I a woman?" Truth was not only speaking directly to the males in the audience but addressing the women too. She was broadening the definition of women's rights to include black and working-class women as well as those women of the upper and middle classes who heretofore had controlled the agendas of women's rights organizations.

Throughout the 1850s, until the outbreak of the Civil War, Truth traveled throughout the East and the Midwest preaching and lecturing against slavery. When the war broke out in April 1861, Truth decided to tour the Midwest and seek support for the Union's war effort. Though now in her mid-sixties, she worked so hard that exhaustion finally caused her to return to her home in Battle Creek, Michigan, where she could rest. Upon regaining her strength, in October 1864 she journeyed to Washington, D.C., where she had an audience with President Abraham Lincoln. She was so impressed with the busy atmosphere in the nation's capital that she decided to stay and help in the war effort. Truth was soon put to work as a counselor for the National Freedman's Relief Association, where she helped the newly freed slaves adjust to the responsibilities that accompanied their liberty.

Slavery was officially abolished in the United States in December 1865, when Congress ratified the Thirteenth Amendment. The Fourteenth Amendment to the Constitution, ratified in 1868, granted African Americans full rights of American citizenship. But Truth was not satisfied. That same year, she began a campaign to encourage Congress to grant western lands to freed blacks. Although she also continued to fight for women's rights and other reforms such as temperance and the rights of workers, her push for the land bill became the major crusade of her final years. Only after the death of her grandson Sammy, who had been helping her with the campaign, and after suffering a minor stroke herself in 1875 did Truth give up hope for passage of the bill. The stroke left her partially paralyzed. In addition, she had developed painful ulcers on her legs.

After two years of illness, Truth's health improved. She was thus able to attend, in 1878, the Woman's Rights Convention in Rochester, New York, as one of only three delegates from Michigan. But by 1882, she was again gravely ill. Truth died November 26, 1883, in Battle Creek, Michigan.

See also: African Americans; Antislavery Movement; Second Great Awakening; Tubman, Harriet Ross; Woman Suffrage
References: Eleanor Flexner, *Century of Struggle: The Woman's Rights Movement in the United States* (1970); Nell Irvin Painter, *Sojourner Truth: A Life, A Symbol* (1996); Martha Ward Plowden, *Famous Firsts of Black Women* (1993); Erlene Stetson and Linda David, *Glorying in Tribulation: The Lifework of Sojourner Truth* (1994); Sojourner Truth and Frances W. Titus, *Narrative of Sojourner Truth* (1875, reprint 1968).

Tubman, Harriet Ross
(c. 1820–1913)

Harriet Ross Tubman, a woman who would become known as the "Moses of

Harriet Ross Tubman (undated photo)

her people," was born into slavery on a Maryland plantation. The precise date of her birth is not known, but she is believed to have been born in 1820 or 1821. Her parents, Ben Ross and Harriet Green, and her ten brothers and sisters shared a small one-room shack on a plantation belonging to the Brodas family. The Brodas family members were quick to punish slaves for any mistakes, and young Harriet received her share of beatings. But Tubman's parents passed on their strong faith in God to their daughter. She almost always felt God's presence and freely prayed to him at any time of day. Her prayers frequently requested relief for herself and others from the toils of slavery.

In the summer of 1831, Nat Turner, a slave from Virginia, led about seventy slaves in a revolt. Although the revolt ultimately failed and Turner was captured, his actions inspired many slaves, including Harriet, to think about freedom for themselves. A possible means of escape was through the Underground Railroad, a network of people who accepted great risk in arranging the transport of runaway slaves to the North and freedom.

Any hope Harriet had of eventual freedom nearly came to an end when she was about fifteen. While in a village store, she deliberately got in the way of a master chasing a runaway slave. When the master threw a heavy lead weight at the runaway, he missed, instead hitting Harriet on the head and knocking her unconscious. She sustained a brain injury and was near death for a couple of months, never fully recovering. Although her strength gradually returned, she suffered spells of falling asleep in the middle of whatever she was doing and waking up, apparently unaware that time had passed.

In 1844, she married John Tubman, a free African American. It is likely that she hoped he would help her escape to the North, but the marriage was not happy. Although they had been separated for several years, Harriet was surprised when she learned, in 1851, that he had taken a second wife.

About five years after her marriage, rumors that she would be sold and sent to the far South reached Tubman's ears. She decided that it was time for her to escape to the North. The Underground Railroad helped her make her way to Pennsylvania and freedom. There she worked for wages, saving them to enable her to bring other slaves, including her own family, north. Over the next several years she traveled back and forth between the North and the South at least nineteen times, bringing back more than three hundred men, women, and children. Slaves loved her and called her "Moses" for leading them out of bondage. However, slaveowners hated and feared her and offered a $40,000 reward for her capture.

After the Fugitive Slave Law (which required people north of the Mason-Dixon Line to returned escaped slaves to bondage) was passed by Congress in 1850, Tubman conducted her people into Canada, fearing that it was too dangerous to leave them in northern states.

Tubman had a number of close calls in which she and her "passengers" on the Underground Railroad were almost captured. But she placed her faith in the Lord for deliverance and prayed whenever she and her companions were in jeopardy. God, she believed, was good to her and carried her through many scrapes. None of the slaves Tubman led to safety were ever captured. She was, however, saddened when John Brown's raid on Harpers Ferry, in October 1859, failed and he was hung for his actions, for she had helped him recruit soldiers for his cause.

In the early days of the Civil War, northern officials invited Tubman to act as a nurse, spy, and scout for the Union army. Through her experience as a conductor on the Underground Railroad, she had become thoroughly familiar with the topography of the borderlands. For all of her work for the Union, which included risking her life on a number of occasions, she received no recompense until more than thirty years after the war ended.

Though poverty-stricken herself, Tubman continued to do all she could following the war to improve living conditions for aged and poor African Americans. In 1869 Sarah Bradford wrote a hurried biography of Tubman in hopes of helping her friend by giving her the proceeds of the book's sales. The same year, Tubman married a Civil War veteran. In her later years, she received many honors, including a medal from England's Queen Victoria.

Harriet Tubman died in Auburn, New York, in March 1913.

See also: African Americans; Antislavery Movement; Truth, Sojourner
References: Sarah H. Bradford, *Harriet Tubman: The Moses of Her People* (1886, reprint 1974); Sarah H. Bradford, *Scenes in the Life of Harriet Tubman* (1869, reprint 1992); Bert James Loewenberg and Ruth Bogin, eds., *Black Women in Nineteenth-Century American Life: Their Words, Their Thoughts, Their Feelings* (1976); Martha Ward Plowden, *Famous Firsts of Black Women* (1993).

Unitarians/Universalists

The Unitarian and Universalist churches, which have historically been among the most liberal of religious organizations in America, produced some prominent and influential feminists of the women's rights movement. Church tenets that favored the equalizing of the sexes, such as the Universalist belief that men and women are to help each other to salvation, appealed to female reformers. In addition, Unitarian and Universalist ministers were among the most outspoken of the mid-nineteenth century males who favored women's rights and other reforms. At a time when few American clergymen accepted the idea of equality of the sexes, Unitarian preachers like James Freeman Clarke, Thomas Wentworth Higginson, and Theodore Parker spoke out in support of women's rights. Among the nineteenth-century feminists to be influenced by Unitarianism and Universalism were Lydia Maria Child, Judith Sargent Murray, Margaret Fuller, Mary Livermore, and Olympia Brown.

Brown, who was ordained into the Universalist ministry in 1863, became the first woman to be fully ordained as a pastor and to continue in that role for a lengthy career. (Congregationalist Antoinette Brown Blackwell preceded Brown as an ordained minister, but her career ended after only a year.) Though refused admission to a Unitarian theological school, Brown was accepted into the Universalist theological school at St. Lawrence University. Eventually Unitarians too began ordaining women to the ministry. In the decade between 1887 and 1897, twenty-three women received Unitarian ordination, with two additional female pastors being received from other denominations. However, a remarkable decline in female ordination occurred during the period 1901 to 1917, when only one woman was ordained and another was received from an outside fellowship.

Although the latter decades of the nineteenth century found increasing numbers of women ordained in both the Universalist and Unitarian faiths, during the earlier years of their histories the women of the two churches performed work that was similar to women's work in other faiths. Assisting in Sunday schools and participating in sewing circles were the primary activities of churchgoing women of the late eighteenth and early nineteenth centuries. In the early nineteenth century, Unitarian women in Boston (which was the center of Unitarianism) participated in fund-raising campaigns in support of the general ministry. By 1827, with the formation of the Tuckerman Sewing Circle, their benevolent work was well underway. When the Civil War erupted in 1861, both Unitarian and Universalist women became active workers for the United States Sanitary Commission, an agency that provided relief for the sick and wounded of the Union army. One of the best known of these women was Mary Livermore, the wife of a Universalist pastor, who during her career with the commission made frequent speaking tours, wrote thousands of letters, and campaigned for the establishment of over three thousand local aid societies in five states.

In addition to their ordination to the Unitarian and Universalist ministries, strides were made in women's progress when, in 1877, the Western Unitarian Conference voted to give women greater responsibility within the conference and placed two women on the board of directors. The Women's Auxiliary Conference was formed in 1880 and grew to eighty branches within a decade, with a membership of between three and four thousand. But as an auxiliary, it had no independent life. Therefore, a new organization was founded in October 1890, the National Alliance of Unitarian and Other Liberal Christian Women. A year later, it had expanded to ninety branches with five thousand members.

Contributing to the growth of Unitarianism during the late nineteenth century was Sallie Ellis of Cincinnati, who launched a post-office mission in 1881. In the four and a half years remaining of her life, she spread information concerning the teachings of Unitarianism around the country, mailing approximately 2,500 letters and 22,000 tracts and papers and selling 286 books. The movement continued to grow after her death, with 200,000 tracts, sermons, books, and periodicals distributed by 1900. At the same time, women were active in aiding missionaries and small struggling churches and in helping to found new ones.

By early in the twentieth century, the overall modernization of American Protestantism hurt both the Unitarian and Universalist churches. Americans seeking liberal denominations had wider choices than they had during the nineteenth century, and Unitarian and Universalist church membership began to decline. By the 1950s, the two churches began to consider a merger. Their differ-

ences in the past had been more sociological than theological, with Unitarians appealing to the urban elite, whereas Universalism had been attracting mostly rural folk. The two denominations united in 1961 to found the Unitarian Universalist Association (UUA). With membership numbering approximately 140,000 in the early 1990s and with congregations drawn mostly from the well-educated and socially progressive members of their communities, the UUA continues to represent the theological far left wing of American Protestantism.

See also: Brown, Olympia; Clarke, James Freeman; Higginson, Thomas Wentworth; Livermore, Mary Ashton Rice; Parker, Theodore

References: George Willis Cooke, *Unitarianism in America: A History of Its Origin and Development* (1902); Kathryn Gleadle, *The Early Feminists: Radical Unitarians and the Emergence of the Women's Rights Movement, 1831–51* (1995); Susan Hill Lindley, *"You Have Stept Out of Your Place": A History of Women and Religion in America* (1996); Edward L. Queen II et al., eds., *The Encyclopedia of American Religious History* (1996); David Robinson, *The Unitarians and the Universalists* (1985); Conrad Wright, ed., *A Stream of Light: A Sesquicentennial History of American Unitarianism* (1975).

Utopian Communities

Many of the utopian communities established in the late eighteenth century and the nineteenth century were based on religion. At the same time, they frequently offered women an opportunity to fulfill roles that were not usually found in mainstream society. It was common for these communities to experiment with male-female sexual relationships. For example, the Shakers' community, founded by Ann Lee in 1776 near Albany, New York, chose to practice celibacy, thus freeing women from sexual demands of husbands as well as reproductive roles. In addition, Lee's perception of God as both a masculine and a feminine deity provided Shakers a theological basis for promoting male-female equality. The Oneida Community, founded in 1848 by religious leader John Humphrey Noyes, sought to relieve women of some of the oppressive practices found in nineteenth-century American society. Members of the community practiced a system of "complex marriage," designed to benefit women since they were no longer considered the property of men. Males practiced early withdrawal during sexual intercourse, greatly lessening chances of unplanned pregnancies. Joseph Smith, founder of Mormonism, instituted the practice of plural marriage, believing polygamy to be necessary if one was to achieve the highest level of celestial marriage in the afterlife. Some Mormon women accepted the practice, but others found it problematic.

Utopian communities also experimented with male-female equality on a broader level. With its emphasis on the liberation and fulfillment of the greatest potential in all human beings, Transcendentalism offered women an ideological base upon which they could claim equal rights. But although some attempts were made to allow women a larger role in decisionmaking, women in the Transcendentalist commune of Brook Farm (1841–1847) soon found themselves relegated to tiresome domestic chores, caring for a male population that outnumbered them three to two. However, speakers like Margaret Fuller, an influential editor and feminist who lectured on the uplifting of her sex, were frequent visitors to Brook Farm and provided communitarians with an opportunity to broaden their outlook. A second Transcendentalist commune, Fruitlands (1844), attempted an experiment with the "consociate family" in place of the nuclear family, but founder Bronson Alcott's reluctance to break away from his own family doomed the experiment before it really got under way. In addition to a degree of sexual freedom, women at Oneida were encouraged to participate in social and work activities usually considered outside the female "sphere." Nevertheless, they maintained their "feminine" roles of domestic worker and caretaker of children.

For many women, the commune experience did not live up to its promises. Although their religious leaders professed their belief in equality of the sexes, women often found themselves restricted to the same roles they had performed in the outside world. Yet the communes gave women the opportunity to explore lifestyles beyond the mainstream.

See also: Church of Jesus Christ of Latter-Day Saints (Mormons); Lee, Ann; Oneida Community; Shakers (United Society of Believers in Christ's Second Coming); Transcendentalism
References: Wendy E. Chmielewski and Karen Gillenwater, "Utopian Communities," in Angela Howard Zophy with Frances M. Kavenik, eds., Handbook of American Women's History (1990); Lawrence Foster, Women, Family and Utopia: Communal Experiments of the Shakers, the Oneida Community, and the Mormons (1990); Spencer Klaw, Without Sin: The Life and Death of the Oneida Community (1993); Carol A. Kolmerten, Women in Utopia: The Ideology of Gender in the American Owenite Communities (1990); Charles Nordhoff, American Utopias (1993); John McKelvie Whitworth, God's Blueprints: A Sociological Study of Three Utopian Sects (1993).

Van Cott, Margaret Newton (1830–1914)

Evangelist Margaret "Maggie" Newton Van Cott, probably the first American woman to receive an official license to preach from the Methodist Episcopal Church, was born in New York City on March 25, 1830. Her father, William K. Newton, a wealthy real estate broker, and her mother, Rachel A. (Primrose) Newton, raised her in the Episcopal faith. Her maternal grandfather, William P. Primrose, was a Methodist, and it seems that he had some influence on Maggie because she was attracted to Methodism from childhood. In 1848, soon after she completed high school, Maggie married merchant Peter P. Van Cott, and they had two daughters. But after only two years, Peter became chronically ill. His poor health caused her to take control of the management of the family business.

In the midst of a great national religious revival in the late 1850s, Van Cott had a conversion experience that led her to attend prayer meetings at the Duane Street Methodist Episcopal Church in New York City. Although she found the church's pietistic enthusiasm compatible with her temperament, she waited until after her husband's death in 1866 to join the church. Her attachment to the church helped ease her grief over the loss of a daughter, her husband, and her father in rapid succession. She soon was an active participant in church work. One of her responsibilities was to lead prayer meetings and Bible study groups at the interdenominational missions in New York's slums that had been founded by Phoebe Palmer. Van Cott's clear, strong speaking voice brought her invitations to preach in outside parishes, including a request in 1868 to lead revival services at the Methodist church in Durham, New York.

Although Van Cott was somewhat reluctant to preach because it meant breaking into a "male" occupation, she was impressed by the many conversions that followed her sermons. Since she lacked theological training, she gave exhortatory rather than doctrinal sermons. The church recognized her gifts as an evangelist, giving her an "exhorter's license" in September 1868. She gave up her business and devoted her life to helping to save souls. In 1869 the Stone Ridge Methodist Episcopal Church in Ellenville, New York, granted her a "local preacher's license" after ample examination. Because she was a woman, this action created controversy within the New York Conference of the Methodist Episcopal Church, but the conference made no move to oppose Van Cott's work. When a minister at Springfield, Massachusetts, became ill in 1870, Van Cott filled the pulpit. As this happened to be the site of the New England Conference's annual meeting, she preached before the conference.

Van Cott continued her evangelistic work for more than three decades, traveling from 3,000 to 7,000 miles a year for over thirty years and conducting religious revivals when she was invited to do so. In contrast to most white clergy of the era, she became known for her willingness to preach, comfort, and work with African Americans. Although the church granted several other women licenses to preach, it refused to ordain them. When Van Cott was recommended for ordination in California in 1874, the conference bishop would not consider the issue. Although she was never ordained, Van Cott continued her work until she retired in 1902. At her retirement, she was credited with having converted seventy-five thousand persons, and she estimated that about half of them had joined the Methodist Church.

Van Cott died in Catskill, New York, on August 29, 1914.

See also: Methodists; Palmer, Phoebe Worrall
References: John Onesimus Foster, *Life and Labors of Mrs. Maggie Van Cott* (1872, microfiche 1978); Edward T. James, ed., *Notable American Women, 1607–1950*, vol. 3 (1971); Susan Hill Lindley, *"You Have Stept Out of Your Place": A History of Women and Religion in America* (1996); J. Gordon Melton, *Religious Leaders of America* (1991); World Methodist Council and the Commission on Archives and History, *The Encyclopedia of World Methodism*, vol. 2 (1974).

Vatican II
See **Second Vatican Council**

Warde, Frances Teresa (1810–1884)

As Mother Mary Frances Xavier Warde, Frances Teresa Warde likely founded more convents and service institutions than any woman in Christian history. She was born in Mountrath, Ireland, in 1810, the youngest child of John and Jane (Maher) Warde. Her mother died soon after her birth. Frances was a socialite until she met fifty-year-old Catherine McAuley, the future founder of Sisters of Mercy. Warde became McAuley's close associate in McAuley's charity work with poor children. When Mother McAuley established the Sisters of Mercy in 1831, Warde was her first postulant.

Warde professed her vows as Sister Mary Frances Xavier in the first Convent of Mercy in Dublin in 1833. Over the next several years, she founded communities in Carlow, Ireland (where she was mother superior from 1837 to 1843), Naas (1839), Wexford (1840), and Westport (1842). In 1843 Bishop Michael O'Connor of Pittsburgh, Pennsylvania, was in Ireland in search of sisters willing to go to the United States and establish the Sisters of Mercy order there. When he returned to Pittsburgh later in the year, Mother Warde and six sisters accompanied him. These women were the first Sisters of Mercy in the United States. Although typhus and tuberculosis decimated their new community, they were soon able to establish parish schools, two academies, a House of Mercy to train young women, an orphanage, and the first hospital in western Pennsylva-

nia. In 1846 Mother Warde founded a convent and school in Chicago, Illinois, and laid plans for an orphan asylum and hospital. The Mercy Hospital opened there in 1853, serving all nationalities and creeds. In 1848 Mother Warde established a convent in Loretto, Pennsylvania. She was appointed superior to a new mission in Providence, Rhode Island, in 1850, which prospered under her leadership. Eight years later, Mother Warde went to Manchester, New Hampshire, where she was superior until her death there in 1884.

During her half-century of religious vocation, Mother Warde helped to expand the Sisters of Mercy into one of the world's largest congregations of religious women. Like many other pioneers, she established the foundations of new institutions and then moved on to create others. After arriving in America, and with great energy and skill, Mother Warde personally founded twenty-five convents, several orphanages, and at least sixty schools. Many of these communities served as motherhouses, from which missionaries and teachers were sent to serve new areas. Mother Warde's influence was carried further by Sisters of Mercy who established convents and academies in a network that spread throughout North America. Under Mother Warde, the Sisters of Mercy were the first and only sisters to do missionary work among the Native Americans of the state of Maine. During the period 1878–1879, she founded three missions in that state and thereafter visited these missions at least once a year until her death. Despite many hardships, including attempts by the government of the state of Maine to expel the sisters from Native American reservations, and despite anti-Catholic bigotry in nineteenth-century American culture overall, Mother Warde's communities and institutions prospered.

Mother Mary Frances Xavier Warde died in Manchester, New Hampshire, on September 17, 1884.

See also: Roman Catholic Women's Orders (Nuns)

References: Henry Warner Bowden, *Dictionary of American Religious Biography,* 2nd ed. (1993); Kathleen Healy, *Frances Warde: American Founder of the Sisters of Mercy* (1973); *New Catholic Encyclopedia,* vol. 14 (1967).

White, Alma Bridwell (1862–1946)

Alma Bridwell White was the first female bishop of any Christian church in the United States. Born in Kinniconick, Kentucky, on June 16, 1862, she spent her youth and young adulthood in that state. She pursued an education beyond the secondary level, studying first at Vanceburg Seminary in about 1880 and at Millersburg Female College from 1882 to 1883. Between 1880 and 1887, she was a schoolteacher.

A devoutly religious person, Alma sought outlets for religious expression. She married Kent White, a Methodist minister, and served as a song leader and a lay adviser in his churches. But in 1893, after an experience in which she felt entirely sanctified, she became determined to preach in her own right. It seems she heard a call to arouse an apathetic piety in Colorado churches. But Methodist officials were critical of Alma's ministering. They considered it inappropriate for a woman to preach and objected to her energetic style. As a result, in 1895, both Alma and her husband left the Methodist Church. Over

the next six years, the couple traveled throughout the mountain states, directing Holiness revivals. Although the camp meetings were much more exuberant in style than traditional Methodist church services, the Whites stressed adherence to the doctrines professed by the founder of Methodism, John Wesley.

In Denver, Colorado, in 1901, Alma White founded the fundamentalist Methodist sect that after 1917 became known as the Pillar of Fire Church. As the head of that religious organization, she held the title of bishop, the first Christian woman to hold such an office. Adherents of the Pillar of Fire faith believed in Christ's imminent second coming, practiced faith healing, and recognized the ordination of both male and female ministers. They adopted strict personal habits, abstaining from alcohol and tobacco and shunning ostentatious dress.

Kent White felt that, as a man, he was entitled to be both head of the White household and of the church. Alma acquiesced to her husband's demands at home but held onto her role as leader of the church. In 1907, Kent embraced Pentecostalism and began to promote speaking in tongues (glossolalia). Alma worried that his promotion of glossolalia would have a negative effect on her church. Kent's Pentecostalism worsened a marital relationship that was already on shaky ground. On August 11, 1901, Kent withdrew from his membership in the Pillar of Fire Church and left his wife two days later. The couple did not reunite until a few years before Kent's death in 1940. Alma moved her church headquarters from Denver to New Jersey in 1907 and there established a prosperous organization. She traveled and preached in the United States and in Europe and soon had established congregations from Los Angeles to London. The Alma White College, founded in New Jersey in 1921, was one of seven schools organized by her.

White was anti-Catholic, a nativist, and a "super-patriot," viewpoints she shared with the Ku Klux Klan of the 1920s. The Klan apparently saw her as an ally, and in 1922 the order made financial contributions to White's church. By fall 1923, members of the Pillar of Fire Church were joining the Klan. Women members enlisted in the Women of the Ku Klux Klan. White often spoke at Klan events, including a gathering of five thousand Klansmen in Princeton, Illinois, in 1923. The Pillar of Fire was the only religious group to publicly endorse the Ku Klux Klan.

In 1932 White began to paint and produced over three hundred mountain landscapes, all in a primitive folk style. She was also a prolific writer, producing a five-volume autobiography, two dramas for radio, several books of poetry, and more than two hundred hymns. White died in Zarephath, New Jersey, on June 26, 1946. At the time of her death, her Pillar of Fire Church had a membership of approximately four thousand. Her two sons succeeded her as directors of the church. Current membership is not known and is not counted, but in 1988 there were twenty congregations in the United States and others in fifty-six foreign countries.

See also: Clergy; Fundamentalism; Methodists

References: Henry Warner Bowden, *Dictionary of American Religious Biography*, 2nd ed. (1993); Edward T. James, ed., *Notable American Women: 1607–1950* (1971); J. Gordon Melton, *Encyclopedia of American Religions*, 4th ed. (1993); Letha Dawson Scanzoni and Susan Setta, "Women in Evangelical, Holiness, and Pentecostal Traditions," in Rosemary Radford Ruether and Rosemary Skinner Keller, eds., *Women and Religion in America, 1900–1968*, vol. 3 (1986); Susie Cunningham Stanley, *Feminist Pillar of Fire: The Life of Alma White* (1993); Caroline Zilboorg, ed., *Women's Firsts* (1997).

White, Anna (1831–1910)

Shaker eldress and reformer Anna White was born in Brooklyn, New York, on January 21, 1831, to Robert and Hannah (Gibbs) White. Hannah belonged to the Society of Friends, and Robert joined the Quaker faith shortly after their marriage. Their children, including Anna, were all raised in the faith. When Anna was in her early teens, she attended the Mansion Square Seminary in Poughkeepsie, New York, a Quaker boarding school. Upon completing school at the age of eighteen, she returned to New York City and worked with her father in his hardware business. Meanwhile, her mother taught her ways to offer benevolence to the poor.

Robert White had business relations with the United Society of Believers in Christ's Second Coming, popularly known as Shakers, in Hancock, Massachusetts. Occasionally his daughter Anna would accompany him on his visits to the Hancock community. Robert joined the Shakers, and after some consideration, Anna did as well. Her father never severed his ties with his wife and family, but Anna, despite the disapproval of her relatives, joined the community at New Lebanon (the name changed to Mount Lebanon in 1861), New York, in September 1849.

Anna White, who was assigned to the North Family section of the community, came under the intellectual tutelage of Elder Frederick Evans and the spiritual leadership of Eldress Antoinette Doolittle. She also had contact with Shaker leader Ruth Landon, who had seen Ann Lee, the religion's founder, years before. Over the following decades, White gradually rose to become a leader of the community. In 1865 she was appointed associate eldress and given the particular responsibility of the care of girls. Following Eldress Doolittle's death in 1887, White succeeded her as first eldress of the North Family. She held this position until her own death in 1910.

During the 1890s, White was drawn to social causes outside the Shaker community. Like the Quakers, the Shakers were pacifists, and White upheld these principles. She was an enthusiastic worker in the cause of international disarmament and was appointed a vice president of the Alliance of Women for Peace. Eldress White was also a member of the National American Woman Suffrage Association and a vice president of the National Council of Women of the United States. She spoke on behalf of these organizations before the Universal Peace Union in Mystic, Connecticut, in 1899 and the Equal Rights Club in Hartford in 1903. In 1905 she led a conference at Mount Lebanon that adopted resolutions on arbitration that were forwarded to The Hague. White personally delivered the resolutions to President Theodore Roosevelt, a prominent proponent of arbitration.

Among the Shakers, Eldress White became well known for her writing of Shaker songs and history. She compiled two books of Shaker music, which included several of her own songs. She coauthored, with Eldress Leila S. Taylor, *Shakerism: Its Meaning and Message* (1904), the only published history of the society written by someone who was a member. Her interests also included vegetarianism and Spiritualism (the Shakers believed in communication with the spirit world). White claimed that on several occasions when she had suffered from injury or illness, the spirits of the departed had visited her and helped bring her back to health. Although she remained devoted to the Shaker faith, White also investigated Christian Science.

Although Eldress White sometimes left the Shaker community to attend meetings, most of her final years were spent at Mount Lebanon. She died there on December 16, 1910.

See also: Lee, Ann; Shakers (United Society of Believers in Christ's Second Coming)
References: Edward T. James, ed., *Notable American Women, 1607–1950*, vol. 3

(1971); J. Gordon Melton, *Religious Leaders of America* (1991); Anna White and Leila S. Taylor, *Shakerism: Its Meaning and Message* (1904).

White, Ellen Gould (1827–1915)

Cofounder of the Seventh-Day Adventist Church, Ellen Gould White was born in Gorham, Maine, on November 26, 1827. The daughter of Robert and Eunice (Gould) Harmon, she grew up in Portland, where her father was a hatmaker. Ellen attended the Brackett Street School until she suffered a severe injury at the age of nine. At that time she was hit on the head with a rock thrown by an older schoolgirl. Ellen recovered consciousness three weeks later but was unable to resume her schoolwork. Her last attempt at formal education was at Westbrook Seminary and Female College in 1839, but dizziness that caused her to be unable to read or write soon forced her to give up.

Ellen was raised in a family of devout Methodists and had her first religious awakening while attending a Methodist camp meeting in 1840. She was baptized into the faith on June 26, 1842. At about this time, William Miller was spreading his Adventist predictions that Christ would be personally returning to earth in about 1843. The Harmons enthusiastically accepted Miller's message, which led to their expulsion from the Methodist Church. Although many discouraged Millerites returned to their former denominations when Christ's second coming did not occur by 1844, Ellen kept the faith. In December 1844, while attending a women's prayer meeting, Ellen fell into what appeared to be a trance. When she revived, she reported having a vision of her fellow believers on a pilgrimage to the City of God. This was the first of over two thousand such visions that she claimed to receive during the course of her life. She began to preach the message

Ellen Gould White (from Life Sketches, *1915)*

that Christ had indeed returned as Miller had predicted—not to earth, but to a heavenly sanctuary that he cleansed to prepare for his later appearance.

Although in frail health, Ellen became an itinerant minister. During her travels, she met Adventist minister James S. White, whom she married in August 1846. Soon after their marriage the Whites founded a periodical, *Present Truth*, which grew to become the *Advent Review and Sabbath Herald*, the official organ of the Seventh-Day Adventist Church. In 1847 the Whites became convinced that Saturday was the true day of worship and began to keep a Saturday Sabbath. Four years later, Ellen published a sixty-four-page book, *A Sketch of the Christian Experience and Views of Ellen G. White,* an autobiography designed to persuade others to accept her theology. In it she presented grand accounts of her visions.

In 1855 the Whites moved to Battle Creek, Michigan, which was to become the base for what was emerging as the Seventh-Day Adventist movement. The name of the denomination combined two distinctive beliefs—the Saturday Sabbath and the advent of Christ's imminent return. Guided by her visions, Ellen supervised the organization of the new church. Soon after her move to Battle Creek, Ellen had a vision of the battle of good versus evil, which led to what is considered her most important book, *The Great Controversy between Christ and His Angels and Satan and His Angels* (1858).

During her career as leader of the Seventh-Day Adventist Church, Ellen White wrote more than twenty-five books and two hundred shorter works. Though revered as a visionary, she made no claims to be a prophet. Nevertheless, her visions have been accepted by her congregants as being of divine origin, and her interpretations of the Scriptures have largely determined Seventh-Day Adventist orthodoxy.

Reflecting the reforming spirit of the times, White's views on African-American slavery, health, education, and temperance became a part of her religious instruction. During the years prior to the Civil War, she opposed slavery and urged her followers to disobey the Fugitive Slave Law. With the help of Quakers, Battle Creek became a station on the Underground Railroad. In the matter of health, White gradually became convinced that tea, coffee, drugs, and meats were harmful and advocated fresh air and exercise. Early in her career, she had brought about what her followers believed to be some miracles of healing by relying on prayer. In 1848 she advised Adventists to avoid going to regular physicians but by 1860 was suggesting that medical doctors might be necessary in some cases. Drawing on a vision experienced in December 1865, White played a principal role in the establishment of the Health Reform Institute in Battle Creek in 1866. Under the direction of John Harvey Kellogg, a protégé of the Whites, it became the well-known Battle Creek Sanitarium and the prototype for similar institutions founded by Seventh-Day Adventists throughout the world.

Anxious that a practical education should be open to children of all social and economic backgrounds, White founded Battle Creek College in 1874, with James White as principal. Although she did not become involved in most of the social and economic reforms of the post–Civil War period, White did speak out in favor of temperance. It was during her temperance lectures that she drew her largest audiences. At Groveland, Massachusetts, in 1876, twenty thousand people gathered to hear her deliver two discourses on the subject.

James White died in 1881. Following his death, his wife increased her efforts to enlarge the church. In addition to work in the United States, she traveled extensively in her efforts to spread Seventh-Day Adventism. White was in Europe from 1885 to 1888 and in Australia from 1891 to 1899. When she returned, she was instrumental in moving the church's headquarters from Battle Creek to Takoma Park, Maryland, outside Washington, D.C., in 1903. Also that year, she moved to St. Helena, California, where she died on July 16, 1915. By the last quarter of the twentieth century, Seventh-Day Adventism had spread around the world, with a church membership of well over two million.

References: Henry Warner Bowden, *Dictionary of American Religious Biography*, 2nd ed. (1993); Edward T. James, ed., *Notable American Women, 1607–1950* (1971); Gary Land, ed., *Adventism in America: A History* (1986); Gary Land, ed., *The World of Ellen G. White* (1987); J. Gordon Melton, *Religious Leaders of America* (1991); Francis D. Nichol, *Ellen G. White and Her Critics* (1951); Ronald L. Numbers, *Prophetess of Health: A Study of Ellen G. White* (1976).

Whitman, Narcissa Prentiss (1808–1847)

Teacher and missionary to Native Americans of the Pacific Northwest, Narcissa Prentiss Whitman was born March 14, 1808, in Prattsburg, New York. She was the third of the nine children of Stephen and Clarissa (Ward) Prentiss, both Presbyterians. Following a winter revival in 1818–1819, Narcissa joined her parents' church. A later religious experience in January 1824 inspired her to decide that she would someday become a missionary. In 1827 Narcissa was among the first class of girls to be admitted to the Presbyterian-sponsored Franklin Academy, a secondary school in Prattsburg. She was remembered as a popular, vivacious, and sentimentally religious young woman. Following graduation from the academy, Narcissa was still intent on becoming a missionary but worked as a teacher for several years while she awaited God's guidance.

In the fall of 1834, it seemed that Narcissa's hopes might be realized. Reverend Samuel Parker was in New York state, attempting to raise funds and recruits for a mission to take Christianity to the Native Americans of the far West. Marcus Whitman, a thirty-two-year-old physician and Presbyterian elder, was one of the first to volunteer. But when Narcissa Prentiss offered her services, she was rejected because she was an unmarried woman. Her disappointment was brief, however, for before he embarked on an exploratory journey to the West in February 1835, Whitman proposed marriage to Narcissa, and she accepted. The couple was married February 18, 1836, and almost immediately began their long trek to the West. Together with Eliza Hart Spalding, the wife of missionary Henry Spalding (whose proposal of marriage Narcissa had once rejected), Narcissa Whitman was one of the first white women to cross the Continental Divide.

When they reached Fort Walla Walla near the Columbia River in September 1836, the Whitmans chose to establish their mission at Waiilatpu, which was close by. They made their decision despite warnings from other tribes that the local Cayuse could be treacherous. The Spaldings settled about 125 miles away at Lapwai, among the Nez Percé. While her husband led religious services, provided medical care, erected mission buildings, and instructed the natives on the basics of irrigation and the domestication of livestock, Narcissa conducted the mission school and supervised the domestic economy at the mission. The Whitmans' only child, Alice Clarissa, was born on March 14, 1837, but accidentally drowned in July 1839. Her child's death caused Narcissa to enter a long period of depression. At about the same time, Narcissa's eyesight had begun to fail, eventually bringing her close to blindness.

Compounding Narcissa's unhappiness was her disillusionment with her mission work. There was growing dissension at the Oregon missions after missionary Asa Smith arrived in 1838. With the backing of Spalding and other missionaries, Smith had made a move to take over the Waiilatpu mission, but the Whitmans refused to leave. In 1842 the Mission Board in Boston, having heard about problems in Oregon, ordered that the missions at both Waiilatpu and Lapwai be closed. But by that time Smith had left, and the other missionaries had reconciled. Marcus Whitman decided that he must travel to Boston to present his case, and Narcissa agreed.

In October 1842 Narcissa was the only white person left at the mission. She later was frightened when about a week after Marcus departed, a Native American entered the Whitman home around midnight and tried to force his way into her bedroom. But Narcissa screamed and awakened a Hawaiian man, John, who slept at the Whitman home. John helped to scare away the intruder, who was never captured or identified. Overall, Narcissa had become disenchanted with frontier mission life. The Native Americans seemed ill-mannered and dirty to this woman who grew up in East Coast society. But what bothered her most of all was the fact that they were not responding to the Whitmans' teachings of the Gospel. Roman Catholics who had begun to compete in the Oregon country were having greater success in winning converts.

The Whitmans' relationships with the Cayuse grew worse as more white immigrants began flocking to the region. The Native Americans became suspicious that the Whitmans were fostering the white invasion. Their suspicions appeared confirmed in late 1847, when a measles epidemic reached Oregon. Although white children responded to the Whitmans' medical care, the Native American children, who had no immunity, died. The natives believed that Whitman had killed their children with white witchcraft. On November 29, 1847, a small band of Cayuse raided the mission at Waiilatpu, killing fourteen whites, including the Whitmans, and taking forty-seven prisoners.

Though her venture as a missionary resulted in disappointment and martyrdom, Narcissa Whitman helped open the way West for other women, both missionaries and ordinary settlers.

See also: Missionaries; Spalding, Eliza Hart
References: Opal Sweazea Allen, *Narcissa Whitman: An Historical Biography* (1959); Henry Warner Bowden, *Dictionary of American Religious Biography,* 2nd ed. (1993); Clifford M. Drury, *Marcus and Narcissa Whitman and the Opening of Old Oregon* (1986); Edward T. James, ed., *Notable American Women, 1607–1950* (1971).

Wicca

Believed to be an Old English term for "witchcraft," the word "Wicca" is often preferred by twentieth-century practitioners of the religion of neo-Pagan witchcraft because it does not carry the negative stereotypes associated with "witch." The terms "Wicca" and its plural form "Wiccan" distinguish practitioners of neo-Pagan witchcraft from those who practice folk magic and other forms of witchcraft. They connote an organized religion with its own set of beliefs, values, laws, holy days, and rituals. With a focus on Goddess worship and on nature as the primary source of spiritual meaning, some of Wicca's advocates are convinced that they have restored a distinctive religious tradition of Western culture. Practitioners believe that the ancient craft went underground for centuries in order to escape the domination of an oppressive, patriarchal Christianity.

See also: Adler, Margot; Ecofeminism; Fox, Selena; Frost, Yvonne; Handfasting; Witchcraft

References: Margot Adler, *Drawing Down the Moon: Witches, Druids, Goddess-Worshippers and Other Pagans in America Today* (1986); Rosemary Ellen Guiley, *The Encyclopedia of Witches and Witchcraft* (1989); Susan Hill Lindley, *"You Have Stept Out of Your Place": A History of Women and Religion in America* (1996); George A. Mather and Larry A. Nichols, *Dictionary of Cults, Sects, Religions and the Occult* (1993); Leslie Shepard, ed., *Encyclopedia of Occultism and Parapsychology,* 3rd ed. (1991); Charlene Spretnak, ed., *The Politics of Women's Spirituality: Essays on the Rise of Spiritual Power within the Feminist Movement* (1982).

Wilcox, Ella Wheeler (1850–1919)

Ella Wheeler Wilcox, a popular late-nineteenth- and early-twentieth-century poet and an advocate of New Thought metaphysics, was born in Johnstown Center, Wisconsin, on November 5, 1850. She was the youngest daughter of Sarah (Pratt) and Marius Hartwell Wheeler. From childhood, Ella loved to read and write and apparently wrote her first novel, designed for the enjoyment of

Ella Wheeler Wilcox (undated portrait)

her sisters, before she was ten years old. Her first published work, an essay, appeared in the *New York Mercury* when Wheeler was in her early teens. She was also in her teens when *Waverly Magazine* published the first poem under her name. From 1867 to 1868, Wheeler attended the University of Wisconsin but left the university after studying for only one year because she did not feel her classes offered her instruction that would benefit her as a poet. By this time, she had become a successful poet and was making a substantial contribution to her family's income.

She continued to achieve success during the 1870s, with *Drops of Water* (1872), a volume of temperance poetry; *Shells* (1873); and *Maurine* (1876), a narrative poem. A fourth work, *Poems of Passion,* was written during the 1870s, but her publisher, Jansen and McClung of Chicago, refused to publish it, stating that it was immoral. The conflict became public, so that when it was finally published by another company in 1883, the book was highly successful.

Wheeler married Robert Maius Wilcox on May 1, 1884, and moved with him to Meridian, Connecticut. Their only child, a son born in the spring of 1887, survived only a few hours. In 1887 she enrolled in a class given by Emma Curtis Hopkins, the founder of New Thought, a religion that emphasized idealistic healing. Soon Wheeler was caught up in the New Thought movement, and she began to fill her poems with New Thought themes. Early in the twentieth century, she wrote three books with New Thought as their major focus: *The Heart of New Thought* (1902); *New Thought and Common Sense: What Life Means to Me* (1908); and *The Art of Being Alive: Success through Thought* (1914). She also became involved in the women's rights movement and frequently combined the two themes. *Every-Day Thoughts in Prose and Verse* (1901) is one example.

Wilcox had become a well-known and popular writer by the turn of the century. In addition to seeing her work in mass circulation magazines, she wrote a syndicated newspaper column. In 1901 she went to London on an assignment to write a poem commemorating the death of Queen Victoria. When Wilcox visited London again twelve years later, she received the honor of being presented at court.

Both Wilcox and her husband believed in the possibility of communication with the dead. After her husband died in 1916, she believed that she was able to contact him by using a Ouija board. She was in Bath, England, in 1919 when she became severely ill. Wilcox was in a Bath nursing home for three months before returning to her home at Short Beach, Connecticut. She died in Short Beach on October 30, 1919. Her autobiography, *The Worlds and I,* had just been published the previous year.

See also: Hopkins, Emma Curtis; New Thought Movement
References: *Dictionary of American Biography,* vol. 20 (1936); J. Gordon Melton, *Religious Leaders of America* (1991); Ella Wheeler Wilcox, *Maurine and Other Poems* (1888); Ella Wheeler Wilcox, *Poems of Pleasure* (1902).

Wilkinson, Jemima (1752–1819)

Jemima Wilkinson, the first native-born American to found a religious community, was born in Cumberland, Rhode Island, on November 29, 1752. She was the eighth of the twelve children of Jeremiah Wilkinson, a prosperous farmer, and Amey (Whipple) Wilkinson. Little is known of Wilkinson's early life, but traditional accounts report that she was known for her self-indulgence, avoidance of hard work, and time spent reading romances. Other reports state that she was also an avid reader of the Bible and Quaker theology and history. She became especially excited about religion when she was about eighteen, after listening to the sermons of Great Awakening revivalist George Whitefield during his last visit to America and attending meetings of the New Light Baptists, a noisy evangelizing sect that emphasized individual inspiration and enlightenment through the Holy Spirit. Her presence at the meetings of the latter group led to her dismissal from the Society of Friends. Wilkinson was under emotional stress, and in 1776 she became ill with a fever. During this time, she fell into a lengthy trance. When she awoke, she claimed that she had died, that her original body had gone to heaven, and that her present body was now inhabited by the "Spirit of Life," which God intended to use to lead sinners to salvation.

Wilkinson began calling herself the "Public Universal Friend"; refused to recognize the name Jemima Wilkinson; and began to hold religious meetings in her home, outdoors, and in private and public places. These meetings drew increasingly large audiences. Clad in a long, flowing black robe over masculine dress, she led her followers on a series of processions on horseback through Rhode Island. It was not the substance of her preaching that attracted the crowds, for her sermons offered nothing the people had not heard before. Instead, the Friend became known for her charismatic personality and for her beauty. She was tall and graceful, with lovely dark hair and hypnotic black eyes. Her claims that she had been restored to life to become God's messenger, or Jesus Christ in a woman's form, attracted crowds of curious onlookers. Wilkinson sought and successfully won converts from the wealthier and more educated segments of the community. In a time when women were generally deemed incapable of public speaking, Wilkinson proved that she was an effective preacher before large crowds. As people from Massachusetts to Pennsylvania gathered around her, they created a society of Universal Friends. Between 1777 and 1782, as the Americans fought for independence from Britain, she founded meeting halls in New Milford, Connecticut, and in East Greenwich and South Kingston, Rhode Island, all in the name of Universal Friends. A wealthy Kingston judge built a fourteen-room addition to his mansion to accommodate her.

Meanwhile, in her preaching Wilkinson had begun to emphasize celibacy as being superior to marriage and the importance of subordinating family responsibilities to the support of her sect. As a result, she was blamed for the breakup of many families. These circumstances, combined with the claims of her disciples that she was Jesus Christ come again and her own secretiveness in regard to her relations with the divine spirit, completely scandalized the orthodox churches of New England. In 1783 she transferred

her headquarters to Philadelphia. A year later, she published her only printed guide for her followers, *The Universal Friend's Advice to Those of the Same Religious Society,* which consisted mainly of quotations from the Bible. She met with considerable opposition in Philadelphia, including being stoned at one of her meetings. In 1785 she returned to New England.

In 1788 Wilkinson established a colony for her group on a large tract of land in Yates County, near Seneca Lake in western New York. The colony, which was called "Jerusalem," began to prosper under her leadership. Members of the sect raised wheat and built a sawmill, a gristmill, and also a school. Most likely influenced by her Quaker background, the Friend urged her followers to wear plain clothing, practice pacifism, and oppose slavery. She encouraged believers to seek forgiveness for their sins and to prepare themselves for judgment day. Her ministry also included prophecy and dream interpretation, and early in her career she made several attempts at faith healing. By 1800 the population of Jerusalem reached 260 people. The Friend got along well with the neighboring Native Americans, who named her "Squaw Shinnewanagistawge," or Great Woman Preacher, and she helped to create a peaceful coexistence between the Native Americans of western New York and the white newcomers.

As the community grew, so did dissension. Some members of her sect were unhappy with the division of property in the colony and brought unsuccessful lawsuits against the Friend. According to some reports, she was constantly demanding that her followers present her with gifts and grew increasingly dictatorial in her leadership as time passed. Others state that she remained a kindly woman throughout her life, devoting her time and energies to educating, preaching to, and caring for her followers. The Friend had set aside 12,000 acres of the property for herself, and on it she built a large home. She frequently had guests staying with her, and approximately sixteen to eighteen needy members of her society regularly resided in her home. As she aged, Wilkinson developed dropsy and died from that illness on July 1, 1819. It was not long after her death that the society she had founded completely disintegrated.

See also: Great Awakening; Lee, Ann; Society of Friends (Quakers)
References: Henry Warner Bowden, *Dictionary of American Religious Biography* (1977); *Dictionary of American Biography*, vol. 10 (1936); Edward T. James, ed., *Notable American Women: 1607–1950*, vol. 3 (1971); Herbert A. Wisbey, Jr., *Pioneer Prophetess: Jemima Wilkinson, the Publick Universal Friend* (1964).

Willard, Frances Elizabeth Caroline (1839–1898)

Temperance leader and feminist Frances Elizabeth Caroline Willard was born September 28, 1839, in Churchville, New York. When Willard was seven, she moved with her parents to Janesville, Wisconsin. The Willards, who were Congregationalists, found there was no Congregationalist church in Janesville, so they joined the Methodists, who had built a church. Both of Willard's parents, especially her mother, encouraged her to acquire a solid education. In 1857 she enrolled in Northwestern Female Academy, a Methodist-affiliated school in Evanston, Illinois. She graduated from the college in 1859 as class valedictorian. In 1860 she had a bout with typhoid fever that led to a religious conversion and to her formally joining the Methodist Episcopal Church.

Over the next several years, Willard's life was unsettled. She entered the teaching profession, teaching at various academies between 1860 and 1867. For a while

she was engaged to be married to Charles Henry Fowler, the pastor of a Chicago Methodist church, but for unknown reasons the engagement was suddenly broken off. Willard never did marry. In 1865 she became corresponding secretary for the American Methodist Ladies Centennial Association, assuming the major responsibilities for the organization's goal to raise funds for the building of Heck Hall at Northwestern University.

Between 1868 and 1870, Willard traveled for two years in Europe, Russia, Greece, Turkey, the Holy Land, and Egypt. To help her meet expenses for her lengthy excursion, she wrote weekly articles for local newspapers back home. Willard was already interested in uplifting members of her sex, and her travels increased her enthusiasm. Upon her return to Illinois, she settled with her mother in Evanston and began to search for ways to improve women's status. In 1871 Willard was appointed president of the new Evanston College for Ladies, which was associated with Northwestern University. Unfortunately, her former fiancé, Charles Fowler, became president of Northwestern University in 1872 and soon made it clear that he would extend his authority over the female students and their college president. Willard remained at Northwestern from 1873 to 1874 as dean of women and professor of English and art. In October 1873 she accepted an invitation to participate in the founding of the Association for the Advancement of Women in New York City and was elected a vice president of that organization.

At about the same time, a movement to control liquor consumption had begun to grow. The antisaloon crusade was having some success, closing up to three thousand saloons in six months in the Midwest and East. Although she had not been a temperance crusader, Willard recognized in the movement a means to help advance the cause of women. In the summer of 1874, she was elected president of the Chicago Temperance League and in November 1874 was elected the first corresponding secretary of the national Woman's Christian Temperance Union (WCTU). From that position, she campaigned to build support for woman suffrage. The union's first president, Annie Wittenmyer, opposed Willard's attempts to commit the WCTU to endorse this political issue. Nevertheless, Willard created a strong backing for her agenda by lecturing across the country and expressing her arguments in the WCTU journal, *Our Union*. In 1879 Willard was elected president of the WCTU and held that post for the rest of her life.

In her first presidential address, Willard proclaimed her "Do Everything" policy. She envisioned the WCTU as an organization gathering strength to pursue numerous reforms in addition to temperance. Woman suffrage, labor conditions, public health, prison reform, prostitution, race relations, and narcotics were among the many issues that Willard believed should be addressed by the WCTU. Under her leadership, thirty-nine departments were established within the organization to deal with issues affecting society. With Willard at the helm, the WCTU became the largest women's rights organization in the United States.

Willard also had interests outside the WCTU. In 1887 she was one of the first women elected by local church conferences as delegates to the Methodist General Conference. However, when the five women delegates arrived at the conference, a small majority led by Charles Fowler (now Bishop Fowler) would not allow them to be seated. The conference did, however, adopt a resolution in praise of Willard's temperance work.

As president of the WCTU, Willard attempted to press national political parties to endorse WCTU causes. In the 1880s,

she unsuccessfully tried to get suffrage and prohibition accepted as planks of the Republican Party platform and suffrage accepted as part of the platform of the National Prohibition Party. Then in 1892, she attempted to unite the Populists with prohibitionists, suffragists, and labor but met with defeat. Her disappointment over this latest defeat, coupled with the death of her mother, led Willard to seek a period of rest in England.

From the summer of 1892 until the end of 1896, Willard spent most of her time in England. While there, she became interested in socialism and came to embrace the opinion that intemperance was primarily caused by poverty. Further, she adopted the view that education rather than prohibition was a better solution to the liquor problem. Her new ideas and frequent absences brought unrest to the WCTU, but most members remained loyal. When Willard died in New York City on February 18, 1898, her friend and associate Lillian M. N. Stevens succeeded her as president (1898–1914).

While she led the WCTU, Willard wrote several books, including *Woman and Temperance* (1883); her autobiography, *Glimpses of Fifty Years* (1889); and *A Classic Town: The Story of Evanston* (1892).

See also: Wittenmyer, Annie Turner; Woman's Christian Temperance Union
References: Ruth Bordin, *Frances Willard: A Biography* (1986); Henry Warner Bowden, *Dictionary of American Religious Biography*, 2nd ed. (1993); Edward T. James, ed., *Notable American Women, 1607–1950* (1971); Randall C. Jimerson, F. X. Blouin, and C. A. Isetts, eds., *Guide to the Microfilm Edition of Temperance and Prohibition Papers* (1977); J. Gordon Melton, *Religious Leaders of America* (1991); Frances E. Willard, *Woman and Temperance* (1883, reprint 1972).

Witchcraft

Witchcraft has been defined in the Christian tradition as the human attempt to manipulate supernatural forces toward evil ends. Witches were held responsible for disease and other misfortunes and were said to have acquired their evil powers from the devil. For hundreds of years witchcraft has falsely been identified with Satanism, and in the fourteenth through seventeenth centuries, witch-hunting epidemics prevailed in Europe and to some extent were carried over to North America. More women than men were accused of being witches, largely because they were perceived as being more impressionable than men and thus were more easily tempted by Satan. Perhaps of greater importance was the fact that women did not have the power to protect themselves against charges leveled at them by male clerical and governmental officials. Witch hunting in America reached its climax in 1692, when 141 people living in the area surrounding Salem, Massachusetts, were accused of witchcraft, and twenty men and women were executed.

The witch portrayed as an old female hag with warts on her nose, wearing a pointed black hat, riding on a broomstick, and casting spells, is mostly folklore and myth. But witchcraft has existed in various forms since ancient times. In I Samuel 28:7, Saul sought guidance from the witch of Endor; shamans and priests in preindustrial societies were popularly called "witch doctors" and their practice "witchcraft;" and voodoo is usually equated with witchcraft. In modern times, witchcraft is a religion that centers around worship of the Great Mother Goddess and focuses on nature worship and fertility rituals. To distinguish their practices from the older forms of witchcraft, witches frequently refer to themselves as "neo-Pagans" and their Craft as "Wicca."

Egyptologist, folklorist, anthropologist, and self-proclaimed witch Margaret Murray (1863–1963) helped to keep alive an interest in witchcraft, largely through her books *Witchcraft in Western Europe* (1921) and *The God of the Witches* (1933), but Gerald Gardner (1884–1964) is usually credited with launching modern witchcraft. Gardner accumulated extensive occult knowledge while working as an archaeologist in Southeast Asia. After returning to his native England in 1939, he met a woman, Dorothy Clutterbuck, who introduced him to witchcraft. In *Witchcraft Today* (1954), Gardner endorsed Murray's argument that a Goddess religion had been in existence since a number of centuries before Christ. With the last of the Witchcraft Acts having been repealed in Britain in 1951, Gardner urged witches to come out and to speak to the world about their rituals and beliefs, and he wrote about the traditions and rites that he had learned as a member of an English coven. Controversy has surrounded Gardner as to whether he was initiated into an authentic surviving coven from ancient times and whether the practices he described are truly centuries-old rituals and traditions. Despite the controversy, most modern witchcraft, commonly known as Wicca, has developed from the teachings of Gardner. During the 1960s, Gardnerian and other independent variations of Wiccan groups began to establish themselves in the United States. Most of these groups incorporated at least some of Gardner's rituals.

Foremost in the religion of Wicca is the belief in the Great Mother Goddess who throughout history has been revealed in many forms, including Artemis, Aphrodite, and Diana. Pan, the Horned God and the Goddess's consort, is the male principal of Wicca. Minor deities become prominent during the religion's seasonal festivals. Each year Wiccans celebrate eight major festivals, known as "sabbats." Believing that they are in harmony with nature, Wiccans celebrate the phases of the seasons on earth. These festivals are occasions for several covens to gather together, and witches who otherwise practice individually often join with others during the sabbats.

When not celebrating a festival, many witches meet in small autonomous groups known as "covens." Ideally, a coven is made up of thirteen people, and most covens usually have between four and twenty-six members. They meet about every two weeks, during the new and full moons.

Magic is a part of modern witchcraft and is practiced in various forms, including healing. Witches consider healing to be a natural process of Mother Earth. Nature provides herbs for healing, and knowledge of herbs is an area in which many witches specialize. Witches believe that the effects of magic will be returned threefold upon the person practicing it, which is a deterrent against the pronouncing of curses. Also, they follow a principle of ethics known as the Wiccan Rede: "An' it harm none, do what ye will" (Guiley, 1989, p. 363).

During the mid-1970s, a number of women combined witchcraft with feminist ideology. Moderate feminists found witchcraft to be a religion that recognized male-female equality, but the more radical of the group viewed witchcraft as "wimmin's religion" and advocated all-female covens. And although witchcraft is normally considered a polytheistic religion, some radical feminists are monotheists, believing that only the Great Mother Goddess is worthy of worship.

The exact number of witches in the United States is not known, though in 1986 J. Gordon Melton estimated that there were over thirty thousand witches and neo-Pagans in North America. A slight majority of these were female.

See also: Adler, Margot; Fox, Selena; Frost, Yvonne; Starhawk; Wicca
References: Margot Adler, *Drawing Down the Moon: Witches, Druids, Goddess-Worshippers, and Other Pagans in America Today* (1986); Rosemary Ellen Guiley, *The Encyclopedia of Witches and Witchcraft* (1989); George A. Mather and Larry A. Nichols, *Dictionary of Cults, Sects, Religions and the Occult* (1993); J. Gordon Melton, *Encyclopedic Handbook of Cults in America* (1986); Charlene Spretnak, ed., *The Politics of Women's Spirituality: Essays on the Rise of Spiritual Power within the Feminist Movement* (1982); Starhawk, *The Spiral Dance: A Rebirth of the Ancient Religion of the Great Goddess,* 10th anniversary edition (1989).

Wittenmyer, Annie Turner (1827–1900)

Annie Turner Wittenmyer, relief worker, leader in church and charitable work, and the first president of the Woman's Christian Temperance Union (WCTU), was born August 26, 1827, in Sandy Springs, Ohio. She was the daughter of John G. and Elizabeth (Smith) Turner. Annie grew up in Ohio and Kentucky and is believed to have completed her formal education at a seminary in Ohio. She married wealthy merchant William Wittenmyer of Jacksonville, Ohio, in 1847. They had five children, of whom all but one died in infancy. During the 1850s, the Wittenmyers moved to Keokuk, Iowa, where Annie helped organize a Methodist Episcopal church and established a free school for poor children. William died in the late 1850s, leaving his wife a wealthy widow.

The Civil War erupted shortly after William's death, and Annie turned to social service work. She comforted sick and wounded solders and was secretary of the Soldiers' Aid Society of Keokuk. Her travels around Iowa in pursuit of hospital supplies were publicized in the press, and she was soon well known. The publicity brought other women to the cause and resulted in the state hiring Wittenmyer as a sanitary agent. But there were rivalries among the social service workers. The all-male Iowa Army Sanitary Commission attempted a takeover of the work performed by Iowa women. In an effort to resist the takeover, in 1863 Wittenmyer assisted in the organizing of the Iowa State Sanitary Commission, and she was elected its president. Nevertheless, tensions persisted and, although she continued her work, Wittenmyer had to devote considerable time to refuting charges of corruption. Although she was later cleared of the charges, she resigned from her position in May 1864.

Still determined to help the wounded soldiers, Wittenmyer devised a plan for special diet kitchens that would be attached to hospitals and would provide patients with alternatives to army rations. With the assistance of the U.S. Christian Commission, she established the first of several of these kitchens at an army hospital in Nashville, Tennessee.

After the war, Wittenmyer worked to help war orphans and others in need. She persuaded the government to turn over some barracks and hospital supplies to the Iowa Orphans' Home Association. Also, she played a leading role in the establishment of the Ladies' and Pastors' Christian Union (later the General Conference Society) in 1868. This was a Methodist social agency through which women, under the guidance of their pastors, would visit the sick and the needy. Wittenmyer was the corresponding secretary for the organization until 1871 and traveled widely as a lecturer on its behalf.

In 1871 Wittenmyer moved to Philadelphia. There she began to publish a successful periodical, the *Christian Woman,* which continued for eleven years. Through this work, she was able to develop her ideas surrounding the role of women in society. Her first book, *Woman's Work for Jesus* (1874), exhorted women to engage in social service. At about the same time, Wittenmyer became caught up in the largely unorganized "Woman's Crusade" against alcohol. As a leader of Methodist churchwomen, she attended the found-

ing meeting of the WCTU in Cleveland, Ohio, in November 1874 and was elected the organization's first president. She threw herself into the crusade, making extensive lecture tours in the company of the WCTU's corresponding secretary, Frances E. Willard. Together they persuaded women to found local unions. Wittenmyer supervised the establishment of the WCTU's periodical, *Our Union,* and she wrote a book recounting the crusade's early years, *History of the Woman's Temperance Union* (1878).

Soon after her election to the presidency of the WCTU, Wittenmyer came into conflict with Willard, who wanted to broaden the agenda of the organization to include suffrage and other political issues of importance to women. As she revealed in her history of the crusade, Wittenmyer saw the WCTU as a divinely inspired gospel temperance movement and was not about to deviate from that mission. After several attempts to unseat Wittenmyer, Willard finally won the presidency at the 1879 convention. During the five years of Wittenmyer's presidency, more than a thousand local unions, with a total of some twenty-six thousand members, had been organized. After her defeat, Wittenmyer remained active with the WCTU until it endorsed the Prohibition Party in 1890. At that time, Wittenmyer joined with some of Willard's opponents who broke with the WCTU to form the Non-Partisan Woman's Christian Temperance Union. She was president of this organization from 1896 to 1898.

The final crusade for the aging Wittenmyer was with the Woman's Relief Corps, the woman's auxiliary of the Grand Army of the Republic. As president of the organization from 1889 to 1890, she successfully led a campaign to establish in Ohio a National Woman's Relief Corps Home for female victims of war—nurses, widows, and mothers of veterans. Wittenmyer served as director of the home and of a similar one in Pennsylvania. Also, she lobbied Congress on behalf of a bill to grant pensions to nurses of the Civil War, and in 1898 she herself received a special pension. In 1895 she published *Under the Guns,* an autobiography of her war years. Wittenmyer died in Pennsylvania on February 2, 1900.

See also: Willard, Frances Elizabeth Caroline; Woman's Christian Temperance Union
References: Edward T. James, ed., *Notable American Women, 1607–1950* (1971); Susan Hill Lindley, *"You Have Stept Out of Your Place": A History of Women and Religion in America* (1996); Robert McHenry, ed., *Liberty's Women* (1980); J. Gordon Melton, *Religious Leaders of America* (1991).

Woman, Church and State

Although it was highly controversial at the time of its publication, Matilda Joslyn Gage's *Woman, Church and State* (1893) has come to be viewed as "one of the most important theoretical documents produced by the nineteenth century woman's movement" (Wagner, 1990, p. 225). Angered over the continued oppression of the female sex, Gage challenged the contemporary assumption that Christianity elevated women. She argued that, on the contrary, the church had throughout history created an alliance with the state, and together they had degraded and maltreated women.

Gage's opening chapter, "The Matriarchate," drew upon anthropological studies to support her argument that some pre-Christian societies lived under a matriarchate, or mother-rule wherein women were superior to men in religion, government, and society. In her eyes, the fall of matriarchy and the growth of patriarchy resulted in a decline of world civilization. Following chapters on celibacy, canon law, and marquette (the medieval custom by which feudal lords claimed marital rights over new brides)

point out ways in which women have been perceived as inherently sinful and unholy and how they have suffered degradation under male rule. Chapters on witchcraft, wives, polygamy, and woman and work reveal women to be persecuted and, with the sanction of the church, treated as virtual slaves.

In her final chapters, "The Church of To-Day" and "Past, Present, Future," Gage acknowledged that among the general public women were steadily being recognized as having religious rights. Yet she contended that the theories of the Christian churches in regard to the place of women remained much the same as they had been in centuries past. Gage predicted that women would eventually launch a rebellion "against the tyranny of Church and State" that would "overthrow every existing form of these institutions," and from that would emerge a "regenerated world" (p. 545).

See also: Gage, Matilda Joslyn; Woman Suffrage; *The Woman's Bible*
References: Kathryn Cullen-DuPont, with Annelise Orleck, *The Encyclopedia of Women's History in America* (1996); Matilda Joslyn Gage, *Woman, Church and State* (1893; reprint 1972); Edward T. James, ed., *Notable American Women, 1607–1950*, vol. 2 (1971); Susan Hill Lindley, *"You Have Stept Out of Your Place": A History of Women and Religion in America* (1996); Sally Roesch Wagner, "Gage, Matilda Joslyn," in Angela Howard Zophy with Frances M. Kavenik, eds., *Handbook of American Women's History* (1990).

Woman Suffrage

On the issue of woman's suffrage, the position of the churches and of their female congregants varied from church to church and from woman to woman. From the time that a suffrage resolution was passed at the Seneca Falls Convention of 1848 until late in the nineteenth century, female suffrage was considered a radical idea by most women as well as by men. Religious leaders and the women in their congregations usually shared this opinion. Nevertheless, among those religions whose theologies emphasized egalitarianism, it was more likely that women and some men would become agitators for the cause of female suffrage. For example, during the nineteenth century, Quaker women (whose religion stressed an "inner light" experienced equally by both sexes) made up a disproportionately large number of the forces within the movement for woman suffrage. During the 1910s, Quaker Alice Paul led the National Woman's Party, one of the two leading suffrage organizations.

There were some instances in which religious prejudices influenced a denomination's stand on the issue of woman suffrage. An example is the Mormons, who gave women the vote in the Utah Territory in 1870 while feeling pressure from much of the rest of America to eliminate the practice of polygamy. Roman Catholics, who perceived female suffrage as a Protestant reform, were influential in the antisuffrage movement. In 1900 the National American Woman Suffrage Association could count only six Catholic clergymen in the nation who openly supported suffrage.

For many men and women across the religious spectrum, the idea of women voting seemed "unfeminine." Even those women, like those in missions work, who had pushed for greater opportunities and influence within their churches often considered it unwomanly for females to participate in political life. But the reluctance of many female antisuffragists to speak in public because it was an unfeminine thing to do hurt their cause. Roman Catholic women Ellen Ewing Sherman and Madeline Vinton Dahlgren, who during the last quarter of the nineteenth century founded the first antisuffrage organization, opposed the ballot largely because they felt it would lure women from their homes and their wifely duties. Also believing that speaking in public violated female modesty, they often had to resort to letter-writing campaigns to spread their message. When the Nineteenth Amendment became law in 1920, most antisuffragists accepted the status quo, though many clergymen reminded women to uphold traditional feminine values and virtues.

See also: Church of Jesus Christ of Latter-Day Saints (Mormons); Edmunds-Tucker Act; Equal Rights Amendment; Roman Catholic Church; Society of Friends (Quakers)
References: Eleanor Flexner, *Century of Struggle: The Woman's Rights Movement in the United States* (1970); Karen Kennelly, ed., *American Catholic Women: A Historical Exploration* (1989); Susan Hill Lindley, "*You Have Stept Out of Your Place*": *A History of Women and Religion in America* (1996); Marilyn Warenski, *Patriarchs and Politics: The Plight of the Mormon Woman* (1978).

The Woman's Bible

Convinced that the traditional Bible was not the direct word of God and that it was the root cause of centuries of oppression of women, women's rights activist Elizabeth Cady Stanton wrote *The Woman's Bible*. She intended her work to cause women to question the theological doctrine that was so derogatory to them. Stanton had hoped to involve other women in the research and construction of her *Bible*, especially Latin, Greek, and Hebrew scholars, but she failed to interest others in her project. Many women considered the idea sacrilegious. Therefore, she had little help with her two-volume work. Volume 1 was published in 1895, when Stanton was eighty years of age. The second volume was published three years later.

Stanton explains the purpose of *The Woman's Bible* in her introduction:

The canon and civil law; church and state; priests and legislators, all political parties and religious denominations, have alike taught that woman was made after man, of man, and for man, an inferior being subject to man. (p. 7).

She continues:

The Bible teaches that woman brought sin and death into the world, that she precipitated the fall of the race, that she was arraigned before the judgment seat of Heaven, tried, condemned, and sentenced. Marriage for her was to be a condition of bondage, maternity a period of suffering and anguish, and in silence and subjection, she was to play the role of dependent on man's bounty for all her material wants. (p. 12)

Stanton questions why women are willing to review secular law and to make changes but are not comfortable doing the same with religious law. If legislatures can purge laws that denigrate women, why, she asks, cannot councils of bishops and revising committees do the same within the churches? Stanton did not believe "that any man ever saw or talked with God," nor that God inspired the Mosaic code, nor told historians "what they say he did about woman" (p. 14).

In the body of *The Woman's Bible*, Stanton cites various biblical verses from both the Old and New Testaments and then comments upon and analyzes their significance to women. For example, she begins with a look at Genesis: "So God created man in his own image, of God created he him, male and female created he them." Here, she writes, is

the sacred historian's first account of the advent of woman; a simultaneous creation of both sexes, in the image of God. It is evident from the language that there was consultation

in the Godhead, and that the masculine and feminine elements were equally represented. (p. 14)

For people who had been raised believing that the Bible was the direct word of God, *The Woman's Bible* was shocking and was considered a work of Satan. Clergymen preached sermons denouncing the work, and many among the women's movement objected, both on religious grounds and because they felt it harmed their campaign. Nevertheless, both volumes became best-sellers, and Stanton felt that she had accomplished much. The controversy surrounding the book told her that people were at least thinking about the subject, and this was a first step toward action. *The Woman's Bible* planted the seed for what has become known as feminist theology.

See also: Feminist Theology; Stanton, Elizabeth Cady; Woman Suffrage
References: Lois W. Banner, *Elizabeth Cady Stanton: A Radical for Woman's Rights* (1980); Elisabeth Griffith, *In Her Own Right: The Life of Elizabeth Cady Stanton* (1984); Alma Lutz, *Created Equal: A Biography of Elizabeth Cady Stanton, 1815–1902* (1974); Elizabeth Cady Stanton, *Eighty Years and More: Reminiscences, 1815–1897* (1898, republished 1993); Elizabeth Cady Stanton, *The Woman's Bible: Parts I and II* (1895, 1898).

Woman's Christian Temperance Union

Founded in 1874 over the concern that alcohol consumption had a deleterious effect upon families, the Woman's Christian Temperance Union (WCTU) emerged as a national women's movement. The WCTU was born from a series of meetings held in 1874 and, in the words of former president Frances Willard, formed "of Christ's gospel and cradled at His altars." In August 1874, during the National Sunday School Assembly in Chautauqua, New York, women from a dozen states gathered for temperance meetings. By the end

Members of the Woman's Christian Temperance Union, who believed alcohol had a harmful effect on families, worked closely with the woman suffrage movement in their determination to improve the conditions of women's lives (woodcut from Elizabeth Putnam Gordon's Women Torch-Bearers, *1924).*

of the meetings, they had decided to call for a national temperance convention of women to meet in Cleveland, Ohio, the following November. One hundred and thirty-five women attended the November 18–20, 1874, convention, representing seventeen states. They adopted a plan of organization for the national WCTU and its state branches, ratified a constitution, and elected national officers. Annie Wittenmyer became president; Frances E. Willard, corresponding secretary; Mary Johnson, recording secretary; and Mary Ingham, treasurer.

The organization's primary purpose was to protect the home from the troubles caused by alcohol. Wife and child beatings and the family breadwinner's wages being wasted on drink were among the reasons cited for abstinence. The WCTU's slogan, "For God and Home and Native Land" (later changed to "Every Land") expressed the group's priorities. By 1900, membership in the WCTU had grown to half a million, and it was the largest women's organization in the United States.

Under the leadership of Wittenmyer (1874–1879), the WCTU remained strictly focused upon the issue of temperance. When, at its 1876 convention, Frances Willard challenged the organization to broaden its agenda to include woman suffrage, her resolution was voted down. However, three years later Willard was elected president, and under her leadership the WCTU broadened its objectives. Willard, who served as president until her death in 1898, was determined to improve conditions for women in a variety of ways. With her at the helm, the WCTU campaigned for various reforms, including suffrage for women, equal pay for equal work, the eight-hour day, and the elimination of prostitution, in addition to crusades to close neighborhood saloons and to make all liquor sales illegal. In her first presidential address at the 1880 Boston convention, Willard contended that the temperance movement was slowly showing women the necessity of voting and the need to vote against "grog shops."

Upon Willard's death, her loyal friend, Lillian M. N. Stevens, succeeded her as president (1898–1914). The WCTU continued to promote a variety of reforms, including woman's suffrage, the Pure Food and Drug Act (1906), and the Mann Act (1910), which prohibited interstate transport of women for immoral purposes. The passage of the Eighteenth Amendment (1919), prohibiting the manufacture, sale, import, export, and transportation of intoxicating liquors, occurred during the presidency of Anna Gordon (1914–1925). It was a major victory for the WCTU.

Following the ratification of the Eighteenth Amendment the WCTU involved itself in other reforms, especially child welfare, social purity, and the Americanization of foreign immigrants. Membership drives kept numbers on the rise or at least on an even level until 1933. In 1933 the Prohibition amendment was repealed, which no doubt disillusioned many WCTU members. Since then, membership has declined. Currently, the national WCTU has approximately four thousand local branches in forty-eight states, with a total membership of about fifty thousand.

See also: Reform Movements; Willard, Frances Elizabeth Caroline
References: Ruth Bordin, *Frances Willard: A Biography* (1986); Randall C. Jimerson, F. X. Blouin, and C. A. Isetts, eds., *Guide to the Microfilm Edition of Temperance and Prohibition Papers* (1977); Frances E. Willard, *Woman and Temperance* (1883, reprint 1972).

Woman's Home and Foreign Mission Society

The Woman's Home and Foreign Mission Society, a national organization administered by the Advent Christian Church, was established in Friendship, Maine, by Sarah K. Taylor on July 31, 1897. During its first year, the society grew from an active membership of four, plus two honorary members, to about three hundred. In 1997 there were approximately 1,750 members in 136 local groups.

The goals of the society are "to engage and unite the efforts of Christian women of the Advent Church Denomination in sending the Gospel of the Kingdom throughout the world," to encourage "the deepening of the spiritual life among believers in Christ," and, by organization, "to render more efficient the work of the women of the churches" (Wooton, 1997).

Since its beginning more than a hundred years ago, the Woman's Home and Foreign Mission Society has been very much involved in the support of missions, both in the United States and abroad. Between 1906 and 1958, it oversaw all of the Advent Christian work in India. (In 1958 the India work was placed under the American Advent Mission Society.) Over the past four decades, the women have continued their involvement in outreach work, both at home and abroad.

See also: Missionary Societies
References: Jacqueline K. Barrett, ed., *Encyclopedia of Women's Associations Worldwide* (1993); Luree Wooton, Coordinator of Women's Ministries, letter to author (September 10, 1997).

Woman's Missionary Union

Led by Martha McIntosh and Annie Walker Armstrong, who became the organization's first president and corresponding secretary, respectively, the Woman's Missionary Union (WMU) of the Southern Baptist Convention was established in 1888 by a small group of women who felt called to support missionary work. Since that time the WMU has worked to teach, support, and pro-

mote individual involvement in missions. The WMU now has a membership of over a million Southern Baptist women. During the years since its founding, the WMU has raised over $2 billion for home and foreign missions. It is a self-supporting, self-governing auxiliary of the Southern Baptist Convention, receiving its revenue from the sales of the organization's magazines and products and from investments.

The WMU is involved in numerous projects. The organization publishes thirteen magazines, each directed at different audiences, including *Dimension,* for pastors, WMU directors, or other church staff; *Missions Mosaic,* for women on missions age eighteen and over; *Accent Member,* for Acteens, the missions organization for girls in grades seven to twelve; and *Nuestra Tarea,* a Spanish-language publication for adults and leaders of youth and children organizations. The WMU's national ministry project for 1995–1996 was Project HELP:AIDS. Through this project the women worked to break down barriers of preconception, inexperience, and fear within local churches in regard to the disease. They also donated funds, foods, and supplies to benefit people suffering from AIDS. In 1996 the WMU participated in a program that collected and shipped food to relieve hunger in famine-ravaged North Korea, and during the Summer Olympics in Atlanta that year, the WMU volunteered for a variety of jobs. In addition to performing evangelism and ministry, the women interpreted for international visitors; prepared gift bags and religious tracts for distribution; and cleaned restrooms, floors, and eating areas.

New Hope, a publishing arm of WMU, issues books that are targeted to the broader Christian market. Some recent releases include *Precious in His Sight,* 2nd ed. (1996), by Diana Garland, an outspoken supporter of child advocacy; and

Lose the Halo, Keep the Wings (1996), by Virginia Wilson, a book filled with humor and wisdom directed at ministers' wives.

See also: Armstrong, Annie Walker; Missionaries
References: "Armstrong, Annie Walker," in J. Gordon Melton, *Religious Leaders of America* (1991); Jacqueline K. Barrett, ed., *Encyclopedia of Women's Associations Worldwide* (1993); Woman's Missionary Union, *Annual Report 1996* (n.d., c. 1997).

Woman's Sphere

The idea of men and women functioning in separate spheres became popular during the nineteenth century. Writers characterized men and women as polar opposites, depicting men as strong and independent and women as weak and dependent. In the churches, clergymen frequently preached on the subject. Although woman's sphere centered around her home and away from the public arena, it expanded to include her church. Church-associated volunteer work that put into use a woman's "feminine" qualities, including nurturance and self-sacrifice, was accepted by most nineteenth-century Americans as an extension of woman's sphere. Some historians have contended that women's experiences within their churches' prayer groups, missions, and charitable organizations greatly contributed to their developing a desire for increased power and influence within their churches and society as a whole. It has been argued that as women acquired more power within their churches, American religion became "feminized." Others have asserted that church activity led to the women's rights movement by teaching women to organize and by creating in them the desire to break out of their "sphere" and to become active participants in the wider world.

See also: The "Feminization" of American Religion
References: Nancy F. Cott, *The Bonds of Womanhood: "Woman's Sphere" in New*

England, 1780–1835 (1977); Ann Douglas, *The Feminization of American Culture* (1977); Nancy A. Hewitt, *Women's Activism and Social Change: Rochester, New York, 1822–1872*; Barbara Welter, "The Feminization of American Religion: 1800–1860," in Mary S. Hartman and Lois Banner, eds., *Clio's Consciousness Raised: New Perspectives on the History of Women* (1974).

Women's League for Conservative Judaism

Established by Mathilde Schechter in 1918, the Women's League for Conservative Judaism is the national organization of Conservative sisterhoods. At its founding, Schechter envisioned an organization that would be the coordinating body of Conservative synagogue sisterhoods and would promote the perpetuation of traditional Judaism in America through the home, synagogue, and community. During the early years of the Women's League, its leaders spread its message through the publication of educational materials in English, which helped young immigrant women as they assimilated into the American culture. An early project of the Women's League was the establishment of a rooming house that offered Jewish students in New York a homelike atmosphere and kosher board. The program later expanded to other large cities.

Throughout most of its history, the Women's League has involved itself in social action on such issues as human rights and care for the poor. It developed a program for helping blind Jews through the Jewish Braille Institute. In 1954 the Women's League underwrote the first Hebrew-English prayer book in Braille. Especially concerned with women's issues, in recent decades the league has endorsed the Equal Rights Amendment as well as abortion rights and laws to protect battered women. In addition to its support for women's rights in the secular community, the Women's League has long been a vocal advocate for egalitarianism in Conservative Jewish religious life.

With an initial membership of approximately one hundred women in twenty-six sisterhoods, the Women's League grew steadily until it reached a peak of membership of 200,000 in 1968. After a consolidation resulting from changing demographics, in 1997 the league counted 150,000 members in seven hundred affiliated sisterhoods in Conservative synagogues in the United States, Canada, Puerto Rico, Mexico, Israel, and other parts of the world. The Women's League continues its work to perpetuate traditional Judaism and to translate its ideals into practice. Education is of prime importance to the league, and it offers guidance and service to lay and professional Jewish leaders so that they can be better equipped to educate others. Headquartered in New York City, the Women's League is an important arm of the Conservative/Masorti movement, and it maintains close ties to the Jewish Theological Seminary of America, the University of Judaism, and all other programs of the movement.

See also: Jews; Schechter, Mathilde Roth
References: Jacqueline K. Barrett, ed., *Encyclopedia of Women's Associations Worldwide* (1993); Shuly Rubin Schwartz, "Women's League for Conservative Judaism," in Paula Hyman and Deborah Dash Moore, eds., *Jewish Women in America* (1997); Women's League for Conservative Judaism, "Mathilde Schechter: Founder of Women's League for Conservative Judaism" (n.d., c. 1997); Women's League for Conservative Judaism, "Women's League for Conservative Judaism: What it is . . . What it does!" (n.d., c. 1997).

Women's Missionary and Service Commission of the Mennonite Church

The Women's Missionary and Service Commission of the Mennonite Church (WMSC), founded in 1915, was created out of Mennonite women's desire to play more active roles within the church. Since the 1860s, Mennonite women had taught Sunday school, and by the 1890s, they were sometimes speaking at Sunday school conferences and young people's meetings and were writing for the new church periodicals. However, the only area in which women were active in proportion to their numbers was in missions, where women accounted for more than half of the missionaries. Within the missions women led sewing schools, taught Sunday school, distributed Bibles, nursed the sick, and made home visits. Women were particularly effective in reaching other women.

By the turn of the twentieth century, sewing circles were springing up to bolster the new mission efforts of the Mennonite church. Women both sewed for the poor in their localities and provided supplies for the home mission stations. In addition to their sewing activities, the meetings included Bible reading, prayer, and a hymn. Although the women were enthusiastic over their work, the men of the church were not always supportive. When in 1908 seventeen women of Weavers Church in Harrisonburg, Virginia, organized a sewing circle, some of the men opposed it. They believed the women were unable to manage such a project and that it would turn out to be a regular place of gossip, and they ridiculed the entire idea. But the women persisted until, in the early 1910s, a movement began to organize women churchwide, building on the already established circles and urging the creation of others.

Beginning in 1911, Clara Eby Steiner of Bluffton, Ohio, sought to organize churchwide women's work. The widow of M. S. Steiner, a well-known leader of the Mennonite Church, Steiner's interest in missions had grown through working with her husband in Chicago missions. She had also hosted missionaries and listened to conversations of mission board members visiting in her home. As a woman, she was troubled over the difficulties members of her sex faced when they tried to be accepted for foreign mission work. Steiner had a vision of what she described as "a general organization of home and foreign missionary endeavor, including sewing circles, mothers' meetings, ladies aids, missionary societies, young people's and children's circles or societies, and individual Sunday school classes" (MacMaster, February 1990, p. 9).

The women's groups held their first general meeting in August 1915 near Wauseon, Ohio. After much debate, they eventually called their organization the Mennonite Woman's Missionary Society. Most of the leaders of the society were wives or widows of church leaders or were women with mission experience in Chicago and India and were accustomed to leadership. The organization immediately began to grow. American entry into World War I in 1917 further stimulated the growth of the society, and almost all of the circles participated in relief work. By March 1921 there were twelve regional branches, 131 circles, and 3,721 members. Also that year, the women made 17,201 garments, gave $20,853.64 in cash, and sent 32 tons of new and used clothing for relief in Turkey and Russia.

Although the work of Mennonite women was welcome in the mission field, at home they were more restricted. They could teach children and younger women but not men; they could not serve as song leaders or as leaders of Sunday school conferences; they could be writers but not editors; nor could they be elders, ministers, or leaders in the congregation. Even within their own organizations, the women were frequently subject to male authority. For example, the Lancaster Conference had an early established sewing circle on the district level, but this women's organization was administered by men. Between 1926 and 1928 the

mission board of the Mennonite church successfully moved to take over the Woman's Missionary Society. Although the society had been the largest and most active lay movement in the church, the male leaders were not prepared for the idea of women initiating and managing their affairs even if the work was within the parameters of what was generally considered "woman's sphere."

Throughout the mid-twentieth century, the women struggled to regain control of their organization. During this period, the name of the society went through various changes, from General Sewing Circle Committee, to Women's Missionary and Sewing Circle Organization (WMSO), to Women's Missionary and Service Auxiliary (WMSA), to Women's Missionary and Service Commission (WMSC). The latter name change came during the churchwide restructuring of 1971, at which time the WMSC moved from association with the Board of Missions to the Board of Congregational Ministries. During the 1970s, the tide turned for women as they acquired increasingly more power within the church, including positions on church boards and in congregational leadership.

During the 1990s a major function of the WMSC was to encourage spiritual growth in women through prayer, Bible study, and community service. In the summer of 1997, delegates of the WMSC voted to merge with Women in Mission of the General Conference of the Mennonite Church. Beginning August 1, 1997, the two groups formed one organization, calling it Mennonite Women.

See also: Mennonites
References: Jacqueline K. Barrett, ed., Encyclopedia of Women's Associations Worldwide (1993); Lara J. Hall, ed., "WMSC Newsletter" (April 15, 1997); Eleanor Graber Kreider, "Rekindling the Vision," WMSC Voice (May–June 1990); Eve MacMaster, "The Story of Clara Eby Steiner and the Beginnings of WMSC," WMSC Voice (January–April 1990); Dorothy McCammon and Beulah

Kauffman, as told to Saralyn Yoder, "Cautious Progress in a Time of Change, WMSC in the '60s and '70s," *WMSC Voice* (July–August 1990); Kathryn Rodgers, note to author (n.d., c. August 1997).

Women's Missionary Society of the African Methodist Episcopal Church

The founding meeting of the Women's Missionary Society of the African Methodist Episcopal (AME) Church was held on May 8, 1874, in the home of Reverend J. A. Handy in Washington, D.C. Two forerunners of the Women's Missionary Society, the Dorcas Society, founded in 1824, and the Daughters of the Conference, established several years later, did not survive. However, the leader of these earlier groups, Sarah Bass Allen, is revered as the first missionary of the AME Church. Although their early organizations faltered, the women of the AME Church became increasingly visible as benevolent and humanitarian service workers as the nineteenth century progressed. Bishop James A. Shorter issued a call that gave rise to the formation of the Women's Missionary Society in 1874. From humble beginnings, the society (known initially as the Mite Missionary Society) grew to become one of the first associations, black or white, to be organized by women on a national scale with affiliations in foreign lands.

The first convention of the missionary society was held at Bethel AME Church in Philadelphia in 1895. At this time, the Women's Parent Mite Missionary Society was organized. Over the next twenty-one years, the society grew as women established groups in local churches. The society sponsored mission work in Haiti, Santo Domingo, West Africa, Sierra Leone, Barbados, the Virgin Islands, Trinidad, Jamaica, and the British West Indies. In 1915, the society formally adopted a Young People's Department and, a year later, the Juvenile Society was organized. The juvenile group is currently known as the Young People's and Children's Division of the Women's Missionary Society.

As membership in the Women's Parent Mite Missionary Society grew, some women in the southern and western United States felt isolated from the organization's center in the Northeast. They therefore petitioned Bishop Henry McNeal Turner to allow them to organize as the Women's Home and Foreign Missionary Society (WHFMS) of the AME. The General Conference gave its official approval of the group's constitution in May 1896. Over the next forty-seven years, the two women's missionary organizations worked diligently with similar goals and interests. Eventually the two groups decided that they could work better if they united into one organization. The merging of the women's associations was approved at the General Conference in Philadelphia in 1944, giving birth to the Women's Missionary Society of the African Methodist Episcopal Church.

Although the society of today has broader goals than those of the women of the nineteenth century, its primary purpose remains much the same: "To help people to grow in the knowledge and experience of God through His Son, Jesus Christ, through continual Christian training, as well as individual and collective mission work, thus challenging them to respond to God's redemptive plan in the world" (McLloyd and Peck, n.d., p. 5). Led by President Dorothy Adams Peck, the Women's Missionary Society has a membership of over 800,000 women, with operations in the United States, the Bahamas, and England as well as in several countries in the Caribbean and in Africa. The society will be observing the 125th anniversary of its missionary movement in 1999.

See also: Missionary Societies

References: Shawn Brennan, ed., *Women's Information Directory* (1993); Edna W. McLloyd and Dorothy Adams Peck, "The Women's Missionary Society Journey from Vision to Reality," unpublished paper (n.d., c. 1997).

Women's Studies

Women's studies, an interdisciplinary field that developed during the 1970s, has played an important role in bringing to light the experiences of women over the ages. It has challenged the practice of looking at history from a male-oriented perspective and has placed greater emphasis upon examining history through a study of the lives of ordinary people rather than their leaders. Over the past two decades, scholars have greatly enlarged their exploration of women in religion, both past and present. In addition to having a scholarly aspect, women's studies seeks to explain women's statuses and help liberate their potentialities. Much of the research has been performed by feminists such as Carol P. Christ, Rosemary Radford Ruether, and Mary Daly, who have questioned the objectivity of earlier religious histories. They have looked beyond the male hierarchies and into the religious experiences of women. Thus they have enlarged our perspective on religious history.

See also: Daly, Mary; Feminist Theology; Ruether, Rosemary Radford
References: Carol P. Christ, "Toward a Paradigm Shift in the Academy and in Religious Studies," in Christie Farnham, ed., *The Impact of Feminist Research in the Academy* (1987); Howard Eilberg-Schwartz and Wendy Doniger, *Off with Her Head! The Denial of Women's Identity in Myth, Religion and Culture* (1995); Jean Fox O'Barr, *Feminism in Action* (1994); Rosemary Radford Ruether, *Sexism and God-Talk: Toward a Feminist Theology* (1983); Ruether and Rosemary Skinner Keller, eds., *Women and Religion in America* (1986); Charlene Spretnak, ed., *The Politics of Women's Spirituality: Essays on the Rise of Spiritual Power within the Feminist Movement* (1982).

Woodhull, Victoria Claflin (1838–1927)

Unconventional reformer and spiritual medium Victoria Claflin Woodhull was born September 23, 1838, in Homer, Ohio. One of ten children, Victoria was raised under squalid conditions, and her schooling was crude and intermittent. As she was growing up, Spiritualism was sweeping into the Midwest, and Victoria was prone to trances. Her younger sister, Tennessee Celeste Claflin, recognized in Victoria an opportunity for success as a spiritual medium. The girls joined with their brother Hebern and set up a traveling medicine show. Tennessee held seances, Hebern posed as a cancer doctor, and Victoria entertained audiences as a trance medium. When she was fifteen years old, Victoria married Canning Woodhull, a physician, with whom she had two children during the course of their eleven-year marriage. The Woodhulls divorced in 1864. In 1866 Victoria met and may have married Colonel James Harvey Blood of St. Louis, but she retained the name Woodhull.

At the direction of the spirit of Demosthenes, whom Victoria claimed to have spoken with during one of her trances, she, Tennessee, Colonel Blood, her parents, and her other sisters all moved to Manhattan in 1868. There Victoria and Tennessee met multimillionaire Cornelius Vanderbilt. The commodore had recently been widowed and found the sisters' mediumship to be a comfort. He treated the young women generously, starting them in a stock brokerage firm in January 1870—the Woodhull, Claflin and Company—which achieved some success. Not long after her move to New York, Victoria became involved with Pantarchy, the philosophy of a group headed by Stephen Andrews. Andrews envisioned a perfect state in which free love reigned among individuals and children and property were held in common. Victoria had long considered marriage to be a form of female enslavement and was eager to spread Andrews's views. In 1870 she began expounding the philosophy of Pantarchy in the sisters' new publication, the *Woodhull and Claflin's Weekly.* She also used the newspaper to express her support for women's rights, the elimination of the double standard on morality, and legalized prostitution. The *Weekly* was the first journal in America to publish Karl Marx's *Communist Manifesto* in English.

Victoria also gave lectures on the subject of women's rights. Her impassioned speeches on behalf of woman suffrage, especially those before the House Judiciary Committee in January 1871, won her at least tentative acceptance by woman suffrage leaders Susan B. Anthony and Elizabeth Cady Stanton. But her attempts to take over leadership of the movement, combined with her proposal to found a new political party, resulted in a split with the established leaders.

Victoria's interests in reform and her popular notoriety led her to consider running for the presidency. In the spring of 1872 she organized a convention of the Equal Rights Party, and on May 10, 1872, she was nominated as the party's candidate for president of the United States. African-American leader Frederick Douglass was named her running mate, but he refused to campaign because he preferred to support President Ulysses S. Grant. The American public did not take her candidacy seriously, and her detractors focused upon her personal sexual behavior, which offered an abundance of material for scandal. Victoria countered by publishing an exposé of powerful Congregational minister Henry Ward Beecher's alleged affair with married parishioner Elizabeth Tilton. Although the scandal caused problems for Beecher, Victoria and Tennessee were arrested as a result of publishing and circulating the report, and they were charged with sending obscene materials through the mail. The sisters were acquitted the following year, but their actions had served to alienate former friends and allies, and their careers in America came to an end.

In 1877 Victoria moved to England, where she met John B. Martin, a wealthy banker. They married in the fall of 1883, and Victoria was introduced into British society. Not to be outdone, in 1885 Tennessee married Sir Francis Cook, the head of a large dry goods firm. Although Victoria's activism was now muted, it did continue. Between 1888 and 1892 she wrote four books: *Stirpiculture, or the Scientific Propagation of the Human Race* (1888); *Garden of Eden Allegorical Meaning Revealed* (1889); *The Human Body: The Temple of God* (1890); and *Humanitarian Money: The Unsolved Riddle* (1892). From 1892 to 1901, with the assistance of her daughter, Zula Maud, she published a journal, the *Humanitarian,* which focused on eugenics. Victoria made occasional visits to the United States but resided in England until her death on June 10, 1927, at her home at Bredon's Norton in Tewkesbury.

References: Edward T. James, ed., *Notable American Women, 1607–1950,* vol. 3 (1971); Robert McHenry, ed., *Liberty's Women* (1980); J. Gordon Melton, *Religious Leaders of America* (1991); Jennifer S. Uglow, *The Continuum Dictionary of Women's Biography* (1989); Lois Beachy Underhill, *The Woman Who Ran for President: The Many Lives of Victoria Woodhull* (1995).

Woodworth-Etter, Maria Beulah Underwood (1844–1924)

Evangelist Maria Beulah Underwood Woodworth-Etter was born to Samuel and Matilda Underwood on their farm near Lisbon, Ohio, on July 22, 1844. When she was twelve, her father died of sunstroke. As one of eight children, Maria was forced to leave school and find work to help support herself. The balance of her education came through self-study.

Maria had her first religious conversion at the age of thirteen, and from then on, she was interested in ministering in some capacity. But it was her attendance at a revival meeting in Damascus, Ohio, in 1879 at the age of thirty-five that changed her life. At that time she underwent a second religious conversion and was soon having visions along with calls to begin preaching. Within a year of her religious awakening and after the death of the fifth of her six children with husband Philo Harrison Woodworth, Maria felt released and able to respond to the calls. From 1880 to 1884, she was affiliated with the United Brethren and, from 1884 to 1904, with the Churches of God. She then declared herself independent but remained generally associated with Pentecostal congregations.

As a woman, and one who had little formal education and virtually no theological background, Maria faced many obstacles to her career as an itinerant evangelist. Nevertheless, she won converts. Beginning with successful revivals in the Midwest, within five years she was conducting campaigns in the largest cities on both the east and west coasts and was drawing crowds of thousands. Her strong convictions helped her to express herself with power and authority, which in turn brought respect to herself and to other female preachers.

During her twenty years with the Churches of God, Maria was proclaimed by many people as the greatest woman evangelist in the history of the Christian church. She has been credited with winning an amazing number of converts and with enjoying spectacular results from her prayers for the sick. But Maria was also the most criticized of the evangelists. Much of that criticism came from within the Churches of God. The divine healing aspect of her ministry caused concern that she was not devoting enough of her time to evangelism.

The Woodworths, who for years had been living a stormy marriage, divorced in 1891, and Philo died a year later. In 1902 Maria married Samuel P. Etter and began using the hyphenated surname Woodworth-Etter. Along with fame came criticism. Mostly she was reproached for her faith healing and for encouraging her audiences to be "slain in the spirit" during worship services in which they went into trancelike states. She also viewed divine healing and the gift of prophecy as manifestations of God's blessing. When large groups gathered to hear her, Woodworth-Etter would often speak in tongues. The poor and uneducated made up a majority of her congregants, and she upset white southerners by welcoming African Americans into her revival tent. She was also criticized for her misinterpretations of the Scriptures, her fanaticism, and her false prophesies. Although she happily did not experience the physical abuse suffered by many Pentecostal ministers, Woodworth-Etter did receive a number of threatening letters.

Woodworth-Etter's ministry was in peril in 1913 and 1920 when she faced legal charges over obtaining money under false pretenses (1913) and practicing medicine without a license (1920). Both charges arose as a result of her faith healing. She was brought to trial on the charge of obtaining money under false pretenses, accused of misleading people by promising healing that did not occur and receiving money for it. After a four-day trial, the charge was dismissed. The charge of practicing medicine without a license was dismissed before the case went to trial. Despite her legal problems, Woodworth-Etter continued to evangelize. Although she limited her activities when old age, illness (including a serious case of pneumonia in 1914), and the death of her last surviving child marred her final years, she was minister at Woodworth-Etter Tabernacle, which she established in Indianapolis, from 1918 until her death there on September 16, 1924. Woodworth-Etter helped to blaze a trail for women in evangelical ministry. She served as a role model for Aimee Semple McPherson and Kathryn Kuhlman, who became popular evangelists in the twentieth century.

See also: Kuhlman, Kathryn; McPherson, Aimee Semple
References: Henry Warner Bowden, *Dictionary of American Religious Biography*, 2nd ed. (1993); Susan Hill Lindley, *"You Have Stept Out of Your Place": A History of Women and Religion in America* (1996); Wayne E. Warner, *The Woman Evangelist* (1986).

Wright, Frances (1795–1852)

Born into wealth, Frances (Fanny) Wright grew up to become a writer, a reformer, an opponent of organized religion, an advocate for equal rights for women, and a defender of the working classes. She was born in Dundee, Scotland, on September 6, 1795, the daughter of James Wright, a well-to-do merchant and political radical, and Camilla (Campbell) Wright. When she was two years old, her parents died and left Fanny, her brother Richard, and her sister Camilla a fortune. Fanny was raised by relatives in England until she was twenty-one. At that time, she returned to Scotland to live with a great-uncle, a professor of philosophy at Glasgow College. Fanny spent much of her time reading and did some writing of her own.

In 1818, Fanny and Camilla traveled to America, for Fanny was curious to see if the new republic held as much promise as she anticipated. While she was in America, *Altorf,* a play Fanny had written on the subject of Swiss independence, was produced in New York City. Her identity was kept secret, and critics believed it had been written by a man. The play was not a success. Fanny traveled around the country and encountered slavery in action. She hated it. Yet upon her return to England in 1820, she wrote "The Stranger's Farewell," which ignored slavery and praised the United States as the home of freedom.

In 1821 she published *Views of Society and Manners in America,* which was basically laudatory, although she did note faults, such as slavery, the farmer's constant struggle to survive, and problems experienced by American women. Her book won her the respect and friendship of the Marquis de Lafayette, and they became very close. When Lafayette traveled to the United States in 1824, Fanny and Camilla followed. The sisters' friendship with the hero of the American Revolution opened doors for them. Among their hosts were former presidents Thomas Jefferson and James Madison.

Robert Owen, socialist and pioneer of the cooperative movement, was also in America, and Fanny went to hear him speak. She then traveled with him to the future site of his New Harmony town. The visit inspired her to consider experimenting in communal living. Fanny had also been weighing a plan for the gradual emancipation of slaves. In 1825 she published *A Plan for the Gradual Abolition of Slavery in the United States without Danger of Loss to the Citizens of the South,* presenting the idea that the government should set land aside for African Americans. She thought that blacks and whites could be separated, with blacks in Texas and the lower South and whites to the north. Slaves, she thought, would work very hard if they had emancipation for a goal, and Wright believed that they could earn enough money to buy their freedom.

In 1825, Wright, along with coplanner George Flower, began an experiment that combined her ideas on the emancipation of slaves with her notions on communal living. She purchased a 640-acre tract in western Tennessee (near present-day Memphis) and called it Nashoba. Then, she purchased slaves and established a community, with the promise that the slaves would eventually be freed. Wright and Flowers treated their slaves as responsible men and women, viewing them as capable of directing their own lives. Wright came to believe that black and white could live together without conflict if they were raised as equals.

In the beginning, Wright was pleased with the progress of her project. But while she was absent from the commune due to ill health and a trip to England, where she had hopes of persuading new recruits, a scandal broke out over accusations of miscegenation and free love at Nashoba. When she returned in early 1828, she found the commune in ruin. Wright published a newspaper article in which she defended her ideas for Nashoba, and then she joined Robert Owen's socialist community at New Harmony, Indiana. Shortly thereafter, she became an editor for the New Harmony *Gazette*.

In July 1828, Wright began a lecture tour, speaking in favor of equality and against clericalism and the way women—especially in regard to sex and marriage—were treated within religion. At a time when the Second Great Awakening was gaining force, Wright was speaking against it. Religion, she said, was a belief, whereas virtue was a practice. She also lectured against power, such as man over woman and priest over communicant. Her lectures drew large crowds. Wright was the first white woman in America to speak before large secular audiences, and she drew intense criticism for her "unladylike" behavior as well as for her radical ideas that defied the moral standards of the nineteenth century. Ministers referred to her as the "High Priestess of Infidelity" and not one news editor came to her defense (Eckhard, 1984, p. 184).

Wright essentially ignored the attacks and continued to speak her mind on a variety of issues, including birth control and the replacement of legal marriage by a union based on moral obligation. She also voiced support for the working man and, in 1829, assisted in the creation of the Association for the Protection of Industry and for the Promotion of National Education, a pioneer working men's organization.

In 1830, Wright freed the slaves at Nashoba and arranged for their colonization in Haiti. Later that year, she sailed to France with her ailing sister. Fanny was pregnant with the child of her companion on her journey to Haiti, Guillaume Sylvan Casimir Phiquepal D'Arusmont. Camilla died in February 1831, and Wright married D'Arusmont in July. She remained in France until 1836, cut off from friends and family. In 1836, she and D'Arusmont returned to the United States with the idea that Wright would return to the lecture circuit. But her notoriety led to some of her lectures being canceled, and some mayors would not allow her to speak in their towns. At first, her public appearances created havoc, but later her audiences drifted away. Wright was beginning to bore them.

In March 1839, she admitted defeat and returned to Paris with her daughter and husband. Her marriage steadily deteriorated, and in 1846, she became involved in a legal battle with her husband that lasted until her death. The couple divorced in 1850, and Wright returned to America. She died in Cincinnati on December 13, 1852. Despite the controversy during her lifetime, Wright left a legacy for the next generation of women reformers. Both Elizabeth Cady Stanton and Susan B. Anthony kept her writing near at hand.

See also: Utopian Communities
References: Celia Morris Eckhard, *Fanny Wright: Rebel in America* (1984); Robert McHenry, ed., *Liberty's Women* (1980); A. J. G. Perkins and Theresa Wolfson, *Frances Wright: Free Enquirer: The Study of a Temperament* (1972).

Young Women's Christian Association

Founded in London, England, in 1855, the Young Women's Christian Association (YWCA) was established in New York City in 1858 (it was initially known as the Ladies' Christian Association). Its beginnings were slow, but from 1866 onward the YWCA was attracting hundreds of members, and branches were soon opening in cities across the country. The primary early goal of the organization was to assist young women who were working away from home by helping them to lead religious and moral lives. In the early decades of the twentieth century, the YWCA broadened its agenda, promoting "missions" at home and abroad, and recruiting young, college-educated women who were dedicated to Christian service. The organization provided residences as well as recreational and educational programs for young women in the cities. By the 1910s, the "Y" was promoting reforms of the period, emphasizing humanitarian aid for women and children and helping to break down class barriers among women.

During the 1920s, the YWCA endorsed the Federal Council of Churches' Social Creed, including its strong pro-labor position. It also held a liberal position in regard to foreign affairs, advocating U.S. cooperation with the League of Nations, the World Court, and the International Labor Organization. During the 1930s, the YWCA organized a Federation of Industrial Clubs to aid working women. These clubs were particularly effective in organizing textile workers in the South. Its continued liberal stands during the 1930s and 1940s against lynching and in support of the labor movement led to accusations from the far right that the "Y" was a "fellow traveler" with communism.

Despite its progressive attitudes, it took the YWCA several decades to become an interracial organization. Although black branches dated from the late nineteenth century in the North and Midwest and from 1906 in the South, the "Y" did not adopt an interracial charter until 1946. Nevertheless, under the able leadership of Eva del Vakia Bowles, the African-American branches provided important services to black women and children. After years of prodding, throughout the 1920s, 1930s, and 1940s, the YWCA eventually developed an interracial position in its own work and began to speak out on racial issues.

Membership in the American YWCA in the 1990s stands at about two million, in almost 450 local groups. The organization offers women and their families programs of recreation and education and provides counseling and assistance to girls and women in the areas of employment, education, human sexuality, self-improvement, voluntarism, citizenship, emotional and physical health, and juvenile justice. Although the YWCA continues its fight against racism, it also

The Young Women's Christian Association (YWCA) was founded in the mid-nineteenth century to help young girls living and working away from home to lead religious and moral lives. This New York advertisement by artist Neysa McMein captures the idealism of the YWCA's image (1919).

sponsors programs that promote international peace and justice, and rights and liberties for individuals.

See also: Bowles, Eva del Vakia

References: Jacqueline K. Barrett, ed., *Encyclopedia of Women's Associations Worldwide* (1993); Eleanor Flexner, *Century of Struggle: The Woman's Rights Movement in the United States* (1970); Elizabeth Frost-Knappman, *Women's Progress in America* (1994); Susan Hill Lindley, *"You Have Stept Out of Your Place": A History of Women and Religion in America* (1996); Marion O. Robinson, *Eight Women of the YWCA* (1966).

Zell, Morning Glory (1948–)

Morning Glory Zell, a priestess in the Church of All Worlds and a leader in the neo-Pagan community, was born Diana Moore on May 27, 1948. Born and raised in Long Beach, California, Morning Glory attended both the Methodist and Pentecostal churches. During her early childhood she attended the Methodist Church, the church of her father, but eventually became disenchanted with the Methodists. At about age twelve, she joined her mother's Pentecostal church. She was actively involved with the church until her pastor told her that women were subordinate to men and that they were to obey their husbands even if the men were abusive, for such was the will of God. At thirteen, Zell was a budding feminist, and she could not accept her pastor's position. For the next three years, she sought a religion that could accommodate her feminism. Dissatisfied with the status of women within the Christian tradition, she studied Buddhism and Zen Buddhism and joined the Vedanta Society. She found the same sexism in these religions, though the Vedanta Society did introduce her to the worship of the Goddess. As a lover of animals, Zell was attracted to the message of the Goddess, and she became a Pagan.

During high school, Zell read Sybil Leek's autobiography, *Diary of a Witch,* which had a tremendous impact upon her. After she graduated from high school, she embarked upon a vision quest. When she returned, she was convinced that she was a witch. In 1968 she changed her name to Morning Glory because in studying mythology she had learned that her Goddess namesake, Diana, had demanded her human daughters all practice celibacy. Zell wanted to eventually become a mother and feared that her given name might be a hindrance.

In 1969, on her way to join a commune in Eugene, Oregon, Morning Glory met a hitchhiker named Gary who traveled to the commune with her. They married, and in 1970 she gave birth to a daughter. In 1973, while attending the Gnosticon Aquarian festival in St. Paul, Minnesota, Morning Glory met the keynote speaker, Timothy (later Otter) Zell, founder of the Church of All Worlds. She divorced Gary in 1973 and married Zell the following year. After the traditional year and a day of training, Morning Glory became a priestess for the Church of All Worlds. In 1974 she began coediting the *Green Egg,* an important early neo-Pagan magazine, continuing to do so until the Zells left St. Louis in 1976. The publication was revived in 1988 with Morning Glory as coeditor.

After traveling for some time, the Zells settled in Ukiah, California in 1985. Three years later, Morning Glory became vice president of a reorganized Church of All Worlds. In addition to her work for the church, in 1977 she founded the Ecosophical Research Association, a church subsidiary for the research and exploration of history, mythology, and science.

She and Otter Zell both volunteer for Critter Care, a wildlife animal rescue organization. Morning Glory says that she serves the aspect of the Goddess known as Potnia Theron, "Our Lady of the Beasts." In addition to other activities, she writes nonfiction, fiction, and poetry and has written pamphlets and articles on neo-Pagan theology.

See also: Wicca; Witchcraft
References: Rosemary Ellen Guiley, *The Encyclopedia of Witches and Witchcraft* (1989); J. Gordon Melton, *Religious Leaders of America* (1991).

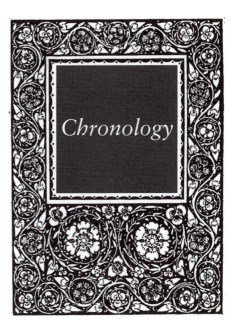

1637 Anne Hutchinson is brought to trial before the General Court of the Massachusetts Bay Colony on charges of heresy. She is found guilty and is banished from the colony.

1656 The first Quakers, Ann Austin and Mary Fisher, arrive in America. Despite persecution, others follow.

1660 Quaker Mary Dyer is hanged for preaching "heresy" in the Puritan-dominated Massachusetts Bay colony.

1676 Mary Rowlandson, a minister's wife, is taken captive by the Narragansett Indians during King Philip's War. Her faith in God helps her to survive her ordeal. After her release, her story reaches the public, and she is held in great esteem for her faith and godliness.

1692 One hundred and forty-one people are indicted in Salem Village (later Danvers, Massachusetts) on charges of witchcraft. Twenty people are put to death before the hysteria ends.

1697 Hannah Duston escapes captivity by killing (with the help of another woman and a boy) and scalping ten of her Native American captors. Puritan minister Cotton Mather compares Duston with a biblical heroine and uses her as an example to illustrate God's desire for the New England settlers to prevail over the Native Americans.

1753 Elizabeth Ashbridge, who will become a renowned Quaker minister, carries her message from America back to her birthplace, England, and to Ireland.

1766–1767 Sarah Haggar Wheaten Osborn's Female Society, which has met in her home since the early 1740s, becomes the center of a great religious revival in Newport, Rhode Island.

1768 The first Methodist church building opens for services in New York City. Much of the credit for the construction of the large stone chapel goes to Barbara Ruckle Heck, "the Mother of American Methodism."

1776 Ann Lee, founder of the United Society of Believers in Christ's Second Coming (Shakers) in America, establishes a commune in Niskeyuna, near Albany, New York.

1788 Jemima Wilkinson establishes a colony, "Jerusalem," for her society of Universal Friends near Seneca Lake in western New York. Wilkinson is the first native-born American to found a religious community.

1790 Methodists become the first denomination in the United States to adopt the Sunday school as official policy, though throughout the early decades of the 1800s, the movement is largely interdenominational.

The Carmel Convent, the first Roman Catholic convent in the United States, is founded in Port Tobacco, Maryland. Mother Bernardina Teresa Xavier of St. Joseph (formerly Ann Teresa Matthews) becomes the convent's first prioress. Most of the later Carmelite convents in the United States trace their origins to this convent or its branches.

1808   Jane Aitken, an early woman publisher, publishes the four-volume Thomson Bible, a translation by Charles Thomson of the Septuagint (the Greek version of the Old Testament).

1809   Elizabeth Ann Seton pronounces her vows and forms a Roman Catholic sisterhood, the Sisters of Charity, in Emmitsburg, Maryland.

1811   The General Assembly of the Presbyterian Church in the U.S.A. announces its support for women in benevolent work. Clergymen suggest, however, that women provide services to women and children only.

1812   The Roman Catholic Sisters of Loretto at the Foot of the Cross, a teaching community, is founded in Kentucky. It is the first American sisterhood without foreign affiliation.

    Ann Hasseltine Judson and her husband, Adoniram Judson, leave for India. She is believed to be the first American woman to become a foreign missionary.

1818   Although she never receives a license to preach, with the approval of Bishop Richard Allen, Jarena Lee begins preaching for the African Methodist Episcopal Church. She is the groundbreaker for further preaching among African-American women.

1819   The Female Hebrew Benevolent Society, the first of hundreds of Jewish women's societies to be established in the United States, is founded in Philadelphia.

1825   Reformer Frances Wright, along with coplanner George Flower, establishes a commune in western Tennessee. An experimental community designed to substantiate Wright's belief that blacks and whites can live together, it fails due to poor organization and scandal.

1827   A pioneer among women preachers, Salome Lincoln begins her career as an itinerant minister.

1829   The Oblate Sisters of Providence, which will become the first successful foundation of African-American sisters in America, is established in Baltimore.

1830   Joseph Smith founds the Church of Jesus Christ of Latter-Day Saints (Mormons). Women will have important roles in the early Mormon Church and Mormon society. As with some other churches, after 1920, with the church firmly established, women's roles will be gradually restricted.

1831   Robert Dale Owen publishes the first important book that discusses birth control, *Moral Physiology; or, a Brief and Plain Treatise on the Population Question*. This leads to a prolonged national debate in which the churches are deeply involved.

1832   African-American Maria Stewart becomes probably the first American-born woman to speak before a "promiscuous" audience of both men and women when she gives her first lecture for the abolitionist cause.

1833   Lucretia Mott, a Quaker minister, leads in founding the Philadelphia Female Anti-Slavery Society. Like its sister society in Boston (founded in 1832), it includes both black and white women.

1834   The Female Moral Reform Society is founded in New York City for the purpose of converting the city's prostitutes to evangelical Protestantism and closing New York's many brothels. The society also hopes to battle the double standard that condemns female sexual transgressions but condones male sexual freedom.

1835   Phoebe Worrall Palmer begins her career as an evangelist with the launching of the "Tuesday Meetings for the Promotion of Holiness." Continuing for thirty-seven years, by 1858 the meetings become broadly evangelical and attract laymen and ministers from a variety of denominations.

1836   Missionaries Eliza Hart Spalding and Narcissa Prentiss Whitman become the first white women to cross the Continental Divide and the Rocky Mountains.

Mary Lyon receives a charter for Mount Holyoke Seminary (later College), the first women's seminary in the United States.

1837   Congregational ministers of the General Association of Massachusetts issue a "Pastoral Letter" that berates abolitionists for speaking on "agitating subjects" in churches and is particularly critical of female abolitionists. Although they are not mentioned by name, it is believed that the "letter" is directed at Angelina and Sarah Grimké.

1838   Rebecca Gratz, an Orthodox Jew, founds the Hebrew Sunday School Society in Philadelphia. It is the first Sunday school for Jewish children in the United States.

Quaker Angelina Grimké, speaking on behalf of the abolitionist movement, becomes the first woman in history to address an American legislative body when she addresses the Massachusetts state legislature in Boston.

Quaker Sarah Grimké publishes *Letters on the Equality of the Sexes,* which attacks biblical arguments frequently used to advance theories of women's inferiority. Her *Letters* help ignite the women's rights movement.

1840   World Anti-Slavery Convention in London, England, excludes female delegates from active participation in the proceedings. Their reception motivates women like Lucretia Mott and Elizabeth Cady Stanton to launch a women's rights movement in 1848.

1841   Dorothea Dix begins a Sunday school class for women at a prison in East Cambridge, Massachusetts. What she sees inspires her to make prison re-

form and mental institution reform her life's work.

1843   Former slave Sojourner Truth embarks on her career as an itinerant minister. She will soon become known as a talented and inspired preacher and, later, as an advocate for the causes of abolitionism and women's rights.

1844   Ellen Gould White falls into a trance and experiences a vision that will lead to her cofounding, with future husband James S. White, the Seventh-Day Adventist Church.

1845   Transcendentalist Margaret Fuller publishes *Woman in the Nineteenth Century,* a book that will become a feminist classic.

1846   The American Missionary Association is founded. It promotes abolition and after the Civil War will become the most influential northern, Protestant religious association working among African Americans.

Mother Mary Frances Xavier Warde founds a convent and school in Chicago and lays plans for an orphan asylum and hospital. During her lifetime she personally establishes twenty-five convents, several orphanages, and at least sixty schools, probably founding more service institutions than any woman in Christian history.

1847   A small band of Cayuse raid the mission at Waiilatpu, killing Presbyterian missionaries Narcissa Whitman and her husband, Marcus Whitman.

1848   John Humphrey Noyes founds the Oneida Community, a religious-based commune that offers women opportunities not found in mainstream American society.

Sisters Margaret and Kate Fox report unusual rapping sounds in their home, which they begin to connect with the spirit world. These events mark the beginning of the Spiritualist movement that becomes popular in the United States during the second half of the nineteenth century.

The *Declaration of Rights and Sentiments and Resolutions* is presented at the first women's rights convention at Seneca Falls, New York. Included in the document are references to the intent of "God," or the "Creator," regarding women's place in the world as well as grievances concerning women's subordinate position in the church.

1849–1850 Lutheran pastor William Passavant of Pittsburgh, Pennsylvania, establishes the first female diaconate in America. It soon founders but is revived in Milwaukee, Wisconsin, in 1893, after the deaconess movement begins to attract larger numbers of Lutherans.

1852 Anne Ayres founds the first Episcopal sisterhood in the United States, the Sisterhood of the Holy Communion in New York City. By 1880 there are six major sisterhoods within the Episcopal Church.

1853 Antoinette Blackwell, a Congregationalist, becomes the first woman to be ordained a minister of a nationally recognized Protestant denomination. Serious theological differences with her congregation cause her to resign a year later.

1858 Initially founded in England in 1855, the Young Women's Christian Association (YWCA) is established in New York City. Its beginnings are slow, but from 1866 onward the YWCA will attract hundreds of members, and branches will open in cities across the country.

1860 The first national interdenominational women's society, the Woman's Union Missionary Society, is established. However, soon various groups begin to break away as new women's societies are created within individual denominations.

1862 Julia Ward Howe's "Battle Hymn of the Republic" is published in the *Atlantic Monthly* and soon becomes the semiofficial song of the Union army.

1863 Olympia Brown is ordained into the ministry of the Universalist Church, becoming the first woman to be fully ordained as a pastor and to continue in that role for a lengthy career.

1865 Harriet Starr Cannon and three or four other Episcopal women found the Community of St. Mary, the first new community to be formally established by the Episcopal Church since the English monasteries were dissolved in the sixteenth century. Cannon becomes the community's first superior.

1866 A turning point is reached in Mary Baker Eddy's life when she is injured in a fall on ice. During the course of her recovery, she undergoes a religious conversion that leads to the formation of the theology she calls "Christian Science."

1869 The Stone Ridge Methodist Episcopal Church in Ellenville, New York, grants Margaret Newton Van Cott a "local preacher's license." Though she will never be ordained to the ministry, she is most likely the first American woman to receive an official license to preach from the Methodist Episcopal Church.

The U.S. government becomes directly involved with the churches and their efforts to assimilate Native Americans with the establishment of the Board of Indian Commissioners. Members of the board are wealthy churchmen, and Christian churches are given control over reservations.

Former slave Amanda Berry Smith launches her career as an evangelist within the Holiness movement. She soon becomes a popular figure within the movement, spreading her message beyond the United States to Britain, India, and Africa.

1870   Phebe Ann Coffin Hanaford accepts a call to become pastor at the First Universalist Church in New Haven, Connecticut. While there, she becomes the first American woman to serve as chaplain in a state legislative body.

1872   Unconventional reformer and spiritual medium Victoria Claflin Woodhull runs for president of the United States on the Equal Rights Party ticket. The American public does not take her candidacy seriously.

1873   Charlotte (Lottie) Diggs Moon embarks for China, where she will serve as a missionary until her death in 1912. During that time she will work in areas where no female missionary has journeyed before.

The Comstock Law is enacted, prohibiting the circulation of materials about female and male sexuality and birth control.

1874   The Women's Missionary Society of the African Methodist Episcopal (AME) Church is founded in Washington, D.C. It will grow to become one of the first associations, black or white, to be organized by women on a national scale with affiliations in foreign lands.

The Woman's Christian Temperance Union (WCTU) is founded. Annie Wittenmyer is elected president, and Frances E. Willard is elected corresponding secretary.

1875   Helena Petrovna Blavatsky, along with Henry Steel Olcott and William Q. Judge, forms the Theosophical Society in New York City.

Hannah Whitall Smith publishes her major work, *The Christian's Secret of a Happy Life,* which becomes a classic among Protestant Christians, eventually selling about two million copies worldwide.

1877   Mormon Susa Amelia Young Gates becomes the first person to be baptized for the dead in the new Saint George Temple. Gates will later become one of the most powerful women in the Mormon Church.

1879   Frances E. Willard is elected president of the Woman's Christian Temperance Union (WCTU). Envisioning the WCTU as an organization gathering strength to pursue numerous reforms in addition to temperance, she announces her "Do Everything" policy.

1880   The Salvation Army, founded by William Booth and his wife, Catherine, in London, England, in 1865, expands to the United States. The army is one of the few nineteenth-century religious groups to offer women leading positions.

1881   Preacher, writer, editor, and social worker Carrie Judd (later Montgomery) publicly enters the ministry when she launches the periodical *Triumphs of Faith*. The magazine will bridge the gap between the Holiness and Pentecostal movements and will provide a nonsectarian forum for other denominations to communicate with one another.

With the aid of black leader Reverend Frank Quarles, Sophia B. Packard and Harriet E. Giles open a school for African Americans in the basement of Friendship Baptist Church. It will be renamed Spelman Seminary in 1884 and will become known as Spelman College in 1924.

1883   Jewish poet Emma Lazarus's sympathy for Jewish immigrants inspires her to write "The New Colossus," which is eventually inscribed on the pedestal of the Statue of Liberty in New York's harbor.

1884   Belle Harris Bennett, a Southern Methodist, has a religious experience of sanctification. Along with numerous other activities, she will go on to be a leader in foreign mission work and found home missions among both blacks and whites.

The Society of the Companions of the Holy Cross, whose members are Episcopal laywomen, is founded. The society preaches and practices the Social Gospel and has notable influence.

1885   Norwegian deaconess Elizabeth Fedde opens a small hospital in Brooklyn, New York, and begins a training program for deaconesses. In 1892, after considerable growth, the society is reincorporated as the Norwegian Lutheran Deaconesses' Home and Hospital. It later becomes the Lutheran Medical Center.

Methodist Lucy Jane Rider Meyer opens the Chicago Training School for City, Home, and Foreign Missions, designed for women wishing to enter religious work. The school helps to make the deaconess program within the Methodist Church the most successful among American Protestants.

Anna Sarah Kugler, working under the sponsorship of the Women's Home and Foreign Mission Society of the General Synod of the Evangelical Lutheran Church in the U.S.A., is officially designated a medical missionary. She is the first Lutheran woman to hold that position.

1887   Congress passes the Edmunds-Tucker Act, which declares plural marriages illegal and disenfranchises Mormon men who practice polygamy. The act also includes a clause that revokes female suffrage in the Utah Territory.

Due to rivalries among the various religious denominations associated with the Board of Indian Commissioners, the organization is replaced, and Native Americans are forced into acculturation through the Dawes Act.

Ann Eliza Worcester Robertson completes the translation of the New Testament into the Creek language, a work that she began with her husband, Presbyterian minister William Schenck Robertson, many years before.

1888   Martha E. McIntosh and Annie Walker Armstrong lead a small group of women to found the Woman's Missionary Union of the Southern Baptist Convention. By the late twentieth century, the organization will have a membership of over a million Southern Baptist women.

Emma Curtis Hopkins establishes a permanent headquarters in Chicago for what will become known as the New Thought movement.

The General Conference of the Methodist Episcopal Church authorizes the use of deaconesses and imposes general rules upon them. Soon Methodist deaconess centers are found in many of the nation's larger cities.

1889   Mother Frances Xavier Cabrini is sent by the pope to the United States to work with Italian immigrants. Founder of more than sixty-seven charitable institutions and a leader in efforts to create opportunities for Catholic women as missionaries, she will be canonized as the first American saint in 1946.

1891   Mary Katharine Drexel takes her vows as the first of the Sisters of the Blessed Sacrament for Indians and Colored People, which she has just founded. The order will grow to found many schools and a university. A case will later be made for her beatification.

1892   Joanna Patterson Moore, who has been working among African Americans as a Baptist missionary since the end of the Civil War, establishes the Fireside School. A family-oriented program, it is considered her greatest contribution to the evangelism of southern blacks.

1893 The first person is converted to Buddhism on American soil. By the 1950s, thousands of men and women convert. For women, Buddhism offers what some see as a nonsexist philosophy, but in practice men have traditionally dominated.

Hannah Greenebaum Solomon, a prominent Jewish woman, establishes the National Council of Jewish Women for the purpose of furthering the cause of religious education and philanthropy.

Matilda Joslyn Gage publishes *Woman, Church and State,* a work that is later praised as one of the most important theological documents of the early women's movement.

1894 Sarah Jane Farmer organizes the first Greenacre Institute, which becomes a summer conference center where lecturers from various religions can speak. In 1913 the center is taken over by the Baha'i faith.

Julia Foote becomes the first woman in the African Methodist Episcopal Zion Church to be ordained a deacon.

Harriet Emilie Cady begins writing a series of lessons that set forth the principles of divine healing. Twelve of these lessons are later published in one volume, *Lessons in Truth,* which becomes a standard text for the Unity School of Christianity (founded by Myrtle and Charles Fillmore in 1903).

1895 African-American Baptist congregations unite to form the National Baptist Convention.

Believing that the traditional Bible is not the direct word of God and convinced that it is the root cause of centuries of oppression of women, women's rights leader Elizabeth Cady Stanton publishes the first volume of her two-volume *The Woman's Bible.* Both volumes (the second will be published in 1898) prove to be extremely controversial, but both are best-sellers.

1897 Maud Nathan is probably the first woman to play a major role in an American Jewish worship service when she reads a paper, "The Heart of Judaism," in lieu of the sermon at Temple Beth-El in New York City.

1899 Eminent Roman Catholic writer and artist Eliza Allen Starr publishes *The Three Archangels and the Guardian Angels in Art.* In recognition of this work, she will receive a medallion from Pope Leo XIII.

1900 Temperance zealot Carry Nation, claiming that God has called upon her to lead the fight against liquor trafficking, begins using a hatchet in her crusade to destroy and close all liquor-distributing establishments.

1901 Alma Bridwell White establishes a fundamentalist Methodist sect that after 1917 will become known as the Pillar of Fire Church. As head of the church, she holds the title of bishop, the first Christian woman to hold such an office.

At a Pentecostalist Bible school in Topeka, Kansas, Agnes N. Ozman becomes the first student to speak in tongues.

1903 Myrtle Page Fillmore and her husband, Charles Fillmore, incorporate the Unity School of Practical Christianity. Theirs will become the largest of the movements collectively known as New Thought.

Twenty-five American Protestant denominations form an Inter-Church Conference on Marriage and Divorce in an attempt to formulate a common policy in regard to remarriage. Although their work leads to broader discussion of the issue, no uniform agreement is reached among the states.

Sister Mary Magdalen (Eliza Healy) is appointed superior of Villa Barlow at St. Albans, Vermont. She is the first African American to hold a position of leadership in a religious order in North America.

1904   Shaker eldress Anna White coauthors, with eldress Leila S. Taylor, *Shakerism: Its Meaning and Message,* the only published history of the society written by someone who has been a member.

After twenty years' affiliation with the Churches of God, evangelist Maria Beulah Underwood Woodworth-Etter declares herself independent.

Mary McLeod Bethune founds the Daytona Literary and Industrial School for Girls. From these roots Bethune-Cookman College will develop, with Methodist support. Bethune, the first African-American woman to found and head such an institution in the United States, will later hold many other important posts.

Evangeline Booth, whose parents founded the Salvation Army, becomes commander of the Salvation Army in the United States, a position she will hold until 1934.

1906   Florence Louise Crawford founds the Apostolic Faith Church in Portland, Oregon. A Pentecostal church, it will grow throughout the Pacific Northwest, Canada, and Scandinavia.

1908   Mary Magdalena Lewis Tate establishes the Church of the Living God, the Pillar and Ground of the Truth, and becomes its chief apostle, elder, president, and first chief overseer. The church is one of the earliest predominantly black Pentecostal denominations in the United States.

1909   The first of a series of pamphlets, *The Fundamentals,* is published. This series, lasting to 1914, stressed among other things the divine inspiration of every word in the Bible. The fundamentalist movement takes its name from the title of these pamphlets.

1911   Kate Harwood Waller Barrett, an Episcopalian and founder of a mission that establishes over fifty homes for women in need, is elected to the presidency of the National Council of Women.

1912   Henrietta Szold and a group of Jewish women gather in New York City to form an organization they call the "Hadassah Chapter of Daughters of Zion," later shortened to "Hadassah." The organization's purpose is to promote Jewish religious and social ideals through education in America and to establish public health facilities and nurses' training in Palestine.

Kathleen Moore Mallory is elected to the post of corresponding secretary of the Woman's Missionary Union of the Southern Baptist Convention. She will capably lead that organization for thirty-six years.

1915   Under the direction of Clara Eby Steiner, individual Mennonite women's sewing circles are organized into the churchwide Mennonite Woman's Missionary Society.

1916   Prominent New Thought advocate Annie Rix Militz establishes the University of Christ in Los Angeles to train New Thought leaders.

1918   Mother Marie Joseph Butler, the first American to head a Catholic congregation whose motherhouse is in a foreign land, opens Marymount College in New York. Other Marymount Colleges will be created later.

Mathilde Roth Schechter establishes the Women's League for Conservative Judaism. The initial purpose of the organization is to perpetuate traditional Judaism in America through the home, synagogue, and community.

1919   The International Association of Women Ministers is founded for purposes of promoting the development of an international and ecumenical fellowship among women ministers and equal ecclesiastical rights for women.

1920   The National Council of Catholic Women is founded under the direction of Catholic bishops. The motivating force behind the formation of this organization is concern over the changing morals of American society.

After four years of trying to persuade male Catholic leaders that women are capable of becoming foreign missionaries, the Maryknoll Sisters of St. Dominic are granted official recognition as a diocesan religious community. They immediately open an orphanage and school for Japanese Americans, and in 1921 they begin mission work in China.

1921   Baptist Helen Barrett Montgomery becomes the first woman to head a major American religious denomination by being elected to the presidency of the Northern Baptist Convention.

1923   Evangelist Aimee Semple McPherson opens the Angelus Temple in Los Angeles, California, which will house her Church of the Foursquare Gospel.

1924   The New England Conference of the Methodist Episcopal Church, North, recognizes the ordination of female clergy.

Ida Bell Robinson founds the Mount Sinai Holy Church of America, the largest African-American Pentecostal denomination to be headed by a woman.

1933   Christian educator Henrietta Cornelia Mears launches the Gospel Light Press (later Publishers). By 1940 Gospel Light will become the fourth-largest independent publisher of Sunday school literature in the United States.

Dorothy Day, with Peter Maurin, establishes the *Catholic Worker,* a newspaper that promotes social justice for the oppressed.

1934   Gospel singer Mahalia Jackson makes her first recording, "God Gonna Separate the Wheat from the Tares."

1938   Edith Elizabeth Lowry, who directs an international ministry to migrant workers, publishes *They Starve That We May Eat.* This book opens the eyes of many Americans to the difficult conditions faced by migrant workers.

1941   Church Women United is founded. It is an ecumenical movement of Roman Catholic, Protestant, Eastern Orthodox, and other Christian women who work on social issues in a Christian context.

1943   Kateri Tekakwitha, who converted to Catholicism in 1676, becomes the first Native American convert to Roman Catholicism to be venerated by the church and was beatified in 1980.

1946   Mother Frances Xavier Cabrini, who in the late nineteenth century and early twentieth century founded numerous charitable institutions throughout the world, is canonized, becoming the first American saint.

1948   The African Methodist Episcopal Church gives women full ordination rights.

1949   Writer Sarah Catherine Wood Marshall publishes *Mr. Jones, Meet the Master,* the first of her best-selling religious books.

1950   Mary Reddington Ely Lyman is appointed Morris K. Jessup Professor of English Bible and dean of women students at Union Theological Seminary. She is the first woman to hold a faculty chair at Union and one of the first women to be a full professor in any American seminary.

1951   Paula Ackerman becomes the first woman to perform the functions of a rabbi. She serves a Reform congregation in Mississippi after her rabbi husband dies, but only until 1954, when a "regular" rabbi will be selected.

1954   The Colored Methodist Episcopal Church recognizes the ordination of women clergy.

1956   The United Methodist Church grants women full ordination rights.

1959   Gloria Lee, who has claimed to have had contacts with aliens from outer space since 1953, founds the Cosmon Research Foundation.

1962   In *Schempp v. School District of Abington Township* (Pennsylvania), the Supreme Court rules that Bible reading and the Lord's Prayer are religious exercises, and therefore their use in public schools is unconstitutional under the First and Fourteenth Amendments.

1962– The documents emerging from the
1965   Second Vatican Council, or Vatican II, present some strong statements on the equality of men and women, which gives feminists some encouragement. However, along with these statements are some qualifications, including the arguments of bishops that a person's role in society must be in accordance with his or her nature and that the woman's domestic role must be preserved. Overall, the council creates a new, enlightened spirit among Catholic men and women.

1965   Yvonne Frost and her future husband, Gavin Frost, found the Church and School of Wicca in St. Louis, Missouri.

Rachel Henderlite receives approval to become the first woman to be ordained a minister of the Southern Presbyterian Church in the United States. A year later, she becomes the first female professor of Christian education at the Austin (Texas) Presbyterian Theological Seminary.

1966   Evangelist Kathryn Kuhlman launches a weekly television program. She tapes

five hundred programs before her death ten years later.

1968   Mary Daly, a Roman Catholic theologian, publishes *The Church and the Second Sex,* in which she charges that the church has long promoted the idea of women being inferior and must take much of the responsibility for the oppression of women within society. The book is one of the first major works to be written from the perspective of feminist theology since Elizabeth Cady Stanton's *The Woman's Bible* was published at the end of the nineteenth century.

The National Black Sisters' Conference, an organization of African-American Catholic women, is established. Headquartered in Washington, D.C., its stated purpose is "to strive to provide ongoing communication and dialogue that focus on the education and support of African-American women religious."

1969   Coretta Scott King becomes the first woman to preach at a regular service at St. Paul's Cathedral in London, England.

1970   Well-known atheist Madalyn Mays Murray O'Hair founds the Society of Separationists (later renamed American Atheists) and opens the Charles E. Stevens American Atheist Library and Archives. American Atheists soon develops into a national organization.

The General Convention of the Episcopal Church votes to make women full deacons, allowing them the same privileges as male deacons.

Both the Lutheran Church in America and the American Lutheran Church (later united as the Evangelical Lutheran Church in America) approve the ordination of women.

1971   Fifty nuns from eight states gather in Houston to address the problem of the underrepresentation of Hispanic sisters among their own people. The result is the founding of Las Hermanas for the purpose of providing more active service to the Hispanic people.

1972   In the case of *Eisenstadt v. Baird*, the U.S. Supreme Court declares the "Crimes against Chastity" law of the state of Massachusetts unconstitutional. The Court rules that by allowing only married persons to obtain contraceptives, the law discriminates against persons who are unmarried.

The Reform branch of Judaism ordains Sally Jane Priesand to the rabbinate. She becomes the first female rabbi in the United States.

With the publication of *Women in Church and Society: A Historical and Theological Inquiry,* Georgia Elma Harkness becomes one of the first to link history with theology in an attempt to take a broad look at woman's historical place in church and society.

In its decision in the case of *Wisconsin v. Yoder,* the U.S. Supreme Court rules that the Amish have the right to educate their own children.

Phyllis Schlafly launches a Stop ERA (Equal Rights Amendment) crusade. Within six years, she will establish branches of the organization in forty-five states.

For her recording of "Put Your Hand in the Hand of the Man from Galilee," Shirley Caesar becomes the first African-American female gospel singer to win a Grammy Award.

1973   The U.S. Supreme Court issues its decison in *Roe v. Wade,* holding that laws restricting abortion during the first trimester of pregnancy are unconstitutional.

1974   Selena Fox founds the Church of Circle Wicca, later known as Circle Sanctuary, or simply Circle. Fox practices a form of Wiccan-shamanism, an eclectic form of neo-Pagan Goddess worship.

The Reconstructionist branch of Judaism ordains its first female rabbi, Sandy Eisenberg Sasso.

A group of eleven female deacons of the Episcopal Church, who will become known as the "Philadelphia 11," are ordained by three retired Episcopal bishops. The House of Bishops declares the ordinations invalid and censures the ordaining bishops.

1975   Theologian Rosemary Radford Ruether publishes *New Woman/New Earth.* It is the first ecofeminist book, written before the concept had a name, and is considered a classic.

The National Conference of Catholic Bishops initiates the Pastoral Plan for Pro-Life Activities for the purpose of enlisting the aid of American Roman Catholics in putting an end to legalized abortion.

Mother Elizabeth Ann Seton, founder of Sisters of Charity in 1809, is canonized, becoming the first American-born Roman Catholic saint.

1976   Disillusioned with Madalyn O'Hair's American Atheists, Anne Nicol Gaylor and her supporters found the Freedom from Religion Foundation.

The General Convention of the Episcopal Church passes a resolution opening both the priesthood and the episcopate to women.

1978   Sonia Harris Johnson and three other women found Mormons for the ERA.

1979   Starhawk (Miriam Simos) publishes *The Spiral Dance: A Rebirth of the Ancient Religion of the Great Goddess,* which becomes the most popular introduction to Wicca and neo-Paganism of the 1980s.

Beverly LaHaye founds Concerned Women for America, an organization that enjoys rapid growth. With a claimed membership of more than half a million by the late 1980s, it is considered the most influential group among the religious right.

1980 Marjorie Swank Matthews becomes the first woman to be elected bishop of a major American denomination when she is elected to the bishopric of the United Methodist Church.

1982 The Equal Rights Amendment, which had been passed in Congress, goes down to defeat when it fails to be ratified by the required number of the states. Religious groups are divided in their attitudes toward the amendment.

1984 Leontine Turpeau Current Kelly is elected a bishop of the United Methodist Church, becoming the first African-American woman to be elected bishop in any major religious denomination in the United States.

1985 Amy Eilberg becomes the first woman to be ordained as a rabbi in the Conservative branch of Judaism.

1988 The Diocese of Massachusetts elects Reverend Barbara Clementine Harris suffragan (assisting) bishop. She becomes the first female to be elected to the bishopric of the Episcopal Church.

1997 The Woman's Home and Foreign Mission Society, a national organization administered by the Advent Christian Church, celebrates its one hundredth anniversary.

Books and Manuscripts

Abbott, Walter M. *Documents of Vatican II.* New York: Guild Press, 1966.

Abraham, Ken. *Who Are the Promise Keepers? Understanding the Christian Men's Movement.* New York: Doubleday, 1997.

Adams, Carol J., ed. *Ecofeminism and the Sacred.* New York: Continuum, 1993.

Adams, Grace, and Edward Hutter. *The Mad Forties.* New York: Harper and Brothers, 1942.

Adler, Margot. *Drawing Down the Moon: Witches, Druids, Goddess-Worshippers and Other Pagans in America Today.* New York: Penguin Books, 1986.

Allen, Catherine B. *Laborers Together with God: 22 Great Women in Baptist Life.* Birmingham, Ala.: Woman's Missionary Union, 1987.

Allen, Clifton Judson, et al., eds., *Encyclopedia of Southern Baptists.* Nashville: Broadman Press, 1958.

Allen, Gay Wilson. *Waldo Emerson: A Biography.* New York: Viking, 1981.

Allen, Opal Sweazea. *Narcissa Whitman: An Historical Biography.* Portland, Oreg.: Binfords and Mort, 1959.

Alonso, Harriet Hyman. *Peace as a Woman's Issue: A History of the U.S. Movement for World Peace and Women's Rights.* Syracuse, N.Y.: Syracuse University Press, 1993.

American Colleges and Universities. 13th ed. New York: Walter deGruyter, 1987.

Ammerman, Nancy Tatom. *Baptist Battles: Social Change and Religious Conflict in the Southern Baptist Convention.* New Brunswick, N.J.: Rutgers University Press, 1990.

Anderson, Robert, and Gail North. *Gospel Music Encyclopedia.* New York: Sterling Publishing, 1979.

Andrews, Edward Deming, and Faith Andrews. *Work and Worship: The Economic Order of the Shakers.* Greenwich, Conn.: New York Graphic Society, 1974.

Andrews, Lynn V. *Crystal Woman: The Sisters of the Dreamtime.* New York: Warner Books, 1987.

_____. *Medicine Woman.* San Francisco: Harper and Row, 1981.

Andrews, William L., ed. *Sisters of the Spirit: Three Black Women's Autobiographies of the Nineteenth Century.* Bloomington: Indiana University Press, 1986.

Apostolic Faith Mission. *A Historical Account of the Apostolic Faith.* Portland, Oreg.: Apostolic Faith Mission, 1965.

Arendt, Hannah. *Eichmann in Jerusalem: A Report on the Banality of Evil.* New York: Viking, 1963.

_____. *The Human Condition.* Chicago: University of Chicago Press, 1958.

_____. *On Revolution.* New York: Viking, 1963.

_____. *The Origins of Totalitarianism.* 1951. New ed., San Diego: Harcourt Brace Jovanovich, 1973.

Armstrong, O. K., and Marjorie M. Armstrong. *The Indomitable Baptists: A Narrative of Their Role in Shaping American History.* Garden City, N.Y.: Doubleday, 1967.

Arrington, Leonard J., and Davis Bitton. *The Mormon Experience: A History of the Latter-Day Saints.* New York: Alfred A. Knopf, 1979.

Arvind, Sharma. *Today's Woman in World Religions.* Albany: State University of New York Press, 1994.

Asals, Frederick. *Flannery O'Connor: The Imagination of Extremity*. Athens: University of Georgia Press, 1982.

Asbury, Herbert. *Carry Nation*. New York: Alfred A. Knopf, 1929.

Axtell, James. *The European and the Indian: Essays in the Ethnohistory of Colonial North America*. Oxford: Oxford University Press, 1981.

Ayres, Anne. *The Life and Work of William Augustus Mühlenberg*. New York: Harper and Brothers, Franklin Square, 1880.

Bacon, Margaret Hope. *Mothers of Feminism: The Story of Quaker Women in America*. San Francisco: Harper and Row, 1986.

_____. *Valiant Friend: The Life of Lucretia Mott*. New York: Walker and Company, 1980.

Baer, Hans A. *The Black Spiritual Movement: A Religious Response to Racism*. Knoxville: University of Tennessee Press, 1984.

Baer, Hans A., and Singer, Merrill. *African-American Religion in the Twentieth Century: Varieties of Protest and Accommodation*. Knoxville: University of Tennessee Press, 1992.

Banner, Lois W. *Elizabeth Cady Stanton: A Radical for Woman's Rights*. San Francisco: HarperCollins, 1980.

Barbour, Hugh, and J. William Frost. *The Quakers*. New York: Greenwood Press, 1988.

Barnhart, Joe E. *Jim and Tammy: Charismatic Intrigue inside PTL*. Buffalo, N.Y.: Prometheus Books, 1988.

Barr, Amelia E. *All the Days of My Life: An Autobiography*. New York: D. Appleton, 1915.

Barrett, Harrison D. *Life Work of Mrs. Cora L. V. Richmond*. Chicago: Hack and Anderson, 1895.

Barrett, Jacqueline K., ed. *Encyclopedia of Women's Associations Worldwide*. London: Gale Research International, 1993.

Barrett, Kate Waller. *Some Practical Suggestions on the Conduct of a Rescue Home*. Washington, D.C.: National Florence Crittenton Mission, 1903.

Bartlett, Irving H. *The American Mind in the Mid-Nineteenth Century*. 2nd ed. Arlington Heights, Ill.: Harlan Davidson, 1982.

Bataille, Gretchen M. *Native American Women: A Biographical Dictionary*. New York: Garland, 1993.

Bataille, Gretchen M., and Kathleen Mullen Sands. *American Indian Women: Telling Their Lives*. Lincoln: University of Nebraska Press, 1984.

Bates, Stephen. *Battleground: One Mother's Crusade, the Religious Right, and the Struggle for Control of Our Classrooms*. New York: Poseidon Press, 1993.

Battis, Emery. *Saints and Sectaries: Anne Hutchinson and the Antinomian Controversy in the Massachusetts Bay Colony*. Chapel Hill: University of North Carolina Press, 1962.

Baum, Charlotte, Paula Hyman, and Sonya Michel. *The Jewish Woman in America*. New York: Dial Press, 1976.

Beckford, James J. *The Trumpet of Prophecy: A Sociological Study of Jehovah's Witnesses*. New York: John Wiley and Sons, 1975.

Beecher, Maureen Ursenbach, ed. *The Personal Writings of Eliza Roxcy Snow*. Salt Lake City: University of Utah Press, 1995.

Bender, Sue. *Plain and Simple: A Woman's Journey to the Amish*. San Francisco: HarperSanFrancisco, 1989.

Bendroth, Margaret Lamberts. *Fundamentalism and Gender: 1875 to the Present*. New Haven: Yale University Press, 1993.

Bengtson, Gloria E., ed. *Lutheran Women in Ordained Ministry, 1970–1995*. Minneapolis: Augsburg, 1995.

Benhabib, Seyla. *The Reluctant Modernism of Hannah Arendt*. Thousand Oaks, Calif.: Sage Publications, 1996.

Benowitz, June Melby. "Speaking Out: Right-Wing American Women, 1933 to 1945." Ph.D. diss., University of Texas at Austin, 1996.

Berg, Barbara. *The Remembered Gate: Origins of American Feminism—The Woman and the City, 1800–1860*. New York: Oxford University Press, 1976.

Bergman, Jerry. *Jehovah's Witnesses and Kindred Groups: A Historical Compendium and Bibliography*. New York: Garland, 1984.

Billson, Janet Mancini. *Keepers of the Culture: The Power of Tradition in Women's Lives.* New York: Lexington Books, 1995.

Blackburn, Thomas C., ed. *December's Child: A Book of Chumash Oral Narratives.* Berkeley: University of California Press, 1975.

Blake, Nelson Manfred. *The Road to Reno: A History of Divorce in the United States.* New York: Macmillan, 1962.

Blanchard, Dallas A., and Terry J. Prewitt. *Religious Violence and Abortion: The Gideon Project.* Gainesville: University Press of Florida, 1993.

Blumhofer, Edith W. *Aimee Semple McPherson: Everybody's Sister.* Grand Rapids, Mich.: W. B. Eerdmans, 1993.

Boles, Janet K. *The Politics of the Equal Rights Amendment: Conflict and the Decision.* New York: Longman, 1979.

Bordin, Ruth. *Frances Willard: A Biography.* Chapel Hill: University of North Carolina Press, 1986.

_____. *Women and Temperance: The Quest for Power and Liberty, 1873–1900.* Philadelphia: Temple University Press, 1981.

Bormann, Ernest G., ed. *Forerunners of Black Power: The Rhetoric of Abolition.* Englewood Cliffs, N.J.: Prentice-Hall, 1971.

Boucher, Sandy. *Turning the Wheel: American Women Creating the New Buddhism.* Boston: Beacon Press, 1993.

Bowden, Henry Warner. *Dictionary of American Religious Biography.* Westport, Conn.: Greenwood Press, 1977; 2nd ed., 1993.

Boyd, Lois A., and R. Douglas Brackenridge. *Presbyterian Women in America: Two Centuries of a Quest for Status.* 2nd ed. Westport, Conn.: Greenwood Press, 1996.

Boyer, Paul, and Stephen Nissenbaum. *Salem Possessed: The Social Origins of Witchcraft.* Cambridge: Harvard University Press, 1976.

Boylan, Anne M. *Sunday School: The Formation of an American Institution, 1790–1880.* New Haven: Yale University Press, 1988.

Bozarth-Campbell, Alla. *Womanpriest: A Personal Odyssey.* New York: Paulist Press, 1978.

Braden, Charles S. *Spirits in Rebellion: The Rise and Development of New Thought.* Dallas: Southern Methodist University Press, 1984.

Bradford, Sarah H. *Harriet Tubman: The Moses of Her People.* 1886. Reprint, New Jersey: Citadel Press, 1974.

_____. *Scenes in the Life of Harriet Tubman.* 1869. Reprint, Salem, N.H.: Ayer Company, 1992.

Bremer, Francis J. *The Puritan Experiment: New England Society from Bradford to Edwards.* London: St. James Press, 1977.

Brennan, Shawn, ed. *Women's Information Directory.* Detroit: Gale, 1993.

Burgess, Standley M. *Dictionary of Pentecostal and Charismatic Movements.* Grand Rapids, Mich.: Regency Reference Library, 1988.

Burgess-Olson, Vicky. *Sister Saints.* Provo, Utah: Brigham Young University Press, 1978.

Burns, Deborah E. *Shaker Cities of Peace, Love, and Union: A History of the Hancock Bishopric.* Hanover, N.H.: University Press of New England, 1992.

Burton, Katherine. *Mother Butler of Marymount.* New York: Longmans, Green and Company, 1944.

Bushman, Claudia L., ed. *Mormon Sisters: Women in Early Utah.* Cambridge: Emmeline Press, 1976.

Butler, Jon. *Awash in a Sea of Faith: Christianizing the American People.* Cambridge: Harvard University Press, 1990.

Butterworth, John. *Cults and New Faiths.* Elgin, Ill.: David C. Cook Publishing Company, 1981.

Bynum, Caroline Walken. *Jesus as Mother: Studies in the Spirituality of the High Middle Ages.* Berkeley: University of California Press, 1982.

Cabot, Laurie, with Jean Miller. *Celebrate the Earth: A Year of Holidays in the Pagan Tradition.* New York: Delta Books, 1994.

Cady, H. Emilie. *God, a Present Help.* New York: R. F. Fenno, 1912.

_____. *Lessons in Truth.* Kansas City, Mo.: Unity School of Christianity, 1919.

Calvin, John. *On the Christian Faith: Selections from the Institutes, Commentaries, and Tracts,* ed. John T. McNeill. Indianapolis: Bobbs-Merrill, 1957.

Campion, Nardi Reeder. *Ann the Word: The Life of Mother Ann Lee, Founder of the Shakers.* Boston: Little, Brown, 1976.

Cantor, Aviva. *Jewish Women/Jewish Men: The Legacy of Patriarchy in Jewish Life.* San Francisco: HarperSanFrancisco, 1995.

Capper, Charles. *Margaret Fuller, an American Romantic Life: The Private Years.* New York: Oxford University Press, 1992.

Carlson, Carole C. *Corrie ten Boom: Her Life, Her Faith.* Old Tappan, N.J.: Fleming H. Revell, 1983.

Carmody, Denise Lardner. *Women and World Religions.* 2nd ed. Englewood Cliffs, N.J.: Prentice-Hall, 1989.

Carr, Anne E. *Transforming Grace: Christian Tradition and Women's Experience.* San Francisco: Harper and Row, 1988.

Carroll, Jackson W., Barbara Hargrove, and Adair T. Lummis. *Women of the Cloth: A New Opportunity for the Churches.* San Francisco: Harper and Row, 1981.

Carson, Mina. *Settlement Folk: Social Thought and the American Settlement Movement, 1885–1930.* Chicago: University of Chicago Press, 1990.

Cazden, Elizabeth. *Antoinette Brown Blackwell: A Biography.* Old Westbury, N.Y.: Feminist Press, 1993.

Champagne, Duane, ed. *The Native North American Almanac.* Detroit: Gale, 1994.

Chevigny, Bell Gale. *The Woman and the Myth: Margaret Fuller's Life and Writings.* Old Westbury, N.Y.: The Feminist Press, 1976.

Christ, Carol P., and Judith Plaskow, eds. *Womanspirit Rising: A Feminist Reader in Religion.* San Francisco: Harper and Row, 1979.

Clarke, James Freeman. *Ten Great Religions: An Essay in Comparative Theology.* Boston: Houghton Mifflin, 1897.

Clifford, Deborah Pickman. *Mine Eyes Have Seen the Glory: A Biography of Julia Ward Howe.* Boston: Little, Brown, 1979.

Coles, Robert. *Dorothy Day: A Radical Devotion.* Reading, Mass.: Addison-Wesley, 1987.

Commager, Henry Steele, ed. 7th ed. *Documents of American History.* New York: Appleton-Century-Crofts, 1962.

_____. *Theodore Parker.* Boston: Beacon Press, 1947, 1960.

Cooke, George Willis. *Unitarianism in America: A History of Its Origin and Development.* Boston: American Unitarian Association, 1902.

Costa, Marie. *Abortion.* 2nd ed. Santa Barbara: ABC-CLIO, 1996.

Coté, Charlotte. *Olympia Brown: The Battle for Equality.* Racine, Wis.: Mother Courage Press, 1988.

Cott, Nancy F. *The Bonds of Womanhood: "Woman's Sphere" in New England, 1780–1835.* New Haven: Yale University Press, 1977.

Cranston, Sylvia. *HPB: The Extraordinary Life and Influence of Helena Blavatsky, Founder of the Modern Theosophical Movement.* New York: G. P. Putnam's Sons, 1993.

Cromwell, Otelia. *Lucretia Mott.* New York: Russell and Russell, 1958.

Cross, Mary Bywater. *Quilts and Women of the Mormon Migration.* Nashville: Rutledge Hill Press, 1996.

Cullen-DuPont, Kathryn, with Annelise Orleck. *The Encyclopedia of Women's History in America.* New York: Facts on File, 1996.

Curti, Merle. *The Growth of American Thought,* 2nd ed. New York: Harper and Row, 1951.

Curtiss, Harriette Augusta, and F. Homer Curtiss. *The Key of Destiny.* New York: E. P. Dutton, 1919.

Daly, Mary. *Beyond God the Father: Toward a Philosophy of Women's Liberation.* Boston: Beacon Press, 1973.

_____. *Pure Lust: Elemental Feminist Philosophy.* Boston: Beacon Press, 1984.

Daly, Mary, and Jane Caputi. *Webster's First New Intergalactic Wickedary of the English Language.* Boston: Beacon Press, 1987.

Davidson, James West, et al. *Nation of Nations: A Narrative History of the American Republic.* 2 vols. New York: McGraw-Hill, 1990.

Davis, Allen F. *Spearheads for Reform: The Social Settlements and the Progressive Movement.* New York: Oxford University Press, 1967. Reprint, New Brunswick, N.J.: Rutgers University Press, 1984.

Davis, Almond H. *The Female Preacher or Memoir of Salome Lincoln.* 1843. Reprint, New York: Arno Press, 1972.

Davis, Cyprian. *The History of Black Catholics in the United States.* New York: Crossroad Publishing, 1992.

Davis, Flora. *Moving the Mountain: The Women's Movement in America since 1960.* New York: Touchstone, 1991.

Day, Dorothy. *The Long Loneliness: The Autobiography of Dorothy Day.* 1952. Reprint, San Francisco: Harper and Row, 1981.

DeBerg, Betty A. *Ungodly Women: Gender and the First Wave of American Fundamentalism.* Minneapolis: Fortress Press, 1990.

Deen, Edith. *Great Women of the Christian Faith.* New York: Harper and Brothers, 1959.

Demos, John Putnam. *Entertaining Satan: Witchcraft and the Culture of Early New England.* Oxford: Oxford University Press, 1982.

_____. *A Little Commonwealth: Family Life in Plymouth Colony.* New York: Oxford University Press, 1970.

_____. *Past, Present and Personal: The Family and the Life Course in American History.* New York: Oxford University Press, 1986.

Díaz-Stevens, Ana María, and Anthony M. Stevens-Arroyo. *Recognizing the Latino Resurgence in U.S. Religion: The Emmaus Paradigm.* Boulder, Colo: Westview Press, 1998.

Dictionary of American Biography, 20 vols. and 10 supps. New York: Charles Scribner's Sons, 1928–1936, 1944–1995.

Dinnerstein, Leonard. *Antisemitism in America.* New York: Oxford University Press, 1994.

Dirvin, Joseph I. *Mrs. Seton: Foundress of the American Sisters of Charity.* New York: Farrar, Straus, and Giroux, 1975.

Dolan, Jay P., and Allan Figueroa Deck, eds. *Hispanic Catholic Culture in the U.S.: Issues and Concerns.* Notre Dame: University of Notre Dame Press, 1994.

Donovan, Mary Sudman. *A Different Call: Women's Ministries in the Episcopal Church, 1850–1920.* Wilton, Conn.: Morehouse-Barlow, 1986.

Douglas, Ann. *The Feminization of American Culture.* New York: Alfred A. Knopf, 1977.

Douglas, William. *Ministers' Wives.* New York: Harper and Row, 1965.

Dresser, Horatio W. *A History of the New Thought Movement.* New York: Thomas Y. Cromwell, 1919.

Driedger, Leo. *Mennonite Identity in Conflict.* Lewiston, N.Y.: E. Mellen Press, 1988.

Drury, Clifford M. *Marcus and Narcissa Whitman and the Opening of Old Oregon.* 2 vols. Seattle, Wash.: Pacific Northwest National Parks and Forests Association, 1986.

DuBois, Ellen Carol. *Feminism and Suffrage: The Emergence of an Independent Women's Movement in America, 1848–1869.* Ithaca, N.Y.: Cornell University Press, 1978.

DuBois, Ellen Carol, and Vicki L. Ruiz, eds. *Unequal Sisters: A MultiCultural Reader in U.S. Women's History.* New York: Routledge, 1990.

Duffy, Consuela Marie. *Katharine Drexel: A Biography.* Cornwells Heights, Penn.: Mother Katharine Drexel Guild, 1972.

DuPree, Sherry Sherrod, ed. *Biographical Dictionary of African-American Holiness-Pentecostals, 1880–1990.* Washington, D.C.: Middle Atlantic Regional Press, 1989.

Ebaugh, Helen Rose Fuchs. *Women in the Vanishing Cloister: Organizational Decline in Catholic Religious Orders in the United States.* New Brunswick, N.J.: Rutgers University Press, 1993.

Eckhard, Celia Morris. *Fanny Wright: Rebel in America.* Cambridge, Mass.: Harvard University Press, 1984.

Eddy, Mary Baker. *Science and Health with Key to the Scriptures.* Boston: Trustees under the Will of Mary Baker Eddy, 1934.

Edgar, Kathleen J., Terrie M. Rooney, and Jennifer Gariepy, eds. *Contemporary Authors.* Vol. 151. Detroit: Gale, 1996.

Effendi, Shoghi. *God Passes By.* Wilmette, Ill.: Baha'i Publishing Trust, 1957.

Eilberg-Schwartz, Howard, and Wendy Doniger. *Off with Her Head! The Denial of Women's Identity in Myth, Religion and Culture.* Berkeley: University of California Press, 1995.

Elkholy, Abdo A. *The Arab Moslems in the United States.* New Haven: College and University Press, 1966.

Ellwood, Robert S., Jr. *Religious and Spiritual Groups in Modern America.* Englewood Cliffs, N.J.: Prentice-Hall, 1973.

Epstein, Barbara Leslie. *The Politics of Domesticity: Women, Evangelism, and Temperance in Nineteenth Century America.* Middletown, Conn.: Wesleyan University Press, 1981.

Epstein, Daniel Mark. *Sister Aimee: The Life of Aimee Semple McPherson.* New York: Harcourt Brace Jovanovich, 1993.

Evory, Ann, and Linda Metger, eds. *Contemporary Authors.* New Revision Series. Detroit: Gale Research, 1984.

Falwell, Jerry. *Listen America!* Garden City, N.Y.: Doubleday, 1980.

_____. *Strength for the Journey: An Autobiography of Jerry Falwell.* New York: Simon and Schuster, 1987.

Farnham, Christie, ed. *The Impact of Feminist Research in the Academy.* Bloomington: Indiana University Press, 1987.

Fass, Paula S. *The Damned and the Beautiful: American Youth in the 1920's.* New York: Oxford University Press, 1977.

Faux, Marian. *Crusaders: Voices from the Abortion Front.* New York: Carol Publishing Group, 1990.

_____. *Roe v. Wade: The Untold Story of the Landmark Supreme Court Decision That Made Abortion Legal.* New York: Macmillan, 1988.

Feeney, Leonard. *Mother Seton: Saint Elizabeth of New York.* Cambridge: Ravengate Press, 1938. Rev. ed., 1991.

Felsenthal, Carol. *The Sweetheart of the Silent Majority: The Biography of Phyllis Schlafly.* Garden City, N.Y.: Doubleday, 1981.

Fields, Rick. *How the Swans Came to the Lake: A Narrative History of Buddhism in America.* 3rd ed. Boston: Shambhala, 1992.

Fillmore, Myrtle. *How to Let God Help You.* Comp. Warren Meyer. Unity Village, Mo.: Unity Books, 1956.

_____. *Myrtle Fillmore's Healing Letters.* 14th ed. Comp. Frances W. Foulkes. Unity Village, Mo.: Unity Books, 1978.

Fink, Greta. *Great Jewish Women: Profiles of Courageous Women from the Maccabean Period to the Present.* New York: Menorah Publishing Company, and Bloch Publishing Company, 1978.

Fishburn, Janet Forsythe. *The Fatherhood of God and the Victorian Family: The Social Gospel in America.* Philadelphia: Fortress Press, 1981.

Fishel, Leslie H., Jr., and Benjamin Quarles. *The Negro American: A Documentary History.* Glenview, Ill.: Scott, Foresman and Company, 1967.

Flammonde, Paris. *The Age of Flying Saucers.* New York: Hawthorn Books, 1971.

Flexner, Eleanor. *Century of Struggle: The Woman's Rights Movement in the United States.* New York: Atheneum, 1970.

Foster, Catherine. *Women for All Seasons: The Story of the Women's International League for Peace and Freedom.* Athens: University of Georgia Press, 1989.

Foster, John Onesimus. *Life and Labors of Mrs. Maggie Van Cott.* Cincinnati: Hitchcock and Walden, 1872. Beltsville, Md.: American Theological Association Board of Microtext; filmed by NCR Corp, 1978.

Foster, Lawrence. *Women, Family and Utopia: Communal Experiments of the Shakers, the Oneida Community, and the Mormons.* Syracuse, N.Y.: Syracuse University Press, 1990.

Frankel, Noralee, and Nancy S. Dye, eds. *Gender, Class, Race, and Reform in the Progressive Era.* Lexington: University Press of Kentucky, 1991.

Fredrickson, George M., ed. *William Lloyd Garrison.* Englewood Cliffs, N.J.: Prentice-Hall, 1968.

Friedman, Jean E., comp. *Our American Sisters: Women in American Life and Thought.* Boston: Allyn and Bacon, 1973.

Frost-Knappman, Elizabeth. *Women's Progress in America*. Santa Barbara: ABC-CLIO, 1994.

Gage, Matilda Joslyn. *Woman, Church and State*. 1893. Reprint, New York: Arno Press, 1972.

Gardener, Helen H. *Men, Women, and Gods, and Other Lectures*. New York: Truth Seeker Company, 1885.

Gaustad, Edwin S., ed. *A Documentary History of Religion in America to the Civil War*. Grand Rapids, Mich.: William B. Eerdmans Publishing, 1982.

Gaver, Jessyca Russell. *The Baha'i Faith: Dawn of a New Day*. New York: Hawthorn Books, 1967.

Gleadle, Kathryn. *The Early Feminists: Radical Unitarians and the Emergence of the Women's Rights Movement, 1831–51*. London and New York: St. Martin's Press, 1995.

Gollaher, David. *Voice for the Mad: The Life of Dorothea Dix*. New York: Free Press, 1995.

Goodsell, Willystine. *Pioneers of Women's Education in America*. New York: McGraw-Hill, 1931.

Gordon, Linda. *Woman's Body, Woman's Right: A Social History of Birth Control in America*. 1977. Reprint, New York: Penguin Books, 1986.

Goreau, Laurraine. *Just Mahalia, Baby*. Waco, Texas: Ward Books, 1975.

Gottschalk, Stephen. *The Emergence of Christian Science in American Religious Life*. Berkeley: University of California Press, 1973.

Grant, Mary H. *Private Woman, Public Person: An Account of the Life of Julia Ward Howe from 1819 to 1868*. Brooklyn, N.Y.: Carlson Publishing, 1994.

Green, Elizabeth Alden. *Mary Lyon and Mount Holyoke: Opening the Gates*. Hanover, N.H.: University Press of New England, 1979.

Greenbacker, Liz, and Sherry Taylor. *Private Lives of Ministers' Wives*. Far Hills, N.J.: New Horizon Press, 1991.

Griffith, Elisabeth. *In Her Own Right: The Life of Elizabeth Cady Stanton*. New York: Oxford University Press, 1984.

Grimm, Harold J. *The Reformation Era: 1500–1650*. New York: Macmillan, 1954.

Guiley, Rosemary Ellen. *The Encyclopedia of Witches and Witchcraft*. New York: Facts on File, 1989.

Hadden, Jeffrey K., and Anson Shupe. *Televangelism: Power and Politics on God's Frontier*. New York: Henry Holt, 1988.

Hagen, June Steffensen, ed. *Gender Matters: Women's Studies for the Christian Community*. Grand Rapids, Mich.: Academic Books, 1990.

Hale, William Harlan. *Horace Greeley: Voice of the People*. New York: Harper and Brothers, 1950.

Hall, Jacqueline Dowd. *Revolt against Chivalry: Jessie Daniel Ames and the Women's Campaign against Lynching*. New York: Columbia University Press, 1979.

Hamm, Thomas D. *The Transformation of American Quakerism: Orthodox Friends, 1800–1907*. Bloomington: Indiana University Press, 1988.

Hammack, Mary L. *Dictionary of Women in Church History*. Chicago: Moody Press, 1984.

Hanaford, Phebe A. *Life of George Peabody*. Boston: B. B. Russell, 1870.

———. *Lucretia the Quakeress, or Principle Triumphant*. Boston: J. Buffum, 1853.

Hanson, Phillip. *Hannah Arendt: Politics, History and Citizenship*. Stanford, Calif.: Stanford University Press, 1993.

Hardman, Keith J. *Charles Grandison Finney, 1792–1875: Revivalist and Reformer*. Syracuse, N.Y.: Syracuse University Press, 1987.

Hare, Lloyd C. M. *The Greatest American Woman: Lucretia Mott*. American Historical Society, 1937; republished, St. Clare Shores, Mich.: Scholarly Press, 1972.

Harkness, Georgia. *Women in Church and Society: A Historical and Theological Inquiry*. Nashville: Abingdon Press, 1972.

Hartman, Mary S., and Lois Banner. *Clio's Consciousness Raised: New Perspectives on the History of Women*. New York: Harper Torchbooks, 1974.

Harvey, Paul. *Redeeming the South: Religious Cultures and Racial Identities among*

Southern Baptists, 1865–1925. Chapel Hill: University of North Carolina Press, 1997.

Hassey, Janette. *No Time for Silence: Evangelical Women in Public Ministry around the Turn of the Century.* Grand Rapids, Mich.: Zondervan, 1986.

Haven, Kendall. *Amazing American Women.* Englewood, Colo.: Libraries Unlimited, 1995.

Healy, Kathleen. *Frances Warde: American Founder of the Sisters of Mercy.* New York: Seabury Press, 1973.

Henry, Marie. *The Secret Life of Hannah Whitall Smith.* Grand Rapids, Mich.: Chosen Books, 1984.

Henry, Sondra, and Emily Taitz. *Coretta Scott King: Keeper of the Dream.* Hillside, N.J.: Enslow Publishers, 1992.

Hersh, Blanche Glassman. *The Slavery of Sex: Feminist Abolitionists in America.* Urbana: University of Illinois, 1978.

Hewitt, Nancy A. *Women's Activism and Social Change: Rochester, New York, 1822–1872.* Ithaca, N.Y.: Cornell University Press, 1984.

Higginbotham, Evelyn Brooks. *Righteous Discontent: The Women's Movement in the Black Baptist Church, 1880–1920.* Cambridge, Mass.: Harvard University Press, 1993.

Higham, John. *Send These to Me: Jews and Other Immigrants in Urban America,* revised ed. Baltimore: Johns Hopkins University Press, 1984.

Hill, Patricia R. *The World Their Household: The American Women's Foreign Mission Movement and Cultural Transformation, 1870–1920.* Ann Arbor: University of Michigan, 1985.

Hine, Darlene Clark, ed. *Black Women in America: An Historical Encyclopedia.* 2 vols. Brooklyn, N.Y.: Carlson Publishing, 1993.

_____. *Black Women in United States History.* 16 vols. Brooklyn, N.Y.: Carlson Publishing, 1990.

Hirschfelder, Arlene, and Paulette Molin. *The Encyclopedia of Native American Religions.* New York: Facts on File, 1992.

Hoekema, Anthony A. *The Four Major Cults: Christian Science, Jehovah's Witnesses, Mormonism, Seventh-day Adventism.* Grand Rapids, Mich.: William B. Eerdmans Publishing, 1963.

Holt, Rackham. *Mary McLeod Bethune: A Biography.* Garden City, N.Y., 1964.

Hooglund, Eric J., ed. *Crossing the Waters: Arabic-Speaking Immigrants to the United States before 1945.* Washington, D.C.: Smithsonian Institution Press, 1987.

Howe, Susan. *The Birth-Mark: Unsettling the Wilderness in American Literary History.* Hanover, N.H.: Wesleyan University Press and University Press of New England, 1993.

Hubbard, Ethel Daniels. *Ann of Ava.* New York: Friendship Press, 1941. Reprint, Freeport, N.Y.: Books for Libraries Press, 1971.

Hudson, Travis. *Breath of the Sun: Life in Early California as Told by a Chumash Indian, Fernando Librado to John P. Harrington.* Banning, Calif.: Malki Museum Press, 1979.

Hull, Eleanor. *Women Who Carried the Good News.* Valley Forge, Penn.: Judson Press, 1975.

Hunter, Louise H. *Buddhism in Hawaii: Its Impact on a Yankee Community.* Honolulu: University of Hawaii Press, 1971.

Hyman, Paula, and Deborah Dash Moore, eds. *Jewish Women in America.* New York: Routledge Press, 1997.

Isasi-Díaz, Ada María, and Fernando F. Segovia, eds. *Hispanic/Latino Theology: Challenge and Promise.* Minneapolis: Fortress Press, 1996.

Isasi-Díaz, Ada María, and Yolanda Tarango. *Hispanic Women—Prophetic Voice in the Church: Toward a Hispanic Women's Liberation Theology.* San Francisco: Harper and Row, 1988.

Jacobs, Lee. *The Wages of Sin: Censorship and the Fallen Woman Film, 1928–1942.* Madison: University of Wisconsin Press, 1991.

Jaher, Frederic Cople. *A Scapegoat in the Wilderness: The Origins and Rise of Anti-Semitism in America.* Cambridge, Mass.: Harvard University Press, 1994.

James, Edward T., ed. *Notable American Women, 1607–1950.* 3 vols. Cambridge: Harvard University, Belknap Press, 1971.

James, Hunter. *Smile Pretty and Say Jesus: The Last Great Days of PTL*. Athens: University of Georgia Press, 1993.

Jeansonne, Glen. *Women of the Far Right*. Chicago: University of Chicago Press, 1996.

Jimerson, Randall C., F. X. Blouin, and C. A. Isetts, eds. *Guide to the Microfilm Edition of Temperance and Prohibition Papers*. Ann Arbor: University of Michigan Press, 1977.

Johnson, Sonia. *From Housewife to Heretic*. Garden City, N.Y.: Doubleday, 1981.

———. *Going Out of Our Minds: The Metaphysics of Liberation*. Freedom, Calif.: Crossing Press, 1987.

———. *The Ship That Sailed into the Living Room: Sex and Intimacy Reconsidered*. Estancia, N.M.: Wildfire Books, 1991.

Jones, David E. *Sanapia: Comanche Medicine Woman*. New York: Holt, Rinehart & Winston, 1972.

Jones, Rufus M. *The Later Periods of Quakerism*. 2 vols. 1921. Reprint, Westport, Conn.: Greenwood Press, 1970.

Judah, J. Stillson. *The History and Philosophy of the Metaphysical Movements in America*. Philadelphia: Westminster Press, 1967.

Juster, Susan. *"Disorderly Women": Sexual Politics and Evangelicalism in Revolutionary New England*. Ithaca, N.Y.: Cornell University Press, 1994.

Katz, Esther, and Anita Rapone, eds. *Women's Experience in America: An Historical Anthology*. New Brunswick, N.J.: Transaction Books, 1980.

Kauffman, Christopher. *Tradition and Transformation in Catholic Culture: The Priests of Saint Sulpice in the United States from 1791 to the Present*. New York: Macmillan, 1988.

Keller, Rosemary Skinner, Louise L. Queen, and Hilah F. Thomas. *Women in New Worlds: Historical Perspectives on the Wesleyan Tradition*. 2 vols. Nashville: Abingdon, 1981, 1982.

Kelley, Mary. *Margaret Fuller*. New York: Penguin Books, 1994.

Kenneally, James J. *The History of American Catholic Women*. New York: Crossroad, 1990.

Kennelly, Karen, ed. *American Catholic Women: A Historical Exploration*. New York: Macmillan, 1989.

Kimmel, Michael S., and Thomas E. Mosmiller, eds. *Against the Tide: Pro-Feminist Men in the United States, 1776–1990: A Documentary History*. Boston: Beacon Press, 1992.

King, Coretta Scott. *My Life with Martin Luther King, Jr.* New York: Holt, Rinehart & Winston, 1969.

Kirby, James E. *The Methodists*. Westport, Conn.: Greenwood Press, 1996.

Klaw, Spencer. *Without Sin: The Life and Death of the Oneida Community*. New York: Penguin Press, 1993.

Klein, Laura F., and Lillian A. Ackerman, eds. *Women and Power in Native North America*. Norman: University of Oklahoma Press, 1995.

Knowles, James Davis. *Life of Mrs. Ann H. Judson, Late Missionary to Burma*. Microfilm. Philadelphia: American Sunday School Union, 1830.

Koehler, Lyle. *A Search for Power: The "Weaker Sex" in Seventeenth-Century New England*. Urbana: University of Illinois Press, 1980.

Kolmerten, Carol A. *Women in Utopia: The Ideology of Gender in the American Owenite Communities*. Bloomington: Indiana University Press, 1990.

Kuhlman, Erika A. *Petticoats and White Feathers: Gender Conformity, Race, the Progressive Peace Movement, and the Debate over War, 1895–1919*. Westport, Conn.: Greenwood Press, 1997.

Kuron, Victoria Hyunchu. *Entrepreneurship and Religion: Korean Immigrants in Houston, Texas*. New York: Garland, 1997.

Kyle, Richard. *The Religious Fringe: A History of Alternative Religions in America*. Downer's Grove, Ill.: Inter Varsity Press, 1993.

Lagerquist, L. DeAne. *From Our Mothers' Arms: A History of Women in the American Lutheran Church*. Minneapolis: Augsburg Publishing, 1987.

LaHaye, Tim, and Beverly LaHaye. *Against the Tide: How to Raise Sexually Pure Kids* in an *"Anything-Goes" World*. Sisters, Oregon: Questar Publishers, 1993.

Land, Gary, ed. *Adventism in America: A History*. Grand Rapids, Mich.: William B. Eerdmans Publishing, 1986.

_____. *The World of Ellen G. White*. Washington, D.C.: Review and Herald Publishing Association, 1987.

Langley, Winston E., and Vivian C. Fox. *Women's Rights in the United States: A Documentary History*. Westport, Conn.: Greenwood Press, 1994.

Larson, Martin A. *New Thought Religion: A Philosophy for Health, Happiness and Prosperity*. New York: Philosophical Library, 1987.

Lavine, Sigmund A. *Evangeline Booth, Daughter of Salvation*. New York: Dodd, Mead and Company, 1970.

Lawless, Elaine J. *Handmaidens of the Lord: Pentecostal Women Preachers and Traditional Religion*. Philadelphia: University of Pennsylvania Press, 1988.

Lawrence, Alberta, ed. *Who Was Who among North American Authors, 1921–1939*. 2 vols. Detroit: Gale, 1976.

Lawrence, Una Roberts. *Lottie Moon*. Nashville: Sunday School Board of the Southern Baptist Convention, 1927.

Leahy, J. Kenneth. *As the Eagle: The Spiritual Writings of Mother Butler*. New York: P. J. Kenedy and Sons, 1954.

Leonard, Bill J., ed. *Dictionary of Baptists in America*. Downers Grove, Ill.: Inter Varsity Press, 1994.

Leonard, Karen Isaksen. *The South Asian Americans*. Westport, Conn.: Greenwood Press, 1997.

Leopold, Richard William. *Robert Dale Owen: A Biography*. Cambridge: Harvard University Press, 1940. Reprint, New York: Octagon Books, 1969.

Lerner, Gerda. *The Female Experience: An American Documentary*. Indianapolis: Bobbs-Merrill, 1977.

_____. *The Grimké Sisters from South Carolina: Rebels against Slavery*. Boston: Houghton Mifflin, 1967.

Lesniak, James G., ed. *Contemporary Authors New Revision Series*. Vol. 30. Detroit: Gale, 1990.

Levenduski, Cristine M. *Peculiar Power: A Quaker Woman Preacher in Eighteenth-Century America*. Washington, D.C.: Smithsonian Institution, 1996.

Levin, Alexandra Lee. *The Szolds of Lombard Street: A Baltimore Family, 1859–1909*. Philadelphia: Jewish Publication Society of America, 1960.

Levitan, Tina. *First Facts in American Jewish History*. Northval, N.J.: Jason Aronson, 1996.

Lewit, Jane, and Ellen Robinson Epstein. *The Bar/Bat Mitzvah Planbook*. New York: Stein and Day, 1982.

Lienesch, Michael. *Redeeming America: Piety and Politics in the New Christian Right*. Chapel Hill: University of North Carolina Press, 1993.

Lindley, Susan Hill. *"You Have Stept Out of Your Place": A History of Women and Religion in America*. Louisville, Ky.: John Knox Press, 1996.

Linkugel, Wil A., and Martha Solomon. *Anna Howard Shaw: Suffrage Orator and Social Reformer*. New York: Greenwood Press, 1991.

Lippy, Charles H., ed. *Twentieth-Century Shapers of American Popular Religion*. New York: Greenwood Press, 1989.

Lippy, Charles H., and Peter W. Williams, eds. *Encyclopedia of the American Religious Experience: Studies of Traditions and Movements*. 3 vols. New York: Charles Scribner's Sons, 1988.

Lipstadt, Deborah E. *Denying the Holocaust: The Growing Assault on Truth and Memory*. New York: The Free Press, 1993.

Litzenberg, Kathleen, ed. *Who's Who of American Women, 1997–1998*. 20th ed. New Providence, N.J.: Marquis Who's Who, 1996.

Livermore, Mary A. *The Story of My Life*. Hartford, Conn.: A. D. Worthington, 1897.

Locher, Frances C., ed. *Contemporary Authors*, vol. 104. Detroit: Gale Research, 1982.

Loewen, Harry, and Steven Nolt. *Through Fire and Water: An Overview of Mennonite History*. Scottdale, Penn.: Herald Press, 1996.

Loewenberg, Bert James, and Ruth Bogin, eds. *Black Women in Nineteenth-Century American Life: Their Words, Their Thoughts, Their Feelings.* University Park: Pennsylvania State University Press, 1976.

Logan, Rayford W., and Michael R. Winston. *Dictionary of Negro Biography.* New York: W. W. Norton, 1982.

Lorence, James J. *Enduring Voices.* 2nd ed. Lexington, Mass.: D. C. Heath, 1993.

Lowenthal, Marvin. *Henrietta Szold: Life and Letters.* 1942. Reprint, Westport, Conn.: Greenwood Press, 1975.

Lowry, Edith E., ed. *They Starve That We May Eat.* New York: Council of Women for Home Missions and Missionary Education Movement, 1938.

Ludlow, Daniel H., ed. *Encyclopedia of Mormonism.* 5 vols. New York: Macmillan, 1992.

Lueker, Erwin L., ed. *Lutheran Cyclopedia.* St. Louis, Mo.: Concordia Publishing House, 1975.

Lutz, Alma. *Created Equal: A Biography of Elizabeth Cady Stanton, 1815–1902.* New York: Octagon Books, 1974.

Lynn, Robert W., and Elliott Wright. *The Big Little School: The Hundred Years of the Sunday School.* 2nd ed. Birmingham, Ala.: Religious Education Press, 1980.

MacLaine, Shirley. *Dancing in the Light.* Toronto: Bantam Books, 1985.

_____. *Going Within: A Guide for Inner Transformation.* New York: Bantam Books, 1989.

_____. *My Lucky Stars: A Hollywood Memoir.* New York: Bantam Books, 1995.

_____. *Out on a Limb.* New York: Bantam Books, 1983.

_____. *You Can Get There from Here.* New York: W. W. Norton, 1975.

Magill, Frank, ed. *Great Lives from History: American Women Series.* 5 vols. Pasadena, Calif.: Salem Press, 1995.

Malinowski, Sharon, ed. *Notable Native Americans.* Detroit: Gale, 1995.

Malson, Micheline R., et al. *Black Women in America.* Chicago: University of Chicago Press, 1990.

Mansbridge, Jane J. *Why We Lost the ERA.* Chicago: University of Chicago Press, 1986.

Marcus, Jacob R. *The American Jewish Woman: A Documentary History.* New York: KTAV Publishing, 1981.

_____. *The American Jewish Woman, 1654–1980.* New York: KTAV Publishing, 1981.

Marshall, Catherine. *Christy.* New York: McGraw-Hill, 1967.

_____. *Julie.* New York: McGraw-Hill, 1984.

_____. *A Man Called Peter.* New York: McGraw-Hill, 1951.

_____. *Mr. Jones, Meet the Master: Sermons and Prayers of Peter Marshall.* Old Tappan, N.J.: Fleming H. Revell, 1949. Reprint, 1982.

_____. *To Live Again.* New York: McGraw Hill, 1957.

Marshall, Helen E. *Dorothea Dix: Forgotten Samaritan.* New York: Russell and Russell, 1937.

Marshall, Peter. *The Best of Peter Marshall.* Comp. and ed. Catherine Marshall. Carmel, N.Y.: Guideposts, 1983.

Martin, Carter W. *The True Country: Themes in the Fiction of Flannery O'Connor.* Nashville: Vanderbilt University Press, 1969.

Mather, George A., and Larry A. Nichols. *Dictionary of Cults, Sects, Religions and the Occult.* Grand Rapids, Mich.: Zondervan Publishing, 1993.

Matsuoka, Fumitaka. *Out of Silence: Emerging Themes in Asian American Churches.* Cleveland, Ohio: United Church Press, 1995.

Maynard, Theodore. *A Fire Was Lighted: The Life of Rose Hawthorne Lathrop.* Milwaukee, Wis.: Bruce Publishing, 1948.

McFague, Sallie. *The Body of God: An Ecological Theology.* Minneapolis: Fortress Press, 1993.

McHenry, Robert, ed. *Liberty's Women.* Springfield, Mass.: G. and C. Merriam Company, 1980.

McLloyd, Edna W., and Dorothy Adams Peck. "The Women's Missionary Society Journey from Vision to Reality." Unpublished paper. Washington, D.C.: Women's Missionary Society, African Methodist Episcopal Church, n.d., c. 1997.

McLoughlin, William G. *Soul Liberty: The Baptists' Struggle in New England, 1630–1833.* Hanover and London: University Press of New England, 1991.

McNamara, Jo Ann Kay. *Sisters in Arms: Catholic Nuns through Two Millennia.* Cambridge: Harvard University Press, 1996.

Melton, J. Gordon. *Biographical Dictionary of American Cult and Sect Leaders.* New York: Garland, 1986.

_____. *Encyclopedia of American Religions.* 4th ed. Detroit: Gale, 1993.

_____. *Encyclopedic Handbook of Cults in America.* New York: Garland, 1986, revised 1992.

_____. *New Age Encyclopedia.* Detroit: Gale, 1990.

_____. *Religious Leaders of America.* Detroit: Gale, 1991.

Melton, J. Gordon, et al. *New Age Almanac.* New York: Visible Ink, 1991.

Melville, Annabelle M. *Elizabeth Bayley Seton, 1774–1821.* New York: Charles Scribner's Sons, 1976.

Merrill, Walter M. *Against Wind and Tide: A Biography of Wm. Lloyd Garrison.* Cambridge, Mass.: Harvard University Press, 1963.

Miller, Perry. *The New England Mind: From Colony to Province.* Boston: Beacon Press, 1953.

Miller, Randall M., and Paul A. Cimbala, eds., *American Reform and Reformers: A Biographical Dictionary.* Westport, Conn.: Greenwood Press, 1996.

Miller, William D. *A Harsh and Dreadful Love: Dorothy Day and the Catholic Worker Movement.* New York: Liveright, 1973.

Miller, William McElwell. *The Baha'i Faith: Its History and Teachings.* South Pasadena, Calif.: William Carey Library, 1974.

Miura, Isshu, and Ruth Fuller Sasaki. *The Koan Zen.* New York: Harcourt, Brace and World, 1965.

Modesto, Ruby, and Guy Mount. *Not for Innocent Ears: Spiritual Traditions of a Desert Cahuilla Medicine Woman.* Arcata, Calif.: Sweetlight Books, 1980.

Mohr, James. *Abortion in America: The Origins and Evolution of National Policy.* New York: Oxford University Press, 1978.

Moore, Joanna P. *"In Christ's Stead": Autobiographical Sketches.* Chicago: Woman's Baptist Home Mission Society, 1903.

Moore, R. Laurence. *In Search of White Crows: Spiritualism, Parapsychology, and American Culture.* New York: Oxford University Press, 1977.

Morantz-Sanchez, Regina Markell. *Sympathy and Science: Women Physicians in American Medicine.* New York: Oxford University Press, 1985.

Morgan, Edmund S. *The Puritan Dilemma: The Story of John Winthrop.* New York: HarperCollins, 1958.

Mountain Wolf Woman, with Nancy Oestreich Lurie, ed. *Mountain Wolf Woman: Sister of Crashing Thunder.* Ann Arbor: University of Michigan Press, 1966.

Murdoch, Norman H. *Origins of the Salvation Army.* Knoxville: University of Tennessee Press, 1994.

Murphy, Larry G., et al. *Encyclopedia of African-American Religions.* New York: Garland, 1993.

Myers, Gloria E. "The Apostolic Faith through the Lens of Sociology." Unpublished paper. Portland, Oreg.: Portland State University, 1989.

Nasso, Christine, ed. *Contemporary Authors.* Vols. 21–24, first revision. Detroit: Gale, 1977.

Nathan, Maud. *Once Upon a Time and Today.* New York: G. P. Putnam's Sons, 1933.

Nation, Carry A. *The Use and Need of the Life of Carry A. Nation.* Rev. ed. Topeka, Kan.: F. M. Stevest Sons, 1909.

Neidle, Cecyle S. *America's Immigrant Women.* Boston: Twayne, 1975.

Nelson, E. Clifford, ed. *The Lutherans in North America.* Philadelphia: Fortress Press, 1975.

_____. *Lutheranism in North America, 1914–1970.* Minneapolis: Augsburg Publishing House, 1972.

Nelson, Geoffrey K. *Spiritualism and Society.* New York: Schocken Books, 1969.

New Catholic Encyclopedia. 17 vols. New York: McGraw-Hill, 1967.

Nichol, Francis D. *Ellen G. White and Her Critics.* Takoma Park, Md.: Review and Herald, 1951.

Nichols, Mary (Sargeant). *Mary Lyndon, or Revelations of a Life.* New York: Stringer and Townsend, 1855.

Nolt, Steven M. *A History of the Amish.* Intercourse, Penn: Good Books, 1992.

Nordhoff, Charles. *American Utopias.* Stockbridge, Mass.: Berkshire House, 1993.

Noveck, Simon, ed. *Great Jewish Personalities in Modern Times.* Clinton, Mass.: Colonial Press, 1960.

Numbers, Ronald L. *Prophetess of Health: A Study of Ellen G. White.* New York: Harper and Row, 1976.

O'Barr, Jean Fox. *Feminism in Action.* Chapel Hill: University of North Carolina Press, 1994.

Occhiogrosso, Peter. *The Joy of Sects: A Spirited Guide to the World's Religious Traditions.* New York: Doubleday, 1994.

O'Connor, Flannery. *The Habit of Being: Letters of Flannery O'Connor,* ed. Sally Fitzgerald. New York: Farrar, Straus, and Giroux, 1979.

O'Connor, June. *The Moral Vision of Dorothy Day.* New York: Crossroad, 1991.

O'Faolain, Julia, and Lauro Martines, eds. *Not in God's Image: Women in History from the Greeks to the Victorians.* 2nd ed. New York: Harper Torchbooks, 1973.

O'Hair, Madalyn M. *What on Earth Is an Atheist?* New York: Arno Press and the New York Times, 1969, 1972.

Olasky, Marvin N. *The Tragedy of American Compassion.* Wheaton, Ill: Crossway Books, 1992.

O'Neil, Robert. *Classrooms in the Crossfire: The Rights and Interests of Students, Parents, Teachers, Administrators, Librarians, and the Community.* Bloomington: Indiana University Press, 1981.

O'Neill, William L. *Everyone Was Brave.* Chicago: Quadrangle Books, 1969.

Painter, Nell Irvin. *Sojourner Truth: A Life, A Symbol.* New York: W. W. Norton, 1996.

Parker, Julie F. *Careers for Women as Clergy.* New York: Rosen Publishing Group, 1993.

Parry, Melanie, ed. *Larousse Dictionary of Women.* New York: Larousse, 1996.

Paul, Diana Y. *Women in Buddhism: Images of the Feminine in Mahayana Tradition.* 2nd ed. Berkeley: University of California Press, 1985.

Pavlos, Andrew J. *The Cult Experience.* Westport, Conn.: Greenwood Press, 1982.

Peabody, Lucy. *Henry Wayland Peabody, Merchant.* West Medford, Mass.: M. H. Leavis, 1909.

Peare, Catherine Owens. *Mary McLeod Bethune.* New York: Vanguard Press, 1951.

Peel, Robert. *Mary Baker Eddy: The Years of Authority.* New York: Holt, Rinehart & Winston, 1977.

_____. *Mary Baker Eddy: The Years of Discovery.* New York: Holt, Rinehart & Winston, 1966.

_____. *Mary Baker Eddy: The Years of Trial.* Boston: Christian Science Publishing Society, 1971.

Penton, M. James. *Apocalypse Delayed: The Story of Jehovah's Witnesses.* Toronto: University of Toronto Press, 1986.

Perkins, A. J. G., and Theresa Wolfson. *Frances Wright: Free Enquirer: The Study of a Temperament.* Philadelphia: Porcupine Press, 1972.

Peterson's Guide to Four-Year Colleges, 1997. 27th ed. Princeton, N.J.: Peterson's, 1996.

Phelps, Shirelle, ed., *Who's Who among African Americans, 1996/97.* Detroit: Gale, 1996.

Phillips, Roderick. *Putting Asunder: A History of Divorce in Western Society.* Cambridge: Cambridge University Press, 1988.

_____. *Untying the Knot: A Short History of Divorce.* Cambridge: Cambridge University Press, 1991.

Piehl, Mel. *Breaking Bread: The Catholic Worker and the Origin of Catholic Radicals in America.* Philadelphia: Temple University Press, 1982.

Pieper, Jeanne. *The Catholic Woman: Difficult Choices in a Modern World.* Los Angeles: Lowell House, 1993.

Pivar, David J. *Purity Crusade: Sexual Morality and Social Control, 1868–1900.* Westport, Conn.: Greenwood Press, 1973.

Ploski, Harry A., and James Williams, comp. and ed. *The Negro Almanac: A Reference*

Work on the African American. 5th ed. Detroit: Gale, 1989.

Plowden, Martha Ward. *Famous Firsts of Black Women*. Gretna, La.: Pelican Publishing, 1993.

Podell, Janet, ed. *The Annual Obituary, 1981*. New York: St. Martin's Press, 1982.

Porucker, Gottfried de. *H. P. Blavatsky: The Mystery*. San Diego: Point Loma Publications, 1974.

Powell, Lyman P. *Mary Baker Eddy: A Life Size Portrait*. London: Nisbet and Co., 1930. Reprint, Boston: Christian Science Publishing Society, 1950.

Powers, Richard Gid. *Not without Honor: The History of American Anticommunism*. New York: Free Press, 1995.

Prebish, Charles S. *American Buddhism*. North Scituate, Mass.: Duxbury Press, 1979.

Priesand, Sally. *Judaism and the New Woman*. New York: Behrman House, 1975.

Proctor, Priscilla, and William Proctor. *Women in the Pulpit: Is God an Equal Opportunity Employer?* Garden City, N.Y.: Doubleday, 1976.

Prucha, Francis Paul. *American Indian Policy in Crisis: Christian Reformers and the Indian, 1865–1900*. Norman: University of Oklahoma Press, 1976.

Pruitt, Anna Seward. *Up from Zero*. Richmond, Va.: Rice Press, 1938.

Qoyawayma, Polingaysi (Elizabeth Q. White). *No Turning Back*. Albuquerque: University of New Mexico Press, 1964.

Quarles, Bernard. *Black Abolitionists*. New York: Oxford University Press, 1969.

Queen, Edward L., II, et al., eds. *The Encyclopedia of American Religious History*. New York: Facts on File, 1996.

Read, Phyllis J., and Bernard L. Witlieb. *The Book of Women's Firsts*. New York: Random House, 1992.

Reed, James. *From Private Vice to Public Virtue: The Birth Control Movement and American Society since 1830*. New York: Basic Books, 1978.

Ribuffo, Leo P. *The Old Christian Right: The Protestant Far Right from the Great Depression to the Cold War*. Philadelphia: Temple University Press, 1983.

Rice, Edwin Wilbur. *The Sunday School Movement, 1780–1917 and the American Sunday-School Union, 1817–1917*. New York: Arno Press, 1971.

Richardson, Marilyn. *Black Women and Religion: A Bibliography*. Boston: G. K. Hall, 1980.

Richardson, Robert D., Jr. *Emerson: The Mind on Fire*. Berkeley: University of California Press, 1995.

Robbins, Thomas. *Cults, Converts, and Charisma: The Sociology of New Religious Movements*. London: Sage Publications, 1988.

Robinson, David. *The Unitarians and the Universalists*. Westport, Conn.: Greenwood Press, 1985.

Robinson, Marion O. *Eight Women of the YWCA*. New York: National Board of the Young Women's Christian Association of the U.S.A., 1966.

Rogal, Samuel J. *Sisters of Sacred Song*. New York: Garland, 1981.

Rogers, Horatio. *Mary Dyer of Rhode Island: The Quaker Martyr*. Providence, R.I.: Preston and Rogers, 1896.

Rose, Anne C. *Transcendentalism as a Social Movement, 1830–1850*. New Haven: Yale University Press, 1981.

Rowbotham, Sheila. *Women in Movement: Feminism and Social Action*. New York: Routledge, 1991.

Rubin, Eva R., ed. *The Abortion Controversy: A Documentary History*. Westport, Conn.: Greenwood Press, 1994.

Ruether, Rosemary Radford. *Gaia and God: An Ecofeminist Theology of Earth Healing*. San Francisco: Harper, 1992.

_____. *Religion and Sexism: Images of Women in the Christian and Jewish Tradition*. New York: Simon and Schuster, 1974.

_____. *Sexism and God-Talk: Toward a Feminist Theology*. Boston: Beacon Press, 1983.

Ruether, Rosemary Radford, and Eleanor McLaughlin, eds. *Women of Spirit: Female Leadership in the Jewish and Christian Traditions*. New York: Simon and Schuster, 1979.

Ruether, Rosemary Radford, and Rosemary Skinner Keller, eds. 3 vols. *Women and Re-*

ligion in America. San Francisco: Harper and Row, 1981–1986.

Rugg, Winnifred King. *Unafraid: A Life of Anne Hutchinson.* Boston: Houghton Mifflin, 1930.

Ruiz, Vicki L. *From out of the Shadows: Mexican Women in Twentieth-Century America.* New York: Oxford University Press, 1998.

Rutledge, Paul. *The Role of Religion in Ethnic Self-Identity: A Vietnamese Community.* Lanham, Md.: University Press of America, 1985.

Ryan, Mary P. *Cradle of the Middle Class: The Family in Oneida County, New York, 1790–1865.* Cambridge: Cambridge University Press, 1981.

Salem, Dorothy C., ed. *African American Women: A Biographical Dictionary.* New York: Garland, 1993.

Sandoval, Moises. *On the Move: A History of the Hispanic Church in the United States.* Maryknoll, N.Y.: Orbis Books, 1990.

Sasaki, Ruth Fuller. *Zen: A Method for Religious Awakening.* Kyoto: First Zen Institute of America in Japan, 1959.

Schlafly, Phyllis. *The Power of the Positive Woman.* New Rochelle, N.Y.: Arlington House, 1977.

Schneider, Susan Weidner. *Jewish and Female: Choices and Changes in Our Lives Today.* New York: Simon and Schuster, 1985.

Schwerin, Jules. *Got to Tell It: Mahalia Jackson, Queen of Gospel.* New York: Oxford University Press, 1992.

Selvidge, Marla J. *Notorious Voices: Feminist Biblical Interpretation, 1500–1920.* New York: Continuum Publishing Company, 1996.

Shakir, Evelyn. *Bint Arab: Arab and Arab American Women in the United States.* Westport, Conn.: Praeger, 1997.

Shaw, Anna Howard. *The Story of a Pioneer.* New York: Harper and Brothers, 1915. Reprint, Kraus Reprint, 1970.

Shea, Daniel B. *Spiritual Autobiography in Early America.* Princeton: Princeton University Press, 1968.

Shepard, Leslie, ed. *Encyclopedia of Occultism and Parapsychology.* 2 vols. 3rd ed. Detroit: Gale, 1991.

Shim, Steve S. *Korean Immigrant Churches Today in Southern California.* San Francisco: R & E Associates, 1977.

Sicherman, Barbara, and Carol Hurd Green, eds. *Notable American Women: The Modern Period.* Cambridge, Mass.: Belknap Press, 1980.

Silberger, Julius, Jr., M.D. *Mary Baker Eddy: An Interpretive Biography of the Founder of Christian Science.* Boston: Little, Brown, 1980.

Skardon, Alvin W. *William Augustus Mühlenberg.* Philadelphia: University of Pennsylvania Press, 1971.

Sklar, Kathryn Kish, and Thomas Dublin. *Women and Power in American History: A Reader, Vol. 1 to 1880.* Englewood Cliffs, N.J.: Prentice-Hall, 1991.

Slater, Elinor, and Robert Slater. *Great Jewish Women.* Middle Village, N.Y.: Jonathan David Publishers, 1994.

Smith, Betsy Covington. *Breakthrough: Women in Religion.* New York: Walker and Company, 1978.

Smith, Hannah Whitall. *The Christian's Secret of a Happy Life.* Old Tappan, N.J.: Fleming H. Revell, 1875.

Smith, Jessie Carney, ed. *Epic Lives: One Hundred Black Women Who Made a Difference.* Detroit: Visible Ink Press, 1993.

_____. *Notable Black American Women.* Detroit: Gale, 1992.

_____. *Notable Black American Women, Book II.* New York: Gale, 1996.

Smith, Jonathan Z., ed. *The HarperCollins Dictionary of Religion.* San Francisco: HarperCollins, 1995.

Smith, Logan Pearsall, ed. *Philadelphia Quaker: The Letters of Hannah Whitall Smith.* New York: Harcourt, Brace and Company, 1950.

_____. *Unforgotten Years.* Boston: Little, Brown, 1939.

Smith-Rosenberg, Carroll. *Disorderly Conduct: Visions of Gender in Victorian America.* New York: Alfred A. Knopf, 1985.

Smylie, James H. *A Brief History of the Presbyterians.* Louisville, Kent.: Geneva Press, 1996.

Spretnak, Charlene, ed. *The Politics of Women's Spirituality: Essays on the Rise of*

Spiritual Power within the Feminist Movement. Garden City, N.Y.: Anchor Press, 1982.

Stanley, Susie Cunningham. *Feminist Pillar of Fire: The Life of Alma White.* Cleveland, Ohio: Pilgrim Press, 1993.

Stansell, Christine. *City of Women: Sex and Class in New York, 1789–1860.* Urbana: University of Illinois Press, 1987.

Stanton, Elizabeth Cady. *Eighty Years and More: Reminiscences, 1815–1897.* T. Fisher Unwin, 1898. Republished, Boston: Northeastern University Press, 1993.

_____. *The Woman's Bible: Parts I and II.* New York: European Publishing Company, 1895 and 1898. Reprint, New York: Arno Press, 1972.

Stanton, Elizabeth Cady, et al., eds. *History of Woman Suffrage.* 6 vols. New York: Arno Press, 1969.

Starhawk. *The Spiral Dance: A Rebirth of the Ancient Religion of the Great Goddess.* San Francisco: HarperCollins, 10th anniversary ed., 1989.

Steele, Robert V. P. *Storming Heaven: The Lives and Turmoils of Minnie Kennedy and Aimee Semple McPherson.* New York: Morrow, 1970.

Stein, Gordon, ed. *The Encyclopedia of Unbelief.* Buffalo, N.Y.: Prometheus Books, 1985.

Stember, Charles Herbert. *Jews in the Mind of America.* New York: Basic Books, 1966.

Stetson, Erlene, and Linda David. *Glorying in Tribulation: The Lifework of Sojourner Truth.* East Lansing: Michigan State University Press, 1994.

Stewart, James Brewer. *Holy Warriors: The Abolitionists and American Slavery.* New York: Hill and Wang, 1976.

Stewart, Maria W. *Maria W. Stewart: America's First Black Woman Political Writer.* Bloomington: Indiana University Press, 1987.

Stewart, Walter Sinclair. *Later Baptist Missionaries and Pioneers.* 2 vols. Philadelphia: Judson Press, 1928–1929.

Stoehr, Taylor. *Free Love in America: A Documentary History.* New York: AMS Press, 1979.

Stoltzfeus, Louise. *Amish Women: Lives and Stories.* Intercourse, Penn.: Good Books, 1994.

Stroup, Herbert. *Social Welfare Pioneers.* Chicago: Nelson-Hall Publishers, 1986.

Sullivan, Mary Louise. *Mother Cabrini: "Italian Immigrant of the Century."* New York: Center for Migration Studies, 1992.

Swander, Mary. *Out of the World: A Woman's Life among the Amish.* New York: Viking, 1995.

Sweet, Leonard I. *The Minister's Wife: Her Role in Nineteenth-Century American Evangelicalism.* Philadelphia: Temple University Press, 1983.

Sweet, William Warren. *Methodism in American History.* New York: Methodist Book Concern, 1933.

Synan, Vinson. *The Holiness-Pentecostal Tradition: Charismatic Movements in the Twentieth Century.* 2nd ed. Grand Rapids, Mich.: William B. Eerdmans Publishing, 1997.

Tarry, Ellen. *Katharine Drexel: Friend of the Oppressed.* Nashville: Winston-Derek Publishers, 1990.

Taylor, Anne. *Annie Besant: A Biography.* Oxford: Oxford University Press, 1992.

_____. *Visions of Harmony: A Study in Nineteenth-Century Millenarianism.* Oxford: Clarendon Press, 1987.

Taylor, Robert Lewis. *Vessel of Wrath: The Life and Times of Carry Nation.* New York: New American Library, 1966.

Taylor, Samuel W. *Rocky Mountain Empire: The Latter-Day Saints Today.* New York: Macmillan, 1978.

ten Boom, Corrie, with C. C. Carlson. *In My Father's House: The Years before "The Hiding Place."* Carmel, N.Y.: Guideposts, 1976.

ten Boom, Corrie, with John Sherrill and Elizabeth Sherrill. *The Hiding Place.* Washington Depot, Conn.: Chosen Books, 1971.

Trotsky, Susan M., ed. *Contemporary Authors.* Vol. 39. New Revision Series. Detroit: Gale, 1992.

_____. Vol. 129. *Contemporary Authors.* Detroit: Gale, 1990.

Truth, Sojourner, and Frances W. Titus. *Narrative of Sojourner Truth.* 1875. Reprint,

New York: Arno Press and the New York Times, 1968.

Tyms, James D. *The Rise of Religious Education among Negro Baptists.* Washington, D.C.: University Press of America, 1979.

Tyrell, Ian. *Sobering Up: From Temperance to Prohibition in Antebellum America.* Westport, Conn.: Greenwood Press, 1979.

Uglow, Jennifer S. *The Continuum Dictionary of Women's Biography.* New York: Continuum, 1989.

Ulrich, Laurel Thatcher. *Good Wives: Image and Reality in the Lives of Women in Northern New England, 1650–1750.* New York: Alfred A. Knopf, 1982.

Underhill, Lois Beachy. *The Woman Who Ran for President: The Many Lives of Victoria Woodhull.* Binghamton, N.Y.: Bridge Works Publishing, 1995.

Ussery, Annie Wright. *The Story of Kathleen Mallory.* Nashville: Broadman Press, 1956.

Utter, Glenn H., and John W. Storey. *The Religious Right: A Reference Handbook.* Santa Barbara, Calif.: ABC-CLIO, 1995.

Van de Sande, Wendy S., ed. *Black Americans Information Directory, 1994–95.* 3rd ed. Detroit: Gale, 1993.

Van Doren, Mark, ed. *The Portable Emerson.* New York: Viking, 1946.

Van Wagoner, Richard S., and Steven C. Walker. *A Book of Mormons.* Salt Lake City: Signature Books, 1982.

Vecsey, Christopher, ed. *Handbook of American Indian Religious Freedom.* New York: Crossroad, 1991.

Vogel, Dan. *Emma Lazarus.* Boston: Twayne, 1980.

Walls, William J. *The African Methodist Episcopal Zion Church: Reality of the Black Church.* Charlotte, N.C.: A.M.E. Zion Publishing, 1974.

Walsh, Frank. *Sin and Censorship: The Catholic Church and the Motion Picture Industry.* New Haven: Yale University Press, 1996.

Warenski, Marilyn. *Patriarchs and Politics: The Plight of the Mormon Woman.* New York: McGraw-Hill, 1978.

Warner, Wayne E. *The Woman Evangelist.* Metuchen, N.J.: Scarecrow Press, 1986.

Westoff, Charles F., and Norman B. Ryder. *The Contraceptive Revolution.* Princeton, N.J.: Princeton University Press, 1977.

White, Anna, and Leila S. Taylor. *Shakerism: Its Meaning and Message.* Columbus, Ohio: Press of Fred J. Heer, 1904.

Whitworth, John McKelvie. *God's Blueprints: A Sociological Study of Three Utopian Sects.* New York: Allen Lake, 1993.

Wilcox, Ella Wheeler. *Maurine and Other Poems.* Chicago: W. B. Conkey, 1888.

_____. *Poems of Pleasure.* Chicago: W. B. Conkey, 1902.

Willard, Frances E. *Woman and Temperance.* Hartford, Conn.: Park Publishing, 1883. Reprint, New York: Arno Press, 1972.

Williams, Delores S. *Sisters in the Wilderness: The Challenge of Womanist God-Talk.* Maryknoll, N.Y.: Orbis Books, 1993.

Williams, Michael. *The African American Encyclopedia.* 6 vols. New York: Marshall Cavendish, 1993.

Williams, Norma. *The Mexican American Family: Tradition and Change.* Dix Hills, N.Y.: General Halls, 1990.

Williams, Selma R. *Divine Rebel: The Life of Anne Marbury Hutchinson.* New York: Holt, Rinehart, & Winston, 1981.

Wilson, Otto, with Robert South Barrett. *Fifty Years' Work with Girls, 1883–1933: A Story of the Florence Crittenton Homes.* 1933. Reprint, New York: Arno Press, 1974.

Wilson, Philip Whitwell. *General Evangeline Booth of the Salvation Army.* New York: Scribner's, 1948.

Wisbey, Herbert A., Jr. *Pioneer Prophetess: Jemima Wilkinson, the Publick Universal Friend.* Ithaca, N.Y.: Cornell University Press, 1964.

_____. *Soldiers without Swords: A History of the Salvation Army in the United States.* New York: Macmillan, 1955.

Woloch, Nancy. *Women and the American Experience.* New York: Alfred A. Knopf, 1984.

World Methodist Council and the Commission on Archives and History. *The Encyclopedia of World Methodism.* 2 vols.

Nashville: United Methodist Publishing, 1974.

Wright, Conrad, ed. *A Stream of Light: A Sesquicentennial History of American Unitarianism*. Boston: Unitarian Universalist Association, 1975.

Wuthnow, Robert. *The Struggle for America's Soul: Evangelicals, Liberals and Secularism*. Grand Rapids, Mich.: William B. Eerdmans Publishing, 1989.

Young, Bette Roth. *Emma Lazarus in Her World: Life and Letters*. Philadelphia: Jewish Publication Society, 1995.

Zilboorg, Caroline, ed. *Women's Firsts*. Detroit: Gale, 1997.

Zophy, Angela Howard, with Frances M. Kavenik, eds. *Handbook of American Women's History*. New York: Garland, 1990.

Articles

Associated Press. "Promise Keepers Ready to Atone." *Sarasota Herald-Tribune* (October 4, 1997): 3A.

Briggs, Kenneth A. "Methodists Elect 19 to Leadership." *New York Times* (July 29, 1984): 19.

Cantor, Aviva. "Rabbi Eilberg." *Ms.* 14, no. 6 (December 1985): 45–46.

"The Drive against Lynching." *Woman's Home Companion* (August 1935).

"End of a Vigil." *Time* 125 (February 25, 1985): 61.

"Feminists to Protest Promise Keepers." *Fort Worth Star-Telegram*, reprinted in *Sarasota Herald-Tribune* (September 21, 1997): 4A.

Hambrick-Stowe, Charles E. "The Spiritual Pilgrimage of Sarah Osborn (1714–1796)." *Church History* 61 (December 1992): 408–421.

Hampson, Rick. "Movement Builds to Canonize Dorothy Day." *USA Today* (March 12, 1998): 4.

Harder, Mary W. "Sex Roles in the Jesus Movement." *Social Compass* 21, no. 3 (1974): 345–353.

Haywood, Carl. "The Authority and Empowerment of Women among Spiritualist Groups." *Journal for the Scientific Study of Religion* 22, no. 2 (June 3, 1983): 156–166.

Kreider, Eleanor Graber. "Rekindling the Vision." *WMSC Voice* (May–June 1990).

Lyles, Jean Caffey. "An Improbable Episcopal Choice." *Christian Century* (August 13–20, 1980): 779–780.

MacMaster, Eve. "The Story of Clara Eby Steiner and the Beginnings of WMSC." *WMSC Voice* (January–April 1990).

Marshall, Marilyn. "Leontine T. C. Kelly: First Black Woman Bishop." *Ebony* 40, no. 6 (November 1984): 164.

Maser, Frederick E. "The Day America Needed Bibles." *Religion in Life* 45 (1976): 138–145.

McCammon, Dorothy, and Beulah Kauffman, as told to Saralyn Yoder. "Cautious Progress in a Time of Change, WMSC in the '60s and '70s. *WMSC Voice* (July–August 1990).

Moore, Harry Thornton. "The Lady Patriot's Book." *The New Republic* 85 (January 8, 1936).

Niebuhr, Gustav. "Wives Urged to Follow Lead of Husbands." New York Times News Service in *Sarasota Herald-Tribune* (June 19, 1998).

Norton, Mary Beth. "'My Resting Reaping Times': Sarah Osborn's Defense of Her 'Unfeminine' Activities, 1767." *Signs* 2 (winter 1976): 516–529.

"Rachel Henderlite: First Woman Ordained by Presbyterian Church, U.S. Taught Six Years at Austin Seminary." Obituary (c. November 19, 1991).

"Rachel Henderlite: 1905–1991." *The Presbyterian Outlook* (December 2–9, 1991).

"Rachel Henderlite Dies at Her Austin Home." *Windows*. Austin Presbyterian Theological Seminary (November 1991).

Smith-Rosenberg, Carroll. "Beauty, the Beast, and the Militant Woman: A Case Study in Sex Roles and Social Stress in Jacksonian America." *American Quarterly* 23 (1971): 562–584.

Testa, Karen. "Christian Women Form Praise Keepers Group." *Sarasota Herald-Tribune* (December 7, 1996): 4E.

Van Gelder, Lindsy. "A Yahoo's Guide to Mary Daly." *Ms.* (February 1979).

Weisenfeld, Judith. "'Who Is Sufficient for These Things?' Sara G. Stanley and the American Missionary Association, 1864–1868." *Church History* 60, no. 4 (December 1991): 493–507.

White, Ann. "Counting the Cost of Faith: America's Early Female Missionaries." *Church History* 57: no. 2 (March 1988): 19–30.

Wooten, Dudley G. "A Noble Ursuline." *Catholic World* 111 (August 1920): 588–602.

"Words of the Week." *Jet* 75, no. 15 (January 16, 1989): 40.

Primary Sources

Association of Southern Women for the Prevention of Lynching. "The Business of Lynching." Bulletin No. 4, n.d.

Chappell, Sister Patricia J. Letter to author (July 21, 1997).

Church Women United. Pamphlet. "Church Women United." N.d., c. 1996.

_____. Pamphlet. "Church Women United Legislative Office, Washington, D.C." N.d., c. 1996.

_____. *Directory and Information Handbook.* N.d., c. 1996.

Concerned Women for America. Information packet with letter (March 7, 1997).

Hall, Lara J., ed. "WMSC Newsletter." Women's Missionary and Service Commission of the Mennonite Church (April 15, 1997).

International Association of Women Ministers. Brochure, N.d., c. 1996.

National Black Sisters' Conference. Pamphlet. "National Black Sisters' Conference." N.d., c. 1997.

National Black Sisters' Conference. Statement. "National Black Sisters' Conference." N.d., c. 1997.

National Council of Catholic Women. *Catholic Woman* (May/June 1997 and July/August 1997).

Rodgers, Kathryn, Women's Missionary Service and Commission of the Mennonite Church. Note to author. N.d., c. August 1997.

Woman's Missionary Union. *Annual Report 1996.* N.d., c. 1997.

Women's League for Conservative Judaism. "Mathilde Schechter: Founder of Women's League for Conservative Judaism." N.d., c. 1997.

_____. "Women's League for Conservative Judaism: What it is . . . What it does!" N.d., c. 1997.

Wooten, Luree, Coordinator of Women's Ministries, Woman's Home and Foreign Mission Society. Letter to author (September 10, 1997).

Chapters in Books

Armstrong, Thomas F. "The American Missionary Association." In Angela Howard Zophy with Frances M. Kavenik, eds., *Handbook of American Women's History.* New York: Garland, 1990.

Assensoh, A. B. "Coretta Scott King." In Jessie Carney Smith, ed., *Epic Lives: One Hundred Black Women Who Made a Difference.* Detroit: Visible Ink Press, 1993.

Barnes, Nancy J. "Women in Buddhism." In Sharma Arvind, *Today's Woman in World Religions.* Albany: State University of New York Press, 1994.

Beck, Martha Nibley. "Roles of Women." In Daniel H. Ludlow, ed., *Encyclopedia of Mormonism.* Vol. 4. New York: Macmillan, 1992.

Bonde, Deborah Dawson. "Spalding, Eliza Hart." In Angela Howard Zophy with Frances M. Kavenik, eds., *Handbook of American Women's History.* New York: Garland, 1990.

Boyer, Horace Clarence. "Shirley Caesar." In Darlene Clark Hine, ed., *Black Women in America: An Historical Encyclopedia.* Brooklyn, N.Y.: Carlson Publishing, 1993.

Cazier, Shirley A. "Aurelia Spencer Rogers." In Daniel H. Ludlow, ed., *Encyclopedia of Mormonism.* Vol. 3. New York: Macmillan, 1992.

Chineworth, M. A. "Oblate Sisters of Providence." In *New Catholic Encyclopedia.* Vol. 10. New York: McGraw-Hill, 1967.

Cott, Nancy F. "Divorce and the Changing Status of Women in Eighteenth-Century Massachusetts." In Kathryn Kish Sklar and Thomas Dublin, *Women and Power in*

American History: A Reader, Vol. 1 to 1880. Englewood Cliffs, N.J.: Prentice-Hall, 1991.

Cutler, Su A. "Rosemary Radford Ruether." In Frank Magill, ed., *Great Lives from History: American Women Series*. Pasadena, Calif.: Salem Press, 1995.

Díaz-Stevens, Ana María. "Latinas and the Church." In Jay P. Dolan and Allan Figueroa Deck, eds., *Hispanic Catholic Culture in the U.S.: Issues and Concerns*. Notre Dame: University of Notre Dame Press, 1994.

Diehl, David W. "Theology and Feminism." In June Steffensen Hagen, ed., *Gender Matters: Women's Studies for the Christian Community*. Grand Rapids, Mich.: Academic Books, 1990.

Dykes, DeWitt C., Jr. "Leontine Kelly." In Jessie Carney Smith, ed., *Epic Lives: One Hundred Black Women Who Made a Difference*. Detroit: Visible Ink Press, 1993.

Endy, Melvin B., Jr. "The Society of Friends." In Charles H. Lippy and Peter W. Williams, eds., *Encyclopedia of the American Religious Experience: Studies of Traditions and Movements*. Vol. 1 of 3. New York: Charles Scribner's Sons, 1988.

Estep, Kimberly K. "Amy Eilberg." In Frank Magill, ed., *Great Lives from History: American Women Series*. 5 vols. Pasadena, Calif.: Salem Press, 1995.

———. "Frances Xavier Cabrini." In Frank Magill, ed., *Great Lives from History: American Women Series*. 5 vols. Pasadena, Calif.: Salem Press, 1995.

———. "Sarah Jane Farmer." In Frank Magill, ed., *Great Lives from History: American Women Series*. 5 vols. Pasadena, Calif.: Salem Press, 1995.

Fitzgerald, Maureen. "Transcendentalism." In Angela Howard Zophy, ed., with Frances M. Kavenik, *Handbook of American Women's History*. New York: Garland, 1990.

Foote, Julia A. "A Brand Plucked from the Fire." *Spiritual Narratives*. New York: Oxford University Press, 1988.

Gilkes, Cheryl Townsend. "'Together in Harness': Women's Traditions in the Sanctified Church." In Micheline R. Malson, et al.,

Black Women in America: Social Science Perspectives. Chicago: University of Chicago Press, 1990.

Gillenwater, Karen. "The Oneida Community." In Angela Howard Zophy, ed., with Frances M. Kavenik, *Handbook of American Women's History*. New York: Garland, 1990.

Gordon, Sarah. "Flannery O'Connor." In Angela Howard Zophy, ed., with Frances M. Kavenik, *Handbook of American Women's History*. New York: Garland, 1990.

Graves, Lawrence L. "Brown, Olympia." In Edward T. James, ed., *Notable American Women, 1607–1950*. 3 vols. Cambridge: Harvard University, Belknap Press, 1971.

Grindal, Gracia. "How Lutheran Women Came to Be Ordained." In Gloria E. Bengtson, ed., *Lutheran Women in Ordained Ministry, 1970–1995*. Minneapolis: Augsburg, 1995.

Hardesty, Nancy, Lucille Sider Dayton, and Donald W. Dayton. "Women in the Holiness Movement: Feminism in the Evangelical Tradition." In Rosemary Radford Ruether and Eleanor McLaughlin, eds., *Women of Spirit: Female Leadership in the Jewish and Christian Traditions*. New York: Simon and Schuster, 1979.

Hewitt, Nancy A. "Drexel, Mother Mary Katharine." In Barbara Sicherman and Carol Hurd Green, eds., *Notable American Women: The Modern Period*. Cambridge, Mass.: Harvard University, Belknap Press, 1980.

Jensen, Joan M. "Native American Women and Agriculture: A Seneca Case Study." In Ellen Carol DuBois and Vicki L. Ruiz, eds., *Unequal Sisters: A Multicultural Reader in U.S. Women's History*. New York: Routledge, 1990.

Keller, Rosemary Skinner. "Lay Women in the Protestant Tradition." In Rosemary Radford Ruether and Rosemary Skinner Keller, eds., *Women and Religion in America*. Vol. 1, *The Nineteenth Century*. San Francisco: Harper and Row, 1986.

Lasch-Quinn, Elizabeth. "Dorothea Dix and Mental Health Reform." In Randall M. Miller and Paul A. Cimbala, eds., *Ameri-*

can Reform and Reformers: A Biographical Dictionary. Westport, Conn.: Greenwood Press, 1996.

Lee, Jarena. "Religious Experience and Journal of Mrs. Jarena Lee." In Spiritual Narratives. New York: Oxford University Press, 1988.

Levenduski, Cristine M. "Elizabeth Sampson Ashbridge." In Angela Howard Zophy, ed., with Frances M. Kavenik, Handbook of American Women's History. New York: Garland, 1990.

Life of Dr. Kate Waller Barrett. In Otto Wilson, with Robert South Barrett, eds., Fifty Years' Work with Girls, 1883–1933: A Story of the Florence Crittenton Homes. 1933. New York: Arno Press, reprint 1974.

Marti, Donald B. "Methodist Women in the Nineteenth Century." In Angela Howard Zophy, ed., with Frances M. Kavenik, Handbook of American Women's History. New York: Garland, 1990.

Moore, Joan. "The Social Fabric of the Hispanic Community since 1965." In Jay P. Dolan and Allan Figueroa Deck, eds., Hispanic Catholic Culture in the U.S.: Issues and Concerns. Notre Dame: University of Notre Dame Press, 1994.

Moore, R. Laurence. "The Spiritualist Medium: A Study of Female Professionalization in Victorian America." In Esther Katz and Anita Rapone, eds., Women's Experience in America: An Historical Anthology. New Brunswick, N.J.: Transaction Books, 1980.

National Conference of Catholic Bishops. "Pastoral Plan for Pro-Life Activities" (1975). In Eva R. Rubin, ed., The Abortion Controversy: A Documentary History. Westport, Conn.: Greenwood Press, 1994.

Nicholson, Aleathia Dolores. "Barbara Harris." In Jessie Carney Smith, ed., Epic Lives: One Hundred Black Women Who Made a Difference. Detroit: Visible Ink Press, 1993.

Oates, Mary J. "Catholic Laywomen in the Labor Force, 1850–1950." In Karen Kennelly, ed., American Catholic Women: A Historical Exploration. New York: Macmillan, 1989.

Owen, Robert Dale. "Moral Physiology" (1831). In Michael S. Kimmel and Thomas E. Mosmiller, eds., Against the Tide: Pro-Feminist Men in the United States. Boston: Beacon Press, 1992.

Parker, Theodore. "A Sermon of the Public Function of Women" (1853). In Michael S. Kimmel and Thomas E. Mosmiller, eds., Against the Tide: Pro-Feminist Men in the United States. Boston: Beacon Press, 1992.

Perkins, Linda M. "The Black Female American Missionary Association Teacher in the South, 1861–1870." In Darlene Clark Hine, ed., Black Women in United States History. Vol. 3. Brooklyn, N.Y.: Carlson Publishing, 1990.

Plummer, Louise. "Susa Young Gates." In Daniel H. Ludlow, ed., Encyclopedia of Mormonism. Vol. 2. New York: Macmillan, 1992.

Podolsky, Marjorie J. "Elizabeth Ann Seton." In Frank Magill, ed., Great Lives from History: American Women Series. Pasadena, Calif.: Salem Press, 1995.

Sandersen, Diana Ruby. "Presbyterian Women's Groups." In Angela Howard Zophy, ed., with Frances M. Kavenik, Handbook of American Women's History. New York: Garland, 1990.

Scanzoni, Letha Dawson, and Susan Setta. "Women in Evangelical, Holiness, and Pentecostal Traditions." In Rosemary Radford Ruether and Rosemary Skinner Keller, eds., Women and Religion in America. 1900–1968, Vol. 3. San Francisco: Harper and Row, 1986.

Schneider, Beth. "Harris, Barbara C." In Dorothy C. Salem, ed., African American Women: A Biographical Dictionary. New York: Garland, 1993.

Schwartz, Shuly Rubin. "Women's League for Conservative Judaism." In Paula Hyman and Deborah Dash Moore, eds., Jewish Women in America. New York: Routledge, 1997.

Shade, William G. "Nichols, Mary Gove." In Angela Howard Zophy, ed., with Frances M. Kavenik, Handbook of American Women's History. New York: Garland, 1990.

"Simos, Miriam." In Frances C. Locker, ed., *Contemporary Authors*. Vol. 104. Detroit: Gale, 1982.

Smith, Barbara B., and Shirley W. Thomas. "Gospel Principles and the Roles of Women." In Daniel H. Ludlow, ed., *Encyclopedia of Mormonism*. Vol. 4. New York: Macmillan, 1992.

Snider, John. "Qoyawayma, Polingaysi." In Angela Howard Zophy, ed., with Frances M. Kavenik, *Handbook of American Women's History*. New York: Garland, 1990.

Thompson, Susan. "Barbara Andrews." In Gloria E. Bengtson, ed., *Lutheran Women in Ordained Ministry, 1970–1995*. Minneapolis: Augsburg, 1995.

Umansky, Ellen M. "Women in Judaism: From the Reform Movement to Contemporary Jewish Feminism." In Rosemary Ruether and Eleanor McLaughlin, eds., *Women of Spirit: Female Leadership in the Jewish and Christian Traditions*. New York: Simon and Schuster, 1979.

Wagner, Sally Roesch. "Gage, Matilda Joslyn." In Angela Howard Zophy, ed., with Frances M. Kavenik, *Handbook of American Women's History*. New York: Garland, 1990.

Welter, Barbara. "The Feminization of American Religion: 1800–1860." In Mary S. Hartman and Lois Banner, eds., *Clio's Consciousness Raised: New Perspectives in the History of Women*. New York: Harper Torchbooks, 1974.

Zikmund, Barbara Brown. "Women in the Clergy." In Sara E. Rix, ed., *The American Woman, 1988–89: A Status Report*. New York: W. W. Norton, 1988.

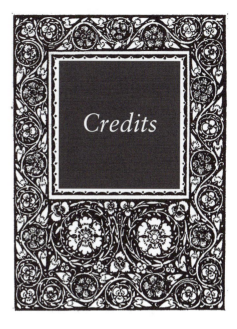

Credits

Index